PARDON MY FRENCH!

POCKET FRENCH SLANG DICTIONARY

ENGLISH-FRENCH/FRENCH-ENGLISH

This third edition published
by Chambers Harrap Publishers Ltd 2007
7 Hopetoun Crescent
Edinburgh EH7 4AY
Great Britain

Previous (second) edition published in 2003

ISBN 978 0245 50657 4 (France)
ISBN 978 0245 60764 6 (UK)

Dépôt légal : février 2007

Designed and typeset by Chambers Harrap Publishers Ltd, Edinburgh
Printed and bound in Britain by Clays Ltd, St Ives plc

Project Editors/Rédacteurs
Kate Nicholson
Georges Pilard

American Consultant/Consultant pour l'anglais américain
Orin Hargraves

Publishing Manager/Direction éditoriale
Anna Stevenson

Prepress/Prépresse
Heather Macpherson

The editors would like to thank Philip O'Prey and his students at the Université Catholique de l'Ouest in Angers for their suggestions for new French slang.

Les rédacteurs tiennent à remercier Philip O'Prey et ses étudiants de l'Université Catholique de l'Ouest à Angers pour leurs suggestions de termes d'argot français.

Preface

Harrap has a long-standing reputation for excellent coverage of slang and colloquial language, and we were the first major dictionary publisher to offer a bilingual slang dictionary. Now in its third edition, *Pardon My French!* has been fully revised and updated to reflect the ever-changing face of French and English slang. We have retained long-established terms but added a wealth of new material to bring the book firmly into the 21st century, including **bingo wings**, **chav**, **MILF** and **tangoed** for English, and **larver**, **c'est de la louse** and **pipole** for French. Like its predecessors, this book also includes many humorous and colourful expressions and offers an insight into the popular culture of both countries.

What is slang?

The word "slang" is sometimes confused with "jargon", that is, the language used within particular social or professional groups. We have excluded such terms from this book (except for some which have gained common currency), focusing instead on a range of non-standard language from the colloquial to the vulgar – the language heard or used by us all every day in informal contexts.

Labelling

Our labelling system is designed to help the reader choose the right word for the situation and avoid embarrassing faux pas.

All of the language is this book is by definition colloquial, and should not be used in a formal context. There are, however, different degrees of informality, which are indicated as follows: the symbol **[!]** denotes that the word or expression may cause offence and should be used with care, while **[!!]** is reserved for vulgar and taboo expressions which will shock in most contexts and should be used with extreme caution.

Racist and homophobic terms are marked *Offensive/Injurieux*, as these will invariably cause offence. However, certain items like **bird/nana** which could be considered sexist or politically incorrect have not been labelled, as they are open to interpretation depending on the context and the intended meaning.

Where possible, translations have been carefully selected to match the register (level of informality) of the source expression. However, in some cases there is no slang equivalent and a neutral translation has been given, followed by the symbol ▫.

Further information

More than just a dictionary, *Pardon My French!* is enriched with nuggets of linguistic and cultural information that make it a pleasure to browse. The thematic panels from the previous edition have been enlarged and updated, and several more have been added, exploring slang-rich fields such as **alcohol/alcool, body parts/parties du corps** and **seduction/séduction**. Other panels focus on particular types of slang, for example **Australian slang, insults/insultes, tabloid speak, argot des banlieues, verlan**.

In addition, hundreds of usage notes throughout the text give more background on items that require more than a simple translation:
▸ explanation of the subtleties of racist and homophobic terms [**fag, Paki, weegie, bouseux, Rital, tantouze**]
▸ interesting etymologies [**bunny boiler, Delhi belly, muffin top, bébert, neuf-trois, jacky**]
▸ information on typical gestures [**to give sb the finger, talk to the hand**]
▸ productive prefixes and suffixes [**-a-go-go, fest, -aille, -ard, -ouse**]
▸ explanations of set phrases that are hard to translate [**beam me up Scotty!, to have a blonde moment, faire avancer le schmilblick**]
▸ cultural items that need fuller explanation [**Chelsea tractor, Croydon facelift, soccer mom, trainspotter, beauf, jacky**].

An international outlook

Although many slang terms are used on both sides of the Atlantic, some remain typically British or North American. These are indicated with the labels *Br* and *Am*, both at headword and at translation level. We would like to thank Orin Hargraves, lexicographer and expert on American English, for checking all the existing American material and suggesting a wealth of new words and expressions.

In addtition, the English-French side includes words and phrases of Scottish (*Scot*), Irish (*Ir*), Australian (*Austr*) and Black American (*Noir Am*) origin, while the French-English side covers French from Belgium (*Belg*), Switzerland (*Suisse*) and Canada (*Can*).

Préface

Les dictionnaires Harrap se sont toujours distingués par la place qu'ils accordent à l'argot et à la langue parlée en général. De toutes les grandes maisons d'édition, Harrap fut la première à publier un dictionnaire bilingue entièrement consacré à cet aspect de la langue.

Ceci est la troisième édition du *Harrap's Slang*, revue, augmentée et entièrement mise à jour de façon à refléter l'évolution des argots anglais et français. Nous avons conservé l'essentiel des mots et expressions des éditions précédentes auxquels nous avons ajouté des termes très récents comme **bingo wings**, **chav**, **MILF** et **tangoed** pour le côté anglais, et **larver**, **c'est de la louse** et **pipole** pour le côté français. Comme les précédentes éditions, cet ouvrage propose de nombreuses expressions savoureuses et pleines d'humour ainsi qu'un certain regard sur les cultures populaires française et britannique.

Qu'entend-on par argot ?

Le terme « argot » est parfois confondu avec le terme « jargon », à savoir la langue propre à certains groupes professionnels ou sociaux. Nous n'avons inclu que les termes de jargon qui ont été absorbés par la langue populaire. Notre ouvrage est donc un dictionnaire d'argot au sens le plus large du terme : un dictionnaire du français et de l'anglais non conventionnels, dont le registre s'étend du familier au très vulgaire.

Les indications d'usage

Des indicateurs d'usage éviteront au lecteur de se mettre dans des situations embarrassantes en utilisant à son insu des mots qui ne manqueraient pas de choquer.

Ceci étant un dictionnaire d'argot, le fait même qu'un terme (ou une expression) y soit traité est le signe qu'il appartient à la langue familière, et qu'il ne doit donc pas être utilisé dans un contexte formel. Il existe cependant différents registres au sein de la langue familière, que nous avons choisi d'indiquer de la façon suivante : le symbole **[!]** indique qu'un mot ou une expression risque de choquer et doit être utilisé(e) avec circonspection ; le symbole **[!!]** est réservé aux termes et expressions vulgaires ou tabous. Les termes accompagnés de ce symbole doivent être utilisés avec la plus grande prudence.

Les termes racistes et homophobes sont accompagnés de la mention *Offensive/Injurieux* car ils sont intrinsèquement injurieux ; des termes tels que **bird/nana** ne sont accompagnés d'aucune mention particulière car leurs connotations dépendent surtout du contexte dans lequel ils sont employés.

Nous nous sommes efforcés, dans nos traductions, de respecter le niveau de langue des mots et expressions de la langue source. Cependant, lorsque ceci s'est avéré impossible, nous avons indiqué que la traduction donnée est neutre en lui accolant le symbole ⊓.

Pour aider l'utilisateur

Le *Harrap's Slang* est plus qu'un simple dictionnaire : en effet, il propose des informations linguistiques et culturelles qui en font un ouvrage très agréable à feuilleter. Cette nouvelle édition compte plus d'une douzaine de nouveaux encadrés thématiques et ceux déjà présents dans l'édition précédente ont été mis à jour. Parmis les thèmes abordés dans les deux parties du dictionnaire, citons l'**alcohol** (alcohol), les **parties du corps** (body parts) et la **séduction** (seduction). D'autres encadrés se concentrent sur différentes variétés d'argot (**Australian slang, tabloid speak, verlan, argot des banlieues**).

Par ailleurs, des centaines de notes d'usage donnent un complément d'information sur les termes pour lesquels une simple traduction est insuffisante :

▶ explication des nuances d'usage des différents termes racistes, xénophobes ou homophobes [**fag, Paki, weegie, bouseux, Rital, tantouze**]
▶ des explications sur certaines étymologies intéressantes [**bunny boiler, Delhi belly, muffin top, bébert, neuf-trois**]
▶ des préfixes et des suffixes particulièrement générateurs [**-a-go-go, fest, -aille, -ard, -ouse**]
▶ des explications sur des expressions et des formules toutes faites posant des problèmes de traduction particuliers [**beam me up Scotty!, to have a blonde moment, faire avancer le schmilblick**]
▶ des explications sur certains termes indissociables d'un contexte culturel ou social donné [**Chelsea tractor, Croydon facelift, soccer mom, trainspotter, beauf, jacky, bidochon**].

Une perspective internationale

Bien que l'argot britannique subisse l'influence toujours croissante de l'anglais parlé aux États-Unis, il existe de nombreux termes et expressions qui n'ont cours que d'un côté ou de l'autre de l'Atlantique. Ces termes sont précédés de la mention *Br* (britannique) et *Am* (américain) ; ces indications figurent aussi bien du côté anglais/français, que dans les traductions, dans la partie français/ anglais. Notre spécialiste en américanismes, Orin Hargraves, a vérifié tous les termes d'argot américain qui figurent dans cet ouvrage et a suggéré l'inclusion de très nombreuses nouvelles entrées et expressions.

Par ailleurs, l'argot des autres pays anglophones et francophones est également bien représenté. Les termes et expressions d'anglais d'Écosse sont indiqués par la mention *Scot*, l'anglais d'Irlande est signalé par la mention *Ir*, l'australien par *Austr*, les termes d'argot noir américain par *Noir Am*, le français de Belgique par *Belg*, les termes suisses par *Suisse* et les termes de français du Canada par *Can*.

Symboles phonétiques de l'anglais

Consonnes

[b] bimbo ['bɪmbəʊ]
[d] dishy ['dɪʃɪ]
[dʒ] ginormous [dʒaɪ'nɔːməs]; jiffy ['dʒɪfɪ]
[f] flunk [flʌŋk]
[g] gaga ['gɑːgɑː]
[h] hunky ['hʌŋkɪ]
[j] yonks [jɒŋks]
[k] conk [kɒŋk]
[l] legless ['leglɪs]
[m] manky ['mæŋkɪ]
[n] naff [næf]
[ŋ] banger ['bæŋə(r)]
[p] prat [præt]
[r] reefer ['riːfə(r)]
[(r)] (seulement prononcé en cas de liaison avec le mot suivant) rotter ['rɒtə(r)]
[s] scran [skræn]
[ʃ] shooter ['ʃuːtə(r)]
[t] tenner ['tenə(r)]
[tʃ] chow [tʃaʊ]
[θ] thicko ['θɪkəʊ]
[ð] brother ['brʌðə(r)]
[v] vibes [vaɪbz]
[w] wacko ['wækəʊ]
[z] zilch [zɪltʃ]
[ʒ] casual ['kæʒʊəl]

Voyelles

[æ] slammer ['slæmə(r)]
[ɑː] barf [bɑːf]
[e] preggers ['pregəz]
[ɜː] hurl [hɜːl]
[ə] gotcha ['gɒtʃə]
[iː] geek [giːk]
[ɪ] dippy ['dɪpɪ]
[ɒ] pong [pɒŋ]
[ɔː] awesome ['ɔːsəm]
[ʊ] footie ['fʊtɪ]
[uː] loony ['luːnɪ]
[ʌ] junkie ['dʒʌŋkɪ]

Diphtongues

[aɪ] wino ['waɪnəʊ]
[aʊ] lousy ['laʊzɪ]
[eə] yeah [jeə]
[eɪ] flake [fleɪk]
[əʊ] loaded ['ləʊdɪd]
[ɪə] weirdo ['wɪədəʊ]
[ɔɪ] boyf [bɔɪf]

French Phonetic Symbols

Consonants

[b]	bagnole [baɲɔl]
[d]	draguer [drage]
[f]	frangin [frãʒɛ̃]
[g]	greluche [grəlyʃ]
[ʒ]	gerber [ʒɛrbe]
[k]	costaud [kɔsto]
[l]	larguer [large]
[m]	mioche [mjɔʃ]
[n]	nul [nyl]
[ŋ]	feeling [filiŋ]
[ɲ]	guignol [giɲɔl]
[p]	pépé [pepe]
[r]	reum [rœm]
[s]	speeder [spide]
[ʃ]	chiper [ʃipe]
[t]	taré [tare]
[v]	vachement [vaʃmã]
[z]	zonard [zonar]

Vowels

[a]	aprème [aprɛm]
[ɑ]	pâlichon [pɑliʃɔ̃]
[e]	bourré [bure]
[ə]	peler [pəle]
[ø]	dégueu [degø]
[œ]	gueule [gœl]
[ɛ]	craignos [krɛɲos]
[i]	nippes [nip]
[ɔ]	hosto [ɔsto]
[o]	dope [dop]
[u]	roupiller [rupije]
[y]	nunuche [nynyʃ]
[ã]	lambin [lãbɛ̃]
[ɛ̃]	joint [ʒwɛ̃]
[ɔ̃]	défoncé [defɔ̃se]
[œ̃]	parfum [parfœ̃]

Semi-vowels

[w]	boîte [bwat]
[j]	flicaille [flikɑj]
[ɥ]	puissant [pɥisã]

Labels
Indications d'usage

gloss	=	glose
[introduces a brief explanation]		[introduit une explication]
cultural equivalent	≃	équivalent culturel
[introduces a translation which has a roughly equivalent status in the target language]		[introduit une traduction dont les connotations dans la langue cible sont comparables]
very familiar	[!]	très familier
vulgar	[!!]	vulgaire
neutral translation	▫	traduction neutre
abbreviation	*abbr, abrév*	abréviation
adjective	*adj*	adjectif
adverb	*adv*	adverbe
American English	*Am*	anglais d'Amérique du Nord
Australian English	*Aust*	anglais d'Australie
auxiliary	*aux*	auxiliaire
Belgian French	*Belg*	français de Belgique
British English	*Br*	anglais britannique
Canadian French	*Can*	canadianisme
exclamation	*exclam*	exclamation
feminine	*f*	féminin
humorous	*Hum*	humoristique
offensive	*Injurieux*	injurieux
[denotes a racist or homophobic term]		[signale un terme raciste ou homophobe]
invariable	*inv*	invariable
Irish English	*Ir*	anglais d'Irlande
ironic	*ironic, ironique*	ironique
masculine	*m*	masculin
modal auxiliary verb	*modal aux v*	auxiliaire modal
noun	*n*	nom
feminine noun	*nf*	nom féminin
feminine plural noun	*nfpl*	nom féminin pluriel
masculine noun	*nm*	nom masculin
masculine and feminine noun	*nmf*	nom masculin et féminin
[same form for both genders]		[formes identiques]
masculine and feminine noun	*nm,f*	nom masculin et féminin
[different form in the feminine]		[formes différentes]

Black American English	*Noir Am*	anglais noir américain
plural noun	*npl*	nom pluriel
proper noun	*npr*	nom propre
offensive	*Offensive*	injurieux
[denotes a racist or homophobic term]		[signale un terme raciste ou homophobe]
pejorative	*Pej, Péj*	péjoratif
prefix	*prefix, préfixe*	préfixe
preposition	*prep, prép*	préposition
pronoun	*pron*	pronom
something	*qch*	quelque chose
somebody	*qn*	quelqu'un
registered trademark	®	marque déposée
somebody	*sb*	quelqu'un
Scottish English	*Scot*	anglais d'Écosse
something	*sth*	quelque chose
suffix	*suffix, suffixe*	suffixe
Swiss French	*Suisse*	helvétisme
verb	*v*	verbe
intransitive verb	*vi*	verbe intransitif
impersonal verb	*v imp*	verbe impersonnel
reflexive verb	*vpr*	verbe pronominal
transitive verb	*vt*	verbe transitif
inseparable transitive verb	*vt insép*	verbe transitif à particule inséparable
[phrasal verb where the verb and the adverb or preposition cannot be separated, eg **bunk off**; he **bunked off** school]		[par exemple : **bunk off** (sécher) ; he **bunked off** school (il a séché l'école)]
separable transitive verb	*vt sép*	verbe transitif à particule séparable
[phrasal verb where the verb and the adverb or preposition can be separated, eg **chuck in**; he **chucked** his job **in** or he **chucked in** his job]		[par exemple : **chuck in** (plaquer) ; he **chucked** his job **in** ou he **chucked in** his job (il a plaqué son travail)]

Thematic panels
Encadrés thématiques

English - French

Aa

Abo, abo ['æbəʊ] *n Austr Injurieux* (*abrév* **Aboriginal**) Aborigène[□] *mf*

AC/DC [eɪsiː'diːsiː] *adj* (*bisexual*) à voile et à vapeur, bi

ace [eɪs] **1** *adj* (*excellent*) super, génial
2 *vt Am* **to ace an exam** réussir un examen les doigts dans le nez

aces ['eɪsəs] *adj Am* (*excellent*) super, génial

acid ['æsɪd] *n* (*LSD*) acide *m*; **to drop acid** prendre de l'acide; **acid house** (*music*) acid house *f*

acidhead ['æsɪdhed] *n* **to be an acidhead** consommer beaucoup de LSD[□]

act [ækt] *n* (**a**) **to get one's act together** se prendre en main[□]; **to clean up one's act** s'acheter une conduite (**b**) *Am* **to queer the act** tout faire foirer ▸ *voir aussi* **riot**

actress ['æktrɪs] *n Br Hum* **he's got a huge one… as the actress said to the bishop** il en a une énorme, si j'ose dire…

ⓘ "As the actress said to the bishop" est une formule humoristique prononcée lorsque l'on se rend compte que ce qui vient d'être dit peut être interprété de façon grivoise.

adam ['ædəm] *n* (*ecstasy*) ecstasy[□] *f*, exta *f*

adam and eve ['ædəmən'iːv] *vt Br* (*rhyming slang* **believe**) croire[□]; **would you adam and eve it!** tu te rends compte?

aggro ['ægrəʊ] *n Br* (*abrév* **aggravation**) (*violence*) castagne *f*; (*hassle*) problèmes[□] *mpl*; **my Mum's giving me so much aggro at the moment** ma mère est toujours sur mon dos en ce moment

-a-go-go [ə'gəʊgəʊ] *suffixe* **it was cocktails-a-go-go last night!** ça y allait, les cocktails, hier soir!; **there were celebs a-go-go at the party** ça grouillait de célébrités à la soirée

aid [eɪd] *n* **what's that in aid of?** pourquoi tu fais/dis ça, exactement?

ain't [eɪnt] *contraction* (**a**) (*abrév* **am not**) **I ain't interested** ça m'intéresse pas (**b**) (*abrév* **is not**) **he ain't too bright** il est pas très futé (**c**) (*abrév* **are not**) **you ain't coming with me** tu viens pas avec moi (**d**) (*abrév* **have not**) **I ain't seen him** je l'ai pas vu (**e**) (*abrév* **has not**) **she ain't got the cash** elle a pas l'argent

air biscuit [eə'bɪskɪt] *n Br* (*fart*) perle *f*, prout *m*; **to float** *or* **launch an air biscuit** lâcher une perle, larguer une caisse

airhead ['eəhed] *n* = jolie nana pas très futée

alky ['ælkɪ] *n* (**a**) (*abrév* **alcoholic**) alcolo *mf*, poivrot(e) *m,f* (**b**) *Am* (*abrév* **alcohol**) gnôle *f*

all [ɔːl] *adv* (**a**) **the team was all over the place** l'équipe a joué n'importe comment[□]; **at the interview he was all over the place** *or* **shop** il a complètement foiré son entretien; **he was pretending to be sober but he was all over the place** il était visiblement complètement bourré même s'il faisait tout son possible pour le dissimuler (**b**) **he's not all there** il n'a pas toute sa tête

---

Pleins feux sur...

Alcohol

Il existe de multiples façons de désigner la boisson et l'ivresse dans les pays anglophones dont les habitants sont réputés pour aimer boire, notamment en Grande-Bretagne et en Australie. Pour parler de quelqu'un qui sort avec l'intention explicite de s'enivrer, on utilisera entre autres les expressions **to go on a bender**, **to go on the piss** ou **to go on the bevvy**. À partir du mot **booze** (à la fois substantif = alcool, et verbe = picoler), de nombreux dérivés ont été créés : **boozehound** en anglais américain signifie "poivrot" ; un **boozer** désigne un ivrogne et, en anglais britannique uniquement, un pub ; on emploiera **booze-up** pour une beuverie, et on dira d'une soirée qu'elle est **boozy** s'il y a beaucoup d'alcool à consommer. Le mot **piss** est également générateur de termes vulgaires liés à l'ivresse tels que **piss-up** (beuverie) et **pisshead** et **piss-artist** (termes qui signifient "poivrot"). Parmi les autres termes désignant un ivrogne, citons **alky**, **lush** et, en anglais américain, **juicer**. Il existe en anglais de très nombreux adjectifs argotiques pour dire d'une personne qu'elle est ivre. En anglais britannique, les plus courants sont **legless**, **hammered**, **wrecked**, **smashed**, **pissed** (ce dernier étant un peu plus vulgaire) et plus récemment sont apparus les termes **bladdered**, **trashed** et **trolleyed**. En Écosse, on emploie fréquemment l'adjectif **steaming**. Le mot **wasted** s'emploie aussi aux États-Unis. Les expressions **off one's face**, **out of it** et **far gone** s'utilisent couramment, tout comme les expressions humoristiques (bien qu'un peu vulgaires) **pissed as a fart** et **pissed as a newt** ("bourré comme un triton"). Dans un registre encore plus vulgaire, on trouvera **shit-faced** et **fucked**. L'expression issue de l'argot rimé ("rhyming slang") **Brahms and Liszt** (= pissed) est pittoresque bien qu'en réalité rarement utilisée. **Blotto** s'employait souvent autrefois, mais ce terme est aujourd'hui vieilli.

Le symbole [!] dénote un terme très familier, [!!] un terme vulgaire.

(c) she was all over him at the party elle l'a dragué tout le temps qu'a duré la soirée; *Hum* **he was all over her like a rash** *or* **a cheap suit** il l'a draguée de façon flagrante

(d) it's all good aucune raison de s'inquiéter

(e) *(reporting speech, thoughts)* **she's all "no way!" and I'm like, "yeah, I swear to god…"** elle me fait "pas possible!" et moi je lui fais "si, je te jure…"; **so he comes over to me and I'm all "oh my God, what do I say?!"** alors il s'approche de moi, et moi je suis là à me demander: "oh là là, qu'est-ce que je vais dire?!"

alley ['ælɪ] *n* **that club sounds like it'll be right up my alley** d'après ce que j'ai entendu dire, ce club devrait me botter; **the film's really gory, it should be right up your alley** le film est très gore, je crois que c'est tout à fait le genre de truc qui devrait te plaire

all right [ɔːl'raɪt] **1** *adj* **an "I'm all right Jack" attitude** un comportement du style "moi d'abord, les autres ensuite"

2 *exclam* **(a)** *(as greeting)* salut, ça va? **(b)** *(in approval)* super!, cool! ▶ *voir aussi* **bit**

all that [ɔːl'ðæt] *adj (excellent)* super, génial; **she thinks she's all that** elle ne se prend pas pour n'importe qui

already [ɔːl'redɪ] *adv esp Am* **enough, already!** ça suffit comme ça!; **will you just shut up, already?** tu vas pas un peu la fermer?

amber ['æmbə(r)] *n Br & Austr* **amber nectar** bière⁰ *f*, mousse *f*

ambulance chaser ['æmbjʊlənstʃeɪsə(r)] *n Am Péj* = avocat qui ne s'occupe que d'affaires de demandes de dommages et intérêts pouvant rapporter gros

angel dust ['eɪndʒəldʌst] *n* PCP *f*, phéncyclidine⁰ *f*

ankle-biter ['æŋkəlbaɪtə(r)] *n* gosse *mf*

ankle-swingers ['æŋkəlswɪŋəz] *npl* pantalon *m* trop court⁰; **to be wearing ankle-swingers** avoir un feu de plancher

anorak ['ænəræk] *n Br Péj (person)* ringard(e) *m,f*

ⓘ Ce terme désigne une personne généralement solitaire dont les activités vont à l'encontre de ce qui est considéré comme "cool". Un "anorak" ne s'intéresse pas à la mode (d'où le terme "anorak", symbole de l'absence de goût en matière vestimentaire) ni à l'actualité musicale ou sportive, et ne fréquente aucun endroit branché.

---

antsy ['æntsɪ] *adj Am (nervous)* agité⁰, nerveux⁰, sur des charbons ardents⁰; *(irritable)* à cran

A-OK [eɪəʊ'keɪ] *Am* **1** *adj* super, génial; **everything's A-OK** tout baigne dans l'huile

2 *adv* **to go A-OK** se passer vachement bien

ape [eɪp] *adj* **to go ape (over)** *(lose one's temper)* piquer une crise, péter les plombs (à cause de); *(enthuse)* s'emballer (pour)

apeshit [!] ['eɪpʃɪt] *adj* **to go apeshit (over)** *(lose one's temper)* piquer une crise, péter les plombs (à cause de); *(enthuse)* s'emballer (pour)

apple ['æpəl] *n* **(a) the (Big) Apple** New York⁰ **(b)** *Br* **apples and pears** *(rhyming slang* **stairs***)* escaliers⁰ *mpl* **(c)** *Austr* **she'll be apples!** tout baignera dans l'huile!

-arama [ə'rɑːmə] *suffixe Hum* **you**

should have seen how much we ate, it was pigarama! t'aurais vu tout ce qu'on a mangé, une vraie orgie!; **try that new bar, it's babe-arama!** essaye ce nouveau bar, il y a toujours plein de canons!

ⓘ Ce suffixe dénote l'abondance de ce qui le précède. On peut l'ajouter à presque n'importe quel nom, verbe ou adjectif pour introduire la notion de foisonnement.

argy-bargy [ˈɑːdʒɪˈbɑːdʒɪ] *n* chamailleries *fpl*; **there was a bit of argy-bargy over who should do it** il y a eu des histoires pour

savoir qui devait le faire

arm [ɑːm] *n* (**a**) **to cost an arm and a leg** coûter la peau des fesses (**b**) *Hum* **arm candy** = personne séduisante qui joue un rôle purement décoratif au bras d'une autre personne

armpit [ˈɑːmpɪt] *n* **the armpit of the universe** *(place)* un coin paumé, un trou

arse [!] [ɑːs] *Br* **1** *n* (**a**) *(buttocks)* cul *m*; **a kick up the arse** un coup de pied au cul; **to make an arse of sth** complètement foirer qch; **to get one's arse in(to) gear** se remuer le cul; **to work one's arse off** bosser comme un nègre; **to talk out of one's arse** dire des conneries; **his**

Pleins feux sur...

Anger

Bien des expressions liées à la colère sont également liées à la folie (voir l'encadré p. 178) ; c'est le cas de **to go nuts** et **to go mental** (devenir fou ou bien fou de rage), **to drive sb nuts**, **to drive sb up the wall** et **to drive sb round the bend** (rendre quelqu'un fou ou bien fou de rage). D'autres expressions telles que **to go ballistic**, **to hit the roof/ceiling**, **to have a fit**, **to flip one's lid**, **to freak (out)**, **to flip (out)** et **to do one's nut** (cette dernière s'employant uniquement en anglais britannique) signifient uniquement "piquer une colère". Être agacé se dit **to be pissed off**, expression que les Américains abrègent souvent en **to be pissed** (attention, "pissed" signifie "ivre" en argot britannique). On peut préciser l'origine de son agacement en utilisant les prépositions **at** et **with** s'il s'agit d'une personne (**I'm pissed off with** ou **at him**) et **about** s'il s'agit d'une chose (**I'm pissed off about that**). **To be fucked off** est une variante plus grossière de "to be pissed off". "Crier après quelqu'un" se dit **to bawl somebody out**, et, en anglais britannique, **to give someone an earbashing** et **to give somebody a bollocking** (plus vulgaire). Toujours en argot britannique, **to throw a strop** et **to throw a wobbler** signifient "piquer une colère".

Le symbole [!] dénote un terme très familier, [!!] un terme vulgaire.

head's completely up his arse il se prend vraiment pas pour de la merde; **to be out on one's arse** *(get fired)* se faire virer; **to go arse over tit** *or* **tip** ramasser une gamelle; **my arse!** mon cul!; **aromatherapy my arse!** aromathérapie mon cul!; **to kiss** *or* **lick sb's arse** faire du lèche-cul à qn; **kiss my arse!** va te faire foutre!; **get your arse over here!** ramène ta fraise!, amène-toi!; **move** *or* **shift your arse!** pousse ton cul!; **come on, park your arse, mate!** allez, pose ton cul, vieux!; **stick** *or* **shove it up your arse!** tu peux te le mettre au cul!; **a nice piece of arse** une nénette bandante; **he's been sitting on his arse all day** il a rien foutu de la journée; **he doesn't know his arse from his elbow** il est complètement nul; **she thinks the sun shines out of his arse** elle le prend pour un dieu; **it's my arse that's on the line** ça risque de me retomber sur la gueule; **we had a Ford Fiesta sitting on our arse** *or* **up our arse the whole way** une Ford Fiesta nous a collé au cul pendant tout le trajet

(b) *(person)* crétin(e) *m,f*; **to make an arse of oneself** se ridiculiser□

2 *vt* **why don't you come with us? – I can't be arsed** tu viens avec nous? – non, j'ai trop la flemme; **he can't be arsed doing it himself** il a pas envie de se faire chier à le faire lui-même

3 *exclam* **oh, arse! I've left my brolly in the pub** merde, j'ai oublié mon pébroque au pub! ▸ *voir aussi* **pain**

arse about [!], **arse around** [!] *vi Br (act foolishly)* faire le con, déconner; *(waste time)* glander, glandouiller

arse up [!] *vt sép* **to arse sth up** foirer qch

arse-bandit [!] ['ɑːsbændɪt] *n Br Injurieux* pédale *f*, tapette *f*

arsehole [!] ['ɑːshəʊl] *n Br* **(a)** *(anus)* trou *m* du cul; **the arsehole of nowhere** *or* **of the universe** *(place)* un coin paumé, un trou **(b)** *(person)* trou *m* du cul; **to make an arsehole of oneself** se ridiculiser□

arseholed [!] ['ɑːshəʊld] *adj Br (drunk)* bourré comme un coing, complètement pété

arse-kisser [!] ['ɑːskɪsə(r)] *n Br* lèche-cul *mf*

arse-kissing [!] ['ɑːskɪsɪŋ] *Br* **1** *n* lèche *f*

2 *adj* **he's nothing but an arse-kissing bastard!** c'est qu'un lèche-cul!

arse-licker [!] ['ɑːslɪkə(r)] = **arse-kisser**

arse-licking [!] ['ɑːslɪkɪŋ] = **arse-kissing**

arsewipe [!] ['ɑːswaɪp] *n Br (person)* raclure *f*

arsey [!] ['ɑːsɪ] *adj Br* **(a)** *(stupid)* débile; *(not trendy)* ringard; **that was a bit of an arsey thing to say** c'est un peu débile de dire un truc pareil **(b)** *(bad-tempered)* de mauvais poil, d'une humeur massacrante; **the bus driver got really arsey with me when I didn't have any change** le chauffeur du bus a été super désagréable avec moi parce que je n'avais pas la monnaie

Arthur or Martha ['ɑːθər ɔːˈmɑːθə] *adj Br & Austr Hum* **he doesn't know if he's Arthur or Martha** *(is confused)* il est *ou* marche à côté de ses pompes; *(is unsure about his sexuality)* il ne sait pas trop lui-même s'il marche à voile ou à vapeur

arty-farty ['ɑːtɪˈfɑːtɪ], *Am* **artsy-fartsy** ['ɑːtsɪˈfɑːtsɪ] *adj (person)* qui

The symbol □ indicates that a translation is neutral.

se donne un genre artiste[□]; *(film, activities)* qui se veut artistique[□]

arvo ['ɑːvəʊ] *n* Austr *(afternoon)* après-midi[□] *mf*, aprème *mf*

as if [æz'ɪf] *exclam* **am I a nag? – as if!** est-ce que je suis une emmerdeuse? – mais non! *(dit ironiquement)*; **I'm going on a diet tomorrow – as if!** je commence un régime demain – c'est ça! *(dit ironiquement)*

ass [!] [æs] *n Am* cul *m*; **a kick in the ass** un coup de pied au cul; **to get one's ass in gear** se remuer le cul; **to work one's ass off** bosser comme un nègre; **to be on sb's ass** être sur le dos de qn; **to do sth ass backwards** faire qch à l'envers[□]; **to get one's ass in a sling** avoir des emmerdes; **to go ass over teakettle** ramasser une gamelle; **my (aching) ass!** mon cul!; **I don't want to put my ass on the line** je veux pas que ça me retombe sur la gueule; **to be out on one's ass** *(get fired)* se faire virer; **to haul** *or* **tear ass** se grouiller; **to kiss sb's ass** faire du lèche-cul à qn; **kiss my ass!** va te faire foutre!; **get your ass over here!** ramène ta fraise!, amène-toi!; **move your ass!** pousse ton cul!; **stick** *or* **shove it up your ass!** tu peux te le mettre au cul!; **a nice piece of ass** une nénette bandante; **he's been sitting on his ass all day** il n'a rien foutu de la journée; **he doesn't know his ass from his elbow** *or* **from a hole in the ground** il est complètement nul; **it's my ass that's on the line** ça risque de me retomber sur la gueule; **to kick sb's ass** *(defeat)* ratatiner qn; **to kick ass** assurer un max; **to break** *or* **bust one's ass** se casser le cul; **to be up to one's ass in work** crouler sous le travail; **up your ass!** va te faire mettre!; **you can bet your ass I will!** un peu que

je vais le faire!; **your ass is grass!** tu vas voir ce que tu vas prendre!; **they oughta fire his sorry ass!** ils devraient le virer!; **if you don't pay up they'll get their lawyers on your ass** si tu payes pas, ils vont te mettre leurs avocats aux trousses; **I was just kidding, don't get all political on my ass!** je disais ça pour plaisanter, alors commence pas à me faire une leçon de politique! ▸ *voir aussi* **bite, pain, rat**

ass-bandit [!] ['æsbændɪt] *n Am Injurieux* pédale *f*, tapette *f*

asshole [!] ['æshəʊl] *n Am* **(a)** *(anus)* trou *m* du cul; **the asshole of the universe** *or* **world** *(place)* un coin paumé, un trou **(b)** *(person)* trou *m* du cul

ass-kisser [!] ['æskɪsə(r)] *n Am* lèche-cul *mf*

ass-kissing [!] ['æskɪsɪŋ] *Am* **1** *n* lèche *f*
2 *adj* **he's nothing but an ass-kissing bastard!** c'est qu'un lèche-cul!

ass-licker [!] ['æslɪkə(r)] *Am* = **ass-kisser**

ass-licking [!] ['æslɪkɪŋ] *Am* = **ass-kissing**

asswipe [!] ['æswaɪp] *Am* = **arsewipe**

at [æt] *prép* **that club is where it's at** c'est la boîte in; **that's not where I'm at** c'est pas mon truc; **to be at it** *(having sex)* être en train de faire des galipettes ▸ *voir aussi* **rabbits**

attitude ['ætɪtjuːd] *n (self-assurance, assertiveness)* assurance[□] *f*; **to have attitude** avoir du caractère; **a car with attitude** une voiture qui a du caractère

Auntie ['ɑːntɪ] *n Br* **Auntie (Beeb)** la BBC

Le symbole **[!]** dénote un terme très familier, **[!!]** un terme vulgaire.

ⓘ "Auntie" se traduit littéralement "tatie" ; c'est le surnom affectueux donné à la BBC par les Britanniques, qui met en relief l'at-titude quelque peu paternaliste de l'institution vis-à-vis du public, et un style qui manque parfois d'audace.

away [ə'weɪ] **1** *adj Br* **well away** *(drunk)* bourré, beurré, pété

2 *adv* **to be away with the fair-** **ies** *(senile)* être complètement gaga; *(eccentric)* être farfelu; *(daydreaming)* être dans les nuages; *Br* **to play away** *(be unfaithful)* être infidèle[□]

ⓘ L'expression "to play away" provient du vocabulaire sportif : elle signifie "jouer à l'extérieur".

awesome ['ɔːsəm] *adj Am* super, génial

AWOL ['eɪwɒl] *adj Hum* **he goes AWOL whenever it's time to**

D'où tu me parles ?

Australian slang

L'Australie (dont le surnom est **Oz**) a la réputation d'être un pays fort décontracté ; ce n'est pas pour rien que l'expression **no worries!** (y'a pas de soucis!) est emblématique de ce pays. Les Australiens (ou **Ozzies**) emploient un type d'argot que l'on appelle **strine** (un mot qui imite la façon dont certains Australiens prononcent "Australian"). L'argot australien ressemble à l'argot traditionnel de Londres du fait que les gens ont tendance à beaucoup employer le terme **mate** quand ils s'adressent les uns aux autres, et ils utilisent également de nombreux termes de rhyming slang (voir l'encadré p. 145). L'argot australien est aussi très influencé par l'argot américain.

Les Australiens se saluent en disant **g'day!** (qui est une contraction de "good day", bonjour). Les hommes sont des **blokes** (comme en Grande-Bretagne) et les femmes des **sheilas**. Un repas typique consiste en un **barbie** (un barbecue), accompagné de **stubbies** (des canettes) de **amber nectar** (la bière). La création de mots par abréviation et ajout du suffixe **-o** ou **-ie** est caractéristique de l'argot australien, par exemple **arvo** (diminutif de "afternoon", après-midi), **garbo** (de "garbage collector", éboueur), **surfie** (de "surfer", surfeur(euse)), **schoolie** (de "schoolboy/schoolgirl", écolier(ère)). D'autres exemples typiques de l'argot d'Australie sont : **bonzer** (génial(e)); **dag** (un(e) ringard(e); l'adjectif est **daggy**); **dunny** (chiottes); **chook** (un poulet/ une femme); **crook** (mal fichu(e)); **rack off!** (casse-toi!) et la fameuse expression de surprise **strewth!**.

---

do the washing-up il se débine à chaque fois qu'il s'agit de faire la vaisselle; **my keys have gone AWOL again** encore une fois, impossible de mettre la main sur mes clés

ⓘ Il s'agit à l'origine d'un acronyme utilisé dans l'armée, dont la forme développée est "absent without leave" (absent sans permission).

awright [ɔː'raɪt] *exclam Br* (**a**) *(as greeting)* salut, ça va? (**b**) *(in approval)* super!, cool!

axe, *Am* **ax** [æks] *n* (**a**) *(guitar)* gratte *f*, râpe *f* (**b**) **to get the axe** *(person)* être viré; *(programme, plan etc)* être annulé[□] *ou* supprimé[□]

Ayrton ['eətən] *n Br* (*rhyming slang* **Ayrton Senna** = **tenner**) = billet de dix livres

Aztec two-step ['æztek'tuːstep] *n Am* **to have the Aztec two-step** avoir la turista

ⓘ Dans cette expression, les Américains emploient le mot "Aztec" (aztèque) car dans l'esprit de nombre d'entre eux, tout séjour en Amérique latine (et notamment au Mexique) s'accompagne fatalement d'une crise de gastro-entérite. Le "two-step" est une danse. En Grande-Bretagne, c'est l'expression "Delhi belly" que l'on emploie (voir cette entrée).

Bb

babe [beɪb] *n* (**a**) *(attractive woman)* canon *m*, bombe *f*; *(attractive man)* canon *m*, beau mec *m*; **his sister's friends are all absolute babes** les copines de sa sœur sont toutes des canons; **check out that total babe over there!** regarde un peu le canon là-bas! (**b**) *(term of address)* chéri(e) *m,f* ▸ *voir aussi* **magnet**

babyfather [ˈbeɪbɪfɑːðə(r)], **baby-daddy** [ˈbeɪbɪdædɪ] *n* = père d'un enfant, dans un couple séparé; **he's her babyfather** *or* **babydaddy** c'est le père de son enfant

ⓘ Ce terme s'emploie essentiellement en Jamaïque et dans la communauté Afro-antillaise britannique.

babymother [ˈbeɪbɪmʌðə(r)] *n* = mère d'un enfant, dans un couple séparé; **she's his babymother** c'est la mère de son enfant

ⓘ Ce terme s'emploie essentiellement en Jamaïque et dans la communauté Afro-antillaise britannique.

backside [bæk'saɪd] *n* derrière *m*

bad [bæd] **1** *adj* (**a**) *(not good)* **I'm having a bad hair day** *(my hair's a mess)* je n'arrive pas à me coiffer aujourd'hui[□]; *(I'm having a bad day)* aujourd'hui c'est un jour sans; **he's bad news** c'est quelqu'un de pas

fréquentable[□] (**b**) *(excellent)* super, génial; **this music's so bad** cette musique est vraiment super

2 *n Am* **my bad!** c'est ma faute!; **we've missed the start of the movie! – sorry, my bad! I got the time wrong** on a raté le début du film! – désolé, c'est ma faute, je me suis trompé d'heure

badass [!] [ˈbædæs] *Am* **1** *n (person)* dur(e) *m,f* (à cuire)

2 *adj* (**a**) *(intimidating, tough)* **to be badass** être un(e) dur(e) à cuire; **her husband's some badass Mob guy** son mari est une espèce de dur à cuire qui bosse pour la Mafia (**b**) *(excellent)* super, génial; **her new sneakers are so badass** ils sont super, ses nouveaux tennis

badmouth [ˈbædmaʊθ] *vt* débiner

bag¹ [bæg] *n* (**a**) *Péj (woman)* **old bag** vieille bique *f* (**b**) *(quantity of drugs)* dose *f (en sachet ou dans un papier plié)* (**c**) *(interest)* dada *m*; **he has a new bag** il a un nouveau dada; **it's not my bag** c'est pas mon truc (**d**) **it's in the bag** c'est dans la poche ▸ *voir aussi* **bum**

bag² *vt (seize)* mettre le grappin sur; *(steal)* piquer, faucher; **she's bagged herself this gorgeous young doctor** elle s'est dégoté un jeune docteur hyper craquant

bag off *vi Br* **did you bag off last night?** t'as emballé hier soir?; **to**

bag off with sb lever *ou* emballer qn

bahookie [bə'hʊkɪ] *n Scot (buttocks)* miches *fpl*, cul *m*

bail [beɪl] *vi Am* se décommander□, annuler□; **my brother set me up on a blind date but I bailed at the last minute** mon frère m'avait arrangé un rendez-vous avec une fille que je n'avais jamais rencontrée mais à la dernière minute j'ai décidé de ne pas y aller

bail on *vt insép Am* faire faux bond à; **I should've known he'd bail on me when I needed the car** j'aurais dû me douter qu'il me ferait faux bond quand j'aurais besoin de la voiture

ball [!!!] [bɔːl] *Am* **1** *vt (have sex with) (of man)* baiser, tringler, troncher; *(of woman)* baiser avec, s'envoyer
2 *vi (have sex)* baiser

ball up [!] *Am* = **balls up**

ball-breaker [!] ['bɔːlbreɪkə(r)], **ball-buster** [!] ['bɔːlbʌstə(r)] *n Am* **(a)** *(woman)* femme *f* de tête□ **(b)** *(problem, situation)* casse-tête *m*

baller ['bɔːlə(r)] *n Noir Am* flambeur (euse) *m,f*

ballistic [bə'lɪstɪk] *adv* **to go ballistic** piquer une crise, péter une durite

balls [!] [bɔːlz] *npl* **(a)** *(testicles)* couilles *fpl*; **to have blue balls** avoir les couilles pleines et douloureuses; **she's been breaking** *or* **busting my balls about it** elle arrête pas de me casser les couilles avec ça; **they've got us by the balls** ils nous tiennent à la gorge **(b)** *(nonsense)* conneries *fpl* **(c)** *(courage)* cran *m*; **to have the balls to do sth** avoir assez de cran pour faire qch; **his balls are bigger than his brains** il est pas bien, il est complètement malade

balls up [!] *vt sép Br* **to balls sth up** *(interview, exam)* foirer qch, se planter à qch; *(plan, arrangement)* faire foirer qch; **you've ballsed everything up** tu as tout fait foirer

balls-up [!] ['bɔːlzʌp] *n Br* merdier *m*; **to make a balls-up of sth** *(interview, exam)* foirer qch, se planter à qch; *(plan, arrangement)* faire foirer qch

ballsy ['bɔːlzɪ] *adj* qui en a; **his wife is one ballsy lady** elle a des couilles, sa femme

ball-up [!] ['bɔːlʌp] *Am* = **balls-up**

baloney [bə'ləʊnɪ] **1** *n (nonsense)* foutaises *fpl*; **don't talk baloney!** arrête de raconter n'importe quoi!
2 *exclam* foutaises!

baltic ['bɔːltɪk] *adj Br (weather)* **it's baltic** il fait un froid de canard

bampot ['bæmpɒt] *n Scot (idiot)* andouille *f*

bananas [bə'nɑːnəz] *adj (mad)* dingue, cinglé, timbré; **to go bananas** devenir dingue *ou* cinglé *ou* timbré

bang [bæŋ] **1** *n* **(a)** *(sexual intercourse)* **to have a bang** [!!] baiser **(b)** *Am* **to get a bang out of sb/sth** s'éclater avec qn/en faisant qch
2 *adv Br* **(a)** *(exactly)* **bang on time** pile à l'heure; **bang up-to-date** hyper-moderne; **bang in the middle** en plein milieu; **you were bang out of order calling him a fool in front of everybody!** tu n'avais pas à le traiter d'imbécile devant tout le monde! **(b)** **bang on** *(guess, answer, calculation)* qui tombe pile; *(arrive, start)* pile à l'heure **(c)** **bang goes that idea** c'est râpé; **bang goes my holiday** c'est foutu pour mes vacances
3 [!!] *vt (have sex with) (of man)* baiser, tringler, troncher; *(of woman)* baiser avec, s'envoyer

4 [!!] *vi (have sex)* baiser

bang on *vi Br (talk at length)* rabâcher; **he's forever banging on about** *Lord of the Rings* il n'arrête pas de nous rebattre les oreilles avec *Le Seigneur des anneaux*

bang up *vt sép Br (imprison)* boucler, coffrer

banger ['bæŋə(r)] *n Br* (a) **(old) banger)** *(car)* tas *m* de ferraille, vieille bagnole *f* (b) *(sausage)* saucisse⁰ *f*; **bangers and mash** saucisses-purée *f*

banging ['bæŋɪŋ] *adj Br (club, party)* hyper animé; **this is a banging tune!** c'est trop puissant comme morceau!

bang-up ['bæŋʌp] *adj Br (excellent)* super, génial; **Heath Ledger's done a bang-up job of portraying the character** Heath Ledger est vraiment entré à fond dans la peau du personnage; **she did a bang-up job of throwing a good party** elle avait organisé une super soirée

banjax ['bændʒæks] *vt Scot & Ir (break)* bousiller

banjaxed ['bændʒækst] *adj Scot & Ir* (a) *(broken)* bousillé (b) *(drunk)* bourré, pété

baps [bæps] *npl Br (breasts)* nichons *mpl*, nibards *mpl*, roberts *mpl*

barbie ['bɑːbɪ] *n Br & Austr (barbecue)* barbecue⁰ *m*, barbeuk *m*; **to have a barbie** se faire un barbeuk; **chuck another steak on the barbie!** balance un autre steak sur le barbeuk!

bar-crawl ['bɑːkrɔːl] *n* tournée *f* des bars⁰; **to go on a bar-crawl** faire la tournée des bars

bare [beɪ(r)] *Br* **1** *adj (a lot of)* des tas de, vachement de; **there was bare people at the party** c'était bourré de monde à la soirée

2 *adv (very)* vachement; **that guy is bare fit!** ce mec est vachement craquant!

bareback ['beəbæk] *adv Br Hum* **to ride bareback** *(have unprotected sex)* faire l'amour sans capote

barf [bɑːf] **1** *n* dégueulis *m*

2 *vi* dégueuler, gerber; **barf bag** sac *m* pour vomir⁰

barfly ['bɑːflaɪ] *n Am* pilier *m* de bistrot

barhop ['bɑːhɒp] *vi Am* faire la tournée des bars⁰

barking ['bɑːkɪŋ] *adj Br* **barking (mad)** cinglé, toqué, taré

barmy ['bɑːmɪ] *adj Br* barjo

barnet *n Br (rhyming slang Barnet fair = hair)* tifs *mpl*

Barney ['bɑːnɪ] *n (ugly man)* mocheté *f*

ⓘ Barney Rubble est l'un des personnages de la bande dessinée américaine *Les Flintstones*.

barney ['bɑːnɪ] *n Br (argument)* prise *f* de bec

Barry White [!] [bærɪ'waɪt] *n Br (rhyming slang shite)* **to have a Barry White** couler un bronze

bar steward ['bɑːstjʊəd] *n Hum* salaud *m*, salopard *m*

ⓘ Il s'agit d'un jeu de mots sur "bastard".

base [beɪs] *n (speed)* amphet *f*

bash [bæʃ] **1** *n* (a) *(party)* fiesta *f* (b) *Br (attempt)* **to have a bash (at sth/ at doing sth)** essayer (qch/de faire qch)⁰; **I'll give it a bash** je vais essayer un coup

The symbol ⁰ indicates that a translation is neutral.

2 vt (hit) cogner; (dent) cabosser
▸ voir aussi **bishop**

basket case ['bɑːskɪtkeɪs] n cinglé(e)
m,f, barjo mf

bastard [!] ['bɑːstəd] n (a) (contemptible person) salaud (salope)
m,f; **some bastard traffic warden
gave me a parking ticket** une salope de contractuelle m'a collé un
papillon
(b) (any man) **poor bastard!** le pauvre!; **lucky bastard!** le veinard!;
you sad bastard! pauvre mec ou
type, va!; **he's a clever bastard** il en
a dans le ciboulot; **her boyfriend's
a big bastard** son copain est un sacré mastard; **all right, you old bastard?** (as greeting) ça va, vieux?
(c) (thing) truc m chiant; **a bastard of
a job** un travail à la con; **this oven is
a bastard to clean** ce four est vraiment chiant à nettoyer; **I can't get
the bastard thing to start** j'arrive
pas à faire démarrer cette saloperie
(d) **it hurts like a bastard** ça fait
super ou vachement mal; **I raced
round the shops like a bastard all
day looking for a present** je me
suis tapé tous les magasins au pas
de course pendant toute la journée à
la recherche d'un cadeau; **I've been
working like a bastard while
you've been lying in your pit all
day** j'ai bossé comme un dingue
alors que toi tu t'es prélassé dans ton
pieu toute la journée

bat¹ [bæt] n (a) Péj (woman) **old bat**
vieille bique f (b) Am (drinking spree)
to be on a bat sortir prendre une
cuite ▸ voir aussi **hell**

bat² vi **to bat for the other side**
or **team** (of gay man) en être, être
pédé; (of lesbian) être gouine; **to
bat for both sides** or **teams** (of
bisexual) marcher à voile et à
vapeur

battered ['bætəd] adj Br bourré,
beurré, pété

battleaxe, Am **battleax** ['bætəlæks]
n (woman) dragon m, virago f

batty ['bætɪ] adj Br (a) (crazy) fêlé,
timbré (b) Injurieux (gay) pédé; **batty
boy** pédé m, tarlouze f, tantouze f

ⓘ Dans les sens (b), il s'agit à
l'origine d'un terme d'argot jamaïcain. L'homosexualité est toujours
un sujet tabou en Jamaïque, et
l'homophobie y est très prononcée.

bawl out [bɔːl] vt sép **to bawl sb
out** enguirlander qn, passer un
savon à qn

beak [biːk] n (a) (nose) quart de brie
m (b) (judge) juge□ m

beam [biːm] vt Hum **beam me up,
Scotty!** que quelqu'un me sorte de
là!

ⓘ Il s'agit de l'expression utilisée
par les membres d'équipage du vaisseau "Starship Enterprise" dans la
série télévisée américaine culte Star
Trek pour demander au technicien
de l'équipe (nommé Scotty) de les
ramener à bord du vaisseau grâce
à un rayon spécial. Aujourd'hui, on
utilise cette expression lorsque l'on
se trouve dans une situation très
désagréable, dont on voudrait bien
être sorti comme par miracle.

bean [biːn], **beaner** [biːnə(r)] n Am
Injurieux métèque mf (d'origine latino-
américaine)

bear [beə(r)] n (a) **he's like a bear
with a sore head** il est d'une humeur massacrante; Hum **does a
bear shit in the woods?** [!] ça me
paraît évident (b) (gay man) pédé m
macho et velu, bear m

beard [bɪəd] *n (woman going out with gay man)* = femme que fréquente un homosexuel de façon à dissimuler son homosexualité

beast [biːst] *n Am (ugly woman)* boudin *m*, cageot *m*

beat [biːt] *vt* (**a**) **to beat it,** *Am* **to beat feet** *(go away)* se tirer, se barrer (**b**) **to beat one's meat [!!]** *(masturbate)* se branler ▸ *voir aussi* **rap**

beat off [!!] *vi (masturbate)* se branler

beat-'em-up [ˈbiːtəmʌp] *n* = film ou jeu vidéo comportant de nombreuses bagarres

beater [ˈbiːtə(r)] *n Am (car)* (vieille) bagnole *f*, (vieux) tacot *m*

beaut [bjuːt] **1** *n (beautiful thing)* splendeur *f*; **his new hi-fi's a beaut** sa nouvelle chaîne est géniale
     2 *adj Austr* super, génial

beauty [ˈbjuːtɪ] **1** *n (beautiful thing)* splendeur *f*; **his new hi-fi's a beauty** sa nouvelle chaîne est géniale; **that black eye is a real beauty!** quel beau coquard!
     2 *exclam Br* **(you) beauty!** super!

beaver [!!] [ˈbiːvə(r)] *n (woman's genitals)* chatte *f*, cramouille *f*, chagatte *f*

bed [bed] *vt (have sex with)* coucher avec

beef [biːf] **1** *n (complaint)* **what's your beef?** c'est quoi, ton problème?; **my beef is with him** c'est avec lui que j'ai un problème
     2 *vi (complain)* râler (**about** à propos de)

beef up 1 *vt (army, campaign)* renforcer□; *(report, story)* étoffer□
     2 *vi (gain muscle)* se muscler□; **Jake Gyllenhaal has really beefed up for his latest role** Jake Gyllenhaal s'est vachement musclé pour son dernier rôle

beefcake [ˈbiːfkeɪk] *n (attractive men)* beaux mecs *mpl* musclés; *Br* **he's a real beefcake** il est vraiment bien foutu

beemer [ˈbiːmə(r)] *n (BMW)* BM *f*

beer goggles [ˈbɪəɡɒɡəlz] *npl* **are you telling me you shagged her?! did you have your beer goggles on?** [!] quoi? tu l'as sautée? t'étais bourré ou quoi?

ⓘ "Beer goggles" signifie littéralement "lunettes de bière". Cette expression fait référence au fait qu'après avoir consommé quelques bières, un individu est susceptible de trouver du charme même aux personnes qui en sont presque totalement dépourvues.

---

bee stings [ˈbiːstɪŋz] *npl (breasts)* œufs *mpl* sur le plat *(petite poitrine)*

beezer [ˈbiːzə(r)] *n Am (nose)* tarin *m*, blaire *m*

bell [bel] *n Br (phone call)* **to give sb a bell** passer un coup de fil à qn, bigophoner qn

bell-end [!!] [ˈbelʹend] *n* (**a**) *(head of penis)* gland *m* (**b**) *(contemptible man)* gland *m*, trou du cul *m*

bellyache [ˈbelɪeɪk] *vi* râler (**about** à propos de)

bellyful [ˈbelɪfʊl] *n* **to have had a bellyful of sb/sth** en avoir ras le bol de qn/qch

belt [belt] **1** *n (blow)* gnon *m*, pain *m*; **to give sb a belt in the face** flanquer un gnon *ou* un pain dans la tronche à qn
     2 *vt (hit) (person)* flanquer un gnon *ou* un pain à; *(ball)* flanquer un grand coup dans

3 vi (move quickly) **to belt along** aller à fond la caisse ou à toute blinde; **to belt down the stairs** descendre les escaliers à fond la caisse ou à toute blinde

belt up vi Br (be quiet) la fermer, la boucler; **belt up!** la ferme!, ta gueule!

belter ['beltə(r)] n Br **a belter of a goal** un but magnifique; **that last song was a belter** la dernière chanson était super

bend [bend] n **to be round the bend** être dingue ou cinglé; **to go round the bend** devenir dingue ou cinglé; **to drive sb round the bend** rendre qn dingue ou cinglé ▸ voir aussi **ear, elbow**

bender ['bendə(r)] n **(a)** (drinking session) beuverie f; **to go on a bender** aller se cuiter **(b)** Injurieux (homosexual) pédale f, tantouze f

ⓘ Dans la catégorie (b), ce terme perd son caractère injurieux quand il est utilisé par des homosexuels.

benjamins ['bendʒəmɪnz] npl Am fric m, blé m, maille f; **it's all about the benjamins** tout ça, c'est une question de fric

ⓘ Le billet de cent dollars représente Benjamin Franklin.

bent [bent] adj **(a)** Br Injurieux (homosexual) pédé; **as bent as a nine bob note** or **as a three pound note** pédé comme un phoque **(b)** Br (corrupt, dishonest) pourri, ripou; **he's as bent as a nine bob note** or **as a three pound note** c'est un vrai pourri **(c)** Am **bent out of shape** (angry, upset) dans tous ses états **(d)** Am **get bent!** [!] va te faire voir!

ⓘ Dans la catégorie (a), ce terme perd son caractère injurieux quand il est utilisé par des homosexuels.

berk [bɜːk] n Br andouille f, débile mf

bet [bet] vi **you bet!** y a intérêt!, un peu!; **he says he's sorry – I bet!** il dit qu'il regrette – c'est ça! ou mon œil, oui!

Betty ['betɪ] n canon m, bombe f

ⓘ Il s'agit à l'origine d'un terme de l'argot des surfeurs. Betty est l'un des personnages féminins de la bande dessinée américaine Les Flintstones.

bevvied ['bevɪd] adj Br bourré, beurré; **to get bevvied** se cuiter, prendre une cuite

bevvy ['bevɪ] n Br **(a)** (alcohol) alcool□ m, bibine f **(b)** (alcoholic drink) **to have a bevvy** boire un coup **(c)** (drinking session) beuverie f; **to go on the bevvy** aller se cuiter, aller prendre une cuite

bezzy ['bezɪ] Br **1** adj (best) meilleur□; **she's my bezzy mate** c'est ma meilleure pote

2 n (best friend) pote mf; **I hung out with my bezzies all weekend** je suis sorti avec mes potes tout le week-end

bi [baɪ] adj (abrév **bisexual**) bi

Bible-basher ['baɪbəlbæʃə(r)], **Bible-thumper** ['baɪbəlθʌmpə(r)] n grenouille f de bénitier

bi-curious [baɪ'kjʊərɪəs] adj = se dit d'une personne souhaitant, par simple curiosité, avoir des expériences homosexuelles

biddy ['bɪdɪ] n **old biddy** vieille bique f

biff [bɪf] *vt (person)* foutre un pain *ou* un gnon à; *(object)* foutre un grand coup dans

biffa, biffer ['bɪfə(r)] *n Br* mocheté *f*

big [bɪg] *adj* **(a) to be into sb/sth big time** *or* **in a big way** être dingue de qn/qch; **he's been doing smack big time** *or* **in a big way** depuis quelque temps il arrête pas de prendre de l'héro; **he's messed everything up big time** il a tout fait foirer dans les grandes largeurs; **did you have fun? – big time!** vous vous êtes bien amusés? – oui, vachement bien!

(b) to make a big deal out of sth faire tout un fromage de qch; **it's no big deal** c'est pas grave; *Ironique* **big deal!** la belle affaire!

(c) *Br* **big girl's blouse** *(wimp)* femmelette *f*

(d) to have big hair = avoir une coiffure bouffante tenue par une grande quantité de laque

(e) *Am* **big hitter** poids *m* lourd; **big house** *(prison)* taule *f*, placard *m*; **he's gone to the big house** on l'a mis à l'ombre

(f) big up to everyone in my class! un grand bonjour à tous mes camarades de classe! ▸ *voir aussi* **cheese, E, enchilada, mama, shot, smoke, wheel**

big up *vt sép* faire du battage à propos de; **to big oneself up** se faire mousser; **all the radio stations are bigging up his new album** toutes les stations de radio font un sacré battage autour de son dernier album

biggie, biggy ['bɪgɪ] *n* **it's going to be a biggie** *(new film, CD)* ça va faire un carton!; *(storm)* ça va faire mal!; **no biggie!** pas de problème!

bigwig ['bɪgwɪg] *n* huile *f*, grosse légume *f*, gros bonnet *m*

bike [baɪk] *n* **(a)** *Br* **on your bike!** *(go away)* casse-toi!, tire-toi!; *(don't talk nonsense)* n'importe quoi!; *(I don't believe you)* c'est ça! **(b) she's the town bike [!]** *(promiscuous)* il n'y a que le train qui ne lui soit pas passé dessus

Bill [bɪl] *n Br* **the (Old) Bill** les flics *mpl*

Billy No Mates [bɪlɪ'nəʊmeɪts] *n Br Hum* = individu peu populaire; **nobody's called me for days, what a Billy No Mates...** ça fait des jours que personne m'a appelé; j'ai pas d'amis...

bimbo ['bɪmbəʊ] *n (woman)* bimbo *f*

bin¹ [bɪn] *n (psychiatric hospital)* maison *f* de fous

bin² *vt Br (throw away)* flanquer à la poubelle; *(boyfriend, girlfriend)* larguer, plaquer

bingo wings ['bɪŋgəʊwɪŋz] *npl Br* **she's got really bad bingo wings** elle a le haut des bras tout flasque

ⓘ Le terme "bingo wings" signifie littéralement "ailes de bingo". Ceci s'explique par le fait qu'au bingo les gagnants doivent lever la main pour attirer l'attention de l'animateur et également parce que ce jeu est surtout prisé par les dames d'un certain âge, dont le haut des bras a parfois perdu sa fermeté initiale.

bint [bɪnt] *n Br* greluche *f*; **you stupid bint!** espèce d'andouille!

bird [bɜːd] *n* **(a)** *Br (woman, girlfriend)* nana *f*, gonzesse *f* **(b)** *Am (man)* mec *m* **(c)** *Am* **to give sb the bird** *(make fun of)* se foutre de la gueule de qn; *(gesture at)* faire un doigt d'honneur à qn; **to flip sb the bird** *(gesture at)* faire un doigt d'honneur à qn **(d)** *Br*

to do bird (serve a prison sentence) faire de la taule

birdbrain ['bɜːdbreɪn] n cervelle f d'oiseau

bishop ['bɪʃəp] n **to bang** or Br **bash the bishop [!]** (masturbate) se branler, se taper sur la colonne ▶ voir aussi **actress**

bit [bɪt] n (a) Br **a bit on the side** (man) amant♢ m; (woman) maîtresse♢ f; **she's a bit of all right!** elle est gironde! (b) Am (term of imprisonment) peine f de prison♢; **he did a bit in Fort Worth** il a fait de la taule à Fort Worth ▶ voir aussi **stuff**

bitch [bɪtʃ] 1 n (a) (nasty woman) salope f, garce f; **she's a real bitch to her husband** c'est une vraie garce avec son mari (b) (any woman) Br **the poor bitch** la pauvre; **the lucky bitch** la veinarde; **bitch fight** crêpage m de chignon (c) (thing) truc m chiant; **life's a bitch!** chienne de vie!; **I've had a bitch of a day** j'ai passé une sale journée; **her place is a bitch to find** sa maison est vraiment chiante à trouver

2 vi (a) Br (say nasty things) déblatérer (**about** contre) (b) (complain) râler (**about** à propos de)

bitch up vt sép **to bitch sth up** saloper qch

bitchface ['bɪtʃfeɪs] n connasse f; **I'm not going to the party if bitchface is gonna be there** je vais pas à la soirée si cette connasse y va aussi

bitchin' ['bɪtʃɪn] adj Am super, génial

bitch-slap ['bɪtʃslæp] Noir Am 1 n = gifle donnée avec la main grande ouverte

2 vt (a) (hit) = gifler quelqu'un avec la main grande ouverte (b) (publicly humiliate) foutre la honte à; **they got totally bitch-slapped by the under-18s side** ils se sont fait

dérouiller par l'équipe des moins de 18 ans

bitchy ['bɪtʃɪ] adj (person) salaud, dégueulasse; (remark) dégueulasse; **that was a bitchy thing to do** c'est vraiment salaud ou dégueulasse d'avoir fait ça

bite [baɪt] Am 1 vt **bite me!, bite my ass! [!]** va te faire voir!

2 vi (be bad) craindre; **this really bites!** ça craint vraiment!

biz [bɪz] n Br (abrév **business**) **it's the biz!** c'est impec'!

bizzies ['bɪzɪz] npl Br **the bizzies** (the police) les flics mpl

BJ [!!] [biː'dʒeɪ] n (abrév **blow-job**) pipe f; **to give sb a BJ** faire une pipe à qn

blab [blæb] 1 vt (tell) raconter♢

2 vi (a) (tell secret) vendre la mèche (b) (chatter) bavarder, jacasser

blabbermouth ['blæbəmaʊθ] n **he's a blabbermouth** il ne sait pas tenir sa langue

black [blæk] n (cannabis resin) hasch m, charas m, kif m

black man's wheels [blækmænz-'wiːlz] npl Br (BMW) BM f

Black Stump ['blæk'stʌmp] n Austr **beyond the Black Stump** en pleine cambrousse

bladdered ['blædəd] adj Br bourré, beurré, pété

blade [bleɪd] n (knife) lame f, surin m

blag [blæg] Br 1 n (robbery) braquage m

2 vt (a) (steal) piquer (b) (con) **to blag oneself sth** obtenir qch au culot; **to blag one's way in** resquiller

blah [blɑː] 1 n (a) (meaningless remarks, nonsense) blabla m, baratin m (b) **blah, blah, blah** (to avoid rep-

D'où tu me parles ?
Black American slang

Il existe de nombreux termes d'argot Noir américain, qui, bien que désormais largement utilisés en Amérique du Nord et en Grande-Bretagne, retiennent néanmoins leur identité afro-américaine. Ces termes portent la mention *Noir Am* dans ce dictionnaire. C'est dans le monde des musiciens, et particulièrement le monde des jazzmen des années trente, que tout un pan de l'argot Noir américain trouve ses origines. Le jargon des musiciens de jazz a par la suite été progressivement adopté par la jeunesse américaine.

Depuis le début des années 80, c'est le rap qui est une source importante de termes d'argot. L'orthographe de ces termes est souvent modifiée de façon à en transcrire fidèlement la prononciation (par ex. **ho**, **nigga**, **gangsta**). Le rap, en tant que forme d'expression d'une communauté défavorisée qui connaît un taux de criminalité très élevé, est une musique souvent violente, qui véhicule volontiers des clichés empreints de misogynie. Ceci dit, les paroles des chansons de rap portent souvent sur des sujets tels que le **bling**, à savoir les signes extérieurs de richesse clinquants (tout un pan de la "culture" rap fait l'apologie de la richesse). Certains rappers aiment parler du luxe de leur **crib** (maison), de leur **ice** (diamants) ainsi que de leurs **pimped-up rides** (voitures customisées).

Le rap continue d'exercer une très grande influence sur la façon dont s'expriment les jeunes – comme en témoigne l'apparition récente du terme **wigger** (qui est la contraction de "white nigger"), que l'on emploie de manière péjorative pour parler des Blancs qui adoptent le langage et la culture des Noirs.

---

etition) etc etc; **he went on for half an hour about how we all had to work harder, blah, blah, blah** il nous a rabâché pendant une demi-heure qu'il fallait qu'on fasse tous plus d'efforts, etc etc
2 *adj (dull)* sans intérêt⁰

blank [blæŋk] *n* **to shoot** *or* **fire blanks** *(of man)* être stérile⁰

blarney ['blɑːnɪ] *n Br* **to have a blarney (with sb)** tailler une bavette (avec qn)

blast [blɑːst] **1** *n Am (good time)* **it was a blast** c'était l'éclate; **we had a blast** on s'est éclatés
2 *exclam Br* **blast (it)!** crotte!, zut!

blasted ['blɑːstɪd] **1** *adj* (a) *(drunk)* bourré, beurré; *(on drugs)* défoncé (b) *(for emphasis)* **the blasted car** cette saleté de voiture; **the blasted child** ce sale môme; **it's a blasted nuisance** c'est sacrément embêtant
2 *adv (for emphasis)* **don't go so**

The symbol ⁰ indicates that a translation is neutral.

blasted fast! ne va pas si vite, bon sang!

blazes ['bleɪzɪz] *npl* (**a**) **to run/work like blazes** courir/travailler comme un(e) fou (folle) (**b**) **what/who/why the blazes...?** que/qui/pourquoi diable...? (**c**) **go** *or* Br **get to blazes!** va au diable!

bleeder ['bliːdə(r)] *n* Br (person) salaud (salope) *m,f*; **the poor bleeder** le pauvre; **you lucky bleeder!** sacré veinard!

bleeding ['bliːdɪŋ] *Br* **1** *adj* (for emphasis) **you bleeding idiot!** espèce de con!; **what a bleeding nuisance!** quelle saloperie!

2 *adv* (for emphasis) foutrement; **you're bleeding (well) coming with me!** tu viens avec moi, un point c'est tout!; **that was bleeding stupid!** c'est vraiment con, ce que tu as fait/dit!

blighter ['blaɪtə(r)] *n* (person) zigoto *m*; (thing) truc *m*, bidule *m*; **you cheeky blighter!** tu as un sacré culot toi!; **there's a wasp in the room and I'm terrified of the little blighters!** il y a une guêpe dans la pièce et j'ai horreur de ces bestioles!

Blighty ['blaɪtɪ] *n* Br Hum (Britain) Grande-Bretagne□ *f*; **it's great to be back in good old Blighty!** ça fait du bien d'être rentré au pays!

blimey ['blaɪmɪ] *exclam* Br zut alors!, la vache!

blinder ['blaɪndə(r)] *n* Br (**a**) (drinking session) beuverie *f*; **to go on a blinder** aller se cuiter, aller prendre une cuite (**b**) (excellent performance) sacrée prestation *f*; **to play a blinder** faire un match/une partie d'enfer

blinding ['blaɪndɪŋ] *adj* Br (excellent) super, génial

bling (bling) [blɪŋ('blɪŋ)] **1** *n* (jewellery) bijoux□ *mpl*, quincaillerie *f*

2 *adj* (ostentatious) tape-à-l'œil; **that car is so bling (bling)!** cette voiture est vraiment tape-à-l'œil!

3 *vi* (show off) frimer, taper la frime

ⓘ Il s'agit d'une onomatopée censée reproduire le bruit de bijoux que l'on agite. Il s'agit à l'origine d'un terme d'argot Noir américain mais on le rencontre également dans d'autres pays anglophones.

---

blingin' ['blɪŋɪn] *adj* tape-à-l'œil; **that car is blingin'!** cette voiture est vraiment tape-à-l'œil!

blink [blɪŋk] *n* Br **to be on the blink** (of TV, machine) déconner

blinking ['blɪŋkɪŋ] *Br* **1** *adj* (for emphasis) sacré; **the blinking thing won't work!** pas moyen de faire marcher cette saloperie!

2 *adv* (for emphasis) sacrément; **you're so blinking stubborn!** ce que tu peux être têtu!

blitzed [blɪtst] *adj* (drunk) bourré, beurré; (on drugs) défoncé

bloater ['bləʊtə(r)] *n* Br (male) gros bonhomme *m*; (female) grosse bonne femme *f*

blob [blɒb] *n* Br **to be on the blob [!]** avoir ses ragnagnas *ou* ses ours

block [blɒk] *n* (**a**) Am (neighbourhood) quartier□ *m* (**b**) **to have been around the block a few times** avoir roulé sa bosse (**c**) (head) caboche *f*; **I'll knock your block off!** je vais te démolir le portrait!

bloke [bləʊk] *n* Br type *m*, mec *m*

blokeish ['bləʊkɪʃ], **blokey** ['bləʊkɪ] *adj* Br = typique d'un style de vie caractérisé par de fréquentes sorties entre copains, généralement copieu-

sement arrosées, et un goût prononcé pour le sport et les activités
de groupe

blonde [blɒnd] *adj* **a blonde joke**
une histoire de blondes; *Hum* **to
have a blonde moment** avoir un
passage à vide

ⓘ Dans le monde anglo-saxon, les
blondes sont la cible de très nombreuses plaisanteries où elles apparaissent généralement comme
des femmes séduisantes mais peu
intelligentes et manquant de bon
sens, d'où l'expression "to have a
blonde moment" (avoir un passage
à vide).

bloody [!] ['blʌdɪ] *Br* **1** *adj (for emphasis)* **you bloody idiot!** espèce de
con!; **bloody hell!** putain!; **where's
my bloody pen?** où est ce putain
de stylo?

2 *adv (for emphasis)* foutrement;
it's bloody hot! il fait foutrement
chaud!, il fait une chaleur à crever!;
it was bloody brilliant! putain,
c'était génial!; *Ironique* **that's just
bloody marvellous!** il manquait
plus que ça!; **I wish he'd bloody
stop it!** quand est-ce qu'il va
s'arrêter, merde!

blooming ['bluːmɪŋ] *Br* **1** *adj (for emphasis)* **I've lost my blooming keys**
j'ai perdu ces saletés de clefs

2 *adv (for emphasis)* sacrément;
he's blooming useless! il est vraiment nul!

blooper ['bluːpə(r)] *n Am* gaffe *f*,
faux pas□ *m*

blooter ['bluːtə(r)] *vt Scot* = donner
un grand coup de pied dans

blootered ['bluːtəd] *adj Scot (drunk)*
pété, bourré, beurré

blotto ['blɒtəʊ] *adj* complètement

paf *ou* pété, bourré comme un
coing

blow [bləʊ] **1** *n Br (cannabis)* shit *m*;
Am (cocaine) coke *f*, neige *f*; *(heroin)*
héro *f*, blanche *f*

2 *vt* **(a) to blow a gasket** *or* **a fuse**
(of person) péter une durite, péter
les plombs; **to blow one's top** *or*
one's stack péter une durite, péter
les plombs; **it blew my mind!** *(of
film, experience)* ça m'a complètement emballé!

(b) *(reveal)* **to blow the gaff** vendre
la mèche

(c) to blow the whistle on sb balancer qn; **to blow the whistle on
sth** dénoncer qch□

(d) *(waste) (chance)* gâcher; **we
should have won but we blew it**
on aurait dû gagner mais on a tout
fait foirer; **that's blown it!** ça a tout
fait foirer!

(e) *(money)* claquer; **he blows all his
salary on holidays/Playstation®
games** il claque tout son salaire en
voyages/jeux de Playstation®; **they
blew £2,000 on an engagement
ring** ils ont claqué 2 000 livres dans
une bague de fiançailles

(f) [!!] *(fellate)* tailler une pipe à

(g) *Am (leave)* **let's blow this joint!**
allez, tirons-nous de là!, allez, on se
casse!

(h) *Am* **to blow chunks** *(vomit)* gerber, dégobiller

3 *vi* **(a)** *(be bad)* craindre, être nul
ou merdique; **this bar/movie really
blows** ce bar/film est vraiment nul

(b) *(leave)* se tirer, se casser; **c'mon
guys, let's blow!** allez, tirons-nous!,
allez, on se casse!

blow away *vt sép* **(a)** *Am* **to blow
sb away** *(shoot dead)* flinguer qn,
descendre qn; *(defeat)* flanquer une
raclée à qn **(b) to blow sb away**
(impress) complètement emballer
qn; **the Grand Canyon just blew**

me away le Grand Canyon m'a coupé le souffle

blow off *vt sép Am* **(a)** **to blow sb off** *(not turn up)* poser un lapin à qn; *(ignore)* snober qn□ **(b)** **to blow sth off** *(abandon, forget about)* laisser tomber qch, oublier qch; **let's blow that meeting off and go shoot some pool!** oublions cette réunion et allons faire un billard!

blower ['bləʊə(r)] *n Br (telephone)* bigophone *m*

blow-job [!!] ['bləʊdʒɒb] *n* pipe *f*; **to give sb a blow-job** tailler une pipe à qn

blub [blʌb] *Br* **1** *vi* chialer comme un veau

2 *n* **I had a bit of a blub at the end of the film** j'ai un peu chialé à la fin du film

blubber ['blʌbə(r)] **1** *vi Br* chialer comme un veau

2 *n* **(a)** *Br (cry)* **I had a bit of a blubber at the end of the film** j'ai un peu chialé à la fin du film **(b)** *(fat)* graisse *f*, gras *m*; **I really need to shift some of this blubber before my holiday** il faut vraiment que je perde un peu de gras avant mes vacances

bludge [blʌdʒ] *vi Austr* **(a)** *(shirk responsibilities)* se défiler **(b)** *(cadge)* quémander□ **(c)** *(live off the State)* vivre en parasite de la société□

bludger ['blʌdʒə(r)] *n Austr* **(a)** *(shirker)* tire-au-flanc *m* **(b)** *(cadger)* pique-assiette *mf inv*, parasite□ *m* **(c)** *(who lives off the State)* parasite *m* de la société□

blue [bluː] *adj* **(a)** **to feel blue** *(depressed)* avoir le cafard **(b)** *(obscene)* **to tell blue jokes** en raconter des vertes et des pas mûres; **blue movie** film *m* porno **(c)** *(idioms)* **I've told you so until I'm blue in the face** je

me tue à te le dire; **to scream blue murder** crier comme un putois; *Am* **he talks a blue streak** il n'arrête pas de jacasser

blue-arsed fly [!] ['bluːɑːstˈflaɪ] *n Br* **to run about** *or* **around like a blue-arsed fly** courir dans tous les sens

blues [bluːz] *npl* **to have the blues** *(be depressed)* avoir le cafard; *Am* **to sing the blues** *(complain)* geindre□, pleurnicher

BM [biːˈem] *n Am (abrév* **bowel movement***)* **to have a BM** aller à la selle□

boak [bəʊk] *vi Scot* dégueuler, gerber

boat [bəʊt] *n Br* **boat (race)** *(rhyming slang* **face***)* tronche *f*, trombine *f*

Bob [bɒb] *npr Br* **...and Bob's your uncle!** ...et le tour est joué!

bobby ['bɒbɪ] *n Br* flic *m*

bobo ['bəʊbəʊ] *n (abrév* **bohemian bourgeois***)* bobo *mf*

bockety ['bɒkətɪ] *adj Ir* de traviole; **the bike's got a bockety wheel** le vélo a une roue voilée

bod [bɒd] *n (abrév* **body***)* **(a)** *Br (person)* individu□ *m*; **he's a bit of an odd bod** c'est un drôle de numéro ou de zèbre **(b)** *(physique)* corps□ *m*; **she's got a great bod** elle est super bien roulée ou foutue

bodacious [bəʊˈdeɪʃəs] *adj Am* incroyable

bog [!] [bɒg] *n Br (toilet)* chiottes *fpl*; **bog roll** papier cul *m*, PQ *m*

bog off [!] *vi Br* se barrer, se casser; **bog off!** *(go away)* barre-toi!, casse-toi!; *(expressing contempt, disagreement)* va te faire voir!

bogan ['bəʊgən] *n Austr* prolo *mf* beauf

bogart [ˈbəʊɡɑːt] *vt* **to bogart a joint** squatter un joint, bogarter

bogey [ˈbəʊɡɪ] *n Br (nasal mucus)* crotte *f* de nez

boggin' [ˈbɒɡɪn] *adj Scot* dégueulasse; **that pizza was boggin'!** cette pizza était vraiment dégueulasse!; **I don't know why you fancy him, he's boggin'** je ne vois pas ce que tu lui trouves, c'est une vraie mocheté; **she was wearing these really boggin' shoes** elle portait des chaussures hyper moches

bog-standard [bɒɡˈstændəd] *adj Br* tout ce qu'il y a d'ordinaire

bog-trotter [ˈbɒɡtrɒtə(r)] *n* (**a**) *Injurieux (Irish person)* Irlandais(e)□ *m,f* (**b**) *(country bumpkin)* plouc *m*, péquenaud *m*

Pleins feux sur...

Body parts

En argot anglais il existe des termes argotiques pour désigner de nombreuses parties du corps et pas seulement les organes sexuels (ceux-ci font l'objet d'un encadré p. 156). Tout en haut se trouve votre **nut**, **noggin**, ou encore **bonce** (tête), sur laquelle pousse votre **barnet** ("Barnet Fair" = "hair" = cheveux, en "rhyming slang"), à moins, bien entendu, que vous ne soyez un **slaphead** (chauve). Sur votre **boat race** (terme de "rhyming slang" qui remplace "face" = visage) se trouvent vos **peepers** (yeux, du verbe "to peep"), votre **conk**, **beak**, ou **hooter** (nez), ainsi que votre **gob** ou **cakehole** (bouche); de part et d'autre se dressent vos **lugs** ou **lugholes** (oreilles). Un peu plus bas, les femmes possèdent une paire de **boobs**, **tits**, **jugs**, **knockers**, **baps**... et la liste n'est pas exhaustive. La plupart d'entre elles tâchent d'éviter le **muffin top** (bourrelet de graisse au niveau de la taille, qui dépasse du pantalon), ainsi que les **thunderthighs** (jambonneaux) et les **bingo wings** (haut des bras flasque); les hommes, pour leur part, rêvent d'avoir des **pecs** (pectoraux) et un **six-pack** (tablette de chocolat) et redoutent le **spare tyre** (pneu de secours) et les **love handles** (poignées d'amour). À l'extrémité des bras se trouvent les **paws** ou **mitts**. Toujours en descendant, on trouvera le **butt** (postérieur), que les Britanniques appellent également **bum** (attention, ce terme signifie "clochard" en anglais américain), et dans un registre plus grossier **arse**; en anglais américain on dit **ass**, **can** ou encore **fanny** (terme qui désigne le sexe de la femme en anglais britannique !). Enfin viennent les **pins** (jambes), à l'extrémité desquelles se trouvent les **plates** (en "rhyming slang", "plates of meat" = "feet"), que les Américains nomment **dogs**.

The symbol □ indicates that a translation is neutral.

bogus ['bəʊgəs] *adj Am (unpleasant)* chiant; *(unfashionable)* ringard

bohunk ['bəʊhʌŋk] *n Am* **(a)** *Injurieux (Eastern European immigrant)* = terme désignant un Américain originaire d'un pays d'Europe de l'Est ou ses descendants **(b)** *(country bumpkin)* bouseux(euse) *m,f*

boiler ['bɔɪlə(r)] *n Péj* **(old) boiler** vieille peau *f* ▸ *voir aussi* **bunny**

boink [bɔɪŋk] *Am* **1** *n* **to have a boink** faire une partie de jambes en l'air
2 *vt* s'envoyer en l'air avec
3 *vi* faire une partie de jambes en l'air

Bolivian marching powder [bə-'lɪvɪən'mɑːtʃɪŋpaʊdə(r)] *n Hum (cocaine)* coco *f*, coke *f*, reniflette *f*

bollock [!] ['bɒlək] *Br* **1** *adv* **bollock naked** à poil, le cul à l'air
2 *vt* **to bollock sb** engueuler qn, passer un savon à qn

bollocking [!] ['bɒləkɪŋ] *n Br* engueulade *f*, savon *m*; **to give sb a bollocking** engueuler qn, passer un savon à qn; **to get a bollocking** se faire engueuler, se faire passer un savon

bollocks [!] ['bɒləks] *Br* **1** *npl* **(a)** *(testicles)* couilles *fpl* **(b)** *(nonsense)* conneries *fpl*; **the film was a load of bollocks** c'était de la merde, ce film **(c) bollocks to him!** qu'il aille se faire foutre! **it's the (dog's) bollocks** c'est super *ou* génial
2 *exclam* **(a)** *(expressing annoyance)* quelles conneries!; **oh, bollocks, I've got no money on me!** quelle merde *ou* quelle connerie, je n'ai pas d'argent sur moi! **(b)** *(nonsense)* des conneries, tout ça!

bollocks up [!] *vt sép* **to bollocks sth up** *(interview, exam)* foirer qch, se planter à qch; *(plan, arrangement)* faire foirer qch

bolshie, bolshy ['bɒlʃɪ] *adj Br* râleur

bomb [bɒm] **1** *n* **(a)** *Br* **to go like a bomb** *(of fast car)* être un vrai bolide; *(of party)* se passer super bien; **he/the car was going like a bomb** il/la voiture roulait à fond la caisse **(b)** *Br (large sum of money)* **to cost a bomb** coûter bonbon *ou* la peau des fesses; **to make a bomb** se faire un fric fou **(c)** *Am (failure)* bide *m* **(d) she's da** *or* **the b.** elle est super; **that's da bomb!** c'est super!, c'est le top!
2 *vt Am (fail) (test)* se planter complètement à
3 *vi* **(a)** *(fail) (of film)* faire un four *ou* un bide; *Am (of student)* se planter complètement **(b) to bomb along** aller à fond la caisse *ou* à toute blinde

bomb out 1 *vt sép Br* **to bomb sb out** poser un lapin à qn
2 *vi (fail)* se faire sortir; **to bomb out of sth** se faire éjecter de qch

bombed [bɒmd] *adj (drunk)* bourré, beurré; *(on drugs)* défoncé

bomber ['bɒmə(r)] *n (cannabis cigarette)* cône *m*

bonce [bɒns] *n Br* caboche *f*, ciboulot *m*

bone [!!] [bəʊn] **1** *vt* baiser, troncher, tringler
2 *vi* baiser, s'envoyer en l'air

bone up on *vt insép* **to bone up on sth** potasser qch

bonehead ['bəʊnhed] *Am* **1** *n* débile *mf*, crétin(e) *m,f*
2 *adj* débile

boner ['bəʊnə(r)] *n* **(a)** *(erection)* **to have a boner** [!!] bander, avoir la trique **(b)** *Am (mistake)* bourde *f*, boulette *f*

bong [bɒŋ] *n* pipe *f* à eau□, bang *m*

bonk [bɒŋk] *Br* **1** *n* **to have a bonk**

faire une partie de jambes en l'air

2 vt s'envoyer en l'air avec

3 vi faire une partie de jambes en l'air

bonkers ['bɒŋkəz] adj cinglé, fêlé, dingue, tapé

bonzer ['bɒnzə(r)] Austr **1** adj vachement bien, super, génial

2 exclam **bonzer!** super!, génial!

bonzo ['bɒnzəʊ] adj Am cinglé, fêlé, dingue, tapé

boob [buːb] **1** n (a) (breast) nichon m; **to have a boob job** se faire refaire les nichons; **boob tube** (garment) bustier m extensible□; Hum **he's got man boobs** on dirait qu'il a des nichons (b) Br (mistake) boulette f, bourde f; **to make a boob** faire une boulette (c) Am (person) abruti(e) m,f, andouille f, courge f; **boob tube** (television) téloche f

2 vi Br (make mistake) faire une bourde ou une boulette

boo-boo ['buːbuː] n Am boulette f, bourde f; **to make a boo-boo** faire une boulette ou une bourde

booger ['buːgə(r)] n Am (a) (nasal mucus) crotte f de nez (b) (person) garnement□ m (c) (thing) bidule m, machin m, truc m

boogie ['buːgɪ] **1** n (dance) **to have a boogie** danser□, guincher

2 vi (a) (dance) danser□, guincher (b) Am (leave) mettre les bouts, se casser, s'arracher; **let's boogie on out of here** on met les bouts, on se casse

book [bʊk] Am **1** vt **to book it** (leave) mettre les bouts, se casser, s'arracher; **let's book it!** on se casse!, on s'arrache!

2 vi (a) (leave) mettre les bouts, se casser, s'arracher (b) (move quickly) foncer

boondocks ['buːndɒks], **boonies**

['buːnɪz] npl Am **the boondocks, the boonies** la cambrousse; **in the boondocks** or **the boonies** en pleine cambrousse

boost [buːst] Am **1** vt (a) (steal) piquer, faucher (b) (break into) cambrioler□

2 vi (steal) voler□

boot [buːt] **1** n (a) (kick) **to give sth a boot** donner un coup de latte dans qch; Br **he was trying to get up when they put the boot in** il essayait de se relever quand ils se sont mis à lui donner des coups de latte; Br **he'd already apologized, you didn't have to put the boot in like that** il s'était excusé, tu n'avais pas besoin d'insister à ce point□

(b) **to give sb the boot** (fire) virer qn; **to get the boot** (get fired) se faire virer

(c) Br Péj (ugly woman) **(old) boot** boudin m, cageot m

(d) **fill your boots!** prends-en autant que tu veux!; **can I have some more cake? – fill your boots, there's loads left!** est-ce que je peux reprendre du gâteau? – vas-y, sers-toi, il en reste plein!

2 vt (kick) donner un coup de latte/des coups de latte à

3 vi (vomit) dégueuler, gerber

boot out vt sép **to boot sb out** foutre qn à la porte, vider qn

booty ['buːtɪ] n (a) (buttocks) cul m, derche m; **to shake one's booty** s'éclater en dansant (b) (sexual intercourse) **to get some booty** s'envoyer en l'air; **to make a booty call** = passer un coup de fil à son ami ou amie dans l'espoir qu'il ou elle sera d'humeur pour une partie de jambes en l'air; **to send sb a booty text** = envoyer un SMS à son ami ou amie dans l'espoir qu'il ou elle sera d'humeur pour une partie de jambes en l'air

bootylicious [buːtɪˈlɪʃəs] *adj* bien foutu

booze [buːz] **1** *n* (a) alcool⁰ *m*, bibine *f*; **to be on the booze** picoler; *Br* **booze cruise** *(to buy alcohol in France)* = excursion d'une journée pour aller acheter de l'alcool en France; *(boat trip)* = croisière au cours de laquelle les participants s'enivrent systématiquement (b) *Austr* **booze bus** = patrouille de police qui arrête les automobilistes au hasard pour leur faire passer l'alcootest
   2 *vi* picoler

boozed up [buːzdˈʌp] *adj Br (drunk)* bourré, beurré, pété; **to get boozed up** prendre une cuite

boozehound [ˈbuːzhaʊnd] *n Am* ivrogne *mf*, poivrot(e) *m,f*

boozer [ˈbuːzə(r)] *n* (a) *Br (pub)* pub⁰ *m*, troquet *m* (b) *(person)* ivrogne *mf*, poivrot(e) *m,f*

booze-up [ˈbuːzʌp] *n* beuverie *f*; **to have a booze-up** prendre une cuite

boozy [ˈbuːzɪ] *adj (person)* qui aime picoler; *(occasion)* où l'on picole beaucoup

bop¹ [bɒp] *Br* **1** *n (dance)* **to have a bop** danser⁰, guincher
   2 *vi (dance)* danser⁰, guincher

bop² **1** *n (punch)* coup *m* de poing⁰, ramponneau *m*; **she gave him a bop on the head** elle lui a donné un coup de poing dans la tête
   2 *vt (hit)* frapper⁰; **she bopped him on the head** elle lui a donné un coup de poing dans la tête

boracic [bəˈræsɪk] *adj Br (rhyming slang* **boracic lint = skint**) fauché, à sec, sans un

boss [bɒs] *adj Br (excellent)* super; **you're looking boss!** tu es superbe!

bottle [ˈbɒtəl] **1** *n* (a) *Br (courage)* courage⁰ *m*, cran *m*; **he lost his bottle** il s'est dégonflé (b) *(alcohol)* **the bottle** l'alcool⁰ *m*; **to be on the bottle** picoler; **to hit the bottle** se mettre à picoler
   2 *vt Br* **to bottle it** se dégonfler; **he was going to ask her out but he bottled it** il allait lui demander de sortir avec lui mais il s'est dégonflé

bottle out *vi Br* se dégonfler; **he bottled out of the fight** il s'est dégonflé au dernier moment et a refusé de se battre; **he bottled out of telling her the truth** finalement il a eu la trouille de lui dire la vérité

bottom feeder [ˈbɒtəmfiːdə(r)] *n (person)* moins *mf* que rien

---

ⓘ Au sens littéral, ce terme désigne les poissons qui se nourrissent d'organismes se trouvant au fond des lacs, des rivières ou des océans.

---

botty [ˈbɒtɪ] *n* fesses⁰ *fpl*

bounce [baʊns] *n Br* **on the bounce** de suite; **they won three games on the bounce** ils ont gagné trois matchs de suite

bouncer [ˈbaʊnsə(r)] *n (doorman)* videur *m*

Bourke [bɔːk] *n Austr* **in the back of Bourke** en pleine cambrousse

---

ⓘ Bourke est une petite ville au fin fond de la Nouvelle-Galles du Sud, en Australie.

---

bowfin' [ˈbaʊfɪn] *adj Scot* dégueulasse; **that meal she cooked was bowfin'!** le repas qu'elle a préparé était vraiment dégueulasse!; **it's bowfin' in here!** *(smelly)* qu'est-ce que ça schlingue ici!

Le symbole [!] dénote un terme très familier, [!!] un terme vulgaire.

box | 25 | **breeder**

box [bɒks] *n* (a) *Br* **to be out of one's box** *(drunk)* être complètement pété, être plein comme une barrique; *(on drugs)* être complètement défoncé (b) **the box** *(television)* la télé, la téloche (c) **[!!]** *(vagina)* chatte *f*, con *m*

boyf [bɔɪf] *n Br (abrév* **boyfriend)** **my/her boyf** mon/son mec

boy [bɔɪ] *n* (a) **the boys** *(friends)* les copains; **he's gone out for a couple of drinks with the boys** il est sorti boire un coup avec les copains; **pay up or we'll send the boys round!** *(tough guys)* donne le fric sinon on envoie nos malabars!; *Br* **the boys in blue** les flics *mpl*, les poulets *mpl*; **Our Boys** *(armed forces)* nos soldats⁰ *mpl*; *(national sports team)* nos joueurs⁰ *mpl* (b) *Br & Austr* **boy racer** jeune conducteur *m* imprudent (c) *Am Hum* **boy toy** jeune amant⁰ *m (d'une femme plus âgée)*

ⓘ Le "boy racer" est un jeune homme qui vient d'obtenir son permis de conduire et dont l'activité principale consiste à faire des tours en voiture avec ses copains, sans destination précise, pied au plancher, toutes vitres baissées tout en écoutant de la musique à plein volume.

boyz [bɔːz] *nmpl Am* **the boyz** les flics *mpl*, les poulets *mpl*

bozo ['bəʊzəʊ] *n Am* crétin(e) *m,f*, andouille *f*, cruche *f*

bracelets ['breɪslɪts] *npl (handcuffs)* menottes⁰ *fpl*, bracelets *mpl*

Brahms and Liszt ['brɑːmzən'lɪst] *adj Br (rhyming slang* **pissed)** bourré, pété, fait

brain [breɪn] **1** *n* (a) **to have brains** en avoir dans le ciboulot; *Br* **to have** sth on the brain faire une fixette sur qch; *Am* **brain bucket** casque⁰ *m (de soldat)* (b) *(person)* tête *f*; **he's a real brain** c'est une vraie tête

2 *vt (hit)* donner un coup sur la cafetière à

brand new ['brænd'njuː] *adj Scot* super, génial, géant; **his new girl-friend's brand new** sa nouvelle copine est une perle

brass [brɑːs] *n Br* (a) *(money)* blé *m*, flouze *m* (b) **brass (neck)** *(cheek, nerve)* culot *m*, toupet *m*; **to have a brass neck** être culotté; **to have the brass (neck) to do sth** avoir le culot de faire qch (c) **it's brass monkeys** *or* **brass monkey weather** *(very cold)* il fait un froid de canard (d) **the top brass** les huiles *fpl* (e) *(prostitute)* pute *f*

brass off *vt sép* **to brass sb off** gonfler qn; **to be brassed off (with)** en avoir marre (de)

brassic ['bræsɪk] *Br* = **boracic**

bread [bred] *n* (a) *(money)* blé *m*, oseille *f* (b) *Br* **it's the best thing since sliced bread** c'est ce qu'on a fait de mieux depuis l'invention du fil à couper le beurre (c) *Br* **bread knife** *(rhyming slang* **wife)** bonne femme *f*, bourgeoise *f*, moitié *f*

break [breɪk] *n* **give me a break!** *(don't talk nonsense)* dis pas n'importe quoi!; *(stop nagging)* fiche-moi la paix! ▸ *voir aussi* **balls**

breeder ['briːdə(r)] *n Péj (heterosexual)* hétéro *mf*

ⓘ Il s'agit d'un terme dont la traduction littérale est "reproducteur". Ce mot n'est utilisé que par certains homosexuels par dérision envers les hétérosexuels.

breeze [briːz] *n* it was a breeze *(simple)* c'était du gâteau ▸ *voir aussi* **shoot**

brekky, brekkie ['brekɪ] *n Br (abrév* **breakfast**) petit déj *m*

brew [bruː] *n* (**a**) *Br (tea)* thé⁰ *m*; **fancy a brew?** tu veux un thé? (**b**) *Am (beer)* mousse *f*

brewer's droop ['bruːəz'druːp] *n Br Hum* = impuissance temporaire due à l'alcool; **he had brewer's droop** il bandait mou parce qu'il avait trop picolé

brewski ['bruːskɪ] *n Am* mousse *f*

brick [brɪk] **1** *n* **to be one brick short of a load** ne pas être net
2 *vt Br* **to brick it** les avoir à zéro; **they were absolutely bricking it when they saw the cops coming** ils les avaient vraiment à zéro quand ils ont vu les flics approcher

brill [brɪl] *adj Br (abrév* **brilliant**) super, génial

bring off [!!] ['brɪŋ] *vt sép (masturbate)* **to bring sb off** branler qn; **to bring oneself off** se branler

bristols ['brɪstəlz] *npl Br (rhyming slang* **Bristol Cities** = **titties**) nichons *mpl*, roberts *mpl*

ⓘ Bristol City est le nom d'une équipe de football de Bristol.

Brit [brɪt] **1** *n (abrév* **Britisher**) Angliche *mf*
2 *adj (abrév* **British**) angliche

Britneys ['brɪtnɪz] *npl Br (rhyming slang* **Britney Spears** = **beers**) bibines *fpl*, bières⁰ *fpl*

bro [brəʊ] *n (abrév* **brother**) (**a**) *(family member)* frangin *m*, frérot *m* (**b**) *Am (male friend)* pote *m*; **yo, bro!** salut mon pote! (**c**) *Am (black man)* = Noir américain; **go ask that bro**

over there va demander au Noir, là-bas

broad [brɔːd] *n Am (woman)* gonzesse *f*, nana *f*

broke [brəʊk] *adj (having no money)* fauché, raide; **to go for broke** jouer le tout pour le tout

brolly ['brɒlɪ] *n Br* pébroc *m*, pépin *m*

brother ['brʌðə(r)] *n Noir Am (black male)* = Noir américain; **a brother got capped last night** un des nôtres s'est fait buter hier soir ▸ *voir aussi* **soul**

brown bread ['braʊn'bred] *n Br (rhyming slang* **dead**) clamsé, crevé

browned-off ['braʊnd'ɒf] *adj Br* **to be browned-off (with)** en avoir marre (de); **to be browned-off with doing sth** en avoir marre de faire qch

brown-nose [!] ['braʊnnəʊz] **1** *n* lèche-cul *mf*
2 *vi* faire de la lèche

bruiser [bruːzə(r)] *n* (**a**) *(big man)* malabar *m* (**b**) *(fighter)* cogneur⁰ *m*

Brum [brʌm] *npr Br (abrév* **Birmingham**) = surnom donné à la ville de Birmingham

Brummie ['brʌmɪ] **1** *n Br* = natif de la ville de Birmingham
2 *adj* de Birmingham

bruv [brʌv] *n Br* (**a**) *(brother)* frangin *m*, frérot *m* (**b**) *(male friend)* pote *m*; **hey, bruv!** salut mon pote!

BS [biː'es] *n Am (abrév* **bullshit**) conneries *fpl*

bubba ['bʌbə] *n Am* (**a**) *(term of address)* mec *m*, vieux *m*; **hey bubba, gimme a smoke!** hé, vieux! file-moi une clope! (**b**) *Péj (redneck)* plouc *m (du sud des États-Unis)*

bubbly ['bʌblɪ] *n Br (champagne)* champ' *m*

buck [bʌk] n Am (dollar) dollar‍□ m; **bucks** fric m; **to make a buck** gagner sa croûte; **to make a fast buck** faire du fric facilement

Buckley's ['bʌklɪz] n Austr **you don't have a Buckley's (chance)** tu n'as aucune chance

buck-naked [bʌk'neɪkɪd] adj à poil, le cul à l'air

buddy ['bʌdɪ] n (a) (friend) pote m (b) (term of address) **thanks, buddy** (to friend) merci, vieux; (to stranger) merci, chef; **hey, buddy!** hé, toi!

buddy up vi **to buddy up to sb** faire de la lèche à qn

buddy-buddy ['bʌdɪbʌdɪ] adj Am Péj copain-copain; **they're very buddy-buddy** ils sont très copain-copain

buff [bʌf] **1** n **in the buff** à poil
2 adj (attractive) canon inv; (muscular) balèze, qui a des biscoteaux; **he's down the gym trying to get buff for his new girlfriend** il est à la salle de gym, il travaille ses biscoteaux pour plaire à sa nouvelle copine

bug [bʌg] **1** vt (annoy, nag) enquiquiner, emmerder (**about** à cause de); (bother) turlupiner; **what's bugging him?** qu'est-ce qui le turlupine?
2 n Am **bug doctor** (psychiatrist) psychiatre‍□ m

bug off vi Am (leave) se casser, s'arracher; **bug off!** casse-toi!

bug out vi Am (a) (leave) se casser, s'arracher (b) (go mad) déjanter

bugger [!] ['bʌgə(r)] Br **1** n (a) (person) salaud m; **the poor bugger** le pauvre; **the silly bugger** cet espèce d'imbécile; **to play silly buggers** faire le con (b) (thing) truc m chiant; **a bugger of a job** un travail à la con; **her house is a bugger to find** sa maison est vachement dure à trouver (c) **bugger all** (nothing) que

dalle; **bugger all money/thanks** pas un sou/un merci; **that was bugger all help** ça n'a servi à rien (d) **I don't give a bugger!** je m'en fous pas mal!
2 exclam **bugger (it)!** merde!, bordel!
3 vt (a) (exhaust) mettre sur les genoux, crever (b) (ruin, break) bousiller (c) (for emphasis) **bugger me!** putain!; **bugger the expense, let's buy it!** et puis merde, tant pis si c'est cher, achetons-le!

bugger about [!], **bugger around** [!] Br **1** vt sép **to bugger sb about** or **around** (treat badly) se foutre de la gueule de qn; (waste time of) faire perdre son temps à qn‍□
2 vi (waste time) glander, glandouiller

bugger off [!] vi Br se barrer, se casser, s'arracher; **they've buggered off to Spain for two weeks and dumped the kids on us** ils se sont barrés en Espagne pour deux semaines et ils nous ont refilé les gosses; **bugger off!** (go away) barre-toi!, casse-toi!; (expressing contempt, disagreement) va te faire foutre!

bugger up [!] vt sép **to bugger sth up** (ruin) foutre qch en l'air; (break) bousiller qch

buggeration [bʌgə'reɪʃən] exclam Br bordel!, putain!, merde!

buggered [!] ['bʌgəd] adj Br (a) (exhausted) crevé, naze (b) (broken) foutu, naze (c) (amazed) **well, I'm buggered!** ben merde alors! (d) (in trouble) foutu; **if we don't get the money soon, we're buggered** si on n'a pas l'argent rapidement, on est foutus (e) (for emphasis) **I'll be buggered if I'm going to apologize!** plutôt crever que de m'excuser!; **I'm buggered if I know!** j'en sais foutre rien!

The symbol □ indicates that a translation is neutral.

buggery [!] ['bʌgərɪ] n Br **like buggery!** ouais, mon cul!; **to run like buggery** courir comme un(e) dératé(e); **is he a good cook? – is he buggery!** il fait bien la cuisine? – tu veux rire!

builder's bum ['bɪldəz'bʌm] n Br = phénomène censé se produire communément chez les ouvriers du bâtiment, dont le pantalon a tendance à tomber, exposant le haut de leur postérieur

bull [bʊl] **1** n (nonsense) conneries fpl; **he's talking bull** il raconte des conneries, il dit n'importe quoi
2 exclam n'importe quoi! ▸ voir aussi **shoot**

bulldyke ['bʊldaɪk] n Injurieux gouine f (d'apparence masculine)

bullshit [!] ['bʊlʃɪt] **1** n conneries fpl
2 exclam des conneries, tout ça!
3 vt **to bullshit sb** raconter des conneries à qn; **she bullshitted her way into the job** elle a eu le boulot au culot
4 vi raconter des conneries

bullshitter ['bʊlʃɪtə(r)] n (smooth talker) baratineur(euse) m,f; **he's a bullshitter** (he talks nonsense) il raconte des conneries

bum [bʌm] **1** n **(a)** (buttocks) fesses fpl, derrière m; **bum bag** banane f (sac); **bum fluff** (beard) barbe f très peu fournie□ **(b)** Am (tramp) **(stew) bum** clodo mf **(c)** (enthusiast) **to be a beach/ski bum** passer son temps à la plage/sur les pistes□ **(d) to give sb the bum's rush** (dismiss) envoyer paître qn; (from work) virer qn; **to give sth the bum's rush** (idea, suggestion) rejeter qch□; **my idea got the bum's rush** mon idée est passée à la trappe
2 adj (worthless) merdique; **to get a bum deal** se faire avoir; **a bum rap** (false charge) une fausse accusation□
3 vt **(a)** (scrounge) **to bum sth (from** or **off sb)** taxer qch (à qn); **to bum a lift** or **a ride** se faire emmener en voiture□; **can I bum a lift** or **a ride to the station?** est-ce que tu peux me déposer à la gare? **(b)** [!] (have anal sex with) enculer, entuber; **I walked in on him bumming his boyfriend** je suis entré et je suis tombé sur lui en train d'enculer son petit copain

bum about, bum around 1 vt insép (spend time in) **to bum around Australia/the country** parcourir l'Australie/le pays sac au dos□; **to bum about the house** rester chez soi à glander
2 vi (hang around) glander

bum out vt sép gonfler, enquiquiner; **her constant whining really bums me out** elle me gonfle, à se plaindre sans arrêt

bum-freezer ['bʌmfriːzə(r)] n Br Hum (jacket) veste f ultra-courte□; (skirt) jupe f ultra-courte□, jupe f ras la touffe

bummed [bʌmd] adj **to be bummed (out)** l'avoir mauvaise

bummer ['bʌmə(r)] n (situation) **what a bummer!** la poisse!, c'est chiant!; **it was a real bummer being stuck at home all day** c'était vraiment la poisse ou chiant de devoir rester enfermé toute la journée; **she failed her driving test again – bummer!** elle a encore raté son permis de conduire – oh merde! ou ça craint!

bump off [bʌmp] vt sép **to bump sb off** (murder) supprimer ou zigouiller ou buter qn

bumwad ['bʌmwɒd] n papier cul m, PQ m

bun [bʌn] n (a) **to have a bun in the oven** (be pregnant) être en cloque (b) Am **buns** (buttocks) fesses fpl, miches fpl

bundle ['bʌndəl] n (a) (large sum of money) **to cost a bundle** coûter bonbon ou la peau des fesses; **to make a bundle** se faire un fric fou (b) Br **to go a bundle on sb** en pincer drôlement pour qn; **to go a bundle on sth** être fan de qch

bung [bʌŋ] Br 1 n (bribe) pot-de-vin[□] m
2 vt (put) flanquer; (throw) balancer

bunk [bʌŋk] n Br **to do a bunk** (from home) fuguer, faire une fugue; (from prison) se faire la belle

bunk off vt insép & vi Br sécher

bunny ['bʌni] n (a) Am **ski** or **snow bunny** jeune minette f qui fait du ski (b) **bunny boiler** = femme obsessionnelle qui poursuit quelqu'un de ses assiduités ▸ voir aussi **jungle**

ⓘ C'est le film américain Liaison fatale qui est à l'origine de l'expression "bunny boiler". Dans une scène devenue célèbre, un personnage féminin assoiffé de vengeance (joué par l'actrice Glenn Close) fait cuire le lapin du fils de l'amant qui l'a délaissée (ce dernier étant incarné par Michael Douglas).

bupkis ['bʌpkɪs] n Am que dalle; **he knows bupkis about it** il y connaît que dalle

burbs [bɜːbz] npl Am (abrév suburbs) banlieue[□] f; **they live in the burbs** ils habitent en banlieue

burl [bɜːl] n Austr (attempt) essai[□] m; **give it a burl!** essaye![□]

burn [bɜːn] vt Am (a) (swindle) arnaquer (b) (anger) foutre en rogne

burn up vt sép Am (anger) foutre en rogne

bush [bʊʃ] n (a) [!] (woman's pubic hair) barbu m (b) (marijuana) herbe f

bushed [bʊʃt] adj crevé, lessivé, naze

business ['bɪznɪs] n **like nobody's business** (sing, tell jokes) vachement bien; (work) comme une bête; Br **it's the business** c'est impec'; **that new DVD player of his is the business** son nouveau lecteur de DVD est vraiment super; **did you do the business with her?** (have sex) est-ce que t'as couché avec elle? ▸ voir aussi **monkey**

bust [bʌst] 1 n (police raid) descente f; **drug bust** descente f des stups
2 adj (a) (broken) foutu (b) (having no money) fauché; **to go bust** (of person, business) boire un bouillon
3 vt (a) (arrest) agrafer (**for** pour) (b) (raid) faire une descente dans (c) **to bust a gut** (work hard) bosser comme un dingue; (laugh) être mort de rire, être plié en quatre; **I bust a gut trying to get that report done on time** j'ai bossé comme un dingue pour finir ce rapport dans les temps (d) Am (catch) découvrir[□]; **you're busted!** je t'y prends!, je t'ai eu! (e) Am (demote) dégrader[□]; **he got busted to sergeant** il est repassé sergent ▸ voir aussi **ass, balls**

buster ['bʌstə(r)] n Am (term of address) mec m; **who are you looking at, buster?** tu veux ma photo, Ducon?

bust-up ['bʌstʌp] n (a) (quarrel) engueulade f; **to have a bust-up** s'engueuler (b) (of relationship) rupture[□] f

butch [bʊtʃ] 1 n (masculine lesbian)

The symbol [□] indicates that a translation is neutral.

lesbienne *f* à l'allure masculine[!]

2 *adj (woman)* hommasse; *(man)* macho

butcher's ['bʊtʃəz] *n Br (rhyming slang* **butcher's hook = look**) **to have a butcher's (at sb/sth)** mater (qn/qch)

butt [bʌt] *n (buttocks)* fesses *fpl*; **move your butt!** bouge-toi!

butt out *vi* s'occuper de ses fesses; **butt out!** occupe-toi de tes fesses!; **just butt out of my life!** laisse-moi vivre!

butthead ['bʌthed] *n Am* crétin(e) *m,f*, andouille *f*, cruche *f*

buttinski [bʌt'ɪnskɪ] *n Am* fouille-merde *mf*

butt-naked [bʌt'neɪkɪd] *adj* à poil, le cul à l'air

button ['bʌtən] *vt* **to button it** *(be quiet)* la fermer; **button it!** ferme-la!

butt-ugly [bʌt'ʌglɪ] *adj* hyper moche

butty ['bʌtɪ] *n Br* sandwich[!] *m*, casse-dalle *m*; **bacon/chip butty** sandwich *m* au bacon/aux frites

buy [baɪ] *vt Am* **to buy the farm** *(die)* clamser, calancher, avaler son bulletin de naissance

buzz [bʌz] *n* (**a**) *(phone call)* **to give sb a buzz** passer un coup de fil à qn, bigophoner qn (**b**) *(thrill)* **to give sb a buzz** exciter qn[!]; **to get a buzz out of doing sth** prendre son pied à faire qch

buzz off *vi* dégager, mettre les bouts, se tirer; **buzz off!** dégage!, tire-toi!

buzzing ['bʌzɪŋ] *adj* (**a**) *(party, night-club)* hyper animé (**b**) *(hyper)* speed, speedé

buzz-kill ['bʌzkɪl] *n Am* rabat-joie[!] *mf*

Cc

cabbage ['kæbɪdʒ] *n* (**a**) *Br* (*brain-damaged person*) légume *m*; (*dull person*) larve *f* (**b**) *Am* (*money*) fric *m*, blé *m*, oseille *f*

cabbaged ['kæbɪdʒd] *adj Br* pété, bourré

cable ['keɪbəl] *n* **to lay (a) cable** couler un bronze

cack [kæk] *Br* **1** *n* (**a**) (*excrement*) caca *m* (**b**) (*nonsense*) conneries *fpl*; **don't talk cack!** arrête de raconter n'importe quoi! (**c**) (*worthless things*) camelote *f*; **the film was a load of cack** le film était nul

2 *adj* (*bad*) nul; **her music is cack** sa musique est nulle

3 *vt* **he was cacking himself** (*scared*) il faisait dans son froc

cack-handed [kæk'hændɪd] *adj Br* maladroit□, manche

cadge [kædʒ] **1** *n Br* (**a**) (*person*) pique-assiette *mf*, parasite□ *m* (**b**) **to be on the cadge** jouer les parasites

2 *vt* (*food, money*) se procurer□ (*en quémandant*); **he cadged a meal from** *or* **off his aunt** il s'est fait inviter à manger par sa tante; **she cadged £10 off me** elle m'a tapé de 10 livres; **they cadged a lift home** à force de quémander ils se sont fait ramener en voiture

3 *vi* quémander□; **she's always cadging off her friends** elle est toujours en train de taper ses amis

cahoots [kə'huːts] *n* **to be in cahoots** (**with sb**) être de mèche (avec qn)

cakehole ['keɪkhəʊl] *n Br* bouche□ *f*, clapet *m*; **shut your cakehole!** ferme-la!, ferme ton clapet!

calaboose ['kæləbuːs] *n Am* taule *f*, placard *m*; **in the calaboose** en taule, au placard, à l'ombre

camp [kæmp] *adj* efféminé; *Hum* **he's as camp as a row of tents** *or* **as Christmas** il fait très grande folle ▸ *voir aussi* **fat**

can¹ [kæn] **1** *n* (**a**) *Am* (*toilet*) chiottes *fpl* (**b**) *Am* (*prison*) taule *f*, placard *m*; **in the can** en taule, au placard, à l'ombre (**c**) *Am* (*buttocks*) fesses *fpl*; **to kick sb in the can** botter les fesses à qn (**d**) *Br* **to carry the can** (*take the blame*) porter le chapeau

2 *vt Am* (**a**) (*dismiss*) virer, saquer (**b**) **to can it** (*shut up*) la fermer, la boucler; **can it!** ferme-la!, boucle-la!

can² *modal aux v* **no can do!** impossible!; *Am* **can do!** pas de problème!

cancer stick ['kænsəstɪk] *n* clope *f*

cane [keɪn] *vt Br* **to cane it** se bourrer *ou* se pinter la gueule

caned [keɪnd] *adj Br* (*drunk*) bourré comme un coing; (*on drugs*) complètement défoncé

caner ['keɪnə(r)] *n* poivrot *m*, alcoolo *m*

cankles ['kænkəls] *npl Hum* **she's got cankles** elle a des mollets tellement gros qu'on ne voit pas ses chevilles

ⓘ Il s'agit d'un mot-valise formé à partir de "calf" (mollet) et "ankles" (chevilles).

canned [kænd] *adj (drunk)* beurré, bourré, pété

cap [kæp] *Am* **1** *n (bullet)* bastos *f* **2** *vt (shoot)* descendre

capper ['kæpə(r)] *n Am* **that was the capper!** c'est la goutte d'eau qui a fait déborder le vase!

cark [kɑːk] *vt Br* **to cark it** calancher, casser sa pipe, passer l'arme à gauche

carnage ['kɑːnɪdʒ] *n Br* **I got to the party at midnight and it was absolute carnage in there** je suis arrivé à la soirée à minuit et c'était le chaos absolu

carpet ['kɑːpɪt] **1** *n* (a) **to be on the carpet** *(in trouble)* être dans le caca; **to put sb on the carpet** *(reprimand)* enguirlander qn, passer un savon à qn (b) **to eat** *or* **munch carpet [!!]** pratiquer le cunnilingus□ **2** *vt Br (reprimand)* enguirlander, passer un savon à

carve up [kɑːv] *vt sép* **to carve sb up** *(attack with knife)* donner des coups de couteau au visage à qn□; *(in car)* faire une queue de poisson à qn

case [keɪs] **1** *n* **he's always on my case** je l'ai tout le temps sur le dos; **get off my case!** lâche-moi les baskets!, oublie-moi! **2** *vt* **to case the joint** repérer les lieux *(avant un cambriolage)*

cash [kæʃ] *n* fric *m*

cash in *Am* **1** *vt sép* **to cash in one's chips** *(die)* calancher, clamser,

passer l'arme à gauche **2** *vi (die)* calancher, clamser, passer l'arme à gauche

casual ['kæʒʊəl] *n Br* jeune supporter *m* de foot

ⓘ Ce terme désigne un certain type de supporter de football. Le "casual" est un jeune homme, généralement issu d'un milieu modeste, qui dépense beaucoup d'argent en vêtements mais ne fait pas preuve d'un goût très sûr (ainsi les chaussures de sport et survêtements de marque côtoieront-ils les polos en laine vierge de coupe classique). Le "casual" se déplace le plus souvent en bande, consomme de la bière en grande quantité et est souvent l'auteur de violences lors des matchs.

cat [kæt] *n* (a) *Am (man)* mec *m*; *(woman)* nana *f*, gonzesse *f* (b) **to look like something the cat dragged in** ne ressembler à rien; **it's like herding cats** ce n'est vraiment pas une mince affaire (c) **cat fight** crêpage *m* de chignon (d) *Br* **to be the cat's pyjamas** *or* **whiskers**, *Am* **to be the cat's pajamas** *or* **meow** être génial ▶ *voir aussi* **fat**

catch [kætʃ] *vt* (a) *(see, experience)* voir; **shall we catch a movie?** on va voir un film?; **did you catch that Angelina Jolie interview last night?** tu as vu l'interview d'Angelina Jolie hier soir?; **to catch some rays** *(sunbathe)* se faire bronzer; **catch you later!** à plus tard! (b) *Br* **to catch it**, *Am* **to catch hell** se faire engueuler; **you'll** *Br* **catch it** *or Am* **catch hell when you get home!** tu vas te faire drôlement engueuler quand tu rentreras!

cathouse ['kæthaʊs] *n* bordel *m*, claque *m*

cattle market ['kætəlmɑːkɪt] *n Br Péj (nightclub)* = boîte réputée pour être un lieu de drague

chalfonts ['tʃælfɒnts] *npl Br (rhyming slang* **Chalfont St Giles = piles**) hémorroïdes□ *fpl*, émeraudes *fpl*

ⓘ Chalfont St Giles est une ville du Buckinghamshire.

champers ['ʃæmpəz] *n Br (abrév* **champagne**) champ' *m*

champion ['tʃæmpjən] **1** *adj* super, génial
2 *exclam* super!, génial!

chance [tʃɑːns] **1** *n* **no chance!** des clous!
2 *vt* **to chance one's arm** *(take a risk)* risquer le coup; *(push one's luck)* exagérer□, pousser

chancer ['tʃɑːnsə(r)] *n Br* opportuniste□ *mf*

chang [tʃæŋ] *n (cocaine)* coke *f*, neige *f*

char [tʃɑː(r)] *n Br (tea)* thé□ *m*

charge [tʃɑːdʒ] *n Am (thrill)* **to get a charge out of sth/doing sth** s'éclater *ou* prendre son pied avec qch/en faisant qch

charidee ['tʃærɪdiː] *n Br Hum* association *f* caritative; **he's shaved his head for charidee** il s'est rasé la tête pour collecter des fonds pour une association caritative□; **I met her at some boring charidee dinner** je l'ai rencontrée à un dîner organisé par une association caritative

charlie ['tʃɑːlɪ] *n* (**a**) *(cocaine)* coke *f*, neige *f* (**b**) *Br (person)* andouille *f*, crétin(e) *m,f*; **to look/feel a right charlie** avoir l'air/se sentir con

chase [tʃeɪs] *vt* **to chase the dragon** chasser le dragon

chaser ['tʃeɪsə(r)] *n* = homosexuel aimant les hommes corpulents, chaser *m*

chassis ['ʃæsɪ] *n (woman's body)* châssis *m*; *Hum* **she's got a classy chassis** elle est super bien foutue *ou* balancée *ou* carrossée

chat up [tʃæt] *vt sép Br* **to chat sb up** baratiner qn, draguer qn

chat-up line ['tʃætʌplaɪn] *n Br* = formule d'entrée en matière pour commencer à draguer quelqu'un; **"are you a model?"! what a lousy chat-up line!** "vous êtes mannequin?"! c'est vraiment une réplique á deux balles!

chav [tʃæv] *n Br* jeune lascar *m*, racaille *f*

chavvy ['tʃævɪ] *adj Br* qui fait racaille

cheapo ['tʃiːpəʊ] *adj* merdique; **he's bought some cheapo mobile** il a acheté une espèce de portable merdique; **don't go to that cheapo supermarket, it's gross!** ne va pas dans ce supermarché au rabais, c'est vraiment nul!

cheapskate ['tʃiːpskeɪt] *n* radin(e) *m,f*

check [tʃek] *vt* **check this!** mate un peu ça!

check out 1 *vt sép (look at)* **to check sb/sth out** mater qn/qch; **there's a new club we could check out** il y a une nouvelle boîte qu'on pourrait essayer; **check it/her out!** mate-moi ça!
2 *vi Am (die)* passer l'arme à gauche

cheeky ['tʃiːkɪ] *adj Br* **fancy a cheeky pint on the way home?** ça te dirait d'aller boire une petite pinte rapide avant de rentrer à la maison?; **he's just nipped out for a cheeky**

fag il est sorti se fumer une petite clope en douce

cheers [tʃɪəz] *exclam* (**a**) *(as toast)* santé!, à la tienne/vôtre! (**b**) *Br (thank you)* merci![□] (**c**) *Br (goodbye)* salut!, ciao!

cheese [tʃiːz] *n* (**a**) *Br* **hard cheese!** pas de pot *ou* veine! (**b**) **big cheese** *(important person)* huile *f* ▸ *voir aussi* **cut**

cheese off *vt sép* **to cheese sb off** gonfler qn; **to be cheesed off (with)** en avoir marre (de)

cheesecake [ˈtʃiːzkeɪk] *n (attractive women)* belles nanas *fpl; Br* **she's a real cheesecake** elle est vraiment bien foutue *ou* balancée *ou* carrossée

cheesy [ˈtʃiːzɪ] *adj* (**a**) *(tasteless)* ringard (**b**) **cheesy grin** large sourire[□] *m*

cheggers [ˈtʃegəz] *adj Br* en cloque

Chelsea tractor [ˈtʃelsɪˈtræktə(r)] *n Hum* = 4x4 utilisé en ville

ⓘ Ce terme signifie littéralement "tracteur de Chelsea", Chelsea étant un quartier bourgeois de Londres. Cette appellation humoristique souligne l'absurdité qui consiste à se doter d'un véhicule tout terrain lorsqu'on habite en ville.

cherry [ˈtʃerɪ] **1** *n* (**a**) *(virginity)* berlingot *m;* **to lose one's cherry** perdre son berlingot; **to pop sb's cherry** dépuceler qn (**b**) *(virgin)* puceau (pucelle) *m,f* (**c**) *Am (newcomer)* bleu *m*
2 *adj Am (in perfect condition)* en parfait état[□], impec'

Chevvy [ˈʃevɪ] *n* Chevrolet®[□] *f*

chew [tʃuː] *vt* **to chew the fat** *or* **the rag** tailler une bavette

chew out *vt sép* **to chew sb out** souffler dans les bronches à qn, passer un savon à qn; **to get chewed out** se faire souffler dans les bronches, se faire passer un savon

chib [tʃɪb] *Scot* **1** *nm (knife)* schlass *m,* lame *f,* surin *m*
2 *vt* suriner

chick [tʃɪk] *n (woman)* nana *f,* gonzesse *f;* **chick flick** = film qui plaît particulièrement aux femmes; **chick lit** = genre romanesque destiné à un public de jeunes femmes et qui est censé refléter leurs préoccupations ▸ *voir aussi* **magnet**

chicken [ˈtʃɪkɪn] **1** *n* (**a**) *(coward)* dégonflé(e) *m,f* (**b**) *(attractive young male)* jeune mec *m* canon
2 *adj (cowardly)* dégonflé ▸ *voir aussi* **spring**

ⓘ L'acception 1(b) de ce terme appartient à l'argot homosexuel.

chicken out *vi* se dégonfler; **he chickened out of the fight** il s'est dégonflé au dernier moment et a refusé se se battre; **he chickened out of telling her the truth** finalement il a eu la trouille de lui dire la vérité

chickenfeed [ˈtʃɪkɪnfiːd] *n (small amount of money)* cacahuètes *fpl*

chickenshit [!] [ˈtʃɪkɪnʃɪt] *adj Am* dégonflé

chill (out) [tʃɪl] *vi* se détendre[□]; **I wish he'd chill out a bit** ça serait bien qu'il soit un peu plus cool; **he likes chilling out at home** il aime bien être chez lui, peinard; **what are you doing? – just chilling** qu'est-ce que tu fais? – rien, je me détends; **chill (out)!** relax!, calmos!

chilled [tʃɪld] *adj* relax

chillin ['tʃɪlɪn] adj Am super, génial, cool

chill pill ['tʃɪlpɪl] n **take a chill pill!** relax!, calmos!

china ['tʃaɪnə] n Br (rhyming slang **china plate = mate**) pote m; **all right, me old china?** ça va, mon pote?

Chink [tʃɪŋk] n Injurieux Chinetoc mf, Chinetoque mf

Chinky ['tʃɪŋkɪ] n Injurieux **(a)** (person) Chinetoc mf, Chinetoque mf **(b)** Br (meal) repas m chinois▫; (restaurant) (resto m) chinois m; **to go for a Chinky** manger chinois

ⓘ Lorsqu'il est question de nourriture, de cuisine, de restaurants, le terme "chinky" perd sa connotation raciste. Il est toutefois déconseillé de l'utiliser.

chinless wonder ['tʃɪnləs'wʌndə(r)] n Br = individu de bonne famille dépourvu de volonté et d'intelligence

ⓘ Ce terme signifie littéralement "merveille au menton fuyant", ce trait physique étant censé être le signe d'un caractère faible et d'un patrimoine génétique peu enviable.

chintzy ['tʃɪntsɪ] adj Am **(a)** (cheap, of poor quality) toc et tape-à-l'œil **(b)** (miserly) radin

chinwag ['tʃɪnwæg] n Br converse f; **to have a chinwag (with sb)** tailler une bavette (avec qn)

chip in [tʃɪp] **1** vt sép (contribute) donner▫; **everyone chipped in a fiver** tout le monde a donné cinq livres▫
2 vi (contribute money) participer▫,

donner▫; **they all chipped in to buy her a present** ils se sont cotisés pour lui offrir un cadeau▫

chippy ['tʃɪpɪ] n Br = boutique qui vend du poisson frit et des frites

chisel ['tʃɪzəl] vt (cheat) arnaquer; **to chisel sb out of sth** arnaquer qn de qch

chiseller ['tʃɪzələ(r)] n Ir gosse mf, môme mf

chocka ['tʃɒkə], **chock-a-block** [tʃɒkə'blɒk] adj Br plein à craquer

choke vt Hum **to choke the chicken [!!]** (masturbate) se taper sur la colonne, se polir le chinois

chocolate ['tʃɒklət] n Br & Austr **she thinks he's chocolate!** elle le trouve génial!; **that guy really thinks he's chocolate!** ce mec ne se prend vraiment pas pour n'importe qui!

chook [tʃʊk] n Austr (chicken) poulet▫ m; (woman) nana f, gonzesse f

chop [tʃɒp] n **to get the chop** (of person) se faire virer; (of plan) passer à la trappe

chopper ['tʃɒpə(r)] n **(a)** (helicopter) hélico m **(b)** Br (penis) pine f, queue f

chops [tʃɒps] npl Br (mouth) gueule f; (face) gueule f, tronche f; **you're going to get a smack in the chops if you're not careful!** tu vas te prendre une baffe dans la gueule si tu fais pas gaffe!

chow [tʃaʊ] n (food) bouffe f

chow down vi Am attaquer

chowderhead ['tʃaʊdəhed] n Am crétin(e) m,f, imbécile mf

chowhound ['tʃaʊhaʊnd] n Am morfale mf

Christ [kraɪst] exclam **Christ (Almighty)!** nom de Dieu!; **for Christ's sake!** bon sang!; Hum **Christ on a**

bike! bon sang!, nom de Dieu!

chrome dome ['krəʊmdəʊm] *n Br* **he's a chrome dome** il a une casquette en peau de fesse

chronic ['krɒnɪk] *adj Br (very bad)* nul; **my back's hurting something chronic** mon dos me fait un mal de chien

chub [tʃʌb], **chubby** ['tʃʌbɪ] *n =* homosexuel corpulent, chub *m*

chuck [tʃʌk] **1** *n Br* **to give sb the chuck** plaquer qn
  2 *vt* (**a**) *(throw)* balancer (**b**) *(boyfriend, girlfriend)* plaquer

chuck down *vt sép* **it's chucking it down** *(raining)* il tombe des cordes

chuck in *vt sép* **to chuck sth in** *(job, studies)* plaquer qch; *(habit)* se débarrasser de qch□

chuck out *vt sép* **to chuck sb out** flanquer qn à la porte; **to chuck sth out** balancer qch

chuck up *vi Br (vomit)* dégobiller, gerber, dégueuler

chucker-out [tʃʌkə'raʊt] *n Br (doorman)* videur *m*

chucking-out time ['tʃʌkɪŋ'aʊtaɪm] *n Br (in pub)* heure *f* de la fermeture□

chuddies ['tʃʌdɪz] *npl Br (underpants)* slibar *m*, calbute *m*

ⓘ "Chuddies" est un terme d'argot britannique d'origine indienne. Il a été popularisé par la série télévisée humoristique *Goodness Gracious Me* par le biais de la formule "kiss my chuddies, man" (embrasse mon slip).

chuff [!] [tʃʌf] *n Br* (**a**) *(vagina)* craquette *f*, fente *f*; **to be as tight as a nun's chuff** *(miserly)* avoir des oursins dans le porte-monnaie, les

lâcher avec des élastiques (**b**) *(anus)* trou *m* de balle (**c**) **for chuff's sake!** bordel de merde!

chuffed [tʃʌft] *adj Br* content□; **I was chuffed to bits** j'étais vachement content

chuffer [!] ['tʃʌfə(r)] *n Br* trou *m* du cul, trouduc *m*

chuffing ['tʃʌfɪŋ] *adj Br* foutu, sacré; **that chuffing idiot** ce sombre crétin

chug [tʃʌg] **1** *n Br* **to have a chug** [!] *(masturbate)* se branler
  2 *vt (drink quickly)* descendre
  3 [!] *vi Br (masturbate)* se branler

chug down *vt sép* **to chug sth down** descendre qch

chump [tʃʌmp] *n* (**a**) *(idiot)* abruti(e) *m,f* (**b**) *Br* **to be off one's chump** être cinglé *ou* timbré; **to go off one's chump** perdre la boule, disjoncter (**c**) *Am* **chump change** *(small amount of money)* cacahuètes *fpl*

chunder ['tʃʌndə(r)] *vi Br & Austr* dégobiller, gerber, dégueuler

cig [sɪg] *n (abrév* **cigarette***)* clope *f*, tige *f*

cigar [sɪ'gɑː(r)] *n* **close, but no cigar!** c'est presque ça, mais pas tout à fait!

ⓘ Il s'agit d'une expression humoristique utilisée lorsqu'une personne à qui l'on a posé une devinette donne une réponse inexacte mais très proche de la réponse juste, le cigare étant la récompense fictive à laquelle cette personne aurait eu droit si elle avait deviné juste. Cette expression a été popularisée par les animateurs de jeux télévisés.

ciggy ['sɪgɪ] *n* (*abrév* **cigarette**) clope *f*, tige *f*

cinch [sɪntʃ] *n* **it was a cinch** c'était du gâteau, c'était simple comme bonjour; **it's a cinch to use** c'est hyper facile à utiliser

cissy ['sɪsɪ] *Br* = **sissy**

city ['sɪtɪ] *n* **you should see the people at the gym – it's fat city!** si tu voyais les gens qui vont au club de gym – c'est tous des gros lards!; **try the park, it's dope city!** va voir au parc, c'est pas les dealers qui manquent! ▸ *voir aussi* **fat**

ⓘ Ce mot dénote l'abondance de ce qui le précède. On peut l'ajouter à presque n'importe quel nom, verbe ou adjectif pour introduire la notion de foisonnement.

clam [klæm] *n Am* (*dollar*) dollar⁰ *m*

clap [klæp] *n* **the clap** la chaude-pisse; **to have (a dose of) the clap** avoir la chaude-pisse

clapped-out [klæpt'aʊt] *adj Br* (*person*) crevé, lessivé, naze; (*car, TV*) fichu

clappers ['klæpəz] *npl Br* **to do sth like the clappers** faire qch comme un dingue

claret ['klærət] *n* (*blood*) raisiné *m*, sang⁰ *m*

clart [klɑːt] *n Scot* (*dirty person*) = personne sale et négligée; **he's a pure clart!** ce qu'il peut être crade *ou* cradingue!

clarty ['klɑːtɪ] *adj Scot* (*dirty*) crade, cradingue, dégueulasse

class [klɑːs] *adj Br* (*excellent*) classe; **a class car/hi-fi** une voiture/chaîne classe

classic ['klæsɪk] **1** *n* **it was a classic!** ça payait!

   2 *adj* **it was classic!** ça payait!

clean [kliːn] *adj* **to be clean** (*not carrying drugs*) ne pas avoir de drogue sur soi⁰; (*not carrying weapons*) ne pas être armé⁰; (*no longer addicted to drugs*) avoir décroché ▸ *voir aussi* **nose**

clean out *vt sép* **to clean sb out** (*leave penniless*) nettoyer qn

clean up *vi* (*make large profit*) gagner gros

cleaner ['kliːnə(r)] *n* **to take sb to the cleaners** nettoyer *ou* plumer qn

clear off [klɪə(r)] *vi Br* dégager, se tirer; **clear off!** dégage!, tire-toi!

clear out *vi* dégager, se tirer; **clear out!** dégage!, tire-toi!

clever clogs ['klevəklɒgz], **clever dick** ['klevədɪk] *n Br* gros (grosse) malin(igne) *m,f*; **OK, clever clogs** *or* **dick, what do we do now?** alors, gros malin, qu'est-ce qu'on fait maintenant?

clink [klɪŋk] *n* (*prison*) taule *f*, placard *m*; **in the clink** en taule, à l'ombre, en cabane

clip [klɪp] **1** *n* (a) *Br* (*blow*) **to give sb a clip round the ear** flanquer une calotte à qn (b) **clip joint** = bar *ou* boîte de nuit où l'on se fait es croquer

   2 *vt Br* **to clip sb round the ear** flanquer une calotte à qn

clipe [klaɪp] *Scot* **1** *n* (*person*) mouchard(e) *m,f*

   2 *vi* moucharder, cafarder; **to clipe on sb** moucharder qn

clit [!!] [klɪt] *n* (*abrév* **clitoris**) clito *m*, clit *m*

clobber¹ ['klɒbə(r)] *n Br* (*clothes*) frusques *fpl*; (*belongings*) barda *m*

Pleins feux sur...

Class

La Grande-Bretagne est un pays où les différences entre classes sociales sont très marquées. Les gens d'origine modeste aiment se moquer des **toffs** (les rupins). Les jeunes bourgeois exubérants sont qualifiés de **Hooray Henrys**, ou de **rugger buggers** s'ils jouent au rugby (sport qui se pratique traditionnellement dans les écoles privées les plus prestigieuses). Leurs équivalents féminins sont les **Sloanes** ou **Sloane Rangers** (Sloane Square étant un quartier chic de Londres). Aux États-Unis, ces jeunes privilégiés se nomment les **preppies** (terme dérivé de "preparatory school", genre d'école privée d'élite). Les classes supérieures britanniques aiment les plaisirs de la campagne, ce qui leur vaut le surnom de **the green welly brigade** (la brigade des bottes de caoutchouc vert).

À l'autre extrémité du spectre social se trouvent les **chavs** (la racaille), issus de la classe ouvrière, qui aiment les vêtements de sport de marque et les bijoux clinquants. Le terme "chav" a cours dans toute la Grande-Bretagne mais il existe des variantes régionales telles que **scally**, **ned**, **kev**, **townie** et **pikey**. Les termes **Essex Boy** et **Essex Girl**, qui existent depuis les années 1980, ont un sens similaire, ce qui est également le cas des termes **Kevin** (pour les garçons) et **Sharon and Tracy** (pour les filles). Les cousins américains des "chavs" sont qualifiés de **white trash**, et les Australiens ont leurs **bogans**.

clobber² vt (**a**) *(hit) (once)* flanquer un pain *ou* gnon à; *(repeatedly)* flanquer une raclée à (**b**) *(defeat)* flanquer une raclée à (**c**) *(penalize)* écraser□, accabler□

clock [klɒk] **1** n (**a**) Br *(face)* gueule f, tronche f (**b**) Am **to clean sb's clock** *(attack)* rentrer dans qn; *(defeat)* écraser qn, battre qn à plates coutures
2 vt Br (**a**) *(hit)* flanquer un pain *ou* un gnon à (**b**) *(notice)* repérer

clogs [klɒgz] npl Br **to pop one's clogs** passer l'arme à gauche, calancher ▸ *voir aussi* **clever clogs**

closet ['klɒzɪt] **1** n **to come out of the closet** *(of homosexual)* faire son comeout
2 adj **closet communist/alcoholic** communiste *mf*/alcoolique *mf* honteux(euse); **closet queen** homo *m* honteux

clot [klɒt] n Br *(person)* nouille f, courge f, andouille f

cloud-cuckoo-land ['klaʊd'kʊkuː-lænd] n Br **to be living in cloud-cuckoo-land** ne pas avoir les pieds sur terre

clout [klaʊt] **1** n (**a**) *(influence)* influence□ f; **to have a lot of clout** avoir le bras long (**b**) *(blow)* calotte *f*; **to give sb a clout** flanquer une calotte à qn; **to give sth a clout** flanquer un coup dans qch

2 *vt (hit) (person)* flanquer une calotte à; *(thing)* flanquer un coup dans

clown [klaʊn] *n Hum* **to be one clown short of a circus** ne pas être net

club [klʌb] *n* (**a**) *Br* **to be in the (pudding) club** *(pregnant)* être en cloque (**b**) **join the club!** t'es pas le (la) seul(e)!

clueless ['kluːlɪs] *adj* nul

clued-up ['kluːd'ʌp], *Am* **clued-in** [kluːd'ɪn] *adj* informé▫; **to be** *Br* **clued-up** *or Am* **clued-in on sth** s'y connaître en qch▫

c'mon [kə'mɒn] *exclam (abrév* **come on***)* allez!

C-note ['siːnəʊt] *n Am* billet *m* de cent dollars▫

cobber ['kɒbə(r)] *n Austr* copain *m*, pote *m*

cobblers [!] ['kɒbləz] *Br* **1** *npl* (**a**) *(testicles)* balloches *fpl*, boules *fpl* (**b**) *(nonsense)* foutaises *fpl*; **it's a load of cobblers** tout ça, c'est des foutaises

2 *exclam* n'importe quoi!, des foutaises, tout ça!

cock [kɒk] *n* (**a**) [!!] *(penis)* queue *f*, bite *f*; *Hum* **cock rock** rock *m* macho (**b**) [!!] *(man)* trou *m* du cul, trouduc *m* (**c**) *Br (term of address)* mon pote; **all right, me old cock!** salut, mon pote!

cock up *vt sép* **to cock sth up** *(interview, exam)* foirer qch, se planter à qch; *(plan, arrangement)* faire foirer qch

cocksucker [!!] ['kɒksʌkə(r)] *n* enculé *m*

cocktease [!!] ['kɒktiːz], **cockteaser** [!!] ['kɒktiːzə(r)] *n* allumeuse *f*

cock-up ['kɒkʌp] *n Br* foirade *f*; **to make a cock-up of sth** *(interview, exam)* foirer qch, se planter à qch; *(plan, arrangement)* faire foirer qch

coco ['kəʊkəʊ] *vi Br* **I should coco!** tu l'as dit!

cod [kɒd] *n Br (nonsense)* foutaises *fpl*

codger ['kɒdʒə(r)] *n* **old codger** vieux croulant *m*

codswallop ['kɒdzwɒləp] *n Br* foutaises *fpl*; **it's a load of codswallop** tout ça, c'est des foutaises

coffin ['kɒfɪn] *n* (**a**) *Br Péj* **coffin dodger** *(old person)* croulant(e) *m,f* (**b**) **coffin nail** *(cigarette)* clope *f*, tige *f*

coke [kəʊk] *n (abrév* **cocaine***)* coke *f*

coked up [kəʊkt'ʌp] *adj* défoncé à la coke

cokehead ['kəʊkhed] *n* **to be a cokehead** marcher à la cocaïne

coldcock ['kəʊldkɒk] *vt Am* assommer▫, estourbir

cold turkey [kəʊld'tɜːkɪ] *n* **to go cold turkey** décrocher d'un seul coup; **to be cold turkey** être en manque

comatose ['kəʊmətəʊs] *adj (drunk)* ivre mort▫

combi ['kɒmbɪ] *n Austr* **combi (van)** camping-car▫ *m*

combo ['kɒmbəʊ] *n (abrév* **combination***)* mélange▫ *m*; **she was wearing this weird skirt and jeans combo** elle était accoutrée bizarrement d'un jean et d'une jupe

come [kʌm] **1** [!] *n (semen)* foutre *m* **2** *vi* (**a**) [!] *(reach orgasm)* jouir (**b**) **come again?** hein?, quoi? (**c**) *Br* **to come it** bluffer; **don't come it with**

me! arrête ton cinéma! ▸ *voir aussi* **prawn**

come off 1 *vt insép* **come off it!** arrête ton char!

  2 [!] *vi (reach orgasm)* jouir

come on *vi* (**a**) **to come on to sb** faire du rentre-dedans à qn (**b**) *Br (start menstruating)* avoir ses ragnagnas; **I came on this morning** les Anglais ont débarqué ce matin

come out *vi (reveal homosexuality)* faire son comeout ▸ *voir aussi* **closet**

come up *vi Br* (**a**) [!] *(ejaculate)* décharger (**b**) *(after taking drugs)* décoller

come-on [ˈkʌmɒn] *n* **to give sb the come-on** faire du rentre-dedans à qn

commando [kəˈmɑːndəʊ] *n Hum* **to go commando** ne pas porter de slip/de culotte

commie [ˈkɒmɪ] *n (abrév* **communist**) coco *mf*

con[1] [kɒn] **1** *n (abrév* **confidence trick**) *(swindle)* arnaque *f*; **con man** arnaqueur *m*

  2 *vt* arnaquer; **to con sth out of sb** arnaquer qn de qch; **to con sb into doing sth** persuader qn de faire qch par la ruse ▸ *voir aussi* **merchant**

con[2] *n (abrév* **convict**) taulard(e) *m,f*

conk [kɒŋk] *n Br (nose)* tarin *m*, blaire *m*

conk out *vi* (**a**) *(break down)* tomber en rade (**b**) *(fall asleep)* s'endormir□, piquer du nez

connection [kəˈnekʃən] *n Am (drug dealer)* dealer *m*

cook [kʊk] **1** *vt* **to cook a shot** préparer un shoot d'héroïne

  2 *vi* **what's cooking?** *(what's happening?)* quoi de neuf?; **now we're cooking with gas!** maintenant tout

marche comme sur des roulettes!

cook up 1 *vt sép* **to cook up a shot** préparer un shoot d'héroïne

  2 *vi (heat heroin)* préparer un shoot d'héroïne

cookie [ˈkʊkɪ] *n* (**a**) *(person)* **a tough cookie** un(e) dur(e) à cuire; **a smart cookie** une tête (**b**) **that's the way the cookie crumbles** c'est la vie (**c**) **to toss** *or Am* **shoot one's cookies** *(vomit)* gerber, dégueuler

cool [kuːl] **1** *adj* (**a**) *(fashionable, sophisticated)* branché; **Glasgow's a really cool city** Glasgow est une ville hyper-branchée; **he still thinks it's cool to smoke** il pense encore que ça fait bien de fumer

  (**b**) *(excellent)* cool, super; **we had a really cool weekend** on a passé un super week-end; **that's a cool hat** il est cool *ou* super, ce chapeau

  (**c**) *(allowed, acceptable)* **is it cool to skin up in here?** on peut se rouler un joint ici?;

  (**d**) *(accepting, not upset)* **are you cool with that?** ça te va?; **they're not cool about me smoking at home** ils n'aiment pas que je fume à la maison□; **I thought she'd be angry, but she was really cool about it** je pensais qu'elle se fâcherait, mais en fait elle a été très cool

  2 *exclam* cool!, super!

  3 *vt* **to cool it** se calmer□; **cool it!** du calme!, calmos! ▸ *voir aussi* **lose**

cooler [ˈkuːlə(r)] *n (prison)* taule *f*, cabane *f*; **in the cooler** en taule, en cabane, à l'ombre

coon [kuːn] *n Injurieux (black person)* nègre (négresse) *m,f*

cooties [ˈkuːtɪz] *npl Am* poux□ *mpl*; **don't sit beside her, she's got cooties!** ne t'assieds pas à côté d'elle, elle a des poux!

cooze [!!] [kuːz] *n Am (female geni-*

tals) craquette *f*, fente *f*, cramouille *f*; *(women)* nanas *fpl*, cuisse *f*; **I'm gonna go out and get me some cooze tonight** j'ai bien l'intention de me mettre une nana sur le bout ce soir; **that new bar's oozing with cooze!** il y a de la cuisse dans ce nouveau bar!

cop [kɒp] **1** *n* (**a**) *(police officer)* flic *m*; **cop shop** *(police station)* poste *m*; **cop show** *(on TV)* série *f* télévisée policière (**b**) *Br (arrest)* **it's a fair cop!** je suis fait, y a rien à dire! (**c**) *Br* **it's not much cop** *(not very good)* ce n'est pas terrible, ça ne casse pas trois pattes à un canard

2 *vt* (**a**) *(catch)* **to cop sb** pincer qn; **to get copped doing sth** se faire pincer en train de faire qch; **to cop hold of sth** choper qch; **cop (a load of) this!** *(listen)* écoute-moi ça!; *(look)* mate-moi ça! (**b**) *Br* **to cop it** *(be punished)* prendre un savon; *(die)* clamser, calancher; **did he try to cop a feel?** il a essayé de te peloter? (**c**) **to cop some** *Br* **zeds** *or Am* **zees** roupiller

cop off *vi Br* **did you cop off last night?** t'as réussi à lever quelqu'un hier soir?; **to cop off with sb** lever *ou* emballer qn

cop out *vi (avoid responsibility)* se défiler; *(choose easy solution)* choisir la solution de facilité[□]; **to cop out of doing sth** ne pas avoir le cran de faire qch

cop-out ['kɒpaʊt] *n* solution *f* de facilité[□]

copper ['kɒpə(r)] *n (police officer)* flic *m*

corker ['kɔːkə(r)] *n Br (excellent thing)* **their new CD is a corker** leur nouveau CD est vraiment super; **that was a corker of a party** c'était une super soirée

corking ['kɔːkɪŋ] *adj Br* super, génial

cornball ['kɔːnbɔːl] *Am* **1** *n* personne *f* gnangnan

    2 *adj* cucul, gnangnan

cornhole [!!] ['kɔːnhəʊl] *vt Am* enculer, enviander

cossie ['kɒzɪ] *n Br & Austr* maillot *m* de bain[□]

cottage ['kɒtɪdʒ] *n Br (public toilet)* tasse *f*, toilettes publiques[□] *fpl (utilisées comme lieu de rencontre par certains homosexuels)*

cottaging ['kɒtɪdʒɪŋ] *n Br* = drague homosexuelle dans les toilettes publiques

couch potato ['kaʊtʃpə'teɪtəʊ] *n* flemmard(e) *m,f* qui passe sa vie devant la télé

cough up [kɒf] **1** *vt sép (money)* cracher, allonger

    2 *vi* cracher *ou* allonger le fric

coulda ['kʊdə] *contraction (abrév* **could have**) **you coulda told me!** tu aurais pu me le dire!; **coulda, woulda, shoulda** on ne peut rien y changer maintenant, ça ne sert à rien de se lamenter

council ['kaʊnsəl] *n Br Hum* **council telly** = surnom donné aux chaînes de télévision hertziennes, qui ne nécessitent pas d'abonnement payant; **council-house facelift** = queue de cheval, avec les cheveux tirés en arrière

ⓘ Ces deux expressions jouent sur un stéréotype selon lequel les habitants des "council houses" (HLM) seraient pour la plupart pauvres, sans éducation et inélégants. Par exemple, le terme "council-house facelift", qui signifie littéralement "lifting HLM", fait référence à un type de coiffure jugé caractéristique des habitantes des HLM, et qui con-

---

The symbol [□] indicates that a translation is neutral.

siste à se ramener les cheveux très en arrière pour former une queue de cheval, si bien que la personne donne presque l'impression de s'être fait faire un lifting. (Voir aussi l'entrée "Croydon facelift".)

couply ['kʌplɪ] *adj* = caractéristique des couples; **I hate going out with Emma and Nick, they always act so couply** j'aime pas sortir avec Emma et Nick, j'ai toujours l'impression d'être de trop; **I'm staying in this weekend, since my mates are all doing couply stuff with their boyfriends** je ne sors pas ce week-end puisque toutes mes amies restent avec leur copain

coupon ['kuːpən] *n Scot (face)* tronche *f*, face *f*

cow [kaʊ] *n Br Péj (woman)* vache *f*, chameau *m*; **poor cow!** la pauvre!; **lucky cow!** la veinarde!; **you silly cow!** espèce de cloche! ▸ *voir aussi* **holy**

cowabunga [kaʊəˈbʌŋgə] *exclam Am* = cri de joie ou de victoire

ⓘ Il s'agit d'un terme du monde des surfers, rendu célèbre par le dessin animé *Les Tortues Ninja*.

cowboy ['kaʊbɔɪ] *n Br Péj (workman)* mauvais artisan◻ *m*, fumiste *m*; **they're a cowboy outfit** ils sont vraiment pas sérieux dans cette entreprise

crab [kræb] *n (pubic louse)* morpion *m*; **to have crabs** avoir des morpions

crack [kræk] **1** *n* (**a**) **crack (cocaine)** crack *m*; **crack den** = lieu où l'on achète, vend et consomme du crack; **crack whore** = droguée qui se prostitue pour acheter du crack

(**b**) [!!] *(woman's genitals)* chatte *f*, con *m*, cramouille *f* (**c**) [!!] *(anus)* troufignon *m*, trou *m* du cul (**d**) *(attempt)* **to have a crack at sth, to give sth a crack** essayer qch◻ (**e**) = craic

2 *vi* **to get cracking** *(make a start)* se mettre au boulot; *(speed up)* se grouiller, se magner ▸ *voir aussi* **sack**

crack on *vi Br & Austr* (**a**) **to crack on to sb** *(chat up)* faire du rentrededans à qn (**b**) **to crack on with sth** *(make progress)* se mettre à qch; **right, let's crack on!** bon, allez, remuons-nous!

crack up 1 *vt sép* **to crack sb up** *(cause to laugh hysterically)* faire éclater qn de rire

2 *vi* (**a**) *Br (get angry)* péter les plombs (**b**) *(have nervous breakdown)* craquer (nerveusement) (**c**) *(laugh hysterically)* éclater de rire

cracked [krækt] *adj (mad)* cinglé, toqué

cracker ['krækə(r)] *n* (**a**) *Br (excellent thing)* **to be a cracker** être génial; **it was a cracker of a goal** c'était un but magnifique; **she's a cracker** *(gorgeous)* elle est hyper canon (**b**) *Am (poor white person)* = pauvre originaire du sud des États-Unis

crackerjack ['krækədʒæk] *Am* **1** *n* **to be a crackerjack** *(person)* être un crack *ou* un as; *(thing)* être génial **2** *adj (excellent)* génial, du tonnerre

crackers ['krækəz] *adj Br (mad)* cinglé, toqué

crackhead ['krækhed] *n* accro *mf* au crack

crackhouse ['krækhaʊs] *n* = lieu où l'on achète, vend et consomme du crack

cracking ['krækɪŋ] *adj Br (excellent)* super, génial

crackpot ['krækpɒt] **1** *n (person)* allumé(e) *m,f*
2 *adj (scheme, idea)* loufoque

cradle-snatcher ['kreɪdəlsnætʃə(r)] *n* **he's a cradle-snatcher** il les prend au berceau

craic [kræk] *n Ir (fun)* **it was great craic last night!** on s'est bien marré hier soir!; **we did it just for the craic** on l'a fait pour le fun; **what's the craic?** *(what's new?)* quoi de neuf?

crank [kræŋk] *n* **(a)** *(eccentric)* allumé(e) *m,f* **(b)** *Am (grumpy person)* râleur(euse) *m,f* **(c)** *(amphetamine)* speed *m; (methamphetamine)* métamphétamine *f*, crystal meth *m*

crank up 1 *vt sép* **to crank sth up** *(music, volume)* monter qch
2 *vi (inject drugs)* se piquer

cranky ['kræŋkɪ] *adj* **(a)** *Br (eccentric)* excentrique□, loufoque **(b)** *Am (grumpy)* grognon, grincheux

crap [!] [kræp] **1** *n* **(a)** *(excrement)* merde *f*; **to have** *or Am* **take a crap** chier, couler un bronze; **he bores the crap out of me** je le trouve chiant comme la pluie
(b) *(nonsense)* conneries *fpl*; **he's full of crap** il raconte n'importe quoi; **you're talking crap!** tu racontes n'importe quoi!; **cut the crap!** arrête tes conneries!, arrête de dire n'importe quoi!; **don't believe all that crap!** il faut pas écouter toutes ces conneries!; **I can't be doing with all that New Age crap** je ne supporte pas toutes ces conneries New Age; **that's crap, I never said that!** c'est des conneries, j'ai jamais dit ça!; **what he's saying is a load of crap** il raconte n'importe quoi
(c) *(worthless things)* **the film/book was a load of crap** il était

nul, ce film/bouquin
(d) *(useless things)* bazar *m*; **clear all your crap off the bed** enlève ton bazar du lit
(e) *(disgusting substance)* merde *f*, saloperie *f*; **he eats nothing but crap** il bouffe que de la merde
(f) *(unfair treatment)* **I'm not taking that crap from you!** si tu crois que je vais supporter tes conneries, tu te gourres!; **I don't need this crap!** je me passerais bien de ce genre de conneries!
(g) to feel like crap *(ill)* se sentir vraiment patraque
2 *adj (worthless)* merdique; *(nasty)* dégueulasse; **to feel crap** *(ill)* se sentir vraiment mal fichu; *(guilty)* se sentir coupable□; **her work is crap** elle fait de la merde; **he's a crap teacher** il est finalement nul comme prof
3 *vt* **to crap oneself** *(defecate, be scared)* faire dans son froc
4 *vi (defecate)* chier, couler un bronze
5 *exclam* **(oh,) crap!** oh merde!

crap out [!] *vi* se dégonfler; **he crapped out of the fight** il s'est dégonflé au dernier moment et a refusé de se battre; **he crapped out of telling her the truth** finalement il a eu la trouille de lui dire la vérité

crapper [!] ['kræpə(r)] *n (toilet)* chiottes *fpl*, gogues *mpl*

crappy [!] ['kræpɪ] *adj (worthless)* merdique; **to feel crappy** *(ill)* se sentir vraiment mal fichu; *(guilty)* se sentir coupable□; **he's a crappy teacher** il est finalement nul comme prof

crash [kræʃ] **1** *vt (party)* s'inviter à, taper l'incruste à
2 *vi (spend night, sleep)* pieuter; *(fall asleep)* s'endormir□; **can I crash at your place?** est-ce que je

peux pieuter chez toi?

crash out vi *(spend night, sleep)* pieuter; *(fall asleep)* s'endormir*; **he was crashed out on the sofa** il roupillait dans le canapé

crate [kreɪt] n *(old car)* vieille bagnole f; *(old plane)* vieux coucou m

crazy medicine ['kreɪzɪ'medsɪn] n *(drug)* métamphétamine f, crystal meth m

cream [kriːm] **1** vt **(a)** *(defeat)* battre à plates coutures; *Am (beat up)* tabasser **(b) to cream one's jeans [!!]** *(of man)* décharger dans son froc; *(of woman)* mouiller sa culotte
2 [!!] vi **(a)** *(become sexually aroused)* (of woman) mouiller **(b)** *(ejaculate)* décharger

cream crackered [kriːm'krækəd] adj Br *(rhyming slang* **knackered***)* *(exhausted)* crevé, lessivé, naze; *(broken, worn out)* bousillé

crease up [kriːs] Br **1** vt sép **to crease sb up** *(cause to laugh hysterically)* faire se tordre qn de rire
2 vi *(laugh hysterically)* se tordre de rire

cred [kred] n Br *(abrév* **credibility***)* **to have (street) cred** être branché ou dans le coup; **he wants to get some (street) cred** il veut faire branché ou dans le coup

creep [kriːp] n **(a)** *(unpleasant man)* type m répugnant; *Br (obsequious person)* lèche-bottes mf **(b) to give sb the creeps** *(scare)* donner la chair de poule à qn; *(repulse)* débecter qn

creepy ['kriːpɪ] adj **it's creepy** *(scary)* ça me donne la chair de poule; *(repulsive)* ça me débecte

creepy-crawly ['kriːpɪ'krɔːlɪ] n bébête f

cretin ['kretɪn] n *(idiot)* crétin(e) m,f

crew [kruː] n bande f de potes; **I was**

hanging with my crew j'étais avec mes potes

crib [krɪb] n Noir Am *(home)* barraque f, foyer*; **we carried on the party back at my crib** on a continué la soirée chez moi

crikey ['kraɪkɪ] exclam bigre!

crim [krɪm] n Br & Austr *(criminal)* criminel(elle)* m,f

Crimbo ['krɪmbəʊ], **Crimble** ['krɪmbəl] n Br *(Christmas)* Noël* m

crimper ['krɪmpə(r)] n Br merlan m *(coiffeur)*

cringe-making ['krɪndʒmeɪkɪŋ], **cringe-worthy** ['krɪndʒwɜːðɪ] adj Br embarrassant*, gênant*

croak [krəʊk] vi *(die)* calancher, passer l'arme à gauche

croc [krɒk] n *(abrév* **crocodile***)* crocodile* m

crock [krɒk] n Am **to be a crock** or **a crock of shit [!]** *(nonsense)* être des foutaises ou des conneries; **don't believe that crock he told you!** ne crois pas ce qu'il t'a dit, c'est des foutaises!

crone [krəʊn] n **old crone** vieille toupie f

crook [krʊk] adj Austr *(ill)* mal fichu; *(not working)* détraqué

cropper ['krɒpə(r)] n **to come a cropper** *(fall)* prendre une gamelle; *(fail)* se planter

crown jewels [!] ['kraʊn'dʒʊəlz] npl Hum *(man's genitals)* bijoux mpl de famille

Croydon facelift ['krɔɪdən'feɪslɪft] n Br Hum Péj = queue de cheval, avec les cheveux tirés en arriére

ⓘ Croydon est une ville-dortoir située au sud de Londres. Selon certains, elle est l'archétype de la ville de banlieue sans intérêt, peuplée essentiellement de gens issus de la classe ouvrière. Le terme "Croydon facelift", qui signifie littéralement "lifting de Croydon", fait référence à un type de coiffure jugé caractéristique des habitants de cette ville, et qui consiste à se ramener les cheveux très en arrière pour former une queue de cheval, si bien que la personne donne presque l'impression de s'être fait faire un lifting. (Voir aussi l'entrée "council".)

crucial ['kru:ʃəl] *adj Br (excellent)* super, génial; **the DJ at the club last night was well crucial** le DJ de la boîte, hier soir, était vraiment super

crucify ['kru:sɪfaɪ] *vt (defeat, criticize)* démolir

crud [krʌd] *n* (**a**) *(dirt)* crasse *f* (**b**) *(nonsense)* conneries *fpl*; **he was talking some crud about the dangers of drugs** il était en train de raconter des conneries sur les dangers de la drogue (**c**) *(person)* ordure *f*, saloperie *f*

cruddy ['krʌdɪ] *adj* (**a**) *(dirty)* cradingue, dégueulasse (**b**) *(worthless)* merdique

cruise [kru:z] **1** *vt (person)* draguer; *(place)* aller draguer dans
   2 *vi* (**a**) *(look for sexual partner)* draguer (**b**) *Am (leave)* mettre les bouts, se casser, s'arracher; **ready to cruise?** on y va? (**c**) *Hum* **you're cruising for a bruising!** toi, tu cherches les emmerdes!

crumb [krʌm] *n Péj (person)* minable *mf*

crumbly ['krʌmblɪ] *n Br (old person)* croulant(e) *m,f*

crummy ['krʌmɪ] *adj* minable

crumpet ['krʌmpɪt] *n Br (women)* nanas *fpl*, gonzesses *fpl*; **a nice bit of crumpet** une belle nana; **the thinking man's/woman's crumpet** une belle nana/un beau mec intelligent(e)

crunk [krʌŋk] **1** *n (type of music)* crunk *m*
   2 *adj (excited)* surexcité; **let's get crunk!** éclatons-nous!

crunked up [krʌŋkt'ʌp] *adj (excited)* surexcité; **we got crunked up on the dancefloor!** on s'est super éclatés sur la piste de danse!

crust [krʌst] *n Br* **to earn a** *or* **one's crust** gagner sa croûte

crustie, crusty ['krʌstɪ] *n Br* jeune hippie *mf* crado

ⓘ Le type "crusty" est apparu au début des années 90 avec l'émergence du mouvement alternatif des "New Age travellers" (communautés néo-hippies parcourant la Grande-Bretagne dans des caravanes et des autobus aménagés, dont les membres sont de tous les combats pour la défense de l'environnement). Le "crusty" est généralement sans emploi et sans domicile fixes, d'une hygiène pas toujours irréprochable, et il se déplace souvent avec un chien tenu au bout d'une ficelle.

cry out [kraɪ] *vi* **for crying out loud!** c'est pas possible!

cuckoo ['kʊku:] *adj (mad)* cinglé, toqué

cuffs [kʌfs] *npl (abrév* **handcuffs***)* menottes▢ *fpl*, bracelets *mpl*

cum [!!] [kʌm] *n* foutre *m*, jute *m*

cunt [!!] [kʌnt] *n* (**a**) *(woman's genitals)* chatte *f*, con *m* (**b**) *(man)* enculé *m*; *(woman)* sale pute *f*; **he's a stu-**

The symbol ▢ indicates that a translation is neutral.

pid cunt! c'est qu'un enculé!; **the poor cunt's smashed his leg to pieces** le pauvre vieux, il s'est bousillé la jambe (**c**) *(thing)* **that exam was an absolute cunt!** cet examen était une vraie saloperie!

① Il s'agit du terme le plus grossier de la langue anglaise, loin devant "fuck". Même les gens qui ont l'habitude de jurer évitent généralement de l'utiliser, y compris entre amis, car son utilisation ne manquerait pas de choquer. Il est préférable de le bannir complètement de son vocabulaire.

cunted [!!] ['kʌntɪd] *adj Br (drunk)* complètement bourré *ou* pété; *(on drugs)* complètement défoncé

cupcake ['kʌpkeɪk] *n* (**a**) *(eccentric person)* allumé(e) *m, f* (**b**) *Am Injurieux*

(homosexual) pédale *f*, tantouze *f*

curb [kɜːb] ▸ *voir* **kick**

curse [kɜːs] *n* **to have the curse** avoir ses ragnagnas

cushti, cushty ['kʊʃtɪ] *adj Br* super, génial; **he's got a cushti set-up there** il est peinard

cut [kʌt] *vt* **to cut the cloth** *or* **the cheese** *(break wind)* péter, lâcher une caisse ▸ *voir aussi* **slack**

cut out 1 *vt sép* **cut it out!** ça suffit!
  2 *vi Am (leave)* mettre les bouts, calter

cute [kjuːt] *adj (attractive)* mignon

cutesy ['kjuːtsɪ] *adj* cucul *inv*

cutie ['kjuːtɪ] *n (term of affection)* mon chou; **he's such a cutie!** il est mignon comme tout!; **his girlfriend is a real cutie** sa copine est mignonne comme tout

Dd

daffy ['dæfɪ] *adj* loufoque, loufedingue

daft [dɑːft] *Br* **1** *adj* bête□, débile; **don't be daft!** fais pas l'idiot!
2 *adv* **don't talk daft!** dis pas de bêtises!

daftie ['dɑːftɪ] *n Br* cruche *f*, andouille *f*

dag [dæg] *n Austr* (**a**) *(unfashionable)* ringard(e) *m,f* (**b**) *(untidy)* type *m* négligé; *(untidy woman)* bonne femme *f* négligée

daggy ['dægɪ] *adj Austr* (**a**) *(unfashionable)* ringard (**b**) *(untidy)* négligé□

Dago ['deɪgəʊ] *Injurieux* **1** *n* métèque *mf (personne d'origine espagnole, italienne, portugaise ou latino-américaine)*
2 *adj* métèque

daisy ['deɪzɪ] *n* **to be pushing up the daisies** manger les pissenlits par la racine

daisy-chaining [!] ['deɪzɪtʃeɪnɪŋ] *n* partouze *f*

daks [dæks] *n Austr (trousers)* futal *m*, falzar *m*

damage ['dæmɪdʒ] *n* **what's the damage?** *(how much does it cost?)* ça fait combien?□

dame [deɪm] *n Am* gonzesse *f*

dammit ['dæmɪt] **1** *n Br* **as near as dammit** dans ces eaux-là
2 *exclam* merde!

damn [dæm] **1** *n* (**a**) **I don't give a damn** j'en ai rien à cirer, je m'en balance (**b**) *Br* **damn all** *(nothing)* que dalle; **damn all money/thanks** pas un sou/un merci; **they had damn all to do with it** ils n'y étaient pour rien
2 *adj* sacré, foutu; **he's a damn nuisance!** c'est un sacré emmerdeur!; **it's one damn thing after another!** ça n'arrête pas!
3 *adv* vachement; **a damn good idea** une super bonne idée; **you're damn right** t'as parfaitement raison; **he's so damn slow** il est hyper lent; **she knows damn well what I'm talking about** elle sait parfaitement de quoi je parle□
4 *exclam* **damn (it)!** merde!
5 *vt* **damn you!** va te faire voir!; **he lied to me, damn him!** il m'a menti, le salaud!; **damn the expense/the consequences!** tant pis pour les frais/les conséquences!; **well, I'll be damned!** eh ben ça alors!; **I'm** *or* **I'll be damned if I'm going to apologize** plutôt crever que de m'excuser
▶ *voir aussi* **sight**

damnation [dæm'neɪʃən] *exclam* zut!

damned [dæmd] *adj & adv* = **damn**

damnedest ['dæmdəst] **1** *n* **to do one's damnedest (to do sth)** faire tout son possible (pour faire qch)
2 *adj Am* **it was the damnedest thing!** c'était carrément incroyable!

dandy ['dændı] adj super; **everything's just (fine and) dandy!** tout baigne!

darky ['dɑːkı] n Injurieux bronzé(e) m,f

darn [dɑːn] **1** adj sacré, foutu; **the darn car won't start** cette saloperie de voiture ne veut pas démarrer; **you're a darn fool** t'es un vrai con
2 adv vachement; **we were darn lucky** on a eu une sacrée veine; **you know darn well what I mean!** tu comprends parfaitement ce que je veux dire!□; **it's too darn hot** il fait vraiment trop chaud□
3 exclam **darn (it)!** zut!
4 vt **he's late, darn him!** il est en retard, il fait vraiment chier!; **well, I'll be darned!** eh ben ça alors! ▶ voir aussi **sight**

darned [dɑːnd] adj & adv = **darn**

dash [dæʃ] exclam **dash (it)!** zut!, mince!

daylights ['deɪlaɪts] npl **to beat the living daylights out of sb** flanquer une dérouillée ou une raclée à qn; **you scared the living daylights out of me!** tu m'as foutu une de ces trouilles!

dead [ded] **1** adj **(a)** (not alive) **to be dead from the neck up** ne rien avoir dans le citron; **to be dead from the waist down** ne pas s'intéresser du tout au sexe; **to be dead to the world** en écraser; **I wouldn't be seen dead there/in that dress** je préférerais mourir que d'y aller/que de porter cette robe **(b)** (absolute) **to be a dead ringer for sb** être le portrait tout craché de qn; **he's a dead loss** c'est un bon à rien; **it was a dead loss** ça n'a servi à rien□
2 adv Br (very) vachement; **it's dead easy/good** c'est vachement facile/bon; **you were dead lucky** tu as eu une sacrée veine; **I'm dead bored** je m'ennuie à mort ▶ voir aussi **knock, meat, president**

deadbeat ['dedbiːt] n Am (lazy person) glandeur(euse) m,f; (tramp) clodo mf; (parasite) pique-assiette mf

deadly ['dedlı] adj Ir super, génial, d'enfer

death [deθ] n **(a) to look like death warmed up** avoir l'air d'un(e) déterré(e); **to feel like death warmed up** se sentir patraque **(b)** Am & Austr **death seat** (in a vehicle) place f du mort ▶ voir aussi **sick**

deck [dek] **1** n **(a) to hit the deck** (get out of bed) sortir de son pieu, se dépagnoter; (fall) se foutre la gueule par terre; (lie down) se jeter à terre□ **(b)** Hum **he's not playing with a full deck** c'est pas une lumière, il a pas inventé l'eau chaude
2 vt **to deck sb** foutre qn par terre

deep-six ['diːp'sıks] vt Am **(a)** (throw away) balancer, foutre en l'air **(b)** (rule out) mettre au placard

deep-throat [!!] ['diːp'θrəʊt] vt faire une pipe à

ⓘ Il s'agit du titre d'un film pornographique très célèbre, tourné dans les années 70.

def [def] adj super, génial

deffo ['defəʊ] adv Br (abrév **definitely**) absolument□; **are you coming tonight? – deffo!** tu viens ce soir? – je veux!

dekko ['dekəʊ] n Br **to have** or **take a dekko at sb/sth** mater qn/qch

Delhi belly ['delıbelı] n Br **to have Delhi belly** avoir la turista; **I got severe Delhi belly after that curry the other night** j'ai eu une sacrée courante après avoir mangé le curry l'autre soir

ⓘ Dans cette expression ("le ventre de Delhi"), les Britanniques emploient le mot "Delhi" car dans l'esprit de nombre d'entre eux, tout séjour en Inde se solde inévitablement par une crise de gastro-entérite. Aux États-Unis, c'est l'expression "Aztec two-step" que l'on emploie (voir cette entrée).

demo ['deməʊ] n (abrév **demonstration**) (a) (in street) manif f (b) (music sample) démo m (c) (explanation) démonstration□ f

dense [dens] adj (stupid) débile

devil ['devəl] n (a) (person) **the lucky devil!** le veinard!; Br **poor devil!** le pauvre!; Br **go on, be a devil!** allez, laisse-toi tenter!; Hum **the devil's dandruff** (cocaine) la coco (b) (for emphasis) **what/who/why the devil…?** que/qui/pourquoi diable…?; **how the devil should I know?** comment veux-tu que je sache?; **we had a devil of a job getting here on time** on a eu un mal de chien à arriver à l'heure

dexy ['deksɪ] n (abrév **dexamphetamine**) amphé f, amphet f

diabolical [daɪə'bɒlɪkəl] adj Br (very bad) nul

diamond ['daɪəmənd] Br **1** n (man) chic type m; (woman) chic fille f; **cheers, mate, you're a real diamond** merci vieux, t'es vraiment super
2 adj (excellent) super, génial; **he's a diamond geezer** c'est un type super

dibble ['dɪbəl] n Br (police) flics mpl, poulets mpl; **there were loads of dibble around** il y avait des flics partout

ⓘ Ce terme vient du dessin animé américain "Top Cat", dont l'un des personnages, un agent de police, se nomme Dibble.

dick [dɪk] n (a) [!] (penis) bite f, queue f (b) [!] (man) trou m du cul, trouduc m (c) Am (detective) privé m
▸ voir aussi **clever clogs, features**

dick about, dick around [!] **1** vt sép **to dick sb about** or **around** faire tourner qn en bourrique
2 vi glander, glandouiller; **oh, stop dicking around!** arrête donc de glandouiller!

dickface [!] ['dɪkfeɪs] n trou m du cul, trouduc m; **hey, dickface!** hé, trouduc!

dickhead [!] ['dɪkhed] n trou m du cul, trouduc m

dickless [!] ['dɪkləs] adj (worthless) minable, nul; (lacking courage) dégonflé, pétochard m; **dickless wonder** = personne qui parle beaucoup mais agit peu, guignol m, rigolo m

dicky-bird ['dɪkɪbɜːd] n Br (rhyming slang **word**) mot□ m; **not a dicky-bird!** motus et bouche cousue!

diddle ['dɪdəl] vt (a) Br (cheat, swindle) duper, rouler; **to diddle sb out of sth** carotter qch à qn; **I've been diddled!** je me suis fait avoir! (b) Am (have sex with) baiser, se taper, s'envoyer; **he's been diddling his secretary for years** ça fait des années qu'il s'envoie sa secrétaire

diddly ['dɪdəlɪ] n Am **that's not worth diddly** ça ne vaut pas un clou

diddlyshit [!] ['dɪdəlɪˈʃɪt] n Am **I don't give a diddlyshit** je m'en balance, je m'en fous complètement

diddlysquat ['dɪdəlɪskwɒt] *n Am* que dalle; **that's not worth diddlysquat** ça ne vaut pas un clou; **I don't know diddlysquat about computers** l'informatique, j'y connais rien

diesel (dyke) ['diːzəl(daɪk)] *n Injurieux* gouine *f (à l'allure masculine)*

dig [dɪg] **1** *vt* **(a)** *(like)* aimer□, apprécier□; **I really dig that kind of music** ça me branche vraiment, ce genre de musique **(b)** *(look at)* mater; **dig that guy over there** mate un peu le mec, là-bas **(c)** *(understand)* piger
2 *vi (understand)* piger; **you dig?** tu piges?

dig in *vi (start eating)* attaquer *(un repas)*

dike [daɪk] *Am* = **dyke**

dildo [!] ['dɪldəʊ] *n Péj (person)* trou *m* du cul, trouduc *m*

dill [dɪl] *n Austr* andouille *f*, courge *f*

dime bag ['daɪmbæg] *n Am* = dose de marijuana d'une valeur de 10 dollars

dimwit ['dɪmwɪt] *n* andouille *f*, courge *f*

ding-dong ['dɪŋdɒŋ] *n Br* **(a)** *(argument)* engueulade *f* **(b)** *(fight)* bagarre *f*

dinkum ['dɪŋkəm] *Austr* **1** *n* Australien(enne) *m,f* de naissance□
2 *adj (person)* franc (franche)□, sincère□; *(thing)* authentique□; **fair dinkum** régulier, vrai de vrai; **dinkum?** sans blague?; **a dinkum Aussie** un vrai Australien□ (une vraie Australienne□)
3 *adv* franchement□, vraiment□

dip [dɪp] *n Am (idiot)* andouille *f*, courge *f*, cruche *f* ▸ *voir aussi* **wick**

dippy ['dɪpɪ] *adj* loufoque, loufedingue

dipshit [!] ['dɪpʃɪt] *n Am* taré(e) *m,f*, crétin(e) *m,f*

dipso ['dɪpsəʊ] *n (abrév* **dipsomaniac***)* alcolo *mf*, poivrot(e) *m,f*

dipstick ['dɪpstɪk] *n (idiot)* andouille *f*, cruche *f*

dirt [dɜːt] *n* **(a)** **to dish the dirt (about)** tout raconter (sur); **come on, dish the dirt!** allez, dis-moi tout! **(b)** *Am* **to do sb dirt** faire une crasse à qn

dirtbag ['dɜːtbæg] *n Am* nul (nulle) *m,f*, nullard(e) *m,f*

dirtbox [!!] ['dɜːtbɒks] *n Br* trou *m* du cul, boîte *f* à pâté

dirty ['dɜːtɪ] **1** *n Br* **to do the dirty on sb,** *Am* **to do sb dirty** faire une crasse à qn
2 *adj* **the dirty deed** *(sex)* = l'acte sexuel; **have you two done the dirty deed yet?** est-ce que vous avez déjà fait crac-crac tous les deux?; **dirty old man** vieux cochon *m*; **dirty weekend** week-end *m* coquin; *Br Hum* **dirty stop-out** débauché(e) *m,f* qui découche

dis [dɪs] = **diss**

disaster area [dɪˈzɑːstəreərɪə] *n* **your desk's a disaster area!** c'est vraiment le foutoir sur ton bureau!; **to be a walking disaster area** être une catastrophe ambulante

disco biscuit ['dɪskəʊˈbɪskɪt] *n Br* cachet *m* d'ecstasy, bonbec *m*

dishwater ['dɪʃwɔːtə(r)] *n* **this coffee's like dishwater!** c'est vraiment de l'eau de vaisselle, ce café!

dishy ['dɪʃɪ] *adj* mignon

diss [dɪs] *vt Am* débiner

ditch [dɪtʃ] *vt (boyfriend, girlfriend)* plaquer, larguer; *(thing)* balancer, foutre en l'air; *(plan, idea)* laisser tomber

---

Le symbole **[!]** dénote un terme très familier, **[!!]** un terme vulgaire.

ditz [dɪts] *n Am* courge *f*, andouille *f*, cruche *f*

ditzy ['dɪtsɪ] *adj Am* étourdi[□]

div [dɪv] *n Br* andouille *f*, cruche *f*

dive [daɪv] *n (place)* bouge[□] *m*

divvy ['dɪvɪ] *n Br (idiot)* andouille *f*, cruche *f*

DL [diː'el] *n Noir Am* = **downlow**

do [duː] **1** *vt* (**a**) *(take)* **to do drugs** se droguer[□]; **let's do lunch** il faudrait qu'on déjeune ensemble un de ces jours
(**b**) *Br (prosecute)* poursuivre[□]; **to get done for speeding** se faire pincer pour excès de vitesse
(**c**) *Br (rob)* **to do a jeweller's/bank** braquer une bijouterie/une banque
(**d**) *(cheat)* arnaquer; **to do sb out of sth** arnaquer qn de qch; **I've been done!** j'ai été refait!
(**e**) *(visit)* **to do Paris/the sights** faire Paris/les monuments
(**f**) *Br (beat up)* tabasser; **I'll do you!** je vais te casser la gueule!
(**g**) *(kill)* zigouiller, buter
(**h**) *(have sex with) (of man)* baiser, tringler, troncher; *(of woman)* baiser avec, s'envoyer; **to do it (with sb)** faire crac-crac (avec qn); **so have you two done it yet?** alors, vous avez fait la chose?
2 *n Br (party)* fête *f*, boum *f*

do in *vt sép Br* (**a**) *(exhaust)* vanner, pomper, crever; **to feel done in** être crevé *ou* naze *ou* sur les rotules (**b**) *(kill)* **to do sb in** buter *ou* zigouiller qn ▶ *voir aussi* **head**

do over *vt sép Br* (**a**) *(beat up)* **to do sb over** tabasser qn (**b**) *(rob)* **to do sb over** dépouiller qn; **to do sth over** dévaliser qch[□]

do with *vt insép (tolerate)* **I can't be doing with people like that** je peux pas blairer les gens comme ça;

he couldn't be doing with living in London il pouvait pas supporter de vivre à Londres

'do [duː] *n (abrév* **hairdo***)* coiffure[□] *f*; **check out her new 'do** vise un peu sa nouvelle coiffure

dob in [dɒb] *vt sép Austr* moucharder

doddle ['dɒdəl] *n Br* **it's a doddle** c'est hyper fastoche

dodgy ['dɒdʒɪ] *adj Br* (**a**) *(unsafe, untrustworthy)* louche; **he's OK, but all his friends are well dodgy** lui, ça va, mais ses amis craignent vraiment; **the house is nice, but it's in a really dodgy area** la maison est bien mais elle est dans un quartier vraiment craignos; **investing money in a scheme like that is just too dodgy** c'est vraiment trop risqué d'investir dans ce genre de truc; **they were involved in a couple of dodgy business deals** ils ont été impliqués dans des transactions plutôt louches
(**b**) *(not working properly, unstable)* merdique; **don't sit on that chair, it's a bit dodgy** ne t'assieds pas sur cette chaise, elle est un peu branlante[□]; **the ceiling looks a bit dodgy** le plafond n'a pas l'air en très bon état[□]; **my stomach's been a bit dodgy for the last couple of days** ça fait deux jours que j'ai l'estomac un peu dérangé[□]; **we can't go camping while the weather's so dodgy** on ne peut pas aller camper alors que le temps risque de se gâter à tout moment[□]
(**c**) *(unfashionable, ridiculous)* ringard; **look at him in that dodgy shirt!** regarde-le avec sa chemise de ringard!

dog [dɒg] *n* (**a**) *(ugly woman)* cageot *m*, boudin *m*
(**b**) **dog's breakfast** *or* **dinner** *(mess)*

The symbol [□] indicates that a translation is neutral.

merdier *m*; **to make a dog's break-fast** *or* **dinner of sth** complètement foirer qch; *Br* **to be dressed up like a dog's dinner** être attifé de façon ridicule

(c) *Br* **to be the dog's bollocks [!]** *(excellent)* être génial

(d) *Br* **to be like a dog with two dicks [!]** avoir l'air très content de soi▫; **he's been like a dog with two dicks since he got Jennifer Aniston's autograph** il se sent plus depuis que Jennifer Aniston lui a donné son autographe

(e) *Br* (*rhyming slang* **dog and bone** = **phone**) bigophone *m*; **get on the dog (and bone) and order a takeaway** prends le bigophone et fais livrer un repas

(f) *Hum* **I'm going to see a man about a dog** *(going to the toilet)* je vais aux toilettes▫; *(going somewhere unspecified)* j'ai un truc à faire

(g) *Br* **to give sb dog's abuse** traiter qn de tous les noms

(h) *Am (useless thing)* merde *f*

(i) *Am (foot)* arpion *m*, pinglot *m*; **my dogs are barking!** ce que j'ai mal aux arpions! ▸ *voir aussi* **hair**, **sausage**

dog-end ['dɒgend] *n Br* mégot▫ *m*, clope *m*

dogging ['dɒgɪŋ] *n* = partouze improvisée entre inconnus dans des lieux publics tels que parkings et parcs, dogging *m*

doggone ['dɒgɒn] *Am* **1** *adj* sacré, foutu; **I've lost the doggone car keys** j'ai perdu ces saletés de clés de bagnole

2 *adv* vachement; **it's so doggone hot!** il fait une chaleur à crever!

3 *exclam* **doggone (it)!** zut!

doggy-fashion ['dɒgɪfæʃən], **doggy-style** ['dɒgɪstaɪl] *adv (have sex)* en levrette

doghouse ['dɒghaʊs] *n* **to be in the doghouse (with sb)** ne pas être en odeur de sainteté *ou* être en dis-grâce (auprès de qn)▫; **he's in the doghouse with his girlfriend for forgetting their anniversary** sa copine lui fait la gueule parce qu'il a oublié de fêter l'anniversaire de leur rencontre

dog-rough ['dɒgrʌf] *adj* (a) *(ugly)* **she's dog-rough!** elle est hyper mo-che! (b) *(unwell)* **I feel dog-rough this morning** je ne me sens pas dans mon assiette ce matin

doh [dəʊ] *exclam* que je suis bête!

ⓘ Il s'agit d'une expression popu-larisée par Homer Simpson, dans le dessin animé américain *The Simpsons*.

doll [dɒl] *n* (a) *(attractive woman)* canon *m* (b) *(term of address)* poupée *f* (c) *Am (kind person)* trésor *m*, chou *m*

doll up *vt sép* **to doll oneself up, to get dolled up** se faire belle▫

dong [!] [dɒŋ] *n* bite *f*, queue *f*

doobie ['du:bɪ] *n* joint *m*, pétard *m*

doodah ['du:dɑ:], *Am* **doodad** ['du:-dæd] *n* truc *m*, machin *m*

doo-doo ['du:du:] *n* (a) *(excrement)* crotte *f*, caca *m*; **the dog's done a doo-doo on the doormat** le chien a fait sa crotte sur le paillasson (b) *(trouble)* pétrin *m*; **we're in deep doo-doo!** on est vraiment dans le pétrin!

doofus ['du:fəs] *n Am* andouille *f*, cruche *f*, courge *f*

doohickey [du:'hɪkɪ] *Am* = **doodah**

doolally [du:'lælɪ] *adj Br* zinzin, tim-bré

ⓘ Il s'agit à l'origine d'un terme d'argot militaire. Deolali était une ville de garnison britannique située près de Bombay, par où transitaient de nombreux militaires britanniques qui rentraient au pays. Le temps de transit était généralement assez long, et les soldats trompaient leur ennui en fréquentant les bars et les prostituées. Nombre d'entre eux se retrouvaient en prison ou victimes de maladies vénériennes. Le nom Deolali a fini par désigner le comportement étrange de ces soldats désœuvrés.

doo-rag ['du:ræg] *n Noir Am* = sorte de bandana porté sur la tête

doorstep ['dɔ:step] *n Br (slice of bread)* grosse tranche *f* de pain□

dope [dəʊp] **1** *n* **(a)** *(cannabis)* shit *m* **(b)** *(person)* crétin(e) *m,f*, abruti(e) *m,f*
2 *adj Am (excellent)* génial, super

dopehead ['dəʊphed] *n* **to be a dopehead** fumer beaucoup de cannabis□

doper ['dəʊpə(r)] *n Am* **to be a doper** fumer beaucoup de cannabis□

dopey ['dəʊpɪ] *adj* empoté, cruche

do-rag ['du:ræg] = **doo-rag**

do-re-mi [dəʊreɪ'mi:] *n Am (money)* fric *m*, blé *m*, oseille *f*, artiche *f*

dork [dɔ:k] *n* ringard *m*, bouffon *m*

dorky ['dɔ:kɪ] *adj* ringard, nul

Dorothy ['dɒrəθɪ] *npr* **a friend of Dorothy** un homo; **is he a friend of Dorothy, do you think?** tu crois qu'il est homo?

ⓘ Cette expression trouve son origine dans le film américain *Le Magicien d'Oz* (1939) dans lequel Judy Garland, actrice fétiche de la communauté homosexuelle, incarnait la jeune Dorothy.

dose [dəʊs] *n* **(a)** *(venereal disease)* chtouille *f*; **to catch a dose** attraper la chtouille **(b)** *Br* **to get through sth like a dose of salts** faire qch en deux coups de cuillère à pot

dosh [dɒʃ] *n Br* blé *m*, oseille *f*

doss [dɒs] *Br* **1** *n* **(a)** *(bed)* plumard *m* **(b)** *(sleep)* **to have a doss** piquer un roupillon **(c)** **it was a doss** *(easy)* c'était fastoche
2 *vi (sleep)* roupiller

doss about, doss around *vi Br* traîner

doss down *vi Br* pieuter

dosser ['dɒsə(r)] *n Br* **(a)** *(tramp)* clodo *mf* **(b)** *(hostel)* asile *m* de nuit□

doss-house ['dɒshaʊs] *n Br* asile *m* de nuit□

dotty ['dɒtɪ] *adj* maboule, loufedingue; **to be dotty about sb/sth** être dingue de qn/qch

douche-bag ['du:ʃbæg] *n Am (person)* ordure *f*

dough [dəʊ] *n (money)* blé *m*, oseille *f*
▸ *voir aussi* **roll**

down [daʊn] **1** *vt (eat, drink)* s'enfiler; **he downed his pint and left** il a descendu sa pinte puis il est parti
2 *adj* **he's always trying to look like he's down with the kids** il essaie toujours d'avoir l'air cool auprès des jeunes; *Am* **shall we go to the mall tomorrow? – yeah, I'm down with that** on va au centre commercial demain? – ouais, ça me branche

down-and-out ['daʊnən'aʊt] **1** *n* clodo *mf*
2 *adj* à la rue □

The symbol □ indicates that a translation is neutral.

downer ['daʊnə(r)] n (**a**) (drug) barbiturique□ m, downer m (**b**) (depressing experience) **to be on a downer** avoir le bourdon; **it was a real downer** c'était vraiment déprimant□; **the film's a complete downer** c'est un film qui file le bourdon

downlow [daʊn'ləʊ] n Noir Am **on the downlow** (confidentially) confidentiellement□; (in secret) secrètement□; **I'm telling you this on the downlow** je te dis ça, mais c'est entre nous; **he's seeing someone else on the downlow** il a une maîtresse□

dozey, dozy ['dəʊzɪ] adj Br (stupid) couillon; **you dozey plonker!** quel couillon ou quelle andouille tu fais!

drag [dræg] n (**a**) (bore) truc m chiant, galère f; **he's such a drag** c'est vraiment un emmerdeur; **the party was a real drag** la soirée était vraiment chiante; **what a drag!** quelle galère! (**b**) (on cigarette, joint) bouffée f, taffe f; **she took** or **had a drag on her cigarette** elle tira sur sa cigarette (**c**) Am (influence) influence□ f; **to have drag** avoir le bras long

drat [dræt] exclam **drat (it)!** zut!, mince!

dratted ['drætɪd] adj sacré, foutu; **where's that dratted brother of mine?** mais où est passé mon frangin?

draw [drɔː] n Br (cannabis) shit m

dream [driːm] **1** n **in your dreams!** tu peux toujours rêver!
2 vi **dream on!** tu peux toujours rêver!

drink-dialling [drɪŋk'daɪəlɪŋ], Am **drunk-dialing** [drʌŋk'daɪəlɪŋ] n Hum = terme dérivé de "drink-driving" (conduite en état d'ivresse) pour désigner le fait de téléphoner à quelqu'un sous l'effet désinhibant de l'alcool

drip [drɪp] n (person) mollusque m

drippy ['drɪpɪ] adj mollasson

drongo ['drɒŋgəʊ] n Austr (idiot) abruti(e) m,f

drop [drɒp] **1** vt (**a**) **drop it!** (I don't want to talk about it) tu me lâches?; (I don't want to hear about it) change de disque! (**b**) **to drop one** (péter) larguer ou lâcher une caisse
2 vi **drop dead!** ta gueule! ▸ voir aussi **log**

drop-dead gorgeous [drɒpded'gɔːdʒəs] adj hyper canon

dross [drɒs] n (worthless things) **it's (a load of) dross** ça ne vaut pas un clou

druggie, druggy ['drʌgɪ] **1** n camé(e) m,f
2 adj (relating to drugs) **he hangs out with a really druggie crowd** il traîne avec une bande de junkies ou de toxicos; **I wouldn't go there at night, it's a bit of a druggie area** je ne m'y risquerais pas la nuit, il y a pas mal de junkies qui traînent par là-bas

drunk-dialing [drʌŋk'daɪəlɪŋ] Am = **drink-dialling**

dry up [draɪ] vi **dry up!** (be quiet) la ferme!

ducats ['dʌkəts] npl Am fric m, blé m, oseille f

dud [dʌd] **1** adj (**a**) (fake) faux (fausse)□ (**b**) (useless) (object, gadget) qui ne marche pas□; (idea) débile
2 n (**a**) (fake coin) fausse pièce f de monnaie□; (fake note) faux billet□ m (**b**) (useless person) nullité f (**c**) (disappointment) **the party was a real dud** la soirée cassait vraiment pas des briques

Pleins feux sur...

Drugs

Les termes de cette rubrique appartiennent au monde de la drogue, qui est particulièrement riche en argot. Les termes suivants servent tous à désigner le cannabis : **dope**, **weed**, **pot**, **grass**, **hash**, **blow**, **shit**, **Mary Jane**, et **wacky baccy** (littéralement : "tabac qui rend fou"). On peut le fumer en **spliff**, **joint** ou **doobie** (terme américain), ou bien le consommer en **space cake**. Parmi les termes désignant la cocaïne, citons **coke**, **charlie**, **snow**, et dans un registre plus humoristique **nose candy** (littéralement : "sucrerie pour le nez"). Le verbe "sniffer" se dit **to snort** lorsqu'il s'agit de cocaïne (ou d'une autre drogue sous forme de poudre) et **to sniff** lorsqu'il s'agit de produits solvants. "Se faire une ligne" est tout simplement **to do a line**. Parmi les termes désignant l'héroïne, citons **smack**, **skag**, **junk**, **horse** et **H** ; "se préparer un shoot" se dit **to cook up** et "se shooter" se dit **to shoot up**. L'ecstasy se décline sous les noms **E**, **X**, ainsi que **pills**, **adam** et **disco biscuits**. Le LSD se dit **acid** (**to drop acid** signifie "prendre du LSD") et il se présente sous forme de **tabs** (buvards). Parmi les autres types de drogue, citons les amphétamines, connues sous les noms de **whizz** et **base**, la kétamine (**special K**, **vitamin K**), et la méthamphétamine (**ice**, **yada**).

Une personne sous l'influence du cannabis est dite **stoned**. De quelqu'un qui a pris des substances hallucinogènes on dit **he/she's tripping**. Les termes généraux pour désigner l'état d'une personne sous l'emprise d'une drogue sont : **high**, **loaded** ou encore **out of one's box/head/tree**. On peut également employer des termes qui signifient "ivre" tels que **wasted**, **bombed**, **mashed** et **out of it**. Un drogué est un **druggie** ; un héroïnomane est un **junkie** (**junk** étant l'un des nombreux surnoms donnés à l'héroïne). Un grand consommateur de cannabis est un **stoner** ou **dopehead**. On notera que le suffixe "-head" sert également à former les noms **cokehead**, **pillhead**, **crackhead** et **acidhead**.

dude [djuːd, duːd] *n Am* (**a**) *(man)* mec *m* (**b**) *(term of address)* mec *m*, vieux *m*; **hey, dude!** *(as greeting)* salut vieux!; *(to attract attention)* excusez-moi![□]; **dude! this place is amazing!** eh bien mon vieux! c'est vraiment super ici!

duds [dʌdz] *npl (clothes)* fringues *fpl*, frusques *fpl*, nippes *fpl*

duff [dʌf] **1** *n* (**a**) *Br* **up the duff** *(pregnant)* en cloque; **to get sb up the duff** mettre qn en cloque (**b**) *Am*

The symbol [□] indicates that a translation is neutral.

(buttocks) cul *m*, derche *m*; **get up off your duff!** bouge ton cul!
2 *adj (bad, useless)* merdique

duff up *vt sép* **to duff sb up** tabasser qn

duffer ['dʌfə(r)] *n (incompetent person)* branleur(euse) *m,f*; **old duffer** vieux schnock *m*

duh [dɜː] *exclam Ironic* **duh! I've got the map upside down!** que je suis bête! la carte est à l'envers!; **ouch, that dish is really hot! – well, duh! it's just come out of the oven!** aïe, ce plat est brûlant! – évidemment, il sort du four!

dumb [dʌm] *adj Am (stupid)* bête□, débile

dumbass [!] ['dʌmæs] *Am* **1** *n* taré(e) *m,f*, débile *mf*, abruti(e) *m,f*
2 *adj* débile

dumbbell ['dʌmbel] *n (person)* cloche *f*, cruche *f*

dumbfuck [!!] ['dʌmfʌk] *n* connard (connasse) *m,f*

dumbo ['dʌmbəʊ] *n* andouille *f*, gourde *f*, cruche *f*

dump [dʌmp] **1** *n* **(a)** *Péj (house, room)* taudis□ *m*; *(town)* trou *m*, bled *m* **(b) to** *Br* **have** *or Am* **take a dump [!]** *(defecate)* chier, couler un bronze
2 *vt (boyfriend, girlfriend)* plaquer, larguer

dumpling ['dʌmplɪŋ] *n (fat man)* gros patapouf *m*; *(fat woman)* grosse dondon *f*

dunno [dʌ'nəʊ] *contraction (abrév* I don't know*)* j'sais pas!

dunny ['dʌnɪ] *n Austr (toilet)* chiottes *fpl*

dustbins ['dʌstbɪnz] *npl Br (rhyming slang* **dustbin lids = kids)** gosses *mpl*, mômes *mpl*

Dutch [dʌtʃ] **1** *adj* **Dutch courage = courage puisé dans la bouteille; I need some Dutch courage before I phone him** il faut que je boive quelque chose avant de l'appeler□
2 *adv* **to go Dutch** payer chacun sa part□

dweeb [dwiːb] *n Am* crétin(e) *m,f*, abruti(e) *m,f*

dyke [daɪk] *n Injurieux (lesbian)* gouine *f*, gousse *f*

Ee

E [iː] *n* (**a**) (*abrév* **ecstasy**) ecsta *f* (**b**) *Br* (*abrév* **elbow**) **to give sb the big E** plaquer qn, larguer qn

ear [ɪə(r)] *n* (**a**) **to be up to one's ears in work** avoir un boulot dingue *ou* pas possible; **to be up to one's ears in debt** être couvert de dettes (**b**) **to throw sb out on his/her ear** vider qn (**c**) **to bend sb's ear** pomper l'air à qn ▸ *voir aussi* **pig, thick**

earbashing [ˈɪəbæʃɪŋ] *n Br* **to give sb an earbashing** passer un savon à qn, souffler dans les bronches à qn; **to get an earbashing** se faire passer un savon, se faire souffler dans les bronches

earful [ˈɪəfʊl] *n* **to give sb an earful** passer un savon à qn, souffler dans les bronches à qn; **to get an earful** se faire passer un savon, se faire souffler dans les bronches; **get an earful of this!** écoute un peu ça!

early doors [ˈɜːlɪˈdɔːz] *adv Br* tôt◻; **we'll have to get there early doors** il faut qu'on se pointe de bonne heure

earner [ˈɜːnə(r)] *n Br* **a nice little earner** une affaire juteuse

earth [ɜːθ] *n* (**a**) *Hum* **did the earth move for you?** (*after sex*) alors, c'était comment pour toi?; **the earth moved!** c'était divin! (**b**) *Hum* **earth to Jane, earth to Jane, can you hear me?** allô, Jane, est-ce que tu me reçois? (**c**) (*for empha-sis*) **what/who/why on earth...?** que/qui/pourquoi diable...?; **how on earth should I know?** comment veux-tu que je le sache?; **to look like nothing on earth** ne ressembler à rien; **to feel like nothing on earth** n'être vraiment pas dans son assiette ▸ *voir aussi* **scum**

ⓘ Dans la catégorie (b), il s'agit d'une phrase humoristique dont le style rappelle un dialogue de film de science-fiction. On l'utilise pour attirer l'attention d'un interlocuteur distrait.

earwig [ˈɪəwɪg] *Br* **1** *vt* écouter de façon indiscrète◻

   2 *vi* écouter aux portes◻

easy [ˈiːzɪ] **1** *adj* (**a**) *Br* (*promiscuous*) facile (**b**) **to be on easy street** avoir la belle vie; **to be easy on the eye** être canon

   2 *adv* **to take it** *or* **things easy** ne pas s'en faire; **take it easy!** du calme!, calmos!; **easy, tiger!** on se calme! ▸ *voir aussi* **lay**

eat [iːt] *vt* (**a**) (*worry*) **what's eating you?** qu'est-ce qui te tracasse? (**b**) *Am* **eat it** *or* **me** *or* **shit!** [!] va te faire voir! (**c**) [!!] (*perform cunnilingus on*) brouter le cresson à, sucer (**d**) *Am* **to eat sb's lunch** battre qn à plates coutures

eat out *vt sép* (**a**) [!!] (*perform cunnilingus on*) brouter le cresson à, sucer (**b**) **eat your heart out, Victoria Beckham!** ça va faire des jalouses, n'est-ce pas, Victoria Beckham?

eats [iːts] *npl* bouffe *f*

ecofreak ['iːkəʊfriːk] *n* écolo *mf* radical(e)

ecstasy ['ekstəsi] *n (drug)* ecstasy *f*

'ed [ed] *adv Br (abrév* **ahead) go 'ed!** vas-y!; **come 'ed!** allez, viens!

> ⓘ Ce terme s'emploie surtout dans la région de Liverpool.

eejit ['iːdʒɪt] *n Ir & Scot* andouille *f*, couillon *m*

eff [!] [ef] *vi Br* **to eff and blind** jurer comme un charretier

> ⓘ Le terme "eff" est un euphémisme du mot "fuck", dont il représente la première lettre.

eff off [!] *vi* se barrer; **eff off!** va te faire!

effing [!] ['efɪŋ] **1** *n Br* **stop that effing and blinding!** arrête de jurer comme un charretier!

2 *adj* fichu, foutu; **the effing telly's on the blink** cette saloperie de télé déconne!

3 *adv* sacrément, vachement; **don't be so effing lazy!** remue-toi, espèce de feignasse!

egg [eg] *n* **a good egg** *(man)* un chic type; *(woman)* une brave femme; **a bad egg** *(man)* un sale type; *(woman)* une sale bonne femme

eggbeater ['egbiːtə(r)] *n Am (helicopter)* hélico *m*

egghead ['eghed] *n Hum ou Péj* intello *mf*

eightball ['eɪtbɔːl] *n Am* **to be be-** hind the eightball être dans la mouise

> ⓘ Il s'agit à l'origine d'un terme de billard; la boule numéro huit est celle qui doit être jouée en dernier et il est donc très délicat de se retrouver dans une position où l'on risque de toucher cette boule avant la fin de la partie.

eighty-six ['eɪtɪ'sɪks] *Am* **1** *adj* **to be eighty-six on sth** *(in restaurant, bar)* manquer de qch□; **tell the customer we're eighty-six on the chicken** dis au client qu'il n'y a plus de poulet

2 *vt* (**a**) *(eject)* vider (**b**) *(kill)* buter, refroidir

elbow ['elbəʊ] *n* (**a**) *Br* **to give sb the elbow** *(employee)* virer qn; *(boyfriend, girlfriend)* plaquer qn, larguer qn; **to get the elbow** *(of employee)* se faire virer; *(of boyfriend, girlfriend)* se faire plaquer *ou* larguer (**b**) *Hum* **to bend one's elbow** *(drink)* lever le coude ▸ *voir aussi* **arse, ass**

El Cheapo [el'tʃiːpəʊ] *Hum* **1** *n* article *m* bas de gamme□

2 *adj* bas de gamme□; **an El Cheapo restaurant** un resto bon marché; **he bought her some El Cheapo engagement ring** il lui a acheté une bague de fiançailles en toc

elevator ['elɪveɪtə(r)] *n Hum* **the elevator doesn't go up to the top floor** c'est pas une lumière

eliminate [ɪ'lɪmɪneɪt] *vt (kill)* liquider

'em [əm] *pron Br (abrév* **them) tell 'em to hurry up!** dis-leur de se dépêcher!□; **I can't find my fags, I must have left 'em at home** je trouve pas mes clopes, j'ai dû les laisser à la maison

Le symbole [!] dénote un terme très familier, [!!] un terme vulgaire.

enchilada [entʃɪˈlɑːdə] *n* **big enchilada** *(person)* huile *f*; **the whole enchilada** *(everything)* tout le tremblement

end [end] *n Br* (a) **[!] to get one's end away** tremper son biscuit (b) **he doesn't know which end is up** il plane complètement (c) **end of story, end of** un point, c'est tout; **you're not going, end of** *or* **end of story!** tu n'y vas pas, un point, c'est tout! ▸ *voir aussi* **go off**

ends, endz [endz] *n Br (neighbourhood)* quartier[□] *m*; **my ends** mon quartier

eppy [ˈepɪ] *n Br (abrév* **epileptic fit)** **to have an eppy** *(lose one's temper)* péter une durite, péter les plombs

equalizer [ˈiːkwəlaɪzə(r)] *n Am (handgun)* flingue *m*, feu *m*

Essex [ˈesɪks] *npr Br Péj* **Essex Girl** minette *f* de l'Essex; **Essex Boy, Essex Man**[□] beauf *m*

ⓘ Il s'agit de stéréotypes sociaux apparus au cours des années 80. L'"Essex Girl" (originaire de l'Essex, comté situé à l'est de Londres) est censée être une jeune femme d'origine modeste aux mœurs légères, vulgaire, bruyante, et peu intelligente. L'"Essex Boy" ou "Essex Man" est lui aussi vulgaire et bruyant ; de plus, il est réactionnaire et inculte.

---

evils [ˈiːvəlz] *npl Br* **to give sb evils** fusiller qn du regard

eyeball [ˈaɪbɔːl] *vt* mater

eye candy [ˈaɪkændɪ] *n (men)* beaux mecs *mpl*; *(women)* belles nanas *mpl*; **there's plenty of eye candy in here tonight** il y a plein de canons ici ce soir; **his latest piece of eye candy** sa dernière nana

eyeful [ˈaɪfʊl] *n* **to get an eyeful (of sb/sth)** mater (qn/qch); **get an eyeful of that!** mate un peu ça!; **she's quite an eyeful!** elle est vachement bien foutue!

eye-popping [ˈaɪpɒpɪŋ] *adj Am* sensationnel

Eyetie [ˈaɪtaɪ] *Injurieux* **1** *n* Rital(e) *m,f*, macaroni *mf*
2 *adj* rital

Ff

FA [eɪˈfeɪ] *n Br* (*abrév* **Fanny Adams** *or* **fuck all**) **sweet FA** que dalle

fab [fæb] *adj Br* (*abrév* **fabulous**) génial, super

face [feɪs] *n* (**a**) *Br* **to be off one's face** (*drunk*) être pété *ou* bourré; (*on drugs*) être défoncé (**b**) **to have a face like a bag of spanners** *or* **a bulldog chewing a wasp** *or* **the back end of a bus** être laid comme un pou; *Br* **to have a face like a smacked** *or* **slapped arse [!]** avoir l'air furibard percutant◻ ► *voir aussi* **feed, shut, waste**

faceache [ˈfeɪseɪk] *n Br* **to be a faceache** (*ugly*) être une mocheté; (*miserable*) toujours faire la gueule

fade [feɪd] *vi Am* (*leave*) s'esbigner, calter

faff [fæf] *Br* **1** *n* **what a faff!** quelle histoire!
2 *vi* **stop faffing and let me do it!** arrête tes conneries et laisse-moi faire!

faff about, faff around *vi Br* (**a**) (*waste time*) glander (**b**) (*potter*) s'occuper◻, bricoler

fag [fæg] *n* (**a**) *Br* (*cigarette*) clope *f*; **fag end** mégot◻ *m*, clope *m* (**b**) *Am Injurieux* (*homosexual*) pédale *f*, tapette *f*, tantouze *f*; **fag hag** fille *f* à pédés

ⓘ Dans la catégorie (**b**), ce terme perd son caractère injurieux quand il est utilisé par des homosexuels ou par quelqu'un qui utilise ce terme à propos de soi.

fagged (out) [fægd('aʊt)] *adj Br* lessivé, crevé, naze

faggot [ˈfægət] *n Am Injurieux* (*homosexual*) pédale *f*, tapette *f*, tantouze *f*

ⓘ Quand il est utilisé par des homosexuels, ce terme perd son caractère injurieux.

faggy [ˈfægɪ] *adj Am Injurieux* qui fait tapette; **that pink shirt makes you look a bit faggy** tu fais un peu tapette avec cette chemise rose

ⓘ Quand il est utilisé par des homosexuels, ce terme perd son caractère injurieux.

fair do's [ˈfeɪəˈduːz] *exclam Br* **I'll let you watch the football if you come and see that film with me – fair do's!** (*fair enough*) je te laisse regarder le match de foot si tu viens avec voir ce film avec moi – d'accord!; **you're not much of a snowboarder, are you! – fair do's, I've only had one lesson!** (*be fair*) dis donc, tu es plutôt nul au snowboard! – tu es dur, je n'ai pris qu'une leçon!

fairy ['feərɪ] n Injurieux (homosexual) tante f, pédé m ▸ voir aussi **away**

fall guy ['fɔːlgaɪ] n (dupe) pigeon m; (scapegoat) bouc m émissaire◻

fall out [fɔːl] vi Noir Am (fall asleep) s'endormir◻

family jewels [!] ['fæməlɪ'dʒuːəlz] npl Hum (man's genitals) bijoux mpl de famille

fancy ['fænsɪ] **1** adj (a) Br **fancy man** amant◻ m; **fancy woman** maîtresse◻ f (b) Am **Fancy Dan** (dandy) dandy m; (show-off) frimeur m
2 vt Br (a) (be attracted to) **to fancy sb** en pincer pour qn; **to fancy the pants off sb** en pincer drôlement pour qn; **to fancy the arse off sb** [!] trouver qn vachement excitant (b) (have high opinion of) **to fancy oneself** se gober (c) (want) **do you fancy a drink/going to the cinema?** ça te dirait d'aller boire un coup/d'aller au cinéma?

fancy-dan ['fænsɪ'dæn] adj frimeur

fanny ['fænɪ] n (a) [!] Br (woman's genitals) chatte f, foufoune f; **fanny fart** [!!] pet m de chatte (b) Am (buttocks) derrière m; **fanny pack** banane f (sac) ▸ voir aussi **magnet**

fanny about [!], **fanny around** [!] vi Br perdre son temps à des bricoles, glander

farm [fɑːm] n Am **to buy the farm** (die) clamser, claquer; Am **I'd bet the farm that...** je te parie tout ce que tu veux que...; **they're a great team, but I wouldn't bet the farm on them** c'est une super équipe mais je ne parierais pas sur leur victoire ▸ voir aussi **fat**

far-out [fɑː'raʊt] **1** adj (a) (strange) zarbi; (avant-garde) d'avant-garde◻ (b) (excellent) génial, géant
2 exclam super!, génial!

fart [fɑːt] **1** n pet m, prout m; **a boring old fart** (person) un(e) vieux (vieille) con (conne)
2 vi péter ▸ voir aussi **pissed**

fart about, fart around vi perdre son temps à des bricoles, glander

fartsack ['fɑːtsæk] n Am (bed) pieu m, plumard m; (sleeping bag) sac m à viande

fashionista [fæʃə'niːstə] n modeux-(euse) m,f

fashion victim ['fæʃənvɪktɪm] n Péj esclave mf de la mode

fast [fɑːst] adj **to pull a fast one on sb** rouler qn

fat [fæt] adj (a) **fat cat** richard(e) m,f; Am **to be in fat city** avoir la belle vie (b) Ironique (for emphasis) **a fat lot of good that'll do me!** ça me fera une belle jambe!; **you're a fat lot of help!** merci! tu m'aides vachement!; **fat chance!** on peut toujours rêver! (c) Am **fat camp** = colonie de vacances où les enfants suivent une cure d'amaigrissement; **fat farm** centre m d'amaigrissement◻ (d) Noir Am (excellent) super, génial ▸ voir aussi **chew**

fathead ['fæthed] n andouille f, courge f

fatso ['fætsəʊ], **fatty** ['fætɪ] n (man) gros lard m; (woman) grosse dondon f

fave [feɪv] (abbr **favourite**) **1** adj préféré◻
2 n préféré(e)◻ m,f

favour ['feɪvə(r)] n Br **do me a favour!** tu rigoles?; **are you going to buy it? – do me a favour!** tu vas l'acheter? – tu rigoles?

faze [feɪz] vt déconcerter◻

features ['fiːtjəs] npl Br **monkey features** Duchnoque; **dick features** [!] Ducon

feck [fek] *exclam Ir* bordel!, merde!, putain!

ⓘ Il s'agit d'un euphémisme du terme "fuck".

fecking ['fekɪŋ] *Ir* **1** *adj* **fecking hell!** merde alors!, putain!; **where are my fecking cigarettes?** où sont mes putains de cigarettes?; **you fecking idiot!** espèce de crétin!
2 *adv* **it's fecking freezing!** on se les gèle!; **we had a fecking amazing weekend!** on a passé un week-end vraiment génial!; **I don't fecking know!** j'en sais foutre rien!

Fed [fed] *n Am* (**a**) **the Feds** (*abrév* **Federal Government**) = toute agence dépendant du gouvernement fédéral, aux États-Unis (**b**) **the Fed** (*abrév* **Federal Reserve Board**) = agence gouvernementale américaine dont le rôle est de réguler le système bancaire (**c**) (*abrév* **Federal Agent**) agent *m* du gouvernement fédéral[□]

federal case ['fedərəl'keɪs] *n Am* **to make a federal case out of sth** faire toute une histoire de qch

feeb [fi:b] *n Am* crétin(e) *m,f*, débile *mf*

Feebie ['fi:bɪ] *n Am* agent *m* du FBI

feed [fi:d] **1** *n* (*large meal*) gueuleton *m*
2 *vt* **to feed one's face** s'en mettre plein la lampe, se goinfrer

feedbag ['fi:dbæg] *n Am* **to put on the (old) feedbag** bouffer

feel up [fi:l] *vt sép* **to feel sb up** peloter qn

feisty ['faɪstɪ] *adj* (*lively*) plein d'entrain[□]; (*combative*) qui a du cran

fella ['felə] *n Br* (*man*) mec *m*, type *m*; (*husband, boyfriend*) mec *m*; **old fella** (*penis*) zob *m*

fem [fem] *n* lesbienne *f* féminine[□]

fence [fens] **1** *n* (*person*) receleur[□] *m*, fourgueur *m*
2 *vi* faire du recel[□]

fender-bender ['fendəbendə(r)] *n Am* accrochage[□] *m*

fess up [fes] *vi* (*confess*) se mettre à table

-fest [fest] *suffixe* **drinkfest** beuverie *f*; *Br* **shagfest** séance *f* de baise intense; **that club's a total babefest!** la boîte est bourrée de jolies nanas!; **the movie was a real gorefest** le film était vraiment gore

ⓘ Le suffixe "-fest" dénote l'excès.

fierce [fɪəs] *adj* (*excellent*) super, génial, de la balle

fifth wheel ['fɪfθ'wi:l] *n Am* **to be** *or* **to feel like a fifth wheel** tenir la chandelle

figure ['fɪgə(r)] *vi Am* **go figure!** va comprendre!

filth [fɪlθ] *n Br Péj* **the filth** (*the police*) les flics *mpl*, les poulets *mpl*

fin [fɪn] *n* (**a**) *Am* (*five-dollar note*) billet *m* de cinq dollars[□] (**b**) *Br* (*five-pound note*) billet *m* de cinq livres[□]

finagle [fɪ'neɪgəl] *vt Am* obtenir en magouillant

finger ['fɪŋgə(r)] **1** *n* **to pull one's finger out** s'enlever les doigts du cul; **to give sb the finger**, *Br* **to give sb the fingers** *or* **to stick two fingers up at sb** ≃ faire un doigt d'honneur à qn; **to put the finger on sb** (*denounce*) balancer qn; (*blame*) accuser qn[□]
2 *vt* (**a**) **[!]** (*woman*) mettre le doigt dans la chatte de, masturber[□] (**b**) (*denounce*) balancer; (*blame*) accuser[□]

ⓘ En Grande-Bretagne, on utilise l'expression "to give sb the fingers" au pluriel car ce geste se fait à l'aide de l'index et du majeur.

finger-fuck [!!] ['fɪŋgəfʌk] *vt (woman)* mettre le doigt dans la chatte de

fink [fɪŋk] *Am* **1** *n* (a) *(informer)* mouchard *m* (b) *(unpleasant person)* blaireau *m*, enflure *f* (c) *(strikebreaker)* jaune *m*
   2 *vi* moucharder; **to fink on sb** balancer qn

firewater ['faɪəwɔːtə(r)] *n* tordboyaux *m*

fish [fɪʃ] *n* (a) *(person)* **cold fish** pisse-froid *mf*; **queer fish** drôle d'oiseau *m* (b) **to drink like a fish** boire comme un trou

fist [!] [fɪst] *vt* insérer le poing dans l'anus de◻

fist-fuck [!!] ['fɪstfʌk] *vt* insérer le poing dans l'anus de◻, pratiquer le fist-fucking sur

fisticuffs ['fɪstɪkʌfs] *n Br* bagarre *f*; **if he finds out, there'll be fisticuffs!** s'il s'en rend compte il va y avoir de la bagarre *ou* du grabuge

fit [fɪt] **1** *n* **to have** *or* **throw a fit** piquer une crise, péter les plombs; *Br* **to be in fits** se tenir les côtes, hurler de rire; *Br* **to have sb in fits** faire hurler qn de rire
   2 *adj Br (attractive)* bien foutu

fit up *vt sép* **to fit sb up** monter un coup contre qn; **they fitted him up** il a été victime d'un coup monté

fitba ['fɪtbɔː] *n Scot (football)* foot *m*

five [faɪv] *n* (a) **to take five** faire un break de cinq minutes (b) **gimme five!** tape-moi dans la main! ► *voir aussi* **high-five**

ⓘ Dans la catégorie (b), il s'agit d'une façon de signifier à quelqu'un que l'on veut lui taper dans la main pour le saluer, le féliciter, ou en signe de victoire.

five-finger discount ['faɪvfɪŋgə-'dɪskaʊnt] *n Am Hum* **I got a five-finger discount on this CD** j'ai fauché ce CD; **I distracted the security guard while my friend took a five-finger discount** j'ai distrait le surveillant pendant que mon copain fauchait des trucs

five-o [faɪv'əʊ] *n* **the five-o** *(police)* les flics *mpl*; **the place was teeming with five-o** ça grouillait de flics

ⓘ Ce terme trouve son origine dans la série télévisée américaine des années 70 *Hawaii Five-0* (*Hawaii police d'état* en français).

fiver ['faɪvə(r)] *n Br (sum)* cinq livres◻ *fpl*; *(note)* billet *m* de cinq livres◻

five-spot ['faɪvspɒt] *n Am* billet *m* de cinq dollars◻

fix [fɪks] **1** *n* (a) *(of drugs)* fix *m*; **I need my daily fix of chocolate** il me faut ma dose quotidienne de chocolat (b) **to be a fix** *(of election, contest)* être truqué
   2 *vt* (a) *(rig)* truquer (b) *(bribe)* graisser la patte à (c) *(get even with)* régler ses comptes avec; **I'll fix him!** il va me le payer!

fixer ['fɪksə(r)] *n (person)* combinard(e) *m,f*, magouilleur(euse) *m,f*

fizgig ['fɪzgɪg] *n Austr (informer)* mouchard(e) *m,f*

flake [fleɪk] *n* (a) *(person)* allumé(e) *m,f* (b) *(cocaine)* neige *f*

flake out *vi* s'écrouler de fatigue

The symbol ◻ indicates that a translation is neutral.

flaky ['fleɪkɪ] *adj* loufoque, loufe-dingue

flamer ['fleɪmə(r)] *n Am* enflure *f*

flaming ['fleɪmɪŋ] *Br* **1** *adj (for emphasis)* **you flaming idiot!** espèce de crétin!; **he's a flaming pest** c'est un sacré emmerdeur; **flaming hell!** merde alors!

2 *adv (for emphasis)* vachement, super; **it was flaming expensive** c'était vachement cher; **you're flaming well staying here!** tu ne bouges pas d'ici, enfonce-toi bien ça dans la tête!

flap [flæp] **1** *n* **to be in a flap** être dans tous ses états; **to get in a flap** se mettre dans tous ses états, faire un caca nerveux

2 *vi* s'exciter, paniquer; **stop flapping!** du calme!, calmos! ▶ *voir aussi* **jaw**

flash [flæʃ] **1** *adj Br (car, clothes, jewellery)* tape-à-l'œil; *(person)* frimeur; **Flash Harry** frimeur *m*

2 *vt Am (expose oneself to)* s'exhiber devant□

3 *vi (expose oneself)* s'exhiber□; *Br* **to flash at sb** s'exhiber devant qn

flash on *vt insép* **to flash on sth** se remémorer qch□; **I flashed on what had happened** tout d'un coup j'ai revu tout ce qui s'était passé□

flashback ['flæʃbæk] *n (hallucination)* flashback *m*, retour *m* d'acide

flasher ['flæʃə(r)] *n (man)* exhibitionniste□ *m*

flashy ['flæʃɪ] *adj (car, clothes, jewellery)* tape-à-l'œil; *(person)* frimeur

flatfoot ['flætfʊt] *n Am (police officer)* flic *m*, poulet *m*

fleabag ['fliːbæg] *n* (**a**) *Br (person)* pouilleux (euse) *m,f*; *(animal)* sac *m* à puces (**b**) *Am (hotel)* hôtel *m* borgne

fleapit ['fliːpɪt] *n Br (cinema)* = vieux

cinéma de quartier mal tenu

fleece [fliːs] *vt (overcharge)* écorcher; *(cheat)* arnaquer, plumer

flesh [fleʃ] *n* **to press the flesh** = serrer des mains au cours d'un bain de foule

flick [flɪk] *n (film)* film□ *m*; *Br* **the flicks** *(cinema)* le cinoche

fling [flɪŋ] *n* (**a**) *(sexual relationship)* aventure□ *f*, passade□ *f*; **to have a fling (with sb)** avoir une aventure (avec qn) (**b**) *(period of enjoyment)* bon temps□ *m*; **to have a final fling** s'éclater une dernière fois

flip [flɪp] **1** *vt* **to flip one's lid** or *Am* **wig** *(get angry)* piquer une crise, péter les plombs; *(go mad)* devenir cinglé, perdre la boule; *(get excited)* devenir dingue

2 *vi (get angry)* piquer une crise, péter les plombs; *(go mad)* devenir cinglé, perdre la boule; *(get excited)* devenir dingue ▶ *voir aussi* **bird**

flip out *vi (get angry)* piquer une crise, péter les plombs; *(go mad)* devenir cinglé, perdre la boule; *(get excited)* devenir dingue

flipping ['flɪpɪŋ] *Br* **1** *adj (for emphasis)* foutu, fichu; **get that flipping dog out of here!** fous-moi cette saleté de clébard dehors!; **flipping heck!** mince alors!

2 *adv (for emphasis)* sacrément; **he's so flipping annoying!** ce qu'il peut être embêtant!; **don't flipping well talk to me like that!** t'as intérêt à me parler sur un autre ton!

float about, float around [fləʊt] *vi Br* traîner

floater ['fləʊtə(r)] *n* (**a**) *(dead body)* = cadavre à la surface de l'eau (**b**) *(in toilet)* = étron qui flotte dans la cuvette des toilettes

flog [flɒg] *vt Br* (**a**) *(sell)* fourguer (**b**)

Le symbole [!] dénote un terme très familier, [!!] un terme vulgaire.

Hum **to flog one's log [!]** *(masturbate)* se tirer sur l'élastique, se taper sur la colonne

floor [flɔː(r)] **1** *n* **to wipe the floor with sb** *(defeat)* battre qn à plates coutures
     2 *vt* **(a)** *(knock down)* foutre par terre **(b)** *(shock)* secouer; *(baffle)* dérouter⁰

floosie, floozie, floozy ['fluːzɪ] *n* pétasse *f*, roulure *f*

flop [flɒp] **1** *n* **(a)** *(failure)* bide *m* **(b)** *Am (hotel)* hôtel *m* borgne; *(hostel)* asile *m* de nuit⁰
     2 *vi* **(a)** *(fail)* faire un bide **(b)** *Am (sleep)* pioncer, roupiller

flophouse ['flɒphaʊs] *n Am (hotel)* hôtel *m* borgne; *(hostel)* asile *m* de nuit⁰

fluff [flʌf] *n Br* **a bit of fluff,** *Am* **a fluff** une gonzesse, une nana ▶ *voir aussi* **bum**

fluffer ['flʌfə(r)] *n* = personne dont le rôle est de maintenir l'érection d'un acteur de films pornographiques sur le plateau de tournage

flunk [flʌŋk] *Am* **1** *vt (exam)* rater⁰, foirer; *(student)* ne pas accorder d'unité de valeur à⁰
     2 *vi (in exam)* échouer⁰, se planter

flunk out *vi Am* se faire virer *(à cause de ses mauvais résultats)*

flush [flʌʃ] *adj (rich)* **to be flush** avoir des ronds; **I'm feeling flush so I'll pay** j'ai des ronds, donc c'est moi qui paie

fly [flaɪ] **1** *adj Noir Am (excellent)* génial, super, géant; *(stylish, attractive)* chouette
     2 *vt* **to fly the coop** *(escape)* se faire la belle
     3 *vi* **to send sb/sth flying** envoyer qn/qch valser; **to fly off the handle** sortir de ses gonds, piquer une crise

▶ *see also* **kite**

fly-by-night ['flaɪbaɪnaɪt] **1** *n (person)* fumiste *mf*, artiste *m*; *(company)* entreprise *f* pas sérieuse
     2 *adj* pas sérieux

fogey ['fəʊgɪ] *n* **old fogey** *(man)* vieux schnock *m*; *(woman)* vieille bique *f*; *Hum* **young fogey** jeune con (conne) *m,f (vieux avant l'âge)*

foggy ['fɒgɪ] *adj* **I haven't the foggiest (idea)!** aucune idée!

folding ['fəʊldɪŋ] *n Br* biffetons *mpl*, fafiots *mpl*, talbins *mpl*; **got any folding?** t'as pas des biffetons?

fool about, fool around [fuːl] *vi* **(a)** *(act foolishly)* faire l'idiot; **to fool about** *or* **around with sth** jouer avec qch **(b)** *(waste time)* glander, glandouiller **(c)** *(have affairs)* fricoter **(with** avec) **(d)** *(of couple)* se bécoter

foot [fʊt] *n* **my foot!** mon œil!

footie ['fʊtɪ], **footer** ['fʊtə(r)] *n Br (abrév* **football**) foot *m*

footsie ['fʊtsɪ] *n* **to play footsie with sb** faire du pied à qn

footy ['fʊtɪ] *n* **(a)** *Br & Austr (soccer)* foot *m* **(b)** *Austr (rugby union)* rugby *m* à quinze; *(rugby league)* rugby *m* à treize; *(Australian rules football)* football *m* australien

fork out [fɔːk] **1** *vt sép* allonger
     2 *vi* casquer (**for** pour)

foul up [faʊl] **1** *vt sép* **to foul sth up** foirer qch, merder qch
     2 *vi* foirer, merder

foul-up ['faʊlʌp] *n* ratage⁰ *m*, foirade *f*

four-eyes ['fɔːraɪz] *n Péj (term of address)* binoclard(e) *m,f*

fox [fɒks] *n Am (woman)* canon *m*

foxy ['fɒksɪ] *adj (sexually attractive)* sexy

fraidy cat ['freɪdɪkæt] n Am poule f mouillée

frat [fræt] n Am (abrév **fraternity**) club m d'étudiants[□]; **frat boy** = étudiant américain membre d'une confrérie d'étudiants, s'adonnant à la boisson et aux conquêtes féminines; **frat party** = soirée organisée par une confrérie d'étudiants; **frat rat** membre m d'un club d'étudiants[□]

ⓘ Les "fraternities" sont des organisations d'étudiants dont chacune possède ses locaux ("fraternity house") et dont la principale raison d'être est de fournir instantanément à ses membres un cercle d'amis et de connaissances. Les étudiants désireux de faire partie d'une "fraternity" doivent être parrainés par des membres et doivent se soumettre à de nombreuses épreuves souvent aussi stupides qu'humiliantes. Le nom de chaque "fraternity" est composé de trois lettres de l'alphabet grec.

frazzled ['fræzəld] adj (exhausted) naze, flagada; (bothered) à cran

freak [friːk] **1** n (a) (odd person) monstre m (b) (fan) **a computer/tennis freak** un fana d'informatique/de tennis

2 vt (shock, scare) faire flipper

3 vi (panic, become scared) flipper, paniquer; (become angry) piquer une crise, péter les plombs ▸ voir aussi **Jesus**

freak out 1 vt sép **to freak sb out** (shock, scare) faire flipper qn

2 vi (a) (panic, become scared) flipper, paniquer; (become angry) piquer une crise, péter les plombs (b) (abandon restraint) s'éclater; **look at him freaking out on the dancefloor!** regarde-le s'éclater sur la piste de danse!

freaking [!] ['friːkɪŋ] Am **1** adj (for emphasis) sacré, foutu; **where are those freaking kids?** mais où sont passés ces foutus gamins?; **freaking hell!** putain!

2 adv (for emphasis) vachement; **it's freaking cold out there** ça pince vachement dehors; **I don't freaking know!** j'en sais foutre rien!

freak-out ['friːkaʊt] n trip m

freaky ['friːkɪ] adj (strange) bizarre[□], zarbi

freebase ['friːbeɪs] vi = chauffer de la cocaïne et en inhaler la fumée

freebie ['friːbɪ] n (for customer) cadeau[□] m; (perk) à-côté[□] m; **it was a freebie** je l'ai eu gratos

freeload ['friːləʊd] vi vivre au crochet des autres

freeloader ['friːləʊdə(r)] n parasite[□] m

French [frentʃ] **1** n Hum **pardon** or **excuse my French!** (after swearing) passez-moi l'expression!

2 adj **French kiss** baiser m avec la langue[□], pelle f, patin m; **to give sb a French kiss** rouler une pelle ou un patin à qn; Br **French letter** capote f anglaise

ⓘ L'image stéréotypée que se font les Britanniques et les Américains des Français est celle d'un peuple très porté sur le sexe, aux mœurs exotiques. Ces clichés sont à l'origine de nombreuses expressions argotiques. Il est amusant de noter que les "French letters" des Anglais sont les "capotes anglaises" des Français.

french Am **1** vt rouler une pelle ou un patin à

2 vi se rouler une pelle ou un patin

French-kiss [frentʃˈkɪs] **1** *vt* rouler une pelle *ou* un patin à

2 *vi* se rouler une pelle *ou* un patin

fresh [freʃ] *adj Am* (**a**) *(cheeky)* culotté; **don't get fresh with me, young man!** ne soyez pas insolent, jeune homme! (**b**) *(sexually bold)* déluré◻; **to get fresh with sb** faire des avances à qn◻ (**c**) *(excellent)* super, génial

fresher [ˈfreʃə(r)] *n Br* étudiant(e) *m,f* de première année◻

fried [fraɪd] *adj* (**a**) *Am (drunk)* bourré, beurré, pété, poivré; *(on drugs)* raide, parti, défoncé (**b**) *Hum* **fried eggs** *(breasts)* œufs *mpl* sur le plat

frig [!] [frɪg] **1** *exclam* **frig (it)!** merde!

2 *vt* (**a**) *(have sex with) (of man)* baiser, tringler, troncher; *(of woman)* baiser avec, s'envoyer (**b**) *(masturbate)* branler

3 *vi (masturbate)* s'astiquer le bouton, se branler

frig about [!], **frig around** [!] *vi* *(act foolishly)* faire le con, déconner; *(waste time)* glander, glandouiller

frigging [!] [ˈfrɪgɪŋ] **1** *adj (for emphasis)* fichu, foutu; **what a frigging waste of time!** tu parles d'une perte de temps!; **shut your frigging mouth!** ferme-la!, ferme ta gueule!

2 *adv (for emphasis)* **don't frigging lie to me!** ne me mens pas, bordel!; **I'm frigging freezing!** je me les gèle!

frighteners [ˈfraɪtnəz] *npl Br* **to put the frighteners on sb** menacer qn◻

Frisco [ˈfrɪskəʊ] *npr Am* = surnom donné à la ville de San Francisco

fritz [frɪts] *n Am* **to be on the fritz** *(of TV, machine)* déconner, débloquer

fro [frəʊ] *n (abrév **Afro**) (coiffure f)* afro *m*

Frog [frɒg], **Froggy** [ˈfrɒgɪ] *Injurieux* **1** *n* Français(e)◻ *m,f*, fransquillon(onne) *m,f*

2 *adj* français◻; **they've got some Frog** *or* **Froggy playing for them** il y a un joueur français dans leur équipe; **I hate Frog food** j'ai horreur de la cuisine française

ⓘ C'est la réputation de mangeurs de cuisses de grenouilles des Français qui leur valut ce surnom. Selon le ton et le contexte, ce terme peut être soit injurieux, soit humoristique.

front [frʌnt] **1** *adj Br Hum* **front bottom** *(vagina)* chatte *f*, minou *m*

2 *vt Am* (**a**) *(pay in advance)* avancer◻; **the cashier can front you the money** le caissier peut vous faire une avance *ou* vous avancer l'argent (**b**) *(give, lend money to)* filer; **can you front me five bucks?** tu pourrais pas me filer cinq dollars?

3 *vi Noir Am* (**a**) *(show off)* frimer (**b**) *(tell lies)* baratiner, raconter des craques

frosh [frɒʃ] *n Am* étudiant(e) *m,f* de première année◻

frump [frʌmp] *n* femme *f* mal fagotée

frumpy [ˈfrʌmpɪ] *adj* mal fagoté

fruit [fruːt] *n Am Injurieux (homosexual)* pédé *m*, tapette *f*

fruitcake [ˈfruːtkeɪk] *n (person)* dingo *mf*, allumé(e) *m,f* ▸ *voir aussi* **nutty**

fry [fraɪ] *Am* **1** *vt (convict)* faire passer à la chaise électrique◻

2 *vi (of convict)* passer à la chaise électrique◻; **he oughta fry for**

that! il mérite de passer à la chaise électrique!

FUBAR, fubar ['fuːbɑː(r)] *adj* (*abrév* **fucked up beyond all recognition**) **my laptop's FUBAR, I think it's got a virus** mon ordinateur portable déconne complètement, je crois qu'il a un virus; **we were fine after the crash but the car's FUBAR** on est sorti indemnes de l'accident, mais la voiture est bonne pour la casse

ⓘ Il s'agit à l'origine d'une terme d'argot militaire américain, qui a été popularisé au cours de la deuxième guerre mondiale.

fuck [!!] [fʌk] **1** *n* (**a**) *(sexual intercourse)* baise *f*; **to have a fuck** baiser, s'envoyer en l'air; **fuck buddy** compagnon (compagne) *m,f* de baise
(**b**) *(person)* **to be a good fuck** bien baiser, être un bon coup; **you stupid fuck!** espèce d'enculé!
(**c**) *(for emphasis)* **who the fuck left the window open?** quel est le con qui a laissé la fenêtre ouverte?; **why the fuck didn't you tell me?** pourquoi est-ce que tu m'as pas prévenu, bordel!; **what the fuck are you doing?** mais qu'est-ce que tu fous, bordel!; **I can't really afford it, but what the fuck!** c'est un peu cher pour moi, mais je m'en fous!; **it costs a fuck of a lot of money** ça coûte la peau du cul!; **it's been a fuck of a long day!** putain, la journée a été longue!; **shut the fuck up!** ferme ta gueule!; *Br* **get to fuck!** va te faire enculer!; **get the fuck out of here!** fous-moi le camp!, dégage!
(**d**) *(expressing surprise, disbelief)* **for fuck's sake!** merde!, putain!; *Br* **fuck knows where he is!** j'ai pas la moindre idée d'où il peut être!
(**e**) *(in comparisons)* **as stupid as**

fuck con comme la lune; **as boring as fuck** chiant comme la pluie; **he ran like fuck** il a pris ses jambes à son cou
(**f**) **not to give a (flying) fuck (about)** se foutre complètement (de); **who gives a fuck!** tout le monde s'en fout!
(**g**) **can I borrow the car? – like fuck you can** or *Br* **can you fuck!** est-ce que je peux prendre la voiture? – alors là tu peux te brosser!; **are you going to apologize? – like fuck I am** or *Br* **am I fuck!** est-ce que tu vas t'excuser? – des clous!
(**h**) **fuck all** que dalle; *Br* **fuck all money/time** pas un flèche/une min-ute; **she's done fuck all today** elle a rien foutu de la journée; **she knows fuck all about it** elle y connaît que dalle

2 *exclam* **fuck (it)!** bordel de merde!

3 *vt* (**a**) *(have sex with) (of man)* baiser, tringler, troncher; *(of woman)* baiser avec; **he fucked her brains out** il l'a baisée comme il faut
(**b**) *(for emphasis)* **fuck him!** qu'il aille se faire enculer!; **fuck me!** merde alors!; **fuck you!** va te faire enculer!; *Br* **go and fuck yourself,** *Am* **go fuck yourself!** va te faire enculer!

4 *vi* (**a**) *(have sex)* baiser (**b**) **to fuck with sb** jouer au con avec qn; **don't fuck with me!** joue pas au con avec moi!; **to fuck with sb's head** faire tourner quelqu'un en bourrique
▸ *voir aussi* **holy, rabbit**

fuck about [!!], **fuck around** [!!] **1** *vt sép* **to fuck sb about** or **around** *(treat badly)* se foutre de la gueule de qn; *(waste time of)* faire perdre son temps à qn▫
2 *vi* (**a**) *(be promiscuous)* baiser à droite à gauche (**b**) *(act foolishly)* déconner, faire le con; *(waste time)*

glander, glandouiller; **to fuck about with sth** tripoter qch

fuck off [!!] 1 vt sép **to fuck sb off** faire chier qn; **to be fucked off (with)** en avoir plein le cul (de)

2 vi (leave) se casser, calter; **fuck off!** (go away) casse-toi!; (expressing contempt, disagreement) va te faire foutre!

fuck over [!!] vt sép **to fuck sb over** baiser qn, arnaquer qn

fuck up [!!] 1 vt sép (a) (person) rendre cinglé; (plan, situation) faire foirer; **she's totally fucked up** (psychologically) elle est complètement à côté de ses pompes; **you've fucked everything up** tu as tout fait foirer ou merder (b) Am **fucked up** (drunk) bourré, beurré, pété, poivré; (on drugs) raide, parti, défoncé

2 vi merder, foirer

fuckable [!!] ['fʌkəbəl] adj baisable

fucked [!!] [fʌkt] adj (a) (exhausted) naze, crevé, lessivé (b) (broken, not working properly) foutu; **my leg's fucked** j'ai la jambe qui déconne (c) (in trouble) foutu; **if they don't win this game, they're fucked** si ils gagnent pas ce match, ils sont foutus (d) (for emphasis) **I'm fucked if I'm going to apologize!** plutôt crever que de m'excuser!; **I'm fucked if I know!** j'en sais foutre rien! (e) Br (drunk) bourré, beurré, pété

fucker [!!] ['fʌkə(r)] n (a) (man) enculé m, enfoiré m; (woman) connasse f; **some fucker's stolen my bike** il y a un enculé qui m'a piqué mon vélo; **you lazy fucker!** espèce de grosse feignasse!; **you stupid fucker!** pauvre con! (b) (thing) saloperie f; **I can't get the fucker to start** j'arrive pas à faire démarrer cette saloperie

fuckfest [!!] ['fʌkfest] n séance f de baise intense

fuckhead [!!] ['fʌkhed] n connard (connasse) m,f

fucking [!!] ['fʌkɪŋ] **1** adj **fucking hell!** merde alors!, putain!; **where the fucking hell have you been?** où est-ce que t'étais passé, bordel?; **she's here all the fucking time!** elle est toujours fourrée ici!; **where are my fucking cigarettes?** où sont mes putains de cigarettes?; **he's a fucking bastard!** c'est un véritable enculé!; **you fucking idiot!** espèce de crétin!; Am **fucking A!** (absolutely) absolument!, tu parles!; (great) super!, génial!

2 adv **it's fucking freezing!** on se les gèle!; **I'm fucking well going home!** merde! moi je rentre chez moi!; **the film was fucking crap!** c'était de la merde ce film!; **we had a fucking amazing weekend!** on a passé un week-end vraiment génial!; **fucking stop it!** arrête, bordel de merde!; **I don't fucking know!** j'en sais foutre rien!

fuck-me [!!] ['fʌkmiː] adj **fuck-me dress** robe f affriolante; **fuck-me shoes** chaussures fpl de pute

fuck-off [!!] ['fʌkɒf] **1** n Am (person) glandeur(euse) m,f

2 adj Br (for emphasis) mastoc, comac, qui se pose là; **they've got a huge fuck-off house in the country** ils ont une baraque comac à la campagne; **they've got a big fuck-off dog** ils ont un clebs qui se pose là

fuckpad [!!] ['fʌkpæd] n Br baisodrome m

fuck-up [!!] ['fʌkʌp] n (a) (bungle) ratage m, foirade f; **to make a fuck-up of sth** foirer qch (b) Am (bungler) manche m; (misfit) paumé(e) m,f

fuckwad [!!] ['fʌkwɒd] n Am connard (connasse) m,f

fuckwit [!!] ['fʌkwɪt] *n* connard (connasse) *m,f*

fudge-packer [!!] ['fʌdʒpækə(r)] *n Injurieux* tantouze *f*, pédale *f*, tapette *f*

fugly [!!] ['fʌglɪ] *adj* (*abrév* **fucking ugly**) hyper moche; **she's really fugly** c'est un vrai boudin *ou* cageot

funky ['fʌŋkɪ] *adj* (**a**) (*fashionable, ex-cellent*) cool (**b**) *Am* (*smelly*) qui pue, qui schlingue

funny farm ['fʌnɪfɑːm] *n* maison *f* de fous

fur burger [!!] [fɜːˈbɜːgə(r)], **furpie** [!!] [fɜːˈpaɪ] *n* (*woman's genitals*) tarte *f* aux poils

fuzz [fʌz] *n Br* **the fuzz** (*the police*) les flics *mpl*, les poulets *mpl*

Gg

G [dʒiː] n Noir Am (**a**) (abrév **gang-sta**) = membre d'un gang de Noirs américains (**b**) (abrév **grand**) (thousand dollars) mille dollars□ mpl; **Gs** des milliers de dollars

gab [gæb] **1** n to have the gift of the gab avoir du bagout
2 vi jacter, jacasser

gabfest ['gæbfest] n Am converse f

gaff [gæf] n (**a**) Br (home) baraque f; **he's staying at my gaff for the weekend** il crèche chez moi ce week-end (**b**) Am to stand the gaff encaisser ▸ voir aussi **blow**

gaffer ['gæfə(r)] n (boss) patron□ m, taulier m

gag [gæg] **1** vt Am Hum **gag me (with a spoon)!** ça me fout la nausée!
2 vi Br **to be gagging for it** [!] avoir envie de se faire tirer

gaga ['gɑːgɑː] adj (**a**) (deranged) toqué, timbré; Br (senile) gaga (**b**) (besotted) **to be gaga about** or **over sb** être dingue de qn

gak [gæk] n (cocaine) coke f

gal [gæl] n Am nana f, gonzesse f

galah [gə'lɑː] n Austr (idiot) truffe f, andouille f; **you great** or **flaming galah!** mais quelle truffe tu fais!

gallus ['gæləs] adj Scot culotté

game [geɪm] n Br (**a**) to be on the game se prostituer□, michetonner

(**b**) **fuck** [!!] or **sod** [!] or **bugger** [!] **this for a game of soldiers!** bon ça va, j'arrête les frais! (**c**) **game on!** (let's start playing) ça joue!; (here we go) ça roule!; **game over** c'est foutu; **if we don't get that money by tonight, it's game over for us** si on n'a pas l'argent d'ici ce soir, on est foutu ▸ voir aussi **mug, skin**

gander ['gændə(r)] n to have a gander (at sb/sth) jeter un œil (à qn/qch), mater (qn/qch)

ganga ['gændʒə] n herbe f

gang-bang ['gæŋbæŋ] **1** n = coïts entre une femme et plusieurs hommes à la suite, gang bang m; (rape) viol m collectif□
2 vt to gang-bang sb baiser qn à tour de rôle; (rape) commettre un viol collectif sur qn□

gangsta ['gæŋstə] n Noir Am = membre d'un gang de Noirs américains

ganja ['gændʒə] = **ganga**

gannet ['gænət] n Br (person) morfal(e) m,f

garbage ['gɑːbɪdʒ] n (**a**) (nonsense) âneries fpl; **don't talk garbage!** ne dis pas n'importe quoi!; **that's garbage, you never said anything of the sort!** tu racontes n'importe quoi, t'as jamais dit ça! (**b**) (worthless things) **their new album is a load of garbage** leur dernier album est vraiment nul; **I've been eating**

too much garbage lately je mange trop de cochonneries en ce moment **(c)** *(useless things)* bazar *m*; **chuck out all that garbage of yours** fous-moi tout ton bazar en l'air, balance-moi tout ton bazar

garbo ['gɑːbəʊ] *n Austr* éboueur⁰ *m*, boueux *m*

garms [gɑːmz] *npl* fringues *mpl*

gas [gæs] **1** *n* **(a)** *(amusing thing, situation)* **what a gas!** quelle rigolade!; **the film was a real gas!** c'était un film vachement marrant!; *Br* **to have a gas** se marrer, s'en payer une tranche **(b)** *(amusing person)* **he's a real gas!** c'est un vrai boute-en-train! **(c)** *Am* **to be out of gas** *(exhausted)* être crevé *ou* naze
2 *vi (chat)* jacter, jacasser ▸ *voir aussi* **cook**

gasbag ['gæsbæg] *n (chatterbox)* moulin *m* à paroles; *(boaster)* fanfaron(onne) *m,f*

gas-guzzler ['gæsgʌzlə(r)] *n* voiture *f* qui bouffe beaucoup d'essence

gash [!!] [gæʃ] *n (woman's genitals)* craquette *f*, fente *f*, cramouille *f*

gasp [gɑːsp] *vi* **to be gasping for a cigarette/a drink** mourir d'envie de fumer une cigarette/de boire un verre

gasper ['gɑːspə(r)] *n Br* clope *f*

gassed [gæst] *adj (drunk)* bourré, pété

gasser ['gæsə(r)] *n Am* **to have a gasser** se marrer, s'en payer une tranche; **what a gasser!** quelle rigolade!; **the film was a real gasser!** c'était un film vachement marrant!

gator ['geɪtə(r)] *n Am (abrév* **alligator)** alligator⁰ *m*

gay [geɪ] *adj (stupid)* nul

gay-basher ['geɪbæʃə(r)] *n* = individu qui attaque des homosexuels

gay-bashing ['geɪbæʃɪŋ] *n* = violences contre des homosexuels; **they got arrested for gay-bashing** ils se sont fait arrêter pour avoir attaqué des homosexuels

gaydar ['geɪdɑː(r)] *n Hum* = sixième sens que certaines personnes sont censées posséder et qui leur permettrait de savoir qui est homosexuel et qui ne l'est pas

ⓘ Il s'agit d'un jeu de mots sur "radar".

gaylord ['geɪlɔːd] *n Péj* grande folle *f*

gay plague ['geɪ'pleɪg] *n* sida⁰ *m*

ⓘ L'expression signifie littéralement "peste gay". Elle est aujourd'hui politiquement incorrecte, mais désignait le sida dans les années 80, à une époque où l'on pensait que cette maladie n'affectait que les homosexuels.

gazillion [gə'zɪljən] *n Hum* **a gazillion** *or* **gazillions (of)** des millions et des millions (de)

GBH [dʒiːbiː'eɪtʃ] *n Br (abrév* **grievous bodily harm)** **he got done for GBH** il s'est fait arrêter pour coups et blessures⁰; *Hum* **to give sb GBH of the earholes** raser qn

GD [dʒiː'diː] *adj Am (abrév* **goddamn(ed))** foutu, sacré; **he's a GD fool** c'est un sacré con

gear [gɪə(r)] *n* **(a)** *(equipment)* matos *m*; *(belongings)* barda *m* **(b)** *(clothes)* fringues *fpl* **(c)** *Br (drugs)* dope *f* **(d)** *Am* **to get it in gear** se magner ▸ *see also* **arse, ass**

gearhead ['gɪəhed] *n Am* fou (folle) *m,f* de bagnoles

gee [dʒiː] *exclam Am* **gee (whizz)!** ça alors!

gee-gee ['dʒiːdʒiː] *n Br Hum (horse)* dada *m*; **I won a few quid on the gee-gees at the weekend** j'ai gagné quelques livres aux courses ce week-end□

geek [giːk] *n* (**a**) *(misfit)* ringard(e) *m,f* (**b**) *(strange person)* zarbi(e) *m,f*, allumé(e) *m,f*; **he's a real comic book geek** c'est un dingue de bandes dessinées

geeky ['giːkɪ] *adj* ringard, débile

geezer ['giːzə(r)] *n* (**a**) *Br (man)* mec *m*, type *m*; *(nice man)* chic type *m*; *(streetwise man)* type *m* débrouillard (**b**) *Am (old person)* vioque *mf*

gelt [gelt] *n Am* fric *m*, flouze *m*, pognon *m*

gender-bender ['dʒendəbendə(r)] *n* travesti□ *m*, travelo *m*

Geordie ['dʒɔːdɪ] **1** *n Br* = natif de Newcastle-upon-Tyne ou de ses environs
2 *adj* de Newcastle-upon-Tyne ou de ses environs

get [get] **1** *n Br (man)* connard *m*; *(woman)* connasse *f*; **you stupid get!** espèce de connard!
2 *vt* (**a**) *(annoy)* énerver□, prendre la tête à; **it really gets me the way he's late for everything** il me gonfle de toujours être en retard (**b**) *(understand)* comprendre□, piger; **get it?** tu piges?; **I get it!** j'ai pigé! (**c**) **to get it** *(be reprimanded)* se faire passer un savon; *(be beaten up)* prendre une raclée (**d**) **to get it together** se remuer le cul; *(in one's life)* se prendre en main□ (**e**) **get you!** *(listen to)* écoute-toi!; *(look at)* regarde-toi! (**f**) **to get some** *(sex)* s'envoyer en l'air, baiser; **he's in a bad mood cos**

he's not getting any il est de mauvaise humeur parce qu'il ne baise pas
3 *exclam (go away)* casse-toi!, dégage! ▸ *voir aussi* **life, room**

get away *exclam (expressing disbelief)* tu déconnes! ▸ *voir aussi* **end**

get by *vi (manage)* y arriver□, se démerder

get down 1 *vt sép* **to get sb down** foutre le bourdon à qn
2 *vi* (**a**) *(abandon restraint)* s'éclater; *(dance with abandon)* s'éclater en dansant (**b**) *Am (get to work, begin)* s'y mettre, attaquer (**c**) *Am (have sex)* s'envoyer en l'air

get in *exclam Br (expressing triumph)* super!, c'est gagné!; **five nil! get in!** cinq zéro! super!

get off *vi* (**a**) *(reach orgasm)* jouir□ (**b**) **to tell sb where to get off** envoyer balader qn; **where does he get off telling me how to raise my kids?** pour qui il se prend, lui, à me dire comment élever mes gosses? (**c**) *Br Hum* **to get off at Edge Hill** *or* **Gateshead** *or* **Haymarket** *or* **Paisley** = pratiquer le coït interrompu

ⓘ L'expression humoristique (c) joue sur la métaphore du voyageur descendant du train à la station qui précède la gare principale. Il est donc possible d'adapter l'expression en fonction de l'endroit où l'on habite. Edge Hill, Gateshead, Haymarket et Paisley sont des gares qui se trouvent respectivement à Liverpool, Newcastle, Édimbourg et Glasgow.

get off on *vt insép* **to get off on sth** prendre son pied avec qch; **to get off on doing sth** prendre son pied à faire qch

get off with vt insép **to get off with sb** faire une touche avec qn

get on vt sép (a) **to get it on (with)** (have sex) s'envoyer en l'air (avec); Am (fight) se friter (avec) (b) Am **to get it on** (get started, get busy) s'y mettre

get to vt insép **to get to sb** déprimer qn□, foutre le bourdon à qn; **don't let it get to you** il faut pas que ça te sape le moral

get up [!] vt sép **to get it up** bander; **he couldn't get it up** il a pas réussi à bander ▸ voir aussi **nose**

get up to vt insép se livrer à□; **what have you been getting up to?** qu'est-ce que tu deviens?

get with vt insep (a) (person) **to get with sb** (become emotionally involved with) se lier avec qn□; (have sex with) coucher avec qn (b) **get with it!, get with the programme!** essaye donc de suivre!

get-go ['getgəʊ] n Noir Am **from the get-go** (from the beginning) dès le début□; **he's a crook from the get-go** (completely) c'est un escroc total, c'est un véritable escroc

get-together ['gettəgeðə(r)] n réunion f entre amis□

get-up ['getʌp] n accoûtrement m

gig [gɪg] n (a) (concert) concert□ m, gig m (b) (job) boulot m

gimme ['gɪmɪ] contraction (abrév **give me**) donne-moi□; Am **the gimmes** la cupidité□ ▸ voir aussi **five**

gimp [gɪmp] n (a) (idiot) andouille f, crétin(e) m,f (b) (sado-masochist) sado-maso mf

ginge [dʒɪndʒ] n Br rouquin(e) m,f; **oi, ginge!** hé, le rouquin/la rouquine!

ginger¹ ['gɪŋə(r)] n Br rouquin(e) m,f

ⓘ Normalement, le terme "ginger" se prononce ['dʒɪndʒə(r)] et n'a aucune connotation particulière. Par contre, prononcé ['gɪŋə(r)], il prend une connotation argotique quelque peu péjorative.

---

ginger² ['dʒɪndʒə(r)] n Scot = boisson gazeuse

ginormous [dʒaɪ'nɔːməs, Am dʒɪ'nɔː-məs] adj énorme□, mastoc

gippo ['dʒɪpəʊ] = **gyppo**

giraffe [dʒɪ'rɑːf] n Br (rhyming slang **laugh**) **you're having a giraffe, mate!** tu rigoles, vieux!

girl [gɜːl] n **you go, girl!** vas-y, ma grande!

girlfriend ['gɜːlfrend] n Am (term of address) = terme utilisé par les Américaines pour s'adresser les unes aux autres; **yo, girlfriend!** salut frangine!; **you go, girlfriend!** vas-y, ma grande!

ⓘ À l'origine, ce terme n'était utilisé que par les Noires américaines. Aujourd'hui, son usage s'est généralisé.

---

girlie ['gɜːlɪ] n fille□ f, nana f; **girlie mag** revue f porno; Br **to have a girlie chat** bavarder entre filles□; **she's out seeing some girlie film with her mates** elle est allée voir un film pour les gonzesses avec ses copines

gism ['dʒɪzəm] = **jism (a)**

git [gɪt] n (man) connard m; (woman) connasse f; **you clumsy git!** espèce de manche!

give [gɪv] vi **who gives?** qu'est-ce que ça peut foutre?; Am **what gives?** quoi de neuf? ▸ voir aussi **finger, one**

Le symbole **[!]** dénote un terme très familier, **[!!]** un terme vulgaire.

give out *vi Ir* **he came in and started giving out about how hard it is to find a parking space round here** il est arrivé et il commencer à râler parce que c'est toute une histoire pour trouver à se garer dans le quartier; **to give out to sb** engueuler qn; **the boss is always giving out to me for coming in late** le patron est toujours en train de m'engueuler parce que j'arrive en retard

give over *Br* **1** *vt insép* **give over shouting!** arrête de gueuler comme ça!
2 *vi* arrêter◻

giz [gɪz] *contraction Br* (abrév **give us**) donne-moi; **giz a kiss!** donne-moi un bisou!

gizmo ['gɪzməʊ] *n* gadget *m*, truc *m*

glaikit ['gleɪkɪt] *adj Scot* (stupid, vacant) débile

glam [glæm] *adj Br* glamour◻

glam up *vt sep Br* (**a**) (person) **to get glammed up** (with clothes) se saper; (with make-up) se faire une beauté (**b**) (building) retaper; (place) embellir◻; (outfit) ajouter une touche glamour à

Glasgow ['glɑːzgəʊ] *n* **Glasgow kiss** coup *m* de boule; **Glasgow handshake** marron *m*, patate *f*; **Glasgow shower** = fait de s'asperger de déodorant ou de parfum pour éviter de se laver

ⓘ En Grande-Bretagne, Glasgow a la réputation d'être une ville violente.

glitterati [glɪtə'rɑːti] *npl* **the glitterati** le beau monde

glitz [glɪts] *n* clinquant *m*, tape-à-l'œil *m*

glitzy ['glɪtsɪ] *adj* tape-à-l'œil

globes [gləʊbz] *npl* (breasts) nichons *mpl*, nénés *mpl*; **check out the globes on that!** mate un peu les nichons!

glom [glɒm] *vt Am* (seize) arracher◻

glom onto *vt insép Am* (**a**) (seize) arracher◻ (**b**) (catch sight of) apercevoir◻

Glorias ['glɔːrɪəz] *npl Br* (rhyming slang **Gloria Gaynors = trainers**) tennis◻ *mpl or fpl*

ⓘ Gloria Gaynor est une chanteuse américaine de style disco des années 70, connue essentiellement pour sa chanson "I Will Survive".

G-man ['dʒiːmæn] *n Am* agent *m* du FBI◻

gnarly ['nɑːlɪ] *adj Am* (excellent, awful) mortel

gnat [næt] *n Br* **gnat's piss [!]** (drink) eau *f* de vaisselle, pipi *m* de chat

go [gəʊ] *vt* (**a**) (say) dire; **so she goes "you're lying!" and I go "no, I'm not!"** alors elle me fait "tu mens!" et je lui fais "non, je mens pas!" (**b**) *Br* **I could really go a beer/ciggy** je me taperais bien une bière/une clope ▸ *voir aussi* **way**

go down *vi* (**a**) (go to prison) aller en taule; **he went down for ten years** il en a pris pour dix ans (**b**) *Br* (be received) **to go down like a ton of bricks** *or* **a lead balloon** faire un bide total, se casser la gueule (**c**) *Am* (fall) **to go down like a ton of bricks** se casser la gueule (**d**) (happen) se passer◻, avoir lieu◻; **what's going down?** quoi de neuf?

go down on [!!] *vt insép* **to go down on sb** (fellate) sucer qn, tailler une pipe à qn; (perform cunnilingus on) sucer qn, brouter le cresson à qn

go for *vt insép* **go for it!** vas-y!

go into *vt insep Br* **to go into one** se mettre en pétard, voir rouge

go off *vi Br* **to go off on one** se mettre en pétard, voir rouge; **to go off (at) the deep end** péter les plombs, péter une durite

go over *vi Am* *(be received)* **to go over like a ton of bricks** *or* **a lead balloon** faire un bide total, se casser la gueule

go under *vi (of company)* se casser la gueule

go with *vt insép* **(a)** *(be romantically involved with)* sortir avec□ **(b)** **to go with the flow** suivre le mouvement□

goat [gəʊt] *n* **(a)** *Br* **to act the goat** *(act foolishly)* faire l'imbécile, déconner **(b)** **to get sb's goat** *(annoy)* irriter qn□, prendre la tête à qn **(c)** *Péj* **old goat** *(lecherous man)* vieux *m* cochon; *Am (old man)* vieux schnock *m*; *(old woman)* vieille toupie *f*

gob [gɒb] *Br* **1** *n (mouth)* gueule *f*, **shut your gob!** ferme ta gueule!; **to give sb a gob job [!!]** tailler *ou* faire une pipe à qn
2 *vi (spit)* mollarder **(at/on** vers/sur)

gobble [!!] ['gɒbəl] *vt (fellate)* sucer, tailler une pipe à

gobbledygook ['gɒbəldıguːk] *n* **(a)** *(jargon)* charabia *m* **(b)** *(nonsense)* conneries *fpl*

gobby ['gɒbı] *adj Br* **to be gobby** être une grande gueule

gobshite [!] ['gɒbʃaıt] *n Br (man)* trouduc *m*; *(woman)* connasse *f*

gobsmacked ['gɒbsmækt] *adj Br* estomaqué

God [gɒd] *n* **(my) God!** mon Dieu!; **for God's sake!** bon Dieu!; **God**

knows va savoir; **what in God's name are you doing?** mais qu'est-ce que tu es en train de faire?□; **he thinks he's God's gift (to women)** il s'imagine que toutes les femmes sont folles de lui; **the God squad** les culs bénis

godawful ['gɒdɔːfəl] *adj* dégueulasse, nul

godbotherer ['gɒdbɒðərə(r)] *n* cul béni *mf*

godbothering ['gɒdbɒðərıŋ] **1** *adj* cul béni
2 *n* activités *fpl* de culs bénis

goddammit [!] [gɒd'dæmıt] *exclam* bordel!

goddamn [!] ['gɒd'dæm], **goddamned [!]** ['gɒd'dæmd] **1** *adj* foutu, fichu; **he's a goddamn** *or* **goddamned fool!** c'est un pauvre con!
2 *adv* vachement; **that was goddamn** *or* **goddamned stupid!** c'est vraiment pas malin!
3 *exclam* **goddamn (it)!** bordel!

goer ['gəʊə(r)] *n Br (woman)* **she's a bit of a goer** elle couche à droite à gauche

gofer ['gəʊfə(r)] *n* larbin *m*

ⓘ Le terme "gofer" est une altération des termes "go for" qui signifie "aller chercher", ce qui résume le genre de tâches confiées aux employés subalternes.

goldbrick ['gəʊldbrık] *Am* **1** *n (malingerer)* tire-au-flanc *m*
2 *vi (malinger)* tirer au flanc

gold-digger ['gəʊld'dıgə(r)] *n Péj (woman)* croqueuse *f* de diamants

golden showers [!!] [gəʊldən'ʃaʊəz] *npl* uro *f*, = pratique sexuelle qui consiste à uriner sur son ou sa partenaire

golly ['gɒlɪ] *exclam* bon Dieu!

gone [gɒn] *adj* (**a**) **to be gone on sb** être dingue de qn (**b**) **to be well gone** *(drunk)* être beurré *ou* bourré *ou* pété

goner ['gɒnə(r)] *n* **to be a goner** être foutu

gong [gɒŋ] *n (medal)* médaille□ *f*, breloque *f*; *(prize)* prix□ *m*, récompense□ *f*

gonna ['gɒnə] *contraction (abrév* **going to**) **I'm gonna kill him!** je vais le buter!

ⓘ Cette contraction n'est utilisée que pour exprimer le futur proche.

gonzo ['gɒnzəʊ] *adj Am* dingue, dément

goober ['gu:bə(r)] *n Am* crétin(e) *m,f*, andouille *f*, tache *f*

goods [gʊdz] *npl Am* **to have the goods on sb** avoir la preuve de la culpabilité de qn□

goof [gu:f] *Am* **1** *n* (**a**) *(person)* crétin(e) *m,f*, andouille *f*, tache *f* (**b**) *(mistake)* boulette *f*, bourde *f*
2 *vi* (**a**) *(make mistake)* faire une boulette *ou* une bourde (**b**) *(joke)* rigoler; **to goof with sb** *(tease)* faire enrager qn (**c**) *(stare)* **to goof at sb/sth** regarder qn/qch bêtement□

goof about, goof around *vi Am* (**a**) *(act foolishly)* faire le con, déconner (**b**) *(waste time)* glander, glandouiller

goof off *Am* **1** *vt insép* **to goof off school** sécher l'école; **to goof off work** ne pas aller bosser
2 *vi* glander, glandouiller

goof up *Am* **1** *vt sép* **to goof sth up** foirer qch, merder qch
2 *vi* foirer, merder

goofball ['gu:fbɔ:l] *n Am* (**a**) *(person)* crétin(e) *m,f*, andouille *f*, tache *f* (**b**) *(barbiturate)* mélange *m* de barbituriques et d'amphétamines□

goofy ['gu:fɪ] *adj* (**a**) *(stupid)* débile, abruti (**b**) *Br* **to have goofy teeth** avoir les dents qui courent après le bifteck

gook [gu:k] *n Am Injurieux* bridé(e) *m,f*

goolies [!] ['gu:lɪz] *npl Br* couilles *fpl*, valseuses *fpl*

goon [gu:n] *n* (**a**) *(idiot)* andouille *f*, cruche *f*, courge *f* (**b**) *(hired thug)* gorille *m*

goose [gu:s] *vt* **to goose sb** mettre la main au cul à qn

gooseberry ['gʊzbərɪ] *n Br* **to play gooseberry** tenir la chandelle

gorblimey [gɔ:'blaɪmɪ] *exclam Br* nom de Dieu!, merde alors!

Gordon Bennett ['gɔ:dən'benɪt] *exclam Br* nom d'une pipe!

ⓘ Il s'agit d'un euphémisme du mot "God" utilisé comme juron. Gordon Bennett était un journaliste américain du 19ème siècle haut en couleurs.

gorilla [gə'rɪlə] *n Péj (man)* grosse brute *f*

gosh [gɒʃ] *exclam* la vache!

goss [gɒs] *n Br (abrév* **gossip**) cancans *mpl*, potins *mpl*; **what's the goss?** quels sont les derniers potins?

gotcha ['gɒtʃə] *exclam (abrév* **I got you**) *(I understand)* je comprends□, d'accord□; *(when catching hold of someone)* pris!□; *(when catching some-one doing something)* je t'y prends!□; *(when one has an advantage over someone)* je te tiens!□

The symbol □ indicates that a translation is neutral.

gotta ['gɒtə] *contraction* (**a**) (*abrév* **got to**) **I('ve) gotta go** (il) faut que j'y aille; **it's gotta be done** il faut que ce soit fait▫ (**b**) (*abrév* **got a**) **he's gotta new girlfriend** il a une nouvelle copine▫

grand [grænd] *n* (*thousand pounds*) mille livres▫ *fpl*; (*thousand dollars*) mille dollars▫ *mpl*; **a grand** mille livres/dollars▫; **five grand** cinq mille livres/dollars▫

grapes [greɪps] *npl* (*haemorrhoids*) hémorroïdes▫ *fpl*, émeraudes *fpl*

grass [grɑːs] **1** *n* (**a**) (*marijuana*) herbe *f* (**b**) *Br* (*informer*) mouchard *m*, balance *f*
2 *vi Br* (*inform*) moucharder; **to grass on sb** balancer qn, moucharder qn

grass up *vt sép* **to grass sb up** balancer qn, moucharder qn

gravy ['greɪvɪ] *n* (**a**) *Am* (*easy money*) argent *m* facile▫; **to get on the gravy train** profiter d'un filon (**b**) **it's all gravy** tout baigne

greased lightning [griːst'laɪtnɪŋ] *n* **like greased lightning** à tout berzingue, à fond la caisse

grease monkey ['griːsmʌŋkɪ] *n* mécano *m*

greaser ['griːsə(r)] *n* (**a**) (*biker*) motard *m* (**b**) *Am Injurieux* (*Latin American*) métèque *mf* (*d'origine latino-américaine*)

greasy spoon [griːsɪ'spuːn] *n* (*café*) boui-boui *m*

greedy-guts ['griːdɪɡʌts] *n* morfal(e) *m,f*

green [griːn] *n Am* (*money*) fric *m*, flouze *m*, blé *m*; **let's see your green** aboule ton fric

greenback ['griːnbæk] *n Am* fafiot *m*

greenhorn ['griːnhɔːn] *n* bleu *m*

green-welly [griːn'welɪ] *adj Br Hum* **the green-welly brigade** la grande bourgeoisie rurale▫

ⓘ Le terme "green welly" signifie littéralement "botte de caoutchouc verte". Par métonymie, il désigne les aristocrates et les grands bourgeois vivant à la campagne, que l'on voit souvent chaussés de bottes de caoutchouc vertes et vêtus de vestes de chasse.

greeny ['griːnɪ] *n Br* (**a**) (*phlegm*) mollard *m* (**b**) (*nasal mucus*) morve *f*

grief [griːf] *n* (*trouble, inconvenience*) embêtements▫ *mpl*; **to give sb grief** embêter qn▫; **I'm getting a lot of grief from my parents** mes parents n'arrêtent pas de m'embêter▫ *ou* de me prendre la tête

grifter ['grɪftə(r)] *n Am* escroc▫ *m*, arnaqueur *m*

grill [grɪl] *vt* (*interrogate*) cuisiner

grip [grɪp] *n* **to get a grip** se ressaisir▫; **get a grip!** ressaisis-toi!, assure!

grody ['grəʊdɪ] *adj Am* dégueulasse

grogshop ['grɒɡʃɒp] *n Austr* magasin *m* de vins et spiritueux▫

groovy ['gruːvɪ] **1** *adj* super, cool
2 *exclam* super!, cool!

gross [grəʊs] *adj* (*disgusting*) dégueulasse

gross out *vt sép* **to gross sb out** dégoûter qn▫, débecter qn

gross-out ['grəʊsaʊt] **1** *n Am* = chose ou situation répugnante; **what a gross-out!** c'est vraiment dégueulasse!
2 *adj* **gross-out movie** comédie *f* lourde▫, film *m* à l'humour lourd▫

grot [grɒt] *n Br* crasse□ *f*

grotty ['grɒtɪ] *adj* dégueulasse, dégueu

groupie ['gruːpɪ] *n* groupie *f*

growler [!!] ['grəʊlə(r)] *n Br (woman's genitals)* cramouille *f*, craque *f*

grub [grʌb] *n (food)* bouffe *f*; **grub's up!** à la soupe!

grundle [!!] ['grʌndəl] *n Am* = zone située entre le scrotum et l'anus

grungy ['grʌndʒɪ] *adj Am (dirty)* dégueulasse, dégueu

grunt [grʌnt] *n Am (soldier)* bidasse *m*

gubbins ['gʌbɪnz] *n Br* bêtises *fpl*; **I don't have time to read all this gubbins** je n'ai pas le temps de lire toutes ces bêtises; **that programme's a load of gubbins** cette émission est débile

guff [gʌf] **1** *n* (**a**) *(nonsense)* âneries *fpl*; **don't talk guff!** ne dis pas d'âneries!; **the film was a load of guff** le film était vraiment débile (**b**) *(fart)* pet *m*, prout *m*

2 *vi* péter, larguer une caisse, lâcher une perle; **who just guffed?** qui est-ce qui vient de larguer une caisse?

guinea ['gɪnɪ] *n Am Injurieux (Italian)* Rital(e) *m,f*, macaroni *mf*

gunk [gʌŋk] *n* saloperie *f (substance)*

gutless ['gʌtlɪs] *adj* **to be gutless** ne rien avoir dans le bide; **a gutless performance** une prestation sans intérêt□; **gutless wonder** = personne qui parle beaucoup mais agit peu, guignol *m*

gutrot ['gʌtrɒt] *n* (**a**) *(drink)* tord-boyaux *m* (**b**) *(stomach upset)* mal *m* de bide

guts [gʌts] *npl* (**a**) *(insides)* **to hate sb's guts** ne pas pouvoir blairer qn; **to work** *or* **slog one's guts out** travailler comme un nègre (**b**) *(courage)* cran *m*; **to have guts** en avoir dans le bide, avoir du cran; **to have the guts to do sth** avoir le cran de faire qch ► *voir aussi* **spew, spill**

gutsy ['gʌtsɪ] *adj* (**a**) *(courageous)* **to be gutsy** en avoir dans le bide, avoir du cran (**b**) *(greedy)* morfal

gutted ['gʌtɪd] *adj Br (disappointed)* dégoûté, hyper déçu

guttered ['gʌtəd] *adj Br (drunk)* bourré, pété, beurré, poivré

guv [gʌv], **guvnor** ['gʌvnə(r)] *n Br* (**a**) *(boss)* **the guv** *or* **guvnor** le patron, le chef (**b**) *(term of address)* chef *m*, patron *m*

guy [gaɪ] *n* (**a**) *(man)* mec *m*, type *m* (**b**) *(person)* **hi, guys!** salut vous!; **what are you guys doing tonight?** qu'est-ce vous faites ce soir? ► *voir aussi* **tough**

gyp [dʒɪp] **1** *n* (**a**) *Br (pain)* **to give sb gyp** faire déguster qn (**b**) *Am (swindler)* escroc□ *m*, arnaqueur *m*

2 *vt Am (swindle)* arnaquer

gyppo ['dʒɪpəʊ] *n Br* romano *mf*

Hh

H [eɪtʃ] *n* (*abrév* **heroin**) blanche *f*, héro *f*

habit ['hæbɪt] *n* (*drug addiction*) accoutumance□ *f*; **to have a drug habit** être toxico; **to have a coke/ smack habit** être accro à la coke/à l'héro; **to kick the habit** décrocher

hack [hæk] **1** *n* (**a**) *Péj* (*writer*) pissecopie *mf* (**b**) *Am* (*taxi*) taxi□ *m*, tacot *m*; (*taxi driver*) chauffeur *m* de taxi□
  2 *vt* (*cope with*) **he can't hack the pace** il n'arrive pas à tenir le rythme; **he can't hack it** il s'en sort pas

hack off *vt sép* **to hack sb off** prendre la tête à qn; **to be hacked off (with)** en avoir marre (de)

hackette [hæ'ket] *n Br Péj* pissecopie *f*

hag [hæg] *n* (*ugly woman*) **(old) hag** vieille peau *f* ▸ *voir aussi* **fag**

hair [heə(r)] *n* **to get in sb's hair** taper sur les nerfs à qn; **get out of my hair!** fous-moi la paix!; **to let one's hair down** se laisser aller; **keep your hair on!** du calme!, calmos!; *Hum* **this'll put hairs on your chest!** tiens, bois/mange ça, c'est bon pour la santé!; **I need a hair of the dog (that bit me)** j'ai besoin d'un verre pour soigner ma gueule de bois

hairpie [!!] [heə'paɪ] *n* (*woman's genitals*) tarte *f* aux poils

half [hɑːf] **1** *n* (**a**) **a party/day/hangover and a half** une sacrée nouba/

journée/gueule de bois (**b**) **my other** or **better half** ma moitié
  2 *adv Br* (*for emphasis*) **you don't half talk rubbish** tu racontes vraiment n'importe quoi; **it's not half bad** c'est pas mal du tout; **he hasn't half changed** il a vachement changé; **not half!** et comment!

half-arsed [!] [hɑːf'ɑːst], *Am* **half-assed** [!] [hæf'æst] *adj* foireux

half-cut [hɑːf'kʌt] *adj Br* (*drunk*) bourré, pété, fait

half-inch [hɑːf'ɪntʃ] *vt Br* (*rhyming slang* **pinch**) piquer, faucher, chouraver; **he got his wallet half-inched** il s'est fait piquer son portefeuille

halfwit ['hɑːfwɪt] *n* abruti(e) *m,f*, débile *mf*

halfwitted [hɑːf'wɪtɪd] *adj* abruti, débile

ham-fisted [hæm'fɪstɪd] *adj* maladroit□, manche

hammer ['hæmə(r)] **1** *n Am* **to let the hammer down** appuyer sur le champignon, mettre les gaz
  2 *vt* (**a**) (*beat up*) tabasser (**b**) (*defeat*) écraser, battre à plates coutures (**c**) (*criticize*) éreinter, démolir

hammered ['hæməd] *adj* (*drunk*) bourré, beurré, pété, fait

hammering ['hæmərɪŋ] *n* (**a**) (*beating*) **to give sb a hammering** tabasser qn; **to get a hammering** se faire tabasser (**b**) (*defeat*) branlée *f*, pâtée f; **to give sb a hammering** battre qn à plates coutures, foutre la pâtée à qn; **to get a hammering** être battu à plates coutures **(c)** *(criticism)* **to give sb/sth a hammering** éreinter *ou* démolir qn/qch; **to get a hammering** se faire éreinter *ou* démolir

hand [hænd] *n* **(a) talk to the hand (cos the face ain't listening)!** parle à mon cul, ma tête est malade **(b)** *Br Hum* **to have a hand shandy [!!]** se branler, faire cinq contre un; **to give sb a hand shandy [!!]** branler qn

ⓘ L'expression "talk to the hand" s'emploie lorsque quelqu'un veut montrer à la personne qui lui parle qu'elle perd son temps ; elle est généralement accompagnée d'un geste de la main demandant à la personne de se taire, tout en regardant ailleurs.

hand-job [!!] ['hænddʒɒb] *n* **to give sb a hand-job** branler qn

handsome ['hændsəm] *exclam Br* super!, génial!

hang [hæŋ] **1** *vt Am* **to hang a left/a right** tourner à gauche/à droite⁰
2 *vi* **(a)** *Am (spend time)* traîner; **he's hanging with his friends** il traîne avec ses copains; **what are you up to? – just hanging** qu'est-ce que tu fais? – oh, rien de spécial **(b) how's it hanging?** *(how are you?)* comment ça va? **(c)** *Am* **to hang loose** rester cool; **hang loose!** détends-toi!, cool!; **to hang tough** s'accrocher

hang about, hang around *vi* **(a)** *(spend time)* traîner; **who does she hang about or around with?** avec qui est-ce qu'elle sort? **(b)** *(wait)* poireauter; **to keep sb hanging**

about *or* **around** faire poireauter qn; **hang about, that's not what I meant!** attends voir, c'est pas ce que je voulais dire!

hang in *vi* **to hang in there** tenir bon, tenir le coup; **hang in there!** tiens bon!

hang on *vt sép* **to hang one on** *(get drunk)* prendre une cuite

hang out *vi* **(a)** *(spend time)* traîner; **he hangs out at the local bar** c'est un habitué du café du coin; **who's that guy she hangs out with?** c'est qui ce mec avec qui elle sort? **(b) to let it all hang out** être relax

hang up *vt sép* **(a) to be hung up on sb/sth** *(obsessed)* être obsédé par qn/qch⁰ **(b)** *Am* **to hang it up** *(stop)* laisser tomber

hang-out ['hæŋaʊt] *n* **that bar's my favourite hang-out** c'est le bar où je vais d'habitude⁰; **it's a real student hang-out** c'est un endroit très fréquenté par les étudiants⁰

hang-up ['hæŋʌp] *n* complexe⁰ *m*; **she's got a real hang-up about her weight** elle fait un complexe sur son poids

Hank Marvin [hæŋk'mɑːvɪn] *adj Br (rhyming slang* **starving**) **I'm Hank Marvin** j'ai la dalle *ou* les crocs

ⓘ Hank Marvin est un guitariste britannique, membre fondateur des Shadows.

hanky-panky ['hæŋkɪ'pæŋkɪ] *n (sexual activity)* galipettes *fpl*; *(underhand behaviour)* coups *mpl* fourrés

happening ['hæpənɪŋ] *adj* branché, dans le coup

happy ['hæpɪ] *adj Hum* **he's not a happy camper** *or Br* **chappy** *or* **bunny** il est pas jouasse; **to be**

happy as a pig in clover or **shit [!]** être heureux comme un poisson dans l'eau□, se la couler douce

happy-clappy [hæpɪ'klæpɪ] *Br Hum Péj* **1** *adj* = agaçant de par sa joie exubérante *(appliqué aux Chrétiens évangéliques)*; **I hate him and his happy-clappy friends** je le déteste lui et ses copains, ces grenouilles de bénitier avec leur sourire béat

2 *n* chrétien(enne) *m,f* évangélique□

hard-ass [!] ['hɑːdæs] *n Am (person)* dur(e) *m,f* à cuire

hard-on [!] ['hɑːdɒn] *n* **to have a hard-on** bander; **to get a hard-on** se mettre à bander

hard-up [hɑːd'ʌp] *adj* fauché, raide, sans un

hash [hæʃ] *n* **(a)** *(abrév* **hashish)** hasch *m* **(b)** *(mess)* **to make a hash of sth** saloper qch

hassle ['hæsəl] **1** *n (trouble, inconvenience)* embêtements *mpl*; **to give sb hassle** harceler qn□; **it's too much hassle** c'est trop de tintouin, c'est trop galère; **moving house is such a hassle** c'est vraiment galère de déménager

2 *vt* **to hassle sb** harceler qn□; **to hassle sb into doing sth** harceler qn jusqu'à ce qu'il fasse qch□

hatchet ['hætʃɪt] *n* **(a) hatchet job** très mauvaise critique□ *f*; **to do a hatchet job on sb/sth** éreinter *ou* démolir qn/qch **(b) hatchet man** *(hired killer)* tueur *m* à gages□; *(in industry, politics)* = personne dont le rôle est de restructurer une entreprise ou une organisation, le plus souvent à l'aide de mesures impopulaires

hatstand ['hætstænd] *adj Br (mad)* toqué, timbré, cinglé

haul [hɔːl] ▶ *voir* **ass**

have [hæv] *vt* **(a) to have had it** *(be ruined, in trouble)* être foutu; *Am (be exhausted)* être crevé *ou* naze *ou* lessivé; **to have had it up to here (with)** en avoir marre (de), avoir eu sa dose (de); **to let sb have it** *(physically)* casser la gueule à qn; *(verbally)* souffler dans les bronches à qn; **I tried to convince her but she wasn't having any of it** j'ai essayé de la convaincre, mais elle n'a pas voulu en entendre parler; **he had it coming** il l'a cherché **(b)** *(beat up)* casser la gueule à; **I could have you!** si tu me cherches tu vas te trouver! **(c)** *(cheat)* **to be had** se faire avoir **(d) [!]** *(have sex with) (of man)* baiser, s'envoyer; *(of woman)* baiser avec, s'envoyer

have away *vt sép* **to have it away (with sb) [!]** s'envoyer en l'air (avec qn)

have in *vt sép* **to have it in for sb** avoir qn dans le nez

have off *vt sép Br* **to have it off (with sb) [!]** s'envoyer en l'air (avec qn)

have on *vt sép* **to have sb on** faire marcher qn

hay [heɪ] *n* **to hit the hay** *(go to bed)* se pieuter, se bâcher

hayseed ['heɪsiːd] *n Am & Austr* bouseux(euse) *m,f*, péquenaud(e) *m,f*

head [hed] *n* **(a) to get one's head together** se mettre en train□; **to laugh one's head off** être mort de rire; **to shout one's head off** gueuler comme un sourd; *Br* **to do sb's head in** prendre la tête à qn; *Br* **go and boil your head!** va te faire cuire un œuf! **(b)** *Br* **to be off one's head** *(mad)* être cinglé *ou* toqué; **to be out of one's head** *(mad)* être cinglé *ou* toqué; *(drunk)* être bourré *ou* beurré *ou* pété; *(on drugs)* être défoncé *ou* parti (**c**) **to give sb head [!!]** sucer qn ▸ *voir aussi* **hole, honcho, knock, lose, rush, upside**

-head [hed] *suffixe* **she's a bit of a whiskyhead** elle a un faible pour le whisky; **he's a real jazzhead** c'est un vrai fana de jazz

ⓘ Le suffixe "-head" dénote l'enthousiasme de quelqu'un pour une activité ou une substance.

headbanger ['hedbæŋə(r)] *n* (**a**) *(heavy metal fan)* hardeux(euse) *m,f* (**b**) *Br (mad person)* cinglé(e) *m,f*, toqué(e) *m,f*

headcase ['hedkeɪs] *n* cinglé(e) *m,f*, toqué(e) *m,f*

header ['hedə(r)] *n Ir* cinglé(e) *m,f*, toqué(e) *m,f*

headfuck [!!] ['hedfʌk] *n* (**a**) *(man)* mec *m* pas net; *(woman)* nana *f* pas nette (**b**) *(thing, experience)* épreuve□ *f*; **this movie is a bit of a headfuck** c'est un peu le bad trip, ce film

headshrinker ['hedʃrɪŋkə(r)] *n Am* psy *mf*

heap [hiːp] *n (car)* poubelle *f*

heaps [hiːps] *Br* **1** *npl (a lot)* **I've got heaps to do** j'ai un tas de trucs à faire; **heaps of time/money** vachement de temps/d'argent
2 *adv* **I like him heaps** je l'aime vachement

heart-throb ['hɑːtθrɒb] *n* idole *f*

heat [hiːt] *n Am* (**a**) **the heat** les flics *mpl* (**b**) **to be packing heat** *(carrying a gun)* porter un flingue sur soi, être enfouraillé

heave [hiːv] **1** *n* **to give sb the heave** *(employee)* virer qn, sacquer qn; *(boyfriend, girlfriend)* plaquer qn, larguer qn; **to get the heave** *(of*

employee) se faire virer *ou* sacquer; *(of boyfriend, girlfriend)* se faire plaquer *ou* larguer
2 *vi (retch)* avoir un haut-le-cœur□; *(vomit)* gerber, dégueuler, dégobiller

heave-ho [hiːv'həʊ] *n* **to give sb the (old) heave-ho** *(employee)* virer qn, sacquer qn; *(boyfriend, girlfriend)* plaquer qn, larguer qn; **to get the (old) heave-ho** *(of employee)* se faire virer *ou* sacquer; *(of boyfriend, girlfriend)* se faire plaquer *ou* larguer

heaving ['hiːvɪŋ] *adj Br (extremely busy)* hyper animé

heavy ['hevɪ] **1** *n (man)* balaise *m*, grosse brute *f*
2 *adj* (**a**) *(frightening, troublesome)* craignos; **to get heavy with sb** devenir agressif avec qn□; **things started to get a bit heavy** ça a commencé à craindre (**b**) *(profound, affecting)* profond□; **to get heavy with sb** prendre la tête à qn ▸ *voir aussi* **hot**

hebe [hiːb] *n Am Injurieux* youpin(e) *m,f*; youtre *mf*

heck [hek] **1** *n* **who the heck said you could borrow my car?** bon sang! qui t'a dit que tu pouvais prendre ma voiture?; **why the heck didn't you tell me?** pourquoi est-ce que tu m'as pas prévenu, nom de nom!; **what the heck are you doing?** mais qu'est-ce que tu fous, nom de nom!; **there were a heck of a lot of people there** il y avait un maximum de monde; **he misses her a heck of a lot** elle lui manque vachement; **I can't afford it, but what the heck!** c'est un peu cher pour moi mais je m'en fous!; **to do sth just for the heck of it** faire qch juste pour le plaisir; *Br* **so did you pay him?** – **did I heck!** alors, tu l'as payé? – tu rigoles?
2 *exclam* mince alors!

The symbol □ *indicates that a translation is neutral.*

heebie-jeebies ['hi:bɪ'dʒi:bɪz] *npl* **to have the heebie-jeebies** avoir la trouille *ou* les chocottes; **to give sb the heebie-jeebies** *(scare)* foutre la trouille à qn; *(repulse)* débecter qn

heel [hi:l] *n (person)* chameau *m*

heifer ['hefə(r)] *n Péj (fat woman)* grosse dondon *f*

Heinz [haɪnz] *n Hum (dog)* bâtard□ *m*

ⓘ C'est parce que la marque Heinz se vantait jadis d'offrir une gamme de 57 variétés de produits différents que l'on gratifie parfois un chien bâtard de cette appellation. Le sous-entendu est que l'animal est issu d'un nombre comparable de variétés canines.

heist [haɪst] **1** *n (robbery)* cambriolage□ *m*; *(hold-up)* braquage *m*, casse *m*

2 *vt (money)* rafler; *(bank)* braquer

hell [hel] **1** *n* **(a)** **the boyfriend/flatmate/neighbours from hell** un petit ami/un colocataire/des voisins de cauchemar; **to give sb hell** engueuler qn; **to knock hell out of sb** tabasser qn; **all hell broke loose** ça a chié; **this weather plays hell with my joints** ce temps est mauvais pour mes articulations□; **there'll be hell to pay** on va avoir des embêtements; **hell for leather** à fond la caisse, à tout berzingue; **like a bat out of hell** comme une furie; **the environment is going to hell in a handcart** l'environnement est en train d'être saccagé; **this company is going to hell in a handcart** cette entreprise est en train de sombrer; **go to hell!** va te faire voir!

(b) *(for emphasis)* **what the hell** *or* **in hell's name are you doing?** mais qu'est-ce que tu fous, nom de Dieu!; **who the hell are you talking about?** mais tu parles de qui, nom de Dieu!; **why the hell did you say that?** pourquoi t'as dit ça, nom de Dieu!; **how the hell should I know?** mais comment veux-tu que je le sache?; **what the hell, you only live once!** et puis merde, on ne vit qu'une fois!; **are you going? – like** *or* **the hell I am!, am I hell!** est-ce que tu y vas? – tu rigoles!; **get the hell out of here!** fous-moi le camp!; **I did it just for the hell of it** je l'ai fait rien que pour le plaisir; **to hell with it!** et puis merde!; **I wish to hell I knew** c'est ce que j'aimerais bien savoir; **it was hell on wheels** c'était l'enfer; **hell's bells** *or Br* **teeth!** nom de Dieu!

(c) **he's in a hell of a bad mood** il est d'humeur massacrante; **he had a hell of a job carrying the wardrobe** il en a chié pour porter l'armoire; **to have a hell of a time** *(very good)* s'éclater; *(very bad)* passer un très mauvais moment; **he likes her a hell of a lot** il est dingue d'elle; **it could have been a hell of a lot worse** ça aurait pu être bien pire; **it's a hell of a cold day outside** il fait un froid de canard dehors

(d) *(in comparisons)* **to work/run like hell** travailler/courir comme un dingue; **as jealous as hell** hyper jaloux; **as mad as hell** fou à lier; **I'm as sure as hell not going** il est pas question que j'y aille

2 *exclam* bon Dieu!

hella ['helə] *Am* **1** *adj (a lot of)* **there are hella chicks in here man!** c'est bourré de nanas là-dedans, vieux!

2 *adv (very)* **the club was hella cool!** la boîte de nuit était super cool!

hellacious [hel'eɪʃəs] *adj Am* **(a)** *(bad, unpleasant)* infernal **(b)** *(excellent)* super, génial

hellhole ['helhəʊl] *n* trou *m* à rats

hellish ['helɪʃ] *adj (very bad)* infernal; **the weather was hellish** il a fait un temps dégueulasse; **I feel hellish** je me sens vraiment pas dans mon assiette

hellishly ['helɪʃlɪ] *adv* vachement

hello [he'ləʊ] *exclam (expressing disbelief)* **of course he's not my boyfriend, I mean, hello? the guy's a total loser!** bien sûr que non, ce n'est pas mon petit ami, ne dis pas n'importe quoi, il est complètement nul, ce mec-là!; **you think you're going to pull wearing that hideous shirt? hello?** tu crois que tu vas avoir du succès si tu sors avec cette chemise affreuse? tu rêves ou quoi?; **so they're all discussing my future and I'm like hello? I AM still here you know!** ils étaient tous là à discuter de mon avenir, alors je leur ai fait "hé ho, je suis toujours là, au cas où vous l'auriez pas remarqué!"

ⓘ Il s'agit d'un usage du terme "hello" d'origine américaine. Ce terme se prononce "hell-*o*?"; il faut insister sur le "o" tout en lui donnant une intonation ascendante. Cette exclamation est souvent accompagnée d'une mimique exprimant l'indignation ou l'incrédulité.

helluva ['heləvə] *contraction (abrév* **hell of a)** **they're making a helluva noise** ils font un boucan pas possible; **he's a helluva nice guy** c'est un type formidable; **I miss him a helluva lot** il me manque vachement; **it costs a helluva lot of money** ça coûte vachement cher, ça coûte bonbon; **we had a helluva time getting there** on en a chié pour arriver là-bas

helmet [!] ['helmɪt] *n (head of penis)* gland[□] *m*

hen [hen] *n* Scot *(term of address) (to customer)* ma petite dame; *(to relative, friend)* ma chérie

Henry ['henrɪ] *n Br* = un huitième d'once *(environ 3,5 grammes)*

ⓘ C'est un terme de l'argot de la drogue. Il s'agit d'une référence à Henri VIII ("the Eighth").

herb [hɜːb] *n (marijuana)* herbe *f*

her indoors [hɜːrɪn'dɔːz] *n Br Hum* la patronne, ma bourgeoise; **I wanted to go down the boozer, but her indoors wasn't having any of it** je voulais aller au pub mais la patronne *ou* ma bourgeoise n'a pas voulu en entendre parler

hey [heɪ] *exclam* salut!

hick [hɪk] *n Am* bouseux(euse) *m,f*, péquenaud(e) *m,f*

hickey ['hɪkɪ] *n Am* suçon *m*

hide [haɪd] *n* **to tan sb's hide** tanner le cuir à qn

high [haɪ] *adj* **(a)** *(on drugs)* défoncé, parti, raide; **to get high** se défoncer; **as high as a kite** complètement parti, raide; *Br (very excited)* surexcité[□] **(b)** *Br* **he's for the high jump** *(in trouble)* son compte est bon **(c)** **high roller** richard(e) *m,f* ▶ *voir aussi* **hog**¹

high-five ['haɪ'faɪv] *n* **(a)** *(type of handshake)* = tape amicale donnée dans la paume de quelqu'un, bras levé, pour le saluer, le féliciter, ou en signe de victoire; **high-five!** tape-moi dans la main! **(b)** *Noir Am (HIV)* **he's got the high-five** il est séropo

hightail ['haɪteɪl] *vt* **to hightail it** décamper, mettre les bouts en vitesse; **he hightailed it home** il est rentré chez lui à fond de train

hike [haɪk] *n Am* **take a hike!** va te faire voir!

hillbilly ['hɪlbɪlɪ] *n Péj* péquenaud(e) *m,f*, plouc *mf*; **hillbilly heroin** = surnom donné à des antalgiques qui ont un effet similaire à celui de l'héroïne

himbo ['hɪmbəʊ] *n Hum* beau mec *m* pas très futé

ⓘ Il s'agit d'un jeu de mots sur le terme "bimbo" et le pronom "him".

hinky ['hɪŋkɪ] *adj (suspect)* louche

hip [hɪp] **1** *adj (fashionable)* branché, tendance; **that's the hippest bar in town** c'est le bar le plus branché *ou* tendance de la ville

   2 *vt Am* **to hip sb to sth** mettre qn au courant de qch□; **let me hip you to the latest** je vais te mettre au parfum

hipped [hɪpt] *adj Am* **to be hipped on sb/sth** être dingue de qn/qch

hissy fit ['hɪsɪfɪt] *n* **to have a hissy fit** faire une crise

history ['hɪstərɪ] *n* **he's history!** *(in trouble)* il est fini!; *(no longer in my life)* avec lui, c'est terminé

hit [hɪt] **1** *n* **(a)** *(of hard drugs)* fix *m*; *(of joint)* taffe *f*; *(effect of drugs)* effet□ *m (procuré par une drogue)*; **you get a good hit off that grass** cette herbe fait rapidement de l'effet **(b)** *(murder)* meurtre *m* sur commande□

   2 *vt* **(a)** **to hit the road** *or Am* **the bricks** *(leave)* mettre les bouts, se barrer, s'arracher

(b) **to hit the roof** *or Am* **the ceiling** *(lose one's temper)* piquer une crise, péter les plombs

(c) *(go to)* **to hit the shops** aller faire du shopping; *Br* **to hit the town**

aller faire la fête en ville; *Br* **to hit the pub** aller au pub

(d) *(murder)* buter, zigouiller, refroidir

(e) **to hit sb for sth** *(borrow)* emprunter qch à qn□; *(scrounge from)* taper qch à qn

(f) **that hit the spot** *(was satisfying, refreshing)* ça fait du bien par où que ça passe

(g) *Am* **to hit the bricks** *(be released from prison)* sortir de taule

(h) *Am* **to hit sb on the hip** *(page)* biper qn□; *(call his/her mobile)* appeler qn sur son portable□ ▶ *voir aussi* **deck, hay, rack, sack**

hit off *vt sep* **to hit it off** bien accrocher; **to hit it off with sb** bien accrocher avec qn

hit on *vt insép* **to hit on sb** draguer qn, faire du plat à qn

hit up *vt sép* **(a)** **to hit it up** *(inject drugs)* se piquer, se shooter **(b)** *Am (ask to borrow money)* **she hit me up for a hundred bucks** elle m'a demandé de lui prêter cent dollars□

hitch [hɪtʃ] *vt* **to get hitched** *(married)* se maquer, se passer la corde au cou

hitman ['hɪtmæn] *n* tueur *m* à gages□, tueur professionnel□

hiya ['haɪjə] *exclam Br* salut!

ho [həʊ] *n Noir Am (abrév* **whore***)* pouffiasse *f*, grognasse *f*

ⓘ Il s'agit de la transcription phonétique du mot "whore", tel que le prononcent certains Noirs américains. C'est un terme sexiste très employé par les chanteurs de rap et qui désigne une fille ou une femme.

hoaching ['həʊtʃɪŋ] *adj Scot* archibondé; **the town was hoaching**

with rugby fans la ville grouillait de supporters de rugby

hog¹ [hɒg] n (**a**) Am (person) goinfre m, porc m (**b**) Am (motorbike) grosse bécane f, gros cube m (**c**) Noir Am (luxury car) voiture f de luxe□ (généralement une Cadillac ou une Lincoln Continental) (**d**) Am **to live high on the hog** se la couler douce; **to be in hog heaven** être au septième ciel

hog² vt monopoliser□; **he always hogs the TV** il monopolise toujours la télé; **stop hogging all the wine for yourself** ne garde pas tout le vin pour ta poire

hogwash ['hɒgwɒʃ] n foutaises fpl; **that's a lot of hogwash!** tout ça c'est des foutaises!

hokey ['həʊkɪ] adj Am (nonsensical) absurde□; (sentimental) à la guimauve

hokum ['həʊkəm] n Am (nonsense) foutaises fpl; (sentimentality) guimauve f

hole [həʊl] n (**a**) (house, room) taudis□ m; (town) trou m, bled m (**b**) (difficult situation) **to be in a hole** être dans la mouise; **to get sb out of a hole** sortir qn de la mouise; **to dig oneself (into) a hole** aggraver son cas, s'enferrer (**c**) **hole in the wall** (restaurant) petit restaurant□ m; (shop) petite boutique□ f; (cash dispenser) distributeur m automatique de billets□, crache-thunes m; Am (apartment) appartement m minuscule□ (**d**) **I need that like a hole in the head!** j'ai vraiment pas besoin de ça!; **do you miss him? – like a hole in the head!** il te manque? – mais alors pas du tout! (**e**) [!!] (vagina) chagatte f, chatte f; Br **to get one's hole** baiser

hole up vi (hide) se planquer

-holic ['hɒlɪk] suffixe Hum **chocoho-**lic accro mf au chocolat; **workaholic** bourreau m de travail; **shopaholic** maniaque mf du shopping

holy ['həʊlɪ] adj Am (**a**) **holy cow** or **smoke** or **mackerel!** ça alors!; **holy shit** [!] or **fuck!** [!!] putain de merde! (**b**) **holy Joe** cul m béni

homeboy ['həʊmbɔɪ] n Noir Am (**a**) (man from one's home town) compatriote m (**b**) (friend) pote m (**c**) (fellow gang member) = membre de la même bande

homegirl ['həʊmgɜːl] n Noir Am (**a**) (woman from one's home town) compatriote f (**b**) (friend) copine f (**c**) (fellow gang member) = membre de la même bande

homegrown ['həʊmgrəʊn] n = cannabis cultivé chez soi ou dans son jardin

homer ['həʊmə(r)] n Br = séance de travail au noir effectuée chez un particulier par un artisan, généralement le soir ou le week-end

homey ['həʊmɪ] = **homeboy, homegirl**

homo ['həʊməʊ] n Injurieux (abrév **homosexual**) tapette f, pédale f

---

ⓘ Attention, il s'agit d'un terme injurieux, qui n'est pas l'équivalent du français "homo".

---

hon [hʌn] n Am (abrév **honey**) (term of address) chéri(e) m,f

honcho ['hɒntʃəʊ] n Am chef m; **head honcho** grand chef m

honey ['hʌnɪ] n (**a**) (term of address) chéri(e) m,f (**b**) (attractive woman) canon m; (attractive man) beau mec m (**c**) (nice person) **he's a honey** il est vachement gentil; (nice thing) **a honey of a car/dress** une voiture/robe très chouette

honeypot [!] ['hʌnɪpɒt] *n Am (vagina)* chatte *f*, foufoune *f*

honk [hɒŋk] *vi Br* (a) *(smell bad)* schlinguer, fouetter (b) *(vomit)* gerber, dégueuler

honker ['hɒŋkə(r)] *n Am* (a) *(nose)* blaire *m*, tarin *m*, pif *m* (b) *(breast)* nichon *m* (c) *(device)* bécane *f*

honkie, honky ['hɒŋkɪ] *n Noir Am Injurieux* sale Blanc (Blanche) *m,f*

hooch [huːtʃ] *n Am* alcool *m* de contrebande⁰

hood [hʊd] *n* (a) *(abrév* **hoodlum**) *(delinquent)* voyou *m*, loubard *m*; *Am (gangster)* truand *m*, gangster⁰ *m* (b) *Noir Am (abrév* **neighborhood**) quartier⁰ *m*

hoodie ['hʊdɪ] *n* (a) *(hooded sweatshirt)* sweat *m* à capuche⁰ (b) *Péj (person wearing a hooded sweatshirt)* = personne portant un sweatshirt à capuche; **he was mugged by a gang of hoodies** il s'est fait dévali-ser par un groupe de jeunes voyous à capuche

---

ⓘ Le terme "hoodie" est l'abréviation de "hooded sweatshirt" (sweatshirt à capuche). Récemment, ce terme a pris une connotation négative du fait de la popularité de ce genre de vêtement parmi les jeunes délinquants qui souhaitent éviter d'être reconnus par le biais de caméras de sécurité. Aujourd'hui le terme "hoodie" désigne à la fois le vêtement et la personne qui le porte.

---

hoodlum ['huːdləm] *n (delinquent)* voyou *m*, loubard *m*; *Am (gangster)* truand *m*, gangster⁰ *m*

hooey ['huːɪ] *n* foutaises *fpl*

hoof [huːf] *vt* **to hoof it** aller à pinces

hoo-ha ['huːhaː] *n (fuss)* raffut *m*, barouf *m*

hook [hʊk] **1** *n Br* **to sling one's hook** mettre les bouts, foutre le camp, se casser; **sling your hook!** fous le camp!, casse-toi!

2 *vt Am* **to hook school** faire l'école buissonnière

3 *vi Am (work as prostitute)* faire le trottoir

hook up *vi esp Am* (a) *(meet)* **let's hook up later and go see a movie** retrouvons-nous plus tard pour aller voir un film⁰ (b) *(get together)* **they hooked up at Alex's party and they've been together ever since** il se sont rencontrés à la soirée d'Alex et ils sont ensemble depuis; **did you hook up with anyone last night?** tu as fait une rencontre hier soir?

hooked [hʊkt] *adj* **to be hooked (on)** être accro (à)

hooker ['hʊkə(r)] *n* (a) *(prostitute)* pute *f* (b) *Am (of drink)* **a hooker of gin/bourbon** un bon coup de gin/de bourbon

hookey, hooky ['hʊkɪ] *n Am & Austr* **to play hookey** faire l'école buissonnière

hoon [huːn] *n Austr* loubard *m*

hoops [huːps] *npl Am (basketball)* basket *m*; **to shoot hoops** jouer au basket

Hooray Henry ['hɒreɪ'henrɪ] *n Br* fils *m* à papa *(exubérant et bruyant)*

ⓘ Il s'agit d'un homme issu de la grande bourgeoisie, généralement jeune, qui parle très fort et aime se faire remarquer lorsqu'il s'amuse.

---

hoosegow ['huːsgaʊ] *n Am* taule *f*; **in the hoosegow** en taule, en cabane

hoot [huːt] *n* (a) **I don't give a hoot**

or **two hoots (about)** j'en ai rien à fiche (de) (**b**) *(amusing person, situation)* **to be a hoot** être marrant *ou* crevant; **and then he fell over, what a hoot!** et puis après il est tombé par terre, quelle rigolade!

hooter ['huːtə(r)] *n* (**a**) *(nose)* pif *m*, blaire *m*, tarin *m* (**b**) *Am (breast)* nichon *m*

hop [hɒp] *vt* **to hop it** mettre les bouts, foutre le camp, se casser; **hop it!** casse-toi!, fous le camp!

hophead ['hɒphed] *n Am* toxico *mf*

hopper ['hɒpə(r)] *n Austr* kangourou[□] *m*

horn [hɔːn] *n* (**a**) **(!)** *Br (erection)* érection[□] *f*; **to have the horn** avoir la trique *ou* le gourdin; **to give sb the horn** *(arouse)* exciter qn (**b**) *Am (telephone)* bigophone *m*; **to get on the horn to sb** passer un coup de fil *ou* de bigophone à qn

hornbag ['hɔːnbæg] *n Austr* super canon *m*

horny ['hɔːnɪ] *adj* (**a**) *(sexually aroused)* excité (**b**) *Br (sexually attractive)* sexy

horror ['hɒrə(r)] *n* (**a**) *(person, thing)* horreur *f*; **that kid's a little horror** ce gosse est un petit monstre (**b**) *Br* **to have the horrors** faire dans son froc; **to give sb the horrors** donner le frisson à qn

horse [hɔːs] *n (heroin)* blanche *f*, héro *f* ▸ *voir aussi* **hung**

horseshit **[!]** ['hɔːsʃɪt] *n Am (nonsense)* conneries *fpl*

hot [hɒt] *adj* (**a**) *(sexually aroused)* excité; **to be hot to trot** *(of man)* être en rut; *(of woman)* être en chaleur; **I saw her getting hot and heavy with her boyfriend in the cinema** je l'ai vue qui n'arrêtait pas de bécoter son copain dans le cinéma (**b**) *(sexually attractive)* chaud, sexy (**c**)

(excellent) génial, super (**d**) *(stolen)* volé[□] (**e**) *Am* **the hot seat** *(electric chair)* la chaise électrique[□]; *Fig* **to be in the hot seat** être sur la sellette; **the Prime Minister's in the hot seat over the hostage crisis** le Premier ministre est sur la sellette à propos de l'affaire des otages

hot-knife ['hɒtnaɪf] *vi* se droguer au hasch *(en coinçant un morceau de haschich entre deux lames de couteau préalablement chauffées)*

hotrod ['hɒtrɒd] *n* bagnole *f* trafiquée

hots [hɒts] *npl* **to have the hots for sb** craquer pour qn

hotshot ['hɒtʃɒt] **1** *n (expert)* crack *m*; *Br (important person)* huile *f*; *Am Péj (self-important person)* personne *f* suffisante[□]

2 *adj* **a hotshot lawyer** un super avocat; **a hotshot pool player** un as du billard

hottie ['hɒtɪ] *n (attractive woman)* canon *m*; *(attractive man)* beau mec *m*

hound [haʊnd] *n Br (ugly woman)* cageot *m*, mocheté *f*

house ape ['haʊs eɪp] *n Am Hum (child)* môme *mf*, chiard *m*

how's-your-father [haʊzjə'fɑːðə(r)] *n Br Hum (sexual intercourse)* **a bit of how's-your-father** une partie de jambes en l'air

hubba-hubba ['hʌbə'hʌbə] *exclam Am* la super gonzesse!

hubby ['hʌbɪ] *n* mari[□] *m*, bonhomme *m*, jules *m*

huff [hʌf] **1** *n* **to be in a** *or* **the huff** faire la tête, bouder[□]; **to take the huff, to go in a huff** se mettre à bouder[□]

2 *vt Am (glue, solvents)* sniffer

huffy ['hʌfɪ] *adj* **to be huffy** *(in a bad*

mood) faire la tête, bouder⁰; *(by nature)* être susceptible⁰, être chatouilleux

hum [hʌm] **1** *n* (**a**) *Br (bad smell)* puanteur⁰ *f*; **there's a bit of a hum in here!** ça coince *ou* ça fouette ici! (**b**) *Am* **hum job** [!!] pipe *f*; **to give sb a hum job** tailler *ou* faire une pipe à qn
  2 *vi Br (smell bad)* coincer, fouetter

humdinger [hʌm'dɪŋə(r)] *n* **to be a humdinger** être génial; **a humdinger of a football match** un match de foot magnifique; **she's a humdinger!** elle est hyper canon!

hummer [!!] ['hʌmə(r)] *n Am (fellatio)* pipe *f*, turlute *f*; **to give sb a hummer** faire *ou* tailler une pipe à qn, piper qn

humongous [hjuː'mʌŋgəs] *adj* énorme⁰, mastoc

hump [hʌmp] **1** *n* (**a**) *Br* **to have the hump** être de mauvais poil; **to get** *or* **take the hump** se mettre à faire la gueule; **to give sb the hump** mettre qn de mauvais poil (**b**) *Am (person)* crétin(e) *m,f*, andouille *f*
  2 *vt* (**a**) [!] *(have sex with) (of man)* baiser, se taper; *(of woman)* baiser avec, se taper (**b**) *(carry)* trimballer
  3 [!] *vi (have sex)* baiser, s'envoyer en l'air

humungous [hjuː'mʌŋgəs] = **humongous**

hung [hʌŋ] *adj* **to be hung like a horse** *or* **a whale** *or Br* **a donkey** *or Am* **a mule** [!] être monté comme un âne *ou* un taureau *ou* un bourricot

hunk [hʌŋk] *n (man)* beau mec *m*

hunky ['hʌŋkɪ] *adj* bien foutu

hunky-dory [hʌŋkɪ'dɔːrɪ] *adj* au poil; **everything's hunky-dory** tout baigne

hurl [hɜːl] *vi (vomit)* dégobiller, gerber

hurting ['hɜːtɪŋ] *adj Am* (**a**) *(in need)* **to be hurting for sth** avoir méchamment besoin de qch (**b**) *(in trouble)* dans la mouise

hush money ['hʌʃmʌnɪ] *n* = argent versé à quelqu'un pour acheter son silence

hustle ['hʌsəl] *Am* **1** *n (swindle)* arnaque *f*
  2 *vt* (**a**) *(swindle)* arnaquer; **to hustle sb out of sth** soutirer qch à qn; **to hustle some pool** jouer au billard pour de l'argent⁰ (**b**) *(sell)* fourguer (**c**) *(obtain dishonestly)* soutirer; *(steal)* piquer, faucher
  3 *vi (work as prostitute)* faire le tapin

hustler ['hʌslə(r)] *n Am* (**a**) *(energetic person)* battant(e) *m,f* (**b**) *(swindler)* magouilleur(euse) *m,f* (**c**) *(prostitute)* pute *f*

hype¹ [haɪp] **1** *n* (**a**) *(abrév* **hypodermic**) shooteuse *f*, pompe *f* (**b**) *(drug addict)* toxico *mf*, camé(e) *m,f*
  2 *adj Noir Am (excellent)* super, génial, grand

hype² *n (publicity)* battage *m*, matraquage *m*

hype up *vt sép* **to hype sth up** faire du battage autour de qch

hyper ['haɪpə(r)] *adj (excited)* surexcité⁰

hypo ['haɪpəʊ] *n (abrév* **hypodermic**) shooteuse *f*, pompe *f*

Ii

ice [aɪs] **1** n (**a**) (diamonds) diams mpl (**b**) (drug) ice f
2 vt (kill) buter, refroidir, zigouiller

icky ['ɪkɪ] adj (repulsive) dégueulasse; (sticky) poisseux; (sentimental) mièvre□, à la guimauve

idea [aɪ'dɪə] n **what's the big idea?** à quoi tu joues?

idiot box ['ɪdɪətbɒks] n Am (television) téloche f

iffy ['ɪfɪ] adj (**a**) (doubtful, unreliable) **our holidays are looking very iffy** nos vacances risquent de tomber à l'eau; **the brakes are a bit iffy** les freins déconnent un peu; Br **my stomach's been a bit iffy lately** je me sens un peu barbouillé ces temps-ci (**b**) (suspicious) louche, chelou; **it all sounded rather iffy** tout ça m'avait l'air plutôt louche; **her new man sounds really iffy** son nouveau copain a l'air vraiment louche

ill [ɪl] adj Noir Am (excellent) super, top, génial

illin' ['ɪlɪn] adj Noir Am (**a**) (unpleasant) merdique (**b**) (mad) cinglé, toqué, timbré

in [ɪn] **1** adj (fashionable) in, branché; **it's the in place** c'est l'endroit le plus branché; **it's the in thing/colour** c'est le truc/la couleur à la mode; **the in crowd** les gens branchés
2 adv (**a**) **to be in on a secret/a**

plan être au courant d'un secret/d'un projet□; **I wasn't in on it** j'étais pas dans la confidence; **I want in** (include me) ça me branche (**b**) **you're going to be in for it!** tu vas voir ce que tu vas prendre!

inhale [ɪn'heɪl] vt Am **to inhale sth** (eat quickly) engouffrer qch; (drink quickly) descendre qch

innit ['ɪnɪt] adv Br (**a**) (isn't it) hein?; **it's great, innit?** c'est super, hein? (**b**) (general question tag) hein?; **that was a kicking night out, innit?** on a passé une super soirée, hein?; **you fancy her, innit?** elle te plaît, hein?

ⓘ "Innit?" est la contraction de "isn't it?" Dans la région de Londres, cependant, cette forme s'utilise de plus en plus pour toutes les personnes du singulier et du pluriel.

----

inside 1 adj ['ɪnsaɪd] **it was an inside job** c'est quelqu'un de l'intérieur qui a fait le coup
2 adv [ɪn'saɪd] (in prison) en taule, à l'ombre, au frais; **to put sb inside** mettre qn en taule ou à l'ombre

into ['ɪntʊ] prép (keen on) **to be into sb** en pincer pour qn; **to be into sth** être branché qch; **to be into doing sth** s'éclater à faire qch; **he's into drugs** il se drogue□; **I'm not into that sort of thing** c'est pas mon truc

Pleins feux sur...
Insults

Son but principal étant de choquer, l'insulte est sans
doute la forme la plus pure et la plus immédiate d'utilisation de la langue familière. On trouvera ci-dessous certains
des mécanismes de formation les plus répandus en anglais.
La forme d'insulte la plus simple est un substantif utilisé comme
exclamation (cf. colonne "nom") et parfois précédé de "you".
Cette combinaison peut à son tour être renforcée par un
adjectif. Le tableau ci-dessous illustre ce procédé à l'aide de
quelques mots très communs. Il faut remarquer que, bien que les
combinaisons soient en principe multiples, certaines sont plus fixes que
d'autres.

	ADJECTIF	NOM
(you)	**stupid**□	**idiot**□
	Br **bleeding**	*Br* **pillock**
	goddamn	**bitch**
	Br **bloody [!]**	**prat**
	Br **sodding [!]**	**bastard [!]**
	Am **dumbass [!]**	*Br* **arsehole,** *Am* **asshole [!!]**
	fucking [!!]	*Br* **wanker [!!]**
	motherfucking [!!]	**motherfucker [!!]**
		cunt [!!]

Pour un effet tout aussi percutant, on pourra utiliser un impératif, tel
que **get lost**, **push off**, *Br* **bugger off [!]**, **piss off [!]** ou
fuck off [!!].

L'expression **go (and)...** est également très productive lorsqu'elle
précède un infinitif, comme dans :

> **go (and) boil your head!**
> **go (and) jump in the lake!**
> **go (and) play in the traffic!**
> **go (and) fuck yourself! [!!]**

Enfin, et notamment lorsque le locuteur veut être sarcastique,
l'expression **Why don't you...** revient souvent dans la formation
d'insultes : elle peut servir à introduire n'importe laquelle des tournures
impératives ci-dessus.

Le symbole [!] dénote un terme très familier, [!!] un terme vulgaire.

in-your-face [ˌɪnjɔːˈfeɪs] *adj* (*unsubtle*) **percutant**▢

irie [ˈaɪrɪ] *adj* cool, impec; **everything's irie** tout baigne

ⓘ Il s'agit d'un terme d'origine jamaïcaine, fréquemment employé par les Britanniques de la communauté afro-antillaise. Il sert à décrire toute chose jugée positive ou agréable. Il évoque un sentiment de bien-être et de bonheur (qui peut être en rapport avec la prise de cannabis) et est censé refléter la mentalité décontractée des Jamaïcains.

Irish [ˈaɪrɪʃ] *adj Br* (*contradictory, illogical*) loufoque

ⓘ "Irish" signifie littéralement "irlandais". En Grande-Bretagne les Irlandais sont la cible de nombreuses plaisanteries où ils apparaissent généralement comme des gens peu intelligents et manquant de bon sens. Bien que ce terme ne témoigne pas nécessairement d'une attitude xénophobe de la part de celui qui l'utilise, il est préférable de ne pas l'employer.

iron [ˈaɪən] *n Br Injurieux* (*rhyming slang* **iron hoof** = **poof**) pédale *f*, tantouze *f*, tapette *f* ▸ *voir aussi* **pump**

ish [ɪʃ] *adv* plus ou moins; **is he good-looking? – ish** est-ce qu'il est beau? – mouais...

ⓘ Il s'agit du suffixe "-ish", dénotant l'approximation, utilisé en tant qu'adverbe.

it [ɪt] *pron* **she thinks she's IT** elle se prend pas pour de la merde; **it girl** jeune mondaine▢ *f*

item [ˈaɪtəm] *n* **they're an item** (*of couple*) ils sont maqués

Jj

J [dʒeɪ] *n (abrév* **joint***) (cannabis cigarette)* joint *m*

Jack [dʒæk] *npr Am Péj (term of address)* Duchnoque ▸ *voir aussi* **all right**

jack [dʒæk] *n* (**a**) **every man jack (of them)** absolument tout le monde (**b**) **jack, jack shit [!]** que dalle; **he doesn't do jack** *or* **jack shit [!] around here** il en rame pas une ici

jack around *Am* **1** *vt sép* **to jack sb around** *(treat badly)* se ficher de qn; *(waste time of)* faire perdre son temps à qn□
2 *vi (waste time)* glander, glandouiller

jack in *vt sép* **to jack sth in** laisser tomber qch, plaquer qch; **to jack it all in** tout plaquer

jack off [!] **1** *vt sép* **to jack sb off** branler qn
2 *vi* se branler, se palucher

jack up **1** *vt sép* (**a**) *Br (drugs)* s'injecter□, se piquer à (**b**) *(prices, profits)* gonfler
2 *vi Br* se piquer, se shooter

jackaroo [dʒækə'ruː] *n Austr* = apprenti dans un ranch

jackass ['dʒækæs] *n Am* andouille *f*, cruche *f*, crétin *m*

jacksie, jacksy ['dʒæksɪ] *n Br (buttocks)* fesses *fpl*, popotin *m*; *(anus)* troufignon *m*, trou *m* de balle

Jack-the-lad [dʒækðə'læd] *n Br* = jeune homme exubérant et insolent d'origine modeste

jaffa ['dʒæfə] *n Br Hum* homme *m* stérile□

ⓘ Cet usage vient du fait que les oranges de la marque Jaffa n'ont pas de pépins.

Jag [dʒæg] *n (abrév* **Jaguar***)* Jaguar□ *f*

jailbait ['dʒeɪlbeɪt] *n* fille *f* mineure□, poids *m* mort

jake [dʒeɪk] *n Br* joint *m*, pétard *m*

jakey ['dʒeɪkɪ] *n Scot* clodo *m* alcolo

jalopy [dʒə'lɒpɪ] *n Am* vieille bagnole *f*, guimbarde *f*

jam [dʒæm] **1** *n* (**a**) *(music)* **jam (session)** bœuf *m*, jam-session *f*; **to have a jam (session)** faire un bœuf *ou* une jam-session (**b**) *Br* **jam jar** *(rhyming slang car)* bagnole *f*, caisse *f* (**c**) *Br* **jam rag [!]** serviette *f* hygiénique□ (**d**) *Br* **jam sandwich** voiture *f* de police□
2 *vi* faire un bœuf *ou* une jam-session

ⓘ Dans la catégorie 1(d) le terme "jam sandwich" s'utilise en Grande-Bretagne pour désigner les voitures de police, car celles-ci sont souvent ornées d'une bande rouge en leur milieu.

D'où tu me parles ?
Jafaikan

Jafaikan (ou **Jafaican**) est un mot créé récemment pour décrire la façon dont parlent de nombreux jeunes Londoniens. C'est un mot-valise formé à partir des mots "Jamaican" et "African" et qui témoigne de l'impact de ces communautés sur la langue parlée à Londres. (Il se trouve également que lorsqu'on prononce ce mot on entend le terme "fake" (faux), ce qui souligne l'absurdité du fait que certains Blancs adoptent ce type d'accent de façon à se donner un genre jamaïcain). Le traditionnel accent cockney se raréfie, le **rhyming slang** (voir encadré) n'a plus la cote parmi les jeunes, qui préfèrent employer des termes d'origine jamaïcaine tels que **nang** et **sick** (cool), **bare** (très/beaucoup de), **yard** (maison), **ends** (quartier), **bruv** (frère/pote), **rude boy/girl** (voyou, gangster) et **buff** (bien foutu(e)). Notons également le fait que le son "th" devient "d" ; ainsi les termes "that" et "them" deviennent "dat" et "dem". Par ailleurs, le Jafaikan fait de nombreuses entorses à la grammaire : on entendra par exemple "I/they is" au lieu de "I am/they are", et l'expression "innit" (isn't it) à la suite de n'importe quelle affirmation, du type : "Dem boys is buff innit!" (Ces garçons sont bien foutus, pas vrai?).

---

jammy ['dʒæmɪ] *adj Br (lucky)* veinard; **you jammy devil** *or* **bugger! [!]** sacré veinard!

Jane Doe ['dʒeɪn'dəʊ] *npr Am* = l'Américaine moyenne

ⓘ Aux États-Unis Jane Doe est le nom attribué aux femmes dont on ne connaît pas, ou dont on ne veut pas dévoiler, l'identité.

JAP [dʒæp] *n Am Péj (abrév* **Jewish American Princess)** = jeune Américaine juive issue de la grande bourgeoisie

Jap [dʒæp] *Injurieux (abrév* **Japanese)** **1** *n* Jap *mf* **2** *adj* jap

jar [dʒɑː(r)] *n Br (drink)* pot *m*, godet *m*; **let's go out for a couple of jars** allons boire un pot

jarhead ['dʒɑːhed] *n Am Péj* marine□ *m*

ⓘ Ce mot, qui signifie littéralement "tête de pot", trouve son origine dans la ressemblance de la tête des marines américains (cheveux rasés sur les côtés et brosse sur le dessus) avec la forme d'un pot muni d'un couvercle.

java ['dʒɑːvə] *n Am (coffee)* kawa *m*

jaw [dʒɔː] **1** *n Am* **to flap one's jaw** gueuler **2** *vi* tailler une bavette

jazz [dʒæz] *n* **(a)** **...and all that jazz** ...et tout le tremblement **(b)** jazz

mag bouquin *m* de cul

jeepers (creepers) [ˈdʒiːpəz(ˈkriːpəz)] *exclam* bon Dieu!, bon sang!

Jeez [dʒiːz] *exclam* bon Dieu!, bon sang!

jelly [ˈdʒelɪ] *n Br (drug)* gélule *f* de Temazepam□

jerk [dʒɜːk] *n (person)* abruti(e) *m,f*, crétin(e) *m,f*

jerk about [!!], **jerk around** [!] *vt sép* **to jerk sb about** *or* **around** faire tourner qn en bourrique

jerk off [!] **1** *vt sép* **to jerk sb off** branler qn
2 *vi* se branler, se palucher

jerk-off [!] [ˈdʒɜːkɒf] *n Am (person)* connard (connasse) *m,f*

jerky [ˈdʒɜːkɪ] *adj Am (stupid)* débile, abruti

jessie [ˈdʒesɪ] *n Scot (feeble man)* mauviette *f*; **stop pretending you're hurt, you big jessie!** arrête de faire semblant d'avoir mal, espèce de mauviette!

Jesus [ˈdʒiːzəs] **1** *n* **Jesus freak** chrétien(enne) *m,f* hippie
2 *exclam* **Jesus (Christ)!** nom de Dieu!; *Br* **Jesus wept!** bon sang!

jiff [dʒɪf], **jiffy** [ˈdʒɪfɪ] *n* seconde□ *f*, instant□ *m*; **in a jiff** *or* **jiffy** dans une seconde

jiggered [ˈdʒɪɡəd] *adj Br (exhausted)* naze, crevé, lessivé

jiggy [ˈdʒɪɡɪ] *adj Am* **to get jiggy (with it)** s'envoyer en l'air

jillaroo [dʒɪləˈruː] *n Austr* = apprentie dans un ranch

jimjams [ˈdʒɪmdʒæmz] *npl* (**a**) **to have the jimjams** être sur les nerfs (**b**) *Br (pyjamas)* pyjama□ *m*

Jimmy [ˈdʒɪmɪ] *npr Br (rhyming slang* **Jimmy Riddle** = **piddle**) **to have a**

Jimmy pisser; **to go for a Jimmy** aller pisser

jism [ˈdʒɪzəm] *n* (**a**) [!!] *(semen)* foutre *m* (**b**) *Am (energy)* ressort□ *m*

jive [dʒaɪv] *Noir Am* **1** *n (nonsense)* foutaises *fpl*; *(insincerity)* craques *fpl*
2 *adj (phoney)* à la noix

jive-ass [!] [ˈdʒaɪvæs] *adj Noir Am* à la noix

jizz [!!] [dʒɪz] *n (semen)* foutre *m*

joanna [dʒəʊˈænə] *n Br (rhyming slang* **piano**) piano□ *m*

job [dʒɒb] *n* (**a**) *(thing)* truc *m*; **her new car is one of those sporty jobs** sa nouvelle voiture est un de ces modèles style "sport"; **their latest hi-fi is a lovely job** leur nouvelle chaîne stéréo est super (**b**) *(crime)* coup *m*; **to do** *or* **pull a job** faire un coup; **he did** *or* **pulled that bank job** c'est lui qui a braqué la banque (**c**) *Br* **to be on the job** [!] *(having sex)* être en train de baiser (**d**) *Br (excrement)* caca *m* (**e**) *Am* **to do a job on sth** *(ruin, damage)* bousiller qch ▸ *voir aussi* **boob, hatchet, nose, snow**

jobby [ˈdʒɒbɪ] *n* (**a**) *(thing)* truc *m*; **the sofa's one of them fold-out jobbies** le sofa est un de ces trucs qui se déplient (**b**) *Scot (excrement)* caca *m*

Jock [dʒɒk] *npr Injurieux (Scotsman)* Écossais□ *m*

① "Jock" est un diminutif un peu désuet de "John" qui est parfois utilisé en Écosse. Bien que ce terme ne témoigne pas nécessairement d'une attitude xénophobe de la part de celui qui l'utilise, il est préférable de ne pas l'employer.

jock [dʒɒk] *n Am* (**a**) *(athlete)*

sportif(ive) *m,f* *(pas très brillant intellectuellement)* **(b)** *(abrév* **disc jockey)** disc-jockey *mf*

Joe [dʒəʊ] *npr* **(a)** *Am (man)* mec *m*, type *m*; **a good Joe** *(man)* un chic type; *(woman)* une brave femme; **he's just an ordinary Joe** c'est un type comme les autres **(b)** *Br* **Joe Public, Joe Bloggs, Joe Soap,** *Am* **Joe Blow, Joe Schmo, Joe Six-Pack** Monsieur Tout-le-Monde; *Am* **Joe College** = l'étudiant typique ▶ *voir aussi* **holy**

John [dʒɒn] *npr Br (term of address)* chef; **got a light, John?** t'as du feu, chef?

ⓘ Il s'agit d'un terme qui s'utilise surtout à Londres.

john [dʒɒn] *n Am* **(a)** *(toilet)* chiottes *fpl* **(b)** *(prostitute's client)* micheton *m*

John Doe ['dʒɒn'dəʊ] *npr Am* = l'Américain moyen

ⓘ Aux États-Unis John Doe est le nom attribué aux individus dont on ne connaît pas, ou dont on ne veut pas révéler, l'identité.

johnny ['dʒɒnɪ] *n Br (condom)* **(rubber) johnny** capote *f*

johnson ['dʒɒnsən] *n Am* quéquette *f*

joint [dʒɔɪnt] *n* **(a)** *(cannabis cigarette)* joint *m* **(b)** *(place)* turne *f*; **we ate at some fancy joint** on a mangé dans un resto super classe **(c)** *Am (prison)* taule *f*, placard *m*; **in the joint** en taule, à l'ombre **(d)** **[!]** *Am (penis)* pine *f*, bite *f* ▶ *voir aussi* **case, clip**

jollies ['dʒɒlɪz] *npl Am* **to get one's jollies (doing sth)** prendre son pied

(en faisant qch), s'éclater (en faisant qch)

jolly ['dʒɒlɪ] *n* voyage *m* aux frais de la princesse; **my job's great, we're always off on jollies to nice hotels** j'ai un super boulot, on est toujours en voyage et logés dans des hôtels de luxe

jones [dʒəʊnz] *n Am* **to have a jones for sth** adorer qch□; **I've always had a jones for a challenge** j'ai toujours adoré les défis□

journo ['dʒɜːnəʊ] *n Br (abrév* **journalist)** journaleux(euse) *m,f*

joypop ['dʒɔɪpɒp] *vi* = prendre de la drogue sans devenir dépendant

Juan Doe ['hwæn'dəʊ] *npr Am* = l'Hispanique moyen

ⓘ Il s'agit d'une adaptation humoristique du terme John Doe (voir cette entrée), qui s'applique aux Américains d'origine latino-américaine.

jug [dʒʌg] *n* **(a)** *(prison)* taule *f*, cabane *f*; **in (the) jug** en taule, à l'ombre **(b)** **jugs [!]** *(breasts)* nichons *mpl*, lolos *mpl*

juice [dʒuːs] *n* **(a)** *(petrol)* essence□ *f*; *(electricity)* jus *m*; *Br (gas)* gaz□ *m* **(b)** *Noir Am (popularity, recognition)* succès□; **to have a lot of juice** faire un tabac ▶ *voir aussi* **jungle**

juiced [dʒuːst] *adj Am (drunk)* pété, bourré, beurré

juicer ['dʒuːsə(r)] *n Am* alcolo *mf*, poivrot(e) *m,f*

jump [dʒʌmp] *vt* **(a)** *(attack)* **to jump sb** sauter sur le paletot à qn; **to get jumped** se faire agresser□ **(b)** **to jump sb** *or* **sb's bones** *(sexually)* sauter sur qn

2 *vi* **go jump (in the lake)!** va te faire voir!; **if he thinks I'm going**

to pick him and his drunk mates up at 2 a.m. he can go jump! si il s'imagine que je vais aller le chercher, lui et ses copains bourrés, à deux heures du mat', il peut aller se faire voir!

3 n (**a**) **go take a (running) jump!,** Am **take a running jump at the moon!** va voir ailleurs si j'y suis!, va te faire cuire un œuf! (**b**) Am **from the jump** depuis le début□; **I knew from the jump he was lying** je savais qu'il mentait depuis le début
▸ voir aussi **high, throat**

jumping ['dʒʌmpɪŋ] adj (party, night-club) hyper animé

jungle ['dʒʌŋgəl] n (**a**) Injurieux **jungle bunny** nègre (négresse) m,f (**b**) **jungle juice** tord-boyaux m (le plus souvent produit artisanalement)

junk [dʒʌŋk] **1** n (**a**) (worthless things) **his new book is a pile of junk** son nouveau bouquin ne vaut pas un clou; **she eats nothing but junk** elle mange que des saloperies (**b**) (useless things) bazar m; **move all that junk of yours off the bed** enlève ton bazar du lit (**c**) (drug) drogue f dure□ (le plus souvent héroïne)

2 vt (**a**) (throw away) balancer, foutre en l'air (**b**) (criticize) débiner, éreinter

junker ['dʒʌŋkə(r)] n Am (old car) vieille bagnole f

junkie ['dʒʌŋkɪ] n junkie mf; **a chocolate/soap opera junkie** un accro du chocolat/des feuilletons télé

juve [dʒuːv] Am & Austr n mineur m délinquant□

juvie ['dʒuːvɪ] Am & Austr **1** n centre m pour mineurs délinquants□

2 adj (court) pour mineurs délinquants□

Kk

Kaffir ['kæfə(r)] *n Br Injurieux* nègre (négresse) *m,f* d'Afrique du Sud

Kappa Slappa, Kappa Slapper ['kæpəslæpə] *n* = jeune fille d'origine modeste, peu raffinée, qui porte toujours des vêtements de sport

ⓘ Il s'agit d'un stéréotype social britannique. Une Kappa Slappa (Kappa®) est une marque de vêtements de sports et "slapper" signifie "traînée") est une jeune fille plutôt vulgaire et sans éducation qui ne s'habille qu'avec des vêtements de sport de marque et qui porte des bijoux clinquants. Bien souvent elle a également un "Croydon facelift" (voir cette entrée).

kaput [kə'pʊt] *adj* kaput; **the TV's kaput, we can't watch the match!** la téloche est kaput; impossible de regarder le match!

karsey, karzey, kazi ['kɑːzɪ] *n Br* chiottes *fpl*, gogues *mpl*

kazoo [kə'zuː] *n Am (buttocks)* derrière *m*, arrière-train *m*; **to have problems/debts up the kazoo** *(in excess)* avoir des problèmes/des dettes jusqu'au cou

kecks [keks] *npl Br* fute *m*, falzar *m*

keel over [kiːl] *vi* (**a**) *(faint)* tourner de l'œil (**b**) *(die)* calancher, passer l'arme à gauche

keister ['kiːstə(r)] *n Am (buttocks)* fesses *fpl*, derrière *m*, derche *m*

keks [keks] = kecks

ker-ching [kɜː'tʃɪŋ] *exclam* = exclamation imitant le bruit d'une caisse enregistreuse, pour parler de quelqu'un qui est sur le point de s'enrichir, d'une idée lucrative, etc; **I hear she's marrying a professional footballer – ker-ching!** il paraît qu'elle va se marier avec un footballeur professionnel – ouah, par ici les picaillons!

Kevin ['kevɪn], **Kev** [kev] *npr Br Péj* jeune beauf *m*

ⓘ Il s'agit d'un stéréotype social popularisé au cours des années 90, comparable à celui de l'"Essex Man" et plus récemment au "chav" (voir ces entrées). Le "Kevin" est jeune, d'origine modeste, peu cultivé, parfois violent, et ne fait pas toujours preuve d'un goût très sûr. Kevin est un prénom très courant dans les milieux populaires et, de ce fait, est considéré comme vulgaire par beaucoup de gens. Ces termes peuvent s'écrire avec un "k" minuscule.

kick [kɪk] **1** *n (thrill)* **to get a kick out of sth/doing sth** prendre son pied avec qch/en faisant qch; **to do sth for kicks** faire qch histoire de rigoler

2 vt (**a**) **to kick the bucket** (die) calancher, passer l'arme à gauche (**b**) **to kick sb into touch, to kick sb to the curb** larguer qn, plaquer qn; **she got sick of her boyfriend lying to her and kicked him into touch** or **to the curb** elle en a eu marre que son petit ami lui mente alors elle l'a largué; **to kick sth into touch, to kick sth to the curb** laisser tomber qch, abandonner qch[□]; **the idea got kicked into touch** or **to the curb when the company started running out of money** ils ont laissé tomber cette idée quand la société s'est mise à avoir des difficultés de trésorerie

3 vi Am (die) calancher, passer l'arme à gauche ▸ voir aussi **ass, shit**

kick about, kick around 1 vt insép (spend time in) **to kick about the world/Africa** rouler sa bosse ou traîner ses guêtres autour du monde/ en Afrique; Br **is my purse kicking around the kitchen somewhere?** est-ce que mon porte-monnaie traîne quelque part dans la cuisine?

2 vi (hang around) traîner (**with** avec); Br **have you seen my lighter kicking about?** t'as pas vu mon briquet (traîner) quelque part?

kick off vi (**a**) Am (die) calancher, passer l'arme à gauche (**b**) Br (get violent) **it's going to kick off** ça va bastonner

kick out vt sep **I wouldn't kick him/her out of bed (for eating** Br **biscuits** or **crisps** or Am **crackers)!** si il/elle était dans mon lit, j'irais pas coucher dans la baignoire!

kick-ass ['kɪkæs] adj super; **he's got this new stereo with these big kick-ass speakers** il a une nouvelle chaîne avec de grosses enceintes su-

per-puissantes; **the DJ played some real kick-ass tunes last night** le DJ a passé de la musique trop cool hier soir

kickback ['kɪkbæk] n (bribe) pot-de-vin m

kicker ['kɪkə(r)] n Am (**a**) (hidden drawback) os m, hic m (**b**) (worst part of situation) **the work's tough and the kicker is the pay's lousy** le travail est dur, et en plus de ça, c'est payé avec un lance-pierres

kicking ['kɪkɪŋ] **1** n Br **to give sb a kicking** tabasser qn à coups de latte; **to get a kicking** se faire tabasser à coups de latte

2 adj (**a**) (party, nightclub) hyper animé (**b**) (excellent) super, génial

kicky ['kɪkɪ] adj Am (excellent) super, génial, géant

kid [kɪd] n (child) gosse mf; (young adult) jeune[□] mf, gamin(e) m,f; Br **our kid** (brother) le petit frère; (sister) la petite sœur

kiddie, kiddy n Br (child) gosse mf

kiddy-fiddler [!] n Br pédophile[□] mf

kike [kaɪk] n Am Injurieux youpin(e) m,f, youtre mf

kill [kɪl] **1** vt Br **to kill oneself (laughing)** être mort de rire; Ironique **you kill me!** toi alors!

2 vi **I'd kill for a beer** je me damnerais pour une bière

killer ['kɪlə(r)] **1** n (**a**) (difficult thing) **those steps were a killer!** ces marches m'ont lessivé!; **the English exam was a killer** l'examen d'anglais était vraiment coton (**b**) (excellent thing) **their new album's a killer** leur dernier album est vraiment génial ou mortel; **this one's a killer** (joke) elle est bien bonne, celle-là

2 *adj* (**a**) *Am (excellent)* d'enfer (**b**) **killer heels** talons *mpl* vertigineux

killing ['kɪlɪŋ] *adj Br* (**a**) *(very amusing)* marrant, crevant, mortel (**b**) *(exhausting)* crevant, tuant

kinda ['kaɪndə] *contraction (abrév* **kind of**) **this is my kinda party!** c'est le genre de soirée que j'aime!ᵈ; **that kinda thing** ce genre de truc; **you look kinda tired** t'as l'air un peu fatigué; **I kinda expected this** je m'y attendais un peuᵈ; **do you like it? – kinda** tu trouves ça comment? – pas mal

kinky ['kɪŋkɪ] *adj (person) (sexually)* qui a des goûts spéciaux; *(eccentric)* loufoque; *(clothing, sex)* très spécial

kip [kɪp] *Br* **1** *n* **to have a kip, to get some kip** piquer un roupillon, pioncer; **to get an hour's kip** piquer un roupillon d'une heure; **I didn't get much kip last night** j'ai pas beaucoup roupillé la nuit dernière
2 *vi* roupiller, pioncer

kip down *vi Br* pieuter

kiss [kɪs] *vt* **to kiss sth goodbye, to kiss goodbye to sth** faire une croix sur qch; **you can kiss your money/ promotion goodbye!** tu peux faire une croix sur *ou* dire adieu à ton argent/ta promotion! ▸ *voir aussi* **arse, ass, French**

kiss off *vt sép Am* (**a**) **to kiss sb off** *(dismiss)* envoyer balader *ou* promener qn; *(kill)* buter *ou* zigouiller qn (**b**) **to kiss sth off** *(give up hope of)* faire une croix sur qch; **you can kiss off your promotion!** tu peux faire une croix sur *ou* dire adieu à ta promotion!

kisser ['kɪsə(r)] *n (mouth)* bec *m*, museau *m*

kiss-off ['kɪsɒf] *n Am* **to give sb the kiss-off** envoyer balader *ou* promener qn

kit [kɪt] *n Br (clothes)* **to get one's kit off** se désaper, se mettre à poil; **get your kit off!** à poil!

kite [kaɪt] *n* **go fly a kite!** va voir ailleurs si j'y suis! ▸ *voir aussi* **high**

kittens ['kɪtənz] *npl* **to have kittens** *(become agitated)* faire un caca nerveux

Kiwi ['kiːwiː] *n (person)* Néo-Zélandais(e)ᵈ *m,f*, kiwi *mf*

klutz [klʌts] *n Am (clumsy person)* manche *m*

knacker ['nækə(r)] *Br* **1** *n* **knackers** [!] *(testicles)* couilles *fpl*, balloches *fpl*
2 *vt* (**a**) *(exhaust)* crever, lessiver (**b**) *(break, wear out)* bousiller

knackered ['nækəd] *adj Br* (**a**) *(exhausted)* crevé, lessivé, naze (**b**) *(broken, worn out)* bousillé

knackering ['nækərɪŋ] *adj Br* crevant

knees-up ['niːzʌp] *n Br (party)* sauterie *f*

knee-trembler ['niːtremblə(r)] *n Br* **to have a knee-trembler** baiser debout

knickers ['nɪkəz] *Br* **1** *npl* **to get one's knickers in a twist** *(become agitated)* s'affoler, s'exciter; *(become angry)* piquer une crise, se mettre en pétard; **to get into sb's knickers** s'envoyer qn
2 *exclam* n'importe quoi!

knife [naɪf] *n* **he isn't the sharpest knife in the drawer** il n'a pas inventé l'eau chaude *ou* le fil à couper le beurre

knob [nɒb] *Br* **1** *n* (**a**) [!] *(penis)* bite *f*, queue *f* (**b**) [!] *(man)* trou *m* du cul (**c**) **the same to you with knobs on!** toi-même!
2 [!] *vt (have sex with)* baiser, tringler, troncher

The symbol ᵈ indicates that a translation is neutral.

knobhead [!] ['nɒbhed] *n Br* trou *m* du cul, trouduc *m*

knock [nɒk] *vt* (**a**) *(criticize)* éreinter, débiner; **don't knock it till you've tried it!** n'en dis pas de mal avant d'avoir essayé□ (**b**) *Br (have sex with) (of man)* baiser, tringler, troncher; *(of woman)* baiser avec, s'envoyer (**c**) *Br* **to knock sth on the head** *(put a stop to)* faire cesser qch□; **knock it on the head, will you!** c'est pas bientôt fini? (**d**) **to knock sb for six,** *Am* **to knock sb for a loop** *(amaze)* scier qn, en boucher un coin à qn (**e**) **to knock sb dead** *(impress)* en mettre plein la vue à qn; **Snow Patrol knocked them dead last night** hier soir, Snow Patrol ont fait un tabac

knock about, knock around 1 *vt insép (spend time in)* **to knock about the world/Africa** rouler sa bosse *ou* traîner ses guêtres autour du monde/en Afrique; *Br* **are my keys knocking around the kitchen somewhere?** est-ce que mes clés traînent quelque part dans la cuisine?
2 *vi (hang around)* traîner (**with** avec); *Br* **are my fags knocking about?** est-ce que mes clopes sont dans le coin?

knock back *vt sép* (**a**) *(drink)* descendre (**b**) *Br (cost)* coûter à□; **it knocked me back a few hundred pounds** ça m'a coûté quelques centaines de livres; **that must have knocked you back a bit!** ça a dû te coûter un paquet de fric! (**c**) *Br (reject)* **to knock sb back** rejeter qn□; **to knock sth back** *(offer, invitation)* refuser qch□; **she knocked him back** il s'est pris une veste

knock off 1 *vt sép* (**a**) *(stop)* **knock it off!** arrête! (**b**) *(steal)* piquer, faucher; **to knock off a bank/jeweller's** *(rob)* braquer une banque/une bijouterie (**c**) *(murder)* buter, refroidir, zigouiller (**d**) *(have sex with) (of man)* baiser, tringler, troncher; *(of woman)* baiser avec, s'envoyer
2 *vi (stop working)* dételer

knock out *vt sép* **to knock oneself out** *(indulge oneself)* se faire plaisir; **there's plenty food left, knock yourself out!** il reste plein de nourriture, sers-toi autant que tu veux!□

knock over *vt sép Am (rob)* braquer

knock up *vt sép* **to knock sb up** *(make pregnant)* engrosser qn

knockback ['nɒkbæk] *n Br (rejection)* veste *f*; **to get a knockback** prendre une veste

knockers [!] ['nɒkəz] *npl (breasts)* nichons *mpl*, roberts *mpl*

knocking shop ['nɒkɪŋʃɒp] *n Br* bordel *m*, boxon *m*, claque *m*

knockout ['nɒkaʊt] **1** *n (excellent thing)* merveille□ *f*; **she's a knockout** *(gorgeous)* elle est vachement sexy
2 *adj* super

knockover ['nɒkəʊvə(r)] *n Am (robbery)* casse *m*

knot [nɒt] **1** *n* **to tie the knot** *(get married)* se maquer, se passer la corde au cou
2 *vt Br* **get knotted!** *(go away)* casse-toi!, va te faire voir ailleurs!; *(expressing contempt, disagreement)* la ferme!

knucklehead ['nʌkəlhed] *n* andouille *f*, nouille *f*

kook [kuːk] *n Am* zigoto *m*, zigomar *m*

kooky ['kuːkɪ] *adj Am* loufoque, loufedingue

Kool-Aid® ['kuleɪd] *n* **to drink the Kool-Aid®** être crédule□; **don't**

drink the Kool-Aid®! ne gobe pas tout ce qu'on te raconte!

ⓘ Kool-Aid® est une marque de boisson non alcoolisée américaine. L'expression "to drink the Kool-Aid®" remonte au suicide collectif qui avait eu lieu au Guyana en 1978, lorsque les adeptes de la secte du Temple du peuple (People's Temple) avaient absorbé du cyanure dilué dans du Kool-Aid®.

---

kosher [ˈkəʊʃə(r)] *adj (legitimate, honest)* réglo, régulier

Kraut [kraʊt] *Injurieux* **1** *n* Boche *mf* **2** *adj* boche

kvetch [kvetʃ] *vi Am* râler, geindre

L1

lad [læd] *n Br* (**a**) *(young man)* garçon⁰ *m*, petit gars *m*; **he's a bit of a lad** c'est un sacré fêtard; **he's one of the lads** on se marre bien avec lui (**b**) **the lads** *(friends)* les copains; **he's gone out for a couple of drinks with the lads** il est sorti boire un coup avec les copains ▸ *voir aussi* **new**

laddish ['lædɪʃ] *adj Br* = typique d'un style de vie caractérisé par de fréquentes sorties entre copains, généralement copieusement arrosées, un comportement arrogant et macho et un goût prononcé pour le sport et les activités de groupe

ladette [læ'det] *n Br* jeune femme *f* délurée⁰ *(qui se revendique l'égale des hommes pour ce qui est des sorties, de la vulgarité, etc)*

la-di-da [lɑːdɪ'dɑː] **1** *adj (person, attitude)* prétentieux⁰, snobinard; *(voice)* affecté⁰
2 *adv* d'une façon prétentieuse⁰

lager lout ['lɑːgəlaʊt] *n Br* = jeune voyou buveur de bière

lagered (up) ['lɑːgəd('ʌp)] *adj Br* bourré à la bière; **he gets lagered up with his mates every Friday night** il se bourre la gueule à la bière avec ses potes tous les vendredi soir

lah-di-dah [lɑːdɪ'dɑː] = **la-di-da**

laid-back [leɪd'bæk] *adj* décontracté⁰, relax

lairy ['leərɪ] *Br adj* (**a**) *(noisy, obnoxious)* **they get a bit lairy after a few pints** ils deviennent assez lourds et bruyants après quelques pintes (**b**) *(garish)* **a lairy shirt** une chemise très tape-à-l'œil

La-la land ['lɑːlɑːlænd] *n* (**a**) *Am Péj* = surnom donné à la ville de Los Angeles (**b**) **to be in La-la land** être dans le coaltar

laldy ['lældɪ] *adv Scot* **to give it laldy** s'en donner; **check him out giving it laldy on the dancefloor!** regarde comme il s'en donne sur la piste de danse!; **they were giving it laldy next door again** *(arguing)* ils étaient encore en train de s'engueuler à côté, et ils faisaient pas semblant

lame [leɪm] *Am* **1** *n (stupid person)* andouille *f*, cruche *f*, courge *f*
2 *adj (stupid)* cloche, nouille

lamebrain ['leɪmbreɪn], **lamo** ['leɪməʊ] *n Am* andouille *f*, cruche *f*, courge *f*

lamp [læmp] *vt Scot (hit) (once)* filer un gnon à; *(more than once)* dérouiller, filer une raclée à

land [lænd] *vt* (**a**) *Br* **to get landed with sb/sth** se retrouver avec qn/qch sur les bras; **I got landed with doing the dishes** c'est moi qui me suis tapé *ou* coltiné la vaisselle (**b**) *(hit)* **to land sb a punch** coller une châtaigne *ou* un ramponneau à qn; **he landed me one on the chin** il m'a envoyé un marron dans le menton

langered ['læŋəd] *adj Ir* bourré, pété

lardarse [!] ['lɑːdɑːs], *Am* **lardass** [!] ['lɑːdæs] *n (man)* gros *m* plein de soupe; *(woman)* grosse vache *f*

lardy ['lɑːdɪ] *adj* gros□; **get off your lardy arse and give me a hand!** lève ton gros cul et viens me donner un coup de main!

large [lɑːdʒ] **1** *adj* **it was a large one last night** on a passé une soirée bien arrosée hier

2 *adv* (a) *Br (to a large extent)* **Arsenal got thrashed large** Arsenal s'est fait ratatiner *ou* s'est fait battre à plates coutures; **we got pissed large last night** [!] on s'est pris une cuite maison hier soir; **to have it large** s'éclater *(généralement en consommant de grandes quantités d'alcool)* (b) *Noir Am* **to live large** mener la belle vie□

3 *vt* **to large it** s'éclater *(généralement en consommant de grandes quantités d'alcool)*

lark [lɑːk] *n Br* (a) *(joke)* rigolade *f*; **to do sth for a lark** faire qch histoire de rigoler (b) *(activity)* **I'm fed up with this dieting lark** j'en ai marre de ce régime que je suis en train de faire; **I can't be doing with that fancy dress lark** je n'aime pas du tout cette histoire de bal masqué

lark about, lark around *vi Br* faire l'idiot

larrikin ['lærɪkɪn] *n Austr* vaurien *m*

lash [læʃ] *n Br* **to be on the lash** se péter, se bourrer la gueule, prendre une cuite; **to go on the lash** aller se bourrer la gueule, aller prendre une cuite

lashed [læʃt] *adj Br (drunk)* bourré, pété, fait

lasties ['lɑːstɪz] *npl Br* dernières commandes□ *fpl (au pub)*; **if we go now, we can get down the local for lasties** si on part maintenant, on arrivera juste avant qu'ils arrêtent de servir

later ['leɪtə(r)], *Br* **laters** ['leɪtəz] *exclam* salut!, à la prochaine!

laugh [lɑːf] **1** *n* **to have a laugh** se marrer; **to do sth for a laugh** faire qch histoire de rigoler; **he's always good for a laugh** c'est un marrant; **you're having a laugh, aren't you?** tu déconnes?

2 *vi* (a) **don't make me laugh!** ne me fais pas rigoler!, laisse-moi rire! (b) *Br* **if we win this match, we'll be laughing** si on gagne ce match, on n'a plus de souci à se faire; **if your offer's accepted, you'll be laughing** s'ils acceptent ta proposition, ce sera super pour toi

laughing gear ['lɑːfɪŋgɪə(r)] *n Br* bouche□ *f*, clapet *m*, bec *m*; **get your laughing gear round this!** *(food, cigar)* fourre-toi ça dans le bec!

lav [læv], **lavvy** ['lævɪ] *n Br (abrév lavatory)* vécés *mpl*

law [lɔː] *n* **the law** les flics *mpl*; **I'll get the law on you!** j'appelle les flics!

lay [leɪ] **1** *n* **to be a good lay** être un bon coup; **to be an easy lay** avoir la cuisse légère

2 *vt* (a) *(have sex with)* **to lay sb** s'envoyer qn; **to get laid** s'envoyer en l'air (b) *Am* **to lay one** *(fart)* péter, larguer une caisse

lay off *vt insép* (a) **to lay off sb** *(stop annoying, nagging)* ficher la paix à qn; **just lay off me!** fiche-moi la paix!, fais-moi des vacances! (b) *(abstain from)* **to lay off the chocolate** ne plus manger de chocolat□; **to lay off the cigarettes** s'arrêter

---

The symbol □ indicates that a translation is neutral.

de fumer□; **you'd better lay off the booze for a while** tu devrais t'arrêter de boire pendant quelque temps□

lazybones ['leɪzɪbəʊnz] n flemmard(e) m,f

lead [led] n **to fill** or **pump sb full of lead** plomber qn; Am Hum **to get lead poisoning** (get shot dead) se faire buter

league [liːg] n **he's/she's way out of your league!** il est bien trop beau/elle est bien trop belle pour toi!

leak [liːk] n **to take** or Br **have a leak** (urinate) pisser un coup

leatherboy ['leðəbɔɪ] n cuir m, pédé m cuir

leatherneck ['leðənek] n Am marine□ m (américain), ≈ marsouin m

leave out [liːv] vt sép Br **leave it out!** arrête!

leccy ['lekɪ] n Br (electricity) électricité□ f, jus m; **the leccy got cut off** ils nous ont coupé le jus; **we need to pay the leccy bill** il faut payer la facture d'électricité□

lech [letʃ] **1** n obsédé m
2 vi regarder/agir avec concupiscence□; **to lech after sb** baver devant qn (de concupiscence)

leery ['lɪərɪ] adj **to be leery of sb/sth** se méfier de qn/qch□

left field [left'fiːld] n **to be way out in left field** être complètement loufoque; **it came out of left field** (comment, question) c'est tombé comme un cheveu sur la soupe

left-footer [left'fʊtə(r)] n Br Péj catholique□ mf, catho mf

leftie, lefty ['leftɪ] n gaucho mf

leg [leg] **1** n (**a**) Br **to get one's leg over** s'envoyer en l'air (**b**) **to shake a leg** (get moving) se magner, se

grouiller; **shake a leg!** magne-toi!, grouille-toi!
2 vt Br **to leg it** (run, run away) cavaler

legit [lə'dʒɪt] adj (abrév **legitimate**) réglo, régulier

legless ['leglɪs] adj Br (drunk) pété, bourré, beurré

legover ['legəʊvə(r)] n Br partie f de jambes en l'air; **he's hoping to get a legover tonight** il espère tirer un coup ce soir

lemon ['lemən] n (**a**) Br (person) abruti(e) m,f; **I felt a total lemon** je me suis senti tout con; **everyone was chatting away in Spanish and I was just standing there like a lemon** tout le monde parlait espagnol et moi j'étais là, comme un idiot (**b**) Am (useless thing) **it's a lemon** c'est de la camelote

length [leŋθ] n Br **to slip sb a length** [!] glisser un bout à qn, tringler qn

lesbo ['lezbəʊ] n Injurieux (abrév **lesbian**) gouine f

① Ce terme perd son caractère injurieux lorsqu'il est utilisé par des lesbiennes.

let off [let] vi Br (fart) larguer, lâcher

lettuce ['letɪs] n Am (money) blé m, oseille f, artiche m

level ['levəl] n **on the level** réglo, régulier

lez [lez], **lezza** ['lezə], **lezzy** ['lezɪ] n Injurieux (abrév **lesbian**) gouine f

① Ce terme perd son caractère injurieux lorsqu'il est utilisé par des lesbiennes.

lick [lɪk] **1** vt (defeat) battre à plates coutures, mettre la pâtée à, ratatiner; **to get licked** être battu à plates coutures

2 to give it big licks se donner à fond ▸ *voir aussi* **arse**

lick out [!!] *vt sép* **to lick sb out** brouter le cresson à qn

life [laɪf] *n* **get a life!** t'as rien de mieux à faire de ton temps?; *Br* **my life!** c'est pas vrai!

lifer ['laɪfə(r)] *n* prisonnier *m* condamné à perpète

lift [lɪft] *vt* (**a**) *(steal)* piquer, faucher (**b**) *Br (arrest)* agrafer, alpaguer; **he got lifted for stealing cars** il s'est fait agrafer *ou* alpaguer pour vol de voitures

light [laɪt] *n Hum* **the lights are on but there's nobody home** c'est pas une lumière

lighten up ['laɪtən] *vi* se détendre□; **oh, lighten up will you!** hé ho, relax!

lightweight ['laɪtweɪt] *n* = personne qui ne tient pas l'alcool

like [laɪk] *adv* (**a**) **there were like three thousand people there** il devait y avoir environ trois mille personnes□; **I was busy, like, that's why I didn't call you** j'étais occupé, c'est pour ça que je t'ai pas appelé, tu comprends?; **he just came up behind me, like** il s'est approché de moi par derrière□ (**b**) *(in reported speech)* **I was like "no way"** alors je lui ai fait "pas question"; **so he was like "in your dreams, pal!"** alors il a dit "c'est ça, compte là-dessus mon vieux!"

ⓘ "Like" est très souvent utilisé pour combler les temps morts lorsque l'on parle, ou après une expression peu claire ou inhabituelle.

lils [lɪlz] *npl Br (breasts)* nichons *mpl*, nénés *mpl*

limey ['laɪmɪ] *Am* **1** *n* Angliche *mf*, Rosbif *mf*

2 *adj* angliche

limo ['lɪməʊ] *n (abrév* **limousine**) limousine□ *f*

limp-wristed [lɪmp'rɪstɪd] *adj* efféminé□, chochotte

line [laɪn] *n (of powdered drugs)* ligne *f*; **to do a line** se faire une ligne ▸ *voir aussi* **main**

lionels ['laɪənəl] *npl Br (rhyming slang* **lionel blairs** = **flares**) pantalon *m* pattes d'eph'

ⓘ Lionel Blair est un comédien, danseur et animateur britannique.

lip [lɪp] *n (cheek)* toupet *m*; **don't give me any of your lip!** ne sois pas insolent!□

lipo ['laɪpəʊ] *n (liposuction)* lipo *f*; **to have lipo** se faire faire une lipo

lippy ['lɪpɪ] **1** *n Br (abrév* **lipstick**) rouge *m* à lèvres□

2 *adj (cheeky)* insolent□

lipstick lesbian ['lɪpstɪk'lezbɪən] *n* lesbienne *f* glamoureuse□

liquidate ['lɪkwɪdeɪt] *vt (kill)* liquider, refroidir

load [ləʊd] *n* (**a**) **a load of** un tas de; **it's a load of rubbish** c'est un tas de conneries; **get a load of this!** *(look)* mate-moi ça!; *(listen)* écoute un peu ça! (**b**) **loads of** des tas de; **loads of money/time** vachement d'argent/de temps (**c**) *Am* **to have a load on** être complètement bourré *ou* beurré *ou* pété ▸ *voir aussi* **shoot**

loaded ['ləʊdɪd] *adj* (**a**) *(wealthy)* plein aux as (**b**) *(drunk)* bourré, beurré, pété; *(on drugs)* défoncé, raide

---

The symbol □ indicates that a translation is neutral.

loaf [ləʊf] n Br (rhyming slang **loaf of bread = head**) citron m, cigare m; **use your loaf!** réfléchis une minute!

loaf about, loaf around vi Br traîner

loan shark ['ləʊnʃɑːk] n usurier(ère)[□] m,f

lob [lɒb] vt (throw) balancer

local ['ləʊkəl] n Br (pub) pub m du coin (où l'on a ses habitudes)

loco ['ləʊkəʊ] adj Am timbré, toqué, cinglé

locoweed ['ləʊkəʊwiːd] n (marijuana) herbe f

log [lɒg] n Br **to drop a log [!]** (defecate) couler un bronze ▶ voir aussi **flog**

lolly ['lɒlɪ] n Br (money) oseille f, artiche m, fric m, pognon m

loo [luː] n Br vécés mpl; **loo paper, loo roll** papier m cul, PQ m

loogie ['luːgɪ] n Am mollard m

looker ['lʊkə(r)] n **she's a real looker** elle est vraiment canon; **she's not much of a looker** c'est pas une beauté

loon [luːn] n cinglé(e) m,f, dingue mf, toqué(e) m,f

loonie ['luːnɪ] n Can pièce f d'un dollar

loony ['luːnɪ] **1** n cinglé(e) m,f, dingue mf, toqué(e) m,f; **loony bin** maison f de fous; **he's fit for the loony bin!** il est bon pour le cabanon! **2** adj timbré, dingue, cinglé

loony-tune ['luːnɪtjuːn] n Am cinglé(e) m,f, dingue mf, toqué(e) m,f

loony-tunes ['luːnɪtjuːnz] adj Am cinglé, toqué, timbré

loop [luːp] n **to be out of the loop** ne pas être dans le coup; **to cut sb**

out of the loop mettre qn aux oubliettes; **keep me in the loop** tiens-moi au jus ▶ voir aussi **knock**

loopy ['luːpɪ] adj cinglé, chtarbé, dingue

loose [luːs] adj (promiscuous) fa-cile; **to be loose** être une fille facile ▶ voir aussi **hang, screw**

loot [luːt] n (money) fric m, pèse m, flouze m; (goods) marchandise[□] f; (presents) cadeaux[□] mpl

lorry ['lɒrɪ] n Br Hum **it fell off the back of a lorry** c'est de la marchandise volée[□], c'est du tombé de camion

lose [luːz] vt (**a**) **to lose one's cool** se démonter; **to lose one's head** piquer une crise, voir rouge, se mettre en pétard; **to lose it** (go mad) perdre une boule; (lose one's temper) piquer une crise, péter les plombs; Br **to lose the plot** perdre la boule; Br **to lose the place** devenir gaga (**b**) **get lost!** (go away) casse-toi!, tire-toi!; (expressing contempt, disagreement) n'importe quoi! ▶ voir aussi **lunch, marbles, rag, shirt**

loser ['luːzə(r)] n (man) raté m, loser m; (woman) ratée f

Louis ['luːɪ] n Br = un seizième d'once (environ 1,8 gramme)

ⓘ C'est un terme de l'argot de la drogue. Il s'agit d'une référence à Louis XVI ("the Sixteenth").

lounge lizard ['laʊndʒ'lizəd] n salonnard m

louse [laʊs] n (person) peau f de vache

louse up vt sép **to louse sth up** foirer qch

lousy ['laʊzɪ] adj (**a**) (very bad) merdique; **to feel lousy** (ill) se sentir vraiment mal fichu; (guilty) se sentir

Le symbole **[!]** *dénote un terme très familier,* **[!!]** *un terme vulgaire.*

coupable□, avoir les boules *ou* les glandes; **we had a lousy time** on s'est vraiment fait suer; **he's in a lousy mood** il est d'humeur dégueulasse; **all he gave me was twenty lousy quid** il ne m'a filé que vingt malheureuses livres **(b) to be lousy with sth** être bourré de qch; **the streets were lousy with cops** les rues étaient pleines de flics; **to be lousy with money** être bourré de fric, être plein aux as

love [lʌv] *n* **(a)** *Br (term of address) (to one's spouse, partner, child)* chéri(e) *m,f; (to male stranger)* Monsieur *m; (to female stranger)* Madame *f* **(b) love handles** poignées *fpl* d'amour; **love rat** salaud *m* qui trompe sa compagne

loved up [lʌvd'ʌp] *adj Br* **(a)** *(after taking ecstasy)* tout gentil *(sous l'effet de l'ecstasy)* **(b)** *(in love)* très amoureux□; **she's all loved up with her new boyfriend** elle est folle amoureuse de son nouveau petit copain

lovely jubbly [lʌvlɪ'dʒʌblɪ] *exclam Br* super!, au poil!

ⓘ Il s'agit d'une expression popularisée par Del Boy, le personnage principal d'une série télévisée comique britannique intitulée *Only Fools and Horses* diffusée pendant les années 80 et 90.

lover boy ['lʌvəbɔɪ] *n Ironique* **she's gone out with lover boy** elle est sortie avec son Jules; **when's lover boy coming round to see you?** quand est-ce qu'il vient te voir ton Jules?

lovey-dovey [lʌvɪ'dʌvɪ] *adj (behaviour)* sentimental□; **to be all lovey-dovey** *(of two lovers)* être comme des tourtereaux

luck into [lʌk] *vt insép Am* **to luck into sth** dégoter qch

luck out, luck up *vi Am* décrocher le gros lot

luck up on *vt insép* **to luck up on sth** dégoter qch

lucky ['lʌkɪ] *adj* **to get lucky** emballer

lug[1] [lʌg] *n Am (man)* abruti *m*, crétin *m*

lug[2], **lughole** ['lʌghəʊl] *n Br (ear)* esgourde *f*, portugaise *f*

lulu ['luːluː] *n Am* **to be a lulu** être génial

lumber ['lʌmbə(r)] **1** *vt Br* **to get lumbered with sb/sth** se taper *ou* se coltiner qn/qch; **I got lumbered with doing the dishes** je me suis coltiné *ou* farci la vaisselle

2 *n Scot* **to get a lumber** faire une conquête; **is that your lumber?** c'est ta conquête?

lummox ['lʌməks] *n Br (clumsy person)* empoté(e) *m,f; (stupid person)* cruche *f*, andouille *f*

lunch [lʌntʃ] *n* **to be out to lunch** *(mad)* travailler du chapeau, être cinglé; **to lose** *or Am* **shoot one's lunch** *(vomit)* gerber, dégobiller; **liquid lunch** = alcool qui tient lieu de déjeuner; **the boss has had another of his liquid lunches** le patron a encore passé sa pause déjeuner au pub à picoler

lunchbox ['lʌntʃbɒks] *n Br (man's genitals)* service *m* trois pièces, bijoux *mpl* de famille

lunkhead ['lʌŋkhed] *n Am* cruche *f*, andouille *f*, courge *f*

lurgy ['lɜːgɪ] *n Br Hum* **I've got the (dreaded lurgy)** j'ai chopé quelque chose

lush [lʌʃ] **1** *n* alcolo *mf*, poivrot(e) *m,f*

2 adj Br (attractive) canon, super; (excellent) super, génial

lushed [lʌʃt] adj Am pété, bourré, beurré

luvved up [lʌvd'ʌp] = **loved up**

luvvie, luvvy ['lʌvɪ] n Br Péj (man) acteur m prétentieux□; (woman) actrice f prétentieuse□

Mm

Mac [mæk] *npr Am (term of address)* chef *m*

mack [mæk] *n* (**a**) *Am (pimp)* maquereau *m*, mac (**b**) *Noir Am (expert seducer)* tombeur *m*

mack on *vt insép Noir Am* **to mack on sb** draguer qn

mad [mæd] *adj* (**a**) **to be mad about sb/sth** être dingue de qn/qch; *Br* **to be mad for it** *(raring to go)* être prêt à s'éclater (**b**) **to run/work like mad** courir/travailler comme un dingue

madam ['mædəm] *n* (**a**) *(of brothel)* mère *f* maquerelle (**b**) *Br (arrogant girl)* **she's a little madam** c'est une petite pimbêche (**c**) *Br (term of address)* madame *f*; **that's enough of your cheek, madam!** ça suffit comme ça, petite insolente!

made up [meɪd'ʌp] *adj Br* hyper content

ⓘ Il s'agit d'un terme utilisé surtout dans la région de Liverpool.

---

madhouse ['mædhaʊs] *n (psychiatric hospital, busy place)* maison *f* de fous; **it's like a madhouse in here** c'est une vraie maison de fous ici

mag [mæg] *n (abrév* **magazine**) revue□ *f*, magazine□ *m* ▸ *voir aussi* **girlie, skin, stroke, wank**

magic ['mædʒɪk] *adj* (**a**) *Br (excellent)* super, génial (**b**) **magic mushrooms** champignons *mpl* hallucinogènes□, champignons *mpl*

magnet ['mægnɪt] *n* **his new car's a babe** *or* **chick** *or* **fanny [!] magnet** sa nouvelle voiture est super pour emballer les gonzesses

main [meɪn] *adj* (**a**) *Am* **main man** *(friend)* pote *m*; **yo, my main man, how ya doin'?** salut mon pote, comment ça va?; *Br* **when it comes to scoring goals, Wayne Rooney's the main man** pour ce qui est de marquer des buts, Wayne Rooney est champion (**b**) **main line** *(vein)* veine *f* apparente□ *(choisie pour s'injecter de la drogue)* ▸ *voir aussi* **squeeze**

mainline ['meɪnlaɪn] **1** *vt (drugs)* se faire un shoot de; *(habitually)* se shooter à
2 *vi* se shooter, se piquer

mainliner ['meɪnlaɪnə(r)] *n* junkie *mf*, shooté(e) *m,f*

make [meɪk] **1** *n* **to be on the make** *(financially)* chercher à s'en mettre plein les poches; *(sexually)* draguer
2 *vt Am* **to make sb, to make it with sb** coucher avec qn
3 *vi Am* **to make like sb** *(pass oneself off as)* essayer de passer pour qn□; **he's always making like a tough guy** il essaie toujours de jouer les durs; **make like you don't know anything** fais comme si tu savais pas

make out *vi Am (sexually)* se peloter;

to make out with sb peloter qn

malarkey [mə'lɑːkɪ] *n Br* bêtises◻ *fpl*, sottises *fpl*; **I don't believe in ghosts or any of that malarkey** je ne crois pas aux fantômes et à toutes ces sottises

mama, mamma ['mæmə] *n Am* (**a**) *(woman)* bonne femme *f* (**b**) **big mama** *(large object)* mastodonte *m*

man [mæn] **1** *n* (**a**) *Br (husband, boyfriend)* mec *m*; **she's got a new man** elle a un nouveau mec (**b**) *(term of address)* **hey, man!** *(as greeting)* salut vieux!; **how you doing, man?** comment ça va, vieux?; **come on, man!** allez! (**c**) *Noir Am* **the Man** *(white people)* les Blancs◻ *mpl*; *(the police)* les flics *mpl*; *(drug dealer)* dealer *m*

2 *exclam* la vache!; **man, am I tired!** la vache, je suis crevé!

Manc [mæŋk] **1** *n Br (abrév* **Mancunian)** = natif de la ville de Manchester

2 *adj* de Manchester◻

maneater ['mæniːtə(r)] *n (woman)* mangeuse *f* d'hommes

mank [mæŋk], **manky** ['mæŋkɪ] *adj Br* cradingue, crado

manor ['mænə(r)] *n Br (of police, criminal, gang)* territoire *m*; **my manor** par chez moi

map [mæp] *n Am (face)* tronche *f*, trombine *f*

marbles ['mɑːbəlz] *npl* **to lose one's marbles** perdre la boule; **to have all one's marbles** ne pas être gâteux du tout

mardy ['mɑːdɪ] *adj Br* grincheux; **she's a right mardy cow!** elle a un caractère de cochon!

mare¹ [meə(r)] *n Br Péj (woman)* grognasse *f*; **you silly mare!** espèce d'andouille!

mare² *n Br (abrév* **nightmare)** cauchemar◻ *m*; **it was a total mare!** c'était un vrai cauchemar!; **we had a bit of a mare finding somewhere to park** on a eu vachement de mal pour trouver une place où se garer

mark [mɑːk] *n* pigeon *f*, poire *f*

mashed [mæʃt] *adj Br (drunk)* bourré, pété; *(on drugs)* défoncé, raide

massive ['mæsɪv] **1** *adj Ir (brilliant)* super, génial

2 *n Br (gang)* bande◻ *f*; **the Brighton massive** la bande de Brighton

mate [meɪt] *n Br* (**a**) *(friend)* pote *m* (**b**) *(term of address)* **thanks, mate** *(to friend)* merci vieux; *(to stranger)* merci chef; **watch where you're going, mate!** hé, regarde devant toi!

matey ['meɪtɪ] *Br* **1** *n (term of address)* **how's it going, matey?** comment ça va vieux?; **just watch it, matey!** fais gaffe!

2 *adj (friendly)* **to be matey with sb** être pote avec qn; **they're very matey all of a sudden** ils sont très potes tout d'un coup

max [mæks] *(abrév* **maximum) 1** *n Am* **to the max** *(totally)* un max; **did you have a good time? – to the max!** tu t'es bien amusé? – vachement bien! *ou* un max!

2 *adv (at the most)* maxi; **it'll take three days max** ça prendra trois jours maxi

3 *vt Am* **to max an exam** obtenir le maximum de points à un examen◻

max out *Am* **1** *vt sép* **to max out one's credit card** dépenser le maximum autorisé avec sa carte de crédit◻

2 *vi* **to max out on chocolate** se goinfrer de chocolat; **to max out on booze** picoler un max

---

Le symbole [!] *dénote un terme très familier,* [!!] *un terme vulgaire.*

maxed [mækst] *adj Am (very drunk)* bourré comme un coing, pété à mort

maxed out [mækst'aʊt] *adj Am* **(a) to be maxed out on one's credit card** avoir dépensé le maximum autorisé avec sa carte de crédit□ **(b) to be maxed out on chocolate/sci-fi movies** avoir fait une overdose de chocolat/de films de science-fiction

mean [miːn] *adj (excellent)* super, génial; **she's a mean chess player** elle joue super bien aux échecs, elle touche (sa bille) aux échecs; **he makes a mean curry** il fait super bien le curry

meat [miːt] *n* **(a) you're dead meat!** t'es mort! **(b)** [!!] *(penis)* bite *f*, queue *f* **(c) meat rack** lieu *m* de drague *(en particulier chez les homosexuels)* **(d) meat wagon** *(ambulance)* ambulance□ *f*; *(police van)* panier *m* à salade; *(hearse)* corbillard□ *m* **(e)** *Br Péj* **meat market** *(nightclub)* = boîte réputée pour être un lieu de drague ▸ *voir aussi* **beat**

meatball ['miːtbɔːl], **meathead** ['miːthed] *n Am (person)* crétin(e) *m,f*, truffe *f*, andouille *f*

meatheaded ['miːthedɪd] *adj Am* débile

medallion man [mɪ'dæljənmæn] *n Br* macho *m* à chaîne en or

ⓘ Le "medallion man" est généralement un homme entre deux âges traversant une crise d'identité. Il porte une chemise ouverte sur un torse velu et des bijoux clinquants (dont le fameux médaillon). Il fréquente les boîtes de nuit en compagnie de gens nettement moins âgés que lui, et tente de séduire les jeunes femmes.

mega ['megə] **1** *adj (excellent)* génial, super, géant; *(enormous)* énorme **2** *adv (very)* hyper, méga

mega- ['megə] *préfixe* hyper; **megarich** hyper riche; **mega-famous** hyper célèbre; **mega-angry** hyper en colère

megabucks ['megəbʌks] *n* un fric fou, une fortune

megastar ['megəstɑː(r)] *n* superstar *f*

megilla [mə'gɪlə] *n Am* **the whole megilla** tout le tremblement; **I don't need the whole megilla, just give me the main points** t'as pas besoin de tout me raconter en détail *ou* par le menu, dis-moi le principal

mellow ['meləʊ] **1** *n Noir Am (friend)* pote *m* **2** *adj* **(a)** *Noir Am (attractive)* sexy, craquant **(b)** *Noir Am (fine, acceptable)* cool; **see you at six? – yeah, that's mellow** on se voit à six heures? – ouais, ça marche! **(c)** *(relaxed, unexcited)* cool, décontract, relaxe; **stay mellow!** calmos!, du calme! **(d)** *(on drugs)* **to be mellow** être parti, planer

mellow out *vi (relax)* se calmer

melons ['melənz] *npl (breasts)* nichons *mpl*, roberts *mpl*

mensch [menʃ] *n Am (man)* chic type *m*; *(woman)* brave femme *f*

mental ['mentəl] *adj Br (mad)* dingue, cinglé; **to go mental** *(go mad)* devenir dingue *ou* cinglé, perdre la boule; *(lose one's temper)* péter les plombs, péter une durite, piquer une crise; **Robbie Williams came on stage and the crowd just went mental** Robbie Williams a fait son entrée sur scène et la foule s'est déchaînée; **it was a mental party!** c'était une fête vraiment délire *ou* dingue!; **you should have seen the way they**

were shouting at each other, it was mental! t'aurais vu comme ils se criaient dessus, c'était dingue!

mentalist ['mentəlɪst] *n Br* dingue *mf*

Merc [mɜːk] *n* (*abrév* **Mercedes**) Mercedes[□] *f*

merchant ['mɜːtʃənt] *n* **speed merchant** *Br* (*fast driver*) chauffard *m*; *Am* (*athlete*) = coureur à pied très rapide; *Br* **gossip merchant** commère *f*; *Br* **rip-off** *or* **con merchant** arnaqueur(euse) *m,f*

ⓘ Ce terme peut s'ajouter à de nombreux noms pour désigner quelqu'un qui s'adonne à une activité.

merry ['merɪ] *adj Br* (*slightly drunk*) éméché

meshuga [mə'ʃʊɡə] *adj Am* dingue, taré, cinglé

mess [mes] *vi* (**a**) *Br* **no messing!** sans blagues! (**b**) **to mess with sb** embêter qn; **don't mess with him!** le cherche pas!, te frotte pas à lui!

mess about, mess around 1 *vi* (**a**) (*act foolishly*) faire l'imbécile (**b**) (*waste time*) glander, glandouiller (**c**) (*potter*) bricoler (**d**) **to mess about** *or* **around** (*sexually*) coucher avec qn
2 *vt* **to mess sb about** *or* **around** faire tourner qn en bourrique

metalhead ['metəlhed], **metaller** ['metələ(r)] *n* fan *mf* de heavy metal[□], hardeux(euse) *m,f*

Mex [meks] *Am Injurieux* (*abrév* **Mexican**) **1** *n* Mexicain(e)[□] *m,f*
2 *adj* mexicain[□]

Mick [mɪk] *npr Injurieux* (**a**) (*Irishman*) Irlandais[□] *m* (**b**) *Ir* (*Catholic*) = terme injurieux désignant un catholique, en Irlande du Nord

ⓘ "Mick" est le diminutif de "Michael", l'un des prénoms les plus courants en Irlande. Bien que ce terme ne témoigne pas nécessairement d'une attitude xénophobe de la part de celui qui l'utilise, il est préférable de ne pas l'employer.

mick [mɪk], **mickey** ['mɪkɪ] *n Br* **to take the mick** *or* **mickey out of sb/sth** se ficher de qn/qch; **are you taking the mick** *or* **mickey?** tu te fiches de moi?

Mickey (Finn) ['mɪkɪ('fɪn)] *n* = boisson alcoolisée dans laquelle on a versé un sédatif

Mickey Mouse ['mɪkɪ'maʊs] *adj Péj* à la gomme, à la noix (de coco); **he's got a degree from some Mickey Mouse university** il est titulaire d'un diplôme d'une espèce d'université à la noix; **he works for some Mickey Mouse dotcom company** il travaille pour une espèce de start-up à la gomme

middle finger salute ['mɪdəlfɪŋɡəsə'luːt] *n Br* doigt *m* d'honneur; **to give sb the middle finger salute** faire un doigt d'honneur à qn

middy ['mɪdɪ] *n Austr* (*beer*) ≃ demi *m* de bière[□]

mighty ['maɪtɪ] *adv* vachement, hyper

Mike [maɪk] *npr* **for the love of Mike!** c'est quelque chose!, c'est pas vrai!

miles [maɪlz] *adv Br* (*very much*) vachement; **I feel miles better** je me sens vachement mieux; **it's miles more interesting** c'est vachement plus intéressant; **you're miles too slow** t'es vachement trop lent, t'es mille fois trop lent

MILF [!!] [mɪlf] *n* (*abrév* **mother I'd**

like to fuck) mère f baisable

ⓘ Cet acronyme a été popularisé par le film *American Pie* (1999).

million ['mɪljən] *adj* **to look (like) a million dollars** en jeter; **to feel (like) a million dollars** être au septième ciel

mince pies [mɪns'paɪz] *npl Br (rhyming slang* **eyes)** mirettes *fpl*, calots *mpl*

mind [maɪnd] *n* **to be out of one's mind** être cinglé *ou* dingue *ou* fêlé; **to be bored out of one's mind** mourir d'ennui; **to be out of one's mind with worry** être malade d'inquiétude ▸ *voir aussi* **blow**

mind-blowing ['maɪndbləʊɪŋ] *adj* époustouflant

minder ['maɪndə(r)] *n Br (bodyguard)* garde *m* du corps□, gorille *m*

ming [mɪŋ] *vi Br* puer, coincer, fouetter, schlinguer; **it mings in here!** ça schlingue ici!

minge [!!] [mɪndʒ] *n Br* chatte *f*

minger ['mɪŋə(r)] *n Br (unattractive person)* mocheté *f*

minging ['mɪŋɪŋ] *n Br (unattractive)* moche; *(of poor quality)* merdique; **that wine is absolutely minging!** ce vin est vraiment dégueulasse!; **is she going out with him? he's minging!** elle sort avec lui? il est moche comme un pou!

mingy ['mɪndʒɪ] *adj Br (person)* radin; *(sum, portion, amount)* ridicule□, minable

mint [mɪnt] *Br* **1** *n (fortune)* fortune□ *f*; **to make a mint** faire fortune□
2 *adj (excellent)* génial, dément, top
3 *vt* **to be minting it** rouler sur l'or

minted ['mɪntɪd] *adj Br* plein aux as, bourré de fric

missis, missus ['mɪsɪz] *n Br (wife)* bourgeoise *f*; **the missis** la patronne, ma bourgeoise

mitt [mɪt] *n (hand)* pogne *f*, patte *f*; **get your mitts off me!** bas les pattes!

mix up [mɪks] *vt sép Am* **to mix it up** *(fight)* se castagner, se bastonner

mo¹ [məʊ] *n* **(a)** *Br (abrév* **moment)** instant□ *m*, seconde□ *f*; **half a mo!, wait a mo!** une seconde! **(b)** *Am (abrév* **homosexual)** homo *mf*

mo² [məʊ] *adv Noir Am (very, much)* vachement; **we're gonna play some mo phat sounds** on va vous passer de la super musique

Mob [mɒb] *n* **the Mob** la mafia□

mobbed [mɒbd] *adj* bourré de monde; **the bar was mobbed** le bar était bourré de monde

mobster ['mɒbstə(r)] *n* gangster□ *m (particulièrement de la mafia)*

moby ['məʊbɪ] *n Br (mobile phone)* mobile *m*

Mockney ['mɒknɪ] *Br* **1** *n* = personne issue d'un milieu aisé qui affecte l'accent cockney
2 *adj* = caractéristique des personnes issues d'un milieu aisé qui affectent l'accent cockney

mofo [!] ['məʊfəʊ] *n Noir Am (abrév* **motherfucker)** enfoiré *m*

mog [mɒg], **moggy** ['mɒgɪ] *n Br* greffier *m*

momma ['mɒmm] = **mama**

mondo ['mɒndəʊ] *adv Am* vachement

money ['mʌnɪ] **1** *n* **(a)** **to be in the money** avoir du fric **(b)** *Noir Am (term of address)* chef *m*; **what's up, money?** ça va, chef?
2 *adj Noir Am (cool)* cool

moneybags ['mʌnɪbægz] n *(person)* richard(e) *m,f*, rupin(e) *m,f*; **lend us a fiver, moneybags!** passe-moi cinq livres, toi qui es plein aux as!

money-grubber ['mʌnɪgrʌbə(r)] n rapace *m*, requin *m*

mong [mɒŋ] n *Br (abrév* **mongol**) mongol(e) *m,f*, gol *m*

ⓘ Bien que ce terme soit très injurieux et politiquement incorrect lorsqu'il s'applique à un trisomique, il est relativement anodin lorsqu'il désigne simplement un imbécile.

---

moniker ['mɒnɪkə(r)] n blase *m*

monkey ['mʌŋkɪ] n **(a)** *Br (£500)* cinq cents livres⁰ *fpl* **(b)** *Br* **I don't give a monkey's** je m'en fiche pas mal, j'en ai rien à battre **(c) monkey business** magouilles *fpl* **(d) to spank the monkey** se branler, se taper sur la colonne **(e)** *Am* **to have a monkey on one's back** être accro **(f) monkey suit** *(formal suit)* costard *m* chic; *Am (uniform)* uniforme⁰ *m* ▸ *voir aussi* **brass, features**

monkey about, monkey around *vi* faire l'imbécile

Montezuma's Revenge [mɒntɪ'zuːməzrə'vendʒ] n *Hum* la turista

monty ['mɒntɪ] n *Br* **the full monty** le grand jeu, la totale

moo [muː] n *Br Péj (woman)* vieille bique *f*, vieille toupie *f*; **you silly moo!** espèce d'andouille!; **shut up, you old moo!** la ferme, espèce de vieille toupie!

mooch [muːtʃ] *Am* **1** *vt* taper, taxer; **to mooch sth off sb** taper *ou* taxer qch à qn
2 *vi* taxer

mooch about, mooch around 1 *vt insép* **to mooch about** *or* **around**

the house traîner dans la maison
2 *vi* glander, glandouiller

moocher ['muːtʃə(r)] n *Am* tapeur(euse) *m,f*

moody ['muːdɪ] *adj Br (goods)* volé⁰; *(passport, document)* faux⁰

moola, moolah ['muːlə] n *Am* flouze *m*, fric *m*, pognon *m*

moon [muːn] *vi (expose one's buttocks)* montrer ses fesses

moonshine ['muːnʃaɪn] n *Am* **(a)** *(nonsense)* foutaises *fpl* **(b)** *(illegal alcohol)* alcool *m* de contrebande⁰

moose [muːs] n *(unattractive person)* mocheté *f*

morning glory ['mɔːnɪŋ'glɔːrɪ] n *Br* érection *f* au réveil⁰

moron ['mɔːrɒn] n crétin(e) *m,f*, imbécile *mf*

moronic [mə'rɒnɪk] *adj* débile

mortal ['mɔːtəl] *Br* **1** *adj (very drunk)* complètement bourré *ou* pété
2 *adv* **I was mortal drunk last night!** j'étais complètement bourré hier soir!

mother ['mʌðə(r)] n **(a)** *(large person, thing)* mastodonte *m*; **I've got a mother of a hangover** j'ai une vache de gueule de bois; **her boyfriend's a big mother** son copain est un balaise; **we had the mother of all rows** on a eu une engueulade monstre **(b)** **[!]** *(abrév* **motherfucker**) *(person)* enfoiré *m*; *(thing)* saloperie *f*; **some mother's stolen my drink** il y a un enfoiré qui m'a pris mon verre; **the mother's broken down again** cette saloperie est encore tombée en panne

motherfucker **[!!]** ['mʌðə'fʌkə(r)] n **(a)** *(person)* enculé *m*; **stupid motherfucker** pauvre con **(b)** *(thing)* saloperie *f*; **the motherfucker won't start** cette saloperie

---

Le symbole **[!]** dénote un terme très familier, **[!!]** un terme vulgaire.

Pleins feux sur...

Money

Parmi les termes d'argot qui désignent l'argent, **cash** et **dough** en sont certainement les plus courants, bien que le terme **dosh** s'emploie souvent au Royaume-Uni. Le mot **bread**, autrefois très courant, est aujourd'hui un peu vieillot. Le terme américain **greenback** trouve son origine dans le fait que les billets américains sont tous verts ; ce terme s'emploie pour désigner un billet vert de n'importe quelle valeur. Le yiddish a donné les termes américains **gelt** et **mizuma**. **Dead presidents** et **benjamins** sont d'autres expressions humoristiques pour désigner les billets aux États-Unis ; ils font référence au fait que tous les billets américains portent l'effigie d'un président du pays (Benjamin Franklin pour les billets de 100 dollars). En anglais britannique on emploie parfois le mot **folding** pour parler de billets de banque (**got any folding?**), et les termes **coppers** et **shrapnel** désignent la petite monnaie ; le mot **readies** (abréviation de "ready cash") s'applique à l'argent liquide. Il existe différents termes pour parler de sommes d'argent précises, tels que **a pony** (25 livres) et **a monkey** (500 livres), surtout utilisés à Londres, **a ton** (100 livres), **a grand** (1000 livres ou 1000 dollars), **a tenner** (10 livres ou 10 dollars) et **a fiver** (5 livres). En Grande-Bretagne, **tenner** et **fiver** peuvent aussi désigner le billet lui-même. Un billet de 100 dollars se nomme **a C-note**, du chiffre romain C qui équivaut à cent. **Quid** est le mot le plus utilisé pour désigner la livre sterling ; il est invariable au pluriel (**ten quid**, **a thousand quid**, etc). Le mot **buck**, très courant, signifie "dollar" et se retrouve dans de nombreuses expressions dont **to make a fast buck** (faire du fric facilement). Le terme **bucks** (au pluriel) s'emploie également pour parler de l'argent d'une manière générale. Pour dire que quelqu'un est très riche, on emploiera les expressions **to be loaded**, **to be rolling in it** ou, en anglais américain, **to be rolling in dough**, tandis qu'on dira d'une personne pauvre qu'elle est **broke**, **hard up**, ou en anglais britannique **skint**, **strapped** ou **boracic** (de l'argot rimé **boracic lint** = **skint**). On dira d'un avare qu'il est **tight**. On dit aussi que c'est **a tightwad** ou **a skinflint**. "Coûter très cher" se dit **to cost a packet**, **a bomb** ou **an arm and a leg**. Une très mauvaise affaire est **a rip-off** (terme apparenté aux expressions **to rip somebody off**, arnaquer quelqu'un, et **to get ripped off**, se faire arnaquer).

The symbol □ indicates that a translation is neutral.

ne veut pas démarrer; **I've got a motherfucker of a hangover** j'ai une gueule de bois d'enfer

motherfucking [!!] ['mʌðəˈfʌkɪŋ] *adj* foutu; **where's that motherfucking bastard?** où est passé cet enculé?; **open up or I'll kick the motherfucking door in!** ouvre ou j'enfonce cette putain de porte!

mothering [!] ['mʌðərɪŋ] *adj Am* foutu; **where's that mothering bitch?** où est passée cette conne?

motor ['məʊtə(r)] *Br* **1** *n* (*car*) bagnole *f*
    2 *vi* **to be motoring** (*going fast*) foncer

motormouth ['məʊtəmaʊθ] *n* moulin *m* à paroles

mouth [maʊθ] *n* **to be all mouth** n'avoir que (de) la gueule; *Br Hum* **he's all mouth and no trousers** il a que (de) la gueule; **to shoot one's mouth off** parler à tort et à travers; **me and my big mouth!** j'ai encore perdu une occasion de me taire!
    ▸ *voir aussi* shut

mouth off [maʊð] *vi* (*brag*) se vanter□, crâner; (*talk impudently*) la ramener; (*talk indiscreetly*) parler à tort et à travers

mouthful ['maʊθfʊl] *n* (**a**) (*word*) mot *m* imprononçable□; (*name*) nom *m* à coucher dehors (**b**) *Br* **to give sb a mouthful** traiter qn de tous les noms (**c**) *Am* **you said a mouthful!** tu l'as dit, bouffi!

move [muːv] *n* (**a**) **to get a move on** se magner; **get a move on!** magnetoi! (**b**) **to make a move** (*leave*) y aller□, bouger; **to make a move on sb** faire des avances à qn□

muck [mʌk] *n Br* (**a**) (*dirt*) crasse *f* (**b**) (*worthless things*) **his book's a load of muck** son livre ne vaut pas un clou; **he eats nothing but muck** il

mange que des saloperies

muck about, muck around 1 *vi* (**a**) (*act foolishly*) faire l'imbécile (**b**) (*waste time*) glander, glandouiller (**c**) (*potter*) bricoler
    2 *vt* **to muck sb about** *or* **around** faire tourner qn en bourrique

muck up 1 *vt sép Br* (*make a mess of*) saloper
    2 *vi Austr* (*lark around*) faire des bêtises□

mucker ['mʌkə(r)] *n Br* (**a**) (*friend*) pote *m* (**b**) (*term of address*) vieux *m*; **all right, me old mucker!** salut vieux!, salut mon pote!

mucky ['mʌkɪ] *adj Br* (**a**) (*dirty*) crasseux (**b**) (*obscene*) cochon

muff [!!] [mʌf] *n* (*woman's genitals*) chatte *f*, con *m*, cramouille *f*

muff-diving [!!] ['mʌfdaɪvɪŋ] *n* descente *f* au barbu; **to go muff-diving** faire une descente au barbu, faire minette

muffin top ['mʌfɪntɒp] *n Hum* = bourrelet de graisse qui dépasse du pantalon

ⓘ Ce terme vient du fait que les muffins présentent en leur milieu un renflement qui depasse du moule dans lequel ils cuisent.

mug [mʌg] *n* (**a**) (*face*) tronche *f*, trombine *f*; **mug shot** = photo d'identité prise par la police ou en prison (**b**) (*gullible person*) poire *f*; **it's a mug's game** le jeu n'en vaut pas la chandelle; **the lottery's a mug's game** le loto, c'est un attrape-couillons

muggins ['mʌgɪnz] *n Br* mézigue; **muggins (here) paid the bill as usual** comme d'habitude c'est mézigue qui a payé l'addition

---

Le symbole [!] *dénote un terme très familier,* [!!] *un terme vulgaire.*

mule [mjuːl] n (drug smuggler) mule f ▸ voir aussi **hung**

muller, mullah ['mʊlə] vt (**a**) (defeat heavily) écraser, foutre la pâtée à (**b**) (hit) foutre un gnon à

mullered, mullahed ['mʊləd] adj Br bourré, beurré, pété, fait

munch out [mʌntʃ] vi Am se goinfrer, s'empiffrer

munchies ['mʌntʃiz] npl (**a**) (hunger) fringale f; **to have the munchies** avoir la dalle (**b**) (food) amuse-gueule mpl

munter ['mʌntə(r)] n Br (ugly woman) laideron f, mocheté f, cageot m

muppet ['mʌpɪt] n Br (person) andouille f

murder ['mɜːdə(r)] **1** n (difficult task, experience) **it was murder** c'était l'enfer; **the traffic was murder** il y avait une circulation dingue; **it's murder trying to park in the town centre** c'est l'enfer pour trouver à se garer dans le centre-ville; **standing all day is murder on your feet** ça fait vachement mal aux pieds de rester debout toute la journée

2 vt (**a**) (song, language) massacrer (**b**) Br **I could murder a fag/beer** je me taperais bien une clope/une bière (**c**) (defeat) ratatiner, écrabouiller, foutre la pâtée à

mush [mʊʃ] n Br (term of address) **oi, mush!** hé, Duchenoque!

muso ['mjuːzəʊ] n (abrév **musician**) musico m

mutha ['mʌðə] Noir Am = **mother**

muthafucka ['mʌðəfʌkə] Noir Am = **motherfucker**

mutt [mʌt] n clébard m, clebs m; Br Hum **to be the mutt's nuts** [!] être génial

mutton ['mʌtn] adj Br (rhyming slang Mutt 'n' Jeff = **deaf**) sourdingue

---

ⓘ Mutt et Jeff étaient les personnages d'un dessin animé américain dans les années 30.

Nn

nab [næb] *vt* (**a**) *(catch, arrest)* pincer, alpaguer (**b**) *(steal)* piquer, faucher

nads [!] [nædz] *npl* (*abrév* **gonads**) *Br (testicles)* couilles *fpl*

naff [næf] *adj Br (clothes, place, person)* ringard; *(comment, behaviour)* débile; **naff all** que dalle; **I've got naff all money** j'ai que dalle comme argent

naff off *vi Br* s'arracher, se casser; **naff off!** *(go away)* casse-toi!; *(expressing contempt, disagreement)* va te faire voir!

naffing ['næfɪŋ] *Br* **1** *adj (for emphasis)* foutu, sacré; **shut your naffing mouth!** ferme-la!, ferme ton clapet!; **naffing hell!** putain!
2 *adv (for emphasis)* vachement; **you're so naffing stupid!** t'es vraiment débile!; **you're naffing well coming with me!** tu viens avec moi, un point c'est tout!

nag [næg] *n Br (horse)* bourrin *m*, canasson *m*; **he won a grand and put it all on a nag** il a gagné mille livres et les a misées sur un canasson

Nam [næm] *npr* (*abrév* **Vietnam**) le Vietnam◻

ⓘ Le terme "Nam" n'est utilisé que dans le contexte de la guerre du Vietnam.

nancy (boy) ['nænsɪ(bɔɪ)] *n (effemi-*

nate man) chochotte *f*; *(homosexual man)* homo *m*

nang [næŋ] *adj Br* super, génial, top

narc [nɑːk] *n Am* (*abrév* **narcotics agent**) agent *m* de la Brigade des stups

nark [nɑːk] **1** *n* (**a**) *(informer)* mouchard(e) *m,f* (**b**) *Br (grumbler)* râleur(euse) *m,f*
2 *vt Br (annoy)* foutre en rogne *ou* en boule
3 *vi (inform)* **to nark on sb** balancer qn

narked [nɑːkt] *adj Br* en rogne

narky ['nɑːkɪ] *adj Br* ronchon

nasty ['nɑːstɪ] **1** *n* **to do the nasty** *(have sex)* faire crac-crac; **have you done the nasty yet?** est-ce que vous avez fait crac-crac?
2 *adj Am (excellent)* super, génial; **she makes a nasty pizza** elle fait super bien la pizza

natch [nætʃ] *exclam* (*abrév* **naturally**) bien sûr!◻

natter ['nætə(r)] *Br* **1** *n* converse *f*; **to have a natter** tailler une bavette
2 *vi* papoter

NBF [enbiː'ef] *n Hum* (*abrév* **new best friend**) nouveau meilleur ami (nouvelle meilleure amie◻) *m,f*

neat [niːt] *Am* **1** *adj (excellent)* super, génial
2 *exclam* super!, génial!

neck [nek] **1** *n* (**a**) *Br (cheek)* culot *m*;

she's got some neck! elle a un sacré culot! (**b**) *Br* **to get it in the neck** se faire remonter les bretelles

2 *vi (of couple)* se peloter

3 *vt Br (drink)* descendre; **I necked ten pints last night** j'ai descendu dix pintes hier soir ► *voir aussi* **brass, dead, pain**

ned [ned] *n Scot* racaille *f*, lascar *m*

needful ['niːdfʊl] *n Br (what is necessary)* **to do the needful** faire le nécessaire□; **have you got the needful?** *(money)* t'as du fric?

needle ['niːdəl] **1** *n* **to get the needle** se foutre en boule *ou* en rogne; **to give sb the needle** foutre qn en boule *ou* en rogne

2 *vt (irritate)* foutre en boule *ou* en rogne

3 *vi (inject drugs)* se shooter

neek [niːk] *n* ringard(e) *m,f*

ⓘ Il s'agit d'un mot-valise formé à partir de "nerd" et de "geek" (voir ces entrées).

neeky ['niːkɪ] *adj* ringard

ⓘ Il s'agit d'un mot-valise formé à partir de "nerdy" et de "geeky" (voir ces entrées). .

nelly ['nelɪ] *n* (**a**) *Br* **not on your nelly!** des clous! (**b**) *Am (homosexual man)* folle *f*

nerd [nɜːd] *n* ringard *m*

ⓘ Le "nerd" est une personne, généralement jeune, qui par son désintérêt pour les activités prisées par les gens de son âge, son absence de goût en matière vestimentaire et son incapacité à communiquer de façon satisfaisante avec autrui, se rend impopulaire auprès des au-

tres. Le "nerd" est souvent un passionné d'informatique.

nerdy ['nɜːdɪ] *adj* ringard

never-never ['nevə'nevə(r)] *n Br & Austr* **to buy sth on the never-never** acheter qch à crédit

new [njuː] *adj Br* **new lad** jeune homme *m* moderne□; **new man** homme *m* moderne□

ⓘ Les concepts de "new lad" et de "new man" sont apparus à la fin des années 80. Le "new lad" est un jeune homme dont les centres d'intérêt ne diffèrent en rien de ceux de n'importe quel autre jeune homme (à savoir les sorties, les rencontres, le sport...) mais dont l'attitude témoigne d'une certaine sophistication absente chez le "lad" moyen. Le "new lad" sait boire avec modération et n'est pas sexiste. Le "new man", lui, ne craint pas de laisser s'exprimer sa sensibilité. Il est constamment à l'écoute des besoins de sa compagne et participe équitablement à l'éducation des enfants et aux tâches ménagères.

newbie ['njuːbɪ] *n Am* bleu(e) *m,f (personne nouvellement recrutée)*

newsie ['njuːzɪ] *n Am* (**a**) *(newspaper vendor)* vendeur(euse) *m,f* de journaux□ (**b**) *(journalist)* journaleux(euse) *m,f*

next [nekst] *adv Am* **to get next to sb** *(ingratiate oneself with)* faire de la lèche à qn; *(become emotionally involved with)* se lier avec qn□; *(have sex with)* coucher avec qn

nibs [nɪbz] *n Br* **his/her nibs** son altesse, cézigue

nice [naɪs] *adj Br* **nice one!** bravo!

The symbol □ indicates that a translation is neutral.

▸ *voir aussi* **earner**

nick [nɪk] *Br* **1** *n* **(a)** *(police station)* poste *m*; *(prison)* bloc *m* **(b)** *(condition)* condition[□] *f*, état[□] *m*; **in good/bad nick** en bon/mauvais état[□]
2 *vt* **(a)** *(arrest)* agrafer, alpaguer; **he got nicked for stealing a car** il s'est fait arrêter pour vol de voiture[□] **(b)** *(steal)* piquer, faucher

nickel ['nɪkəl] *n Am* **(a)** *(five cents)* **it's not worth a plugged nickel** ça vaut pas un clou **(b)** *(five dollars)* cinq dollars[□] *mpl*; **to buy a nickel of weed** acheter pour cinq dollars d'herbe

nicker ['nɪkə(r)] *n Br (pounds sterling)* livres *fpl* sterling[□]

niff [nɪf] *Br* **1** *n* puanteur[□] *f*
2 *vi* refouler, schlinguer, fouetter

niffy ['nɪfɪ] *adj Br* qui fouette *ou* refoule

nifty ['nɪftɪ] *adj* **(a)** *(clever) (solution, idea)* astucieux[□]; *(person)* adroit[□], débrouillard; **a nifty little gadget** un petit gadget très astucieux; **a nifty piece of work** du bon travail **(b)** *(quick)* rapide[□]; *(agile)* agile[□] **(c)** *Am (stylish)* chouette, classe; **they've got a nifty house** ils ont une chouette baraque; **that's a nifty sweater** il est chouette, ce pull

nigga ['nɪgə] *n Noir Am* = **nigger**

ⓘ Lorsqu'il est utilisé par des Noirs américains, le terme "nigga" perd son caractère injurieux et acquiert une connotation positive.

nigger ['nɪgə(r)] *n Injurieux* nègre (négresse) *m,f*

ⓘ Lorsqu'il est utilisé par des Noirs américains, le terme "nigger" perd son caractère injurieux et acquiert une connotation positive.

nimrod ['nɪmrɒd] *n Am (fool)* crétin(e) *m,f*, andouille *f*

Nip [nɪp] *n Injurieux* Jap *mf*

nip and tuck [nɪpən'tʌk] *n* **to have a nip and tuck** se faire faire de la chirurgie esthétique[□]

nipper ['nɪpə(r)] *n Br* môme *m*, gosse *m*

nippy ['nɪpɪ] *adj* **(a)** *(weather)* **it's nippy** ça pince, il fait frisquet **(b)** *Br (car)* maniable[□]

nit [nɪt], **nitwit** ['nɪtwɪt] *n Br* andouille *f*, courge *f*

nob [nɒb] *n Br (rich person)* rupin(e) *m,f*, richard(e) *m,f*

no-brainer [nəʊ'breɪnə(r)] *n* **(a)** *Am (stupid person)* crétin(e) *m,f* **(b)** *(obvious thing)* **if you eat less and exercise more, you'll lose weight, it's a no-brainer!** si tu manges moins et que tu fais plus d'exercice, tu maigriras, c'est quand même pas compliqué!

noddle ['nɒdəl] *n Br (head)* caboche *f*, cafetière *f*, ciboulot *m*; **use your noddle!** fais marcher ton ciboulot *ou* tes méninges!

noggin ['nɒgɪn] *n (head)* caboche *f*, cafetière *f*, ciboulot *m*

noise [nɔɪz] *n Br* **shut your noise!** la ferme!, boucle-la!

noise up *vt sép Scot* **to noise sb up** *(tease)* faire enrager qn, taquiner qn; *(annoy)* foutre qn en rogne

no-mark ['nəʊmɑːk] *n (pathetic person) (male)* nul *m*, pauvre type *m*; *(female)* nulle *f*

nonce [nɒns] *n Br (sex offender)* délinquant *m* sexuel[□] *(s'attaquant particulièrement aux enfants)*

no-no ['nəʊnəʊ] *n* **it's a no-no** ça ne se fait pas[□]; **asking him for more money is a definite no-no** il est hors de question de lui demander plus d'argent□

noodle ['nu:dəl] n (head) caboche f, cafetière f, ciboulot m

nookie, nooky ['nʊkɪ] n partie f de jambes en l'air; **to have a bit of nookie** faire une partie de jambes en l'air

nope [nəʊp] adv non□, nan

Norah ['nɔːrə] npr Br **flaming Norah!**, punaise!, purée!; **bloody Norah! [!]** putain!

nork [!] [nɔːk] n Br & Austr (breast) nichon m

north and south ['nɔːθən'saʊθ] n Br (rhyming slang **mouth**) bouche□ f, clapet m

nose [nəʊz] n **to have a nose job** se faire refaire le nez□; Br **to get up sb's nose** taper sur les nerfs à qn; **to keep one's nose clean** se tenir à carreau; **to pay through the nose (for sth)** payer le prix fort (pour qch); **nose candy** (cocaine) coco f, neige f

nose-rag ['nəʊzræg] n tire-jus m

nosey parker [nəʊzɪ'pɑːkə(r)] n Br fouine f

nosh [nɒʃ] **1** n bouffe f
2 vi bouffer

nosh-up ['nɒʃʌp] n Br gueuleton m

not [nɒt] adv **it was a great party…not!** c'était pas vraiment génial comme soirée!; **he's really gorgeous…not!** c'est pas exactement un Apollon!

ⓘ Cette structure a été rendue célèbre par le film comique américain Wayne's World, l'histoire de deux adolescents prolongés. Ce film est à l'origine d'expressions désormais couramment utilisées par de nombreux jeunes, aussi bien en Grande-Bretagne qu'aux États-Unis.

nothing doing ['nʌθɪŋ'duːɪŋ] exclam Br pas question!

nowt [naʊt] pron Br (nothing) rien□, que dalle

nuddy ['nʌdɪ] n Br Hum **in the nuddy** (naked) à poil

nudge nudge wink wink [nʌdʒ-'nʌdʒwɪŋk'wɪŋk] exclam Br vous voyez ce que je veux dire!

ⓘ Cette expression fut popularisée par l'émission de télévision Monty Python's Flying Circus au cours des années 70. On l'emploie pour indiquer à son interlocuteur que ce que l'on dit comporte des sous-entendus, souvent de nature grivoise.

nuke [njuːk] vt (**a**) (attack with nuclear weapons) atomiser□ (**b**) (cook in microwave) faire cuire au four à micro-ondes□ (**c**) (defeat) ratatiner, battre à plates coutures

number ['nʌmbə(r)] n (**a**) (cannabis cigarette) joint m (**b**) **to do a number one/two** (urinate/defecate) faire la petite/grosse commission (**c**) **I've got your number!** j'ai repéré ton manège! (**d**) **to look out for** or **to take care of number one** penser d'abord à soi□ (**e**) Am **to do a number on sth** (spoil, ruin) bousiller qch

numbnuts ['nʌmnʌts] n Hum (idiot) andouille f, crétin(e) m,f, nouille f; **you've gone the wrong way, numbnuts!** tu t'es trompé de route, andouille!

numbskull ['nʌmskʌl] n crétin(e) m,f, andouille f, cruche f

numero uno ['nuːmərəʊ'uːnəʊ] n & adj Am numéro un; **don't forget who's numero uno round here** n'oublie pas qui commande ou qui est le patron ici; **he's the numero uno coke dealer** c'est le principal dealer de coke

numpty ['nʌmptɪ] *n* Scot (*idiot*) crétin(e) *m,f*, cruche *f*, andouille *f*

nut [nʌt] **1** *n* (**a**) (*head*) caboche *f*, cafetière *f*, ciboulot *m*; **to be off one's nut** (*mad*) être dingue *ou* cinglé; **to go off one's nut** (*go mad*) perdre la boule, devenir cinglé; (*get angry*) péter les plombs, péter une durite, piquer une crise; *Br* **to do one's nut** (*get angry*) péter les plombs, péter une durite, piquer une crise (**b**) (*person*) cinglé(e) *m,f*, dingue *mf*; **a football/computer nut** un fana de football/d'informatique; **nut job** cinglé(e) *m,f*, dingue *mf* (**c**) **he can't drive/sing for nuts** il conduit/ chante comme un pied (**d**) **nuts [!]** (*testicles*) boules *fpl*, couilles *fpl*

2 *vt* (*headbutt*) donner un coup de boule à ▸ *voir aussi* **mutt**

nutball ['nʌtbɔːl] *n Am* cinglé(e) *m,f*, dingue *mf*

nutcase ['nʌtkeɪs] *n* cinglé(e) *m,f*, dingue *mf*

nuthouse ['nʌthaʊs] *n* maison *f* de fous

nuts [nʌts] **1** *adj* (*mad*) dingue, cinglé, timbré; **to go nuts** (*go mad*) devenir cinglé, perdre la boule; (*get angry*) péter les plombs, péter une durite; **to drive sb nuts** rendre qn chèvre; **to be nuts about sb/sth** être dingue de qn/qch

2 *exclam* mince!, zut!; **nuts to that!** plutôt crever!

nutso ['nʌtsəʊ] *Am adj* dingue, cinglé, timbré; **to go nutso** (*go mad*) devenir cinglé, perdre la boule; (*get angry*) péter les plombs, péter une durite; **to drive sb nutso** rendre qn chèvre; **to be nutso about sb/sth** être dingue de qn/qch

nutter ['nʌtə(r)] *n Br* cinglé(e) *m,f*, dingue *m,f*

nutty ['nʌtɪ] *adj* (*mad*) dingue, cinglé, timbré; *Hum* **as nutty as a fruitcake** complètement ravagé

nympho ['nɪmfəʊ] *n* (*abrév* **nymphomaniac**) nympho *f*

Oo

-o [əʊ] *suffixe* **sicko** malade *mf*, tordu(e) *m,f*; **thicko** nouille *f*, andouille *f*; **pinko** gaucho *mf*

ⓘ Le suffixe "-o" s'utilise pour construire un nom à partir d'un adjectif. Il s'agit d'un procédé générateur en anglais.

oar [ɔː(r)] *n Br* **to stick one's oar in** ramener sa fraise

oats [əʊts] *npl* **(a)** **to sow one's (wild) oats** jeter sa gourme; *Br* **to get one's oats** tirer un coup **(b)** *Am* **to feel one's oats** *(feel full of energy)* être en pleine forme□; *(be self-important)* faire l'important□

ocker ['ɒkə(r)] *Austr* **1** *n (boor)* beauf *m*
2 *adj* beauf

OD [əʊ'diː] *(abrév* **overdose**) **1** *n* overdose *f*
2 *vi* faire une overdose *(on* de); **I've OD'd on pizzas/soap operas lately** j'ai tellement mangé de pizza/ regardé de feuilletons télé ces derniers temps que j'en suis dégoûté

oddball ['ɒdbɔːl] **1** *n* allumé(e) *m,f*, farfelu(e) *m,f*
2 *adj* loufoque, farfelu

odds [ɒdz] *npl Br (difference)* **it makes no odds** ça change rien; **it makes no odds what I say** ce que je dis ne sert à rien□; **what's the odds?** qu'est-ce que ça peut faire?

ofay [əʊ'feɪ] *n Am Injurieux* sale Blanc (Blanche) *m,f*

off [ɒf] **1** *adj Br (unacceptable)* **that was a bit off** c'est un peu fort de café
2 *vt Am (kill)* buter, refroidir, zigouiller

offie ['ɒfɪ] *n Br (abrév* **off-licence**) magasin *m* de vins et spiritueux□

off-the-wall ['ɒfðə'wɔːl] *adj* bizarroïde

oi [ɔɪ] *exclam* hé!

oik [ɔɪk] *n Br* plouc *mf*

oiled [ɔɪld] *adj* **(well) oiled** *(drunk)* bourré, beurré, pété

OJ ['əʊdʒeɪ] *n Am (abrév* **orange juice**) jus *m* d'orange□

okey-dokey ['əʊkɪ'dəʊkɪ], **okey-doke** ['əʊkɪ'dəʊk] *exclam* OK, d'accord, dac

old [əʊld] **1** *adj* **old lady** *(wife)* bourgeoise *f*; *(mother)* vieille *f*; *Br* **old dear** *(elderly woman)* grand-mère□ *f*; *(mother)* vieille *f*; *Br* **old lag** truand *m*; **old fella, old man** *(husband)* Jules *m*; *(father)* vieux *m*; *(penis)* zob *m*; **old woman** *(wife)* bourgeoise *f*; *(mother)* vieille *f*; *(timid, fussy man)* chochotte *f*
2 *npl* **olds** parents□ *mpl*

oldie ['əʊldɪ] *n (person)* vieux (vieille) *m,f*; **(golden) oldie** *(song)* vieux succès□ *m*; *(film)* classique *m* du cinéma populaire□

on [ɒn] **1** *adj* (**a**) *Br* **it's not on!** *(un-acceptable)* ça va pas du tout! (**b**) **fancy a pint? – you're on!** tu bois une bière? – je veux!; **if you wash the dishes, I'll dry them – you're on!** si tu fais la vaisselle, je l'essuie – ça marche! (**c**) *Br* **to be on** *(men-struating)* avoir ses ragnagnas

2 *adv Br* **to be** *or* **go on about sth** jacter de qch sans arrêt; **what's she (going) on about now?** qu'est-ce qu'elle raconte maintenant?

3 *prép* **what's he on?** il se sent bien? ▸ *voir aussi* **come on**

one [wʌn] *n* (**a**) **to give sb one** [!] *(have sex with)* en glisser une paire à qn (**b**) **to have had one too many** avoir bu un coup de trop (**c**) *(blow)* **to belt/thump sb one** en coller une à qn (**d**) *Br (person)* **you are a one!** toi alors!; **he's a right one, him!** lui alors, il est impayable! ▸ *voir aussi* **go into, lay, nice**

one-eyed trouser snake ['wʌnaɪd-'traʊzəsneɪk] *n Hum* anguille *f* de caleçon

one-night stand [wʌnnaɪt'stænd] *n* aventure *f* sans lendemain□

oodles ['uːdəlz] *npl* **oodles of** un max de, des masses de; **to have oodles of money** avoir un max de fric, être plein aux as; **to have oodles of time** avoir vachement de temps

oomph [ʊmf] *n* (**a**) *(sex appeal)* sex-appeal□ *m*; **she's got plenty of oomph** elle est vachement sexy (**b**) *(vigour)* punch *m*, pêche *f*; **their new album lacks the oomph of the last one** leur nouvel album n'a pas la pêche du précédent; **I use mousse to give my hair a bit of oomph** j'utilise de la mousse pour donner un peu de volume à mes cheveux□

oreo (cookie) ['ɔːriəʊ('kʊki)] *n Am*

Péj (person) = personne de couleur qui adopte les valeurs des Blancs

ⓘ Un "Oreo® cookie" est un type de biscuit au chocolat fourré à la crème : noir à l'extérieur mais blanc à l'intérieur.

orgasmic [ɔː'gæzmɪk] *adj (food, smell, taste)* jouissif

Oscar ['ɒskə(r)] *n Austr (rhyming slang* **Oscar Asche = cash)** pognon *m*, fric *m*

ⓘ Oscar Asche était un acteur et metteur en scène de théâtre australien du début du XXème siècle.

OTT [əʊtiː'tiː] *adj Br (abrév* **over the top)** **the house is nice, but the decor's a bit OTT** la maison est bien, mais la décoration est un peu lourdingue; **it's a bit OTT to call him a fascist** c'est un peu exagéré de le traiter de fasciste; **he went completely OTT when he heard what she'd said** il a pété les plombs quand il a appris ce qu'elle avait dit

out [aʊt] **1** *adj* (**a**) *(not in fashion)* démodé□ (**b**) *(openly homosexual)* ouvertement homosexuel□

2 *adv* (**a**) **to be out of it** *(drunk, on drugs)* être raide; **I felt a bit out of it** *(excluded)* je me sentais un peu de trop (**b**) **out of order** *(unacceptable)* inacceptable□; **that was a bit out of order!** c'est un peu fort de café!; **you were out of order to call her a slut** t'aurais pas dû la traiter de salope (**c**) **I'm out of here** je me casse; **let's get out of here** allez, on se casse (**d**) **out there** loufoque; **listen to him, he's completely out there!** écoute-le, il divague complètement!

3 *vt (homosexual)* dévoiler l'homosexualité de□

outdoorsy [aʊt'dɔːzɪ] *adj (activities)* de plein air; *(person)* qui aime le grand air□, qui aime être dehors□

outta ['aʊtə] *contraction (abrév* **out of)** **let's get outta here!** allez, on se casse!; **you must be outta your mind!** mais t'es complètement dingue!; *Am* **outta sight** *(excellent)* dingue, dément

owt [aʊt] *pron Br (anything)* quelque chose□; **he never said owt** il n'a jamais rien dit□; **is there owt the matter?** il y a quelque chose qui va pas?

Oz [ɒz] *npr (abrév* **Australia)** Australie□ *f*

Ozzie ['ɒzɪ] *(abrév* **Australian) 1** *adj* australien□
2 *n* Australien(enne)□ *m,f*

Pp

pack [pæk] **1** *vt* **to pack a gun** être armé◻, être chargé

2 *vi* **to send sb packing** envoyer qn balader ▸ *voir aussi* **fanny**, **heat**

pack in *vt sép* **to pack sb/sth in** plaquer *ou* laisser tomber qn/qch; **pack it in!** ça suffit!

pack up *vi Br* (**a**) *(stop work)* dételer (**b**) *(break down)* tomber en panne◻; **the telly packed up just as Beckham was about to score** la télé m'a/nous a lâché(s) juste au moment où Beckham allait marquer

package ['pækɪdʒ] *n Br (man's genitals)* service *m* trois pièces

packet ['pækɪt] *n Br* (**a**) *(large amount of money)* **to cost a packet** coûter bonbon; **to earn a packet** gagner des mille et des cents (**b**) *(man's genitals)* service *m* trois pièces

pad [pæd] *n (home)* casbah *f*; **you can crash at my pad** tu peux pieuter chez moi

Paddy ['pædɪ] *npr Injurieux (Irishman)* Irlandais◻ *m*

ⓘ "Paddy" est le diminutif de "Patrick", l'un des prénoms les plus courants en Irlande. Bien que ce terme ne témoigne pas nécessairement d'une attitude xénophobe de la part de celui qui l'utilise, il est préférable de ne pas l'employer.

paddy ['pædɪ] *n* (**a**) *Br* **to be in a paddy** *(angry)* être en rogne (**b**) *Am* **paddy wagon** *(police van)* panier *m* à salade

pain [peɪn] *n* **to be a pain (in the neck)** être casse-pieds; *Am* **to give sb a pain (in the neck)** taper sur le système à qn; **to be a pain in the** *Br* **arse** *or Am* **ass [!]** être casse-couilles *ou* chiant; **it's a real pain in the** *Br* **arse** *or Am* **ass having to get up so early [!]** ça fait vraiment chier de devoir se lever si tôt

Paki ['pækɪ] *n Br Injurieux (abrév* **Pakistani**) *(person)* Pakistanais(e)◻ *m,f*; **Paki shop, Paki's** = épicerie de quartier tenue par un Pakistanais

ⓘ Lorsqu'il est question d'une épicerie de quartier tenue par un Pakistanais, le terme "Paki" perd sa connotation raciste. Il est toutefois déconseillé de l'utiliser.

Paki-basher ['pækɪbæʃə(r)] *n Br* = individu qui attaque des gens d'origine pakistanaise

Paki-bashing ['pækɪbæʃɪŋ] *n Br* = violences à l'encontre d'immigrés pakistanais

pal [pæl] *n* (**a**) *(friend)* pote *m* (**b**) *(term of address)* **thanks, pal** *(to friend)* merci, vieux; *(to stranger)* merci, chef; **watch where you're going, pal** hé, regarde où tu vas!

pal around vi **to pal around with sb** être pote avec qn; **they palled around for a while at high school** il y a un moment où ils étaient potes au lycée

pal up vi devenir copains; **to pal up with sb** devenir copain avec qn

palaver [pə'lɑːvə(r)] n Br (fuss) **what a palaver!** quelle histoire!; **it was a real palaver getting a work permit** ça a été la croix et la bannière pour obtenir un permis de travail; **we had the usual palaver about who was going to pay** ça a été le cirque habituel pour décider qui allait payer

pally ['pælɪ] adj Br **to be pally with sb** être pote avec qn; **they're very pally all of a sudden** ils sont très potes tout d'un coup

palooka [pə'luːkə] n Am (a) (clumsy man) manche m; (stupid man) andouille f, crétin m (b) (inept fighter) mauvais boxeur▢ m

palsy-walsy ['pælzɪ'wælzɪ] adj **to be palsy-walsy with sb** être comme cul et chemise avec qn, être à tu et à toi avec qn; **they're very palsy-walsy all of a sudden** ils sont très potes ou copain-copain tout d'un coup

pan [pæn] **1** n Br **to go down the pan** être foutu en l'air; **that's our holidays down the pan** on peut faire une croix sur nos vacances
2 vt (criticize) éreinter

panic ['pænɪk] n **it was panic stations!** ça a été la panique générale!; Am **to hit the panic button** paniquer, flipper

pansy ['pænzɪ] n (effeminate man) chochotte f; (homosexual man) tante f

pants [pænts] **1** npl (a) **to beat the pants off sb** battre qn à plates cou-

tures; **to scare the pants off sb** foutre une trouille pas possible à qn; **to bore the pants off sb** ennuyer qn à mourir; **he charmed the pants off my parents** il a conquis mes parents▢ (b) **to be caught with one's pants down** être pris sur le fait en train de faire une bêtise

2 n Br (nonsense) foutaises fpl; **don't listen to him, he's talking pants** ne l'écoute pas, il raconte n'importe quoi; **that TV programme's a load** or **a pile of pants!** c'est n'importe quoi, cette émission de télé; **that's pants!** n'importe quoi!

3 adj Br (of poor quality) nul; **that movie was absolute pants!** ce film était particulièrement nul!

4 exclam Br zut! ▸ voir aussi **fancy, pee**

pap [pæp] **1** n (abrév **paparazzi**) **the paps have been camped outside her house all weekend waiting for a picture** les paparazzi ont campé devant sa maison tout le week-end dans l'espoir de pouvoir faire une photo▢

2 vt **he was papped falling out of a London nightclub** des paparazzi l'ont pris en photo alors qu'il sortait d'une boîte de nuit de Londres, complètement bourré

papers ['peɪpəz] npl Am **go peddle your papers!** va voir ailleurs si j'y suis!

paralytic [pærə'lɪtɪk] adj Br (very drunk) pété à mort, bourré comme un coing, rond comme une queue de pelle

pard [pɑːd] n Am mon vieux, mon pote; **hey, pard!** salut, vieux!

ⓘ Il s'agit de l'abréviation du terme "pardner", mot qui imite la prononciation américaine de "partner".

The symbol ▢ *indicates that a translation is neutral.*

park [pɑːk] vt **to park oneself be-side sb/on sth** se poser ou poser ses fesses à côté de qn/sur qch; **park your** Br **bum** or Am **butt over here beside me!** pose-toi ici, à côté de moi! ▸ voir aussi **walk**

parky ['pɑːkɪ] adj Br frisquet; **it's parky today** il fait frisquet aujourd'hui

parp [pɑːp] vi Br péter

party ['pɑːtɪ] **1** n **party animal** fêtard(e) m,f; **party hat** (condom) capote f
2 vi faire la fête

party-pooper ['pɑːtɪpuːpə(r)] n rabat-joie mf

pash [pæʃ] Br & Austr **1** n **to have a pash** se bécoter, se rouler des pelles ou des patins; Hum **I don't even know his name, it was just a pash and dash** je sais même pas comment il s'appelle, je lui ai roulé quelques pelles et puis terminé; Hum **pash rash** = rougeurs sur le visage, provoquées par les baisers d'un homme à la barbe rêche
2 vt bécoter, rouler des pelles ou des patins à
3 vi se bécoter, se rouler des pelles ou des patins

ⓘ Le terme "pash" est l'abréviation de "passion".

---

pass [pɑːs] n **to make a pass at sb** faire du plat à qn

past [pɑːst] prép Br **to be past it** (of person) avoir passé l'âge; (of thing) avoir fait son temps

paste [peɪst] vt (beat up) tabasser; (defeat) battre à plates coutures; **to get pasted** (beaten up) se faire tabasser; (defeated) être battu à plates coutures

pasting ['peɪstɪŋ] n **to give sb a**

pasting (beat up) tabasser qn; (defeat) battre qn à plates coutures; **to** Br **get** or Am **take a pasting** (be beaten up) se faire tabasser; (be defeated) être battu à plates coutures

patch [pætʃ] n Br (of prostitute, salesperson, police officer) territoire m

patsy ['pætsɪ] n Am pigeon m

paw [pɔː] **1** n (hand) pogne m, patte f; Br **paws off!**, Am **keep your (big) paws off!** bas les pattes!
2 vt (touch sexually) peloter

payoff ['peɪɒf] n (bribe) pot-de-vin m

PDA [piːdiːˈeɪ] n (abrév **public display of affection**) séance f de bécotage; **gross, there's a major PDA going on at the back of the bus** beurk, il y en a qui se bécotent à qui mieux mieux à l'arrière du bus

pdq [piːdiːˈkjuː] adv (abrév **pretty damn quick**) illico presto

peach [piːtʃ] n **she's a peach** elle est canon; **a peach of a goal/dress** un but/une robe magnifique□

peachy (keen) ['piːtʃɪ('kiːn)] adj Am super, génial, grand

peanuts ['piːnʌts] npl (small amount of money) cacahuètes fpl

pearl necklace [!!] [pɜːlˈneklɪs] n collier m de perles

pear-shaped ['peəʃeɪpt] adj Br **to go pear-shaped** partir en eau de boudin; **when the neighbours called the police it all began to go pear-shaped** quand les voisins ont appelé la police tout est parti en eau de boudin

pecker ['pekə(r)] n (a) [!] Am (penis) bite f, queue f (b) Br **to keep one's pecker up** ne pas se laisser abattre□

peckerwood ['pekəwʊd] n (a) Noir Am Péj Blanc (Blanche) m,f (b) Am plouc mf

---

pecs [peks] *npl* pectoraux□ *mpl*; **he's got great pecs!** il a des super pectoraux!

pee [!] [piː] **1** *n* pipi *m*; **to have a pee** faire pipi; **to go for a pee** aller faire pipi

2 *vt* **to pee oneself** *or Br* **one's pants** faire pipi dans sa culotte; **to pee oneself (laughing)** rire à en faire dans sa culotte

3 *vi* faire pipi; **it's peeing (it) down** *(raining)* il pleut comme vache qui pisse

pee off [!] *vt sép (annoy)* **to pee sb off** faire chier qn; **to be peed off** être fumasse ou furibard; **to be peed off at sb/about sth** être en pétard contre qn/à cause de qch; **to be peed off with sb/sth** *(have had enough of)* en avoir ras le bol de qn/qch

peeler ['piːlə(r)] *n Br (policeman)* flic *m*

peepers ['piːpəz] *npl* mirettes *fpl*

peeps [piːps] *npl (abrév* **people)** **my peeps** ma bande

peg out [peg] *vi (die)* passer l'arme à gauche, calancher

pen [pen] *n* **(a)** *Am (abrév* **penitentiary)** taule *f*; **in the pen** en taule, en cabane **(b)** *Br (abrév* **penalty)** péno *m*

pen-and-ink [penən'ɪŋk] *n Br (rhyming slang* **stink)** puanteur□ *f*

penguin suit ['pengwɪnsuːt] *n Br* costard *m* chic

penny ['penɪ] *n Br* **to spend a penny** *(urinate)* faire la petite commission

permatan ['pɜːmətæn] *n Hum* bronzage *m* permanent□

perp [pɜːp] *n Am (abrév* **perpetrator)** criminel(elle)□ *m,f*

perv [pɜːv] *Br & Austr* **1** *n (abrév* **per-**

vert) pervers(e)□ *m,f,* détraqué(e) *m,f*; **stop staring at me, you dirty perv!** arrête de me fixer comme ça, espèce de détraqué!

2 *vi* reluquer les nanas/les mecs; **you've got a girlfriend, stop perving!** arrête de reluquer les nanas, rappelle-toi que t'as une copine!

perv over *vt insep* reluquer, mater; **there were all these dirty old men perving over us in the club** il y avait plein de vieux porcs en boîte qui nous mataient grave

pervy ['pɜːvɪ] *adj Br* pervers

pet [pet] *n Br (term of address)* chéri(e) *m,f*; **be a pet and let the cat out, would you?** laisse sortir le chat, tu seras gentil

Pete [piːt] *npr* **for Pete's sake!** bon sang!; *Br* **to go Pete Tong** *(rhyming slang* **wrong)** partir en eau de boudin, se gâter; **it all went a bit Pete Tong when her ex turned up at the party** les choses se sont gâtées quand son ex s'est pointé à la fête

ⓘ Pete Tong est le nom d'un DJ très populaire en Grande-Bretagne.

peter ['piːtə(r)] *n Am (penis)* quéquette *f,* zizi *m*

petrolhead ['petrəlhed] *n Br* dingue *m* de bagnoles

pew [pjuː] *n Br* **take** *or* **have a pew!** *(sit down)* pose-toi quelque part!

phat [fæt] *adj Noir Am* super, génial; **we got some phat tunes for you tonight** on va vous passer de la super musique ce soir

phwoah [fwɔː], **phwoar(gh)** [fwɔː(r)] *exclam Br* wouaouh!; **phwoah! that bird's got some rack on her!** wouaouh! elle a des sacrés nichons, la nana!

The symbol □ indicates that a translation is neutral.

pic [pɪk] *n* (*abrév* **picture**) (*photograph*) photo□ *f*; (*picture*) illustration□ *f*; (*film*) film□ *m*

piccy ['pɪkɪ] *n* (*abrév* **picture**) (*photograph*) photo□ *f*

pick up [pɪk] *vt sép* **to pick sb up** (*sexual partner*) lever qn; (*criminal*) agrafer qn, coffrer qn

pickled ['pɪkəld] *adj* (*drunk*) bourré, pété, beurré

pick-up *adj Am* **pick up joint** lieu *m* de drague; **pick-up line** = formule d'entrée en matière pour commencer à draguer quelqu'un; **"are you a model?"! what a lame pick-up line!** "t'es mannequin?"! c'est vraiment une réplique à deux balles!

picnic ['pɪknɪk] *n* **it was no picnic!** c'était pas de la tarte! ▸ *voir aussi* **sandwich**

picture ['pɪktʃə(r)] *n* (*film*) film□ *m*; *Br* **the pictures** (*the cinema*) le cinoche, le ciné

piddle ['pɪdəl] **1** *n* pipi *m*; **to have a piddle** faire pipi; **to go for a piddle** aller faire pipi
2 *vi* faire pipi

piddling ['pɪdəlɪŋ] *adj* (*details*) insignifiant□; (*amount*) minable

piece [piːs] *n* (**a**) **a piece of cake**, *Br* **a piece of piss [!]** un jeu d'enfant (**b**) *Am* (*gun*) flingue *m*

pie-eyed [paɪ'aɪd] *adj* rond, bourré

pig [pɪg] **1** *n* (**a**) (*greedy person*) goinfre *mf*; **to make a pig of oneself** se goinfrer (**b**) (*ugly person*) mocheté *f*; (*unpleasant person*) chameau *m*; **he's a real pig to her** il est vraiment salaud avec elle (**c**) *Br* (*thing*) truc *m* chiant; **cleaning the oven is a pig of a job** c'est vraiment chiant de nettoyer le four; **the desk was a pig to move** le bureau était vachement chiant à déménager (**d**) (*police officer*) flic *m*,

poulet *m*; **the pigs** les flics *mpl*, les poulets *mpl* (**e**) *Br* **to make a pig's ear of sth** foirer qch; **he made a real pig's ear of laying the carpet** il a posé la moquette comme un vrai sagouin
2 *vt Br* **to pig oneself (on)** se goinfrer (de) ▸ *voir aussi* **happy**

pig out *vi* se goinfrer (**on** de)

pigeon ['pɪdʒɪn] *n Am* (*person*) pigeon *m*, poire *f* ▸ *voir aussi* **stool**

pig-thick ['pɪgˈθɪk] *adj Br* con comme un balai

pig-ugly ['pɪgˈʌglɪ] *adj Br* moche comme un pou

pikey ['paɪkɪ] **1** *n* (**a**) (*yob*) lascar *m*, racaille *f* (**b**) (*gypsy*) romano *m*
2 *adj* de seconde zone; **she must have got those trainers in some pikey shop** elle a probablement acheté ces tennis dans une boutique de seconde zone; **there were all these really pikey kids hanging around** il y avait plein de gamins qui faisaient mauvais genre qui traînaient

pilled-up [pɪld'ʌp] *adj* **to be pilled-up** (*on ecstasy*) être sous ecsta; (*on amphetamines*) être sous amphés

pillhead ['pɪlhed] *n* = personne qui consomme régulièrement des tranquillisants, des speeds ou de l'ecstasy

pillock ['pɪlək] *n Br* andouille *f*, courge *f*

pillow-biter ['pɪləʊbaɪtə(r)] *n Injurieux* pédé *m*, tantouze *f*

pill-popper ['pɪlpɒpə(r)] *n* accro *mf* aux tranquillisants ou aux speeds

pimp [pɪmp] **1** *n* (**a**) (*of prostitute*) maquereau *m* (**b**) *Noir Am* étalon *m* (*homme*)
2 *vt* **to pimp sth (up)** modifier qch pour le rendre plus cool; **he spends**

all his time pimping (up) his ride
il passe son temps à customiser sa
bagnole et à gonfler le moteur

pinch [pɪntʃ] *vt* (**a**) *(steal)* piquer; **to
pinch sth from sb** piquer qch à qn
(**b**) *(arrest)* pincer, alpaguer

pinhead ['pɪnhed] *n* crétin(e) *m,f*, andouille *f*, courge *f*

pinko ['pɪŋkəʊ] **1** *n* gaucho *mf*
2 *adj* gaucho

pins [pɪnz] *npl (legs)* cannes *fpl*, gambettes *fpl*; **she's got a great pair of
pins** elle a des super gambettes

pint-sized ['paɪntsaɪzd] *adj Hum*
tout(e) petit(e)◘, minuscule◘

pish [pɪʃ] *Scot* = **piss**

pished [pɪʃt] *Scot* = **pissed**

piss [!] [pɪs] **1** *n* (**a**) *(urine)* pisse *f*; **to
Br have** *or Am* **take a piss** pisser;
to go for a piss aller pisser; *Br* **piss
flaps** [!!] grandes lèvres◘ *fpl*, esca-
lopes *fpl*; *Am* **to be full of piss and
vinegar** avoir la pêche
(**b**) *Br* **to take the piss out of sb/sth**
se foutre de qn/qch; **are you taking
the piss?** tu te fous de moi?; **to rip
the piss out of sb/sth** se foutre de
qn/qch sans y aller de main morte
(**c**) *Br* **to be on the piss** se péter, se
bourrer la gueule, prendre une cuite;
to go on the piss aller se bourrer la
gueule, aller prendre une cuite
(**d**) *Br (worthless things)* **the film/
book was piss** le film/le bouquin ne
valait pas un clou; **their beer is piss**
leur bière, c'est du pipi de chat
2 *vt* **to piss oneself** se pisser dessus; **to piss oneself (laughing)** rire
à en pisser dans sa culotte
3 *vi* (**a**) *(urinate)* pisser; **it's pissing down, it's pissing with rain** il
pleut comme vache qui pisse (**b**) **to
piss all over sb** *(defeat)* battre qn
à plates coutures (**c**) **to piss sth up
the wall** *(winnings, inheritance, life)*

gaspiller qch◘ (**d**) *Am* **to piss and
moan** geindre, pleurnicher
4 *adv* **piss poor** merdique; *Br* **piss
easy** fastoche ▸ *voir aussi* **gnat,
piece, pot, streak**

piss about [!], **piss around** [!] **1**
vt sép Br **to piss sb about** *or* **around**
(cause problems for) se foutre de la
gueule de qn; *(waste time of)* faire
perdre son temps à qn◘
2 *vi (waste time)* glander, glandouiller

piss away [!] *vt sép* **to piss sth
away** *(winnings, inheritance, life)*
gaspiller qch◘

piss off [!] **1** *vt sép (annoy)* **to piss
sb off** faire chier qn; **to be pissed
off** être fumasse; **to be pissed off
at sb/about sth** être en pétard contre qn/à cause de qch; **to be pissed
off with sb/sth** *(have had enough
of)* en avoir ras le bol de qn/qch
2 *vi (go away)* se casser, se tirer;
piss off! *(go away)* fous le camp!,
tire-toi!, dégage!; *(expressing contempt, disagreement)* va te faire
foutre!

piss-artist [!] ['pɪsɑːtɪst] *n Br* poi-
vrot(e) *m,f*, alcolo *mf*

pissbucket [!] ['pɪsbʌkɪt] *n* (**a**) *(toilet)* chiottes *fpl* (**b**) *(person)* ordure *f*,
raclure *f*

pissed [!] [pɪst] *adj* (**a**) *Br (drunk)*
pété, bourré; **to get pissed** se péter
la gueule; **as pissed as a fart** *or* **a
newt, pissed out of one's head**
bourré comme un coing, plein comme une barrique, rond comme une
queue de pelle (**b**) *Am (annoyed)*
to be pissed être fumasse; **to be
pissed at sb/about sth** être en pétard contre qn/à cause de qch; **to
be pissed with sb/sth** *(have had
enough of)* en avoir ras le bol de
qn/qch

pissed-up [!] ['pɪst'ʌp] *adj Br (drunk)* bourré, pété, beurré

pisser [!] ['pɪsə(r)] *n* **(a)** *(annoying situation)* **what a pisser!** quelle merde!; **it was a real pisser that the weather wasn't better** c'était vraiment chiant qu'il fasse pas plus beau **(b)** *Am (remarkable situation)* **what a pisser!** c'est génial *ou* super! **(c)** *Am (annoying person)* emmerdeur(euse) *m,f*; *(remarkable person)* **to be a pisser** être un mec/une nana génial(e)

pisshead [!] ['pɪshed] *n* **(a)** *Br (drunkard)* poivrot(e) *m,f*, alcolo *mf* **(b)** *Am (unpleasant person)* connard (connasse) *m,f*

pisshole [!] ['pɪshəʊl] *n* **his eyes are like pissholes in the snow** il a des petits yeux

piss-take [!] ['pɪsteɪk] *n Br* satire□ *f*; **the sketch is a piss-take of "Lord of the Rings"** le sketch est une satire du "Seigneur des anneaux"; **this is a piss-take, isn't it?** non mais tu te fous de ma gueule ou quoi?

piss-up [!] ['pɪsʌp] *n Br* beuverie *f*; **to have a piss-up** prendre une cuite, se bourrer la gueule; **to go on a piss-up** aller prendre une cuite *ou* se bourrer la gueule; *Hum* **he couldn't organize a piss-up in a brewery** c'est un incompétent de première

pit [pɪt] *n* **(a)** *(untidy place)* foutoir *m* **(b)** *Br (bed)* plumard *m*, pieu *m* **(c)** **to be the pits** être complètement nul

pixilated ['pɪksɪleɪtəd] *adj Br* bourré, pété, beurré

pizza-face ['piːtsəfeɪs] *n Hum* calculette *f*

PJs ['piːdʒeɪz] *npl (abrév* **pyjamas***)* pyjama□ *m*

plank [plæŋk] *n Br* nouille *f*, andouille *f*; **you plank!** espèce d'andouille!

plant [plɑːnt] *n (person)* taupe *f*; *(thing)* = objet caché dans le but d'incriminer quelqu'un

plastered ['plɑːstəd] *adj (drunk)* bourré, pété, beurré

plastic ['plæstɪk] *n (credit cards)* cartes *fpl* de crédit□; **to put sth on the plastic** payer qch avec une carte de crédit; **do they take plastic?** est-ce qu'ils acceptent *ou* prennent les cartes de crédit?; **can I pay with plastic?** vous prenez les cartes de crédit?

plates [pleɪts] *npl Br (rhyming slang* **plates of meat** = **feet***)* arpions *mpl*, panards *mpl*

play [pleɪ] *vi* **(a)** **to play hard to get** se faire désirer□ **(b)** **to play with oneself** *(masturbate)* se caresser, se toucher **(c)** **to play for the other side** *or* **team** *(of man)* en être, être de la jaquette; *(of woman)* être gouine; **to play for both sides** *or* **teams** marcher à voile et à vapeur ▸ *voir aussi* **deck, hell**

player ['pleɪə(r)], **playa** ['pleɪə] *n* tombeur *m*

pleb [pleb] *n Br Péj (abrév* **plebeian***)* prolo *mf*

plebby ['plebɪ] *adj Br Péj (abrév* **plebeian***)* prolo

plod [plɒd] *n Br (police officer)* flic *m*; **the plod(s)** les flics, les poulets, la flicaille

plonk [plɒŋk] **1** *n Br (wine)* piquette *f* **2** *vt (put, place)* flanquer, coller, foutre; **just plonk your stuff on the table** t'as qu'à foutre tes affaires sur la table; **plonk yourself down over there** pose-toi là-bas

plonker ['plɒŋkə(r)] *n Br* **(a)** *(person)* andouille *f*, courge *f*, truffe *f* **(b)** *(penis)* quéquette *f*, zizi *m*

plowed [plaʊd] *adj Am (drunk)* pété, bourré, beurré

plug [plʌg] **1** *n* **to pull the plug on sth** *(stop financing)* arrêter de financer qch□
2 *vt Am (shoot)* flinguer

plug-ugly ['plʌg'ʌglɪ] *adj* moche comme un pou

plumber's crack ['plʌməz'kræk] *n Am* = phénomène censé se produire communément chez les plombiers, dont le pantalon a tendance à tomber, exposant le haut de leur postérieur

plums [!] [plʌmz] *npl Br (testicles)* couilles *fpl*, valseuses *fpl*

pocket billiards ['pɒkɪt'bɪljədz], *Am* **pocket pool** ['pɒkɪt'puːl] *n Hum* **to play** *Br* **pocket billiards** *or Am* **pocket pool** se caresser les boules à travers sa poche de pantalon

poison ['pɔɪzən] *n* **name your poison!,** *Br* **what's your poison?** qu'est-ce que tu bois?

poke [pəʊk] **1** *n* **(a)** [!] *(sexual intercourse)* **to have a poke** tirer un coup **(b)** *Hum* **it's better than a poke in the eye with a sharp stick** c'est mieux que rien□
2 [!] *vt (have sex with)* tringler, troncher

pokey ['pəʊkɪ] *n Am (prison)* taule *f*, cabane *f*; **in the pokey** en taule, en cabane, à l'ombre

pol [pɒl] *n Am (abrév* **politician)** politicien□ *m*

Polack ['pəʊlæk] *n Injurieux* Polack *mf*

pole [pəʊl] *n* **(a)** *Br* **to be up the pole** *(mad)* être dingue *ou* cinglé; *(pregnant)* en cloque; **to be up the pole with worry** être fou *ou* malade d'inquiétude□; **to drive sb up the pole** rendre qn chèvre **(b)** [!]

(penis) queue *f*, bite *f*

polluted [pə'luːtɪd] *adj Am (drunk)* pété, beurré, bourré, rond

pommie, pommy ['pɒmɪ] *Austr* **1** *n* angliche *mf*
2 *adj* angliche

ponce [pɒns] *n Br* **(a)** *(effeminate man)* chochotte *f* **(b)** *(pimp)* maquereau *m*

ponce about, ponce around *vi Br* **(a)** *(of effeminate man)* faire chochotte **(b)** *(waste time)* glander, glandouiller

poncy ['pɒnsɪ] *adj Br* **(a)** *(effeminate)* qui fait chochotte **(b)** *(pretentious)* chichiteux; **I hate restaurants that serve poncy food** j'ai horreur des restos qui servent de la cuisine chichiteuse

pond [pɒnd] *n* **(a)** **the pond** *(the Atlantic)* l'Océan *m* Atlantique□; **across the pond** outre-Atlantique□ **(b)** **pond life** des moins que rien

pong [pɒŋ] *Br* **1** *n* puanteur□ *f*
2 *vi* schlinguer, fouetter

pony ['pəʊnɪ] *n Br (£25)* vingt-cinq livres□ *fpl*

poo [puː] **1** *n* **(a)** *(excrement)* caca *m*; **to do** *or Br* **have a poo** faire caca **(b)** *Br (worthless things)* **it's a load of poo** ça vaut pas un clou; **he's talking a load of poo** il raconte n'importe quoi
2 *vi* faire caca
3 *exclam* **oh, poo!** oh merde!

pooch [puːtʃ] *n (dog)* clébard *m*, clebs *m* ▸ *voir aussi* **screw**

poof [pʊf], **poofter** ['pʊftə(r)] *n Br Injurieux* pédé *f*, pédale *f*, tantouze *f*, tapette *f*

poofy ['pʊfɪ] *adj Br Injurieux* qui fait tapette; **he's got a really poofy voice** il parle vraiment

Pleins feux sur...

Police

Parmi les termes argotiques les plus anciens pour désigner un policier, citons **bobby** et **peeler**, deux mots formés à partir du nom du fondateur de la police britannique, Robert Peel. Le premier d'entre eux est toujours utilisé mais le deuxième est daté. Aujourd'hui, les termes **copper** et **cop** (provenant sûrement du verbe **to cop** = attraper, arrêter) sont les plus courants. Le mot **plod** s'emploie en Grande-Bretagne pour désigner un policier (**a plod**) ou la police en général (**the plod**) ; ce terme a pour origine le nom du policier de la fameuse série pour enfants d'Enid Blyton *Noddy* (*Oui-Oui* en français). D'autres façons de désigner la police en Grande-Bretagne sont **the boys in blue** (allusion à la couleur de l'uniforme), **the (Old) Bill**, **the fuzz** et l'expression métonymique **the law**. Certains termes sont un peu plus péjoratifs. On appelle souvent un agent de police **a pig** (un cochon). Quant à **flatfoot**, c'est un terme vieilli en anglais britannique, mais il est toujours utilisé aux États-Unis. En Grande-Bretagne, le mot **filth** peut s'employer collectivement pour parler de la police. D'autres expressions permettent de désigner certains éléments spécifiques de la police. Pour la brigade volante de Scotland Yard, on dira **the Sweeney** (de l'argot rimé **Sweeney Todd** = **flying squad**). Aux États-Unis, un membre de la brigade des stupéfiants est appelé un **narc** (de **narcotics agent**) et un agent du FBI, un **Fed** ou **Feebie**. Les expressions signifiant "se faire arrêter" sont **to get nabbed**, **nicked** ou **lifted** en argot britannique, et **to get busted** en argot américain. "Être en prison" se dit **to be in the clink** ou **in the slammer** ou encore **to be inside**. To be **in the nick** et **to be banged up** s'emploient uniquement en anglais britannique. "Purger une peine" se dit **to do time** ou **a stretch**. En argot britannique, l'on dit également **to do porridge**, expression humoristique et un peu vieillotte qui fait référence au régime alimentaire des prisonniers.

---

comme un pédé

Pool [puːl] *npr* (*abrév* **Liverpool**) **the Pool** = surnom donné à la ville de Liverpool

poon [!!] [puːn] *n Am* (**a**) (*female genitals*) chatte *f*, chagatte *f*, cramouille *f* (**b**) (*women*) gonzesses *fpl*, meufs *fpl*; **he's gone out looking for poon** il cherche une meuf à se mettre sur le bout

poontang [!!] ['puːntæŋ] = **poon**

poonani [!] [puːˈnænɪ] *n* chatte *f*, foufoune *f*

poop [puːp] *Am* **1** *n* caca *m*; **to take a poop** faire caca
2 *vi* faire caca

pooped [puːpt] *adj Am* crevé, nase, lessivé

pop¹ [pɒp] **1** *n* (a) *(fizzy drink)* soda☐ *m* (b) **they cost 20 quid a pop** *(each)* ils coûtent vingt livres pièce☐
2 *vt* (a) **to pop the question** proposer le mariage☐ (b) **to pop pills** prendre des pilules☐ ▶ *voir aussi* **cherry, clogs**

pop² *n Am (father)* papa *m*

pop off *vi (die)* calancher, passer l'arme à gauche

Pope [pəʊp] *n Hum* **is the Pope Catholic?** ça me paraît évident

ⓘ Il s'agit d'une expression utilisée lorsque quelqu'un vient de poser une question que l'on juge superflue tant il paraît évident que la réponse ne peut être qu'affirmative.

popper [ˈpɒpə(r)] *n (drug)* popper *m*, nitrate *m* d'amyle☐

pops [pɒps] = **pop²**

popstrel [ˈpɒpstrəl] *n Br Fam* jeune chanteuse *f* pop☐

porcelain [ˈpɔːsəlɪn] **1** *n* **to point Percy at the porcelain** pisser un coup *ou* un bock
2 *adj* **the porcelain throne** le trône *(les toilettes)*

pork [!] [pɔːk] **1** *n Hum* **pork (sword)** *(penis)* queue *f*, bite *f*
2 *vt (have sex with)* tringler, troncher

pork out *vi* grossir☐

porker [ˈpɔːkə(r)] *n (man)* gros lard *m*; *(woman)* grosse vache *f*

porky [ˈpɔːkɪ] **1** *n Br* **porky (pie)** *(rhyming slang* **lie)** mensonge☐ *m*, craque *f*
2 *adj (fat)* gros☐, mastard

porridge [ˈpɒrɪdʒ] *n Br (term of imprisonment)* peine *f* de prison☐; **to do porridge** faire de la taule

posh [pɒʃ] *n Br (cocaine)* coke *f*

Posh 'n' Becks, Posh and Becks [pɒʃənˈbeks] *n Br (rhyming slang* **sex)** baise *f*; **he's hoping to get some Posh 'n' Becks tonight** il espère pouvoir tirer un coup ce soir

ⓘ Posh et Becks sont les surnoms donnés par la presse populaire anglaise à Victoria Beckham (ancienne Spice Girl) et à David Beckman (star du football). "Becks" est l'abréviation de "Beckham" ; Posh était le surnom de Mme Beckham du temps des Spice Girls car elle était considérée comme la plus chic des cinq membres du groupe et le surnom lui est resté depuis.

posse [ˈpɒsɪ] *n* (a) *(group of friends)* bande *f*; **he's out with the posse** il est sorti avec ses potes *ou* avec sa bande (b) *Noir Am (entourage)* clique *f* (c) *Noir Am (criminal gang)* gang *m*

postal [ˈpəʊstəl] *adj Am* **to go postal** péter les plombs

ⓘ Au début des années 90 il y eut plusieurs assassinats qui eurent pour cadre les services postaux américains.

pot [pɒt] *n* (a) *(marijuana)* herbe *f*, beu *f* (b) **to go to pot** *(deteriorate)* aller à vau-l'eau (c) **he hasn't got a pot to piss in [!]** il est complètement fauché ▶ *voir aussi* **shit**

pothead ['pɒthed] *n* **to be a pot-head** marcher au hasch

potted ['pɒtɪd] *adj Am (drunk)* pété, fait, bourré, rond

potty ['pɒtɪ] *adj Br* dingue, cinglé, timbré; **to be potty about sb/sth** être dingue de qn/qch

potty-mouth ['pɒtɪmaʊθ] *n Hum* **to be a potty-mouth** jurer comme un charretier

ⓘ "Potty" signifie "pot de chambre". L'expression évoque une personne dont le langage est tellement ordurier que sa bouche est aussi sale qu'un pot de chambre.

powder ['paʊdə(r)] *vt Hum* **to powder one's nose** *(go to the toilet)* aller se repoudrer le nez; *(snort cocaine)* se poudrer le nez

pox [pɒks] *n Br* **the pox** *(syphilis)* la vérole▫

poxy ['pɒksɪ] *adj Br (worthless)* minable; **he only gave me a poxy five pounds for it** il me l'a acheté cinq malheureuses livres

pram face ['præmfeɪs] *n Br Hum* = jeune femme qui, en dépit de son succès professionnel, a le même style que la plupart des jeunes mères célibataires des cités HLM

prang [præŋ] *Br* **1** *n* accrochage▫ *m*; **to have a prang** avoir un accrochage
2 *vt (vehicle)* bigorner

prat [præt] *n* crétin(e) *m,f*, courge *f*, andouille *f*, cruche *f*

prat about, prat around *vi Br (act foolishly)* faire l'idiot; *(waste time)* glander, glandouiller

prawn [prɔːn] *n Austr* **don't come the raw prawn with me!** n'essaie pas de m'embobiner!

preggers ['pregəz] *adj* en cloque

preppy ['prepɪ] *Am* **1** *n* ≃ BCBG *mf*
2 *adj* ≃ BCBG

president ['prezɪdənt] *n Am* **dead presidents** biffetons *mpl*, fafiots *mpl*

ⓘ Ce terme fait référence au fait que tous les billets américains portent l'effigie d'un président des États-Unis.

pressie ['prezɪ] *n Br (abrév* **present)** cadeau▫ *m*

previous ['priːvjəs] *n (previous convictions)* casier *m* judiciaire▫; **he's got previous for drink-driving** il a déjà été arrêté pour conduite en état d'ivresse

prezzie [prezi] = **pressie**

priceless ['praɪslɪs] *adj (amusing)* impayable, crevant

prick [!!] [prɪk] *n* (**a**) *(penis)* bite *f*, queue *f*, pine *f*; **to feel like a spare prick (at a wedding)** tenir la chandelle (**b**) *(man)* tête *f* de nœud, connard *m*, blaireau *m*; **stop acting like such a prick!** arrête donc de faire le con!

pricktease [!!] ['prɪktiːz], **prick-teaser** [!!] ['prɪktiːzə(r)] *n* allumeuse *f*

private parts ['praɪvɪt'pɑːts], **privates** ['praɪvɪts] *npl* parties *fpl* génitales▫

pro [prəʊ] *n* (**a**) *(abrév* **prostitute)** pute *f* (**b**) *(abrév* **professional)** pro *mf*

prob [prɒb] *n (abrév* **problem)** problème▫ *m*, blème *m*; *Br* **no probs!** pas de problèmes!

Prod [prɒd], **Proddy** ['prɒdɪ] *n Br (abrév* **Protestant)** protestant(e)▫ *m,f*

profile ['prəʊfaɪl] *vi Noir Am (show off)* frimer, crâner

pronto ['prɒntəʊ] *adv* illico (presto), pronto

psyched [saɪkt] *adj Am* super enthousiaste; **I'm really psyched about going to the game!** je suis super content d'aller voir le match!

psycho ['saɪkəʊ] **1** *n (abrév* **psychopath***)* psychopathe□ *mf*, cinglé(e) *m,f*
   2 *adj (abrév* **psychopathic***)* cinglé, timbré, dingue; **to go psycho** devenir dingue

pub-crawl ['pʌbkrɔːl] *n Br* tournée *f* des bars□; **to go on a pub-crawl** faire la tournée des bars

pubes [pjuːbz] *npl (abrév* **pubic hairs***)* poils *mpl* pubiens□

puff [pʌf] *n Br* **(a)** *(marijuana)* herbe *f*, beu *f*; *(cannabis)* shit *m*, hasch *m* **(b)** *(life)* vie□ *f*; **I've never seen him in my puff!** je ne le connais ni d'Ève ni d'Adam! **(c)** *(breath)* souffle□; **to be out of puff** être à bout de souffle

puh-lease [pə'liːz] *exclam* je t'en/vous en prie!□; **oh, puh-lease! did you really think I'd believe that?** oh, je t'en prie! tu croyais vraiment que j'allais avaler ça?

ⓘ Il s'agit en fait du mot "please" prononcé comme s'il comportait deux syllabes au lieu d'une, l'accent tonique portant sur la deuxième. Cette exclamation, généralement accompagnée d'une grimace, exprime le mépris ou l'incrédulité.

---

puke [pjuːk] **1** *n* dégueulis *m*
   2 *vi* dégueuler, gerber

puke up 1 *vt sép* dégueuler, gerber
   2 *vi* dégueuler, gerber

pukey ['pjuːkɪ] *adj* dégueulasse

pukka ['pʌkə] *adj Br* **(a)** *(excellent)* génial, super **(b)** *(genuine)* réglo, régulier□

pull [pʊl] **1** *n* **(a)** **to go out on the pull** sortir draguer; **they're on the pull tonight** *(looking for women)* ils cherchent des nanas; *(looking for men)* elles cherchent des mecs **(b)** *(influence)* piston *m*; **to have a lot of pull** avoir le bras long
   2 *vt* **(a)** *(pick up)* lever, emballer **(b)** *Br Hum* **to pull one's pudding** [!] se tirer sur l'élastique, se taper sur la colonne
   3 *vi (find sexual partner)* faire une touche ▸ *voir aussi* **fast, plug**

pull off [!!] *vt sép* **to pull sb off** branler qn; **to pull oneself off** se branler

pulling power ['pʊlɪŋpaʊə(r)] *n Br* pouvoir *m* de séduction□; **he thinks his new sports car will increase his pulling power** il croit que sa nouvelle voiture de sport l'aidera à lever les nanas

pump [pʌmp] *vt* **to pump iron** faire de la gonflette ▸ *voir aussi* **lead**

pumped [pʌmpt] *adj Am (excited)* surexcité; *(enthusiastic)* emballé

pumped-up [pʌmpt'ʌp] *adj* **(a)** *Am (excited)* surexcité; *(enthusiastic)* emballé **(b)** *(muscular)* qui a de gros biscoteaux

punch out [pʌntʃ] *vt sép Br* **to punch sb's lights out,** *Am* **to punch sb out** amocher qn, arranger le portrait à qn

punk [pʌŋk] *n Am (worthless person)* ordure *f*

punter ['pʌntə(r)] *n Br* **(a)** *(gambler)* parieur(euse)□ *m,f* **(b)** *(consumer, customer)* client(e)□ *m,f* **(c)** *(prostitute's client)* micheton *m*

puppies ['pʌpɪz] *npl (breasts)* nichons *mpl*, roberts *mpl*

pure [pjʊə(r)] *adv Br (for emphasis)* **that party was pure mental!** la soirée était vraiment délire *ou* dingue!; **she's pure freaking out about her driving test** elle flippe complètement à cause de son examen de conduite

push [pʊʃ] **1** *n* (a) *Br* **to give sb the push** *(employee)* virer qn; *(boyfriend, girlfriend)* plaquer qn; **to get the push** *(of employee)* se faire virer; *(of boyfriend, girlfriend)* se faire plaquer (b) *Austr (gang)* bande *f*, clique *f*
2 *vt* (a) *(drugs)* dealer (b) **to be pushing forty/fifty** friser la quarantaine/cinquantaine (c) **it'll be pushing it to finish by five** ça va faire un peu juste pour finir à cinq heures; **that's pushing it a bit** c'est un peu exagéré; **don't push your luck!** fais gaffe à toi! ▸ *voir aussi* **daisy**

push off *vi Br* mettre les bouts, se casser, se tirer; **push off!** tire-toi!, casse-toi!

pusher ['pʊʃə(r)] *n (drug dealer)* dealer *m*

pushover ['pʊʃəʊvə(r)] *n* (a) *(person)* poire *f*, pigeon *m* (b) *(thing)* jeu *m* d'enfant; **the German exam was a pushover** l'examen d'allemand était hyper fastoche

puss [pʊs] *n* (a) *(cat)* minou *m*, minet *m* (b) *(face)* binette *f*, frimousse *f*

pussy ['pʊsɪ] *n* (a) *(cat)* minou *m*, minet *m* (b) [!!] *(woman's genitals)* chatte *f*, chagatte *f*, cramouille *f* (c) [!!] *(women)* nanas *fpl*, cuisse *f*; *(sex)* baise *f*; **they're out looking for pussy** ils cherchent des meufs; **he hasn't had any pussy for weeks** ça fait des semaines qu'il a pas baisé *ou* qu'il a pas tiré un coup (d) [!] *(weak, cowardly man)* lavette *f*

pussy-whipped [!] ['pʊsɪwɪpt] *adj* dominé par sa femme□; **he's totally pussy-whipped** c'est sa femme qui porte la culotte

put [pʊt] *vt Br* **put it there!** *(shake hands)* serrons-nous la pince!

put about *vt sép Br* (a) **to put a rumour about** répandre une rumeur□; **to put it about that…** répandre la rumeur comme quoi… (b) **to put it** *or* **oneself about** *(be promiscuous)* coucher à droite à gauche

put away *vt sép* (a) **to put sb away** *(in prison)* mettre qn à l'ombre; *(in psychiatric hospital)* interner qn□, enfermer qn chez les fous (b) **to put sth away** *(food, drink)* s'envoyer qch; **he can really put it away!** *(food)* il a un sacré appétit!; *(drink)* qu'est-ce qu'il descend!

put on *vt sép* (a) **to put sb on** *(tease)* faire marcher qn (b) **to put it on** *(pretend)* faire du cinéma *ou* du chiqué

put out *vi Am (of woman)* accepter de coucher *(for* avec); **did she put out?** est-ce qu'elle a bien voulu coucher?; **she'd put out for anybody** elle coucherait avec le premier venu

put over *vt sép* **to put one over on sb** gruger qn

putrid ['pju:trɪd] *adj (worthless)* pourri; **that burger was putrid** ce burger était vraiment dégueulasse

put-up ['pʊtʌp] *adj* **a put-up job** un coup monté

putz [pʌts] *n Am* andouille *f*, truffe *f*

putz around *vi Am* (a) *(act foolishly)* faire l'idiot, faire l'imbécile (b) *(waste time)* glander, glandouiller

Qq

q.t. [kjuːˈtiː] *n* **on the q.t.** en douce, en loucedé

quack [kwæk] *n Br Péj (doctor)* toubib *m*

quality [ˈkwɒlɪtɪ] *Br* **1** *adj (excellent)* super, top, génial; **that was a quality night out!** c'était une super soirée!; **that goal was pure quality** le but était absolument génial; **you should have seen his karaoke attempt last night, it was pure quality!** *(very funny)* tu l'aurais vu chanter au karaoke hier soir, c'était tordant!
2 *exclam* super!, génial!

queen [kwiːn] *n* (**a**) *(effeminate homosexual)* folle *f*; **he's a screaming queen** c'est une vraie folle perdue (**b**) *Injurieux (any homosexual man)* pédé *m*, tantouze *f*, tapette *f*

ⓘ Ce terme perd son caractère injurieux lorsqu'il est utilisé par des homosexuels. Par ailleurs, lorsqu'il désigne un individu efféminé (sens (a)), il n'est jamais véritablement injurieux. Il convient toutefois de l'utiliser avec circonspection.

---

queer [kwɪə(r)] **1** *n Injurieux (homosexual)* pédé *m*, pédale *f*, tantouze *f*
2 *adj* (**a**) *Injurieux (homosexual)* pédé, homo (**b**) *Br* **to be in queer street** être dans la mouise *ou* dans la panade ▸ *voir aussi* **act, fish**

ⓘ Ce terme perd son caractère injurieux quand il est utilisé par des homosexuels.

---

queer-basher [ˈkwɪəbæʃə(r)] *n* = individu qui se livre à des violences à l'encontre d'homosexuels

queer-bashing [ˈkwɪəbæʃɪŋ] *n* = violences à l'encontre d'homosexuels; **he's into queer-bashing** il aime bien aller casser du pédé

quickie [ˈkwɪkɪ] **1** *n* **to have a quickie** *(drink)* boire un coup en vitesse; *(sex)* tirer un coup vite fait
2 *adj* **quickie divorce** divorce *m* express

quid [kwɪd] *n Br (pound sterling)* livre *f* sterling□; **a quid/ten quid** une livre/dix livres; **to be quids in** être à l'aise, avoir du fric

quim [!!] [kwɪm] *n* chatte *f*, chagatte *f*, con *m*

Rr

rabbit ['ræbɪt] **1** *n Péj* **rabbit food** *(salad)* verdure *f*; *Br* **rabbit hutch** *(accommodation)* cage *f* à lapins **(b)** **to be at it** *or* **to fuck** [!!] **like rabbits** baiser comme des lapins

2 *vi Br (rhyming slang* **rabbit and pork** = **talk**) jacter, jacasser

rabbit on *vi Br* bavasser (**about** à propos de); **what's he rabbiting on about?** qu'est-ce qu'il bave?

rack [ræk] *n* **(a)** *Am* **to hit the rack** *(go to bed)* se pieuter, se bâcher **(b)** *(breasts)* nichons *mpl*, nénés *mpl*, roberts *mpl*; **check out the rack on that!** mate un peu les nichons de la nana!

rack back *vt sép* **to rack sb back** passer un savon à qn, remonter les bretelles à qn

rack off *vi Austr* se casser; **just rack off, will you!** casse-toi!

racket ['rækɪt] *n* **(a)** *(noise)* boucan *m*, barouf *m*; **to make a racket** faire du boucan *ou* du barouf **(b)** *(criminal activity)* activité *f* criminelle⁼; **protection racket** racket *m*; **drugs racket** trafic *m* de drogue

rad [ræd] *adj (abrév* **radical**) super, génial, géant

radical ['rædɪkəl] *adj* super, génial, géant

rag [ræg] *n* **(a)** *(newspaper)* torchon *m* **(b)** *Br* **to lose one's** *or* **the rag** piquer une crise, péter les plombs **(c)**

to be on the rag [!] avoir ses ragnagnas **(d)** **to feel like a wet rag** *or Am* **a dish rag** se sentir ramollo **(e)** *Am* **rags** *(clothes)* fringues *fpl* ▶ *voir aussi* **chew**

raghead ['ræghed] *n Am Injurieux* raton *m*, bicot *m*

rah [rɑː] *Br* **1** *n* = jeune personne de bonne famille au caractère exubérant; **my uni course was full of rahs** il y avait plein de bourges exubérants dans mes cours, à la fac

2 *adj* **it's an OK bar but it's a bit too rah for me** c'est pas mal comme bar, mais il y a un peu trop de jeunes bourges bruyants à mon goût

rake in [reɪk] *vt sép* **to rake sth in** *(money)* ramasser qch à la pelle; **he must be raking it in!** il doit s'en mettre plein les poches!

rake-off ['reɪkɒf] *n* commission *f* illicite⁼, ristourne *f*

ralph [rælf] *vi* gerber, dégueuler

rammed [ræmd] *adj* bourré de monde, bondé

rancid ['rænsɪd] *adj* dégueulasse, répugnant⁼

random ['rændəm] **1** *n* personne *f* quelconque; **who was that girl you were talking to? – oh, just some random** c'était qui la fille avec qui tu parlais? – oh, personne en particulier, juste une fille; **all these randoms turned up at the party** il y a a plein d'inconnus qui se sont pointés à la soirée

2 adj (**a**) (unknown) quelconque; **I was standing at the bus stop and this random guy came up and asked for my phone number** j'étais à l'arrêt de bus et il y a un type qui est venu me voir et qui m'a demandé mon numéro de téléphone (**b**) (unexpected, strange) bizarre; **it turns out we went to the same school, how random!** il se trouve qu'on est allé à la même école, tu parles d'une coïncidence!

randy ['rændɪ] adj Br excité (sexuellement)

rank [ræŋk] adj (**a**) Br (worthless) merdique; **this wine's absolutely rank!** ce vin est vraiment dégueulasse! (**b**) (ugly) moche; **she is rank!** c'est un vrai cageot!

rank on vt insép **to rank on sb** agonir qn d'injures, traiter qn de tous les noms

rap [ræp] n (**a**) (blame) **to take the rap (for sth)** écoper (pour qch); Am **to beat the rap** échapper à la condamnation□, être acquitté□; Am **rap sheet** casier m judiciaire□ (**b**) Am (speech) **don't give me that rap!** raconte pas n'importe quoi!; **he was laying down some rap about the new model** il était en train de faire un baratin sur le nouveau modèle

2 vt Am (criticize) éreinter, descendre

3 vi Noir Am (talk) causer; **what's he rapping about now?** qu'est-ce qu'il raconte maintenant? ▶ voir aussi **bum**

rare [reə(r)] adj Scot (excellent) super, génial; **we had a rare night out last night** on a passé une super soirée hier

raspberry ['rɑːzbərɪ] n Br (**a**) (rhyming slang **raspberry ripple** = **nipple**) mamelon□ m (**b**) (rhyming slang

raspberry ripple = **cripple**) infirme mf

rat [ræt] n (**a**) (person) salaud m, salopard m, ordure f (**b**) Am **I don't give a rat's ass [!]** je m'en fous pas mal, je m'en balance (**c**) Br **to do sth/go somewhere like a rat up a drainpipe** faire qch/aller quelque part à fond de train; **when he heard the police siren, he was off like a rat up a drainpipe** quand il a entendu la sirène de la police, il est parti comme une flèche ▶ voir aussi **frat**

rat on vt insép **to rat on sb** balancer qn, moucharder qn

rat out vt sép **to rat sb out** balancer qn, moucharder qn

rat-arsed [!] ['rætɑːst] adj Br bourré comme un coing, pété à mort, plein comme une barrique

ratbag ['rætbæg] n Br salaud m, salopard m, ordure f

ratfink ['rætfɪŋk] n Am salaud m, salopard m, ordure f

ratted ['rætɪd] adj Br bourré comme un coing, pété à mort, plein comme une barrique; **to get ratted** se péter, se torcher

ratty ['rætɪ] adj râleur, rouspéteur

raunchy ['rɔːntʃɪ] adj sexy

raver ['reɪvə(r)] n Br (**a**) (socially active person) noceur(euse) m,f (**b**) (person who attends raves) raver mf

rave-up ['reɪvʌp] n Br boum f

razz [ræz] **1** vt Am (jeer at) chambrer

2 n Br **to go on the razz** faire la bringue ou la teuf

razzle ['ræzəl] n Br **to go on the razzle** faire la bringue ou la teuf

readies ['redɪz] npl Br liquide m (argent)

real [rɪəl] **1** adj **is he for real?** il est

sérieux?; **get real!** arrête de rêver!, redescends sur terre!; **to keep it real** rester simple□; **he may be a millionaire but he's keeping it real, still hanging out with his friends from high school** il a beau être millionnaire, il sait rester simple, il fréquente toujours ses copains de lycée

2 *adv Am (very)* vachement; **you were real lucky** t'as eu une sacré veine; **it's real hot** il fait vachement chaud; **we had a real good time** on s'est vachement bien amusés

ream out [riːm] *vt sép Am* **to ream sb out** *(scold)* passer un savon à qn, remonter les bretelles à qn

rear end [rɪər'end] *n (buttocks)* arrière-train *m*

redneck ['rednek] *n Am* plouc *mf*, bouseux(euse) *m,f (du Sud des États-Unis)*; **a redneck politician/cop** un homme politique/un flic tout ce qu'il y a de plus réactionnaire

reefer ['riːfə(r)] *n (cannabis cigarette)* joint *m*, stick *m*

ref [ref] *n (abrév* **referee***)* arbitre□ *m*

rellies ['reliz] *n Br (relatives)* famille□ *f*; **are you seeing your rellies at Christmas?** tu vas voir ta famille à Noël?

rent boy ['rentbɔɪ] *n Br* jeune prostitué *m* homosexuel□

rents [rents] *npl Am (abrév* **parents***)* vieux *mpl*, renps *mpl*

rep [rep] *n (abrév* **reputation***)* réputation□ *f*; **my rep will take a hammering if they find out she dumped me** ma réputation va en prendre un coup s'ils apprennent qu'elle m'a larguée

repo ['riːpəʊ] **1** *n (abrév* **repossession***)* **repo man** huissier□ *m (chargé*

par une société de saisir des biens non payés)

2 *vt (abrév* **repossess***)* saisir□

represent [reprɪ'zent] *vi Noir Am* se pointer

result [rɪ'zʌlt] *n Br* **to get a result** *(in sport)* gagner□, l'emporter□; **he had a result last night, he pulled some gorgeous bird** il a fait fort hier soir, il a levé une super nana; **a 20% pay rise? (what a) result!** 20% d'augmentation? tu as fait fort!

retard ['riːtɑːd] *n* crétin(e) *m,f*, débile *mf* mental(e)

retarded [rɪ'tɑːdɪd] *adj* **(a)** *(person)* débile, gogol **(b)** *(thing)* débile; **this game is so retarded!** ce jeu est complètement débile!

Richard [**!**] ['rɪtʃəd] *npr Br (rhyming slang* **Richard the Third** = **turd***)* étron *m*

ride [raɪd] **1** *n* **(a)** [**!!**] *(sexual partner)* **to be a good ride** être un bon coup **(b)** *Noir Am (car)* bagnole *f*, caisse *f*, tire *f*

2 *vt* [**!!**] *(have sex with) (of man)* baiser, tringler, troncher, sauter; *(of woman)* baiser avec, s'envoyer

rig [rɪg] *n (large truck)* gros-cul *m*

right [raɪt] **1** *adj* **(a)** **too right!** tu l'as dit, bouffi! **(b)** *Am* **a right guy** un chic type

2 *adv* **(a)** *Br (for emphasis)* vachement, drôlement; **I was right angry** j'étais vachement en colère; **it's a right cold day** ça pince drôlement aujourd'hui, il fait drôlement frisquet aujourd'hui **(b)** **right on!** bravo!
▶ *voir aussi* **yeah**

righteous ['raɪtʃəs] *adj Noir Am* **(a)** *(genuine)* authentique□ **(b)** *(excellent)* génial, super, géant

right-on ['raɪt'ɒn] *adj (socially aware)* politiquement correct□

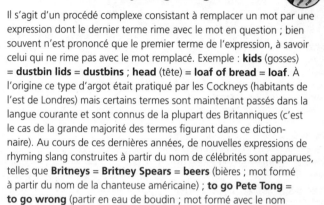

D'où tu me parles ?

Rhyming slang

Il s'agit d'un procédé complexe consistant à remplacer un mot par une expression dont le dernier terme rime avec le mot en question ; bien souvent n'est prononcé que le premier terme de l'expression, à savoir celui qui ne rime pas avec le mot remplacé. Exemple : **kids** (gosses) = **dustbin lids** = **dustbins** ; **head** (tête) = **loaf of bread** = **loaf**. À l'origine ce type d'argot était pratiqué par les Cockneys (habitants de l'est de Londres) mais certains termes sont maintenant passés dans la langue courante et sont connus de la plupart des Britanniques (c'est le cas de la grande majorité des termes figurant dans ce diction-naire). Au cours de ces dernières années, de nouvelles expressions de rhyming slang construites à partir du nom de célébrités sont apparues, telles que **Britneys** = **Britney Spears** = **beers** (bières ; mot formé à partir du nom de la chanteuse américaine) ; **to go Pete Tong** = **to go wrong** (partir en eau de boudin ; mot formé avec le nom d'un DJ britannique) ; **Posh and Becks** = **sex** (relations sexuelles ; il s'agit évidemment du footballeur David Beckham et de sa femme Victoria, surnommée "Posh" lorsqu'elle faisait partie des Spice Girls) ; et enfin **Tonys** = **Tony Blairs** = **flares** (signifiant "pantalon pattes d'éléphant").

Riley ['raɪlɪ] *npr* **to lead the life of Riley** se la couler douce, avoir la belle vie

ring [!!] [rɪŋ], **ringpiece** [!!] ['rɪŋ-piːs] *n* rondelle *f*, troufignon *m*

rinky-dink ['rɪŋkɪdɪŋk] *adj Am* (goods) merdique; (business, busi-nessman) minable

riot ['raɪət] *n* (a) (amusing person, thing) **he's a complete riot** il est vraiment tordant, il est impayable; **the party was a riot** la soirée était vraiment démente (b) **to read sb the riot act** souffler dans les bronches à qn, passer un savon à qn

rip [rɪp] *vi Br* **to let rip** (behave un-restrainedly) se déchaîner; (fart) lar-guer une caisse; **to let rip at sb** se mettre en pétard contre qn ▶ *voir aussi* **piss**

rip off *vt sép* **to rip sb off** (cheat, swindle) arnaquer qn; **to rip sth off** (steal) piquer qch, faucher qch

rip-off ['rɪpɒf] *n* arnaque *f*; **what a rip-off!** quelle arnaque! ▶ *voir aussi* **merchant**

ripped [rɪpt] *adj* (drunk) bourré, beur-ré, pété; (on drugs) raide, défoncé; *Br* **ripped to the tits** [!] (drunk) bourré comme un coing, plein comme une barrique, rond comme une queue de pelle; (on drugs) complètement raide *ou* défoncé

ripper ['rɪpə(r)] *Austr* **1** *n* (excellent person, thing) **he's a ripper** c'est

---

The symbol [□] indicates that a translation is neutral.

quelqu'un de super; **it's a ripper** c'est super *ou* génial; **you little ripper!** super!, génial!

2 *adj* (*excellent*) super, génial

rise [raɪz] *n* **to take** *or* **get a rise out of sb** faire enrager qn

ritzy ['rɪtsɪ] *adj* tape-à-l'œil, clinquant

river ['rɪvə(r)] *n* **to sell sb down the river** trahir qn□, vendre qn□; *Am* **to send sb up the river** (*to prison*) mettre qn à l'ombre *ou* en taule *ou* en cabane

roach [rəʊtʃ] *n* (**a**) (*of cannabis cigarette*) mégot□ *m* (*d'une cigarette de marijuana*) (**b**) (*abrév* **cockroach**) cafard□ *m*

roadhog ['rəʊdhɒɡ] *n* (*man*) chauffard *m*, écraseur *m*; (*woman*) écraseuse *f*

roasting ['rəʊstɪŋ] *n* (**a**) (*telling off*) **to give sb a roasting** souffler dans les bronches à qn, passer un savon à qn; **to get a roasting** se faire souffler dans les bronches, prendre *ou* se faire passer un savon (**b**) [!!] (*sexual practice*) = relations sexuelles entre une femme et plusieurs hommes, simultanément ou successivement

rob [rɒb] *n* **to go on the rob** aller faucher des trucs

robbery ['rɒbərɪ] *n* **it's** *Br* **daylight** *or Am* **highway robbery** c'est de l'arnaque

rock [rɒk] **1** *n* (**a**) (*diamond*) diam *m* (**b**) (*crack cocaine*) crack *m*; *Br* (*cocaine*) coco *f*, neige *f* (**c**) **rocks** [!] (*testicles*) couilles *fpl*, boules *fpl*; **to get one's rocks off** (*have sex*) baiser, s'envoyer en l'air; (*have orgasm*) jouir, prendre son pied; (*enjoy oneself*) s'éclater, prendre son pied; **to get one's rocks off doing sth** s'éclater *ou* prendre son pied en faisant qch (**d**) **on the rocks** (*drink*) aux

glaçons□; (*relationship, marriage, business*) en train de battre de l'aile (**e**) *Am* **to have rocks in one's head** être bête comme ses pieds

2 *vi* **the party was really rocking** il y avait une ambiance d'enfer à la soirée; **his new sound system really rocks!** sa nouvelle chaîne hifi est vraiment super *ou* géniale!; **let's rock!** allez, on y va!

rock up *vi* se pointer; **he rocked up at the party at midnight with some bird** il s'est pointé à la soirée à minuit avec une nana

rocker ['rɒkə(r)] *n* **to be off one's rocker** (*mad*) être cinglé, avoir une araignée dans le plafond; **to go off one's rocker** (*go mad*) perdre la boule, devenir dingue *ou* cinglé; (*lose one's temper*) péter les plombs, péter une durite, piquer une crise

rockhouse ['rɒkhaʊs] *n Am* = lieu où l'on achète, vend et consomme du crack

rocky ['rɒkɪ] *n Br* (*abrév* **Moroccan**) (*cannabis*) marocain *m*

rod [!] [rɒd] *n* (*penis*) pine *f*, bite *f*, tige *f*

roger [!] ['rɒdʒə(r)] *vt Br* baiser, sauter, sabrer

roid [rɔɪd] *n Am* (*abrév* **steroid**) **roids** stéroïdes□ *mpl*; **roid rage** = état d'agressivité extrême causé par l'absorption de stéroïdes

① L'expression "roid rage" est un jeu de mots sur l'expression "road rage", qui signifie "rage au volant".

roll [rəʊl] **1** *n* **to have a roll in the hay** faire une partie de jambes en l'air

2 *vt* (**a**) **to roll one's own** se rouler ses cigarettes□ (**b**) *Am* (*rob*) faire les poches à *(une personne ivre ou en-dormie)*

3 *vi* **to be rolling in it** *or Am* **rolling in dough** *(very rich)* être plein aux as

Roller ['rəʊlə(r)] *n Br* (*abrév* **Rolls Royce®**) Rolls Royce *f*

rollick ['rɒlɪk] *vt Br* engueuler, remonter les bretelles à

rollicking ['rɒlɪkɪŋ] *n Br* **to give sb a rollicking** engueuler qn, remonter les bretelles à qn; **to get a rollicking** se faire engueuler, se faire remonter les bretelles

rollie ['rəʊlɪ] *n Br* cigarette *f* roulée à la main□

Rolls [rəʊlz] = **Roller**

roll-up ['rəʊlʌp], **roll-your-own** ['rəʊljɔːr'əʊn], **rolly** ['rəʊlɪ] *n Br* cigarette *f* roulée à la main□

romp [rɒmp] **1** *n* **to have a romp (with sb)** faire une partie de jambes en l'air (avec qn); **"soap star's three-in-a-bed romp with models"** *(in headline)* la vedette d'un feuilleton télévisé partouze avec deux manne-quins

2 *vi* **to romp with sb** faire une partie de jambes en l'air avec qn

roo [ruː] *n Austr* kangourou□ *m*

roofie ['ruːfɪ] *n* (*abrév* **Rohypnol®**) Rohypnol® *m*

rook [rʊk] *vt Am (cheat)* arnaquer

room [ruːm] *n Hum* **get a room!** *(to couple)* ne faites pas ça en public!

roomie ['ruːmɪ] *n Am* (*abrév* **roommate**) colocataire *mf*, coloc *mf*

root [!] [ruːt] *Austr* **1** *vt (have sex with)* s'envoyer en l'air avec

2 *vi (have sex)* s'envoyer en l'air; **root rat** chaud lapin *m*

rooted [!] ['ruːtɪd] *adj Austr (ex-hausted)* naze, lessivé

rort [rɔːt] *Austr* **1** *n* **(a)** *(trick, fraud)* arnaque *f* **(b)** *(party)* fiesta *f*, bringue *f*

2 *vi* **(a)** *(protest)* gueuler **(b)** *(commit fraud)* faire une arnaque

Rosie Lee, Rosy Lee [rəʊzɪ'liː] *n Br (rhyming slang tea)* thé□ *m*

rot [rɒt] *n Br (nonsense)* foutaises *fpl*; **don't talk rot!** arrête de raconter n'importe quoi!

rotgut ['rɒtgʌt] *n* tord-boyaux *m*, gnôle *f*

rotten ['rɒtən] *adj* **(a)** *(worthless)* nul, pourri, merdique; **he's a rotten cook** il est complètement nul comme cuisinier; **the weather was really rotten** le temps était vraiment pourri; **we had a rotten time** on a passé un moment dégueulasse **(b)** *(unkind)* vache, dégueulasse; **to be rotten to sb** être vache *ou* dégueulasse avec qn; **that was a rotten thing to say/do** c'est vraiment salaud *ou* vache *ou* dégueulasse d'avoir dit/fait ça **(c) to feel rotten** *(ill)* se sentir patraque; *(guilty)* se sentir coupable□ ▶ *voir aussi* **something**

rotter ['rɒtə(r)] *n Br* pourriture *f*, ordure *f*

rough [rʌf] **1** *n* **she likes a bit of rough** *(person)* elle aime s'envoyer un prolo de temps en temps; *(sexual activity)* elle aime qu'on la malmène un peu pendant l'amour

2 *adj* **(a)** *Br (ill)* **to feel/look rough** ne pas être/ne pas avoir l'air dans son assiette; **I feel as rough as a badger's arse [!]** je me sens vraiment pas dans mon assiette **(b)** *Br (disgusting)* dégueulasse **(c) rough trade** *(male prostitute)* = jeune prostitué homosexuel à tendances violentes; *(working-class male homosexual)* homosexuel *m* prolo

rough up *vt sép* **to rough sb up** tabasser qn

roust [raʊst] *vt Am (harass)* harceler; *(arrest)* agrafer, gauler, alpaguer

royal [ˈrɔɪəl] *adj (for emphasis)* sombre, de première; **her whining gives me a royal pain** elle me fait vraiment chier avec ses jérémiades; **he's a royal idiot** c'est un sombre crétin *ou* un crétin de première

royally [ˈrɔɪəlɪ] *adv (for emphasis)* dans les grandes largeurs; **they messed up royally** ils se sont plantés dans les grandes largeurs, ils se sont plantés, et pas qu'un peu

rozzer [ˈrɒzə(r)] *n Br* flic *m*, poulet *m*

rub out [rʌb] *vt sép Am* **to rub sb out** zigouiller *ou* buter *ou* refroidir qn

rubber [ˈrʌbə(r)] *n* (**a**) *(condom)* capote *f* (anglaise) (**b**) **rubber** *Br* **cheque** *or Am* **check** chèque *m* en bois

rubberneck [ˈrʌbənek] *Péj* **1** *n* (**a**) *(at scene of accident)* curieux(euse) *m,f (qui s'attarde sur le lieu d'un accident)* (**b**) *(tourist)* touriste[□] *mf (qui assiste à des visites guidées)*

2 *vi* (**a**) *(at scene of accident)* = faire le curieux sur le lieu d'un accident (**b**) *(of tourist)* faire le touriste[□] *(en assistant à des visites guidées)*

rubbish [ˈrʌbɪʃ] *Br* **1** *n (nonsense)* foutaises *fpl*; **don't talk rubbish!** arrête de raconter n'importe quoi!; **his book's a load of rubbish** son livre ne vaut pas un clou, son livre est vraiment nul

2 *exclam* n'importe quoi!

3 *adj (worthless)* nul, pourri; **that was a rubbish film/meal** le film/repas était nul

4 *vt (criticize)* éreinter

rube [ruːb] *n Am* plouc *mf*, péquenaud(e) *m,f*

rub-out [ˈrʌbaʊt] *n Am* assassinat[□] *m*

ruby [ˈruːbɪ] *n Br (rhyming slang* **Ruby Murray** = **curry**) curry[□] *m*; **fancy going out for a ruby tonight?** ça te dit d'aller manger indien ce soir?

ruck [rʌk] *n Br (fight)* baston *m ou f*; **there was a bit of a ruck after the match** il y a eu du grabuge *ou* du baston après le match

ruddy [ˈrʌdɪ] *Br* **1** *adj (for emphasis)* sacré; **you ruddy idiot!** espèce d'andouille!; **he's a ruddy liar!** c'est un sacré menteur!

2 *adv (for emphasis)* sacrément, vachement, drôlement; **you look ruddy ridiculous** t'as l'air vraiment ridicule

rug [rʌg] *n (hairpiece)* moumoute *f*

rugger bugger [ˈrʌgəbʌgə(r)] *n Br Péj* amateur *m* de rugby[□] *(généralement issu des classes aisées)*

ⓘ Le terme "rugger" est un terme d'argot employé dans les classes aisées et qui signifie "rugby". Du fait que le rugby était très pratiqué dans les écoles privées les plus prestigieuses, ce sport a conservé des connotations élitistes. Le "rugger bugger" typique est un jeune homme arrogant et exubérant issu d'une famille aisée, qui porte le plus souvent un maillot de rugby et qui aime boire et pratiquer des activités viriles (dont le rugby).

rug-rat [ˈrʌgræt] *n (child)* môme *mf*, chiard *m*

rumble [ˈrʌmbəl] **1** *n (fight)* baston *m ou f*, castagne *f*

2 *vt Br (see through) (scheme, plot)* découvrir[□], flairer; *(person)* démasquer[□], voir venir

3 *vi (fight)* se friter, se castagner

rum-dum [ˈrʌmdʌm] *n Am* (**a**) *(idiot)* abruti(e) *m,f*, crétin(e) *m,f* (**b**) *(drun-*

---

ken tramp) **he's a rum-dum** c'est un clodo et un poivrot

rump [rʌmp] *n (buttocks)* croupe *f*; **move your rump!** pousse tes fesses!

rumpy-pumpy ['rʌmpɪ'pʌmpɪ] *n Br Hum* zig-zig *m*, crac-crac *m*; **to have a bit of rumpy-pumpy** faire une partie de jambes en l'air, faire zig-zig *ou* crac-crac

runner ['rʌnə(r)] *n Br* **to do a runner** *(run away)* décaniller, se débiner,

mettre les bouts; *(leave without paying)* partir sans payer□

runs [rʌnz] *npl (diarrhoea)* **the runs** la courante

rush [rʌʃ] *n (after taking drugs)* flash *m*; **I got a real rush from that coffee** ce café m'a donné un coup de fouet; **to get a head rush** avoir la tête qui tourne ▸ *voir aussi* **bum**

rustbucket ['rʌstbʌkɪt] *n (car)* poubelle *f*, tas *m* de ferraille

Ss

sack [sæk] **1** *n* (**a**) *(dismissal)* **to get the sack** se faire virer *ou* sacquer; **to give sb the sack** virer qn, sacquer qn (**b**) *(bed)* pieu *m*, plumard *m*; **to hit the sack** se pieuter, se pagnoter; **to be good/no good in the sack** être/ne pas être une affaire au pieu (**c**) **[!!]** *(scrotum)* bourses□ *fpl*; *Hum* **back, sack and crack** = épilation du dos, des bourses et du sillon fessier (**d**) *Am* **sad sack** *(person)* raté(e) *m,f* **2** *vt (dismiss)* virer, sacquer

sack out *vi Am* se pieuter, se bâcher, se pager

sad [sæd] *adj Péj (pitiful)* pitoyable□; **he's still living with his parents, how sad can you get?** il habite toujours chez ses parents, il est grave *ou* il craint!; **what a sad bastard! [!]** quel branleur!; **he's got really sad taste in music** il écoute de la musique vraiment craignos ▸ *voir aussi* **sack**

saddo ['sædəʊ] *n Br* nul (nulle) *m,f*

safe [seɪf] *adj Br (good)* chouette, cool; **are we still on for tonight? – yeah, safe** ça marche toujours pour ce soir? – ouais, pas de problème; **her boss is a complete tosser, but mine's safe** son patron est un vrai con, mais le mien est cool

salad dodger ['sæləd'dɒdʒə(r)] *n Hum (man)* gros patapouf *m*; *(woman)* grosse vache *f*

salami [sə'lɑːmɪ] *n Hum* **to play hide the salami** *(have sex)* s'envoyer en l'air

sambo ['sæmbəʊ] *n* (**a**) *Br Injurieux (black man)* nègre *m*, bamboula *m*; *(black woman)* négresse *f* (**b**) *Ir (sandwich)* casse-dalle *m*

sandwich ['sændwɪtʃ] *n* (**a**) *Br Hum* **to be one sandwich short of a picnic** ne pas être net (**b**) **knuckle sandwich** coup *m* de poing dans la gueule, bourre-pif *m*; **to give sb a knuckle sandwich** mettre son poing dans la gueule à qn (**c**) *Br Hum* **to give sb a tongue sandwich** rouler une pelle *ou* un patin à qn

sap [sæp] *n (person)* poire *f*

sarky ['sɑːkɪ] *adj Br (abrév* **sarcastic**) sarcastique□

sarnie ['sɑːnɪ] *n Br (abrév* **sandwich**) casse-dalle *m*

sassy ['sæsɪ] *adj* (**a**) *(lively)* plein de pêche (**b**) *Am (cheeky)* culotté

Saturday night special ['sætədɪeɪt'speʃəl] *n Am (gun)* flingue *m*, feu *m (bon marché et de qualité médiocre, que l'on peut se procurer facilement)*

sauce [sɔːs] *n* (**a**) *Br (cheek)* insolence□ *f*; **that's enough of your sauce!** arrête de faire l'insolent! (**b**) *(alcohol)* alcool□ *m*, bibine *f*; **to hit the sauce** se mettre à picoler; **to be on the sauce** s'être mis à picoler; **to be off the sauce** être au régime sec

sauced [sɔːst] *adj (drunk)* beurré, bourré, pété

saucepot ['sɔːspɒt] *n* bombe *f* sexuelle

saucy ['sɔːsɪ] *adj* olé olé, corsé

sausage ['sɒsɪdʒ] *n Br* (**a**) *not a sausage (nothing)* que dalle; *you silly sausage!* espèce de nouille! (**b**) *sausage dog* saucisse *f* à pattes (**c**) *Hum (penis)* chipolata *f*

savvy ['sævɪ] **1** *n* jugeote *f*
2 *adj (well-informed)* calé; *(shrewd)* astucieux□

sawbones ['sɔːbəʊnz] *n* chirurgien□ *m*

sawbuck ['sɔːbʌk] *n Am* billet *m* de dix dollars□

sawed-off [sɔːd'ɒf] *adj Am Hum (person)* petit□, minus

scab [skæb] **1** *n (strikebreaker)* jaune *m (non-gréviste)*
2 *vi Am (work as a strikebreaker)* briser une grève□

scabby ['skæbɪ] *adj Br* (**a**) *(worthless)* merdique; *you can keep your scabby car!* tu peux te la garder, ta caisse de merde! (**b**) *(shabby)* merdique, craignos; *(dirty)* cradingue, crado, dégueu

scads [skædz] *npl Am scads (of)* un paquet (de), des tas (de), une tapée (de)

scag [skæg] *n* (**a**) *(heroin)* héro *f*, blanche *f* (**b**) *Am (ugly woman)* boudin *m*, cageot *m*

scally ['skælɪ] *n* jeune lascar *m*, racaille *f*

ⓘ Il s'agit d'un terme qui s'emploie dans le Nord de l'Angleterre, et principalement à Liverpool.

scam [skæm] **1** *n* arnaque *f*
2 *vt* arnaquer

scammer ['skæmə(r)] *n* arnaqueur(euse) *m,f*

scants [skænts] *npl Br (men's)* calcif *m*; *(women's)* petite culotte *f*

scaredy cat ['skeədɪkæt] *n* poule *f* mouillée

scarf [skɑːf] *vt Am (eat)* bouffer, boulotter

scarper ['skɑːpə(r)] *vi Br (go away)* se casser, se barrer, trisser, se tirer

scat [skæt] *vi (go away)* se casser, se barrer, se tirer, trisser; *scat!* casse-toi!, dégage!

scene [siːn] *n it's not my scene* c'est pas mon truc

schemie ['skiːmɪ] *n Scot* jeune lascar *m*, racaille *f*

ⓘ Il s'agit d'un terme dérivé de "housing scheme" (cité HLM) et qui ne s'emploie que dans la région d'Édimbourg.

schiz [skɪts] *Am* = **schizo**

schizo ['skɪtsəʊ] *(abrév* **schizophrenic**) **1** *n* cinglé(e) *m,f*, dingue *mf*
2 *adj* cinglé, timbré, toqué

schlemiel [ʃlə'miːl] *n Am* minable *mf*

schlep [ʃlep] **1** *n* (**a**) *(person)* lourdaud(e) *m,f* (**b**) *(journey)* trotte *f*; *it's a bit of a schlep to the supermarket* ça fait une trotte jusqu'au supermarché
2 *vt (carry)* trimballer
3 *vi (walk)* crapahuter; *to schlep home* rentrer chez soi à pinces; *I had to schlep to the grocery store* il a fallu que je crapahute jusqu'à l'épicerie

schlep around 1 *vt insép* **to schlep**

around town crapahuter en ville
2 *vi Am* crapahuter

schlock [ʃlɒk] *Am* **1** *n (worthless things)* saloperies *fpl*, daube *f*
2 *adj (worthless)* qui ne vaut pas un clou, nul; **schlock jewelry** bijoux *mpl* en toc

schlong [!] [ʃlɒŋ] *n Am* queue *f*, bite *f*, pine *f*

schlub [ʃlʌb] *n Am* crétin(e) *m,f*, andouille *f*

schmaltz [ʃmɔːlts] *n* guimauve *f*

schmaltzy [ʃmɔːltsɪ] *adj* à la guimauve

schmo [ʃməʊ] *n Am (unlucky person)* guignard(e) *m,f*; *(stupid person)* nul (nulle) *m,f* ▸ *voir aussi* **Joe**

schmooze [ʃmuːz] **1** *vi* **(a)** *(chat)* bavarder, jaspiner, jacasser **(b)** *(socialize)* **he's always schmoozing with celebrities** il est toujours à traîner avec des célébrités
2 *vt* **to schmooze sb** passer de la pommade à qn; **look at him schmoozing the boss** regarde-le en train de passer de la pommade au patron

schmozzle [ʃmɒzəl] = **shemozzle**

schmuck [ʃmʌk] *n Am* andouille *f*, courge *f*

schnook [ʃnʊk] *n Am* poire *f*, pigeon *m*

schnozz [ʃnɒz], **schnozzle** [ʃnɒzəl] *n* blaire *m*, tarin *m*

schoolie [skuːlɪ] *n Austr (abrév* **schoolboy, schoolgirl***)* écolier(ère) *m,f*

schtuk [ʃtʊk] *n Br* **to be in schtuk** être dans le pétrin, être dans la panade

schtum [ʃtʊm] *adj Br* **to keep schtum** ne pas piper mot

schtup [ʃtʊp] *vt* baiser, troncher; **he's**

been schtupping his secretary for years ça fait des années qu'il baise sa secrétaire

schwing [ʃwɪŋ] *exclam* putain, la supernana!

ⓘ Il s'agit d'une onomatopée censée reproduire le son que produirait une érection. Ce terme a été popularisé par le film américain *Wayne's World*.

sci-fi [ˈsaɪfaɪ] *(abrév* **science-fiction***)*
1 *n* SF *f*
2 *adj* de SF

scoff [skɒf] **1** *n Br (food)* bouffe *f*, graille *f*
2 *vt (eat)* bouffer, boulotter

scooby [ˈskuːbɪ] *n Br (rhyming slang* **Scooby Doo** = **clue***)* **he hasn't got a scooby** *(is incompetent)* il est vraiment nul; *(doesn't suspect)* il se doute de rien; *(doesn't know)* il en a pas la moindre idée

ⓘ Ce terme vient du dessin animé américain *Scooby Doo*.

scoop [skuːp] *n* **(a)** *Br (drink)* canon *m*, godet *m*; **we went out for a couple of scoops last night** on est allé boire un coup hier soir **(b)** *Am* **to get the scoop on sth** se renseigner sur qch□; **get the scoop on all your favourite movie stars** découvrez les potins sur tous vos acteurs préférés

scoot [skuːt] *vi* se sauver, filer; **scoot!** du vent!, file!

scoot away, scoot off *vi* se sauver, filer

scope [skəʊp] *vt Am* **(a)** *(look at)* mater, reluquer; **he's at the beach scoping the babes** il est à la plage en train de mater les nanas (**b**) *(see)* voir[□]; **did you scope that ring he was wearing?** t'as vu un peu la bague qu'il avait au doigt?

scope out *vt sép* = **scope**

scorcher ['skɔːtʃə(r)] *n* journée *f* de forte chaleur[□]; **today's been a scorcher** il en a fait un plat aujourd'hui

score [skɔː(r)] **1** *n* (**a**) **to know the score** savoir à quoi s'en tenir[□]; **what's the score?** qu'est-ce qui se passe? (**b**) *Br (20 pounds)* vingt livres[□] *fpl* (**c**) *Am (20 dollars)* vingt dollars[□] *mpl*
    2 *vt (drugs)* acheter[□]
    3 *vi* (**a**) *(buy drugs)* acheter de la drogue[□] (**b**) *(find sexual partner)* faire une touche; **to score with sb** emballer qn

Scouse [skaʊs] *Br* **1** *n (person)* = natif de la ville de Liverpool; *(dialect)* = dialecte de la ville de Liverpool
    2 *adj* de Liverpool

ⓘ Le terme "scouse" vient de "lob-scouse", qui est un plat traditionnel de la région de Liverpool composé de viande bouillie et légumes accompagnés de biscuits, que consommaient les marins.

Scouser ['skaʊsə(r)] *n Br* = natif de la ville de Liverpool

scram [skræm] *vi* se casser, se barrer, trisser, se tirer; **scram!** du vent!, file!

scran [skræn] *n Br* bouffe *f*, graille *f*

scrap [skræp] **1** *n (fight)* baston *m* ou *f*; **to get into a scrap** se bagarrer; **to get into a scrap with sb** se friter ou se castagner avec qn
    2 *vi (fight)* se friter, se castagner

scratch [skrætʃ] *n Am (money)* fric *m*, pognon *m*, flouze *m*, oseille *f*

scream [skriːm] *n* **he's a scream** il est impayable; **it was a scream** c'était tordant, c'était à se tordre de rire; **the book/film's a scream** le livre/le film est tordant; **scream queen** actrice *f* de films d'horreur[□]

screw [skruː] **1** *n* (**a**) [!] *(sexual intercourse)* baise *f*; **to have a screw** baiser, tirer un coup, s'envoyer en l'air; **to be a good screw** *(of person)* être un bon coup (**b**) **to have a screw loose** *(be mad)* avoir une case de vide (**c**) *Br (prison officer)* maton(onne) *m,f* (**d**) *Br (salary)* salaire[□] *m*; **to be on a good screw** avoir un super bon salaire
    2 *vt* (**a**) [!] *(have sex with) (of man)* baiser, troncher, tringler, limer; *(of woman)* baiser avec, s'envoyer (**b**) [!] *(for emphasis)* **screw you!** va te faire foutre!; **screw him!** qu'il aille se faire foutre!; **go (and) screw yourself!** va te faire foutre! (**c**) *(cheat)* arnaquer (**d**) *Am* **to screw the pooch** *(blunder)* faire une gaffe *ou* une boulette
    3 [!] *vi (have sex)* baiser, s'envoyer en l'air

screw around 1 *vt sép* **to screw sb around** *(treat badly)* se foutre de la gueule de qn; *(waste time of)* faire perdre son temps à qn[□]
    2 *vi* (**a**) *(act foolishly)* faire l'andouille; *(waste time)* glander, glandouiller (**b**) [!] *(be promiscuous)* coucher à droite à gauche

screw over *vt sép* **to screw sb over** arnaquer qn, refaire qn

screw up 1 *vt sép (person)* rendre cinglé; *(plan, situation)* faire foirer, foutre en l'air; **she's totally screwed up** elle est complètement à côté de ses pompes; **you've screwed everything up** tu as tout foutu en l'air
    2 *vi* foirer, merder

screwball ['skruːbɔːl] **1** *n* allumé(e)

m,f, barge *mf*
  2 *adj* allumé, barge

screwed [skru:d] *adj (in trouble)* **to be screwed** être foutu

screw-loose ['skru:lu:s] *adj Am* loufoque, loufedingue

screw-up ['skru:ʌp] *n Am (bungler)* manche *m*; *(misfit)* paumé(e) *m,f*

screwy ['skru:ɪ] *adj Am* dingue, cinglé, toqué

scrote [!] [skrəʊt] *n Br (abrév* **scrotum***) (person)* gland *m*, taré *m*

scrubber ['skrʌbə(r)] *n Br (woman)* roulure *f*, salope *f*

scrummy ['skrʌmɪ] *adj Br* délicieux[□], super bon

scum [skʌm] *n* **(a)** *(people)* ordures *fpl*; **he's scum** c'est une ordure;

Pleins feux sur...

Seduction

En Grande-Bretagne, se mettre en quête d'un partenaire sexuel se dit **to go** ou **to be on the pull**, et draguer quelqu'un se dit **to come on to someone** ou encore **to chat someone up** ; aux États-Unis, l'on dira **to hit on someone**. Si les tentatives de séduction se révèlent fructueuses, on dira **he/she scored**, ou bien **he/she pulled** (ce dernier terme – qui s'emploie en argot britannique uniquement – peut également s'utiliser transitivement : **to pull someone**). "Embrasser quelqu'un avec la langue" se dit **to get off** ou **cop off with someone**, ou encore **to snog someone**, tandis que les Américains emploient l'expression **to make out with someone**. Les gens possédant un physique agréable peuvent être qualifiés de **eye candy** ; en Grande-Bretagne on parlera volontiers de **totty** et de **talent** (ex : **there's loads of talent in here tonight!**) ; le terme **beefcake** est réservé aux hommes beaux et musclés. Une personne séduisante (homme ou femme) est un(e) **babe**, **hottie** ou encore **honey**. Les termes **hunk** et **stud muffin** sont réservés aux hommes, tandis que **stunner** et **fox** ne s'appliquent qu'aux femmes. Les adjectifs **fit** (anglais britannique), **hot**, **buff** et **drop-dead gorgeous** (tous unisexes) sont très utiles pour décrire une personne que l'on trouve sexy. Une personne (homme ou femme) n'ayant pas été gâtée par la nature est **a moose** ou **a minger** (argot britannique), ou bien encore **a dog** ou **a boot** (ces deux derniers termes étant réservés aux femmes). Les adjectifs véhiculant la notion de laideur sont **minging**, **rough**, **rank** (tous britanniques) ainsi que **fugly**. Si vous êtes de sortie gare aux **beer goggles**, l'abus d'alcool risquant de vous faire prendre **a moose** pour **a hottie** !

Le symbole [!] dénote un terme très familier, [!!] un terme vulgaire.

he's the scum of the earth c'est le dernier des derniers; **she treats him like scum** elle le traite comme de la merde **(b)** [!] *Am (semen)* foutre *m*

scumbag ['skʌmbæg] *n* **(a)** *(person)* ordure *f*, raclure *f* **(b)** [!] *Am (condom)* capote *f* (anglaise)

scumbucket ['skʌmbʌkɪt] *n Am (person)* ordure *f*, raclure *f*

scummer ['skʌmə(r)] *n Br* jeune lascar *m*, racaille *f*

scuzzy ['skʌzɪ] *adj* dégueulasse, cradingue

search [sɜːtʃ] *vt* **search me!** *(I don't know)* j'en ai pas la moindre idée!

sec [sek] *n (abrév* **second)** seconde□ *f*, instant□ *m*; **half a sec!** une seconde!; **wait a sec!** attends une seconde!

seeing-to ['siːɪŋtuː] *n Br* **to give sb a good seeing-to** *(have sex with)* faire passer qn à la casserole; *(beat up)* tabasser qn

see ya ['siːjə] *exclam* salut!, à plus!

semi ['semɪ] *n (half-erection)* **to have a semi** bander mou

serious ['sɪərɪəs] *adj (for emphasis)* **she makes serious money** elle gagne un fric fou; **we did some serious drinking last night** on a picolé hier soir, et on n'a pas fait semblant; **that is one serious computer** c'est pas de la gnognotte, cet ordinateur

seriously ['sɪərɪəslɪ] *adv (for emphasis)* sérieusement, vachement; **she's getting seriously fat** elle devient énorme; **he was seriously drunk** il était sérieusement éméché; **her boyfriend is seriously gorgeous** son petit ami est super beau

sesh [seʃ] *n Br (abrév* **session)** **to have a drinking sesh** se pinter; **we had a bit of a sesh last night** on s'en est donné hier soir

set back [set] *vt sép (cost)* coûter à□; **it set me back twenty quid** ça m'a coûté vingt livres; **that must have set you back a bit** ça a dû te coûter bonbon

set up *vt sép (trap, trick)* piéger□; **they were set up** ils ont été victimes d'un coup monté; **your flatmate's really cute, d'you think you could set me up with him?** ton coloc est super mignon, tu crois que tu pourrais m'organiser un rancard avec lui?

set-up ['setʌp] *n (trap, trick)* machination□ *f*, coup *m* monté

severe [sɪ'vɪə(r)] *adj Br (for emphasis)* sacré, vache (de); **he is a severe pain** c'est un sacré emmerdeur

severely [sɪ'vɪəlɪ] *adv Br (for emphasis)* sérieusement, vachement; **we were severely drunk last night** on était sérieusement déchirés hier soir; **you are severely annoying me!** tu me cours sérieusement sur le haricot!

sewermouth ['suːəmaʊθ] *n Am* **to be a sewermouth** jurer comme un charretier

sex [seks] *n* **sex god** apollon *m*; **sex goddess** vénus *f*; **sex kitten** nana *f* sexy, joli petit colis *m*; **that girl is just sex on legs** *or* **on a stick** cette nana est vraiment super sexy

sex up *vt sep* **(a)** *(image, style)* rendre plus sexy; **that actress has really sexed up her look** l'actrice a adopté un look beaucoup plus sexy **(b)** *(topic, thing)* rendre plus intéressant□; *(document, story)* enjoliver□

sexploits ['seksplɔɪts] *npl Hum* exploits *mpl* sexuels□; **I'm sick of**

Pleins feux sur...

Sex

On ne compte plus les termes argotiques anglais désignant l'organe sexuel masculin. Parmi les plus fréquents,
on peut citer **dick**, **cock** et **prick**. Les termes **willy** (anglais
britannique) et **peter** (anglais américain) sont moins choquants.
Le yiddish a donné le mot **schlong**. On trouve également des expressions plus humoristiques telles que **one-eyed trouser snake**.
Pour un homme particulièrement "bien équipé", on utilise les
expressions **to be hung like a horse**, **a donkey** ou **a mule**.
Pour parler d'une érection on emploiera les mots **hard-on**, **boner** et, en
argot britannique, **stiffy**. **Balls** est le mot le plus fréquent pour désigner
les testicules, mais il existe d'autres synonymes tels que **nuts**, **bollocks**
(anglais britannique) et **nads** (terme britannique qui vient de "gonads").
Pour désigner le sexe de la femme on emploie **pussy**, **snatch**, **beaver**
et, en anglais britannique, **fanny**. (Il est bon de savoir que **fanny** signifie
"fesses" en anglais américain, une différence qui pourrait entraîner
quelques malentendus...)

"Faire l'amour" a d'innombrables équivalents argotiques en anglais, dont
le verbe **to fuck** (très vulgaire) est le plus courant. On peut citer d'autres
synonymes tels que **to screw**, **to bone**, **to bang**, **to hump** et **to poke**,
tous ces verbes étant plutôt vulgaires. En Grande-Bretagne le verbe **to
shag** est très largement employé, à tel point qu'il choque beaucoup
moins que les termes précédemment cités. Dans un registre encore un peu
moins vulgaire, on trouve **to bonk** en anglais britannique et **to boink** en
américain, ainsi que les expressions **to do it**, **to get it on** et **to have it off**
(anglais britannique). Certaines expressions britanniques sont un peu plus
humoristiques : **hanky-panky**, **rumpy-pumpy**, **nookie**, **a bit of how's
your father** et **a roll in the hay** désignent toutes l'acte sexuel.

Plusieurs expressions imagées, dont beaucoup contiennent des allitéra-
tions ou des rimes, permettent de désigner la masturbation masculine.
Citons par exemple **to bash the bishop**, **to beat one's meat**, **to
spank the monkey** et **to choke the chicken**. Cependant, les expressions les plus communes sont **to jerk off** (surtout utilisé aux États-
Unis) et en Grande-Bretagne **to wank** et **to have a wank** (à l'origine
de la plus commune des insultes en anglais britannique : **wanker**,
"connard"). Une personne en état d'excitation sexuelle est **horny**,
ou encore **gagging for it** ou **randy** (en anglais britannique unique-

Le symbole [!] dénote un terme très familier, [!!] un terme vulgaire.

ment pour ces deux dernières expressions). D'une personne en état de chasteté involontaire, on dira : **he's/she's not getting any** (le complément d'objet étant implicite).

reading about all these celebrity **sexploits!** j'en ai marre de tous ces articles sur les exploits sexuels des célébrités!

sexpot ['sekspɒt] n bombe f sexuelle

sex-starved ['seks'stɑːvd] adj frustré

shack up [ʃæk] vi **to shack up with sb** se mettre à la colle avec qn; **to be shacked up (with sb)** être à la colle (avec qn); **they shacked up together** ils se sont mis à la colle

shades [ʃeɪdz] npl (sunglasses) lunettes fpl noires□

shaft [!] [ʃɑːft] 1 n (a) (penis) chibre m, queue f (b) Am **to get the shaft** (get cheated) se faire baiser ou arnaquer

2 vt (a) Br (have sex with) baiser, tringler, troncher (b) (cheat) baiser, arnaquer; **to get shafted** se faire baiser ou arnaquer

shafted ['ʃɑːftɪd] adj Br beurré, bourré, pété

shag [!] [ʃæg] Br 1 n (a) (sexual intercourse) baise f; **to have a shag** baiser, tirer un coup, s'envoyer en l'air; **to be a good shag** (of person) être un bon coup; **shag buddy** compagnon (compagne) m,f de baise (b) (boring task) plaie f; **it's a real shag having to get up so early every morning** c'est vraiment chiant ou la plaie de devoir se lever si tôt tous les matins

2 vt (have sex with) (of man) baiser, troncher, tringler, limer; (of woman) baiser avec, s'envoyer

3 vi (have sex) baiser, s'envoyer en l'air

shaggable [!] ['ʃægəbəl] adj Br baisable

shagged (out) [!] [ʃægd('aʊt)] adj Br (tired) naze, lessivé

shake [ʃeɪk] 1 n (a) **in two shakes (of a lamb's tail)** en moins de deux, en deux temps trois mouvements, en deux coups de cuiller à pot (b) **it's no great shakes** ça casse pas des briques, ça casse pas trois pattes à un canard

2 vt Austr (rob) piquer, tirer ▶ voir aussi **leg, stick**

shake down vt sép Am (a) (blackmail) **to shake sb down** faire chanter qn□ (b) (search) **to shake sb down** fouiller qn□, palper qn; **to shake sth down** fouiller qch□

shakedown ['ʃeɪkdaʊn] n Am (a) (blackmail) chantage□ m (b) (search) fouille□ f

shampoo [ʃæm'puː] n Hum (champagne) champ' m

shamus ['ʃeɪməs] n Am (private detective) privé m

shank [ʃæŋk] Am 1 n (knife) surin m, lame f

2 vt (stab) planter

Sharon and Tracy ['ʃærənən'treɪsɪ] npr Br = type de jeune femme d'origine modeste aux mœurs légères, vulgaire, bruyante, et peu intelligente

ⓘ L'expression "Sharon and Tracy" a été popularisée au cours des années 90. Ces deux prénoms étaient très courants dans les classes populaires et à ce titre beaucoup de gens les considéraient comme vulgaires. On utilise cette expression de la façon suivante : "the club was full of Sharon and Tracys", "she's a bit of a Sharon and Tracy (type)". Il s'agit d'un stéréotype social comparable à l'"Essex girl" et au "chav" (voir ces entrées).

sharp [ʃɑːp] *adj (stylish)* chicos, classe
▸ *voir aussi* **poke**

sharpish [ˈʃɑːpɪʃ] *adv Br* illico presto, vite fait; **you'd better do it sharpish** t'as intérêt à le faire illico presto, t'as intérêt à faire fissa

shattered [ˈʃætəd] *adj Br (exhausted)* naze, lessivé, crevé, claqué

shebang [ʃəˈbæŋ] *n* **the whole shebang** et tout le tremblement, et tout le bataclan

shedload [ˈʃedləʊd] *n Br* **a shedload of, shedloads of** une tapée de; **she earns a shedload** *or* **shedloads of dosh** elle se fait un fric fou; **he's sold a shedload of albums over the last few years** il a vendu une tapée d'albums ces dernières années

sheep-shagger [!!] [ˈʃiːpʃægə(r)] *n Br Injurieux (Welsh person)* Gallois(e)□ *m,f; (any rural person)* péquenaud(e) *m,f*

sheesh [ʃiːʃ] *exclam (in surprise)* tiens!; *(in exasperation)* allez!

sheets [ʃiːts] *npl Br* livres *fpl* sterling□; **his camera cost him 500 sheets** son appareil photo lui a coûté 500 livres

sheila [ˈʃiːlə] *n Austr* nana *f*

shekels [ˈʃekəlz] *npl (money)* fric *m*, flouze *m*, pognon *m*

shell out [ʃel] **1** *vt sép* raquer
2 *vi* raquer, casquer (**for** pour)

shellac [ʃəˈlæk] *vt Am (defeat)* battre à plates coutures, écrabouiller, filer une raclée *ou* une déculottée à; **to get shellacked** être battu à plates coutures, se faire écrabouiller, prendre une raclée *ou* une déculottée

shellacking [ʃəˈlækɪŋ] *n Am* (**a**) *(beating)* **to give sb a shellacking** tabasser qn, passer qn à tabac; **to take a shellacking** se faire tabasser, se faire passer à tabac, prendre une raclée (**b**) *(defeat)* raclée *f*, déculottée *f*; **to give sb a shellacking** battre qn à plates coutures, écrabouiller qn, filer une raclée *ou* une déculottée à qn; **to take a shellacking** être battu à plates coutures, se faire écrabouiller, prendre une raclée *ou* une déculottée

shemozzle [ʃəˈmɒzəl] *n Am* merdier *m*

sherbet [ˈʃɜːbət] *n Br* (**a**) *(alcoholic drink)* verre□ *m*; **fancy going for a couple of sherbets?** ça te dirait de sortir prendre un verre? (**b**) **sherbet dab** *(rhyming slang* **cab***)* taxi□ *m*, tacot *m*

sherman [!] [ˈʃɜːmən] *n Br (rhyming slang* **Sherman tank = wank***)* branlette *f*; **to have a sherman** se branler, se faire une branlette, faire cinq contre un

shift [ʃɪft] **1** *vt* (**a**) *(sell)* fourguer (**b**) *(eat, drink)* s'envoyer; **hurry up and shift that pint!** dépêche-toi d'écluser ta pinte! (**c**) **shift yourself!** *(move)* pousse tes fesses!; *(hurry up)* magne-toi!, remue-toi!
2 *vi (move quickly)* foncer

shifty [ˈʃɪftɪ] *adj (person)* louche; *(look)* fuyant□

shill [ʃɪl] *Am* **1** *n* baron *m*
2 *vt* (**a**) *(lure into swindle)* arnaquer; **they shilled him into handing over his life savings** ils ont réussi à

lui soutirer toutes ses économies (**b**) *(hype)* faire de la pub pour; **they've got a quarterback shilling their new frozen yoghurt** il y a un joueur de football américain qui fait la pub pour leur nouveau yaourt glacé

shindig ['ʃɪndɪg] *n* (**a**) *(party)* fête□ *f*, fiesta *f*; **to have a shindig** faire la fiesta (**b**) *(commotion)* raffut *m*, ramdam *m*; **to kick up a shindig** faire du raffut

shine [ʃaɪn] **1** *n Am Injurieux (black man)* nègre *m*, bamboula *m*; *(black woman)* négresse *f*

2 *vi* **stick it where the sun don't shine!** [**!**] tu peux te le mettre où je pense! ▸ *voir aussi* **arse**

shiner ['ʃaɪnə(r)] *n (black eye)* œil *m* au beurre noir, coquard *m*

shirt [ʃɜːt] *n* **keep your shirt on!** t'énerve pas!, du calme!; *Br* **to put one's shirt on sth** miser jusqu'à son dernier centime sur qch□; **to lose one's shirt** tout perdre□; **to take the shirt off sb's back** faire cracher jusqu'à son dernier centime à qn; **stuffed shirt** *(person)* collet *m* monté

shirt-lifter ['ʃɜːtlɪftə(r)] *n Br Injurieux* pédé *m*, tantouze *f*, tapette *f*

shit [**!**] [ʃɪt] **1** *n* (**a**) *(excrement)* merde *f*; **to** *Br* **have** *or Am* **take a shit** chier, couler un bronze; **to have the shits** avoir la chiasse; **to be in the shit** être dans la merde; **to drop sb in the shit** foutre qn dans la merde; **I don't give a shit** j'en ai rien à battre *ou* à secouer; **who gives a shit?** qu'est-ce que ça peut foutre?; **to treat sb like shit** traiter qn comme de la merde; **to beat the shit out of sb** défoncer la gueule à qn; **to kick** *or* **beat seven shades of shit out of sb** faire une tête au carré à qn, démolir la gueule à qn; **to scare the shit out of sb** foutre une trouille pas

possible à qn; **to get one's shit together** se ressaisir□; **to be up shit creek (without a paddle)** être dans une merde noire; **when the shit hits the fan** quand ça pètera; **he thinks his shit doesn't stink** il se prend pas pour de la merde; **eat shit (and die)!** va te faire foutre!; **tough shit!** tant pis!; **shit happens** ce sont des choses qui arrivent□; **same shit, different day** c'est toujours la même merde

(**b**) *(nonsense)* conneries *fpl*; **he's full of shit** il dit que des conneries, il sait pas ce qu'il dit; **to talk shit** raconter des conneries; **that's shit!** c'est des conneries!; **don't believe that shit** n'écoute pas ces conneries; **no shit?** sans déconner?, sans dec?; **no shit!** sans déconner!, sans dec!

(**c**) *(worthless things)* **to be a load of shit**, *Am* **to be the shits** être de la merde; **the film was a piece of shit** c'était vraiment de la merde, ce film

(**d**) *(useless things)* bordel *m*, foutoir *m*; **clear all that shit off your desk** vire-moi ce bordel de ton bureau

(**e**) *(disgusting substance)* merde *f*, saloperie *f*; **I can't eat this shit** je peux pas bouffer cette merde

(**f**) *(person)* ordure *f*, bâton *m* merdeux; **he's been a real shit to her** il s'est vraiment conduit en salaud avec elle

(**g**) *(unfair treatment)* **to give sb shit** faire chier qn; **the press have been giving him a lot of shit lately** la presse l'a traîné dans la merde ces derniers temps; **don't take his shit!** le laisse pas te traiter comme de la merde!; **I don't need this shit!** j'ai pas envie de m'emmerder avec ce genre de conneries!; **to be on sb's shit list** ne pas être dans les petits papiers de qn

(**h**) *(anything)* **he doesn't do shit** il en rame pas une, il en fout pas une

The symbol □ *indicates that a translation is neutral.*

rame; **I can't see shit** j'y vois goutte; **they can't sing for shit** ils chantent comme des savates

(i) *Am (things like that)* **he's really smart, he writes poetry and shit** il est vraiment intelligent, il écrit des poèmes, des trucs comme ça; **then he got mad and started yelling and shit** puis il s'est mis en colère et il a commencé à gueuler et tout le bazar

(j) **to feel/look like shit** *(ill)* se sentir/avoir l'air patraque

(k) *(cannabis)* shit *m*, chichon *m*; *(heroin)* héro *f*, blanche *f*

2 *adj (worthless)* merdique; **to feel shit** *(ill)* se sentir patraque; *(guilty)* se sentir coupable□, avoir les boules *ou* les glandes; **I had a really shit time** j'ai passé un moment dégueulasse; **he's a shit driver** il conduit comme un pied

3 *adv* **to be shit out of luck** ne pas avoir de bol *ou* de pot

4 *exclam* merde!

5 *vt* (a) **to shit oneself** *(defecate, be scared)* chier dans son froc; *(react with anger)* piquer une crise; *(react with surprise)* ne pas en revenir; **to shit a brick** *or* **bricks** chier dans son froc

(b) *Am* **to shit sb** *(lie to)* raconter des craques à qn; *(deceive)* se foutre de la gueule de qn; *Hum* **I shit you not!** je déconne pas!

6 *vi* (a) *(defecate)* chier; **shit or get off the pot!** alors, tu te décides?□

(b) **to shit on sb** *(treat badly)* traiter qn comme de la merde; *Br* **to shit on sb from a great height** *(treat badly)* traiter qn comme de la merde; *(defeat)* battre qn à plates coutures, écrabouiller qn, foutre une déculottée à qn; *Am* **shit on that!** et puis merde!

(c) *Am (react with anger)* piquer une crise; *(react with surprise)* ne pas en revenir; **your parents will**

shit when they see what you've done! tes parents vont piquer une crise quand ils se rendront compte de ce que t'as fait ▸ *voir aussi* **bear, crock, eat, holy, jack**

shit-ass [!] ['ʃɪtæs] *n Am (person)* salaud (salope) *m,f*

shit-can [!] ['ʃɪtkæn] *vt Am (discard)* balancer, foutre en l'air; *(disregard, abandon)* laisser tomber

shite [!] [ʃaɪt] *Br* **1** *n* (a) *(excrement)* merde *f* (b) *(nonsense)* conneries *fpl*; **he's full of shite** il raconte que des conneries, il sait pas ce qu'il dit; **to talk shite** raconter des conneries, déconner; **that's shite!** c'est des conneries!; **don't believe that shite!** n'écoute pas ces conneries!

2 *adj (bad)* merdique; **to feel shite** *(ill)* se sentir patraque; *(guilty)* se sentir coupable□, avoir les boules *ou* les glandes; **I had a really shite time** j'ai passé un moment dégueulasse; **he's a shite singer** il chante comme un pied

3 *exclam* merde!

shit-faced [!] ['ʃɪtfeɪst] *adj (drunk)* bourré, pété, beurré; *(on drugs)* défoncé, raide

shit-for-brains [!] ['ʃɪtfəbreɪnz] *n* tache *f*, gogol *mf*

shithead [!] ['ʃɪthed] *n* enfoiré(e) *m,f*

shit-heel [!] ['ʃɪthiːl] *n Am (person)* pécore *mf*, bouseux(euse) *m,f*

shithole [!] ['ʃɪthəʊl] *n (dirty place)* porcherie *f*, taudis *m*; **this town's a complete shithole** *(boring, ugly)* cette ville est un vrai trou

shit-hot [!] [ʃɪt'hɒt] *adj* super, génial

shithouse [!] ['ʃɪthaʊs] *n* chiottes *fpl*, gogues *mpl*; **to be built like a brick shithouse** être une armoire à glace

Le symbole **[!]** dénote un terme très familier, **[!!]** un terme vulgaire.

shitkicker [!] ['ʃɪtkɪkə(r)] *Am n* (**a**) *(farmhand)* garçon *m* de ferme◻; *(rustic)* pedzouille *mf*, pécore *mf* (**b**) **shitkickers** *(heavy boots)* écrase-merde *mpl*

shitless [!] ['ʃɪtlɪs] *adj* **to be bored shitless** se faire chier à mort; **to be scared shitless** être mort de trouille

shitload [!] ['ʃɪtləʊd] *n* **a (whole) shitload (of)** une chiée (de), une tapée (de)

shit-scared [!] [ʃɪt'skeəd] *adj* **to be shit-scared** être mort de trouille

shit-stirrer [!] ['ʃɪtstɜːrə(r)] *n* fouteur(euse) *m,f* de merde

shitstorm [!] ['ʃɪtstɔːm] *n Am* foin *m*; **the announcement caused one hell of a shitstorm** la déclaration a fait un sacré foin

shitter [!] ['ʃɪtə(r)] *n (toilet)* chiottes *fpl*, gogues *mpl*; **that's two whole days' work down the shitter!** c'est deux jours entiers de travail de foutus!

shitty [!] ['ʃɪtɪ] *adj (worthless)* merdique; *(nasty)* dégueulasse; **that was a shitty thing to do/say** c'est salaud *ou* dégueulasse d'avoir fait/dit ça; **to feel shitty** *(ill)* se sentir patraque◻, *(guilty)* se sentir coupable◻, avoir les boules *ou* les glandes; **I wouldn't touch it with a shitty stick!** je n'en voudrais pour rien au monde!◻

shitweasel [!] ['ʃɪtwiːzəl] *n Am* ordure *f*, raclure *f*

shiv [ʃɪv] *Am* **1** *n (knife)* surin *m*, lame *f*
2 *vt (stab)* planter

shiznit ['ʃɪznɪt] *n Noir Am* **it's the shiznit!** c'est super *ou* top!

shizzle ['ʃɪzəl] **1** *adj (sure)* **for shizzle!** c'est clair!
2 *n (shit)* **it's the shizzle!** c'est top

ou génial!; **the gig was off the shizzle!** le concert était super génial!

shock jock ['ʃɒkdʒɒk] *n Am* = animateur ou animatrice de radio au ton irrévérencieux et provocateur

shonky ['ʃɒŋkɪ] *adj Austr* (**a**) *(risky)* risqué◻; **don't get involved in his shonky schemes** ne te laisse pas embringuer dans ses histoires à la gomme (**b**) *(untrustworthy)* louche; **there's something a bit shonky about him** je le trouve un peu louche (**c**) *(not working properly)* qui déconne; **the brakes are a bit shonky** les freins déconnent un peu

shoo-in ['ʃuːɪn] *n* **it's a shoo-in** c'est couru d'avance; **they're a shoo-in to win the next election** ils vont gagner les prochaines élections, c'est couru d'avance

shoot [ʃuːt] **1** *exclam Am* zut!, mince!
2 *vt* (**a**) *Am* **to shoot the breeze** *or* **the bull** *(chat)* papoter (**b**) **to shoot one's load** *or* **wad** [!!] *(ejaculate)* décharger, balancer la purée; *Am* **to shoot one's wad** *or* **the works** *(do all one can)* se donner à fond
3 *vi (speak)* **shoot!** vas-y, je t'écoute! ▸ *voir aussi* **blank, cookie, hoops, lunch, mouth**

shoot up 1 *vt sép (drugs)* se faire un shoot de; *(habitually)* se shooter *ou* se piquer à
2 *vi (inject drugs)* se piquer, se shooter

shoot-'em-up ['ʃuːtəmʌp] *n* = film ou jeu vidéo comportant de nombreux échanges de coups de feu

shooter ['ʃuːtə(r)] *n (gun)* flingue *m*, feu *m* ▸ *voir aussi* **square, straight**

shooting-gallery ['ʃuːtɪŋgælərɪ] *n Am (for buying drugs)* = lieu où l'on achète, vend et consomme de la drogue

shooting-iron [ˈʃuːtɪŋaɪən] n Am (gun) flingue m, feu m

shooting-match [ˈʃuːtɪŋmætʃ] n **the whole shooting-match** tout le bataclan, tout le tremblement

shop [ʃɒp] vt Br (inform on) dénoncer◻, balancer

short [ʃɔːt] adj **to have sb by the short hairs** or Br **the short and curlies** avoir qn à sa merci◻

shortarse [!] [ˈʃɔːtɑːs] n Br rase-bitume mf, bas-du-cul mf

shorts [ʃɔːts] npl (a) **to have the shorts** (have little money) être fauché, être raide (b) Am **eat my shorts!** tu me gonfles!

ⓘ L'expression "eat my shorts!" (mange mon short!) a été popularisée par le dessin animé américain The Simpsons au cours des années 90. Il s'agit d'une expression qu'emploie le jeune Bart Simpson quand il veut qu'on le laisse tranquille.

shorty [ˈʃɔːtɪ] n (a) (short person) rase-bitume mf, bas-du-cul mf; **hey, shorty!** hé, rase-bitume! (b) Noir Am (attractive girl) canon m; (girlfriend) copine f, nana f

shot [ʃɒt] **1** n (a) **to do sth like a shot** (speedily) faire qch à tout berzingue; (with no hesitation) faire qch sans hésiter◻ (b) **big shot** gros bonnet m, huile f (c) Noir Am **the whole shot** tout le tremblement
2 adj (a) Br **to get shot of sb/sth** se débarrasser de qn/qch◻; **I can't wait to be shot of this house** j'ai hâte de me débarrasser de cette maison (b) Am (wasted, ruined) fichu, foutu; **that's another day shot!** en-

core une journée de foutue (en l'air)!
▸ voir aussi **cook, cook up, mug**

shotgun [ˈʃɒtgʌn] **1** adj **shotgun wedding** mariage m forcé◻ (lorsque la future mariée est enceinte)
2 adv **to ride shotgun** (in car) être assis à la place du mort

ⓘ L'expression "to ride shotgun" vient de l'époque où les cochers des diligences de l'Ouest américain étaient accompagnés d'un garde armé d'un fusil ("shotgun"), en cas d'attaque.

shoulda [ˈʃʊdə] contraction = should have ▸ voir aussi **coulda**

shout [ʃaʊt] **1** n (a) Br & Austr (round of drinks) tournée◻ f; **it's my shout** c'est ma tournée; **whose shout is it?** c'est la tournée de qui? (b) Br (chance) **to be in with a good shout of sth** avoir de bonnes chances de décrocher qch
2 vt Austr (treat) **to shout sb a meal** payer le restaurant à qn
3 vi Austr (pay for drinks) **I'll shout** c'est ma tournée◻, c'est moi qui rince

shouty [ˈʃaʊtɪ] adj (person) grande gueule; (singer, music) braillard

shove off [ʃʌv] vi décaniller, se barrer, se tirer; **shove off!** dégage!, fous le camp!

show [ʃəʊ] vi (arrive) se pointer

showboat [ˈʃəʊbəʊt] Am **1** n (show-off) crâneur(euse) m,f, frimeur(euse) m,f
2 vi (show off) crâner, frimer

shower [ˈʃaʊə(r)] n Br Péj (people) **what a shower!** quel bande de nuls!; **you lazy shower!** bande de flemmards!

shrapnel [ˈʃræpnəl] n (loose change)

Le symbole [!] dénote un terme très familier, [!!] un terme vulgaire.

mitraille f, ferraille f

shredded [ˈʃredɪd] adj Am (drunk) bourré, pété, beurré

shreddies [ˈʃredɪz] npl (underwear) calbute m, calcif m

shrink [ʃrɪŋk] n (psychiatrist) psy mf

shroomer [ˈʃruːmə(r)] n = personne qui prend des champignons hallucinogènes

shrooms [ʃruːmz] npl (abrév **mushrooms**) champignons mpl hallucinogènes□, champignons mpl

shtuk [ʃtʊk] = **schtuk**

shtum [ʃtʊm] = **schtum**

shuck [ʃʌk] Noir Am **1** n (trick) arnaque f

2 vt (trick) arnaquer

3 vi **to shuck (and jive)** (act foolishly) faire l'andouille; (speak misleadingly, bluff) baratiner

shucks [ʃʌks] exclam mince!, punaise!

shufty [ˈʃʊftɪ] n Br **to have a shufty at sth** jeter un coup d'œil à qch; **have a quick shufty at this!** regarde un peu ça!

shut [ʃʌt] vt **shut your mouth or face, shut it!** ferme ton clapet!, la ferme! ▶ voir aussi **noise, trap**

shut up 1 vt sép **to shut sb up** clouer le bec à qn; **that shut him up!** ça lui a cloué le bec!

2 vi fermer son clapet, la fermer, la boucler; **shut up!** la ferme!, ferme ton clapet!, boucle-la!

shut-eye [ˈʃʌtaɪ] n **to get some shut-eye** piquer un roupillon, roupiller

shyster [ˈʃaɪstə(r)] n Am (businessman, politician) homme m d'affaires/ politicien m véreux; (lawyer) avocat m marron

sick [sɪk] adj (a) **to be sick (and tired) of sb/sth** en avoir marre ou ras le bol de qn/qch; **to be sick to death or sick of the sight of sb/ sth** en avoir sa claque de qn/qch (**b**) Br **(as) sick as a parrot** (disappointed) déçu□, dégoûté (**c**) (perverse) malsain□ (**d**) Am (excellent) génial, super, top; **that new snowboard is sick!** ce nouveau snowboard est génial! ▶ voir aussi **teeth**

sick up vt sép Br gerber, dégueuler

sickbag [ˈsɪkbæg] n Br **pass the sickbag!** ça me fout la nausée!

sickie [ˈsɪkɪ] n Br & Austr **to take or pull a sickie** se faire porter pâle (lorsqu'on est bien portant)

sicko [ˈsɪkəʊ] n malade mf, tordu(e) m,f

sight [saɪt] n (**a**) **she can't stand or Br stick the sight of him** elle ne peut pas le voir en peinture (**b**) (mess) **to be or Br look a sight** être dans un bel état; Br **what a sight!** quel tableau! (**c**) (for emphasis) **a damn or darn sight better/easier** vachement mieux/plus facile; **a damn or darn sight more/less** vachement plus/moins ▶ voir aussi **outta, sick**

signify [ˈsɪgnɪfaɪ] vi Noir Am = se livrer à des joutes verbales entre amis; **they were signifying back and forth** ils se chambraient, ils s'envoyaient des vannes

ⓘ Le "signifying" est une sorte de joute verbale improvisée au cours de laquelle des amis se lancent des remarques sarcastiques et grotesques.

simoleon [sɪˈməʊlɪən] n Am (dollar) dollar□ m

simp [sɪmp] n Am (abrév **simpleton**) andouille f, crétin(e) m,f

sing [sɪŋ] vi (confess, inform) cracher

ou lâcher le morceau; **he sang like a canary** il a craché le morceau, il s'est mis à table ► *voir aussi* **blues**

singer ['sɪŋə(r)] *n Br (informer)* indic *mf*

sis [sɪs] *n (abrév* **sister**) frangine *f*

sissy ['sɪsɪ] *n* femmelette *f*

sister ['sɪstə(r)] *n* (a) *Noir Am (fellow black woman)* Noire *f* américaine□; **you don't treat your sisters like that!** c'est pas des façons de traiter d'autres Noires! (b) *(fellow feminist)* camarade *f* féministe□

six-pack ['sɪkspæk] *n* (a) *Hum (stomach muscles)* abdos *mpl*; **he's got a great six-pack** il a des super abdos (b) *Br Hum* **to be one can short of a six-pack** ne pas être net

sixty-nine [sɪkstɪ'naɪn] *n (sexual position)* soixante-neuf *m*

skag [skæg] = **scag**

skank [skæŋk] *n* cageot *m*, boudin *m*

skanky ['skæŋkɪ] *adj* cradingue; **he's always wearing those skanky old trainers** il porte toujours les mêmes vieilles baskets cradingues

skate [skeɪt] *n* **to get one's skates on** *(hurry up)* se magner, se grouiller; **get your skates on!** magne-toi!, grouille-toi!

skedaddle [skɪ'dædəl] *vi* décamper, se tailler, décaniller

skeezer ['skiːzə(r)] *n Noir Am* (a) *(ugly woman)* cageot *m*, boudin *m* (b) *(promiscuous woman)* pouffiasse *f*, traînée *f*

sket [sket] *n (promiscuous woman)* pouffiasse *f*, traînée *f*

sketchy ['sketʃɪ] *adj Am (unsafe, untrustworthy)* louche; **it sounds like a pretty sketchy deal to me** ça me paraît un peu louche comme plan; **I live in kind of a sketchy area**

j'habite dans un quartier un peu craignos

skid [skɪd] *n* (a) **to be on the skids** *(of company, marriage)* battre de l'aile; *Am* **to hit the skids** *(of company, sales, prices)* dégringoler (b) *Am* **skid row** bas-fonds□ *mpl*; **to be on skid row** être dans la dèche (c) *Br* **skid lid** casque□ *m (de moto)* (d) **skid marks** [!] traces *fpl* de pneus *(traces d'excrément sur le slip)*

skin [skɪn] **1** *n* (a) *(abrév* **skinhead**) skinhead *mf*, skin *mf* (b) *Br (cigarette paper)* feville *f* de papier à cigarette□ (c) *Am* **gimme some skin!** tape-moi dans la main! (d) **skin flick** film *m* de cul; **skin mag** magazine *m* de cul (e) *Am* **skin game** *(swindle)* arnaque *f*

2 *vt* (a) *(swindle)* arnaquer (b) *Am* **skin me!** tape-moi dans la main!

ⓘ Dans les catégories 1(c) et 2(b), il s'agit d'une façon de signifier à quelqu'un que l'on veut lui taper dans la main pour le saluer, le féliciter, ou en signe de victoire.

skin up *vi Br* rouler un joint

skinflint ['skɪnflɪnt] *n* radin(e) *m,f*

skinful ['skɪnfʊl] *n* **to have had a skinful** tenir une bonne cuite

skinny ['skɪnɪ] *n Am (inside information)* renseignements□ *mpl*; **what's the skinny on the situation?** résume-moi la situation□

skinny-dipping ['skɪnɪdɪpɪŋ] *n* **to go skinny-dipping** se baigner à poil

skin-pop ['skɪnpɒp] **1** *vt (drugs)* se piquer *ou* se shooter à

2 *vi (inject drugs)* se piquer, se shooter

skint [skɪnt] *adj Br* fauché, raide

skirt [skɜːt] *n (women)* nanas *fpl*,

gonzesses *fpl*; **they've gone out looking for skirt** ils sont allés draguer; *Br* **a bit of skirt** une nana, une gonzesse

skite [skaɪt] *Austr* **1** *n (boastful person)* vantard(e)ᵈ *m,f*; *(boasting)* vantardiseᵈ *f*

2 *vi (boast)* se vanterᵈ

skitters ['skɪtəz] *npl Scot* **the skitters** la courante

skive [skaɪv] *Br* **1** *n (easy job)* planque *f*; **she's taking PE because it's such a skive** elle a choisi éducation physique parce que c'est pépère

2 *vi* tirer au flanc, tirer au cul

skive off *Br* **1** *vt insép* **to skive off school** sécher les cours; **to skive off work** ne pas aller bosser

2 *vi* tirer au flanc, tirer au cul

skiver ['skaɪvə(r)] *n Br* tire-au-flanc *mf*, tire-au-cul *mf*

skivvies ['skɪvɪz] *npl Am* calbute *m*, calcif *m*

skoosh [skʊʃ] *n Scot* **(a)** *(easy thing)* **to be a skoosh** être fastoche **(b)** *(carbonated drink)* soda *m*

skull [skʌl] *n* **to be out of one's skull** *(drunk)* être plein comme une barrique, être rond comme une queue de pelle ▸ *voir aussi* **thick**

skunk [skʌŋk] **1** *n* **(a)** *Péj (person)* salaud (salope) *m,f* **(b)** *(type of cannabis)* skunk *m*

2 *vt Am (defeat)* écraser, battre à plate coutures, mettre la pâtée à; **to get skunked** se faire battre à plates coutures

slack [slæk] **1** *n* **cut me some slack!** lâche-moi un peu les baskets!

2 *vi* tirer au flanc; **no slacking!** pas de tire-au-flanc!

slacker ['slækə(r)] *n* bon (bonne) *m,f* à rien, raté(e) *m,f*

ⓘ Il s'agit d'un stéréotype social apparu aux États-Unis, au début des années 90. Ce terme désigne une personne jeune (entre vingt et trente ans), qui a fait des études, mais que le monde du travail et la notion de carrière rebutent, et qui se contente le plus souvent de travaux subalternes qui ne comportent aucune responsabilité.

slag [slæg] *Br* **1** *n* **(a)** *(promiscuous woman)* pouffiasse *f*, traînée *f*; *(promiscuous man)* tombeur *m*, coureur *m* **(b)** *Péj (person)* enfoiré(e) *m,f*; **some slag's stolen my fags** il y a un enfoiré qui m'a piqué mes clopes

2 *vt* **(a)** *(criticize)* débiner, éreinter, descendre en flammes **(b)** *(make fun of)* se foutre de

slag off *vt sép Br* **(a)** *(criticize)* débiner, éreinter, descendre en flammes **(b)** *(make fun of)* se foutre de

slaggy ['slægɪ] *adj Br* qui fait pute; **she looks really slaggy in all that make-up** elle fait vraiment pute avec tout son maquillage; **that's a really slaggy dress she's wearing** elle porte une robe qui fait vraiment pute

slam [slæm] *vt* **(a)** *(criticize)* éreinter, descendre en flammes; **to get slammed** se faire éreinter, se faire descendre en flammes **(b)** [!] *Am (have sex with) (of man)* baiser, s'envoyer; *(of woman)* baiser avec, s'envoyer **(c)** *(drink quickly)* descendre, écluser; **let's go slam some beers** allons écluser quelques bières

slammer ['slæmə(r)] *n (prison)* taule *f*, cabane *f*; **in the slammer** en taule, en cabane, à l'ombre

slanging match ['slæŋɪŋmætʃ] *n Br* prise *f* de bec, engueulade *f*

slant [slɑːnt] *n Injurieux (Oriental)* bridé(e) *m,f*

slap [slæp] *n Br (make-up)* maquillage⬜ *m*

slaphead ['slæphed] *n Br* chauve⬜ *m*; **he's a slaphead** il n'a pas un poil sur le caillou, il a une casquette en peau de fesse

slapper ['slæpə(r)] *n Br* (**a**) *(promiscuous woman)* pouffiasse *f*, traînée *f*, salope *f* (**b**) *Péj (any woman)* gonzesse *f*, grognasse *f*

slash [slæʃ] *n Br* **to have a slash** pisser; **to go for a slash** aller pisser un coup

slasher film ['slæʃəfilm], **slasher movie** ['slæʃəmuːvi] *n* = film d'horreur particulièrement sanglant

slate [sleɪt] *Br* **1** *n* **to have a slate loose** avoir une case de vide, avoir une araignée au plafond
2 *vt (criticize)* éreinter, débiner, descendre en flammes

slaughter ['slɔːtə(r)] *vt (defeat, criticize)* démolir

slaughtered ['slɔːtəd] *adj Br (drunk)* bourré, beurré, pété

slay [sleɪ] *vt (amuse)* faire mourir de rire; *Ironique* **you slay me!** tu es impayable!

sleazebag ['sliːzbæg], **sleazeball** ['sliːzbɔːl], **sleazoid** ['sliːzɔɪd] *n* (**a**) *(despicable person)* ordure *f*, raclure *f* (**b**) *(repulsive man)* gros dégueulasse *m*

sleep around [sliːp] *vi* coucher à droite à gauche

slice-and-dice movie *n* = film d'horreur particulièrement sanglant

slick up [slɪk] *vi Am (dress smartly)* se mettre sur son trente-et-un, se faire beau

slimeball ['slaɪmbɔːl], **slimebag**

['slaɪmbæg], **slimebucket** ['slaɪmbʌkɪt] *n* (**a**) *(despicable person)* ordure *f*, raclure *f* (**b**) *(repulsive man)* gros dégueulasse *m*

slit [!!] [slɪt] *n (vagina)* craque *f*, cramouille *f*

Sloane (Ranger) [sləʊn('reɪndʒə(r))] *n Br* ≃ jeune femme *f* BCBG

ⓘ Une "Sloane Ranger" est une jeune femme à la mode, fille de grands bourgeois ou d'aristocrates. À l'origine, ce terme ne désignait que les jeunes femmes dont la famille habitait Sloane Square (quartier chic du sud-ouest de Londres) ; aujourd'hui, sa sphère géographique s'est étendue au reste de Londres et à ses environs. "Sloane Ranger" est un jeu de mots sur "Lone Ranger", qui est le nom du héros d'une série télévisée américaine des années 50 qui avait pour cadre le Far West.

Sloaney ['sləʊnɪ] *adj Br* ≃ BCBG

slob [slɒb] *n (dirty person)* souillon *mf*; *(lazy person)* flemmard(e) *m,f*; **he's nothing but a big fat slob** ce n'est qu'un gros flemmard

slob about, slob around 1 *vt insép* traînasser; **he just slobs about the house all day** il passe ses journées à traînasser dans la maison
2 *vi* traînasser

slob out *vi* flemmarder; **he spends every night slobbing out in front of the TV** il passe ses soirées affalé devant la télé

slog [slɒg] **1** *n (task)* tâche *f* duraille, corvée *f*
2 *vi (work hard)* trimer; **to slog away (at sth)** travailler comme un dingue (à qch)

slope off [sləʊp] *vi* s'esbigner, se dé-

---

biner, s'esquiver□; **he always slopes off when it's his round** il se débine toujours quand c'est à lui de payer une tournée

sloshed [slɒʃt] *adj* bourré, pété, beurré

slug [slʌg] **1** *n* (**a**) *(of drink)* goulée *f*, lampée *f*; **to take** or **have a slug of sth** boire une lampée de qch (**b**) *(bullet)* pruneau *m*, bastos *f*
2 *vt (hit)* cogner; **to slug it out** se bastonner, se friter, se castagner

slug down *vt sép* siffler *(boire)*

slugfest ['slʌgfest] *n Am* baston *m ou f*, castagne *f*

slut [slʌt] *n* (**a**) *(promiscuous woman)* pouffiasse *f*, traînée *f* (**b**) *(prostitute)* pute *f*

slutty ['slʌti] *adj (promiscuous)* coucheuse; *(clothes, behaviour, make-up)* qui fait pute

smack [smæk] *n (heroin)* héro *f*, blanche *f*

smacker ['smækə(r)] *n* (**a**) *(kiss)* gros bisou *m* (**b**) *(pound sterling)* livre *f* sterling□; *(dollar)* dollar□ *m*; **fifty smackers** cinquante livres/dollars

smalls [smɔːlz] *npl Br* sous-vêtements□ *mpl*

smart [smɑːt] **1** *n Am* **smarts** *(intelligence)* intelligence□ *f*; **to have smarts** en avoir dans le ciboulot; **he's pretty low on smarts** c'est pas une lumière
2 *adj* **smart alec** petit(e) malin(igne) *m,f*, je-sais-tout *mf* ▸ *voir aussi* **cookie**

smartarse [!] ['smɑːtɑːs], *Am* **smartass** [!] ['smɑːtæs] *n* petit(e) malin(igne) *m,f*

smashed [smæʃt] *adj (drunk)* bourré, pété, beurré; *(on drugs)* raide, défoncé

smasher ['smæʃə(r)] *n Br* **to be a smasher** être génial; **that second goal was a smasher** le deuxième but était de toute beauté; **she's a smasher** *(gorgeous)* elle est hyper canon

smashing ['smæʃɪŋ] *adj Br* super, génial, géant

smoke [sməʊk] **1** *n* (**a**) *(cigarette)* clope *f*; *(cannabis cigarette)* joint *m*; *(cannabis)* chichon *m*, shit *m*, teuch *m* (**b**) *Br* **the (Big) Smoke** *(any big city)* la grande ville
2 *vt Am (defeat)* écraser, mettre la pâtée à, battre à plates coutures; **the Bears were smoked for the third time in a row** ça fait trois fois de suite que les Bears se font mettre la pâtée ▸ *voir aussi* **holy**

smooch [smuːtʃ] **1** *n* **to have a smooch** *(kiss)* se bécoter; *(cuddle)* se peloter
2 *vi (kiss)* se bécoter; *(cuddle)* se peloter

smoochy ['smuːtʃɪ] *adj* **her latest song's another smoochy ballad** sa dernière chanson est un slow bien sirupeux, idéal pour se bécoter

smoothie, smoothy ['smuːðɪ] *n* individu *m* mielleux

snaffle ['snæfəl] *vt Br* piquer, faire main basse sur; **who's snaffled my pen?** qui est-ce qui m'a piqué mon stylo?

snafu [snæfuː] *adj (abrév* **situation normal, all fucked up**) en pagaille, bordélique

① Il s'agit à l'origine d'une terme d'argot militaire américain, qui a été popularisé au cours de la deuxième guerre mondiale.

snag [snæg] *n Austr (sausage)* saucisse□ *f*

snail mail ['sneɪlmeɪl] n Hum = terme humoristique désignant les services postaux par opposition aux messageries électroniques

snakebite ['sneɪkbaɪt] n Br (drink) = boisson comprenant une mesure de bière et une mesure de cidre; **snakebite and black** = boisson comprenant une mesure de bière, une mesure de cidre ainsi que du sirop de cassis

snap [snæp] exclam Br **I'm on holiday next week – snap!** je suis en vacances la semaine prochaine – moi aussi!▫

ⓘ "Snap" est un jeu de cartes dans lequel les joueurs retournent leurs cartes une par une et simultanément, jusqu'au moment où deux cartes de la même valeur sont retournées ; le premier à dire "snap" remporte alors les cartes accumulées. On utilise cette expression lorsque l'on remarque deux choses identiques.

snapper ['snæpə(r)] n Ir môme mf, gosse mf

snarky ['snɑːkɪ] adj Am grincheux

snatch [!!] [snætʃ] n (woman's genitals) craque f, cramouille f, chatte f

snazzy ['snæzɪ] adj chicos, classe

sneak [sniːk] **1** n (**a**) Br (tell-tale) cafard(e) m,f, cafteur(euse) m,f (**b**) Am **sneaks** (abrév **sneakers**) baskets fpl
2 vi (tell tales) cafter, cafarder; **to sneak on sb** cafter qn, cafarder qn

snip [snɪp] n (**a**) **to have the snip** (vasectomy) se faire faire une vasectomie▫ (**b**) Br (bargain) occase f, affaire▫ f

snippy ['snɪpɪ] adj (abrupt) pète-sec

snit [snɪt] n Am **to be in a snit** être fumasse ou furibard

snitch [snɪtʃ] **1** n (**a**) (tell-tale) cafard(e) m,f, cafteur(euse) m,f (**b**) Br (nose) blaire m, tarin m, pif m
2 vi (tell tales) cafter, cafarder; **to snitch on sb** cafter qn, cafarder qn

snockered ['snɒkəd] adj Am (drunk) bourré, pété, fait, beurré

snog [snɒg] Br **1** n **to have a snog** se bécoter, se rouler des pelles ou des patins
2 vt bécoter, rouler des pelles ou des patins à
3 vi se bécoter, se rouler des pelles ou des patins

snoggable ['snɒgəbəl] adj Br qu'on a envie de bécoter; **he's the most snoggable boy in our school** de tous les garçons de l'école, c'est celui que je préférerais bécoter

snooker ['snuːkə(r)] vt (**a**) Br (thwart) mettre dans l'embarras▫; **if that doesn't work, we're snookered!** si ça marche pas, on est foutu! (**b**) Am (swindle, trick) arnaquer; **don't get snookered into anything!** te laisse pas arnaquer!

snoot [snuːt] n (nose) blaire m, tarin m, pif m

snoozefest ['snuːzfest] n **that history lecture was a total snoozefest** ce cours d'histoire était hyper rasoir

snort [snɔːt] **1** n (of drug) **to have a snort** se faire une ligne
2 vt (drug) sniffer

snot [snɒt] n (mucus) morve f

snotrag ['snɒtræg] n tire-jus m, tire-moelle m

snotty ['snɒtɪ] adj (**a**) (nose, handkerchief) morveux, plein de morve (**b**) (haughty) bêcheur, prétentiard; (insolent) insolent▫

snout [snaʊt] n Br (**a**) (cigarette) clope

Le symbole [!] dénote un terme très familier, [!!] un terme vulgaire.

f; (tobacco) tabac[□] *m*, foin *m* (**b**) *(informer)* indic *mf*

snow [snəʊ] **1** *n* (**a**) *(cocaine)* coco *f*, neige *f; (heroin crystals)* cristaux *mpl* d'héroïne[□] (**b**) *Am* **snow job** baratin *m*; **to give sb a snow job** baratiner qn, rouler qn dans la farine
2 *vt Am* **to snow sb** *(charm, persuade)* baratiner qn, rouler qn dans la farine; **to snow sb into doing sth** baratiner qn pour qu'il fasse qch
▸ *voir aussi* **bunny, pisshole**

snuff [snʌf] **1** *n* **snuff movie** = film pornographique au cours duquel un participant est réellement assassiné
2 *vt* (**a**) *Br* **to snuff it** *(die)* calancher, passer l'arme à gauche (**b**) *Am (murder)* buter, refroidir, zigouiller

so [səʊ] *adv* (**a**) *(indeed)* **I never said that! – you did so!** je n'ai pas dit ça! – si, tu l'as dit![□] (**b**) *(for emphasis)* **socks with sandals is SO not a good look** porter des chaussettes avec des sandales, ça le fait pas; **I SO don't want to go to work tomorrow** je n'ai, mais alors, aucune envie d'aller bosser demain

soak [səʊk] **1** *n* **old soak** vieux (vieille) poivrot(e) *m,f*
2 *vt Am* **to soak sb** *(charge heavily)* écorcher qn; *(tax heavily)* accabler qn d'impôts[□]

soap-dodger ['səʊpdɒdʒə(r)] *n Br Hum (man)* mec *m* cradingue; *(woman)* bonne femme *f* cradingue

sob [!], **SOB** [!] [esəʊ'biː] *n Am (abrév* **son-of-a-bitch**) salaud *m*, fils *m* de pute

soccer mom [spkə'mɒm] *n Am Péj* = dans une famille bourgeoise, mère qui pousse ses enfants et leur fait faire plein d'activités

ⓘ Aux États-Unis, le football reste un sport relativement peu pratiqué et il est perçu comme un jeu plus élitiste et prétentieux que les sports nationaux tels que le football américain et le base-ball. Les "soccer moms" veulent faire de leurs enfants des "gagnants" et elles sont constamment à les conduire d'une activité extrascolaire à l'autre à bord de leur 4x4.

sock [spk] **1** *n* (**a**) *(blow)* beigne *f*, châtaigne *f*; **she gave him a sock in the face** elle lui a filé une beigne (**b**) **to put a sock in it** la fermer, la mettre en veilleuse, la boucler; **put a sock in it!** la ferme!, ferme ton clapet!, mets-la en veilleuse!
2 *vt* (**a**) *(hit)* filer une beigne *ou* une châtaigne à; **she socked him in the face** elle lui a filé une beigne (**b**) **to sock it to sb** montrer à qn ce que l'on sait faire; **sock it to them!** vas-y, montre-leur ce que tu sais faire!, vas-y, donne le maximum!

sod [!] [spd] *Br* **1** *n* (**a**) *(person)* con (conne) *m,f*; **the poor sod** le pauvre, le pauvre bougre; **you're a lazy sod** t'es vraiment un flemmard (**b**) *(thing)* saloperie *f*; **it's a sod of a job** c'est un boulot vraiment chiant (**c**) **sod all** que dalle; **sod all money** pas un flèche, pas un rond; **there's sod all to eat** il y a que dalle à bouffer
2 *vt* **sod it!** merde!; **sod him!** qu'il aille se faire voir!; **sod the expense, let's just go!** tant pis si ça coûte cher, allons-y!

sod off [!] *vi Br* foutre le camp, décamper, décaniller; **sod off!** fous le camp!, dégage!

sodding [!] ['spdɪŋ] *Br* **1** *adj (for emphasis)* sacré, foutu; **get that sodding dog out of here!** fous-moi cette saleté de clébard dehors!; **he's a sodding nuisance!** c'est un sacré emmerdeur!; **sodding hell!** merde alors!

2 adv (for emphasis) vachement; **you can sodding well do it yourself!** démerde-toi tout seul pour le faire!; **don't be so sodding lazy!** ce que tu peux être flemmard!

Sod's law ['sɒdz'lɔː] n Br la loi de l'emmerdement maximum

softie, softy ['sɒftɪ] n (gentle person) bonne pâte f; (coward) poule f mouillée

solid ['sɒlɪd] Noir Am **1** adj (excellent) génial, super, géant

2 adv (absolutely) absolument□; **I solid gotta do it!** il faut absolument que je le fasse!

some [sʌm] adj (**a**) (for emphasis) **that was some party/meal!** c'était une sacrée fête!/un sacré gueuleton!; **she's some cook!** c'est une sacrée cuisinière! (**b**) Ironique **some friend he is!** tu parles d'un copain!; Br **some hope!** on peut toujours rêver!

something ['sʌmθɪŋ] **1** pron **that meal was something else!** c'était quelque chose, ce repas!; **he really is something else!** il est pas possible!

2 adv Br **something rotten** or **awful** (a lot) vachement; **it hurts something rotten** or **awful** ça fait vachement mal; **he fancies her something rotten** or **awful** il est dingue d'elle

son-of-a-bitch [!!] [sʌnəvə'bɪtʃ] Am **1** n (**a**) (man) salaud m, fils m de pute; **you old son-of-a-bitch, how ya doin'?** comment ça va, enfoiré? (**b**) (object) saloperie f; **this son-of-a-bitch is too heavy to carry** cette saloperie est trop lourde à porter

2 exclam putain!

son-of-a-bitching [!!] [sʌnəvə-'bɪtʃɪŋ] adj Am (for emphasis) foutu, putain de; **where'd that son-of-a-bitching letter go?** où est passée cette putain de lettre?

son-of-a-gun [sʌnəvə'gʌn] Am **1** n salaud m; **hi, you old son-of-a-gun!** salut, vieux bandit!

2 exclam putain!

sook [sʊk] n Austr (weak person) mauviette f

soph [sɒf] n Am (abrév **sophomore**) étudiant(e) m,f de deuxième année□

sorehead ['sɔːhed] n Am (person) ronchon(onne) m,f, grincheux(euse) m,f

sorry-ass [!] ['sɒrɪ'æs], **sorry-assed** [!] ['sɒrɪæst] adj Am (inferior, contemptible) à la con, minable; **your sorry-ass** or **sorry-assed team haven't won a game all season!** ton équipe de minables n'a pas gagné un seul match de toute la saison!

sorted ['sɔːtɪd] Br **1** adj **to be sorted** (psychologically) être équilibré□, être bien dans ses baskets; (have everything one needs) être paré; **she's the most sorted person I know** c'est la personne la plus équilibrée que je connaisse□; **if I get that pay rise, I'll be sorted** si j'obtiens cette augmentation j'aurai plus à m'en faire; **to be sorted for sth** disposer de qch□; **are you sorted for E's/coke?** t'as ce qu'il te faut comme ecsta/coke?

2 exclam super!, génial!

soul [səʊl] n Noir Am **soul brother** Noir m américain□; **soul sister** Noire f américaine□

ⓘ Il s'agit d'expressions utilisées par les Noirs américains pour se désigner eux-mêmes et s'adresser les uns aux autres. Ces expressions sont souvent abrégées en "brother" et "sister".

sound [saʊnd] *Br* **1** *adj* **(a)** *(excellent)* super, génial, géant **(b)** *(trustworthy, nice)* bien□, sympa; **he's a really sound guy** c'est vraiment un mec bien

2 *exclam* super!, génial!, cool!

sounds [saʊndz] *npl (music)* zizique *f*, zicmu *f*

soup [suːp] *n* **to be in the soup** être dans le pétrin *ou* dans la panade

soup-strainer ['suːpstreɪnə(r)] *n Am Hum (large moustache)* grosses bacchantes *fpl*

sourpuss ['saʊəpʊs] *n (ill-tempered person)* grincheux(euse) *m,f*

souse [saʊs] *n Am (person)* alcolo *mf*, poivrot(e) *m,f*

soused [saʊst] *adj Am (drunk)* bourré, pété, fait, beurré

sozzled ['sɒzəld] *adj Br* bourré, beurré, pété, fait

SP [esˈpiː] *n Br (abrév* **starting price**) **to give sb the SP (on)** mettre qn au parfum (à propos de *ou* concernant)

ⓘ Il s'agit au départ d'une expression de turfistes. Le "starting price" est la cote d'un cheval juste avant le départ.

space [speɪs] *n* **(a)** *Hum* **space cadet**, *Am* **space case** allumé(e) *m,f*; **he's a bit of a space cadet** *or Am* **space case** il est toujours en train de planer **(b)** *Br* **space cakes** gâteaux *mpl* au cannabis□, space cakes *mpl*

spaced out [speɪstˈaʊt], **spacey** ['speɪsɪ] *adj* **to be** *or* **feel spaced out** *or* **spacey** *(dazed)* être dans le coaltar; *(after taking drugs)* être raide, planer

spade [speɪd] *n Injurieux (black man)* nègre *m*, bamboula *m*; *(black woman)* négresse *f*

spag bol ['spægˈbɒl] *n Br (abrév* **spaghetti bolognese**) spaghettis *mpl* (à la) bolognaise□

spangled ['spæŋgəld] *adj (drunk)* bourré, fait, beurré; *(on drugs)* raide, défoncé

spare [speə(r)] *adj* **(a)** *(mad) Br* **to go spare** péter les plombs, péter une durite; **to drive sb spare** rendre qn chèvre, faire tourner qn en bourrique **(b)** *Hum Br* **spare tyre,** *Am* **spare tire** *(roll of fat)* poignée *f* d'amour, pneu *m* de secours ▸ *voir aussi* **prick**

sparkler ['spɑːklə(r)] *n (diamond)* diam *m*

sparks [spɑːks] *n Br (electrician)* électricien(enne)□ *m,f*

spastic ['spæstɪk] *n Injurieux* gol *mf*, gogol *mf*

ⓘ Ce terme signifie littéralement "handicapé moteur". Il s'agit d'une injure extrêmement politiquement incorrecte qu'il est préférable de bannir complètement de son vocabulaire.

spaz [spæz] *n Injurieux* gol *mf*, gogol *mf*

ⓘ Il s'agit d'une abréviation du mot "spastic" utilisé comme injure. Bien que cette injure ne soit pas aussi choquante que le mot dont elle est dérivée, il est préférable de l'utiliser avec beaucoup de circonspection.

spaz out *vi* faire le con

spazzy ['spæzɪ] = **spaz**

The symbol □ indicates that a translation is neutral.

speccy ['spekɪ] *Br* **1** *n* binoclard(e) *m,f*
2 *adj* binoclard

special K [speʃəl'keɪ] *n (ketamine)* spécial K *f*, vitamine K *f*

specs [speks] *npl (abrév* **spectacles**) carreaux *mpl*, hublots *mpl*

speed [spiːd] **1** *n* (**a**) *(amphetamines)* amphets *fpl*, speed *m* (**b**) **to be up to speed on sth** être au courant de qch◻
2 *vi* **to be speeding** *(have taken amphetamines)* être sous amphets, speeder ▸ *voir aussi* **merchant**

speedball ['spiːdbɔːl] *n* speedball *m (mélange d'héroïne et de cocaïne)*

speedfreak ['spiːdfriːk] *n* (**a**) *(person who takes amphetamines)* **to be a speedfreak** marcher aux amphets (**b**) *(fast driver)* chauffard *m*

spesh [speʃ] *adj Br (abrév* **special**) (**a**) *(special)* spécial◻ (**b**) *(weird)* **he's a bit spesh** il est un peu zarbi

spew [spjuː] *Br* **1** *vt* dégueuler, gerber; **to spew one's guts up** rendre tripes et boyaux
2 *vi* dégueuler, gerber

spewing ['spjuːɪŋ] *adj Br (angry)* fumasse, furax, en pétard

spic, spick [spɪk] *n Am Injurieux* métèque *mf (d'origine latino-américaine)*

spieler ['spiːlə(r)] *n Austr* escroc◻ *m*, arnaqueur *m; (card-sharp)* tricheur(euse) *m,f* aux cartes◻

spike [spaɪk] **1** *n (hypodermic needle)* shooteuse *f*, pompe *f*
2 *vt* **to spike sb's drink** *(with alcohol)* mettre de l'alcool dans la boisson de qn◻; *(with drugs)* mettre de la drogue dans la boisson de qn◻

spill [spɪl] **1** *vt* **to spill the beans, to spill one's guts** vendre la mèche; *(under interrogation)* cracher

ou lâcher le morceau
2 *vi* vendre la mèche; *(under interrogation)* cracher ou lâcher le morceau; **come on, spill!** allez, accouche!

spin [spɪn] *n Br* **on the spin** *(in a row)* de suite◻; **they've won seven games on the spin** ils ont gagné sept matchs de suite

spins [spɪnz] *npl* **to have the spins** avoir le tournis *(généralement après avoir trop bu)*

spit [spɪt] *n* **1** (**a**) *Br* **to be the (very) spit of sb** être le portrait craché de qn (**b**) *Br* **it's a bit of a spit and sawdust pub** c'est un pub sans prétentions◻ (**c**) *Hum* **to swap spit** se rouler des pelles ou des patins (**d**) *Am* **it doesn't count for spit** ça vaut pas un clou
2 *vt* **to spit the dummy** faire un caprice, piquer une colère

spit out *vt sép* **spit it out!** accouche!

spitroast [!!] ['spɪtrəʊst] **1** *n* = situation où deux hommes pénètrent la même femme simultanément, l'un à chaque extrémité
2 *vt* = pénétrer la même femme simultanément, l'un à chaque extrémité

splatter movie ['splætəmuːvɪ] *n* = film violent et sanglant

spliced [splaɪst] *adj* **to get spliced** *(marry)* se marier◻, se maquer

spliff [splɪf] *n* splif *m*, joint *m*

split [splɪt] **1** *vt* **to split one's sides (laughing)** se tenir les côtes (de rire)
2 *vi* (**a**) *Am (leave)* se casser, se barrer, s'arracher; **come on, let's split** allez, on se casse (**b**) *Br (inform)* **to split on sb** cafarder qn

spondulicks [spɒn'duːlɪks] *npl* fric *m*,

pognon m, flouze m

sponge [spʌndʒ] **1** vt **to sponge sth (off sb)** taper qch (à qn)
  2 vi jouer en parasite; **to sponge off sb** vivre aux crochets de qn

sponger ['spʌndʒə(r)] n pique-assiette mf

spook [spuːk] **1** n (a) (spy) barbouze f (b) Am Injurieux (black man) nègre m, bamboula m; (black woman) négresse f
  2 vt (startle) faire sursauter, foutre la trouille à; (frighten, disturb) donner la chair de poule à

sport [spɔːt] n Austr (term of address) mon pote, mon vieux

spot-on ['spɒtɒn] Br **1** adj (accurate) **his guess was spot-on** il a mis en plein dans le mille; **his remark was spot-on** sa remarque était vachement bien vue
  2 exclam (excellent) super!, génial!

spout [spaʊt] n Br **to be up the spout** (pregnant) être en cloque; (ruined) être foutu; **that's our holidays up the spout** on peut faire une croix sur nos vacances

spread [spred] vt Br **to spread it** or **oneself about a bit** (be promiscuous) avoir la cuisse légère, coucher à droite à gauche

spring [sprɪŋ] **1** n **she's no spring chicken** (no longer young) elle a pas mal d'heures de vol, elle est plus de la première jeunesse
  2 vt (prisoner) faire évader□

sprog [sprɒg] n Br (child) môme mf, gosse mf; **to drop a sprog** avoir un môme

spud [spʌd] n (potato) patate f

spunk [spʌŋk] n (a) [!!] (semen) foutre m (b) Austr (attractive woman) canon m; (attractive man) beau mec m

spunky ['spʌŋkɪ] adj Austr (attractive) canon

squaddie ['skwɒdɪ] n Br bidasse m

square [skweə(r)] **1** n (a) (unfashionable person) ringard(e) m,f (b) Am **square shooter** (candid person) personne f franche□
  2 adj (unfashionable) ringard

square up vi Am (of criminal) raccrocher, se ranger des voitures; (of drug addict) décrocher

squat [skwɒt] n Am (nothing) que dalle; **you don't know squat about my problems!** tu sais que dalle sur mes problèmes!

squawk [skwɔːk] Am **1** n (complaint) plainte□ f; **what's your squawk?** c'est quoi ton problème?
  2 vi (complain) râler

squeal [skwiːl] vi (inform) moucharder; **to squeal on sb** balancer ou moucharder qn

squealer ['skwiːlə(r)] n (informer) indic mf

squeeze [skwiːz] n (a) **(main) squeeze** (boyfriend) mec m, Jules m; (girlfriend) nana f, gonzesse f (b) **to put the squeeze on sb** faire pression sur qn□

squiffy ['skwɪfɪ] adj Br éméché

squillion ['skwɪljən] n Br Hum **squillions (of)** une foultitude (de), une ribambelle (de)

squire ['skwaɪə(r)] n (term of address) chef m, patron m

squirrelly ['skwɪrəlɪ] adj Am (eccentric) loufedingue

squirt [skwɜːt] n (person) avorton m, demi-portion f

squits [skwɪts] npl Br **the squits** la courante

stache [stæʃ] n Am (abrév **mustache**) bacchantes fpl, moustagache f

stack ['stæk] *vt Br* **to stack it** se casser la gueule; **and then I stacked it down the stairs!** et puis je me suis cassé la gueule dans les escaliers!

stacked [stækt] *Am* = **well-stacked**

staggered ['stægəd] *adj (amazed)* estomaqué

stallion ['stæljən] *n* (**a**) *(man)* étalon *m* (**b**) *Noir Am (woman)* canon *m*, bombe *f*

stand up [stænd] *vt sép* **to stand sb up** poser un lapin à qn

star [stɑː(r)] *n* (**a**) **she's not the brightest star in the sky** elle n'a pas inventé l'eau chaude *ou* le fil à couper le beurre (**b**) *(kind, helpful person)* **I've managed to fix your computer for you – oh, thanks, you're a star!** j'ai réparé ton ordinateur – oh, merci, tu es un ange!

starfucker [!!] ['stɑːfʌkə(r)] *n* groupie *f (qui multiplie les aventures avec des stars)*

starkers ['stɑːkəz] *adj Br* à poil

stash [stæʃ] **1** *n* (**a**) *(hidden supply)* provision *f*; *(hiding place)* planque *f* (**b**) *(supply of drugs)* réserve *f* de drogue□; **the police found his stash under the floorboards** la police a trouvé sa réserve de drogue cachée sous le plancher
2 *vt (hide)* planquer

static ['stætɪk] *n Am* (**a**) *(insolence)* insolence□ *f*; **I'm not taking that static from you!** arrête de faire l'insolent! (**b**) *(hassle, interference)* embêtements *mpl*; **you can expect plenty of static from mom** tu vas avoir Maman sur le dos

steal [stiːl] *n (bargain)* occase *f*, affaire□ *f*

steam in [stiːm] *vi Br (join in)* s'en mêler; **when they started to threaten his girlfriend, that was**

when he steamed in quand ils ont commencé à menacer sa copine il a décidé de s'en mêler

steam up [stiːm] *vt sép Am* **to steam sb up** *(infuriate)* mettre qn en pétard *ou* en boule; **to be steamed up** être en pétard *ou* en boule

steamboats ['stiːmbəʊts] *adj Scot (drunk)* rond comme une queue de pelle, plein comme une barrique

steaming ['stiːmɪŋ] *adj* (**a**) *Scot (drunk)* rond comme une queue de pelle, plein comme une barrique (**b**) *Am (angry)* en pétard, en boule

steamy ['stiːmɪ] *adj (erotic)* chaud, sexy

stems [stemz] *npl Am (legs)* quilles *fpl*, gambettes *fpl*, cannes *fpl*

stew [stjuː] **1** *n Am (abrév* **stewardess***)* hôtesse *f* de l'air□
2 *vi Br* **to be stewing** *(of person)* crever de chaleur; **it's stewing in here** il fait une chaleur à crever ici
▸ *voir aussi* **bum**

stewed [stjuːd] *adj* **stewed (to the gills)** rond comme une queue de pelle, plein comme une barrique, pété à mort

stick [stɪk] **1** *n* (**a**) *Br* **up the stick** *(pregnant)* en cloque (**b**) **the sticks** *(place)* la cambrousse; **to live in the sticks** habiter en pleine cambrousse (**c**) *Br* **to give sb stick (for sth)** *(tease)* faire enrager qn, chambrer qn (à cause de qch); **they're giving him stick for buying platform shoes** ils le font enrager parce qu'il a acheté des platform shoes (**d**) *Am (cannabis cigarette)* stick *m* (**e**) *Br Hum* **he's won more awards than you can shake a stick at** on lui a décerné une flopée de prix; **there was more talent than you can shake a stick at** ça grouillait de beaux mecs/de belles nanas

2 *vt* (**a**) *(place, put)* flanquer, coller (**b**) *Br (tolerate) (person)* encadrer, blairer, piffer, encaisser; *(thing)* encaisser; **I can't stick him** je peux pas le blairer; **how have you stuck it for so long?** comment t'as fait pour supporter ça aussi longtemps? (**c**) **you can stick your job!** ton boulot, tu peux te le mettre où je pense!; **he can stick his money!** son fric, il peut se le mettre *ou* coller où je pense!; **stick it!** va te faire voir! ▸ *voir aussi* **arse, ass, oar, poke, shine, sight**

stickybeak ['stıkıbiːk] *Austr* **1** *n* fouineur(euse) *m,f*, fouinard(e) *m,f*
2 *vi* fouiner

sticky fingers ['stıkı'fıŋgəz] *npl* **to have sticky fingers** *(steal things)* avoir tendance à piquer tout ce qui traîne

stiff [stıf] **1** *n* (**a**) *(corpse)* macchabée *m* (**b**) *Br (failure)* bide *m* (**c**) *Am (tramp)* clodo *mf* (**d**) *Am (stupid person)* nul (nulle) *m,f*
2 *adj Am (drunk)* bourré, rond, fait, beurré

stiffy [!] ['stıfı] *n Br* **to have a stiffy** bander, avoir la trique *ou* le gourdin; **to get a stiffy** se mettre à bander

stillies ['stılız] *npl Br (stilettos)* talons *mpl* aiguilles□

sting [stıŋ] **1** *n* (**a**) *(swindle)* arnaque *f* (**b**) *Am (police operation)* coup *m* monté *(dans le cadre d'une opération de police)*
2 *vt (swindle)* arnaquer, refaire; **to get stung** se faire arnaquer, se faire refaire; **they stung him for a hundred quid** ils l'ont arnaqué *ou* refait de cent livres

stink [stıŋk] **1** *n (fuss)* foin *m*, pataquès *m*; **to raise** *or* **make** *or Br* **kick up a stink (about sth)** faire

toute une histoire (de qch)

2 *vi (be bad)* être nul, craindre; **don't bother going to the concert, it stinks!** ne vas pas au concert, c'est nul!; **what do you think of my plan? – it stinks!** qu'est-ce que tu penses de mon projet? – il est nul! ▸ *voir aussi* **shit**

stinker ['stıŋkə(r)] *n* (**a**) *(person)* ordure *f* (**b**) *(difficult thing)* **to be a stinker** être vachement dur, être coton; **the German exam was a real stinker** l'examen d'allemand était vraiment coton (**c**) *(worthless thing)* **to be a stinker** être nul, être merdique; **his new film's a total stinker** son nouveau film est complètement nul (**d**) **to have a stinker of a cold** avoir un sacré rhume *ou* un rhume carabiné

stinking ['stıŋkıŋ] **1** *adj* (**a**) *(worthless)* merdique, nul (**b**) *Br* **to have a stinking cold** avoir un sacré rhume *ou* un rhume carabiné
2 *adv* **to be stinking rich** être plein aux as, être bourré de fric

stinko ['stıŋkəʊ] *adj Am (drunk)* pété, bourré, fait

stir [stɜː(r)] **1** *n (prison)* taule *f*, placard *m*, cabane *f*; **in stir** en taule, en cabane, à l'ombre; **stir crazy** cinglé *(à force d'être en prison)*
2 *vt Br* **to stir it** *(cause trouble)* semer la zizanie
3 *vi (cause trouble)* semer la zizanie

stirrer ['stɜːrə(r)] *n (troublemaker)* fouteur(euse) *m,f* de merde

stitch [stıtʃ] *n* (**a**) *Am (amusing person, thing)* **to be a stitch** être tordant *ou* crevant (**b**) **to be in stitches** *(laugh)* se tenir les côtes (de rire), être plié de rire; **to have sb in stitches** faire rire qn aux larmes

stitch up *vt sép* **to stitch sb up**

(frame) piéger qn□, monter un coup contre qn; **he was stitched up** il a été victime d'un coup monté

stoater ['stəʊtə(r)] *n Scot* (a) *(excellent thing)* **that was a stoater of a goal!** quel but d'enfer!; **we had a stoater of an idea** on a eu une idée géniale (b) *(beautiful person)* canon *m*; **his new girlfriend's a wee stoater!** sa nouvelle copine est canon!

stocious ['stəʊʃəs] *adj Scot (drunk)* bourré, beurré

stogie ['stəʊgɪ] *n Am (cigar)* cigare□ *m*

stoked [stəʊkt] *adj Am (excited, enthusiastic)* emballé

stomach ['stʌmək] *vt (tolerate) (person)* blairer, piffer, encaisser; *(thing)* encaisser; **I like him but I can't stomach his brother** lui, je l'aime bien, mais je peux pas blairer son frère; **I can't stomach the way he looks at me** il a une façon de me regarder qui me débecte ▶ *voir aussi* **throat**

stomp [stɒmp] *vt Am (defeat)* flanquer une peignée *ou* une déculottée *ou* une tannée à

stone [stəʊn] *adj Noir Am (absolute, real)* véritable□, total; **she is a stone fox!** c'est une supernana!; **this is turning into a stone drag!** ça devient vraiment galère!

stoned [stəʊnd] *adj (on drugs)* raide, défoncé; **to get stoned** se défoncer

stoner ['stəʊnə(r)] *n* adepte *mf* de la fumette

stonker ['stɒŋkə(r)] *n Br* (a) *(impressive thing)* **that was a stonker of a goal!** quel but d'enfer!; **their latest album's a complete stonker!** leur dernier album est absolument génial! (b) *(large thing)* mastodonte *m*;

that new skyscraper is a stonker! ce nouveau gratte-ciel est un vrai mastodonte (c) **[!]** *(erect penis)* trique *f*, gaule *f*

stonking ['stɒŋkɪŋ] *adj Br* super, génial, d'enfer; **he scored a stonking goal** il a marqué un but d'enfer

stony (broke) ['stəʊnɪ('brəʊk)] *adj* fauché (comme les blés), raide, à sec

stooge [stuːdʒ] *n* (a) *(dupe)* pigeon *m*, poire *f* (b) *(idiot)* andouille *f*, crétin(e) *m,f*

stool [stuːl], **stoolie** ['stuːlɪ], **stool pigeon** ['stuːlpɪdʒɪn] *n* indic *mf*

storm [stɔːm] *n* **to go down a storm** *(be very successful)* faire un tabac, faire un malheur; **their new sitcom's going down a storm with the critics** leur nouvelle sitcom fait un vrai malheur auprès de la critique

straight [streɪt] **1** *n* (a) *(heterosexual)* hétéro *mf* (b) *Am (conventional person)* personne *f* conventionnelle *ou* sérieuse□; **don't be such a straight!** sois pas si sérieux!

2 *adj* (a) *(heterosexual)* hétéro (b) *(not on drugs)* **to be straight** ne pas avoir pris de drogue□ (c) *(conventional)* conventionnel□, sérieux□; **her dad's really straight, don't swear in front of him** son père n'est pas du genre rigolo, ne dis pas de gros mots devant lui (d) *Am* **a straight arrow** *(man)* un brave type; *(woman)* une brave femme; **a straight shooter** *(person)* une personne franche□ (e) *Am (true)* vrai□ (f) *Am* **to get straight** = prendre une dose d'héroïne (ou d'une drogue comparable) de façon à éviter l'effet de manque

3 *adv* (a) **to go straight** *(of criminal)* se ranger des voitures (b) *Br* **straight up?** sans déconner?, sans dec?; **straight up!** sans déconner!, je t'assure!, sans dec!

straight-edge [streɪt'edʒ] *adj Am* sérieux⁰, rangé⁰

strapped [stræpt] *adj* (**a**) **to be strapped (for cash)** être fauché, ne pas avoir un rond (**b**) *Am (armed)* armé⁰, chargé

streak [striːk] *n Br* **he's a long streak of piss** [!] *(tall and thin)* c'est une grande perche; *(insipid in character)* c'est une lavette ▸ *voir aussi* **blue**

street [striːt] *n* (**a**) **to be on the street** *or* **streets** *(of homeless person)* être à la rue; *(of prostitute)* faire le trottoir *ou* le tapin; **to walk the streets** *(of prostitute)* faire le trottoir *ou* le tapin (**b**) *Br* **this job should be right up your street** ce boulot devrait être dans tes cordes; **there'll be loads of free booze, it'll be right up your street** il y aura plein d'alcool gratuit, c'est tout à fait ton truc ▸ *voir aussi* **cred, easy, queer**

streetwalker [ˈstriːtwɔːkə(r)] *n* prostituée⁰ *f*; **to be a streetwalker** faire le trottoir

strength [strenθ] *n* **give me strength!** pitié!

stretch [stretʃ] *n (term of imprisonment)* peine *f* de prison⁰; **to do a stretch** faire de la taule; **he was given a five-year stretch** il a écopé de cinq ans

strewth [struːθ] *exclam Br & Austr (abrév* **God's truth***)* mince alors!

strides [straɪdz] *npl Br & Austr (trousers)* futal *m*, fute *m*

stringbean [strɪŋˈbiːn] *n Am (person)* grande perche *f*, asperge *f*

stroke [strəʊk] *vt* (**a**) *Am (flatter)* passer de la pommade à (**b**) **stroke mag** bouquin *m* de cul

strop [strɒp] *n Br* **to be in a strop** être mal luné, être de mauvais poil;

we were treated to another of his famous strops il nous a fait la gueule comme il sait si bien le faire

stroppy [ˈstrɒpɪ] *adj Br* mal luné, de mauvais poil; **there's no need to get stroppy!** tu n'as pas besoin d'être désagréable comme ça!

strut [strʌt] *vt* **to strut one's stuff** frimer

stubby [ˈstʌbɪ] *n Br & Austr (bottle of beer)* canette *f*

stuck [stʌk] *adj Br* **to get stuck into sb** *(physically, verbally)* rentrer dans le lard à qn; **to get stuck into sth** *(book, work, meal)* attaquer qch; **get stuck in!** attaque!

stud [stʌd] *n (man)* étalon *m*; *Am* **stud muffin** super beau mec *m*

stuff [stʌf] **1** *n* (**a**) *Br* **she's a lovely bit of stuff** elle est vraiment bien balancée, elle est canon; **he was there with his bit of stuff** il était là avec sa gonzesse (**b**) **go on, do your stuff!** allez, à toi de jouer!; **to know one's stuff** s'y connaître, connaître son affaire; **that's the stuff!** parfait! (**c**) *(drugs)* came *f*

2 *vt* (**a**) **to stuff oneself** *or* **one's face** se goinfrer, s'empiffrer, s'en mettre plein la lampe, s'en mettre jusque-là (**b**) **get stuffed!, stuff you!** va te faire cuire un œuf!; **stuff this, I'm going home!** rien à foutre de ce truc, moi je rentre chez moi!; **I've had enough, he can stuff his job!** j'en ai marre, son boulot il peut se le mettre où je pense! (**c**) *(defeat)* écrabouiller, foutre une déculottée à, battre à plates coutures (**d**) [!!] *(have sex with)* baiser, troncher, tringler

stuffed [stʌft] *adj Br & Austr (in trouble)* cuit, fichu; **if that cheque doesn't arrive soon, we're stuffed** si ce chèque n'arrive pas bientôt, on est cuits

Pleins feux sur...

Stupidity and madness

Il existe en anglais un très grand nombre d'expressions argotiques pour exprimer la bêtise ou la folie. Les expressions employées pour exprimer la bêtise d'une personne sont très souvent originales, comme en témoignent les images suivantes : **the lights are on but there's nobody home** et **the elevator doesn't go up to the top floor**. Certaines expressions humoristiques génèrent de nombreuses variantes, et l'on voit régulièrement apparaître de nouvelles trouvailles, souvent éphémères. Parmi les plus courantes, citons **to be one sandwich short of a picnic**, **one brick short of a load** et **one clown short of a circus**. De même, on peut dire d'une personne **he/she isn't the sharpest knife in the drawer** ou bien **isn't the sharpest tool in the shed** ou encore **isn't the brightest star in the sky**. Un manque de bon sens momentané se dit **a blonde moment**, à cause du stéréotype de la femme blonde séduisante mais peu intelligente. Certains suffixes permettent de former toute une série de mots : par exemple **-head** donne **airhead**, **bonehead**, **butthead**, **dickhead** (plus vulgaire) et **meathead**, pour n'en citer que quelques-uns. Parmi les autres termes qui désignent une personne stupide, citons **a moron**, **a dope**, **a jerk** et les mots d'anglais britanniques **a prat**, **a plonker** et plus récemment **a muppet**.

Pour désigner la folie, on emploie très souvent le terme **nut**, ainsi que ses dérivés. Un fou peut alors être **a nut**, **a nutter**, **a nutcase** ou **a nutso**. On dira d'une personne qu'elle est **nutty** ou **off one's nut**, qu'elle devient **nuts** (**to go nuts**) ou qu'elle va finir dans une **nuthouse** (**to end up in the nuthouse**). Il existe aussi de nombreux adjectifs se terminant en **-y**, surtout en anglais britannique : citons **barmy**, **potty**, **loopy** et **loony** (aussi utilisé comme substantif, **a loony**). **Bonkers** et **mental** sont d'autres termes très employés en Grande-Bretagne. Il existe d'autres façons de décrire un fou, telles que **to be off one's head**, **rocker** ou **trolley**. De la même façon, on emploiera les expressions **to go up the wall**, **to go round the bend** ou **the twist**, **to go bananas** et **to lose the plot** ou **one's marbles** pour parler de quelqu'un qui est en train de perdre la raison.

stumblebum ['stʌmbəlbʌm] n Am (**a**) (drunken vagrant) clodo mf alcolo (**b**) (clumsy, incompetent person) manche m

stump up [stʌmp] Br **1** vt sép cracher, casquer

2 vi casquer, raquer (**for** pour); **come on, stump up!** allez, raque!

stunner ['stʌnə(r)] n Br (woman) canon m, bombe f

stupe [stjuːp] n Am andouille f, truffe f, crétin(e) m,f

style [staɪl] vi Noir Am (show off) frimer, flamber; (do well) bien se démerder

-stylee ['staɪliː] suffixe **he dived in to rescue her, James Bond-stylee** il a plonger pour la sauver, à la James Bond; **they were doing this Saturday Night Fever-stylee dance routine** ils faisaient un numéro de danse à la Saturday Night Fever

sub [sʌb] Br **1** n (abrév **subsistence allowance**) (small loan) prêt□ m; **to give sb a sub** dépanner qn; **to get a sub** se faire dépanner

2 vt (lend) **to sub sb sth** dépanner qn de qch; **can you sub me a fiver?** tu peux me dépanner de cinq livres?

suck [sʌk] **1** vt Am **to suck face** se rouler des pelles ou des patins ou des galoches

2 vi (be bad) craindre, être nul ou merdique; **this bar/film sucks** ce bar/film est vraiment nul; **this sucks, let's do something else** c'est nul, si on faisait autre chose?; **I've got to work all weekend – that sucks!** il faut que je travaille tout le week-end – ça craint!

suck off [!!] vt sép **to suck sb off** sucer qn, tailler une pipe à qn, faire un pompier à qn

suck up vi **to suck up to sb** faire de la lèche à qn, cirer les pompes à qn

sucker ['sʌkə(r)] **1** n (**a**) (gullible person) poire f, pigeon m; **he's a sucker for blondes/chocolate ice-cream** il adore les blondes/la glace au chocolat (**b**) Am (despicable man) blaireau m (**c**) Am (object) truc m, machin m, bitoniau m; **what's this sucker for?** à quoi ça sert, ce truc?

2 vt (trick, swindle) arnaquer

sucky ['sʌkɪ] adj nul; **I have to get up at 5 a.m., which is pretty sucky** il faut que je me lève à 5 heures du mat', ça craint!; **I heard it's a really sucky movie** j'ai entendu dire que c'était nul comme film

sugar ['ʃʊgə(r)] **1** n (**a**) (term of address) chéri(e) m,f (**b**) **sugar daddy** = homme âgé qui entretient une jeune maîtresse

2 exclam miel!, punaise!

suit [suːt] n Péj (person) costard-cravate m, employé(e) m,f de bureau□ (en costume ou tailleur) ▸ voir aussi **monkey**, **penguin suit**

sunnies ['sʌnɪz] npl (abrév **sunglasses**) lunettes fpl de soleil□

sunshine ['sʌnʃaɪn] n Br (term of address) mon coco m, ma cocotte f; **watch it, sunshine!** fais gaffe, mon coco!

supergrass ['suːpəgrɑːs] n Br indic mf de choc

sure [ʃɔː(r)] **1** adj **sure thing!** et comment!

2 exclam (**a**) Am (you're welcome) de rien!□, il n'y a pas de quoi!□ (**b**) **(for) sure!** (of course) bien sûr!

surfie ['sɜːfɪ] n Austr surfeur(euse) m,f

suss[1] [sʌs] adj Br & Austr (abrév **suspicious**) louche□; **he says he's working late but it all seems a bit suss to me** il dit qu'il doit rester

---

tard au travail mais ça m'a l'air un peu louche

suss[2] *vt Br (work out)* découvrir□; *(realize)* se rendre compte de□; **I soon sussed what he was up to** j'ai vite compris son petit manège; **I haven't sussed where the good pubs are yet** j'ai pas encore repéré les bons pubs

suss out *vt sép* **to suss sth out** *(work out)* découvrir□; *(realize)* se rendre compte de□; **I couldn't suss out how the modem worked** j'ai pas pigé comment le modem fonctionnait; **I can't quite suss her out** c'est quelqu'un que j'ai du mal à cerner; **I haven't sussed out his motives yet** j'ai toujours pas pigé ses motivations; **we have to suss out the best places to go at night** il faut qu'on repère les endroits où sortir le soir

sussed [sʌst] *adj* **(a)** *(astute)* rusé, malin **(b) I haven't got her sussed yet** je l'ai pas encore vraiment cernée; **I haven't got this computer sussed yet** j'ai pas encore pigé comment fonctionne cet ordinateur; **he's got it sussed, he does no work and gets paid a fortune** il a trouvé le bon filon, il ne travaille pas et il gagne une fortune

swacked [swækt] *adj Am (drunk)* bourré, fait, beurré

swally ['swælɪ] *n Scot (drinking session)* beuverie *f*; **fancy a swally?** ça te dirait de te pinter?

swamp donkey ['swɒmpdɒŋkɪ] *n* mocheté *f*

swanky ['swæŋkɪ] *adj* **(a)** *(chic, posh)* classe, chicos **(b)** *(boastful)* frimeur

sweat [swet] **1** *n* **no sweat!** pas de problèmes!
2 *vt* **don't sweat it!** calmos!, relax!

sweeney ['swiːnɪ] *n Br (rhyming slang* **Sweeney Todd = flying squad)** = la brigade volante de Scotland Yard

ⓘ Sweeney Todd est un personnage fictif apparu au XVIIIème siècle; il s'agit d'un barbier londonien qui assassinait ses clients pour en faire de la viande hachée.

sweet [swiːt] **1** *adj (excellent)* génial, super
2 *exclam* cool!, génial! ▶ *voir aussi* **FA**

sweet-ass ['swiːtæs] *adj Am (excellent)* génial, super, top

sweetie(-pie) ['swiːtɪ(paɪ)] *n (term of address)* mon (ma) chéri(e) *m,f*

swift [swɪft] *adj* **(a)** *Br* **have we got time for a swift half?** est-ce qu'on a le temps de se boire une petite bière rapidos? **(b)** *Am (clever)* malin; **that was a real swift move** c'était bien joué; **she's not real swift** c'est pas une lumière, elle est pas très maligne

swifty ['swɪftɪ] *n Austr* **to pull a swifty on sb** rouler qn

swine [swaɪn] *n Br (person)* salaud *m*; **he's a lazy swine!** c'est une grosse feignasse!; **oh, you lucky swine!** sacré veinard, va!; **he's a jealous swine, just ignore him** ce n'est qu'un jaloux, ne fais pas attention à lui

swing [swɪŋ] *vi* **(a)** *(be hanged)* être pendu; **he should swing for that!** il mériterait douze balles dans la peau! **(b)** *(exchange sexual partners)* faire de l'échangisme□ **(c) to swing both ways** *(be bisexual)* marcher à voile et à vapeur **(d) to swing for sb** *(hit out at)* essayer d'en coller une à qn

swinger ['swɪŋə(r)] *n* **(a)** *(who ex-*

changes sexual partners) échangiste□ *mf* (**b**) *Am (sociable person)* fêtard(e) *m,f*

swipe [swaɪp] *vt (steal)* piquer, chouraver, barboter; **who's swiped my pen?** qui m'a piqué *ou* chouravé *ou* barboté mon stylo?

swish [swɪʃ] **1** *n Am Injurieux (effeminate homosexual)* folle *f*
   2 *adj Br (chic)* classe, chicos

swishy ['swɪʃɪ] *adj Am Injurieux (ef-*

feminate) chochotte

switch-hitter ['swɪtʃhɪtə(r)] *n Injurieux* **he's a switch-hitter** il marche à voile et à vapeur, il est bi

swizz [swɪz] *n Br* arnaque *f*

swot [swɒt] *Br* **1** *n Péj* bûcheur(euse) *m,f*
   2 *vi* bûcher

swot up on *vt insép Br* bûcher

syrup ['sɪrəp] *n Br (rhyming slang* **syrup of figs = wig**) moumoute *f*

Tt

Tabloid speak

Les tabloids britanniques (du type *The Sun*, *The Daily Mirror*, *The Daily Mail*) sont friands de scandales, de ragots et d'anecdotes sur les célébrités. Leurs sujets préférés sont les écarts de conduite des comédiens de feuilletons télévisés (**soap operas**), des stars d'émissions de télé-réalité et des footballeurs. Il existe un style d'écriture propre aux tabloids (le "tabloidese"), qui se caractérise par une abondance de termes d'argot et certaines expressions récurrentes. À titre d'exemple, une femme séduisante est toujours **a stunner** ou **a babe**, un bel homme est immanquablement **a hunk** ou **a stud**, et les gens au physique avantageux sont désignés collectivement par le terme **totty**. Un homme qui trompe sa compagne est un **love rat**, des relations sexuelles deviennent **a romp** ou bien **some rumpy-pumpy**, une chanteuse de pop est une **popstrel**, l'alcool est invariablement nommé **booze**, les délinquants sont toujours des **yobs**, un scandale est **a shocker** et une journée de grande chaleur **a scorcher**. Se marier avec quelqu'un devient **to tie the knot with someone** ou **to wed someone** ; coucher avec quelqu'un se dit **to bed someone** ou **to romp with someone**, et pour dire "critiquer quelque chose" on évitera le verbe "to criticize" et on lui préférera **to slam**. Les titres sont écrits en style télégraphique et souvent à la première personne pour donner l'impression qu'une célébrité ne manquera pas de révéler des détails de sa vie intime ; on pourra lire par exemple : **My booze-fuelled romp with footie star** (Ma nuit d'amour et d'ivresse avec une star du football). Les tabloids évitent les mots trop longs et compliqués et leur préfèrent les monosyllabes afin de toucher un public pas toujours très éduqué, et aussi pour gagner de la place et créer des titres plus accrocheurs. La plupart des mots longs sont abrégés ; ainsi le football devient **footie**, les célébrités sont des **celebs**, les paparazzi deviennent des **paps**, un délinquant sexuel est un **perv** (abréviation de "pervert") et ses activités sont qualifiées de **pervy**, le mot "holiday" devient **hol**. Une trouvaille récente des tabloids est le terme **WAGs**, abréviation de "wives and girlfriends", à savoir les compagnes des footballeurs de l'équipe de football d'Angleterre. Les jeux de mots sont fréquents et l'allitération fort prisée ; pour désigner de jolies présentatrices de télévision, on pourra dire par exemple **top telly totty**. Voici quelques exemples du genre de titres que l'on peut voir en gros titres des tabloids (à vous de déchiffrer) : **Popstrel's pervy vid slammed** ; **WAGs in boozy bar brawl** ; **Yobs wrecked our dream hol**.

ta [tɑː] *exclam Br* merci!□

tab [tæb] *n* (**a**) *(of LSD)* buvard *m* (**b**) *Br (cigarette)* clope *f*, tige *f*, sèche *f*

table ['teɪbəl] *n* **he drank me under the table** il tenait encore debout alors que j'avais déjà roulé sous la table

tackle ['tækəl] *n Br Hum* **(wedding) tackle** *(man's genitals)* service *m* trois pièces, bijoux *mpl* de famille

tad [tæd] *n* **a tad** un tantinet; **it's a tad expensive** c'est un peu chérot; **it's a tad long** c'est un peu longuet; **it's a tad worrying** c'est un tantinet inquiétant; **I think you're exaggerating a tad** je crois que t'exagères un tantinet; **you were being a tad naive if you believed him** si tu l'as cru, t'as été un tantinet naïf

tadger ['tædʒə(r)] *n Br (penis)* chipolata *f*

Taffy ['tæfɪ] *n Br Péj (Welshman)* Gallois□ *m*

ⓘ "Taffy" est censé être la transcription phonétique du prénom "David" tel que le prononcent les Gallois, et désigne une personne originaire du pays de Galles. Bien que ce terme ne témoigne pas nécessairement d'une attitude xénophobe de la part de celui qui l'utilise, il est préférable de ne pas l'employer.

tail [teɪl] **1** *n* (**a**) *(buttocks)* derrière *m*; **to work one's tail off** bosser comme un malade (**b**) *(person following a criminal)* filocheur *m*; **to put a tail on sb** faire filer le train à qn, faire filocher qn (**c**) **[!]** *Am (woman)* **she's a great piece of tail** c'est une nana super bandante; **he's looking for some tail** il cherche une femme à se mettre sur le bout
2 *vt (follow)* filocher, filer le train à
▶ *voir aussi* **shake**

take [teɪk] *n* **to be on the take** toucher des pots-de-vin, palper

take off *vi (leave)* se barrer, se tirer

take out *vt sép* **to take sb out** *(kill)* buter qn, zigouiller qn, refroidir qn

tale [teɪl] *n* **to tell tales** *(inform)* cafter; **she's been telling tales to the teacher again** elle est encore allée cafter à la maîtresse

talent ['tælənt] *n Br (attractive men)* beaux mecs *mpl*; *(attractive women)* belles nanas *fpl*; **he's out chatting up the local talent** il est en train de draguer les minettes du coin; **it's an OK bar, but there's not much talent** c'est pas mal comme bar, mais question mecs/nanas, ça casse pas des briques

talk [tɔːk] *vi* **talk about lucky!** tu parles d'un coup de bol!; **talk about a waste of time!** tu parles d'une perte de temps; **now you're talking!** à la bonne heure!, voilà, c'est beaucoup mieux!; **you can talk!, look who's talking!** tu peux parler!
▸ *voir aussi* **hand**

tango ['tæŋgəʊ] *vt Br Hum* **to be tangoed** *or* **tango'd** *(wearing too much fake tan)* avoir le visage tartiné d'autobronzant; **she ought to go easy on the fake tan, she looks like she's been tangoed!** elle devrait y aller mollo avec l'autobronzant, elle est carrément orange!

ⓘ Tango® est une boisson gazeuse au goût d'orange, populaire en Grande-Bretagne. Au cours des années 90, ce produit a fait l'objet d'une série de publicités télévisées où l'on voyait un homme entièrement peint en orange faire peur à des gens en train de boire du Tango® ; le slogan publicitaire en était "you know when you've been tangoed!" De nos jours, ce verbe, inventé pour l'occasion, s'emploie à propos de personnes ayant un peu forcé sur l'autobronzant ou ayant passé trop de temps sous la lampe à UV.

tank [tæŋk] **1** *n* **to be built like a tank** être une armoire à glace
2 *vt Br* **to tank it** foncer
3 *vi Am* **(a)** *(fail, do badly)* **the company tanked after the scandal** la société s'est cassé la gueule à la suite du scandale; **my computer just**

tanked mon ordinateur a planté; **the film tanked at the box office** le film a fait un bide *ou* un flop **(b)** *(lose deliberately)* faire exprès de perdre□

tanked [tæŋkt] *adj Am (drunk)* bourré, beurré, pété; **to get tanked** prendre une cuite

tanked up [tæŋkt'ʌp] *adj Br (drunk)* bourré, beurré, pété; **to get tanked up** prendre une cuite

tap [tæp] *vt Br* **to tap sb for sth** taper qch à qn; **he tapped me for a loan but I refused** il a voulu me taper du fric, mais j'ai refusé

tapped out ['tæpt'aʊt] *adj Am* crevé, lessivé, nase

ta-ra [təˈrɑː] *exclam Br* salut!, ciao!

tart [tɑːt] *n Br* **(a)** *(prostitute)* pute *f* **(b)** *Péj (promiscuous woman)* pétasse *f*, traînée *f*; *Hum* **a tart with a heart** une pétasse au grand cœur

tart up *vt sép* **to tart oneself up** se pomponner; **to tart sth up** décorer qch□ *(le plus souvent avec mauvais goût)*

tarty ['tɑːtɪ] *adj Br* qui fait pute; **she looks really tarty with her hair bleached like that** elle fait vraiment pute avec ses cheveux décolorés comme ça

tash [tæʃ] *n Br (abrév* **moustache**) moustache□ *f*, bacchantes *fpl*

tasty ['teɪstɪ] *adj (attractive)* bien foutu, bien balancé

ta-ta [təˈtɑː] = **ta-ra**

tater ['teɪtə(r)] *n Br* patate *f (tubercule)*

taters ['teɪtəz] *adj (cold)* **it's taters today** il fait un froid de canard aujourd'hui

tatt [tæt] *n (abrév* **tattoo**) tatouage□ *m*

tatties ['tætɪz] *npl esp Scot* patates *fpl (tubercules)*

tax [tæks] *vt Br (steal)* taxer, piquer, chouraver

tea leaf ['tiːliːf] *n Br (rhyming slang thief)* voleur(euse)□ *m,f*

technicolour yawn, *Am* **technicolor yawn** ['teknɪkʌlə'jɔːn] *n Hum* **to have a technicolour yawn** *(vomit)* gerber, dégobiller

tee [tiː] *n (T-shirt)* tee-shirt□ *m*

teenybopper ['tiːnɪbɒpə(r)] *n* petite minette *f (qui suit la mode)*

teeth [tiːθ] *npl Br* **to be fed up** *or* **sick to the back teeth of sb/sth** en avoir plus que marre de qn/qch ▸ *voir aussi* **hell**

tell-tale ['telteɪl] *n Br* cafteur(euse) *m,f*

tenner ['tenə(r)] *n Br (ten-pound note)* billet *m* de dix livres□; *Am (ten-dollar note)* billet *m* de dix dollars□; *Br (sum)* dix livres□ *fpl*

ten-spot ['tenspɒt] *n Am* billet *m* de dix dollars□

there [ðeə(r)] *adv* **don't even go there!** ne m'en parle pas!; **been there, done that(, got the T-shirt)** non merci, j'ai déjà donné

thick [θɪk] *adj* **(a)** *(stupid)* bête□, débile; *Br* **to be as thick as two short planks** être bête comme ses pieds *ou* bête à manger du foin; **to be thick as pigshit** [!] être con comme un balai; **will you get that into your thick skull!** tu vas te mettre ça dans la tête, oui ou non? **(b)** *Br (unreasonable)* **that's a bit thick!** c'est un peu fort!; **it's a bit thick expecting us to take them to the airport!** ils exagèrent de compter sur nous pour les conduire à l'aéroport! **(c)** *Br* **to give sb a thick ear** flanquer une taloche à qn

thickie ['θɪkɪ], **thicko** ['θɪkəʊ] *n Br* nouille *f*, andouille *f*

thing [θɪŋ] *n* **(a)** **to have a thing about sb/sth** *(like)* avoir un faible pour qn/qch; *(dislike)* avoir horreur de qn/qch; **he's got a real thing about tidiness/punctuality** il est très à cheval sur la propreté/la ponctualité **(b)** **to have a thing with sb** *(be romantically involved with)* avoir une liaison avec qn□; **we had a thing last summer but it was nothing serious** on a eu une petite liaison l'été dernier mais c'était juste une passade□ **(c)** *(penis)* chose *f* ▸ *voir aussi* **sure**

thingumabob ['θɪŋəmɪbɒb], **thingumajig** ['θɪŋəmɪdʒɪg], **thingummy** ['θɪŋəmɪ], **thingy** ['θɪŋɪ] *n (person)* Bidule *mf*, Machin(e) *m,f*; *(thing)* truc *m*, machin *m*

third degree ['θɜːdɪ'griː] *n* **to give sb the third degree** cuisiner qn

thrash [θræʃ] *vt* **(a)** *(beat up)* tabasser, casser la gueule à **(b)** *(defeat)* foutre la pâtée *ou* une raclée *ou* une déculottée à, écrabouiller, battre à plates coutures **(c)** *Br (car)* conduire comme un dingue

thrashing ['θræʃɪŋ] *n* **(a)** *(beating)* **to give sb a thrashing** tabasser qn, casser la gueule à qn, foutre une raclée à qn; **to get a thrashing** prendre une raclée, se faire tabasser **(b)** *(defeat)* déculottée *f*, dégelée *f*, raclée *f*; **to give sb a thrashing** foutre la pâtée *ou* une raclée *ou* une déculottée à qn, écrabouiller qn, battre qn à plates coutures; **to get a thrashing** prendre une raclée *ou* une déculottée, se faire battre à plates coutures

threads [θredz] *npl (clothes)* fringues *fpl*

throat [θrəʊt] *n* **(a)** *Hum* **my stom-**

The symbol □ indicates that a translation is neutral.

ach thinks my throat's cut je crève la dalle (**b**) **to be at each other's throats** *(arguing)* se disputer, se chamailler; **to jump down sb's throat** *(shout at)* rentrer dans qn, gueuler sur qn

throw [θrəʊ] *vt* (**a**) **to throw one's toys out of the pram** *(get angry)* faire un caprice, piquer une colère (**b**) **to throw shapes** *(dance wildly)* danser comme un dément

ⓘ L'image à l'origine de l'expression "to throw one's toys out of the pram" est celle d'un très jeune enfant qui fait une colère et qui jette ses jouets hors de son landau.

throw up *vi (vomit)* dégobiller

thrupenny bits [!] [ˌθrʌpənɪˈbɪts] *npl Br (rhyming slang* **tits**) nichons *mpl*, nénés *mpl*, roberts *mpl*

thunderthighs [ˈθʌndəθaɪz] *n Hum (cuisses)* jambonneaux *mpl*; *(woman)* = femme aux grosses cuisses; **she's a real thunderthighs** elle a de sacrés jambonneaux

tick [tɪk] *n Br* (**a**) *(moment)* seconde□ *f*, instant□ *m*; **hang on a tick** *or* **two ticks** attends une seconde; **I'll just be a tick** *or* **two ticks** j'en ai pour une seconde *ou* deux secondes (**b**) *(credit)* **to buy sth on tick** acheter qch à crédit□

tick off *vt sép* (**a**) *Br (scold)* passer un savon à (**b**) *Am (annoy)* prendre la tête à; **to be ticked off (with)** en avoir marre (de)

ticker [ˈtɪkə(r)] *n (heart)* palpitant *m*

ticket [ˈtɪkɪt] *n* **that's (just) the ticket!** c'est exactement ce qu'il me/te/*etc* faut!

tiddly [ˈtɪdlɪ] *adj Br* (**a**) *(drunk)* éméché (**b**) *(small)* minus

tie on [taɪ] *vt sép Am* **to tie one on** *(get drunk)* prendre une cuite, se cuiter

tight [taɪt] *adj* (**a**) *(miserly)* pingre, radin (**b**) *(drunk)* pompette (**c**) *(close)* **to be tight** être comme les deux doigts de la main, être super copains/copines

tight-arsed [!] [ˈtaɪtɑːst], *Am* **tight-assed** [!] [ˈtaɪtæst] *adj (uptight)* coincé

tight-fisted [taɪtˈfɪstɪd] *adj* pingre, radin

tightie whities = **tighty whities**

tightwad [ˈtaɪtwɒd] *n* radin(e) *m,f*

tighty whities [ˌtaɪtɪˈwaɪtɪz] *npl* slip *m* kangourou□

time [taɪm] *n* (**a**) **to do time** *(in prison)* faire de la taule (**b**) *Am* **to make time with sb** *(chat up)* draguer qn; *(have sex with)* s'envoyer en l'air avec qn

tinkle [ˈtɪŋkəl] **1** *n* (**a**) *Br (phone call)* **to give sb a tinkle** passer un coup de fil à qn (**b**) *(act of urinating) Br* **to have a tinkle** faire pipi; **to go for a tinkle** aller faire pipi
2 *vi (urinate)* faire pipi

tinnie [ˈtɪnɪ] *n Austr* boîte *f* de bière□

tip [tɪp] *n Br (untidy place)* taudis *m*
▶ *voir aussi* **arse**

tipsy [ˈtɪpsɪ] *adj* éméché

tit [!] [tɪt] *n* (**a**) *(breast)* nichon *m*, robert *m*; *Br* **to get on sb's tits** courir sur le haricot à qn, taper sur les nerfs à qn; **to be off one's tits** *(drunk)* être complètement bourré *ou* pété; *(drugged)* complètement défoncé; **the movie was all tits and ass** il y avait plein de femmes à poil dans ce film; **tit tape** = ruban adhésif double-face appliqué sur la peau et utilisé pour faire tenir une robe très décolletée (**b**) *Br (person)* con (conne) *m,f*; **I felt a right tit** je me suis senti tout con ▸ *voir aussi* **arse, ripped**

titch [tɪtʃ] *n (short person)* microbe *m*

titchy ['tɪtʃɪ] *adj* minuscule, tout petit□

tits up [!] [tɪts'ʌp] *adv Br* **to go tits up** partir en couille

titty [!], **tittie** ['tɪtɪ] *n* (**a**) *(breast)* nichon *m*, robert *m*; **titty bar** bar *m* topless□ (**b**) **tough titty!** dur! dur!

toast [təʊst] *n* **to be toast** *(in trouble)* être foutu; *(exhausted)* être naze *ou* crevé *ou* lessivé *ou* claqué; **if Mum finds out, you're toast** si Maman s'en rend compte, t'es mort *ou* foutu!; **I can't drink any more or I'll be toast tomorrow** il faut que j'arrête de boire, sinon demain je serai dans le coaltar

toasty ['təʊstɪ] *adj* chaud et confortable□

tod [tɒd] *n Br (rhyming slang* **Tod Sloan** = **own)** **on one's tod** tout seul□

ⓘ Tod Sloan était un célèbre jockey américain du début du XXème siècle.

todger ['tɒdʒə(r)] *n Br (penis)* chipolata *f*

to-die-for [tə'daɪfɔː(r)] *adj* craquant

toff [tɒf] *n Br* rupin(e) *m,f*

toffee ['tɒfɪ] *n Br* **he can't sing/act for toffee!** il chante/joue comme un pied!

toffee-nosed ['tɒfɪnəʊzd] *adj Br* bêcheur, snob

together [tə'geðə(r)] *adj (well-adjusted)* équilibré□, bien dans ses baskets

togs [tɒgz] *npl Br* fringues *fpl*, sapes *fpl*

toilet ['tɔɪlɪt] *n* (**a**) **to go down the toilet** *(of plan, career, work)* être foutu en l'air; **that's our holidays down the toilet!** on peut faire une croix sur nos vacances! (**b**) *Br (horrible place)* trou□ *m*; **this town is an absolute toilet** c'est vraiment le trou du cul du monde, cette ville

toke [təʊk] **1** *n (of joint)* taffe *f*; **to take a toke** prendre une taffe
2 *vi* **to toke on a joint** prendre une taffe d'un joint

tom [tɒm] *n Br* (**a**) *(prostitute)* pute *f* (**b**) *(rhyming slang* **tomfoolery** = **jewellery)** quincaillerie *f* (**c**) [!] *(rhyming slang* **tomtit** = **shit)** **to have/go for a tom** couler/aller couler un bronze, faire/aller faire la grosse commission

tomcat around ['tɒmkæt] *vi Am* courir les filles

Tom, Dick and Harry ['tɒm'dɪkən'hærɪ] *npr* **every** *or Br* **any Tom, Dick and Harry** le premier venu, n'importe qui

tomfoolery [tɒm'fuːlərɪ] *n Br (rhyming slang* **jewellery)** quincaillerie *f*

tomtit [!] [tɒm'tɪt] *n Br (rhyming slang* **shit)** **to have/go for a tomtit** couler/aller couler un bronze, faire/aller faire la grosse commission

ton [tʌn] *n Br* cent□ *m*; *(£100)* cent livres□ *fpl*

tonsil hockey ['tɒnsɪl'hɒkɪ], **tonsil tennis** ['tɒnsɪl'tenɪs] *n Hum* **to play tonsil hockey** *or* **tennis** se rouler des pelles *ou* des patins

Tonys ['təʊnɪz], **Tony Blairs** ['təʊnɪ'bleəz] *npl Br (rhyming slang* **flares)** pantalon *m* pattes d'eph'

tool [!] [tuːl] *n* (**a**) *(penis)* engin *m* (**b**) *(man)* con *m*, connard *m* (**c**) **he isn't**

the sharpest tool in the shed il n'a pas inventé l'eau chaude *ou* le fil à couper le beurre

tool around *Am* **1** *vt insép* (*spend time in*) **to tool around Australia/the country** parcourir l'Australie/le pays sac au dos[□]; **to tool around the house** rester chez soi à glander
2 *vi* (*hang around*) glander

tool up *vt sép Br* **to tool oneself up, to get tooled up** s'armer[□], se charger, s'enfourailler

toon [tu:n] *n Am* (*cartoon*) dessin *m* animé[□]

toonie ['tu:ni] *n Can* pièce *f* d'un dollar[□]

toot [tu:t] **1** *n* (**a**) (*of cocaine*) prise *f* de cocaïne[□] (**b**) *Am* (*drinking spree*) cuite *f*; **to go out on a toot** sortir prendre une cuite
2 *vt* (*cocaine*) sniffer
3 *vi* (*sniff cocaine*) sniffer de la coke

toots [tu:ts] *n* (*term of address*) chéri(e) *m,f*

top [tɒp] **1** *adj* (**a**) **to pay top dollar (for sth)** payer le prix fort (pour qch); *Br* **to pay/earn top whack** payer/gagner un max; **we can offer you £50 top whack** on vous propose 50 livres mais pas plus *ou* et c'est notre dernier prix (**b**) *Hum* **top banana** huile *f*, gros bonnet *m*; **their new video's top banana!** leur nouvelle vidéo est super! (**c**) *Br* (*excellent*) top, génial, super; **that was an absolutely top steak!** ce steak était vraiment super bon!; **top plan!** super idée!; **his last movie was top** son dernier film était vraiment top
2 *vt Br* (*kill*) buter, zigouiller, refroidir; **to top oneself** se suicider[□], se foutre en l'air ▶ *voir aussi* **blow, totty, up**

tops [tɒps] *adv* (*at the most*) maxi;

it'll cost a fiver tops ça coûtera cinq livres maxi *ou* à tout casser

torqued [tɔ:kt] *adj Am* (**a**) (*angry*) furibard, furax, fumasse (**b**) (*drunk*) bourré, fait, beurré

tosh [tɒʃ] *Br* **1** *n* foutaises *fpl*; **that's a load of tosh!** c'est des foutaises!
2 *exclam* n'importe quoi!

toss [tɒs] *n Br* **I don't give a toss!** je m'en fiche pas mal!; **who gives a toss?** qu'est-ce que ça peut foutre? ▶ *see also* **cookie**

toss off [!] *Br* **1** *vt sép* **to toss sb off** branler qn; **to toss oneself off** se branler, se palucher, se pogner
2 *vi* se branler, se palucher, se pogner

tosser ['tɒsə(r)], **tosspot** ['tɒspɒt] *n Br* tache *f*, branque *m*

total ['təʊtəl] *vt Am* (*vehicle*) fusiller, bousiller

totally ['təʊtəlɪ] *adv Am* (*very much*) vachement; **I don't smoke but my parents totally smoke** moi je fume pas, mais mes parents ils fument vachement *ou* ils fument comme des malades

totty ['tɒtɪ] *n Br* (*attractive women*) belles nanas *fpl*, belles gonzesses *fpl*; (*attractive men*) beaux mecs *mpl*; **he's at the beach checking out the totty** il est en train de mater les nanas sur la plage; **check out the top totty!** vise un peu les canons!

touch [tʌtʃ] **1** *n* **to be a soft touch** être un pigeon *ou* une poire
2 *vt* **to touch sb for sth** taper qch à qn

touch up *vt sép* **to touch sb up** peloter qn; **to touch oneself up** se toucher

touched [tʌtʃt] *adj* (*mad*) timbré, toqué, cinglé

tough [tʌf] **1** *adj* **a tough guy** un

dur ▶ *voir aussi* **cookie, hang, shit, titty**
  2 *exclam* tant pis!

towelhead ['taʊəlhed] *n Injurieux* raton *m*, bicot *m*

townie ['taʊnɪ] *n Br* lascar *m*, racaille *f*

toyboy ['tɔɪbɔɪ] *n* = jeune amant d'une femme plus âgée

tracks [træks] *npl* (**a**) **to make tracks** *(leave)* mettre les bouts, se casser (**b**) *(on arm)* traces *fpl* de piquouses

tradesman's entrance [!] ['treɪdz-mənz'entrəns] *n Br Hum (anus)* entrée *f* de service

traffic ['træfɪk] *n* **go play in the traffic!** va voir ailleurs si j'y suis!

trainspotter ['treɪnspɒtə(r)] *n Br Péj* ringard(e) *m,f*

ⓘ À l'origine, le terme "trainspotter" désigne un passionné des chemins de fer dont le passe-temps consiste à noter les numéros des locomotives qu'il aperçoit. Au sens large, ce terme désigne une personne généralement solitaire et ennuyeuse, qui ne sait pas s'habiller (il porte le plus souvent un anorak). Un "trainspotter" ne s'intéresse pas à l'actualité musicale ou sportive, et ne fréquente aucun endroit branché.

tramlines ['træmlaɪnz] *npl Br (on arm)* traces *fpl* de piquouses

tramp [træmp] *n (promiscuous woman)* Marie-couche-toi-là *f*, pétasse *f*, traînée *f*

trampy ['træmpɪ] *adj (promiscuous)* coucheuse; *(clothes, behaviour, make-up)* qui fait pute

trank [træŋk], **trankie** ['træŋkɪ] *n (abrév* **tranquillizer**) tranquillisant□ *m*

trannie, tranny ['trænɪ] *n Br (abrév* **transvestite**) travelo *m*

trap [træp] *n (mouth)* clapet *m*; **shut your trap!** ferme ton clapet, ferme-la!; **to keep one's trap shut** la fermer, la boucler

trash [træʃ] **1** *n* (**a**) *(nonsense)* foutaises *fpl*; **his new film's a load of trash** son dernier film ne vaut pas un clou (**b**) *(people)* racaille *f*; **he's just trash** c'est un moins que rien; *Am* **white trash** petits Blancs *mpl* pauvres; *Am* **trailer trash** prolos *mpl* (qui vivent dans des caravanes) (**c**) *Noir Am* **to talk trash** *(converse, gossip)* tailler une bavette
  2 *vt* (**a**) *(vandalize)* foutre en l'air, bousiller (**b**) *(criticize)* éreinter, démolir

trashed [træʃt] *adj (drunk)* rond, fait, bourré; *(on drugs)* défoncé, raide

tree [triː] *n* **to be out of one's tree** *(mad)* être cinglé *ou* givré; *(drunk)* être rond *ou* rétamé *ou* bourré; *(on drugs)* être défoncé *ou* raide

trendy ['trendɪ] **1** *n* branché(e) *m,f*
  2 *adj* branché

trick [trɪk] *n* (**a**) **how's tricks?** comment ça va? (**b**) **to do the trick** faire l'affaire (**c**) *(prostitute's client)* micheton *m*; **to turn a trick** faire une passe; **she's been turning tricks for years** ça fait des années qu'elle fait la pute

trim [trɪm] *n (women)* nanas *fpl*, gonzesses *fpl*; **that's his new bit of trim** c'est sa nouvelle nana *ou* gonzesse

trip [trɪp] **1** *n* (**a**) *(after taking drugs)* trip *m*; **to have a good/bad trip** avoir un bon/mauvais trip (**b**) *(quantity of LSD)* dose *f* de LSD□, trip *m* (**c**) *(experience)* **to be on a guilt trip** culpabiliser; **to be on a power trip** être en plein trip mégalo; **to be on**

an ego trip se faire mousser

  2 *vi* **to be tripping** *(after taking drugs)* triper; *(crazy)* être dingue

trip out *vi (after taking drugs)* triper

tripe [traɪp] *n (nonsense)* foutaises *fpl*, conneries *fpl*; **don't talk tripe!** dis pas n'importe quoi!, raconte pas de conneries!; **what a load of tripe!** n'importe quoi!; **the film is absolute tripe!** il vaut pas un clou, ce film!

trippy ['trɪpɪ] *adj* psychédélique□

trog [trɒg] *n Br (ugly person)* mocheté *f*; **he's going out with a real trog** il sort avec un vrai cageot *ou* un vrai laideron

troll [trəʊl] *n Br (ugly person)* mocheté *f*; **his last bird was well fit but this one's a complete troll** sa dernière nana était canon, mais celle-ci c'est carrément un cageot *ou* un laideron

trolley ['trɒlɪ] *n* **(a) to be off one's trolley** avoir un grain, être cinglé **(b)** *Br Hum Péj* **trolley dolly** *(air hostess)* hôtesse *f* de l'air□ **(c)** *Br* **trolleys** *(underpants)* calbute *m*, calcif *m*

trolleyed, trollied ['trɒlɪd] *adj Br* bourré, pété, beurré

trots [trɒts] *npl* **the trots** *(diarrhoea)* la courante

trouble ['trʌbəl] *n* **(a) man/woman trouble** peines *fpl* de cœur **(b)** *Br* **trouble and strife** *(rhyming slang wife)* femme□ *f*, bourgeoise *f*

trounce [traʊns] *vt* battre à plates coutures, écrabouiller, mettre la pâtée à; **to get trounced** être battu à plates coutures, prendre une déculottée

trousered ['traʊzəd] *adj Br* rond comme une queue de pelle, plein comme une barrique

trout [traʊt] *n* **(a)** *Péj (woman)* **(old) trout** vieille bique *f* **(b)** *Hum* **trout pout** lèvres *fpl* au collagène□

trump [trʌmp] *Br* **1** *vi* péter, lâcher *ou* larguer une caisse

  2 *n* pet *m*, prout *m*

trustafarian [trʌstə'feərɪən] *n Br* = jeune anglais blanc de milieu aisé qui cultive une image rasta

ⓘ Il s'agit d'un mélange des termes "rastafarian" et "trust fund". Un "trust fund" est un fonds en fidéicommis que des parents établissent pour que leurs enfants aient accès à une somme d'argent quand ils atteignent un âge déterminé. Ces produits financiers s'adressent avant tout aux familles aisées et c'est pourquoi le "trustafarian" typique, en dépit de son look quelque peu depenaillé, est certain de ne jamais manquer de rien.

try on [traɪ] *vt sép Br* **to try it on with sb** *(attempt to deceive)* essayer d'embobiner qn; *(attempt to seduce)* faire du rentre-dedans à qn□; *(test someone's tolerance)* essayer de faire le coup à qn

tub [tʌb] *n* **a tub of lard** *(man)* un gros lard, un gros plein de soupe; *(woman)* une grosse dondon, une grosse vache

tube [tjuːb] *n* **(a) to go down the tubes** *(of plans)* tomber à l'eau; **that's £500 down the tubes** ça fait 500 livres de foutues en l'air **(b) the tube** *(television)* la téloche **(c) to have one's tubes tied** *(be sterilized)* se faire ligaturer les trompes□ **(d)** *Scot (idiot)* andouille *f*, courge *f*, cruche *f* **(e)** *Am* **tube steak [!!]** *(penis)* chipolata *f*, bite *f* ▸ *voir aussi* **boob**

tucker ['tʌkə(r)] n Br & Austr (food) bouffe f

tug [!] [tʌg] n Br **to have a tug** (masturbate) se tirer sur l'élastique, se polir le chinois

turd [!] [tɜːd] n (a) (excrement) merde f (b) (person) ordure f

turd-burglar [!] ['tɜːdbɜːglə(r)] n Br Injurieux pédale f, tantouze f, lope f

turf [tɜːf] n (a) (territory) territoire m (b) Am (field of expertise, authority) domaine⁰ m, truc m, rayon m; **that's not my turf** c'est pas mon rayon

turf out vt sép **to turf sb out** vider qn, foutre qn dehors

turkey ['tɜːkɪ] n Am (a) (unsuccessful film, book) bide m (b) (person) crétin(e) m,f, andouille f, courge f (c) **to talk turkey** passer aux choses sérieuses⁰ ▶ voir aussi **cold turkey**

turn off [tɜːn] vt sép **to turn sb off** (repulse) débecter qn

turn on 1 vt sép (excite) **to turn sb on** exciter qn; **to be turned on** être excité; **whatever turns you on!** du moment que tu y trouves ton compte!
2 vi (take drugs) se camer

turn over vt sép Br (rob, burgle) **to turn sth over** (house) cambrioler qch⁰; (bank, shop) cambrioler qch⁰, braquer qch

turn-off ['tɜːnɒf] n (sexually) **it's a turn-off** ça coupe l'envie

turn-on ['tɜːnɒn] n (sexually) **it's a real turn-on for him** il trouve ça super excitant

tush [tʊʃ], **tushy** ['tʊʃɪ] n Am (buttocks) fesses fpl

TV [tiː'viː] n (abrév **transvestite**) travelo m

twat [twæt] **1** n (a) [!] (woman's genitals) chatte f, chagatte f (b) [!]

(person) tache f, taré(e) m,f (c) Br (tap, knock) claque⁰ f; **give him a twat on the head!** donne-lui une claque sur la tête!
2 vt Br (hit) donner une claque à⁰; **he twatted her on the head** il lui a donné une claque sur la tête

twatted ['twætɪd] adj Br (drunk) rond comme une queue de pelle, plein comme une barrique

tweaked [twiːkt] adj Am (drunk) bourré, fait, beurré; (on drugs) raide, défoncé

twenty-four seven ['twentɪfɔː'sevən] adv (constantly) sans arrêt⁰

ⓘ Cette expression (à laquelle on ajoute parfois "365", prononcé "three sixty-five") signifie littéralement 24 heures par jour, 7 jours par semaine (et 365 jours par an).

twerp [twɜːp] n courge f, nouille f

twink [twɪŋk], **twinkie, twinky** ['twɪŋkɪ] n Am Péj (a) (homosexual) = jeune minet homosexuel, le plus souvent blond et pas très futé (b) (Asian person) = Asiatique qui adopte les valeurs des Blancs

ⓘ Le Twinkie® est une sorte de gâteau fourré à la crème, vendu aux États-Unis. L'extérieur est jaune et l'intérieur est blanc.

twist [twɪst] n Br **to be round the twist** être dingue, avoir un grain; **to go round the twist** devenir dingue ou cinglé, perdre la boule; **to drive sb round the twist** rendre qn chèvre ▶ voir aussi **knickers**

twister ['twɪstə(r)] n (a) Br (crook) arnaqueur(euse) m,f (b) Am (tornado) tornade⁰ f

twit [twɪt] *n Br* courge *f*, nouille *f*

twitcher ['twɪtʃə(r)] *n Br* dingue *mf* d'ornithologie

two and eight [tuːən'eɪt] *n Br* (*rhyming slang* **state**) **to be in a two and eight** être dans tous ses états; **he was in a right two and eight when his missis left him** il était dans tous ses états quand sa nana l'a quitté

two-bit ['tuːbɪt] *adj* à la noix (de coco), à la gomme; **he plays for some two-bit team** il joue pour une espèce d'équipe à la noix; **she's nothing but a two-bit secretary** ce n'est qu'une petite secrétaire à la gomme

2CB [tuːsiːˈbiː] *n* 2CB *m*, nexus *m*

twock [twɒk] *vt Br* (*car*) faucher, tirer, chouraver

ⓘ Il s'agit d'un terme formé à partir des initiales de la phrase "Take Without the Owner's Consent".

twonk [twɒŋk] *n* (*fool*) andouille *f*, cruche *f*, cloche *f*

two-time [tuːˈtaɪm] *vt* **to two-time sb** tromper qn□, faire porter des cornes à qn

two-timer [tuːˈtaɪmə(r)] *n* personne *f* infidèle□

tyke [taɪk] *n* (**a**) *Br* (*coarse person*) lourdaud(e) *m,f* (**b**) (*child*) morveux(euse) *m,f*, môme *mf*

Uu

uh-huh [ʌ'hʌ] *exclam* ouais!; **uh-huh?** ah ouais?

uh-oh ['ʌəʊ] *exclam* allons bon!

uh-uh ['ʌʌ] *exclam (no)* non non!; *(in warning)* hé!

umpteen ['ʌmptiːn] *adj* des tas de; **I've told you umpteen times** je te l'ai déjà dit trente-six fois

umpteenth ['ʌmptiːnθ] *adj* énième; **for the umpteenth time** pour la énième fois

'un [ʌn] *pron (one)* **that's a good 'un!** elle est bonne celle-là!; **he's a bad 'un** c'est un sale type; **the little 'uns** les petiots *mpl*

uncool [ʌn'kuːl] *adj (a) (unfashionable, unsophisticated)* ringard; **it's a really uncool place** c'est nul comme endroit; **what an uncool thing to do!** c'est vraiment nul de faire un truc pareil! **(b)** *(not allowed, not accepted)* mal vu□; **I think it's a bit uncool to smoke in here** je pense pas que ce soit permis de fumer ici□ **(c)** *(upset)* **she was a bit uncool about me moving in with them** elle tenait pas trop à ce que je m'installe chez eux

undercrackers ['ʌndəkrækəz] *npl Br* calcif *m*, calbute *m*

undies ['ʌndɪz] *npl (abrév underwear)* sous-vêtements□ *mpl*

unhip [ʌn'hɪp] *adj* ringard

uni ['juːnɪ] *n (a) Br (abrév university)* fac *f*; **he's doing law at uni** il fait une fac de droit **(b)** *Am (abrév uniform)* uniforme□ *m*

unreal [ʌn'rɪəl] *adj (a) (unbelievable)* pas possible, pas croyable, dingue **(b)** *(excellent)* dément, super, génial

up [ʌp] **1** *n (drug)* amphet *f*, amphé *f*
2 *adj (a)* **what's up?** *(what's happening)* qu'est-ce qui se passe?□; *(what's wrong)* qu'est-ce qui va pas?; *Am (as greeting)* salut!; **what's up with him?** qu'est-ce qui lui arrive?□; **there's something up with the TV** la télé débloque **(b)** *Br* **we're going clubbing tonight, are you up for it?** on va en boîte ce soir, ça te branche?; **I'm well up for it tonight!** j'ai la super pêche pour ce soir!; **was she up for it?** *(willing to have sex)* alors, elle a bien voulu coucher?
3 *adv Br* **he doesn't have very much up top** c'est pas une lumière, il a pas inventé l'eau chaude *ou* le fil à couper le beurre; **she's got plenty up top** elle en a dans le ciboulot
4 *prép* **he's totally up himself** il se prend vraiment pas pour de la merde; **up yours! [!!]** va te faire foutre!

upchuck ['ʌptʃʌk] *vi Hum* dégobiller

uphill gardener [!] ['ʌphɪl'gɑːdnə(r)] *n Br Péj Hum* pédale *f*, tantouse *f*

upper ['ʌpə(r)] *n (a) (drug)* amphet *f*, amphé *f*; **he's on uppers** il est sous amphets *ou* amphés (**b**) *Br* **to be on one's uppers** être dans la dèche

upside ['ʌpsaɪd] *prép Noir Am* **to hit sb upside the head** filer un coup sur le ciboulot *ou* la cafetière à qn

upstairs [ʌp'steəz] *adv* (**a**) **he hasn't got much upstairs** c'est pas une lumière, il a pas inventé l'eau chaude *ou* le fil à couper le beurre (**b**) **to kick sb upstairs** *(promote)* se débarrasser de qn en lui donnant de l'avancement□

uptight [ʌp'taɪt] *adj Noir Am (excellent)* super, génial, géant

us [ʌs] *pron Br (me)* **give us a kiss** embrasse-moi□; **give us a look** fais

voir□; **he bought us a drink** il m'a payé un verre□

use [juːz] *vi (take drugs)* se camer

user ['juːzə(r)] *n* (**a**) *(addict)* drogué(e)□ *m,f*; **heroin user** héroïnomane□ *mf*; **cocaine user** cocaïnomane□ *mf* (**b**) *(who uses people)* personne *f* intéressée□; **I dumped him cos he was such a user** je l'ai largué parce qu'il se servait de moi

usual ['juːʒʊəl] *n (drink, food)* **the usual, sir?** comme d'habitude, monsieur?; **I'll just have my usual** je prends comme d'habitude

ute [juːt] *n Austr (abrév **utility vehicle**)* gros pick-up□ *m*

Vv

V [viː] *n Br* **to give sb the V** *or* **Vs** *n* faire un doigt d'honneur à qn

ⓘ Ce geste se fait à l'aide de l'index et du majeur, avec la paume de la main face à soi.

vag¹ [!!] [vædʒ] *n* (*abrév* **vagina**) chatte *f*, cramouille *f*

vag² [væg] *n Am* (*abrév* **vagrant**) clodo *mf*

vamoose [vəˈmuːs] *vi* se tirer, se casser; **vamoose!** tire-toi!, casse-toi!

vamp [væmp] *vi Noir Am* (*leave*) se casser, se tirer, s'arracher

vamp up *vt sep* (*image, style*) rendre plus sexy; **that actress has really vamped up her look** l'actrice a adopté un look beaucoup plus sexy

veep [viːp] *n Am* (*abrév* **vice-president**) vice-président□ *m*

veg [vedʒ] **1** *npl Br* (*abrév* **vegetables**) légumes□ *mpl*, verdure *f*
2 *vi* traîner, glandouiller; **I spent the whole weekend vegging in front of the TV** j'ai passé tout le week-end à glandouiller devant la télé

veg out *vi* traîner, glandouiller; **I spent the whole weekend vegging out, watching DVDs** j'ai passé tout le week-end à glandouiller en regardant des DVD

veggie [ˈvedʒɪ] **1** *n* (**a**) (*abrév* **vegetarian**) végétarien(enne)□ *m,f* (**b**) (*abrév* **vegetable**) **veggies** légumes□ *mpl*, verdure *f*
2 *adj* (*abrév* **vegetarian**) végétarien□

velvet [ˈvelvɪt] *n Am* (*profit*) bénef *m*; (*easy money*) argent *m* facile□

Vera [ˈvɪərə] *n Br* (*rhyming slang* **Vera Lynn = gin**) gin□ *m*; **go out and get a bottle of Vera** va acheter une bouteille de gin

ⓘ Vera Lynn est une chanteuse britannique qui connut son heure de gloire pendant la deuxième guerre mondiale lorsqu'elle alla chanter pour les soldats britanniques.

verbal [ˈvɜːbəl] **1** *n Br* (*insults*) insultes□ *fpl*; **to give sb some verbal** traiter qn de tous les noms
2 *adj Hum* **to have verbal** *Br* **diarrhoea** *or Am* **diarrhea** être atteint de diarrhée verbale

Vette [vet] *n Am* (*abrév* **Corvette®**) Corvette® *f*

vibe [vaɪb] *n* (*abrév* **vibration**) (**a**) (*atmosphere*) atmosphère□ *f*, ambiance□ *f*; **this bar has a nice relaxed vibe** l'ambiance est très cool dans ce bar; **their new album's got a bit of an R&B vibe** leur nouvel album a un petit côté R&B (**b**) (*feeling*) **to get good/bad vibes about sb/sth**

bien/mal sentir qn/qch; **he gives me good/bad vibes** il y a quelque chose chez lui que j'aime/que j'aime pas; **this place gives me strange vibes** cet endroit me donne de drôles de sensations

vid [vɪd] *n* (*abrév* **video**) vidéo◻ *f*

-ville [vɪl] *suffixe* **boresville** hyper chiant; **sleazeville** hyper corrompu

ⓘ Le suffixe "-ville" sert à former des noms et des adjectifs. Il indique que le terme qui le précède caractérise ce dont on parle.

vines [vaɪnz] *npl Noir Am* (*clothes*) fringues *fpl*, sapes *fpl*

vino ['viːnəʊ] *n* pinard *m*, picrate *m*

Pleins feux sur...

Violence

Il existe de nombreux termes pour désigner une arme de poing, notamment **shooter**, **piece** et **equalizer**. L'expression américaine **Saturday night special** désigne un petit pistolet bon marché. Pour parler d'une personne armée, on emploiera les expressions **to be packing heat** ou **to be tooled up**. On appelle un couteau **a blade**, **a chib** ou **a shiv** (ces deux derniers sont issus du mot gitan "chiv" qui signifie "lame" ; ils s'emploient également comme verbes – **to chib** ou **to shiv someone**). De nombreux verbes sont synonymes de "tuer" : **to blow away**, **to bump off**, **to do in**, **to ice**, **to liquidate**, **to waste** et **to whack**. "Se suicider" se dit **to do oneself in** ou **to top oneself** (en anglais britannique uniquement).

Pour désigner une bagarre, on emploie les mots **scrap**, **ruck**, **punch-up** (anglais britannique) ou **rumble**. Il existe un certain nombre de verbes qui signifient "battre", dont les plus courants sont **to hammer**, **to paste** et **to thrash**. On utilise également la forme substantivée de ces verbes. On peut dire, par exemple, **to give someone a thrashing**, **a hammering**, etc. Pour dire "frapper", on emploiera les termes **to bash**, **to belt**, **to clout**, **to whack** et **to wallop**. "Envoyer quelqu'un au tapis" se dit **to flatten** ou **to deck somebody**, ou encore **to punch somebody's lights out** (en anglais britannique) et **to punch somebody out** (en anglais américain).

Pour dire "mourir" (et pas nécessairement de mort violente), on dira **to croak**, **to kick the bucket**, **to pop one's clogs**, **to snuff it** (ces deux dernières expressions étant britanniques), ainsi que **to check out** et **to buy the farm** (en anglais américain). Enfin, on dira d'un défunt **he's/she's six feet under** ou **pushing up the daisies**.

Le symbole [!] dénote un terme très familier, [!!] un terme vulgaire.

virus ['vaɪrəs] *n* **the virus** le dass, le sida□

voddy ['vɒdɪ] *n Br* (*abrév* **vodka**) vodka□ *f*; **a voddy and orange** une vodka-orange

vom [vɒm] (*abrév* **vomit**) **1** *n* dégueulis *m*
   2 *vi* dégueuler, gerber

Ww

wack [wæk] adj Noir Am (**a**) (worthless) nul (**b**) (mad) cinglé, toqué, timbré (**c**) (stupid) débile

wack-job ['wækdʒɒb] n Am cinglé(e) m,f, dingue mf

wacko ['wækəʊ] **1** n cinglé(e) m,f, dingue mf
2 adj cinglé, dingue, timbré, toqué

wacky ['wækɪ] adj loufoque; Hum **wacky baccy** (marijuana) herbe f

wag [wæg] vt Br **to wag it** faire l'école buissonnière

wagon ['wægən] n (**a**) **to be on the wagon** être au régime sec; **to be off** or **have fallen off the wagon** s'être remis à picoler (**b**) Ir (unpleasant woman) chameau m; (ugly woman) cageot m, mocheté f ▸ voir aussi **meat, paddy**

walk [wɔːk] **1** n **take a walk!** va voir ailleurs si j'y suis!, dégage!; **it was a walk in the park** (very easy) c'était un jeu d'enfant; Hum **to do the walk of shame** (after night out) = rentrer chez soi le matin avec les vêtements de la veille, après avoir passé la nuit avec quelqu'un
2 vt **to walk it** gagner les doigts dans le nez ▸ voir aussi **street**

wall [wɔːl] n (**a**) **off the wall** (eccentric) loufoque, zarbi (**b**) **to be up the wall** (mad) être cinglé ou givré, avoir un grain; **to drive sb up the wall** rendre qn chèvre ▸ voir aussi **hole**

wallop ['wɒləp] **1** n **to give sb a wallop** foutre une beigne ou un gnon à qn; **to give sth a wallop** foutre un coup dans qch
2 vt (**a**) (hit) (person) foutre une beigne ou un gnon à; (object) foutre un coup dans (**b**) (defeat) foutre la pâtée ou une raclée ou une déculottée à, écrabouiller, battre à plates coutures

wally ['wɒlɪ] n Br andouille f, nouille f

wank [!!] [wæŋk] Br **1** n branlette f; **to have a wank** se branler, se pogner, se palucher; **wank mag** magazine m de cul
2 vi se branler, se pogner, se palucher
3 adj débile, con

wank off [!!] Br vt sép **to wank sb off** branler qn; **to wank oneself off** se branler, se pogner, se palucher
2 vi se branler, se pogner, se palucher

wanker [!!] ['wæŋkə(r)] n Br (idiot) connard m

wankered [!!] ['wæŋkəd] adj Br (drunk) rond comme une queue de pelle ou comme un boudin, plein comme une barrique, fin plein

wanky [!!] ['wæŋkɪ] adj Br (stupid) débile, con; **he's OK but all his friends are a bit wanky** lui, ça va, mais tous ses copains son assez cons; **he looks really wanky when he dances** il a vraiment l'air con quand il danse; **what are you wearing that wanky T-shirt for?** pourquoi est-ce que tu portes ce tee-shirt à la con?

wannabe ['wɒnəbiː] n (**a**) *(who wants money, success)* arriviste⁰ mf (**b**) *(who wants to be like someone famous)* = personne qui cherche à être comme son idole; **the place was full of Britney Spears wannabes** c'était plein de filles qui se prenaient pour Britney Spears

warpaint ['wɔːpeɪnt] n Hum *(make-up)* maquillage⁰ m; **to put the warpaint on** se maquiller⁰

washed-up [wɒʃt'ʌp] adj **to be (all) washed-up** *(of person)* être fini; *(of plan)* être tombé à l'eau

washout ['wɒʃaʊt] n *(failure)* fiasco m, bide m

waste [weɪst] vt *(attack)* casser la gueule à, démonter le portrait à; *(kill)* buter, refroidir, zigouiller; Br **to waste sb's face** casser ou défoncer la gueule à qn, faire une tête au carré à qn

wasted ['weɪstɪd] adj *(drunk)* pété, bourré, fait; *(on drugs)* défoncé, raide

waster ['weɪstə(r)] n Br glandeur(euse) m,f, glandouilleur(euse) m,f

watering hole ['wɔːtərɪŋhəʊl] n Hum *(bar)* troquet m, rade m

water sports [!] ['wɔːtəspɔːts] npl uro f, = pratique sexuelle qui consiste à uriner sur ou sa partenaire

way [weɪ] **1** n (**a**) **no way!** pas question!; **no way am I going!** il est pas question que j'y aille!; **no way, José!** pas question! (**b**) **to go all the way** or **the whole way with sb** coucher avec qn; **they went all the way** or **the whole way** ils ont couché ensemble; **we haven't gone**

all the way yet on n'a pas encore vraiment fait l'amour (**c**) Am **way to go!** super!

2 exclam Am si! *(en réponse à "no way!")*

3 adv *(very)* vachement; **he's way crazy** il est vachement atteint ▶ *voir aussi* **swing**

ⓘ L'usage figurant dans la catégorie 2 a été popularisé par le film comique américain *Wayne's World.*

way-out [weɪ'aʊt] adj *(eccentric)* loufoque

wazoo [wə'zuː] n Am *(buttocks)* fesses⁰ fpl, miches fpl

wazz [wæz] Br **1** n **to have a wazz** faire la petite commission; **to go for a wazz** aller faire la petite commission

2 vi faire la petite commission

wazzed [wæzd] adj Br bourré, pété, fait

wazzock ['wæzək] n Br andouille f, cloche f, cruche f

wazzup [wɒz'ʌp] exclam Am *(greeting)* quoi de neuf?

ⓘ Il s'agit d'une contraction des termes "what's up?".

wedge [wedʒ] n Br *(money)* fric m, flouze m, pognon m, oseille f

wedgie ['wedʒɪ] n **to have a wedgie** avoir le slip coincé entre les fesses; **to give sb a wedgie** remonter brusquement le slip de quelqu'un pour le lui coincer entre les fesses

wee [wiː] Br **1** n pipi m; **to have a wee** faire pipi

2 vi faire pipi

weed [wiːd] n (**a**) Br *(person)* femmelette f, mauviette f, lavette f (**b**) *(marijuana)* herbe *f* (**c**) *Am (cigarette)* clope *f*, sèche *f*, tige *f*; *(cannabis cigarette)* joint *m* (**d**) **the weed** *(tobacco)* tabac⁰ *m*; **I've given up the weed** j'ai arrêté de fumer⁰

weedgie ['wiːdʒɪ] = **weegie**

weedy ['wiːdɪ] *adj Br (physically)* racho; *(in character)* faible⁰, mou

weegie ['wiːdʒɪ] *Br Péj ou Hum* **1** *n* habitant(e) *m,f* de Glasgow⁰
     2 *adj* de Glasgow⁰

ⓘ Selon le ton et le contexte, le terme "weegie" peut être soit péjoratif, soit humoristique. Bien que la plupart des gens qui l'emploient le fassent sans mauvaise intention, les habitants de Glasgow n'apprécient pas toujours d'être appelés ainsi. Il est donc préférable de ne pas utiliser ce terme si l'on ne sait pas comment il sera accueilli.

---

weener ['wiːnə(r)] = **wiener**

weenie ['wiːnɪ] *n Am* (**a**) *(frankfurter)* saucisse *f* de Francfort⁰ (**b**) *(idiot)* andouille *f*, truffe *f*, courge *f* (**c**) *(student)* bûcheur(euse) *m,f* (**d**) *Hum (penis)* chipolata *f*; **to play hide the weenie** *(have sex)* s'envoyer en l'air

---

ⓘ "Weenie" est le diminutif de "wiener" (qui signifie "viennois" en allemand), qui est le nom donné aux saucisses de Francfort aux États-Unis.

---

weigh into [weɪ] *vt insép Br* rentrer dans le lard à

weird out [wɪəd] *vt sép Am* **to weird sb out** faire flipper qn

weirded out ['wɪədɪd'aʊt] *adj Am* (**a**) *(strange)* loufoque, zarbi; *(mad)* cinglé, dingue, timbré (**b**) *(uncom-*

fortable) mal à l'aise⁰; **I was a bit weirded out by all the questions he was asking** il me foutait un peu mal à l'aise avec toutes ses questions

weirdo ['wɪədəʊ] *n* hurluberlu⁰ *m*

well [wel] *adv Br (very)* vachement; **he looks well dodgy** il a l'air vachement louche; **the club was well cool** la boîte était vachement cool

well 'ard ['welɑːd] *adj Br (very tough)* **he's well 'ard!** c'est un vrai dur (à cuire)!

well-hung [!] ['wel'hʌŋ] *adj (man)* bien monté

wellied ['welɪd] *adj Br* bourré comme un coing, rond comme une queue de pelle *ou* comme un boudin

well-stacked ['wel'stækt] *adj (woman)* qui a de gros nichons; **she's well-stacked** il y a du monde au balcon

welly ['welɪ] *n Br* **to give it some welly** mettre le paquet

wet [wet] **1** *n Br (feeble person)* mauviette *f*, lavette *f*
     2 *adj* (**a**) *Br (feeble)* faible⁰, mou (**b**) **wet blanket** rabat-joie *mf* (**c**) *Am* **to be all wet** *(mistaken)* se gourer
▸ *voir aussi* **rag**

wetback ['wetbæk] *n Am Injurieux* = travailleur clandestin mexicain

---

ⓘ "Wetback" signifie littéralement "dos mouillé". Cette appellation vient du fait que de nombreux Mexicains traversent le Rio Grande à la nage pour aller travailler clandestinement aux États-Unis.

---

whack [wæk] **1** *n (attempt)* essai⁰ *m*, tentative⁰ *f*; **to give sth a whack, to take a whack at sth** essayer qch

2 vt (kill) buter, zigouiller, refroidir
▸ voir aussi **top**

whack off [!] vi se branler, se pogner, se palucher

whacked [wækt] adj (a) crevé, naze, lessivé, claqué (b) **whacked out** parti, raide, défoncé; **to be whacked out on E/acid** il est complètement défoncé à l'ecsta/au LSD

whacky ['wækɪ] = **wacky**

whang [!] [wæŋ] n Am (penis) bite f, zob m, queue f

whatever ['wɒtevə(r)] exclam (not interested) **I'll call you next week – whatever** je t'appellerai la semaine prochaine – comme tu veux; (dismissing) **so my mum's like "finish your homework" and I'm like "yeah, whatever..."** puis ma mère me dit: "finis tes devoirs" et moi je lui réponds: "ouais, c'est ça..."; (not believing) **nothing happened, we're just friends! – yeah, whatever...** il ne s'est rien passé, on est juste amis! – ouais, c'est ça...

what-for ['wɒtfɔː(r)] n **to give sb what-for** (physically) foutre une raclée à qn; (verbally) passer un savon à qn, remonter les bretelles à qn; **to get what-for** (physically) prendre une raclée; (verbally) se faire passer un savon, se faire remonter les bretelles

what's-her-face ['wɒtsɜːfeɪs], **what's-her-name** ['wɒtsɜːneɪm] n Machine f

what's-his-face ['wɒtsɪzfeɪs], **what's-his-name** ['wɒtsɪzneɪm] n Machin m

whatsit ['wɒtsɪt], **whatsitsname** ['wɒtsɪtsneɪm] n machin m, truc m, bidule m

wheel [wiːl] **1** n (a) **(big) wheel** (person) huile f, gros bonnet m (b) **(set of) wheels** (car) bagnole f, caisse f, tire f

2 vi **to wheel and deal** magouiller
▸ voir aussi **fifth wheel, hell**

wheeler-dealer ['wiːlə'diːlə(r)] n magouilleur(euse) m,f

whiffy ['wɪfɪ] adj Br qui schlingue, qui coince, qui fouette; **it's a bit whiffy in here** ça schlingue ici

whipped [wɪpt] adj Am = **pussy-whipped**

whistle ['wɪsəl] n Br (rhyming slang **whistle and flute** = **suit**) costard m
▸ voir aussi **blow**

white [waɪt] adj (a) **white stuff** (heroin) blanche f, héro f; (cocaine) coco f, neige f, coke f (b) **white lightning** tord-boyaux m (distillé illégalement)

whitebread ['waɪtbred] adj Am Péj (dull, conventional) conventionnel et ennuyeux□

whitey ['waɪtɪ] n (a) **to have a whitey** = devenir tout pâle et être sur le point de dégueuler après avoir fumé trop de hasch (b) Noir Am **Whitey** Blanc (Blanche) m,f

whizz [wɪz] **1** n (a) (expert) as m; **a computer whizz** un as de l'informatique; **he's a whizz at chess** c'est un crack aux échecs; **whizz kid** jeune prodige m (b) Br (amphetamines) amphés fpl, amphets fpl (c) Am **to take a whizz** (urinate) faire pipi

2 vi Am (urinate) faire pipi

whizzbang ['wɪzbæŋ] adj Am (excellent) super, génial, géant

whoop [wuːp] n Am Ironique **big whoop!** la belle affaire!□

whopper ['wɒpə(r)] n (a) (impressive thing) mastodonte m; **that's a whopper of a bruise you've got** tu as un sacré bleu; **that salmon he caught was a whopper** c'est un sacré morceau le saumon qu'il a pêché (b) (lie) craque f, bobard m

whopping ['wɒpɪŋ] **1** adj énorme, géant; **it costs a whopping £3,000** ça coûte la coquette somme de trois mille livres; **he scored a whopping forty goals last season** il a carrément marqué quarante buts la saison dernière

2 adv **a whopping great lie** un bobard énorme

whore [hɔː(r)] n (**a**) (prostitute) pute f; **to take a whore's bath** = s'asperger de parfum et de déodorant pour éviter de se laver (**b**) (promiscuous woman) salope f, pétasse f, traînée f

whorehouse ['hɔːhaʊs] n bordel m, claque m

whup [wʊp] vt Noir Am (hit) foutre une beigne ou un gnon à; **to whup sb's ass** (defeat) foutre la pâtée ou une raclée ou une déculottée à qn, battre qn à plates coutures

wick [wɪk] n (**a**) Br **to get on sb's wick** taper sur les nerfs à qn, courir sur le haricot à qn (**b**) **to dip one's wick** [!] tremper son biscuit

wicked ['wɪkɪd] **1** adj (**a**) (excellent) super, génial, géant (**b**) Hum **to have one's wicked way with sb** faire une partie de jambes en l'air avec qn; **so, has he had his wicked way with you yet?** alors, est-ce que tu t'es donnée à lui?

2 exclam super!, génial!

3 adv vachement; **I was wicked drunk last night** j'étais fin plein hier soir

widdle ['wɪdəl] Br **1** n **to have a widdle** (urinate) faire pipi

2 vi faire pipi

wide [waɪd] adj Br (cocky) culotté, gonflé; **wide boy** magouilleur m

widget ['wɪdʒɪt] n (**a**) (thing, object) bidule m, machin m (**b**) (gadget) gadget⁰ m

wiener ['wiːnə(r)] n Am (**a**) (small penis) petite bite f, petite nouille f (**b**) (man) trou m du cul, trouduc m

wife-beater ['waɪfbiːtə(r)] n Am (vest) marcel m

wig out [wɪg] vi Am (get angry) piquer une crise, péter les plombs; (go mad) devenir cinglé, perdre la boule; (get excited) devenir dingue

wigga = **wigger**

wigged (out) [wɪgd('aʊt)] adj Am (crazy) cinglé, tapé, timbré

wigger ['wɪgə(r)] n Péj = Blanc qui cherche à copier le mode de vie des Noirs

ⓘ "Wigger" est la contraction de "white" et de "nigger".

wiggy ['wɪgɪ] adj Am (mad) cinglé, tapé, timbré; (eccentric) loufoque, allumé

wild [waɪld] adj (**a**) (angry) en pétard, fumasse, furibard, furax; **to go wild** se mettre en pétard (**b**) (enthusiastic) **to be wild about sb/sth** être dingue de qn/qch; **I wasn't exactly wild about it** ça ne m'a pas vraiment emballé (**c**) (excellent) super, génial, géant; **that was a wild film!** ce film était génial! (**d**) **to do the wild thing** (have sex) s'envoyer en l'air

willies ['wɪlɪz] npl Br **to give sb the willies** donner la chair de poule à qn

willy ['wɪlɪ] n quéquette f, zizi m

wimp [wɪmp] n mauviette f, femmelette f, lavette f

wimp out vi se dégonfler; **he wimped out of the fight** il s'est dégonflé au dernier moment et a refusé de se battre; **he wimped out of telling her the truth** finalement il a eu la trouille de lui dire la vérité

wimpy ['wɪmpɪ] *adj (physically)* malingre□, racho; *(mentally)* poule mouillée *(inv)*; **he's so wimpy!** quelle mauviette!

wind up [waɪnd] *vt sép Br* **to wind sb up** *(tease)* faire enrager qn, taquiner qn; *(fool)* mettre qn en boîte; *(irritate)* foutre qn en rogne

windbag ['wɪndbæg] *n* moulin *m* à paroles

window ['wɪndəʊ] *n* (**a**) **to go out (of) the window** *(of plans)* tomber à l'eau; **that's my chances of promotion out the window** je peux faire une croix sur mon avancement (**b**) *Péj* **window licker** [!] débile *mf* mental(e)

wind-up ['waɪndʌp] *n Br* mise *f* en boîte; **this has to be a wind-up!** dis-moi que c'est une plaisanterie!

wingding ['wɪndɪŋ] *n Am (celebration)* bringue *f*, bombe *f*, fiesta *f*

winkle ['wɪŋkəl] *n Br (penis)* quéquette *f*, zizi *m*

wino ['waɪnəʊ] *n* poivrot(e) *m,f*, alcolo *mf*

wipe out [waɪp] *vt sép* **to wipe sb out** *(exhaust)* lessiver qn; *(kill)* buter *ou* refroidir *ou* zigouiller qn

wiped (out) [waɪpt('aʊt)] *adj (exhausted)* crevé, naze, lessivé

wired ['waɪəd] *adj (highly strung)* sur les nerfs, à cran; *(after taking drugs)* défoncé *(après avoir pris de la cocaïne ou des amphétamines)*

wise up [waɪz] *vi* **to wise up to sb** voir qn sous son vrai jour□; **to wise up to sth** se rendre compte de qch□; **wise up!** réveille-toi!, ouvre les yeux!

wiseass [!] ['waɪzæs] *n Am* je-sais-tout *mf*

wiseguy ['waɪzgaɪ] *n Am* (**a**) *(know-all)* je-sais-tout *mf* (**b**) *(criminal)* truand *m*

witch [wɪtʃ] *n (nasty woman)* garce *f*, chameau *m*

with it ['wɪðɪt] *adj* (**a**) *(fashionable)* dans le coup, dans le vent (**b**) *(awake)* bien réveillé□ ▶ *voir aussi* **get with**

witter ['wɪtə(r)] *vi Br* **to witter (on)** jacasser, bavasser, parler pour ne rien dire; **he's always wittering on about the army** il n'en finit pas de parler de l'armée

wizz [wɪz] = **whizz**

wobbler ['wɒblə(r)], **wobbly** ['wɒblɪ] *n Br* **to throw a wobbler** *or* **a wobbly** piquer une crise, péter les plombs, péter une durite

wog [wɒg] *n Injurieux (black man)* nègre *m*, bamboula *m*; *(black woman)* négresse *f*

wolf [wʊlf] *n (womanizer)* coureur *m*

wombat ['wɒmbæt] *n Am (man)* hurluberlu□ *m*, drôle de zèbre *m*; *(woman)* hurluberlu□ *m*

wonga ['wɒŋgə] *n Br* fric *m*, flouze *m*, pognon *m*

wonk [wɒŋk] *n Am* (**a**) *(student)* bûcheur(euse) *m,f* (**b**) *(intellectual, expert)* intello *mf (qui ne s'intéresse qu'à sa discipline)*

wood [wʊd] *n* (**a**) *Am* **to put the wood to sb** *(beat up)* tabasser qn; *(defeat)* écrabouiller qn, battre qn à plates coutures, mettre une raclée *ou* une déculottée à qn (**b**) [!!] **to get/have wood** *(erection)* bander; **to put the wood to sb** *(have sex with)* tringler *ou* troncher qn

wooden overcoat ['wʊdən'əʊvəkəʊt] *n Hum (coffin)* costume *m* de sapin

woodie [!!] ['wʊdɪ] *n Am (erection)* érection□ *f*, bandaison *f*; **to have a**

woodie avoir la trique *ou* le gourdin, bander

woof [wʊf] *vi* Noir Am (boast, bluff) frimer, flamber

woofter ['wʊftə(r)] *n* Br Injurieux tante *f*, tapette *f*

wop [wɒp] *Injurieux* **1** *n* Rital(e) *m, f*
2 *adj* rital

word [wɜːd] **1** *n* **(the) word on the street is...** on raconte que...
2 *exclam* Noir Am **word (up)!** (I agree) parfaitement!; (it's true) sans dec!

workie ['wɜːkɪ] *n* Br ouvrier□ *m*

working girl ['wɜːkɪŋgɜːl] *n* Am (prostitute) prostituée□ *f*, putain *f*

work over [wɜːk] *vt sép* **to work sb over** (beat up) tabasser qn, filer une raclée à qn, dérouiller qn

works [wɜːks] *npl* (**a**) **the works** (everything) la totale, tout le toutim (**b**) (drug paraphernalia) matos *m* de drogué ▸ *voir aussi* **shoot**

worm [wɜːm] *n* (person) larve *f*

worry ['wʌrɪ] *n* Austr **no worries!** pas de problème!

wotcha ['wɒtʃə], **wotcher** ['wɒtʃə(r)] *exclam* Br bonjour!□, salut!

would [wʊd] *vi* Br **I know she's getting on a bit, but you would, wouldn't you?** je sais bien qu'elle n'est plus de la première jeunesse, mais tu ne dirais pas non, pas vrai?; **would you? – no way, he's minging!** est-ce que tu te le ferais? – tu rigoles, il est bien trop moche!

woulda ['wʊdə] *contraction* = **would have** ▸ *voir aussi* **coulda**

wow [waʊ] **1** *exclam* oh là là!, la vache!
2 *vt* en mettre plein la vue à, époustoufler; **he wowed me with a bunch of red roses and a marriage proposal** il m'en a mis plein la vue avec un bouquet de roses rouges puis il m'a demandée en mariage

wowser ['waʊzə(r)] *n* Austr (killjoy) rabat-joie *mf inv*; (prude) puritain(e)□ *m, f*

wrap [ræp] *n* (for powdered drugs) sachet *m* de drogue□

wrap up [ræp] *vi* Br (be quiet) la fermer, la boucler; **wrap up!** la ferme!, boucle-la!, écrase!

wrecked [rekt] *adj* (drunk) bourré, pété, beurré, fait; (on drugs) défoncé, raide; (exhausted) crevé, naze, lessivé, claqué

wrinkly ['rɪŋklɪ] *n* Br (old person) croulant(e) *m, f*

wuss [wʊs] *n* mauviette *f*, lavette *f*

wussy ['wʊsɪ] **1** *n* mauviette *f*, lavette *f*
2 *adj* mou, mollasson

Le symbole [!] dénote un terme très familier, [!!] un terme vulgaire.

XYZ

X [eks] *n* (*abrév* **ecstasy**) X *f*, ecsta *f*

X-rated ['eks'reɪtɪd] *adj* (*lewd, erotic*) osé, salé; (*violent*) violent□, saignant

ⓘ "X-rated" signifie littéralement "classé X". Cette appellation n'est plus utilisée par les commissions de censure américaine et britannique mais l'expression perdure.

yaba ['jɑːbə] *n* yaba *m*

yabber ['jæbə(r)] *Austr* **1** *vi* jacasser
2 *n* jacassements *mpl*

yack [jæk] = **yak**

yada ['jædə] *n Am* **yada yada (yada)** et patati et patata

yah [jɑː] *n Br Péj* (**OK**) yah ≃ bourge *mf*

ⓘ "Yah" est la transcription phonétique du mot "yes" tel qu'il est prononcé par certains éléments de la grande bourgeoisie et de l'aristocratie anglaises. Par extension, le mot "yah" désigne une personne d'un milieu très aisé, arrogante et imbue d'elle-même, qui adopte une attitude méprisante avec ceux qu'elle considère comme ses inférieurs.

yak [jæk] **1** *n* (*conversation*) converse *f*; **to have a yak** papoter

2 *vi* (**a**) (*chat*) papoter (**b**) *Am* (*vomit*) gerber, dégueuler

y'all [jɔːl] *pron Am* (*abrév* **you all**) vous; **hey y'all!** salut tout le monde!, salut la compagnie!; **what are y'all up to tonight?** qu'est-ce que vous faites ce soir, tous autant que vous êtes?

Yank [jæŋk] **1** *n* Amerloque *mf*, Ricain(e) *m,f*
2 *adj* ricain

ⓘ Lorsqu'il est utilisé par les Américains eux-mêmes, ce terme n'a aucune connotation péjorative. Lorsqu'il est utilisé par une personne d'une autre nationalité, il peut être soit injurieux, soit humoristique, selon le ton et le contexte.

yank [jæŋk] **1** [!] *n* branlette *f*; **to have a yank** se tirer sur l'élastique, se taper sur la colonne
2 *vt* **to yank sb's chain** faire marcher qn; **hey, I'm only yanking your chain!** je te fais marcher!
3 [!] *vi* se tirer sur l'élastique, se taper sur la colonne

Yankee ['jæŋkɪ] **1** *n* (**a**) *Br Injurieux* (*American*) Amerloque *mf*, Ricain(e) *m,f* (**b**) *Am* (*person from Northern USA*) = natif du Nord des États-Unis
2 *adj* (**a**) *Br Injurieux* (*American*) ricain (**b**) *Am* (*from Northern USA*) du Nord des États-Unis□

ⓘ Dans la catégorie 1(a), ce terme peut être soit injurieux, soit humoristique, selon le ton et le contexte.

yap [jæp] **1** n (**a**) (mouth) clapet m, gueule f; **shut your yap!** ferme ton clapet!, la ferme!, écrase! (**b**) Am (idiot) andouille f, truffe f; (country bumpkin) pécore mf, péquenaud(e) m,f
  2 vi jacasser, bavasser

yard [jɑːd] n **in my/their yard** chez moi/chez eux□

yawn [jɔːn] n (boring person, event) **to be a yawn** être rasoir ▸ voir aussi **technicolour yawn**

yay[1] [jeɪ] n Am (cocaine) coco f, neige f

yay[2] exclam ouais!; **yay! it's the holidays!** ouais! c'est les vacances!

yeah [jeə] exclam ouais!; Ironique **yeah, right!** oui, c'est ça!

yellow ['jeləʊ] adj (cowardly) trouillard; **to have a yellow streak** être un peu trouillard sur les bords

yellow-belly ['jeləʊbelɪ] n (coward) poule f mouillée

yep [jep] exclam ouais!

Yid [jɪd] n Injurieux youpin(e) m,f, youde mf

ying-yang [!] ['jɪŋjæŋ] n Am (**a**) (anus) troufignon m, fion m, rondelle f (**b**) (penis) bite f, biroute f, pine f

yo [jəʊ] exclam Noir Am salut!

yob [jɒb], **yobbo** ['jɒbəʊ] n Br loubard m

yoke [jəʊk] n Ir (thing) machin m, truc m, bidule m

yonks [jɒŋks] npl Br une éternité; **I haven't seen him for yonks** ça fait un bail ou une paye que je l'ai pas vu

youse [juːz] pron vous; **what are youse up to tonight?** qu'est-ce que vous faites ce soir, tous autant que vous êtes?

yummy mummy ['jʌmɪ'mʌmɪ] n Br Hum = mère de famille jeune et séduisante

yup [jʌp] exclam = yep

yuppie, yuppy ['jʌpɪ] n (abrév **young upwardly-mobile professional**) yuppie mf; **yuppie flu** syndrome m de fatigue chronique□

zap [zæp] **1** vt (kill) buter, refroidir, zigouiller
  2 vi (change TV channels) zapper

zapper ['zæpə(r)] n (TV remote control) télécommande□ f, zappette f

zebra ['ziːbrə] n Am (American football referee) arbitre□ m

ⓘ C'est à cause de leur chemise à bandes noires et blanches que l'on donne ce surnom aux arbitres.

zeds [zedz], Am **zees** [ziːz] npl **to catch some** Br **zeds** or Am **zees** piquer un roupillon ▸ voir aussi **cop**

ⓘ C'est la bande dessinée qui est à l'origine de cette expression : "zzzz" est l'onomatopée la plus fréquemment utilisée pour évoquer le sommeil.

zero ['zɪrəʊ] **1** n (person) nul (nulle) m,f
  2 adj aucun□; **he's got zero charm** il a aucun charme; **they've got zero chance of winning** ils ont pas la moindre chance de gagner

zilch [zɪltʃ] n (nothing) que dalle

zillion ['zɪljən] n Hum **a zillion** or

zillions (of) des millions et des millions (de)

zing [zɪŋ] *vt Am (tease)* vanner, chambrer

zinger ['zɪŋə(r)] *n Am (pointed remark)* vanne *f*

zip [zɪp] **1** *n* (**a**) *Am (nothing)* que dalle; *(zero)* zéro *m*; **the score was four-zip** le score était de quatre à zéro (**b**) *(drug)* zip *m*, méthamphétamine[□] *f*

2 *vt* **to zip it** *(be quiet)* la fermer, la boucler; **zip it!** la ferme!, ferme ton clapet!, écrase!

zit [zɪt] *n (pimple)* bouton[□] *m*

zone [zəʊn] *Am n* (**a**) **to be in a zone** *(dazed)* être dans le coaltar; *(after taking drugs)* être raide, planer (**b**) **to be in the zone** être au mieux de sa forme[□], être à son top niveau; **fantastic shot! he's really in the zone now!** quel tir formidable! il tient vraiment la super forme maintenant!

zone out *vi* planer, rêvasser

zoned (out) [zəʊnd('aʊt)] *adj Am* **to be zoned out** *(dazed)* être dans le coaltar; *(after taking drugs)* être raide, planer

zonked (out) [zɒŋkt('aʊt)] *adj (exhausted)* crevé, naze, lessivé, claqué; *(drunk)* bourré, rond, pété, fait; *(on drugs)* défoncé, raide

zoom [zuːm] *vt Am* (**a**) *(fool, deceive)* se foutre de, duper[□] (**b**) *(flirt with)* faire du rentre-dedans à

zooted ['zuːtɪd] *adj Am* (**a**) *(drunk)* bourré, pété, fait (**b**) *(on drugs)* raide, défoncé

zowie ['zaʊɪ] *exclam Am* oh là là!, la vache!

Français - Anglais

Aa

abattis [abati] *nmpl* **t'as intérêt à numéroter tes abattis** start saying your prayers!

abdos-kros [abdokro] *nmpl* beer gut or *Br* belly

ⓘ This is a humorous expression used to describe a less than toned stomach. "Abdos" (short for "abdominaux") means "abs" and "kro" is short for "Kronenbourg" (the French lager).

---

abeilles [abɛj] *nfpl* **avoir les abeilles** to be hacked off or cheesed off

abîmer [abime] *vt* **abîmer qn** to beat sb up, to give sb a hammering or a pasting; **se faire abîmer** to get beaten up, to *Br* get or *Am* take a hammering or a pasting ▸ *see also* **portrait**

abonné, -e [abɔne] *adj* **être abonné à qch** to be prone to sth□; **décidément, je suis abonné!** this is happening to me all the time!

abouler [abule] **1** *vt (apporter)* to bring□; *(passer)* to pass□; **allez, aboule le fric!** come on, cough up!

2 s'abouler *vpr* to turn up, to show up, to roll up; **alors, tu t'aboules?** you coming, then? ▸ *see also* **viande**

accoucher [akuʃe] *vi* **accouche!** spit it out!, out with it!

accro [akro] **1** *adj* **être accro à qch** *(drogué)* to be hooked on sth; *(fanatique)* to be really into sth, to be mad about sth

2 *nmf* **(a)** *(drogué)* addict□, junkie; **être accro à qch** to be hooked on sth **(b)** *(fanatique)* addict□, nut, fanatic□; **un accro du jazz** a jazzhead; **un accro du yoga** a yoga nut

accrocher [akrɔʃe] **1** *vi (bien fonctionner)* **ça n'a pas accroché entre eux** they didn't hit it off; **j'arrive pas à lire ce roman, j'accroche vraiment pas** I just can't get into this novel

2 s'accrocher *vpr* **(a)** *(persévérer)* to stick at it, to hang in there; **accroche-toi Jeannot!** hang in there *Br* mate or *Am* buddy! **(b)** **tu peux te l'accrocher!** you can forget it!; **s'il continue comme ça, sa médaille, il peut se l'accrocher** if he carries on like that he can kiss goodbye to his chances of winning a medal

achaler [aʃale] *vt Can* **achaler qn** to bug sb, to get up sb's nose

acide [asid] *nm (LSD)* acid

activer [aktive] *vi* to get a move on, to move it, to get one's skates on, *Am* to get it in gear; **allez, active!** come on, get a move on!

ado [ado] *nmf (abbr* **adolescent, -e***)* teen

à donf [adɔ̃f] *adv (verlan* **à fond***) (vite) Br* like the clappers, *Am* like sixty; *(très fort)* at full blast; *(beaucoup)* really, like crazy; **je la kiffe à donf, cette nana** *Br* I don't half fancy that bird, *Am* I have a major crush on that chick

affaire [afɛr] *nf* (a) **être/ne pas être une affaire (au pieu)** to be good/ no good in the sack *or* between the sheets ▶ *see also* **faire, juteux²** (b) **lâche l'affaire!** *(laisse-moi tranquille)* give me peace!; *(laisse tomber)* just drop it!; **lâche pas l'affaire!** hang on in there!

afficher [afiʃe] **s'afficher** *vpr* to make an idiot of oneself; **il a fait tomber ses lunettes dans le bol de punch; je te dis pas comment il s'est affiché!** he dropped his glasses in the punch bowl, he looked like such a loser *or Br* he looked a right prat!

affirmatif [afirmatif] *exclam* you bet!, sure thing!

after [aftœr] *nm or nf (soirée)* after party; **on a décidé d'aller faire l'after chez Alex** we finished the night off at Alex's place; **je fais une after après la soirée en boîte, d'accord?** everybody back to mine after the clubs shut, yeah?

agace-pissette [!!] [agaspisɛt] *nf Can* pricktease(r)

agité, -e [aʒite] *nm,f Hum* **agité du bocal** *Br* nutter, headcase, *Am* wacko, screwball

agrafer [agrafe] *vt* (a) *(retenir)* to corner; **la secrétaire m'a agrafé au début de la réception, et elle m'a tenu la jambe toute la soirée!** the secretary cornered me right at the start of the party and bent my ear all night! (b) *(arrêter) Br* to nick, *Am* to bust; **il s'est fait agrafer par les flics en sortant de la banque** he got *Br* nicked *or Am* busted by

the cops just as he came out of the bank

aidé, -e [ɛde] *adj* **il est pas aidé** *(bête)* he's not too bright; *(laid)* he's no oil painting

aile [ɛl] *nf* **avoir un coup dans l'aile** to have had one too many; **battre de l'aile** to be in a bad way, to be struggling

-aille [ɑj] *suffix* **boustifaille** food□, chow, grub; **duraille** tough; **la flicaille** the cops, the pigs, *Br* the filth; **marmaille** kids, brats

ⓘ This suffix is found at the end of many French slang nouns and adjectives and indicates that the word is rather pejorative.

air [ɛr] *nm* **de l'air!** get lost!, get out of here!; **ficher** *ou* **foutre [!] qch en l'air** *(mettre sens dessus dessous)* to turn sth upside down; *(jeter aux ordures)* to chuck sth (out), to bin sth, *Am* to trash sth; **se foutre en l'air [!]** *(se suicider)* to kill oneself□, *Br* to top oneself; *(avoir un accident de la route)* to have a crash□; **avoir l'air con et la vue basse [!]** to look like a real jerk ▶ *see also* **envoyer, jambe, pomper**

airbags [ɛrbag] *nmpl* tits, jugs, knockers, *Am* hooters

aise [ɛz] *nf* **à l'aise** *(facilement)* easily□, no problem, *Br* no probs; **ça coûte 200 euros à l'aise** it's easily worth 200 euros, it's worth 200 euros no problem *or Br* no probs; **et lui il se tournait les pouces, à l'aise, Blaise!** and there HE was, twiddling his thumbs without a care in the world!

alcolo, alcoolo [alkɔlo] *nmf (abbr* **alcoolique)** alky, lush, boozer, *Am* juicer

---

The symbol [!] denotes a very familiar term, [!!] a vulgar one.

aligner [aliɲe] **1** vt (**a**) **les aligner** to pay up, to cough up (**b**) **il s'est fait aligner par un flic en moto** a motorcycle cop slapped a fine on him
2 s'aligner vpr to go without; **tu peux t'aligner pour que je te prête du fric, maintenant!** you can get lost if you think I'm going to lend you any money now!

aller [ale] vi (**a**) **tu peux y aller, c'est ce qui se fait de mieux!** you can take it from me, it's the best there is! (**b**) **où tu vas?** are you mad?, have you got a screw loose?, Br are you off your head?

aller-retour [aleʀətuʀ], **aller et retour** [aleeʀətuʀ] nm slap on the face◻ (first with the palm and then with the back of the hand)

allô [alo] exclam (à quelqu'un qui n'écoute pas) **allô?** hello?

allocs [alɔk] nfpl (abbr **allocations**) Br child benefit◻, Am dependents' allowances◻

allonger [alɔ̃ʒe] **1** vt (**a**) (donner) **allonger une baffe à qn** to give sb a slap◻, to slap sb◻; **allonger un coup de poing à qn** to punch sb◻ (**b**) **les allonger, allonger le fric** to pay up, to cough up

---

Spotlight on:

L'alcool et l'ivresse

In the land of wine and pastis there is no shortage of slang terms to refer to drinking and drunkenness. Tradition dictates that the aperitif, or more familiarly **l'apéro**, is a sacred ritual for many, but there are numerous other occasions, both at home and in bars, to **s'enfiler un verre** or **siffler une bouteille**. **Bourré** is the most common slang term for "drunk"; other very commonly used terms include **pété**, **torché**, **bituré**, and **beurré**. Less crudely, one may describe someone as **rond**, **paf** or **cuit**. The ensuing hangover is known as a **gueule de bois**. "To get drunk" is **prendre une cuite**, and a more recent expression is **se mettre une mine**. Colloquial words for an alcoholic include **alcolo**, **poivrot** and, less commonly, **soûlard**, **pochetron** and **soiffard**. Drink itself is called variously **la bibine** (a somewhat old-fashioned term now), **la picole** (from the verb picoler) and **la tise** (a more recent term which belongs to "l'argot des cités"). Unsurprisingly, wine is the drink best represented in the slang lexicon; **pinard** (from the word **pineau**, which means "grape variety"), **picrate** and **jaja** are all commonly found. A red wine of poor quality may be referred to as **gros rouge** or **gros (rouge) qui tache**. Pastis – the drink favoured by many in the South of France – is known as **pastaga**, while **la gnôle** may refer to alcohol in general or eau-de-vie in particular.

Le symbole ◻ indique que la traduction n'est pas argotique.

2 s'allonger vpr (faire des aveux) to spill the beans

allouf [aluf] nf match□ (for lighting)

allumé, -e [alyme] nm,f crackpot, crank

allumer [alyme] vt (**a**) (battre) to beat up, Br to do over; **se faire allumer** to get beaten up or Br done over (**b**) (tuer) to kill□, to waste, Br to do in (**c**) (exciter) to turn on, to make horny (deliberately)

allumeuse [alymøz] nf pricktease(r)

allure [alyr] nf Hum **à toute allure!** see you later!

ⓘ This expression, which literally means "at full speed", is a pun on the phrase "à tout à l'heure".

alpaguer [alpage] vt to collar, to nab; **se faire alpaguer** to get collared or nabbed

amazone [amazon] nf = prostitute who works from a car

ⓘ This slang word is inspired by the mythical female warriors the Amazons, said to spend all their time on horseback.

amener [amne] **s'amener** vpr (venir) to come□; (arriver) to turn up, to show up, to roll up ▸ see also **viande**

Amerloque [amɛrlɔk] nmf Yank, Yankee

ami [ami] nm **t'as pas d'amis!** you're so unpopular!□, Br what a Billy-no-mates!

amocher [amɔʃe] vt (personne, objet) to smash up

amortisseurs [amɔrtisœr] nmpl tits, jugs, knockers, Am hooters

amourette [!!] [amurɛt] nf **amourettes** balls, nuts, Br bollocks

amphés [ɑ̃fe], **amphets** [ɑ̃fet] nfpl (abbr **amphétamines**) speed, Br whizz

amphi [ɑ̃fi] nm (abbr **amphithéâtre**) lecture room or hall□

ampli [ɑ̃pli] nm (abbr **amplificateur**) amp

anar [anar] nmf (abbr **anarchiste**) anarchist□

andouille [ɑ̃duj] nf dope, Br divvy, Am dork

Anglais [ɑ̃glɛ] nmpl **les Anglais ont débarqué** I've/she's got my/her period□, I'm/she's on the rag

angliche [ɑ̃gliʃ] **1** adj British□, Brit **2** nm (langue) English□ **3** nmf **Angliche** (personne) Brit

anglo [ɑ̃glo] nmf Can Pej English-speaking Quebecker□

angoisse [ɑ̃gwas] nf **c'est l'angoisse!, bonjour l'angoisse!** what a pain or drag or bummer!

angoisser [ɑ̃gwase] vi to be all uptight or worked up

anguille [ɑ̃gij] nf Hum **anguille de caleçon** (one-eyed) trouser snake

antisèche [ɑ̃tisɛʃ] nf Br crib sheet, Am trot

apéro [apero] nm (abbr **apéritif**) aperitif□

à pluss [aplys] exclam see you later!, catch you later!, Br laters!

appart' [apart] nm (abbr **appartement**) pad, Br flat□, Am apartment□

appuyer [apɥije] **s'appuyer** vpr **s'appuyer qn** to get stuck or Br lumbered or landed with sb; **s'appuyer le ménage/la vaisselle** to get stuck or Br lumbered or landed with the housework/the dishes

---

The symbol **[!]** denotes a very familiar term, **[!!]** a vulgar one.

▸ *see also* **champignon**

aprème [aprɛm] *nm or nf (abbr* **après-midi**) **cet** *ou* **cette aprème** this afternoon□, *Austr* this arvo

Arbi [arbi] *nm Offensive* = racist term used to refer to a North African Arab

archi- [arʃi] *prefix* extremely□, seriously, *Br* dead, well, *Am* real; **les magasins sont archibondés le samedi après-midi** the shops are *Br* chock-a-block *or Am* jammed on Saturday afternoons; **c'est faux, archifaux!** it's so□ *or Br* dead wrong!; **c'est un air archiconnu** it's a *Br* dead *or Am* real well-known tune

-ard [ar] *suffix* **connard** [!] stupid bastard, prick, *Br* arsehole, *Am* asshole; **faiblard** weakish, on the weak side; **flemmard** lazy so-and-so; **salopard** [!] bastard

ⓘ This suffix is found at the end of many French slang nouns and adjectives and indicates that the word is rather pejorative.

ardoise [ardwaz] *nf (pour inscrire des dettes)* slate, tab; **laisser une ardoise** to disappear without paying one's debts□, to do a runner

aristo [aristo] *nmf (abbr* **aristocrate**) aristo, *Br* toff, nob

arme [arm] *nf* **passer l'arme à gauche** to croak, to kick the bucket, *Br* to snuff it, *Am* to check out

ⓘ The expression "passer l'arme à gauche", meaning "to die", comes from military terminology, referring to the position in which soldiers hold their weapons when they stand at ease; this is because in

French the expression for "to stand at ease" is "être au repos", which can also mean "to be resting" in a non-military context.

armoire [armwar] *nf* **c'est une armoire à glace** he's built like a tank

arnaque [arnak] *nf* **c'est (de) l'arnaque!** what a rip-off!, it's *Br* daylight *or Am* highway robbery!

arnaquer [arnake] *vt* **arnaquer qn** to rip sb off; **se faire arnaquer** to get ripped off

arnaqueur, -euse [arnakœr, -øz] *nm,f Br* rip-off merchant, *Am* hustler

arpion [arpjɔ̃] *nm* foot□, *Br* plate, *Am* dog

arquer [arke] *vi* to walk□

arracher [araʃe] **1** *vt* **(a)** **ça t'arracherait la gueule de dire merci/de t'excuser?** it wouldn't kill you to say thanks/to apologize! **(b)** **ça arrache (la gueule)** it blows the top of your head off

2 **s'arracher** *vpr* to hit the road, to make tracks; **il faut que je m'arrache** I must be off, I've got to make tracks

arranger [arɑ̃ʒe] *vt* **arranger qn** *(battre)* to beat sb up, to clobber sb, *Br* to kick sb's head in

arroser [aroze] **1** *vt* **(a)** *(fêter)* **arroser qch** to celebrate sth with a few drinks□; **il faut arroser ça** that calls for a celebration *or* a drink **(b)** *(mitrailler)* to spray with bullets

2 **s'arroser** *vpr* **ça s'arrose** that calls for a celebration *or* a drink

arsouille [arsuj] *nm* hood, hooligan, *Br* yob

Arthur [artyr] *npr* **se faire appeler Arthur** to get one's head bitten off,

Spotlight on:

L'argent

Fric is the most common of the numerous slang words for "money". Other frequently encountered terms include **pognon**, **flouse** (from the Arabic "el-flouss" = money), **blé** and **pèze**. Two now slightly old-fashioned terms are **grisbi** (as mentioned in the title of the classic film noir "Touchez pas au grisbi") and **oseille**, while conversely the words **caillasse**, **maille** and **genhar** (the verlan term for "argent") belong to "l'argot des banlieues" (see panel). Some words are used specifically to refer to small change, such as **mitraille** and **ferraille**. The words **bifton** and **fafiot** are used for banknotes. Someone who is completely penniless may be said to be **sans un radis**, **un rond** or **un rotin** whilst a rich person will be described as **plein aux as** or **bourré de fric**. The most common slang word to refer to francs, before the arrival of the euro rendered this currency obsolete, was **balles**. Terms relating to specific amounts of francs have also been common, for example **une patate**, **une brique** and **un bâton**, all used to refer to 10,000 francs and **un sac** (10 francs). **Thune** was originally used to mean the sum of 5 francs, but now refers to money in general. Note too its verlan form **nethu**. It remains to be seen if the euro will have its own slang terms; perhaps "roeu" will soon be heard in the "cités"... Someone with no money is **fauché**, **à sec** or **dans la dèche**, whilst a rich person is **plein aux as** or is said to **rouler sur l'or**. **Casquer**, **raquer** and **cracher** mean "to pay a high price", whilst **radin** and **rat** refer to a miser.

to get bawled out *or Am* chewed out

artiche [artiʃ] *nm* dough, bread, *Br* dosh, *Am* bucks

as [ɑs] *nm* (**a**) *(expert)* whizz, ace; **un as du volant** a crack driver (**b**) **passer à l'as** to go out of the window, to go down the tubes *or Br* pan (**c**) **être fichu** *ou* **foutu** *ou* **fagoté comme l'as de pique** *Br* to be dressed like a scarecrow *or* a tramp, *Am* to look like a bum (**d**) **être plein aux as** to

be loaded, *Br* to be rolling in it, *Am* to be rolling in dough

asperge [aspɛrʒ] *nf (personne)* beanpole, *Am* stringbean

aspi [aspi] *nm (abbr* **aspirant**) = soldier with the rank of lieutenant engaged in military service

assaisonner [asezɔne] *vt* (**a**) *(réprimander)* **assaisonner qn** to give sb a roasting, to bawl sb out, *Am* to chew sb out; **se faire assaisonner** to get a roasting, to get bawled out,

The symbol [!] denotes a very familiar term, [!!] a vulgar one.

Am to get chewed out (**b**) *(malmener)* to rough up

asseoir [aswar] **s'asseoir** *vpr* **s'asseoir sur qch** *(ne pas en tenir compte)* not to give a damn *or* a hoot about sth .

assis, -e [asi, -iz] *adj* **en rester assis** to be stunned *or Br* gobsmacked; **quand il m'a dit qu'il était pédé, j'en suis resté assis** when he told me he was queer, I was completely stunned *or Br* gobsmacked

assoce [asɔs] *nf (abbr* **association)** association□

assurer [asyre] *vi* (**a**) *(être compétent)* **il assure vachement en anglais** he's brilliant at English; **elle assure à la batterie** she's a brilliant drummer; **il assure pas** he hasn't got a clue, he's totally useless; **putain, t'assures pas, merde! on se pointe pas une demi-heure en retard quand on a un rendez-vous avec un client!** you haven't got a fucking clue! you don't turn up half an hour late to meet a client!; **elle assure pas un clou** *ou* **pas une cacahuète** *Br* she's totally bloody clueless, *Am* she doesn't have a goddamn clue (**b**) *(garder son sang-froid)* to stay in control, to keep one's head; **vas-y, assure!** go for it!

astap [astap] *adj inv (abbr* **à se taper le cul par terre)** hysterical, side-splitting; **c'était astap** it was a scream *or* a hoot

astiquer [astike] **s'astiquer** *vpr (se masturber)* to play with oneself, to get oneself off

Athénien [atenjɛ̃] *nm* **c'est là que les Athéniens s'atteignirent** it was at that point that things started to go wrong□ *or Br* pear-shaped

atout [atu] *nm (coup)* clout, thump;

prendre un atout to get clouted *or* thumped

attaque [atak] **d'attaque** *adj* **être d'attaque** to be on top form; **se sentir d'attaque pour faire qch** to feel up to doing sth

attaquer [atake] **1** *vt (entamer)* to tackle, *Br* to get stuck into
2 *vi (commencer à manger) Br* to get stuck in, *Am* to chow down

atteint, -e [atɛ̃, -ɛ̃t] *adj* **être atteint** *(ne pas être sain d'esprit)* to be touched, to have a screw loose

attrape-couillon [atrapkujɔ̃] *nm* scam, swindle, con, *Am* hustle

auberge [obɛrʒ] *nf* **on n'est pas sortis de l'auberge** we're not out of the woods yet

auge [oʒ] *nf (assiette)* plate□

autre [otr] *pron* **qu'est-ce qu'il a, l'autre?** what's up with him *or Br* your man there?; **oh l'autre eh! il sait pas faire du vélo!** the guy can't even ride a bike!; **à d'autres!** gimme a break!, yeah right!, *Br* do me a favour!

avaler [avale] *vt* (**a**) **avaler son bulletin de naissance** to croak, to kick the bucket, *Am* to cash in one's chips (**b**) **avaler la fumée [!!]** *(au cours d'une fellation)* to swallow

avoine [avwan], **avoinée** [avwane] *nf* thrashing, hammering; **prendre une avoine** to *Br* get *or Am* take a thrashing *or* a hammering; **filer une avoine à qn** to give sb a thrashing *or* a hammering

avoir [avwar] *vt* (**a**) **se faire avoir** to be had *or* conned *or* done (**b**) **en avoir** to have guts *or* balls

azimut [azimyt] **tous azimuts** *adv* all over the place *or Br* shop

azimuté, -e [azimyte] *adj* crackers, *Br* barking, *Am* wacko

Bb

baba [baba] **1** *adj (stupéfait)* flabbergasted, *Br* gobsmacked; **j'en suis resté baba** I was flabbergasted *or Br* gobsmacked

2 *nmf (hippie)* baba (cool) hippy

3 *nm* **l'avoir dans le baba** to be had *or* conned

ⓘ "Baba" in sense 2 is a term used to refer to a second-generation hippy who has adopted the image and lifestyle of the original hippy generation of the 60s and 70s.

babos [babos] = **baba 2**

baboune [babun] *nf Can* **faire la baboune** to be in a huff

babtou [babtu] *nmf Cités (verlan* **toubab)** Frenchman, *f* Frenchwoman□

baby [bebi] *nm* = half-measure of spirits

babylone [babilɔn] *nm Cités (policier)* cop, pig

bac [bak] *nm (abbr* **baccalauréat)** = secondary school examinations qualifying for entry to university, *Br* ≃ A-levels□, *Am* ≃ high school diploma□

bacchantes [bakɑ̃t] *nfpl* moustache□, tash

bâche [bɑʃ] *nf* **(a)** *(casquette)* flat cap□ **(b)** **bâches** *(draps)* sheets□; **se mettre dans les bâches** to hit the sack *or* the hay *or Am* the rack

bâcher [bɑʃe] **se bâcher** *vpr* to hit

the sack *or* the hay *or Am* the rack

bachot [baʃo] *nm* = secondary school examinations qualifying for entry to university, *Br* ≃ A-levels□, *Am* ≃ high school diploma□; **attends d'avoir passé ton bachot, après tu verras** wait till you've got your exams, then you can see; **boîte à bachot** crammer

bachotage [baʃɔtaʒ] *nm* cramming, *Br* swotting, *Am* grinding away

bachoter [baʃɔte] *vi* to cram, *Br* to swot, *Am* to grind away

bachoteur, -euse [baʃɔtœr, -øz] *nm,f* = student cramming *or Br* swotting up *or Am* grinding away for an exam

bacon [bekɔn] *nm Can* **avoir du bacon** to be loaded

badloqué, -e [badlɔke] *adj Can Joual* **être badloqué** to have rotten luck

ⓘ This word comes from the English "bad luck".

bâdrage [badraʒ] *nm Can* pain (in the neck)

bâdrant, -e [badrɑ̃, -ɑ̃t] *adj Can* **être bâdrant** to be a pain (in the neck)

bâdrer [badre] *vt Can* **bâdrer qn** to bug sb, *Br* to do sb's head in, *Am* to give sb a pain (in the neck)

baffe [baf] *nf* clout, cuff

baffer [bafe] *vt* to clout, to cuff; **si il continue à m'emmerder, je vais le baffer celui-là!** if he keeps bugging me like that, I'm going to clout him!

bafouille [bafuj] *nf* letter□

bâfrer [bɑfʀe] *vi* to stuff oneself or one's face, to pig out

bâfreur, -euse [bɑfʀœʀ, -øz] *nm, f* pig, *Br* greedy-guts, gannet, *Am* hog

bagne [baɲ] *nm* **c'est le bagne ici** it's like a sweatshop here

bagnole [baɲɔl] *nf* car□, wheels, *Br* motor

bagou [bagu] *nm* gift of the gab; **avoir du bagou** to have the gift of the gab

bagouse [baguz] *nf* (**a**) ring□ *(for finger)* (**b**) **être de la bagouse [!!]** to be *Br* a poof or *Am* a fag

baguenauder [bagnode] **1** *vi* to saunter or wander around□
   2 se baguenauder *vpr* to saunter or wander around□

bahut [bay] *nm* (**a**) *(camion)* lorry□, truck□ (**b**) *(taxi)* taxi□, cab (**c**) *(lycée)* high school□

baigner [beɲe] *vi* (**a**) **tout baigne (dans l'huile)** everything's hunky-dory or *Am* A-OK (**b**) **avoir les dents du fond qui baignent** to have stuffed oneself or one's face, to have pigged out

baigneur [!] [beɲœʀ] *nm* (**a**) *(sexe de la femme)* pussy, snatch, *Br* fanny (**b**) *(postérieur) Br* arse, *Am* ass, fanny

bail [bɑj] *nm* **ça fait un bail** it's been ages or *Br* yonks

baille [bɑj] *nf* water□; **tomber à la baille** to fall in□

bain [bɛ̃] *nm* **être/se mettre dans le bain** to be in/get into the swing of things; **je me suis écouté un petit disque à fond avant d'aller en boîte, histoire de me mettre dans le bain** I put a record on full blast before I went out clubbing, just to get me in the mood

baisable [!!] [bɛzabl] *adj* fuckable, *Br* shaggable

baise [!!] [bɛz] *nf (amour physique)* fucking, screwing, *Br* shagging

baisebeige [bɛzbeʒ] *(abbr* **BCBG**) **1** *adj inv Br* ≃ Sloany, *Am* ≃ preppy
   2 *nmf Br* ≃ Sloane (Ranger), *Am* ≃ preppy

ⓘ This term is a humorous rephrasing of the term "BCBG" (see entry), itself the abbreviation of "bon chic bon genre".

baise-en-ville [bɛzɑ̃vil] *nm inv* overnight bag□

baise-la-piastre [bɛzlapjas] *nmf Can* skinflint, tightwad

ⓘ The word "piastre" is a colloquial term for a dollar in Canadian French.

baiser [!!] [beze] **1** *vt* (**a**) *(faire l'amour avec)* to fuck, to screw, *Br* to shag (**b**) *(duper)* to screw, to shaft; **se faire baiser** to get screwed or shafted (**c**) *(surprendre)* to nab; **se faire baiser** to get nabbed
   2 *vi* to fuck, to screw, *Br* to shag; **il baise bien** he's a great fuck or lay or screw or *Br* shag ► *see also* **couille, lapin**

baiseur, -euse [!!] [bɛzœʀ, -øz] *nm, f* **c'est une sacrée baiseuse** she's a great fuck or lay or screw or *Br* shag

baisodrome [!!] [bɛzɔdʀom] *nm* fuckpad

bakchich [bakʃiʃ] *nm Br* backhander, bung, *Am* payoff

Le symbole □ indique que la traduction n'est pas argotique.

balader [balade] *vi* **envoyer balader qn** to tell sb where to go, *Br* to send sb packing; **envoyer balader qch** *(lancer)* to send sth flying; *(abandonner)* to quit sth, *Br* to chuck or pack sth in

baladeuse [baladøz] *adj* **avoir les mains baladeuses** to have wandering hands

balai [balɛ] *nm* (**a**) *(an)* year⁻; **il a cinquante balais** he's fifty⁻ (**b**) **ce qu'il peut être coincé, ce mec! on dirait qu'il a un balai dans le cul** he can be so uptight, that guy, it's like he's got a poker up his *Br* arse or *Am* ass

---

① In category (a), this word is used only when referring to people's ages.

---

balaise [balɛz] **1** *adj* (**a**) *(fort) (physiquement)* hefty, burly⁻; *(intellectuellement)* brainy; **être balaise en qch** to be brilliant at sth (**b**) *(difficile)* tough, tricky
2 *nm* big guy

balance [balãs] *nf (dénonciateur)* squealer, *Br* grass, *Am* rat

balancé, -e [balãse] *adj* **être bien balancé** to have a great bod, to be in great shape

balancer [balãse] **1** *vt* (**a**) *(dénoncer)* to squeal on, *Br* to grass on, *Am* to rat on (**b**) *(lancer)* to chuck (**c**) *(mettre aux ordures)* to chuck (out), to bin, *Am* to trash
2 *vi (médire)* to dish the dirt, *Br* to bitch
3 s'en balancer [!] *vpr* not to give a shit or *Br* a toss or *Am* a rat's ass
▸ *see also* **purée, sauce**

balcon [balkɔ̃] *nm* **il y a du monde au balcon** she's well-stacked, she's a big girl, *Br* you don't get many of those to the pound

baliser [balize] *vi* to be scared stiff or witless

balle [bal] *nf* (**a**) *(franc)* franc⁻; **t'as pas cent balles?** got any change? (**b**) **une excuse à deux balles** a lame or pathetic excuse; **une blague à deux balles** a lame or crap joke; **le film est plein de clichés à deux balles** the movie's full of corny clichés (**c**) **c'est de la balle!** *Br* it's absolutely wicked!, *Am* it's totally awesome!
▸ *see also* **peau, trou**

---

① It should be noted that in sense of "franc", the word "balle" has been gradually falling into disuse since the introduction of the euro.

---

balloches [!] [balɔʃ] *nfpl* balls, nuts, *Br* bollocks

ballon [balɔ̃] *nm* (**a**) *(Alcootest®)* **faire souffler qn dans le ballon** to get sb to blow into the bag (**b**) **à fond les ballons** *(très vite) Br* like the clappers, *Am* like sixty; *(très fort)* at full blast

ballot [balo] *nm (idiot) Br* prat, wally, *Am* goof, geek

balloune [balun] *nf Can Joual* (**a**) **prendre une balloune, partir une balloune** to get wrecked or wasted (**b**) **être en balloune** *(enceinte)* to be in the (pudding) club

---

① This word comes from the Gallicization of the English word "balloon".

---

baloche [balɔʃ] *nm* local dance⁻

baltringue [baltrɛ̃g] *nmf Cités* wimp, chicken, *Br* big girl's blouse

bambou [bãbu] *nm* **avoir le coup de bambou** *(avoir un accès de folie)*

The symbol **[!]** denotes a very familiar term, **[!!]** a vulgar one.

to crack up, to go nuts, *Br* to go off one's head; *(être épuisé)* to be wiped or *Br* shattered or *Am* pooped; **attraper un coup de bambou** *(avoir une insolation)* to get sunstroke▫; **c'est le coup de bambou** *(c'est très cher)* it costs an arm and a leg or *Br* a bomb or a packet

bamboula [bãbula] **1** *nf (fête)* wild party; **faire la bamboula** to party, *Br* to go on the razzle

  2 *nm Offensive (homme de race noire)* nigger, *Br* wog, *Am* coon

banane [banan] *nf* (**a**) *(coiffure)* quiff (**b**) *(insulte)* **banane!** you moron or *Br* plonker or *Am* jerk! (**c**) **avoir la banane [!!]** to have a hard-on or a boner or *Br* a stiffy

bandaison [!!] [bãdεzɔ̃] *nf* hard-on, boner, *Br* stiffy

bandant, -e [!!] [bãdã, -ãt] *adj* (**a**) *(désirable sexuellement)* **elle est bandante** she's really horny, she really turns me on (**b**) *(enthousiasmant)* thrilling▫, exciting▫

bander [!!] [bãde] *vi* to have a hard-on; **bander mou** to have a semi; **il bande pour elle** he's got the hots for her, she really turns him on, *Br* he thinks she's really horny; **faire bander qn** *(exciter sexuellement)* to turn sb on, to make sb horny, *Br* to give sb the horn; **ce genre de musique, ça me fait pas vraiment bander** I can't really get into this sort of music

bandouiller [!!] [bãduje] *vi* to have a semi

bang [bãg] *nm (pipe à eau)* bong

banquer [bãke] *vi* to cough up, to hand over the cash

baquer [bake] **se baquer** *vpr* to go for a dip

baraka [baraka] *nf* **avoir la baraka** to be lucky▫ or *Br* jammy

---

ⓘ This term comes from an Arabic word meaning "godsend".

---

baraque [barak] *nf (maison)* place, pad; **casser la baraque** *(remporter*

Le symbole ▫ indique que la traduction n'est pas argotique.

un vif succès) to bring the house down; **casser la baraque à qn** *(faire échouer ses projets)* to mess things up for sb

baraqué, -e [barake] *adj* hefty, burly☐

baratin [baratɛ̃] *nm (d'un vendeur)* sales talk *or* pitch; *(pour séduire)* sweet talk, *Br* patter; **c'est du baratin** it's a load of bull *or* tripe *or Br* waffle

baratiner [baratine] *vt* **baratiner qn** *(essayer de convaincre)* to shoot sb a line, to try to talk sb round; *(pour séduire) Br* to chat sb up, *Am* to hit on sb; **baratiner qn pour qu'il fasse qch** to try to talk sb into doing sth☐

baratineur, -euse [baratinœr, -øz] *nm,f* smooth talker

barbant, -e [barbɑ̃, -ɑ̃t] *adj* deadly dull; **c'est barbant, mais il faut le faire** it's a drag, but it's got to be done

barbaque [barbak] *nf* meat☐

ⓘ This word has the same origin as the word "barbecue".

barbe [barb] *nf* **c'est la barbe** it's a drag; **la barbe!** give it a rest!

barber [barbe] **1** *vt* **barber qn** to bore sb stiff *or* to tears
2 se barber *vpr* to be bored stiff *or* to tears

barbeuk [barbœk] *nm (barbecue)* barbecue☐, *Br & Austr* barbie; **on se fait un barbeuk demain soir si il continue à faire beau?** shall we have a barbie tomorrow night if it stays nice?

barbeux, -euse [barbø, -øz] *Can* **1** *adj* **être barbeux** to be a pain (in the neck)
2 *nm,f* pain (in the neck)

barboter [barbɔte] *vt (voler)* to

pinch, *Br* to nick; **barboter qch à qn** to pinch *or Br* nick sth from sb; **se faire barboter qch** to get sth pinched *or Br* nicked

barbouze [barbuz] *nf* **(a)** *(barbe)* beard☐ **(b)** *(espion)* spy☐, spook

ⓘ The "spy" sense of this word is connected to the "beard" sense, as a false beard is considered a typical disguise for a spy.

barbu [!] [barby] *nm (poils pubiens de la femme)* bush

barda [barda] *nm* stuff, gear

ⓘ This word is derived from an Arabic word describing a packsaddle for a donkey. It entered the French language at the time of the colonial expansion in North Africa.

bardeau, -x [bardo] *nm Can* **manquer un bardeau** to be not right in the head, to have a screw loose

ⓘ The literal meaning of "bardeau" is "shingle", so this expression is almost a word-for-word equivalent of "to have a slate loose".

barder [barde] *v imp* **ça va barder!** there's going to be trouble!, *Br* it's going to kick off!

barge [barʒ], **barjo, barjot** [barʒo] **1** *adj* nuts, *Br* bonkers, *Am* wacko
2 *nmf* headcase, nutcase, *Br* nutter, *Am* wacko

baron [barɔ̃] *nm (compère)* plant

barouf [baruf], **baroufle** [barufl] *nm* racket, din

ⓘ This word is derived from the

Italian "baruffa", which means "fight".

━━━━━━━━━━━━━━━━

barre [bar] *nf* **(a) avoir un coup de barre** to be bushed *or* wiped *or Br* shattered *or Am* beat **(b) c'est le coup de barre** it costs an arm and a leg *or* a bundle *or Br* a packet ▸ *see also* **couille**

barré, -e [bare] *adj* **(a) être bien barré** to be looking good; **être mal barré** to be heading for trouble; **on est mal barrés pour y être à huit heures** we're not likely to get there for eight o'clock now⁰; **c'est mal barré** it's got off to a bad start; **entre eux deux, c'est mal barré** they started off on the wrong foot with each other **(b)** *(fou)* **il est bien barré, ce mec-là** that guy's completely nuts *or Br* barmy; **c'est un film bien barré** *(loufoque)* it's a really wacky film; *(étrange)* it's a really weird *or* freaky film **(c)** *Can* **ne pas être barré** *(être plein d'énergie)* to be a livewire

barreau, -x [baro] *nm* **(a) barreau de chaise** *(cigare)* fat cigar⁰, *Am* stogie **(b) être/se retrouver derrière les barreaux** to be/end up behind bars

barrer [bare] **se barrer** *vpr (partir)* to hit the road, to get going, to make tracks; *(se sauver)* to beat it, *Br* to clear off, *Am* to book it; **barre-toi!** get out of here!, beat it!, *Am* take a hike!

barrette [barɛt] *nf (de haschich)* = thin strip

basket [baskɛt] *nf* **(a) être bien dans ses baskets** to be very together *or Br* sorted **(b) lâche-moi les baskets!** get off my back!, don't hassle me!

bassiner [basine] *vt* **bassiner qn** to bug sb, to get up sb's nose, *Br* to do sb's head in

bassinet [basinɛ] *nm* **cracher au bassinet** to cough up, to hand over the cash

basta [basta] *exclam* that'll do!

Bastoche [bastɔʃ] *nf* **la Bastoche** = the Bastille area of Paris

baston [bastɔ̃] *nm or nf* scuffle, *Br* punch-up, *Am* fist fight

bastonner [bastɔne] **1** *v imp* **ça a bastonné** there was a scuffle *or Br* a punch-up *or Am* a fist fight

   2 se bastonner *vpr* to have a scuffle *or Br* a punch-up *or Am* a fist fight

bastos [bastos] *nf* bullet⁰, slug

━━━━━━━━━━━━━━━━

ⓘ Bastos® is a cigarette brand. The meaning of the slang word might be related to the the similarity in shape between a cigarette and a bullet.

━━━━━━━━━━━━━━━━

bastringue [bastrɛ̃g] *nm* **(a)** *(vacarme)* racket, din **(b)** *(désordre)* shambles **(c) et tout le bastringue** blah blah blah

bataclan [bataklɑ̃] *nm* **et tout le bataclan** blah blah blah

bataillon [batajɔ̃] *nm* **inconnu au bataillon** never heard of him, who's he when he's at home?

bâtard [!!] [batar] *nm* bastard

bateau [bato] *adj inv (banal)* hackneyed⁰, trite⁰

bâton [batɔ̃] *nm* Formerly *(dix mille francs)* ten thousand francs⁰

battant [batɑ̃] *nm (cœur)* ticker

battre [batr] **1** *vt* **j'en ai rien à battre [!]** I don't give a shit *or Br* a toss *or Am* a rat's ass

   2 se battre *vpr* **je m'en bats l'œil** I don't give a damn *or* a hoot *or Br* a stuff; **je m'en bats les couilles [!!]**

━━━━━━━━━━━━━━━━

Le symbole ⁰ indique que la traduction n'est pas argotique.

I don't give a (flying) fuck ▸ see also
aile

bavard [bavar] nm (avocat) lawyer□,
brief

bavarde [bavard] nf (langue) tongue□;
tenir sa bavarde to hold one's
tongue, to keep one's mouth shut

bavasser [bavase] vi to yak, Br to
natter

bavasseux, -euse [bavasø, -øz] nmf
Can Pej (bavard) chatterbox; (indis-
cret) gossip(monger)

baver [bave] 1 vt (a) (dire) **qu'est-ce
que tu baves?** what are you ram-
bling or jabbering or Br wittering on
about? (b) **en baver** to have a hard
or tough time of it; **en faire baver
à qn** to give sb a hard time (c) Can
(contrarier) to mess around; **se faire
baver** to be messed around
   2 vi (bavarder) to chat, to yak, Br
to natter; **baver sur qn** to dish the
dirt about sb, to badmouth sb, Br to
bitch about sb

bavette [bavɛt] nf **tailler une
bavette (avec qn)** to have a chat or
Br a natter (with sb)

baveux, -euse [bavø, -øz] 1 nm,f
Can (enfant effronté) brat
   2 nm (a) (savon) soap□ (b) (journal)
paper□ (c) (baiser) sloppy kiss

bazarder [bazarde] vt (a) (jeter) to
chuck (out), to bin, Am to trash (b)
(dénoncer) to squeal on, Br to grass
on, Am to rat on

bazou [bazu] nm Can (voiture) rustbucket, heap

BCBG [besebeʒe] (abbr **bon chic
bon genre**) 1 adj inv Br ≃ Sloany,
Am ≃ preppy
   2 nmf Br ≃ Sloane (Ranger), Am ≃
preppy

ⓘ This term refers to someone

whose classic, elegant style of dress
suggests a wealthy, conservative social background.

BD [bede] nf (abbr **bande dessinée**)
comic strip□, cartoon□

beauf [bof] (abbr **beau-frère**) 1 adj
(caractéristique du Français moyen)
= stereotypically narrow-minded and
middle-class
   2 nm (a) (beau-frère) brother-in-
law□ (b) (Français moyen) = stereotypical narrow-minded, middle-class
man

ⓘ The term "beauf" – short for
"beau-frère" – comes from a character in a comic strip created in
the 1960s by the French cartoonist Cabu. A "beauf" is the average
middle-class Frenchman with a racist, reactionary and jingoistic out-
look on life.

beaujolpif [boʒɔlpif] nm Beaujolais□

bébé [bebe] nm Can Joual (jolie fille)
un beau bébé a babe, a hottie

bébert [bebɛr] nm Cités = stereotypical reactionary Frenchman

ⓘ This word has a dual etymology:
"bébert" comes firstly from the abbreviation "BBR", which stands for
"bleu, blanc, rouge", the colours
of the French flag and a symbol of
French nationalistic pride. In addition, the name Bébert (a nickname
for "Albert") sounds very typically
French.

bec [bɛk] nm (a) (bouche) mouth□, Br
gob, cakehole; **clouer le bec à qn**
to shut sb up; **puer du bec** to have
rotten breath or dogbreath (b) Belg,
Can & Suisse (baiser) peck, kiss□;

donner un bec à qn to give sb a kiss or peck; *Can* **bec pincé** snob ▸ *see also* **claquer**

bécane [bekan] *nf* (a) *(bicyclette, moto)* bike (b) *(machine)* machine□, *Am* honker

because [bikɔz] *prep* because of□, cos of; **je ne peux pas sortir ce soir because les enfants** I can't go out tonight cos of the kids

bècebège [bɛsbɛʒ] = **BCBG**

bêcheur, -euse [bɛʃœr, -øz] **1** *adj* stuck-up, snooty
  2 *nm,f* stuck-up *or* snooty person

bécosses [bekɔs] *nfpl Can Joual Br* bog, *Am* john, can

bécot [beko] *nm* kiss□

bécoter [bekɔte] **1** *vt Br* to snog, *Am* to neck
  2 se bécoter *vpr Br* to snog, *Am* to neck, to suck face

becter [bɛkte] *vt & vi* to eat□

bédave [bedav], **bédaver** [bedave] *vi Cités* to smoke□

bédé [bede] = **BD**

bédo [bedo] *nm Cités* joint, doobie, spliff, number

before [bifɔr] *nm or nf (soirée)* = party attended before going out clubbing; **où est-ce qu'on va faire le before ce soir?** where are we going to go to start things off this evening?

béger [beʒer] *vi (verlan* **gerber**) to puke, to throw up, to barf, *Br & Austr* to chunder

bégueule [begœl] *adj* fussy□

beigne [bɛɲ] *nf* clout, cuff; **flanquer une beigne à qn** to clout *or* cuff sb

belette [bəlɛt] *nf* chick, *Br* bird

belle [bɛl] *nf* (a) **se faire la belle** *(faire une fugue)* to run away□, *Br* to

do a bunk; *(s'évader)* to break out□ (b) *Belg* **avoir belle à faire qch** to have no trouble doing sth; **en avoir une belle avec qn** to go through some hard times with sb; **en faire une (bien) belle** to do something really silly *or* stupid; **ne jamais en faire une belle** to be always putting one's foot in it; **ne pas en faire une belle** to be a total disaster

belle-doche [bɛldɔʃ] *nf* mother-in-law□

bénard [benar], **bène** [bɛn] *nm Br* trousers□, keks, *Am* pants□

bénef [benɛf] *nm (abbr* **bénéfice**) profit□; **c'est tout bénef** it's all profit

béni-oui-oui [beniwiwi] *nm inv* yes-man

berceau [bɛrso] *nm* **les prendre au berceau** to be a cradle-snatcher

Bérézina [berezina] *npr* **c'est la Bérézina** it's a disaster□

ⓘ This expression refers to the Berezina river in Belarus which Napoleon's "Grande Armée" crossed during its hectic retreat from Russia in 1812. Many soldiers lost their lives during the disorganized crossing.

berge [bɛrʒ] *nf (an)* year□; **elle a cinquante berges** she's fifty□

ⓘ This term is used only when referring to people's ages.

berlingot [!] [bɛrlɛ̃go] *nm* (a) *(clitoris)* clit (b) *(virginité)* **avoir son berlingot** to be a virgin□; **perdre son berlingot** to lose one's virginity□ *or* cherry

berlue [bɛrly] *nf* **avoir la berlue** to be seeing things

berzingue [bɛrzɛ̃g] **à tout berzingue** *adv* at top speed, *Br* like the clappers, *Am* like sixty

bésef [bezɛf] *adv* **pas bésef** not a lot□, not much□; **dix euros par jour pour faire vivre une famille; ça fait pas bésef** ten euros a day to feed a family, it's not loads

ⓘ This word is derived from an Arabic word meaning "plentiful". It entered the French language at the time of the colonial expansion in North Africa.

besogner [!] [bəzɔɲe] *vt* to hump, to screw, to shaft

bête [bɛt] *nf* **(a)** *(expert)* **être une bête (en)** to be brilliant (at) **(b) comme une bête** like crazy **(c) faire la bête à deux dos** to make the beast with two backs

béton¹ [betɔ̃] *vi* (*verlan* **tomber**) **laisse béton!** forget it!, drop it!

béton² [betɔ̃] *adj (argument)* cast-iron; **dis que ton train a déraillé, ça c'est une excuse béton!** say that your train was derailed, that's a cast-iron excuse!

bétonner [betɔne] *vt (préparer avec soin)* to work hard on□; **il a bétonné son discours/son dossier** he's worked really hard on his speech/his application

beu [bø] *nf* grass, weed

ⓘ This word is the first syllable of the "verlan" version of the word "herbe".

beur [bœr], **beurette** [bœrɛt] *nm, f (verlan* **arabe***)* = person born and living in France of North African immigrant parents

beurré, -e [bœre] *adj (ivre)* wasted, plastered, *Br* pissed; **beurré comme un petit Lu®** *Br* pissed as a newt, *Am* stewed to the gills

ⓘ Lu® is a popular French brand of biscuits and one of its most famous products is "le Petit Beurre®", a biscuit made with butter, as its name suggests. The expression "beurré comme un petit Lu®" is therefore a play on the word "beurré", which means "buttered" in normal parlance but "drunk" in slang.

bézef [bezɛf] = **bésef**

bi [bi] *adj inv (abbr* **bisexuel, -elle***)* bi

biberonner [bibrɔne] *vi* to be a boozer *or* an alky a; **qu'est-ce qu'il biberonne!** he can really put it away, he's a real boozer *or* alky!

bibi [bibi] **1** *nm (chapeau)* (woman's) hat□

2 *pron (moi)* yours truly; **et qui c'est qu'a payé l'addition? c'est bibi!** and who paid the bill? yours truly *or Br* muggins here!

bibiche [bibiʃ] *nf* sweetheart, honey, sugar

bibine [bibin] *nf (alcool)* gutrot, rotgut, *Am* alky; *(bière)* dishwater

bibite [bibit] *nf Can* animal□; **il fait froid en bibite** it's freezing *or Br* it's baltic; **être en bibite (contre qn)** to be teed off *or* hacked off (with sb)

bibli [bibli] *nf (abbr* **bibliothèque***)* library□

biche [biʃ] *nf* **ma biche** darling, sweetheart

bicher [biʃe] *vi* **(a)** *(bien se passer)* **ça biche?** how's it going?, how's are things? **(b)** *(être satisfait)* to be pleased as Punch *or Br* chuffed (to

Spotlight on:

La bêtise et la folie

The word **con** is one of the most commonly used insults in French. Despite having the same etymology, it is notably less offensive or taboo than the English word "cunt" and is generally used to refer to a stupid person, its nuances ranging from the slightly forgetful to the completely insane. This word may also be used to refer to an object, an attitude or even a situation, in, for example, **c'est con que...** used to mean "it's a pity that…". The word often appears in similes; the construction **con comme...** is very common and one may be, variously, **con comme un balai, ses pieds, pas deux, un manche** or **une bite**, the first expression being very similar to the English "daft as a brush". The term **couillon** (from the word **couille**, a common slang term for "testicle") is found more frequently in the South of France, and may have quite affectionate overtones. Other picturesque expressions to denote stupidity include **il n'a pas inventé la poudre, l'eau chaude** or **le fil à couper le beurre, c'est pas une lumière, il en tient une couche** and **il lui manque une case**. Familiar expressions which are slightly less vulgar than **con** include **andouille, cruche, cloche, nouille** and **banane**, all of which may be used somewhat affectionately. The adjective **grave** is often used to describe someone as stupid, for example, **il est grave, lui...**; its verlan form **vegra** is also commonly used as is **ouf**, the verlan form of "fou". Further down the route to madness, many colourful adjectives are used to describe the state of someone who is not so much stupid as deranged, such as **cinglé, timbré, givré, fêlé, dingue** (and its verlan form **gueudin**), **chtarbé** or **siphonné**. Electricity-related metaphors are popular with the expression **péter les plombs** (literally "to blow the fuses") and, similarly, **disjoncter** ("to short-circuit"). Metaphors connected to transport or driving also exist in terms such as **dérailler** ("to go off the rails", an expression also used figuratively in English, although with a different meaning) and **perdre les pédales** (a variant of **perdre la boule**). Also of note is the term **fada**, a word originating in the Provençal dialect, which is still used exclusively in the South of France.

bits); **ça me fait bicher** that makes me happy□; **ça le fait vraiment bicher d'être passé à la télé** he's as pleased as Punch or Br chuffed to bits that he was on TV

biclo [biklo], **biclou** [biklu] nm bike

bicoque [bikɔk] nf (maison) place, pad

bicot [biko] nm Offensive = racist term used to refer to a North African Arab

bicrave [bikrav], **bicraver** [bikrave] vt Cités to sell□, Br to flog; (drogue) to deal

bidasse [bidas] nm Br squaddie, Am grunt

bide [bid] nm (a) (ventre) belly, gut; **être gras du bide** to have a huge gut; **il n'a rien dans le bide** (il n'a pas de courage) he's got no guts or balls (b) (échec) flop, washout, Am bomb; **faire un bide** to be a flop or a washout, Am to bomb

bidoche [bidɔʃ] nf meat□; **j'ai renoncé à bouffer de la bidoche** I've stopped eating meat; **l'été est arrivé; les touristes déballent leur bidoche sur les plages** summer's here, the tourists are flashing their flesh on the beaches

ⓘ This terme is derived from the word "bidet", which means "mule" and originally refered to bad horse meat.

bidochon [bidɔʃɔ̃] nmf = stereotypical working-class, reactionary person

ⓘ This word is an allusion to Les Bidochon, a comic strip by the cartoonist Binet, about an ordinary French couple who embody the stereotypical behaviour and values of the working class.

bidon [bidɔ̃] **1** adj inv phoney

2 nm (a) (ventre) belly, gut (b) **c'est du bidon** it's a load of baloney or garbage or Br rubbish; **c'est pas du bidon** it's gospel, it's the honest truth; **c'est pas du bidon, il a vraiment mal** he's not putting it on, he's in real pain

3 nmpl Belg **bidons** (habits) togs, gear, threads; (affaires) things□, stuff

bidonnant, -e [bidɔnɑ̃, -ɑ̃t] adj side-splitting, hysterical; **c'était bidonnant!** it was a scream or a hoot!

bidonner [bidɔne] **1** vt to fix; **il est célèbre pour avoir bidonné une interview de Castro** he's famous for his hoax interview with Castro

2 se bidonner vpr to kill oneself (laughing), to crack up, to laugh one's head off

bidouillage [biduja3] nm **c'est du bidouillage** it's been thrown together; **j'appelle pas ça réparer la télé: c'est du bidouillage ce que tu nous as fait là** that's not repairing the TV, that's just patching it up

bidouiller [biduje] vt (bricoler) to tinker with; (trafiquer) to fiddle

bidous [bidu] nmpl Can dough; **avoir des bidous** to be loaded, to be Br rolling in it or Am rolling in dough

bidule [bidyl] **1** nm (chose) thingy, whatsit

2 npr **Bidule** (personne) thingy, what's-his-name, f what's-her-name

biffe [bif] nf **la biffe** the infantry□

biffeton [biftɔ̃] = **bifton**

biffin [bifɛ̃] nm (a) (soldat) infantry-man□ (b) (personne ridicule) buffoon, clown

bifteck [biftɛk] nm **défendre son**

bifteck to look after number one; **j'fais pas grève par plaisir mais pour défendre mon bifteck, mon gars!** I'm not on strike for the fun of it, pal, it's to protect my livelihood!; **gagner son bifteck** to earn one's crust or one's bread and butter

bifton [biftɔ̃] nm (billet de banque) note☐, Am greenback; (de transport, de spectacle) ticket☐

bigler [bigle] **1** vt (observer) to eyeball, to check out
2 vi (loucher) to have a squint☐

bigleux, -euse [biglø, -øz] adj (**a**) (qui louche) cross-eyed (**b**) (qui voit mal) short-sighted☐

bigophone [bigɔfɔn] nm Br blower, Am horn

bigophoner [bigɔfɔne] vi to make a phone call☐; **bigophoner à qn** to give sb a buzz or Br a bell

bigorner [bigɔrne] **1** vt to smash up, Br to prang; **bigorner sa bagnole contre un arbre** to smash one's car into a tree
2 se bigorner vpr to have a scrap or Br a punch-up or Am a fist fight

bijoux [biʒu] nmpl Hum **les bijoux de famille** (sexe de l'homme) the crown or family jewels

bilan [bilɑ̃] nm **déposer le bilan** (mourir) to croak, to kick the bucket, Br to snuff it, Am to check out; (déféquer) to Br have or Am take a crap or a dump

bilingue [bilɛ̃g] **1** adj Can (bisexuel) bi
2 nmf Can (bisexuel) bi

billard [bijar] nm **passer sur le billard** to go under the knife

bille [bij] nf (**a**) (visage) face☐, mug; **une bille de clown** a funny face☐ (**b**) **reprendre** ou **retirer ses billes** to pull out☐ (from a deal) (**c**) **toucher**

sa bille (en ou **à)** to know a thing or two (about)

bimbo [bimbo] nf bimbo

bine [bin] nf Can (**a**) (visage) mug, face☐ (**b**) Joual **être dans les bines** to be out to lunch; **faire qch en criant bine** to do sth in a flash

ⓘ The Joual sense of the word comes from the English word "bean".

binerie [binri] nf Can Joual Pej greasy spoon

ⓘ This sense comes from the English word "bean".

binette [binɛt] nf (visage) face☐, mug

bingo [biŋgo] nm Can (révolte) prison riot☐

biniou [binju] nm (téléphone) Br blower, Am horn; **filer un coup de biniou** to make a phone call☐; **filer un coup de biniou à qn** to give sb a buzz or Br a bell

ⓘ In standard French, a "biniou" is a type of Breton bagpipe.

binoclard, -e [binɔklar, -ard] nm,f four-eyes, Br speccy

binouze [binuz] nf (bière) beer☐; **on se boit une binouze?** fancy a Br pint or Am brew?

binz [bins] nm (**a**) (chose compliquée) **quel binz pour trouver sa maison!** it was a real performance or hassle or Br carry-on finding his house! (**b**) (désordre) shambles

bio [bjo] nf (abbr **biographie**) biog; **une bio d'Elvis** an Elvis biog

bique [bik] **1** *nm Offensive* = racist term used to refer to a North African Arab

2 *nf* **une vieille bique** an old bag

biroute [!] [birut] *nf* dick, cock, *Br* knob, *Am* schlong

biscoteaux [biskɔto] *nmpl* biceps□

biscuit [biskɥi] *nm* (a) **tremper son biscuit [!!]** to dip one's wick (b) *(amende infligée à un automobiliste)* fine□

bisoune [bizun] *nf Can* (a) *(petite fille)* sweetheart; **ma bisoune** sweetheart, sweetie (b) *(pénis) Br* willy, *Am* peter, johnson

bistouquette [bistukɛt] *nf Br* willy, *Am* peter, johnson

bite [!!] [bit] *nf* dick, cock, *Br* knob, *Am* schlong; **rentrer la bite sous le bras** to go home without getting laid *or Br* without getting one's oats

biter [!] [bite] *vt* **j'y bite rien** I don't understand a *Br* bloody *or Am* goddamn thing

bitoniau [bitɔnjo] *nm* thingy, whatsit, *Br* doodah, *Am* doodad

bitos [bitos] *nm* hat□

bitu [bity] *adj Belg (ivre)* plastered, smashed

biture [bityr] *nf* **il tenait une de ces bitures!** he was completely plastered *or* wasted *or Br* legless *or* pissed!; **prendre une biture** to get plastered *or* wasted *or Br* legless *or* pissed

---

ⓘ The expression "prendre une biture" derives from nautical terminology. A "biture" is a length of cable attached to the anchor.

---

biturer [bityre] **se biturer** *vpr* to get plastered *or* wasted *or Br* legless *or* pissed

bizut [bizy] *nm* = first-year student in a "grande école"

bizutage [bizytaʒ] *nm Br* ragging, *Am* hazing *(in "grandes écoles")*

bizuter [bizyte] *vt Br* to rag, *Am* to haze *(in "grandes écoles")*

blabla [blabla] *nm inv* baloney, *Br* waffle

blablater [blablate] *vi* to waffle on, *Br* to witter on

black [blak] **1** *adj* Black

2 *nmf (personne de race noire)* Black

3 *nm* **travailler au black** *(clandestinement)* = to work without declaring one's earnings; *(en plus de son travail habituel)* to moonlight

blackos [blakos] *nmf* Black

blague [blag] *nf* (a) **sans blague!** *(je t'assure)* no kidding!, it's true!; **sans blague?** *(est-ce vrai?)* no kidding?, yeah?; **j'ai fait la connaissance de ta sœur, elle est vachement plus bandante que toi, dis donc! blague!** I've met your sister, she's way sexier *or Br* fitter than you! joke! *or* just kidding! (b) **blagues à tabac** saggy boobs

blair, blaire [blɛr] *nm Br* conk, hooter, *Am* schnozzle

blaireau, -x [blɛro] *nm (individu)* jerk, *Br* prat

blairer [blɛre] *vt* **je peux pas le blairer** I can't stand *or* stomach *or Br* stick him

blanche [blɑ̃ʃ] *nf (héroïne)* smack, scag, skag

Blanche-Neige [blɑ̃ʃnɛʒ] *nm inv Offensive* nigger, *Br* wog, *Am* coon

blase, blaze [blɑz] *nm* name□, handle, moniker

ⓘ This word derives from "blason", which refers to the coat of arms of a noble family or group.

blé [ble] nm (argent) dough, Br dosh, Am bucks

blèche [blɛʃ] adj hideous, Br pig-ugly, Am butt-ugly

bled [blɛd] nm (localité) place[□]; Pej hole, dump, dive

ⓘ This word is derived from an Arabic word meaning "country". It entered the French language at the time of the colonial expansion in North Africa.

blème [blɛm] nm Cités (abbr **problème**) problem, Br prob

bleu [blø] nm (a) (novice) rookie (b) **un petit bleu** a telegram[□] (c) (policier) cop, Br plod, Am flatfoot (d) Suisse (permis de conduire) Br driving licence[□], Am driver's license[□] (e) Can **avoir les bleus** (être triste) to have the blues; **prendre les bleus** (devenir triste) to get the blues; (se mettre en colère) to go crazy; **être dans les bleus** (être ivre) to be wasted

bleubite [bløbit] nm rookie

bleue [blø] nf **la grande bleue** the sea[□]; (la Méditerranée) the Med

bleusaille [bløzaj] nf **la bleusaille** the new recruits[□], the rookies

blinde [blɛ̃d] **à toute blinde** adv at full speed, like lightning, Br like the clappers

blindé, -e [blɛ̃de] adj (a) (ivre) blitzed, plastered, wasted (b) **être blindé (de monde)** to be swarming or Br heaving (with people)

blinder [blɛ̃de] **1** vi to bomb along
2 se blinder vpr (s'enivrer) to get

blitzed or plastered or wasted

bloblote [blɔblɔt] nf **avoir la bloblote** to have the shakes

bloc [blɔk] nm (a) (prison) slammer, clink, Br nick, Am pen (b) Can (tête) head[□], nut (c) Belg (temps exécrable) awful weather[□]; **quel bloc aujourd'hui!** the weather's so lousy today!

bloke [blɔk] nm Can Joual Pej English-speaking Canadian[□]

blondasse [blɔ̃das] nf brassy blonde

blonde [blɔ̃d] nf Can girlfriend[□], Br bird

bloquer [blɔke] **1** vt (a) Belg (examen) to cram for, Br to swot for, Am to grind away for; (matière) to cram, Br to swot up, Am to grind away at (b) Can to fail[□], to flunk
2 vi **bloquer sur qn** to have the hots for sb, Br to fancy sb

blouser [bluze] vt **blouser qn** to put one over on sb, to take sb for a ride; **se faire blouser** to get taken for a ride

bluffer [blœfe] vt (impressionner) to blow away; **ils m'ont vraiment bluffé lors de leur passage à Paris** they really blew me away when they played Paris

bobard [bɔbar] nm fib, Br porky, whopper; **raconter des bobards** to tell fibs or Br porkies or whoppers

bobet [bɔbɛ] Suisse **1** adj dim, thick, Am dumb
2 nm Br prat, Am jackass

bobinard [!] [bɔbinar] nm whorehouse, Br knocking shop

bobine [bɔbin] nf (visage) face[□], mug

bobo [bɔbo] nmf (abbr **bourgeois(e) bohème**) bobo

bobonne [bɔbɔn] nf (a) (épouse) the

old lady, *Br* the missus, her indoors (**b**) *Belg* grandma

boche [bɔʃ] *Offensive* **1** *adj* Kraut
2 *nmf* **Boche** *(personne)* Kraut

ⓘ Depending on the context and the tone of voice used, this term may be either offensive or affectionately humorous. It is nonetheless inadvisable to use it unless one is quite sure of the reaction it will receive.

---

bœuf [bœf] **1** *adj* **faire un effet bœuf** to cause a stir, to make a splash
2 *nm* (**a**) **faire un bœuf** to have a jam session, to jam (**b**) **on n'est pas des bœufs** you can't treat us like slaves

bof [bɔf] *exclam* **c'était bien? – bof** was it good? – not particularly

---

ⓘ Normally accompanied by an expression of utter indifference, this term is used in numerous situations to express a disdainful lack of enthusiasm.

---

bogarter [bɔgarte] *vi* to bogart a joint

bois [bwɑ] *nm* **ça envoie le bois** it's the business

boîte [bwat] *nf* (**a**) *(société)* firm□, company□ (**b**) **boîte (de nuit)** club, nightclub□; **sortir en boîte** to go clubbing (**c**) **boîte à ouvrage [!!]** box, twat, *Br* fanny; **boîte à pâté [!!]** *Br* dirtbox, arsehole, *Am* asshole ► *see also* **bachot**

boit-sans-soif [bwasɑ̃swaf] *nmf inv* alky, lush, boozer, *Am* juicer

bol [bɔl] *nm (chance)* luck□; **un coup de bol** a stroke of luck□; **manque de bol, il était déjà parti** he'd already left, it was too bad ► *see also* **ras**

bombarder [bɔ̃barde] **1** *vt* **on l'a bombardé ministre** he's been made a minister out of the blue
2 *vi (fumer beaucoup)* to smoke like a chimney

bombe [bɔ̃b] *nf* (**a**) *(fête)* **faire la bombe** to party (**b**) *(jolie fille)* babe, hottie, knockout (**c**) **à toute bombe** at top speed, *Br* like the clappers, *Am* like sixty; **aller à toute bombe** to bomb along, to belt along (**d**) **c'est de la bombe!** *Br* it's fab!, *Am* it's awesome!; **c'est de la bombe de balle!** it really rocks!

bomber [bɔ̃be] *vi* to bomb along, to belt along

bomme [bɔm] *nm Can Joual* tramp, *Am* bum

bommer [bɔme] *vi Can Joual* to bum around

bon app' [bɔnap] *exclam (abbr* **bon appétit)** enjoy your meal!, *Am* enjoy!

bonbec [bɔ̃bɛk] *nm (cachet d'ecstasy)* E, *Br* disco biscuit

bonbon [bɔ̃bɔ̃] **1** *adv* **coûter bonbon** to cost an arm and a leg *or* a bundle *or Br* a bomb
2 [!] *nm* (**a**) *(clitoris)* clit (**b**) **bonbons** *(testicules)* balls, *Br* bollocks; **casser les bonbons à qn** to piss sb off, *Br* to get on sb's tits, *Am* to break sb's balls

bonhomme [bɔnɔm] *nm (mari)* old man; **elle a préféré venir sans son bonhomme** she preferred to come without her old man ► *see also* **nom**

bonjour [bɔ̃ʒur] *exclam* **bonjour l'ambiance/l'odeur!** what an atmosphere/a smell!; **bonjour les dégâts!** what a mess!

bonnard [bɔnar] *adj* **c'est bonnard!** cool!

bonne [bɔn] **1** *adj Cités (belle)* gorgeous, hot, *Br* fit; **elle est bonne, la sœur de Frédo** Frédo's sister is a real babe *or Br* is well fit

2 *nf* **avoir qn à la bonne** to like sb▫ ▸ *see also* **pâte, poire**

bonnet [bɔnɛ] *nm* (a) **un gros bonnet (de)** a big shot *or* big cheese (in) (b) **te casse pas le bonnet** don't worry about it▫, don't let it bother you▫

bonniche [bɔniʃ] *nf* servant▫, *Br* skivvy

booké, -e [buke] *adj* booked-up, busy▫

bord [bɔr] *nm* **sur les bords** a bit▫, a tad; **il est un peu menteur sur les bords** he's a bit of a liar

bordel [!!] [bɔrdɛl] **1** *nm* (a) *(maison close)* brothel▫, whorehouse, *Br* knocking shop (b) *(désordre)* shambles, mess; **foutre le bordel (dans)** *(mettre en désordre)* to make a fucking mess (of); **il fout le bordel en classe** he creates fucking havoc in the classroom

2 *exclam* fuck!; **bordel de merde!** fucking hell!; **mais qu'est-ce qu'il fout, bordel!** what the fuck is he doing?

bordélique [bɔrdelik] *adj* **être bordélique** *(endroit, situation)* to be a mess *or* a shambles; *(personne)* to be messy

borgne [bɔrɲ] *nm Hum* **étrangler le borgne** *(se masturber)* to bang *or Br* bash the bishop

borne [bɔrn] *nf (kilomètre)* kilometre▫; **la pompe à essence la plus proche est à quinze bornes** the nearest *Br* petrol station *or Am* gas station is fifteen kilometres away

bosse [bɔs] *nf* **rouler sa bosse** to knock about; **il a roulé sa bosse un peu partout** he's been around a bit

bosser[1] [bɔse] *vi* to work▫; **bosser comme un nègre** to slog one's guts out

bosser[2] [bɔse] *vt Can Joual* to boss around; **arrête de me bosser!** stop bossing me around!

bosseur, -euse [bɔsœr, -øz] **1** *adj* hard-working▫

2 *nm,f* hard worker▫

botcher [bɔtʃe] *vt Can Joual* to botch

botte [bɔt] *nf* **en avoir plein les bottes** to be *Br* knackered *or Am* pooped; **lécher les bottes à qn** to lick sb's boots; **chier dans les bottes à qn** [!!] to piss sb off, *Br* to get on sb's tits, *Am* to break sb's balls; **il lui a proposé la botte** [!] he asked her straight out to sleep with him; *Belg* **être bien dans ses bottes** to have a fair bit (of money) tucked away; *Belg* **être** *or* **se sentir droit dans ses bottes** to have an easy conscience▫; *Belg* **avoir une pièce dans ses bottes** to have had one too many

botter [bɔte] *vt* (a) *(plaire à)* **ça me botte** I like it▫, I dig it; **ça te botterait d'y aller?** do you want to go?▫, *Br* do you fancy going? (b) *(donner des coups de pied à)* **botter le cul à qn** [!] to give sb *Br* a boot up the arse *or Am* a kick in the ass; **botter les fesses** *ou* **le train à qn** to give sb a kick in the pants; **à chaque fois qu'on lui pose une question à propos du scandale, le ministre s'empresse de botter en touche** every time the minister gets asked a question about the scandal, he dodges the issue

bottine [bɔtin] *nf Can* **avoir les**

deux pieds dans la même bottine *(être maladroit)* to be all (fingers and) thumbs; *(trébucher souvent)* to have two left feet; *(être gaffeur)* to be always putting one's foot in it

boucan [bukɑ̃] *nm* racket, din

boucane [bukan] *nf Can* smoke⁰

bouché, -e [buʃe] *adj* **être bouché (à l'émeri)** *Br* to be thick (as two short planks), *Am* to have rocks in one's head

boucher [buʃe] *vt* **en boucher un coin à qn** to leave sb flabbergasted *or Br* gobsmacked

boucler [bukle] *vt* **(a)** *(fermer)* to shut⁰, to close⁰; **boucler la lourde** to shut *or* close the door⁰ **(b)** *(emprisonner)* to lock up⁰, to put away **(c) la boucler** *(se taire)* to shut up, to button it, *Br* to belt up; **tu vas la boucler?** shut up *or* button it *or Br* belt up, will you?

boudin [budɛ̃] *nm* **(a)** *(femme laide)* dog, *Br* boot, *Am* beast **(b) faire du boudin** to be in a huff ▸ *see also* **eau, rond**

bouffarde [bufard] *nf* pipe⁰

bouffe [buf] *nf* **(a)** *(aliments)* food⁰, eats, chow, grub **(b)** *(repas)* meal⁰; **faire la bouffe** to do the cooking⁰; **se faire une bouffe** to have a meal together⁰

bouffer [bufe] **1** *vt (manger)* to eat⁰; **bouffer de l'essence** to be a gas-guzzler; **bouffer du kilomètre** to clock up a lot of miles; **bouffer du curé-/du coco** to be a priest-/commie-hater

2 *vi* to eat⁰

3 se bouffer *vpr* **se bouffer le nez** to have a shouting *or Br* slanging match, *Br* to have a go at each other ▸ *see also* **chancre, vache**

bouffi [bufi] *nm* **tu l'as dit, bouffi!**

you said it!, *Am* you said a mouthful!

bouffon [bufɔ̃] *nm (personne ridicule)* buffoon, clown

bougeotte [buʒɔt] *nf* **avoir la bougeotte** to be fidgety; *(beaucoup voyager)* to have itchy feet

bouger [buʒe] **1** *vi (sortir)* to make a move, to move on; **on bouge?** shall we make a move?

2 se bouger *vpr* **bouge-toi un peu!** *(agis)* get a move on!, shift yourself!, *Br* get up off your backside!; **se bouger le cul [!]** to get off one's *Br* arse *or Am* ass

bougnoul, bougnoule [buɲul] *nm Offensive* = racist term used to refer to a North African Arab

boui-boui [bwibwi] *nm* greasy spoon

bouillave [bujav], **bouillaver** [bujave] *vt Cités* to screw, to hump, *Br* to shag

bouille [buj] *nf (visage)* face⁰, mug; **avoir une bonne bouille** to look nice⁰

bouillie [buji] *nf* **de la bouillie pour les chats** *(texte)* a load of garbage *or Br* rubbish

bouillon [bujɔ̃] *nm (eau)* water⁰; **tomber dans le bouillon** to fall in⁰; **boire le bouillon** *(avaler de l'eau)* to get a mouthful of water⁰; *(faire faillite)* to go bust

boule [bul] *nf* **(a)** *(tête)* **perdre la boule** to crack up, to lose one's marbles, to go round the bend, *Br* to lose the plot; **donner un coup de boule à qn** to headbutt *or Br* nut sb; **prendre un coup de boule** to get headbutted *or Br* nutted; **avoir la boule à zéro** to have a skinhead (haircut) **(b)** *(angoisse)* **avoir les boules** to be upset⁰; **ça me fout les boules** it makes me upset; **les boules!** how

awful! (**c**) **se mettre en boule** to hit the roof *or Am* ceiling, to blow one's top *or Am* stack, to fly off the handle (**d**) **boules [!]** *(testicules)* balls, nuts

bouler [bule] *vi* **envoyer bouler qn** to tell sb where to go, *Br* to send sb packing

boulet [bulɛ] *nm* (**a**) *(imbécile)* jerk, *Br* prat (**b**) *(poids)* **quel boulet, ce mec!** that guy's a total leech!, that guy sticks to you like glue!

boulette [bulɛt] *nf (erreur) Br* boob, *Am* boo-boo; **faire une boulette** to make a *Br* boob *or Am* boo-boo

Boul' Mich' [bulmiʃ] *npr* **le Boul' Mich'** = the Boulevard Saint-Michel in Paris

boulonner [bulɔne] *vi* to work□

boulot [bulo] *nm* work□; *(tâche, emploi)* job□; **se mettre au boulot** to get to work□, to get down to it

boulotter [bulɔte] *vi* to eat□

boum [bum] **1** *nf* party□ *(for young people)*
2 *nm* **être en plein boum** to be up to one's neck, to be rushed off one's feet

boumer [bume] *vi* **ça boume?** how are things?, how's it going?

bounty [bunti] *nm* = black person who has adopted the lifestyle and values of a white person, *Br* Bounty bar, *Am* oreo (cookie)

ⓘ This term, in a similar way to its English equivalents, comes from the fact that a Bounty® chocolate bar is dark on the outside and white on the inside.

bouquin [bukɛ̃] *nm* book□; **bouquin de cul** skin mag, girlie mag

bouquiner [bukine] *vi* to read□

bourdon [burdɔ̃] *nm* **avoir le bourdon** *(être déprimé)* to feel down, to be on a downer

bourge [burʒ] *Pej (abbr* **bourgeois, -e**) **1** *adj* well-off□, *Br* posh
2 *nmf* well-off□ *or Br* posh person

bourgeoise [burʒwaz] *nf (épouse)* old lady, *Br* missis

bourlinguer [burlɛ̃ge] *vi* to knock about

ⓘ This term derives from nautical terminology, where a "bourlingue" is a type of sail.

bourrage [buraʒ] *nm* **bourrage de crâne** *ou* **de mou** brainwashing□, eyewash

bourre [bur] **1** *nm* cop
2 *nf* **être à la bourre** to be running late□; **coup de bourre** busy time□; **entre midi et deux heures c'est le coup de bourre** it's crazy between twelve and two

bourré, -e [bure] *adj* wasted, plastered, *Br* legless, pissed ▸ *see also* **coing**

bourre-pif [burpif] *nm inv* punch on the nose□

bourrer [bure] **1** [!!] *vt (posséder sexuellement)* to hump, to screw, *Br* to shag ▸ *see also* **mou**
2 *vi (aller très vite)* to belt along, to bomb along
3 se bourrer *vpr* **se bourrer la gueule [!]** to get shit-faced *or Br* rat-arsed *or* pissed

bourrichon [buriʃɔ̃] *nm* **monter le bourrichon à qn** to put ideas in sb's head; **se monter le bourrichon** to get carried away

bourrin, -e [burɛ̃, -in] **1** *adj (qui manque de raffinement) (personne)* oafish□; *(musique)* heavy□, hard-core□; **il est un peu bourrin avec ses blagues de cul, mon cousin** he's a bit of a Neanderthal, my cousin, with his dirty jokes; **leur équipe a joué de manière assez bourrine** their team played pretty rough

2 *nm* (a) *(cheval)* horse□ (b) *(policier)* cop, pig (c) *(femme laide)* dog, *Br* boot, *Am* beast

3 *nm,f (personne qui manque de raffinement)* pig, slob; **il conduit comme un bourrin** he drives like a maniac; **c'est de la musique de bourrin** it's real headbanging music

bourrique [burik] *nf* (a) *(personne têtue)* pig-headed person (b) **être soûl comme une bourrique** *Br* to be (as) pissed as a newt *or* a fart, *Am* to be stewed to the gills (c) **faire tourner qn en bourrique** to drive sb round the bend

bouseux, -euse [buzø, -øz] *nm,f Pej* yokel, peasant, *Am* hick, hayseed

ⓘ This term comes from "bouse", a word which means "cow dung".

bousiller [buzije] *vt* to wreck, to bust, *Br* to knacker

boussole [busɔl] *nf* **perdre la boussole** to crack up, to lose one's marbles, to go round the bend *or Br* the twist

boustifaille [bustifɑj] *nf* food□, chow, grub

bout [bu] *nm* (a) **[!!]** *(sexe de l'homme)* dick, prick, cock; **se mettre une femme sur le bout** to get laid, *Br* to get one's end away; **s'astiquer le bout** to jerk off, *Br* to toss oneself off, to wank, to have a wank (b) **tenir le bon bout** to be on the right track; *Can* **dans mon bout** in my neck of the woods, *Br* round

my way; *Can* **au bout** great, *Br* fab ▶ *see also* **mettre**

boutanche [butɑ̃ʃ] *nf* bottle□ *(usually of wine or spirits)*

bouteille [butɛj] *nf (âge)* **avoir de la bouteille** to have been around a long time; **prendre de la bouteille** to be getting on *or Br* knocking on a bit

boutique [butik] *nf* (a) **parler boutique** to talk shop (b) *(sexe de l'homme)* dick, cock, *Br* knob, *Am* schlong

bouton [!] [butɔ̃] *nm (clitoris)* clit; **s'astiquer le bouton** to play with oneself, to get oneself off

boxon [!!] [bɔksɔ̃] *nm* (a) *(maison close)* brothel□, whorehouse, *Br* knocking shop (b) *(désordre)* mess, shambles; **foutre le boxon (dans)** *(mettre en désordre)* to make a fucking mess (of); **il fout le boxon en classe** he creates fucking havoc in the classroom

bracelets [braslɛ] *nmpl (menottes)* cuffs, bracelets

braire [brɛr] *vi* **ça me fait braire** it hacks me off, *Br* it gets up my nose *or* does my head in, *Am* it gives me a pain

branché, -e [brɑ̃ʃe] *adj (bar, discothèque, personne)* hip, trendy; **être branché cinéma/jazz** to be into movies/jazz

brancher [brɑ̃ʃe] **1** *vt* (a) *(plaire à)* **ça me branche** I'm really into it; **ça me brancherait de venir avec vous** I'd be into *or* up for coming with you (b) *(pour séduire) Br* to chat up, *Am* to hit on (c) *(mettre en contact)* **brancher qn avec qn** to hook sb up with sb□ (d) *(faire parler)* **brancher qn sur un sujet** to get sb started *or* to start sb off on a subject

2 se brancher *vpr* to decide□, to

make up one's mind□

branchitude [brɑ̃ʃityd] *nf* hipness, trendiness; **cette boîte est l'un des hauts lieux de la branchitude parisienne** this club is one of the trendiest *or* hippest in Paris

branchouille [brɑ̃ʃuj] *Pej* **1** *adj* hip, trendy

2 *nmf* trendy person, hipster; **le bar était bourré de jeunes branchouilles** the bar was full of bright young things *or* young hipsters

ⓘ The -*ouille* suffix gives this word a pejorative connotation. This word tends to mean "trendy in an irritating way".

branlée [!] [brɑ̃le] *nf (défaite, correction)* thrashing, pasting; **prendre une branlée** to get thrashed, to *Br* get *or Am* take a pasting

branler [brɑ̃le] **1** [!!] *vt* to jerk off, *Br* to toss off; **j'en ai rien à branler** I don't give a shit *or* a (flying) fuck; **mais qu'est-ce qu'il branle?** what the fuck is he doing?, what the fuck is he up to?

2 *vi Can* to hum and haw

3 [!!] **se branler** *vpr* to jerk off, *Br* to toss oneself off, to wank, to have a wank; **s'en branler** not to give a shit *or* a (flying) fuck

branlette [!!] [brɑ̃lɛt] *nf* hand-job, *Br* wank; **se faire une branlette** to jerk off, *Br* to toss oneself off, to wank, to have a wank; **faire une branlette à qn** to give sb a hand-job, to jerk sb off, *Br* to toss sb off

branleur, -euse [!] [brɑ̃lœr, -øz] *nm,f* **(a)** *(bon à rien)* loser, slacker, *Br* waster **(b)** *(fanfaron)* show-off, *Am* hotshot

branleux, -euse [brɑ̃lø, -øz] *Can* **1**

adj (qui hésite) dithering□; *(lâche)* chicken

2 *nm,f (qui hésite)* ditherer□; *(lâche)* chicken

branque [brɑ̃k] **1** *adj (fou)* bonkers, nuts, *Br* off one's head, barking (mad)

2 *nmf (imbécile)* dope, jerk, *Br* prat; *(fou) Br* nutter, headcase, *Am* wacko, screwball

braque [brak] *adj* crazy, off one's rocker, *Br* mental

braquemart [!] [brakmar] *nm* dick, prick, *Br* knob, *Am* schlong

ⓘ In standard French, a "braquemart" is a type of sword of the late Middle Ages.

braquer [brake] *vt* **(a)** *(voler)* **braquer une banque/une bijouterie** to hold up a bank/a jeweller's; **braquer qch à qn** to pinch *or Br* nick sth from sb **(b)** *(rendre hostile)* **braquer qn** *Br* to get sb's back up, *Am* to tick sb off

braqueur, -euse [brakœr, -øz] *nm,f* armed robber□

bras [bra] *nm* **un gros bras** a big guy; **jouer les gros bras** to act the tough guy; **jouer petits bras** to hold back; **ils n'ont aucune chance de gagner si ils jouent petits bras** they've got no chance of winning if they don't give it their all ► *see also* **bite, pine, yeux**

brêle [brɛl] *nf* **(a)** *(cyclomoteur)* (motor) scooter□, moped□ **(b)** *(imbécile)* jerk, *Br* tosspot, *Am* fathead **(c)** *(personne médiocre)* **je suis une brêle en anglais** I'm totally crap at English, I suck at English

Brésilienne [breziljɛn] *nf (prostitué)* = Brazilian transsexual or transvestite male prostitute

bretelles [brətɛl] *nfpl* **remonter les bretelles à qn** to bawl sb out, *Br* to give sb an earful, *Am* to chew sb out; **se faire remonter les bretelles** to get bawled out, *Br* to get an earful, *Am* to get chewed out ▸ *see also* **piano**

bretter [brete] *Can* **1** *vt (chercher)* to look for□, to be after; **qu'est-ce que tu brettes ici?** what are you poking around here for?
2 *vi* to dawdle

bretteux, -euse [bretø, -øz] *Can* **1** *adj (lent)* dawdling; *(fainéant)* lazy□
2 *nm,f (personne lente) Br* slowcoach, *Am* slowpoke; *(fainéant)* slacker, *Br* waster

bricheton [briʃtɔ̃] *nm* bread□

bricole [brikɔl] *nf (chose insignifiante)* little thing□; **il va lui arriver des bricoles** he's heading for trouble

bricoler [brikɔle] *vi* **(a)** *(faire des petits boulots)* to do odd jobs, to do this and that **(b)** *(se livrer à de menus travaux)* to mess around, to potter around

bridé, -e [bride] *nm,f Offensive* slant, *Am* gook

briffer [brife] *vt & vi (manger)* to eat□; **bon, moi j'irais bien briffer** right, I'm up for some grub

brignolet [briɲɔlɛ] *nm* bread□

bringue [brɛ̃g] *nf* **(a)** *(fête)* **faire la bringue** to party, *Br* to go on the razzle **(b)** **une grande bringue** a beanpole, *Am* a stringbean

brioche [brijɔʃ] *nf* **avoir de la brioche** to have a paunch *or* a pot-belly; **prendre de la brioche** to be getting a paunch *or* a pot-belly

brique [brik] *nf Formerly (dix mille francs)* ten thousand francs□ ▸ *see also* **casser**

briser [brize] *vt* **il/ça me les brise (menues)** he/it really bugs me *or* hacks me off *or Br* gets up my nose *or* does my head in

Bronx [brɔ̃ks] *npr* **mettre le Bronx dans qch** to turn sth upside down, to make a mess of sth

bronze [brɔ̃z] *nm* **couler un bronze [!!]** to *Br* have *or Am* take a dump *or* a crap

bronzé, -e [brɔ̃ze] *nm,f Offensive* nigger, *Br* darky, *Am* coon

brosse [brɔs] *nf* **prendre une brosse** to get wrecked *or* smashed *or Br* pissed; **être en brosse** to be wrecked *or* smashed *or Br* pissed

brosser [brɔse] **1** *vt Belg* **brosser un cours** *Br* to skive off, *Am* to cut a class
2 se brosser *vpr* to do without; **tu peux te brosser pour que je te prête ma caisse, maintenant!** if you think I'm going to lend you my car now, you can forget it!

brosseur, -euse [brɔsœr, -øz] *nm,f Belg* truant□, *Br* skiver

broue [bru] *nf Can* lather□; **faire *ou* péter de la broue** to show off; **péteur de broue** show-off

brouille-ménage [brujmenaʒ] *nm inv* red wine□, *Br* plonk

brouter [brute] *vt* **les brouter à qn [!]** to piss sb off, *Br* to get on sb's tits, *Am* to break sb's balls; **brouter la tige à qn [!!]** to go down on sb, to suck sb off, to give sb head; **brouter le cresson à qn [!!]** to go down on sb, *Br* to lick sb out

brouteuse [!!] [brutøz] *nf* dyke

brûlé, -e [bryle] *adj* **être brûlé** *(être compromis)* to be finished

brut [bryt] *adj* **brut de décoffrage** rough and ready; **il est gentil, son père, mais il est un peu brut de**

décoffrage: n'espère pas parler philosophie avec lui his dad's nice but he's a bit rough and ready, don't hope for any philosophical conversations with him

ⓘ "Brut de décoffrage" literally refers to a type of untreated concrete.

bûche [byʃ] *nf* **ramasser une bûche** *(tomber)* to go flying, to measure one's length

bûcher [byʃe] **1** *vt Br* to swot up on, *Am* to bone up on
2 *vi Br* to swot, *Am* to bone up

ⓘ Originally, the word "bûcher" (from "bûche", "a log") that means "to work hard" in slang, used to mean "to fell trees".

bûcheur, -euse [byʃœr, -øz] **1** *adj* hard-working□
2 *nm,f* hard worker□

buffet [byfɛ] *nm (ventre)* belly, gut; **il s'est pris une bastos dans le buffet** he took a bullet right in the belly

bulle [byl] *nf* **(a)** *(à un devoir)* zero□, *Am* goose egg; **prendre une bulle** to get a zero□ or *Am* a goose egg **(b)** **coincer la bulle** to get some shut-eye or some *Br* zeds or *Am* zees
▸ *see also* **chier**

buller [byle] *vi* to laze about

burettes [!] [byrɛt] *nfpl (testicules)* balls, nuts, *Br* bollocks; **se vider les burettes [!!]** to shoot one's load; **casser les burettes à qn** to piss sb off, *Br* to get on sb's tits, *Am* to break sb's balls

ⓘ In standard French, "une burette" is an oil can.

burlingue [byrlɛ̃g] *nm* office□

burnes [!!] [byrn] *nfpl* balls, nuts, *Br* bollocks; **se vider les burnes** to shoot one's load; **casser les burnes à qn** to piss sb off, *Br* to get on sb's tits, *Am* to break sb's balls

buser [byze] *vt Belg (recaler)* **il a été busé** he failed□, *Am* he flunked

buter [byte] *vt* to kill□, *Br* to do in, *Am* to eighty-six; **se faire buter** to get killed□, *Br* to get done in, *Am* to get eighty-sixed

buvable [byvabl] *adj* **pas buvable** *(très antipathique)* unbearable□; **c'est un mec pas buvable** he's a complete pain (in the neck)

buvard [byvar] *nm (dose de LSD)* tab, trip

Byzance [bizɑ̃s] *npr* **c'est Byzance** it's the last word in luxury; **c'est pas Byzance** it's not exactly luxurious

Cc

cabane [kaban] *nf (prison)* slammer, clink, *Br* nick, *Am* joint; **en cabane** in the slammer *or* clink *or Br* nick *or Am* joint

cabanon [kabanɔ̃] *nm* **il est bon pour le cabanon** he should be locked up *or* put away

câble [kɑbl] *nm* **péter un câble** to crack up, to lose it

câblé, -e [kɑble] *adj (à la page)* hip, trendy

cabochard, -e [kabɔʃar, -ard] *adj* pig-headed

caboche [kabɔʃ] *nf* head□, nut

cabot [kabo] *nm (chien)* mutt

caca [kaka] *nm* poo, poop; **il nous fait un caca nerveux, l'autre!** he's having kittens!, he's having a fit!
▶ *see also* **nez**

cacaille [kakɑj] *nf Belg* piece of junk

cacheton [kaʃtɔ̃] *nm* (**a**) *(cachet d'artiste)* fee□; **courir le cacheton** = to try to get little jobs here and there (**b**) *(médicament)* pill□, tablet□; **il prend des cachetons pour dormir** he takes sleeping pills *or* tablets

cachetonner [kaʃtɔne] *vi (artiste)* = to try to get little jobs here and there

ça comme [sakɔm] *adv Cités (verlan comme ça)* like that□; **t'es con ou quoi, faut pas faire ça comme!** are you completely stupid or what, you don't do it like that!

cacou [kaku] *nmf* **faire le/la cacou** to act smart, to show off

cadavre [kadavr] *nm (bouteille vide)* empty, *Br* dead man

cadeau, -x [kado] *nm* **ce mec, c'est pas un cadeau!** that guy's a total pain (in the neck)!

cador [kadɔr] *nm* (**a**) *(chien)* mutt (**b**) *(personne influente)* big shot, big cheese, bigwig; *(d'une bande)* leader□

cafard [kafar] *nm* (**a**) *(tristesse)* **avoir le cafard** *ou* **un coup de cafard** to feel down *or* low; **ça m'a foutu le cafard** it got me down (**b**) *(délateur)* sneak, tell-tale, *Am* snitch

cafarder [kafarde] **1** *vt* **cafarder qn** to sneak on sb, to tell tales on sb, *Am* to snitch on sb
2 *vi* (**a**) *(être triste)* to feel down *or* low (**b**) *(rapporter)* to sneak, to tell tales, *Am* to snitch

cafardeur, -euse [kafardœr, -øz] *nm,f* sneak, tell-tale, snitch

cafardeux, -euse [kafardø, -øz] *adj (personne)* down, low

cafèt' [kafɛt] *nf (abbr cafétéria)* cafeteria□

cafeter [kafte] = **cafter**

cafeteur, -euse [kaftœr, -øz] = **cafteur**

cafetière [kaftjɛr] *nf (tête)* head□, nut

cafouiller [kafuje] *vi* (**a**) *(mal fonctionner)* to be a shambles or a muddle; *(machine)* to play up, to be on the blink or *Am* on the fritz (**b**) *(s'embrouiller)* to get in a muddle, to tie oneself in knots

cafouillis [kafuji] *nm* shambles, muddle

cafter [kafte] *vi* to sneak, to tell tales, to snitch

cafteur, -euse [kaftœr, -øz] *nm,f* sneak, tell-tale, snitch

cage [kaʒ] *nf* (**a**) **cage à lapins** *(logement)* rabbit hutch; **il habite dans les cages à lapin, à côté de la zone industrielle** he lives in those rabbit hutches beside the industrial estate (**b**) *(buts)* goal□ *(posts, nets)*

cageot [kaʒo] *nm (femme laide)* dog, *Br* boot, *Am* beast, skank

cagnard [kaɲar] *nm (soleil)* blazing sunshine□; **quel cagnard!** what a scorcher!, *Br* it's roasting!

ⓘ This word from the South of France originally described a sheltered, sunny area where one could take a nice nap.

cagoule [kagul] *nf (préservatif)* condom□, rubber, *Br* Durex®

ⓘ In standard French this word means "balaclava".

caïd [kaid] *nm (gros bonnet)* big shot, big cheese, bigwig; *(d'une bande)* leader□; **jouer les caïds** to act tough, *Br* to act the hard man

caillassage [kajasaʒ] *nm* throwing *Br* stones or *Am* rocks *(de* at)□; **il a été très souvent question du caillassage des bus dans les banlieues chaudes** the fact that, in the rough

areas, buses often got pelted with *Br* stones or *Am* rocks was much talked about

caillasse [kajas] *nf* (**a**) *Cités (argent)* dough, bread, *Br* dosh, *Am* bucks, gelt (**b**) *(pierre) Br* stone□, *Am* rock□

caillasser [kajase] *vt* to chuck *Br* stones or *Am* rocks at

caille¹ [kaj] *nf* **ma caille** honey, sweetheart

caille² [kaj] *nf Cités (abbr* **caillera**) *(un voyou)* lout, *Br* yob, ≈ chav

cailler [kaje] **1** *v imp* **ça caille** it's freezing or *Br* baltic, *Br* it's brass monkeys
2 se cailler *vpr* to be freezing; **se les cailler [!]** to be freezing one's *Br* arse or *Am* ass off

caillera [kajra] *nf Cités (verlan* **racaille**) *(voyou)* lout, *Br* yob, ≈ chav

caillou, -x [kaju] *nm* (**a**) *(tête)* head□, nut; **il a plus un poil sur le caillou** he's as bald as a coot; **elle en a dans le caillou** she's a smart cookie, she's pretty switched-on (**b**) *(pierre précieuse)* rock, sparkler

cainf [kɛ̃f], **cainfri** [kɛ̃fri] *nmf (verlan* **Africain**) African□

cainri [kɛ̃ri] **1** *adj (verlan* **ricain**) Yank, *Br* Yankee
2 *nm* Yank, *Br* Yankee

caisse [kɛs] *nf* (**a**) *(voiture)* car□, wheels, *Br* motor (**b**) **passer à la caisse** *(être payé)* to collect (**c**) *(pet)* **lâcher** ou **larguer une caisse [!]** to fart, *Br* to let off, *Am* to lay one

cake [kɛk] *nm (imbécile)* dope, jerk, moron, *Br* plonker, *Am* goober

cakos [kɛkos] *nm* (**a**) *(imbécile)* dope, jerk, moron, *Br* plonker, *Am* goober (**b**) **faire le c.** to act smart

calancher [kalɑ̃ʃe] *vi* to croak, *Br* to snuff it, *Am* to check out

calbar [kalbar], **calbute** [kalbyt] *nm* Br scants, Am shorts, skivvies

calcaire [kalkɛr] *nm* **avoir** *ou* **faire un coup de calcaire** to have a fit, to go off (at) the deep end

calcif [kalsif] = **calbar**

calculer [kalkyle] *vt (regarder)* to check out, to eye (up)

calculette [kalkylɛt] *nf* pizza face; **elle sort avec un mec, une vraie calculette!** she's going out with this real pizza face guy!

ⓘ The literal sense of the word is "calculator". People with acne are so called because in French the word "bouton" means both "button" (of a calculator, for example) and "pimple".

---

calebar [kalbar] = **calbar**

calebasse [kalbas] *nf (tête)* head□, nut

calecif [kalsif] = **calbar**

calendos [kalɑ̃dos] *nm* Camembert□

caleter [kalte] = **calter**

calibre [kalibr] *nm (pistolet)* shooter, Am piece

câlice [kalis] Can Joual **1** *nm* bastard; **mon câlice!** you bastard!; **en câlice** Br dead, Am real; **il fait froid en câlice** it's freezing or Br baltic; **être en câlice (contre qn)** to be fuming mad (with sb)
  2 *exclam* shit!

ⓘ Traditionally, French Canadians were deeply Catholic, which explains why several of their most common swearwords are linked to religion: these include "câlice" (derived from "calice", meaning "chalice"), "ciboire", "tabernacle", "hostie" and "criss" (derived from "Christ").

---

câlicer [kalise] *vt Can Joual* **(a)** *(laisser)* to drop; **il a tout câlicé là et il est parti** he dropped everything and left **(b)** *(mettre)* to stick; **je vais te câlicer mon poing dans la face** I'm going to sock you one, Br I'm going to bloody well smack you one

calmos [kalmos] *exclam* chill (out)!, take it easy!

calots [kalo] *nmpl (yeux)* eyes□, peepers

calotte [kalɔt] *nf* **la calotte** *(le clergé)* the clergy□

calter [kalte] *vi* to beat it, Br to clear off, Am to split

calva [kalva] *nm (abbr* **calvados***)* Calvados□

calvaire [kalvɛr] **1** *nm Can Joual (juron)* bastard; **mon calvaire!** you bastard!
  2 *exlam* shit!

cama [kama] *nm Belg (abbr* **camarade***)* pal, Br mate, Am buddy

Camarde [kamard] *nf* **la Camarde** death□

cambrouse [kɑ̃bruz], **cambrousse** [kɑ̃brus] *nf* **la cambrousse** the sticks, Am the boondocks; **en pleine cambrousse** in the sticks, in the middle of nowhere, Br in the back of beyond

cambuse [kɑ̃byz] *nf* dump, hole, hovel

came [kam] *nf* drugs□, stuff, Br gear

camé, -e [kame] **1** *adj* **être camé** to be on something; **il était complètement camé** he was totally loaded or wrecked or wasted
  2 *nm,f* druggie, junkie, Am dope fiend

camelote [kamlɔt] *nf* **(a)** *(marchandise)* stuff, Br gear **(b)** *(objets de mauvaise qualité)* trash, junk, garbage, *Br* rubbish

camer [kame] **se camer** *vpr* to do drugs; **se camer à l'héroïne/à la cocaïne** to be on heroin/cocaine; **il s'est jamais camé à l'héroïne** he's never done heroin

camp [kɑ̃] *nm* **ficher le camp** to clear off, to beat it, *Am* to split; **foutre le camp [!]** to go to hell, *Br* to piss off, to bugger off; **fiche(-moi) le camp!** get lost!, beat it!, *Br* sling your hook!, *Am* take a hike!; **fous(-moi) le camp! [!]** go to hell!, get the hell out of here!, *Br* piss off!, bugger off!

canard [kanar] *nm* (a) *(journal)* rag (b) **il fait un froid de canard** it's freezing, *Br* it's baltic ▸ *see also* **casser**

canarder [kanarde] *vt* to snipe at□, to take pot shots at

canasson [kanasɔ̃] *nm* horse□, nag

cané, -e [kane] *adj (épuisé) Br* knackered, shattered, *Am* beat

caner[1] [kane] *vi (renoncer)* to throw in the towel, to chuck it in

caner[2], **canner** [kane] *vi* (a) *(mourir)* to croak, *Br* to snuff it, *Am* to cash in (one's chips) (b) *(s'enfuir)* to beat it, *Br* to leg it, *Am* to bug out

cannes [kan] *nfpl (jambes)* legs□, pins; **il est tellement crevé qu'il tient plus sur ses cannes** he's so done in he can hardly stand

canon [kanɔ̃] **1** *adj inv* gorgeous, hot, *Br* fit

2 *nm (bel homme, belle femme)* babe, hottie

canter [kɑ̃te] **se canter** *vpr Can* to crash, to hit the sack *or Am* the rack

cantoche [kɑ̃tɔʃ] *nf* canteen□

caoua [kawa] = **kawa**

cap [kap] *adj (abbr* **capable**) **t'es**

pas cap de...! bet you can't...!

capo [kapo] *nm (abbr* **caporal**) *Br* ≃ lance corporal□, *Am* ≃ private first class□

capote [kapɔt] *nf* **capote (anglaise)** condom□, French letter, rubber

capoté, -e [kapɔte] **1** *adj Can* wasted, out of it
2 *nm,f* wacko

capoter [kapɔte] *vi Can (perdre la tête)* to flip, to lose it

capter [kapte] *vt (comprendre)* to get; **répète, j'ai pas capté** say that again, I didn't get it

carabiné, -e [karabine] *adj (café, cocktail)* powerful□; *(rhume)* stinking; *(fièvre)* raging□; **tenir une cuite carabinée** to be totally plastered *or Br* completely legless *or* off one's face

carabistouille [karabistuj] *nf Belg* (a) *(mensonge)* **raconter des carabistouilles** to talk nonsense (b) *(escroquerie)* con

carafe [karaf] **en carafe** *adv* **rester en carafe** to be left stranded□ *or* high and dry; **je comptais sur lui mais il m'a laissé en carafe** I was counting on him but he left me high and dry *or* in the lurch; **tomber en carafe** *(en panne)* to break down□

carafon [karafɔ̃] *nm (tête)* head□, nut; **il a vraiment rien dans le carafon** he's got nothing between his ears, *Br* he's as thick as two short planks, *Am* he's got rocks in his head

carapater [karapate] **se carapater** *vpr* to scram, to make oneself scarce

carat [kara] *nm* **dernier carat** *(dernière limite)* at the very most□, max, tops

carburer [karbyre] *vi* **il carbure au whisky/au café** whisky/coffee keeps him going

---

Le symbole □ indique que la traduction n'est pas argotique.

carne [karn] *nf* bad-quality meat□; **vieille carne** old bag, old witch

caroline [karɔlin] *nf* (**a**) *(homosexuel passif)* bitch (**b**) *(travesti)* TV, *Br* tranny

carotter [karɔte] *vt* **carotter qch à qn** *(dérober)* to pinch *or Br* nick sth from sb; *(escroquer)* to swindle *or Br* do sb out of sth

carpette [karpɛt] *nf (lâche)* doormat; **jamais il tiendra tête à sa bonne femme, c'est une vraie carpette!** he'll never stand up to his wife, he's such a doormat

carreaux [karo] *nmpl (lunettes)* specs

carrément [karemɑ̃] *adv* **t'as carrément raison** you're absolutely right; **c'est carrément du vol!** it's *Br* daylight *or Am* highway robbery!; **sa jupe fait carrément pute** her skirt's downright slutty; **carrément, mec!** *Br* absolutely, mate!, *Am* totally, man!

carrer [kare] *vt* **tu peux te le carrer dans le cul** *ou* **dans l'oignon! [!!]** you can shove *or* stick it up your *Br* arse *or Am* ass!

carte [kart] *nf Belg* **taper la carte** to play cards□

carton [kartɔ̃] *nm* (**a**) **faire un carton** *(tirer sur quelqu'un)* to take pot shots at somebody; *(avoir du succès)* to be a hit (**b**) **(se) prendre un carton** *(essuyer une défaite)* to get thrashed *or Br* trounced; *(avoir une mauvaise note)* to get a bad *Br* mark□ *or Am* grade (**c**) **taper le carton** *(jouer aux cartes)* to have a game of cards□

cartonner [kartɔne] *vi* (**a**) *(avoir une bonne note)* to pass with flying colours (**b**) *(musique)* to be mind-blowing

casbah [kazba] *nf (maison)* place, pad, *Br* gaff

ⓘ This word is derived from an Arabic word meaning "fortress". It entered the French language at the time of the colonial expansion in North Africa.

case [kaz] *nf* **il lui manque une case** he's got a screw loose, he's off his rocker, he's not all there; **retour à la case départ!** back to square one!

cash [kaʃ] *adv* **payer cash** to pay cash□; **y aller cash** *(sans détour)* to get straight to the point, not to mince one's words; **alors je le lui ai dit comme ça, cash** so I just told him straight out

casquer [kaske] *vt & vi* (**a**) *(payer)* to fork out, to cough up (**b**) **être casqué [!]** *(porter un préservatif)* to be wearing a condom□ *or* rubber□ *or Br* Durex®; **faut pas baiser sans être casqué, c'est trop risqué** best not to ride bareback, it's too risky

casquette [kaskɛt] *nf* (**a**) **avoir la casquette de plomb** *ou* **en zinc** to have a hangover□, to be hungover□ (**b**) *Cités (contrôleur dans les transports en commun)* ticket inspector□ ▸ *see also* **ras**

casse [kɑs] **1** *nm* break-in□, heist; **faire un casse chez un bijoutier** to *Br* do over *or Am* rob a jeweller's **2** *nf* trouble; **va y avoir de la casse** there's going to be trouble, *Br* it's going to kick off

cassé, -e [kɑse] *adj (drogué)* stoned, wrecked, flying; *(ivre)* smashed, plastered, *Br* legless

casse-bonbons [!] [kɑsbɔ̃bɔ̃] **1** *adj inv* **être casse-bonbons** to be a pain (in the neck)

2 *nmf inv* pain (in the neck)

casse-couilles [!!] [kɑskuj] **1** *adj inv* **être casse-couilles** to be a pain in the *Br* arse *or Am* ass

2 *nmf inv* pain in the *Br* arse *or Am* ass

casse-cul [!!] [kɑsky] **1** *adj inv* **être casse-cul** to be a pain in the *Br* arse *or Am* ass

2 *nmf inv* pain in the *Br* arse *or Am* ass

casse-dalle [kɑsdal] *nm inv* sandwich□, *Br* butty, sarnie

casse-graine [kɑsgrɛn] *nm inv* snack□

casse-gueule [kɑsgœl] *adj inv* (*sport, acrobaties*) death-defying□; (*entreprise*) risky□, *Br* dodgy

casse-pieds [kɑspje] **1** *adj inv* **être casse-pieds** to be a pain (in the neck)

2 *nmf inv* pain (in the neck)

casse-pipe [kɑspip] *nm inv* **envoyer qn/aller au casse-pipe** (*à la guerre*) to send sb/go to the front□

casser [kɑse] **1** *vt* (**a**) **casser la figure** *ou* **la gueule** [!] **à qn** to smash sb's face in, to waste sb's face; **casser la gueule à une bouteille** to down a bottle in one

(**b**) (*critiquer*) to tear *or* rip to bits

(**c**) (*agresser*) **casser du pédé** [!] to go queer-bashing *or* gay-bashing; **casser du flic** [!] to beat up some cops

(**d**) **les casser à qn** [!] (*l'importuner*) *Br* to get on sb's tits, *Am* to break sb's balls

(**e**) **ça casse pas des briques, ça casse pas trois pattes à un canard, ça casse rien** it's nothing to write home about

(**f**) **à tout casser** (*au maximum*) max, tops; **ça doit coûter cent euros à tout casser** it must cost a hundred euros max *or* tops; **faire une fiesta à tout casser** to have a hell of a party

2 se casser *vpr* (**a**) (*partir*) to clear off, *Am* to split; **bon, faut que je me casse** I'd better be off, I've got to make tracks; **casse-toi!** get lost!, get the hell out of here!

(**b**) **se casser la figure** *ou* **la gueule** [!] (*tomber*) to fall flat on one's face; (*échouer*) to be a flop

(**c**) (*s'inquiéter*) **te casse pas!** take it easy!, chill (out)!

(**d**) **se casser (à faire qch)** to go out of one's way (to do sth); **se casser le cul (à faire qch)** [!] to bust a gut *or Am* one's ass (doing sth) ▶ *see also* baraque, bonbon, bonnet, burettes, burnes, couille, croûte, graine, margoulette, morceau, nénette, pipe, rondelle, sucre, tronc

casserole [kɑsrɔl] *nf* (**a**) **traîner des casseroles** to be dogged by scandal□ (**b**) *Hum* **passer à la casserole** (*subir un rapport sexuel*) *Br* to get a good seeing-to, *Am* to get a balling; (*être assassiné*) to get bumped off

castagne [kastaɲ] *nf* (*coup*) clout, wallop; **va y avoir de la castagne** there's going to be a *Br* punch-up *or Am* fist fight, *Br* it's going to kick off

castagner [kastaɲe] **1** *vt* to clout, to wallop

2 se castagner *vpr* to have a *Br* punch-up *or Am* fist fight

cata [kata] *nf* (*abbr* **catastrophe**) **c'est la cata** it's a disaster□

catho [kato] *adj & nmf* (*abbr* **catholique**) Catholic□; **il vient d'une famille hyper catho** he comes from a really churchy family

causant, -e [kozɑ̃, -ɑ̃t] *adj* **il n'est pas très causant** he's not very chatty, he doesn't have much to say for himself

causer [koze] *vi* to chat

cavale [kaval] *nf* **être en cavale**

to be on the run; **la police n'a toujours pas retrouvé les trois gangsters en cavale** the police still haven't found the three gangsters who are on the run

cavaler [kavale] **1** *vt* **tu commences à me cavaler!** you're starting to *Br* get on my wick *or* on my tits *or Am* tick me off!

2 *vi* (a) *(courir, se dépêcher)* to run around⁰, to charge around (b) *(rechercher les aventures)* to chase after women/men

cavaleur, -euse [kavalœr, -øz] **1** *adj (homme)* womanizing; *(femme)* man-eating

2 *nm,f (homme)* womanizer, skirt-chaser; *(femme)* man-eater

cave [kav] *nm (imbécile)* sucker, *Br* mug, *Am* patsy

céfran [sefrɑ̃] *Cités (verlan français)* **1** *adj* French⁰

2 *nmf* Frenchman, *f* Frenchwoman⁰

ceinture [sɛ̃tyr] *nf* **faire ceinture** *(être privé de nourriture, être forcé à l'abstinence)* to go without; **ce soir, mon vieux, ceinture!** you'll have to go without tonight!

cendar [sɑ̃dar] *nm* ashtray⁰

cerise [səriz] *nf Can Joual* **faire perdre la cerise à qn [!!]** to pop sb's cherry

ceusses [søs] *pron Hum* **les ceusses qui…** them what…

cézigue [sezig] *pron* his lordship, *Br* his nibs

chagatte [!!] [ʃagat] *nf* pussy, snatch, *Br* fanny

ⓘ This word is in fact the word "chatte" after it has been given the "javanais" treatment (see panel on "javanais" p.309).

chambard [ʃɑ̃bar] *nm* (a) *(remue-ménage)* upheaval⁰ (b) *(vacarme)* racket, din; **faire du chambard** to make a racket *or* a din

chambardement [ʃɑ̃bardəmɑ̃] *nm* upheaval⁰

chambarder [ʃɑ̃barde] *vt* **tout chambarder** *(mettre en désordre, bouleverser)* to turn everything upside-down

chambrer [ʃɑ̃bre] *vt (taquiner)* **chambrer qn** to make fun of sb⁰, *Br* to wind sb up, to take the mickey out of sb, *Am* to goof with sb

chameau, -x [ʃamo] **1** *adj* **être chameau** *(homme)* to be a *Br* swine *or Am* stinker; *(femme)* to be a witch *or Br* a cow

2 *nm (homme) Br* swine, *Am* stinker; *(femme)* witch, *Br* cow

champ' [ʃɑ̃p] *nm (abbr* **champagne)** bubbly, *Br* champers

champignon [ʃɑ̃piɲɔ̃] *nm* **appuyer sur le champignon** *(accélérer) Br* to put one's foot down, *Am* to step on the gas

champion, -onne [ʃɑ̃pjɔ̃, -ɔn] *adj* great, *Br* fab, *Am* aces

Champs [ʃɑ̃] *npr* **les Champs** the Champs-Elysées⁰

chancre [ʃɑ̃kr] *nm* **bouffer comme un chancre** to stuff oneself *or* one's face, to pig out

chandelle [ʃɑ̃dɛl] *nf* (a) *(morve)* drip of snot (b) **tenir la chandelle** *(être de trop) Br* to play gooseberry, *Am* to be the fifth wheel ▸ *see also* **trente-six**

chanson [ʃɑ̃sɔ̃] *nf* **c'est toujours la même chanson** it's always the same old story; **ça va, je connais la chanson!** I've heard it all before!

chapeau [ʃapo] **1** *nm* **travailler du chapeau** to have a screw loose, to be off one's rocker, to be not all there

2 *exclam* good for you/him/*etc*!

char [ʃar] *nm* (**a**) **arrête ton char (Ben Hur)!** come off it!, yeah right! (**b**) *Can (voiture)* car□, wheels, *Br* motor; **ça vaut pas les chars** it's not up to much

charas [ʃaras] *nm* cannabis resin□, black

charbon [ʃarbɔ̃] *nm* **aller au charbon** *(à son travail)* to go to work□

charcler [ʃarkle] *vt* to kill□, to waste, *Br* to do in, *Am* to eighty-six; **ça va charcler!** there's going to be trouble!, *Br* it's going to kick off!

charclo [ʃarklo] *nmf (verlan* **clochard**) tramp, *Br* dosser, *Am* hobo, bum

charcuter [ʃarkyte] *vt (sujet: chirurgien)* to butcher, to hack up

chargé, -e [ʃarʒe] *adj (ivre, drogué)* loaded, wrecked, wasted

charger [ʃarʒe] **se charger** *vpr (s'enivrer)* to get wrecked *or* wasted *or Br* legless *or* pissed; *(se droguer)* to get high *or* wasted

charlot [ʃarlo] *nm (personne qui manque de sérieux)* clown

charogne [!] [ʃarɔɲ] *nf (homme méprisable)* bastard; *(femme méprisable)* bitch

charre [ʃar] = **char**

charrette [ʃaret] **1** *adj inv (en retard)* **être charrette** to be working against the clock

2 *nf* (**a**) *(voiture)* car□, wheels, *Br* motor (**b**) *Suisse* **cette charrette de Paul!** that *Br* blasted *or Am* darn Paul!

3 *exclam Suisse* blast!, *Am* shoot!

charrier [ʃarje] **1** *vt (se moquer de)* **charrier qn** to make fun of sb□, *Br*

to take the mickey out of sb, to wind sb up, *Am* to goof with sb; **il s'est fait charrier** he got made fun of□, *Br* he got the mickey taken out of him

2 *vi* **charrier (dans les bégonias)** *(exagérer)* to go too far; **faut pas charrier!** come off it!, gimme a break!

châsses [ʃas] *nmpl (yeux)* eyes□, peepers

châssis [ʃasi] *nm (silhouette)* chassis, bod; **mate un peu le châssis!** check out the chassis *or* bod on that!

chat [ʃa] *nm* **il n'y avait pas un chat** there wasn't a soul ▸ *see also* **pipi**

châtaigne [ʃatɛɲ] *nf* (**a**) *(coup)* clout, thump; **mettre une châtaigne à qn** to clout *or* thump sb (**b**) *(bagarre)* **il va y avoir de la châtaigne** there's going to be a *Br* punch-up *or Am* fist fight, *Br* it's going to kick off (**c**) *(décharge électrique)* **(se) prendre une châtaigne** to get a shock

châtaigner [ʃatɛɲe] **1** *vt* to clout, to thump; **se faire châtaigner** to get clouted *or* thumped

2 **se châtaigner** *vpr* to trade punches

Château [ʃato] *nm* **le Château** the Élysée Palace□ *(official residence of the French President)*

Château-Lapompe [ʃatolapɔ̃p] *nm Hum* **du Château-Lapompe** water□

ⓘ This humorous expression, imitating a typical name for French wine, is used to mean water when served or ordered instead of wine with a meal.

chatte [!!] [ʃat] *nf (sexe de la femme)* pussy, snatch, *Br* fanny; **avoir de la chatte** to be fucking lucky *or Br* jammy

---

Le symbole □ indique que la traduction n'est pas argotique.

chaud, -e [ʃo, ʃod] **1** *adj* **(a)** *(sexuelle-ment)* hot; **être (un) chaud lapin** to be permanently horny; **être chaud de la pince [!]** to be a horny bastard **(b)** *(difficile)* tricky, tough; **on a intérêt à se magner, ça va être chaud pour avoir notre correspondance!** we'd better get a move on, we're going to have a tough time making our connection **(c)** *Can (ivre)* wasted, *Br* pissed

2 *nm* **on a eu chaud (aux fesses)!** we had a narrow escape!

3 [!!] *nf* horny bitch, nympho; **je me suis toujours demandé pourquoi les Angliches ils s'imaginent que toutes les Françaises sont des chaudes** I've always wondered why the Brits seem to think all French girls are total nymphos *or Br* gagging for it ▸ *see also* **eau**

chaudasse [!!] [ʃodas] *nf* horny bitch, nympho

chaude-pisse [!] [ʃodpis] *nf* **la chaude-pisse** the clap

chauffer [ʃofe] *v imp* **ça va chauffer!** there's going to be trouble!, *Br* it's going to kick off!

chausson, -onne [ʃosɔ̃, -ɔn] *adj Can* dimwit, *Am* bozo

chaussure [ʃosyr] *nf* **avoir mis ses chaussures à bascule** *(être ivre)* to be staggering all over the place

chauve [ʃov] *nm Hum* **le chauve à col roulé** one-eyed trouser snake

cheap [tʃip] *adj (peu cher)* cheap□; *(de mauvaise qualité, de mauvais goût)* tacky, cheap and nasty

chébran [ʃebrã] *adj (verlan branché)* hip, trendy

chef [ʃɛf] *nm* **(a)** *(terme d'adresse)* pal, *Br* mate, *Am* buddy **(b)** **se débrouiller comme un chef** to do really well□

chefaillon [ʃefajɔ̃] *nm* little Hitler

chela [ʃəla] *vt (verlan lâche)* **chela oim!** leave me alone!, get off my back *or* case!

chelou [ʃəlu] *adj (verlan louche)* shady, seedy, *Br* dodgy

chèque [ʃɛk] *nm* **chèque en bois** rubber *Br* cheque *or Am* check

chercher [ʃɛrʃe] *vt (provoquer)* to pick a fight with; **tu me cherches, là?** do you want a fight?; **si tu me cherches, tu vas me trouver!** if you're looking for trouble, you've come to the right place!, if you're looking for a fight, you'll get one! ▸ *see also* **crosses, midi, pou**

chérot [ʃero] *adj inv* pricey

chetron [ʃətrɔ̃] *nf (verlan tronche)* face□, mug

cheval, -aux [ʃəval, -o] *nm* **c'est pas le mauvais cheval** he's a nice enough guy

cheveu, -x [ʃəvø] *nm* **se faire des cheveux (blancs)** to worry oneself sick, to give oneself grey hairs; **venir** *ou* **arriver comme un cheveu sur la soupe** to come at the wrong time; **sa question est tombée comme un cheveu sur la soupe** his question couldn't have come at a worse time

cheville [ʃəvij] *nf* **avoir les chevilles qui enflent** to get big-headed, to get too big for one's *Br* boots *or Am* britches

chèvre [ʃɛvr] *nf* **rendre qn chèvre** to drive sb nuts *or* crazy *or* round the bend; **devenir chèvre** to go nuts *or* crazy *or* round the bend

chevrer [ʃəvre] *vi Suisse* **faire chevrer qn** to drive sb up the wall *or* round the bend

chez [ʃe] *prep* **côté humour, ce film, c'est vraiment lourd de**

chez lourd the humour in this film is SO unsubtle; **son nouveau petit copain, c'est le style blaireau de chez blaireau** her new boyfriend is a complete and utter jerk; **il est nul ton lecteur de CD, le son est carrément pourri de chez pourri!** your CD player's useless, the sound's as crap as you can get!

ⓘ This very generative expression imitates the wording used in French perfume advertisements, which give the name of the perfume followed by the name of the perfume house, for example "Coco, de chez Chanel".

chiadé, -e [ʃjade] *adj* elaborate◻

chiader [ʃjade] *vt* to take care over◻; **ce coup-ci j'ai vraiment chiadé ma dissert, j'ai pas envie de me choper une bulle** this time I took loads of care over my essay, I don't want to get a zero *Br* mark *or Am* grade for it

chialer [ʃjale] *vi* (a) *(pleurer)* to blubber, to snivel (b) *(se plaindre)* to whinge

chiâler [ʃjɑle] *vi Can* to whinge

chiant, -e [!] [ʃjɑ̃, -ɑ̃t] *adj* (a) *(monotone) Br* bloody *or Am* goddamn boring; **chiant comme la pluie** as boring as hell, *Br* piss-boring (b) *(agaçant)* **être chiant** *Br* to be a bloody nuisance, to be a pain in the *Br* arse *or Am* ass

chiard [!] [ʃjar] *nm* brat

chiasse [!!] [ʃjas] *nf* (a) *(diarrhée)* **la chiasse** the runs, the shits, the trots; **foutre la chiasse à qn** *(lui faire peur)* to scare sb shitless (b) *(ennui)* **quelle chiasse!** what a fucking pain (in the *Br* arse *or Am* ass)!

chiatique [!!!] [ʃjatik] *adj* **être chia-**

tique to be a pain in the *Br* arse *or Am* ass

chibre [!] [ʃibr] *nm* dick, *Br* knob, *Am* schlong

chicha [ʃiʃa] *nm Cités (verlan* **haschich**) hash, dope, *Br* blow

chichis [ʃiʃi] *nmpl* **faire des chichis** *(faire des simagrées)* to put on airs; *(faire des complications)* to make a fuss; **un dîner sans chichis** an informal dinner◻

chichiteux, -euse [ʃiʃitø, -øz] *adj* affected

chichon [ʃiʃɔ̃] *nm Cités* hash, dope, *Br* blow

chicos [ʃikos] *adj* classy, smart

chié, -e [!] [ʃje] *adj* (a) *(formidable)* shit-hot, *Am* awesome (b) *(qui exagère)* **il est chié, lui!** he's got a *Br* bloody *or Am* goddamn nerve!

chiée [!] [ʃje] *nf* **(toute) une chiée de** a (whole) shitload of

chie-en-culotte [!] [ʃiɑ̃kylɔt] *nm inv Can* coward◻, wimp, wuss

chien, chienne [ʃjɛ̃, ʃjɛn] **1** *adj (méchant)* **être chien avec qn** to be rotten to sb

2 *nm,f* **avoir un mal de chien à faire qch** to have a hell of a job doing sth; **c'est pas fait pour les chiens** it's there for a reason; **les paillassons c'est pas fait pour les chiens!** the doormat's not there for decoration!; **chienne de vie!** what a life!; *Can* **avoir la chienne** *(avoir peur)* to be scared stiff, *Br* to be bricking it; *(être paresseux)* to be bone idle ▸ *see also* **nom**

chienlit [ʃjɑ̃li] *nf (désordre)* shambles, muddle; **c'est la chienlit** what a complete shambles *or* muddle

ⓘ This expression was popularized by French president Charles De

Gaulle in 1968, when he comment-
ed on the rioting and unrest which
marked a turning point in France's
social history.

---

chier [!!] [ʃje] **1** *vt* **tu vas pas nous
chier une pendule!** don't make
such a fuss◻ *or Br* a bloody song and
dance about it!

2 *vi* (**a**) *(déféquer)* to shit, *to Br* have
or Am take a shit *or* a crap *or* a dump
(**b**) **chier dans la colle** to go too
far, *Br* to take the piss; **chier dans
son froc** *(avoir peur)* to shit oneself, to be shit-scared; **à chier** *(très
mauvais)* fucking awful; **y a pas à
chier** there are no two fucking ways
about it; **en chier (pour faire qch)**
to have a hell of a time (doing sth);
ça va chier (des bulles)! the shit's
going to hit the fan!, all hell's going
to break loose!; **va chier!** fuck off!;
faire chier qn *(mettre en colère) Br*
to piss sb off, to get on sb's tits, *Am*
to break sb's balls; *(ennuyer)* to bore
sb shitless; **se faire chier** *(s'ennuyer)*
to be bored shitless; **se faire chier à
faire qch** *(se donner du mal)* to bust
a gut *or Am* one's ass doing sth; **envoyer chier qn** to tell sb where to
get off, *Br* to tell sb to piss off ▸ *see
also* **botte, nul, rat, tortiller**

chierie [!] [ʃiri] *nf* **quelle chierie!**
Br what a bloody pain!, what a pain
in the *Br* arse *or Am* ass!

chieur, -euse [!] [ʃjœr, -øz] *nm,f*
pain in the *Br* arse *or Am* ass

chignon [ʃiɲɔ̃] *nm Can (tête)* head◻,
nut

chinetoc, chinetoque [ʃintɔk] *nmf*
Offensive Chink, Chinky

chinois [ʃinwa] *nm* **se polir le chinois** [!] to beat one's meat, to bang
or Br bash the bishop

chiotte [!] [ʃjɔt] *nf* (**a**) *(voiture)* car◻,

wheels, *Br* motor; *(moto)* bike, *Am*
hog; *(cyclomoteur)* (motor) scooter◻,
moped◻ (**b**) *(ennui)* **quelle chiotte!**
what a pain in the *Br* arse *or Am* ass!
(**c**) **chiottes** *(W-C) Br* bog, *Am* john;
il a un goût de chiottes he's got
shit taste; **aux chiottes, l'arbitre!**
Br ≃ the ref's a wanker!, *Am* ≃ kill
the umpire!

chiper [ʃipe] *vt* **chiper qch à qn** to
pinch *or Br* nick sth from sb

chipolata [!] [ʃipɔlata] *nf (pénis)*
sausage, *Br* pork sword, *Am* salami

chique [ʃik] *nf* **avoir la chique**
(mal aux dents) to have a swollen
cheek◻ *(because of toothache)*; **ça
m'a coupé la chique** *(surpris)* I was
speechless *or Br* gobsmacked; **mou
comme une chique** spineless, *Br*
wet; **tirer sa chique** [!!] to get laid,
Br to have a shag ▸ *see also* **jus**

chiqué [ʃike] *nm* **c'est du chiqué**
it's all put on *or* pretend; **il s'est
pas vraiment fait mal, c'est du
chiqué!** he hasn't really hurt himself,
he's just pretending!

chlass, chlasse, chlâsse [ʃlɑs] =
schlass²

chleu, chleuh [ʃlø] *nm Offensive*
Kraut

ⓘ Depending on the context and
the tone of voice used, this term may
be either offensive or affectionately
humorous. It is nonetheless inadvisable to use it unless one is quite sure
of the reaction it will receive.

chlinguer [ʃlɛ̃ge] *vi* to stink, *Br* to
pong, to hum

chnoc, chnoque [ʃnɔk] = **schnock**

chnouf, chnouffe [ʃnuf] *nf (héroïne)*
junk, horse; *(cocaïne)* snow, charlie,
coke

The symbol **[!]** denotes a very familiar term, **[!!]** a vulgar one.

chochotte [ʃoʃɔt] *nf (personne maniérée)* wimp, wuss; **fais pas ta chochotte** stop mincing *or Br* poncing about!

chocolat [ʃokola] *adj inv* **on est chocolat!** *(on a été dupés)* we've been done!; *(dans une situation sans issue)* we're up shit creek ▸ *see also* **turbine**

chocottes [ʃokɔt] *nfpl* **avoir les chocottes** to be scared witless *or* stiff, to have the wind up; **foutre les chocottes à qn** to scare sb witless *or* stiff, to put the wind up sb

choir [ʃwar] *vi* **laisser choir qn** to let sb down□; **tout laisser choir** to pack it all in, *Br* to jack it all in, *Am* to chuck everything

chôm'du, chômedu [ʃomdy] *nm (chômage)* **être au chôm'du** to be out of work□; **pointer au chôm'du** to be *Br* on the dole *or Am* on welfare□

choper [ʃope] *vt* **(a)** *(saisir)* to grab□ **(b)** *(surprendre)* to catch□, to nab; **se faire choper** to get caught□ *or* nabbed **(c)** *(maladie, coup de soleil)* to catch□; **je crois que j'ai encore chopé une saloperie** I think I've caught something nasty again

chopine [ʃopin] *nf* **boire une chopine** to have a drink□

chose [ʃoz] *nf* **être porté sur la chose** to have a one-track mind, *Br* to have sex on the brain

chou, choute [ʃu, ʃut] **1** *adj inv (mignon)* cute
2 *nm,f* **(a)** **rentrer dans le chou à qn** to give sb an earful *or Br* a mouthful **(b)** **mon (petit) chou, ma (petite) choute** darling, sweetie **(c)** **c'est bête comme chou** it's as easy as pie

chouette [ʃwɛt] **1** *adj* great, fan-

tastic, fabulous; *Ironic* **ah t'as l'air chouette, avec cet anneau dans le nez!** you look something else with that nose ring!
2 *nm* **refiler du chouette [!!]** to take it up the *Br* arse *or Am* ass
3 *nf* **une vieille chouette** *(femme)* an old bag *or* witch
4 *exclam* **chouette (alors)!** great!, fantastic!, fabulous!

chouf [ʃuf] *exclam Cités* check it out!

chougner [ʃuɲe] *vi (pleurnicher)* to whine, *Br* to whinge

chouïa [ʃuja] *nm* **un chouïa (de)** a smidgen (of), a touch (of)

ⓘ This word is derived from an Arabic word meaning "a little". It entered the French language at the time of the colonial expansion in North Africa.

chouille [ʃuj] *nf* party□, bash

chouiller [ʃuje] *vi* to party

choune [!!] [ʃun] *nf (sexe de la femme)* pussy, snatch, *Br* fanny; **avoir de la choune** to be fucking lucky *or Br* jammy

chouraver [ʃurave], **chourer** [ʃure] *vt* to pinch, *Br* to nick; **chouraver** *ou* **chourer qch à qn** to pinch *or Br* nick sth from sb

chrono [kʀono] *adv* **faire du 140 km/h chrono** to be clocked at 140 km/h

chtar [ʃtar] *nm* **(a)** *(cachot)* slammer, clink, *Br* nick, *Am* pen **(b)** *(coup)* clout, wallop **(c)** *(policier)* cop

chtarbé, -e [ʃtarbe] *adj* crazy, nuts, off one's rocker

chtouille [!] [ʃtuj] *nf* **la chtouille** the clap

chum [tʃɔm] *nm Can* pal, *Br* mate, *Am* buddy

cibiche [sibiʃ] *nf* gasper, cig

ciboire [!] [sibwar] *exclam Can* shit!

ⓘ Traditionally, French Canadians were deeply Catholic, which explains why several of their most common swearwords are linked to religion: these include "câlice" (derived from "calice", meaning "chalice"), "ciboire", "tabernacle", "hostie" and "criss" (derived from "Christ").

ciboulot [sibulo] *nm* **en avoir dans le ciboulot** to have brains, to have a lot between one's ears; **se creuser le ciboulot** to rack *or Am* cudgel one's brains; **travailler du ciboulot** to to be off one's rocker *or Br* trolley, *Br* to have lost the plot

cigare [sigar] *nm* (**a**) *(tête)* head□, nut (**b**) **avoir le cigare au bord des lèvres [!!]** to be dying for a shit (**c**) **cigare à moustaches [!!]** *(sexe de l'homme)* (one-eyed) trouser snake

cinglé, -e [sɛ̃gle] **1** *adj* crazy, off one's rocker *or Br* head
   2 *nm,f* nutcase, *Br* nutter, head-case, *Am* screwball

cinoche [sinɔʃ] *nm* **aller au cinoche** to go to the *Br* flicks *or* pictures *or Am* movies□; **faire du cinoche** to cause a scene, to make a fuss

cinoque [sinɔk] *adj* crazy, nuts, off one's rocker

cinq [sɛ̃k] *adj inv* **en cinq sec** in no time at all, in two shakes; *Hum* **faire cinq contre un [!]** *(se masturber)* to beat one's meat, *Br* to have a hand shandy

cintré, -e [sɛ̃tre] *adj* cracked, *Br* barmy, *Am* screwy, wacko

cirage [siraʒ] *nm* **être dans le cirage** *(soûl)* to be out of it *or Br* off one's face; *(étourdi)* to be feeling out of it *or* woozy

cirer [sire] *vt* (**a**) **cirer les pompes à qn** to lick sb's boots (**b**) **j'en ai rien à cirer [!]** I don't give a shit *or Br* a toss *or Am* a rat's ass

citron [sitrɔ̃] *nm* (**a**) *(tête)* head□, nut; **se presser** *ou* **se creuser le citron** to rack *or Am* cudgel one's brains (**b**) *Can Joual (voiture)* useless car□, *Am* lemon

citrouille [sitruj] *nf (tête)* head□, nut

clacos [klakos] *nm* Camembert□

clair [klɛr] *exclam* I get the message!, I hear you!

clamser [klamse] *vi* to croak, to kick the bucket, *Br* to snuff it, *Am* to check out

clando [klɑ̃do], **clandos** [klɑ̃dos] *nm* illegal immigrant□

claouis [!] [klawi] *nmpl* balls, nuts, *Br* bollocks

clapet [klapɛ] *nm* **ferme ton clapet!** shut your trap!, put a lid on it!, *Br* belt up!

claque [klak] **1** *nf* **se prendre une claque** *(subir une défaite cuisante)* to get thrashed; **en avoir sa claque (de)** to have had it up to here (with), to have had a bellyful (of)
   2 *nm (maison close)* whorehouse, *Br* knocking shop ▶ *see also* **clique, tête**

claqué, -e [klake] *adj (épuisé)* bushed, *Br* knackered, shattered, *Am* beat

claque-merde [!!] [klakmɛrd] *nm (bouche)* trap, *Br* gob; **tu vas le fermer ton claque-merde, dis? j'essaye d'écouter la radio, bordel!** will you shut the fuck up? I'm trying to listen to the radio, for fuck's sake!

claquer [klake] **1** *vt* (**a**) *(dépenser)* to blow (**b**) **claquer le beignet à qn** to shut sb up

2 *vi* (**a**) *(mourir)* to croak, to kick the bucket, *Br* to snuff it, *Am* to cash in (one's chips) (**b**) **claquer du bec** to be starving *or* ravenous⁰

classe [klɑs] **1** *adj inv* *(élégant)* classy; *(formidable)* class

2 *adv* **s'habiller classe** to be a classy dresser

3 *nf* **la classe!** classy!

classieux, -euse [klɑsjø, -øz] *adj* classy

clean [klin] **1** *adj inv* clean-cut⁰

2 *adv* **s'habiller clean** to dress in a clean-cut way⁰

clébard [klebar], **clebs** [klɛps] *nm* mutt

clicheton [kliʃtɔ̃] *nm* *(cliché)* cliché⁰; **l'histoire est d'une banalité affligeante; tous les clichetons sont au rendez-vous** the story is as banal as can be and completely cliché-ridden

clim [klim] *nf* (*abbr* **climatisation**) air con

clique [klik] *nf* (**a**) *(bande)* gang, crowd (**b**) **prendre ses cliques et ses claques** to pack one's bags and go

clit [!!] [klit], **clito** [!!] [klito] *nm* clit

cloche [klɔʃ] **1** *adj* daft, thick, *Am* dumb

2 *nf* (**a**) *(imbécile)* jerk, moron, *Br* prat (**b**) **être de la cloche** to be a tramp *or Am* hobo (**c**) **se taper la cloche** to feed one's face, *Br* to have a slap-up meal ▶ *see also* **sonner**

clocher [klɔʃe] *vi* **il y a quelque chose qui cloche** there's something wrong somewhere; **qu'est-ce qui cloche?** what's up?

clodo [klodo] *nmf* tramp, *Am* hobo

clope [klɔp] *nf* smoke, *Br* fag, ciggy

cloper [klɔpe] *vi* to smoke⁰

clopinettes [klɔpinɛt] *nfpl* **des clopinettes** *(presque rien)* peanuts; **des clopinettes!** no way!, no chance!

cloque [klɔk] *nf* **être en cloque** *Br* to be up the duff *or* spout, to be in the club, *Am* to be knocked up

clou [klu] *nm* (**a**) **ça ne vaut pas un clou** it's not worth a *Br* penny *or Am* red cent; *Can* **cogner des clous** to keep nodding off (**b**) **des clous!** no way!, no chance! (**c**) *(bicyclette)* bike

coaltar [kɔltar] *nm* **être dans le coaltar** *(étourdi)* to be in a daze, to be feeling out of it *or* spaced out; **j'ai pas dormi de la nuit, je suis complètement dans le coaltar** I didn't sleep a wink all night, I'm like a complete zombie

cocard [kɔkar] *nm* black eye⁰, shiner

cochonceté [kɔʃɔ̃ste] *nf* (**a**) *(action obscène)* repulsive act⁰; **allez faire vos cochoncetés ailleurs!** go and do that sort of thing somewhere else! (**b**) *(remarque obscène)* obscenity⁰; **dire des cochoncetés** to talk dirty

cochonner [kɔʃɔne] *vt* *(salir)* to dirty⁰, to make a mess of⁰

coco [koko] **1** *nm* (**a**) *(personne)* **un drôle de** *ou* **un sacré coco** a weirdo, an oddball; **toi mon coco, je t'ai à l'œil!** just watch it, pal *or Br* mate *or Am* buddy! (**b**) *(estomac)* **bien se remplir le coco** to stuff oneself *or* one's face, to feed one's face

2 *nmf* (*abbr* **communiste**) commie

3 *nf* *(cocaïne)* coke, snow ▶ *see also* **noix**

cocoter [kɔkɔte] *vi* to stink, *Br* to pong, to hum

cocotte [kɔkɔt] *nf* **ma cocotte** darling, honey

cocotter [kɔkɔte] = **cocoter**

cocu, -e [kɔky] **1** *adj* **je suis cocu** my wife's cheating on me; **un mari cocu** a man whose wife is cheating on him; **faire qn cocu** to cheat on sb
   2 *nm* deceived husband□; **avoir une chance** *ou* **veine de cocu** to have the luck of the devil

cocufier [kɔkyfje] *vt* to cheat on

coffrer [kɔfre] *vt* to put inside *or* away *or* behind bars; **se faire coffrer** to get put inside *or* away *or* behind bars

cogne [kɔɲ] **1** *nm* cop, *Br* plod, *Am* flatfoot
   2 *nf* (*bagarre*) *Br* punch-up, *Am* fist fight; **il va y avoir de la cogne!** there's going to be trouble *or Br* a punch-up *or Am* a fist fight!

cogner [kɔɲe] **1** *vt* to knock about, to beat (up)
   2 *vi* (a) (*puer*) to stink (to high heaven), *Br* to pong, to hum (b) **ça cogne** (*le soleil chauffe*) it's scorching *or Br* roasting
   3 se cogner *vpr* (a) **se cogner qn/qch** (*corvée*) to get stuck *or Br* lumbered *or* landed with sb/sth (b) **se cogner qn** [!!] (*posséder*) to screw sb, *Br* to have it off with *or* shag sb, *Am* to ball sb

coincer [kwɛ̃se] **1** *vt* (*attraper*) to nab, to collar; **se faire coincer** to get nabbed *or* collared
   2 *vi* (*puer*) to stink, *Br* to pong, to hum ▸ *see also* **bulle**

coinços [kwɛ̃sos] *adj* uptight

coing [kwɛ̃] *nm* **bourré comme un coing** trashed, wasted, plastered, *Br* off one's face, legless

coke [kɔk] *nf* (*cocaïne*) coke

coké [kɔke] *adj* (*drogué à la cocaïne*) coked-up

colbac [kɔlbak] *nm* **attraper qn par le colbac** to grab sb by the scruff of the neck

colis [kɔli] *nm* (*fille*) chick, *Br* bird; **un joli petit colis** a knockout, a babe, *Br* a bit of all right

colle [kɔl] *nf* **être à la colle** to be shacked up together ▸ *see also* **chier, pot**

collé, -e [kɔle] *adj Can* **en avoir de collé** to be loaded

coller [kɔle] **1** *vt* (a) (*placer*) to stick, to dump; **il a collé tous les cartons dans un coin** he stuck *or* dumped all the cardboard boxes in a corner (b) (*administrer*) **coller qch à qn** (*claque, baiser, rhume*) to give sb sth□; (*amende*) to slap sth on sb; **il m'a collé une de ces beignes!** he gave me a real wallop!; **il m'a collé les gosses pour le week-end** he dumped the kids on me for the weekend; **son bonhomme lui a encore collé un marmot** her old man's knocked her up again (c) (*retenir à l'école*) (*élève*) to keep in (d) (*suivre*) **coller qn** to stick to sb like glue, to follow sb around
   2 *vi* (a) **ça colle!** OK!, cool!; **ça ne colle pas très bien entre eux** they don't really see eye to eye (b) **il arrête pas de me coller au cul** [!] he keeps following me around like a lost dog; (*en voiture*) *Br* he keeps driving up my arse, *Am* he keeps tailgating me
   3 s'y coller *vpr* **c'est encore moi qui m'y colle!** I'm stuck *or Br* lumbered with it again!; **c'est toi qui t'y colles** it's your turn ▸ *see also* **pain**

collimateur [kɔlimatœr] *nm* **avoir**

qn dans le collimateur to keep one's eye on sb, to keep tabs on sb

colo [kɔlo] nf (abbr **colonie de vacances**) Br (children's) holiday camp□, Am summer camp□

coloc [kɔlɔk] nmf (abbr **colocataire**) Br (en appartement) flatmate□; (dans une maison) housemate□, Am roommate□, roomie

colon [kɔlɔ̃] nm (**a**) (abbr **colonel**) colonel□ (**b**) **ben mon colon!** goodness me!, Br blimey!, Am gee (whiz)! (**c**) Can (rustre) yokel, peasant, Am hick

colonne [kɔlɔn] nf **se taper (sur) la colonne, s'astiquer la colonne**

[!!] to jerk off, beat one's meat

coltiner [kɔltine] **se coltiner** vpr **se coltiner qn/qch** to get stuck or Br lumbered or landed with sb/sth

comac [kɔmak] adj ginormous, humongous, massive

comater [kɔmate] vi (ne rien faire) to veg (out); **j'ai passé le week-end à comater devant la télé** I spent the weekend vegging (out) in front of the TV or Br telly

comme aç [kɔmas] adv Cités (verlan **comme ça**) like that□; **oh l'autre! t'es con ou quoi, faut pas faire comme aç!** are you completely stupid or what, you don't do it like that!

Spotlight on:

La colère

In French slang, quite a few expressions meaning "to get angry" are related to mechanical failure and are formed with the verb **péter** (in the sense of "to break", "to snap"). These expressions include **péter les plombs** (literally "to blow a fuse"), **péter une durite** (literally "to burst a pipe") and **péter un câble** (which translates literally as "to snap a cable"). Other popular expressions include **piquer une colère**, **piquer une crise** (a phrase similar to the English expression "to have a fit"), **se mettre en boule** (an expression which suggests a hedgehog raising its spines) and **se mettre en pétard** (the image here being of someone exploding with anger).When you are angry you can be said to be **furax**, **furibard**, **fumasse** or **en pétard** and if you happen to be in Quebec, you'll be **en câlice**. If you need to let off some steam you can **pousser un coup de gueule** or **pousser une gueulante** ("to kick up a fuss"). To tell somebody off is **passer un savon à quelqu'un** or **souffler dans les bronches à quelqu'un** (the image being of someone yelling so much that it causes a rush of air into the other person's lungs). If you are only in a bad mood, then you can be said to be **de mauvais poil**, **mal luné**, **ne pas à prendre avec des pincettes**, or **mal vissé** (literally "not properly screwed on").

comme d'hab [kɔmdab] *adv* (*abbr* **comme d'habitude**) as per (usual)

commission [kɔmisjɔ̃] *nf* **faire la petite/grosse commission** to do a number one/number two

compagnie [kɔ̃paɲi] *nf* **salut, la compagnie!** hi, guys *or* folks!; **ces mecs, c'est racaille et compagnie** these guys are a bunch of scumbags

compète [kɔ̃pɛt] *nf* (*abbr* **compétition**) competition□ (*in sport*); **faire de la compète** to enter competitions

compil' [kɔ̃pil] *nf* (*abbr* **compilation**) compilation□

comprenette [kɔ̃prənɛt] *nf* **avoir la comprenette un peu dure, être lent à la comprenette** to be a bit slow on the uptake

comprenure [kɔ̃prənyr] *nf Belg & Can* **être dur de comprenure** to be slow (on the uptake)

compte [kɔ̃t] *nm* **avoir son compte** (*être condamné*) to have had it, to be done for; (*être ivre*) to have had enough (to drink)□; **ça va, j'ai eu mon compte** (*j'en ai assez*) that's enough, I've had it; **régler son compte à qn** (*punir sévèrement*) to give sb what for, to give sb what's coming to him/her; (*tuer*) to bump sb off, *Br* to do sb in, *Am* to eighty-six sb; **son compte est bon** he's had it, *Br* he's for it

compteur [kɔ̃tœr] *nm* (**a**) **elle a pas mal de kilomètres au compteur** (*elle n'est plus très jeune*) she's no spring chicken (**b**) **relever les compteurs** (*maquereau*) to collect the girls' takings□

con, conne [kɔ̃, kɔn] **1** [!] *adj* (**a**) (*stupide*) *Br* bloody *or Am* goddamn stupid; **être con comme la lune** *ou* **comme un balai** *Br* to be thick (as two short planks), to be as daft as

a brush, *Am* to have rocks in one's head; **t'es con, tu devrais venir avec nous, on va bien se marrer!** don't be stupid, come with us, it'll be a laugh!
(**b**) (*regrettable*) **c'est con, je ne vais pas pouvoir me libérer** it's a bummer, but I'm not going to be able to get away
(**c**) **à la con** (*médiocre*) crappy, lousy, *Br* poxy

2 [!] *nm,f* (**a**) (*imbécile*) *Br* arsehole, twat, *Am* asshole; **faire le con** (*faire le clown*) *Br* to arse around, to piss about, *Am* to screw around; **faire le con, jouer au con** (*faire semblant de ne pas comprendre*) to act dumb; **fais pas le con, ça va s'arranger** don't do anything stupid, it'll sort itself out; **fais pas le con, viens avec nous, on va bien se marrer!** don't be stupid, come with us, it'll be a laugh!; **se retrouver comme un con** to be left feeling a complete *Br* arsehole *or Am* asshole; **si les cons volaient, tu serais chef d'escadrille** if being an *Br* arsehole *or Am* asshole was an Olympic event, you'd be a gold medallist (**b**) (*homme déplaisant*) bastard; (*femme déplaisante*) bitch

3 [!!] *nm* (*sexe de la femme*) cunt
▸ *see also* **air, gueule, piège, tête**

conard, -asse [kɔnar, -as] = **connard**

conclure [kɔ̃klyr] *vi* (*en matière amoureuse*) to get a result, to close the deal

concombre [kɔ̃kɔ̃br] *nm Can Br* pillock, *Am* bonehead

condé [kɔ̃de] *nm* (*policier*) cop

conduite [kɔ̃dɥit] *nf* **s'acheter une conduite** to turn over a new leaf, to mend one's ways; (*criminel*) to go straight

confiote [kɔ̃fjɔt] *nf* (*confiture*) jam□

congélo [kɔ̃ʒelo] nm (abbr **congéla-teur**) freezer[□]

connard, -asse [!] [kɔnar, -as] nm,f **(a)** (homme stupide) stupid bastard, prick, Br arsehole, Am asshole; (femme stupide) stupid bitch, Br arsehole, Am asshole **(b)** (homme déplaisant) bastard; (femme déplaisante) bitch

connement [!] [kɔnmã] adv stupidly[□]; **il s'est fait connement piquer sa caisse** the stupid idiot got his car pinched; **et connement j'ai accepté** and like the idiot that I am, I said yes

connerie [!] [kɔnri] nf **(a)** (acte stupide) **faire une connerie** to do a Br bloody or Am goddamn stupid thing; **j'ai peur qu'il fasse une connerie** (un acte inconsidéré) I'm scared he's going to do something Br bloody or Am goddamn stupid **(b)** (remarque stupide) **dire** ou **raconter des conneries** to talk crap or bullshit **(c)** (caractère stupide) stupidity[□]; **il est d'une connerie!** he's so Br bloody or Am goddamn stupid!

conso [kɔ̃so] nf (abbr **consommation**) drink[□] (in bar, club)

constipé, -e [kɔ̃stipe] adj (gêné) uptight; (sourire) strained[□]; **ce qu'il peut m'agacer avec son air constipé, ce mec-là!** he really annoys me, the way he's so uptight!

contrat [kɔ̃tra] nm (d'un tueur) contract

contredanse [kɔ̃trədãs] nf (document) ticket; (amende) fine[□]

contrefiche [kɔ̃trəfiʃ], **contreficher** [kɔ̃trəfiʃe] **se contrefiche** ou **contreficher de** vpr not to give a damn or a hoot or Br a stuff about

contrefoutre [kɔ̃trəfutr] **se contrefoutre de** vpr not to give a damn or

a hoot or Br a stuff about

converse [kɔ̃vɛrs] nf (abbr **conversation**) conversation[□], chat[□]; **faire la converse à qn** to chat to sb

cool [kul] **1** adj inv **(a)** (détendu) laid-back, cool; **cool, mon vieux!** chill (out)!, take it easy! **(b)** (bien, beau) cool
  2 exclam cool!

coolitude [kulityd] nf coolness, hipness

coolos [kulos] adj inv **(a)** (détendu) laid-back, cool **(b)** (bien) cool

coopé [kɔpe] nf (abbr **coopération**) (aide aux PVD) aid to developing countries[□]; (service militaire) = voluntary work overseas carried out as an alternative to national service

copion [kɔpjɔ̃] nm Belg (antisèche) Br crib, Am cheat sheet

coq-l'œil [kɔklœj] **1** adj inv cross-eyed[□]
  2 nmf inv cross-eyed person[□]

coquard [kɔkar] = **cocard**

corbeau, -x [kɔrbo] nm **(a)** (auteur de lettres anonymes) poison-pen letter writer[□]; (auteur de coups de téléphone anonymes) anonymous caller[□] **(b)** (personne) Goth

---

ⓘ Sense (a) of the word comes from a 1943 film by Henri-Georges Clouzot entitled "Le Corbeau", in which the inhabitants of a small town start getting suspicious of one another when many of them start receiving poison-pen letters from someone who signs them "le corbeau".

---

corde [kɔrd] nf **(a)** **se passer la corde au cou** to get spliced or hitched **(b)** **être dans les cordes de qn** to be (right) up sb's street **(c)**

il pleut *ou* **tombe des cordes** it's raining cats and dogs, *Br* it's bucketing down, it's chucking it down (**d**) **faire des cordes** *(être très constipé)* to be all bunged up (**e**) *Can* **coucher sur la corde à linge** to have a wild night of it

corneille [!] [kɔrnɛj] *nf Can (religieuse)* nun□, penguin

cornes [kɔrn] *nfpl* **faire porter des cornes à qn** *(tromper)* to cheat on sb

cornet [kɔrnɛ] *nm (estomac)* **qu'est-ce qu'on s'est mis dans le cornet!** we totally stuffed ourselves *or* our faces!, we really pigged out!

corniaud [kɔrnjo] *nm* moron, *Br* twit, *Am* fathead

cornichon [kɔrniʃɔ̃] *nm (niais) Br* plonker, pillock, *Am* lamebrain, meathead

corrida [kɔrida] *nf (agitation)* hassle, *Br* carry-on; **quelle corrida hier soir, pour rentrer chez moi!** what a hassle *or Br* carry-on I had getting home last night!

cossard, -e [kɔsar, -ard] **1** *adj* lazy□
2 *nm,f* lazybones

cossin [kɔsɛ̃] *nm Can* thingy, whatsit

costard [kɔstar] *nm* suit□ *(clothing)*
▶ *see also* **tailler**

costard-cravate [kɔstarkravat] *nm (personne)* suit

costaud, -e [kɔsto, -od] **1** *adj* (**a**) *(personne)* big□, hefty; *(objet)* sturdy□ (**b**) *(café, alcool)* strong□
2 *nm* big guy

costume-cravate [kɔstymkravat] *nm (personne)* suit; **tous ces sales hippies qui se sont transformés en costumes-cravates** all these bloody hippies who sold

out and became suits

cote [kɔt] *nf* **avoir la cote (avec qn)** to be popular (with sb)□; **j'ai plus la cote avec le patron depuis notre engueulade de l'autre jour** I haven't been in the boss's good books since that row we had the other day

côte [kot] *nf* (**a**) **avoir les côtes en long** to be bone idle (**b**) **se tenir les côtes** to be in stitches, to kill oneself (laughing), to split one's sides

coton [kɔtɔ̃] **1** *adj inv* tough, tricky
2 *nm* **filer un mauvais coton** to be in a bad way

couche [kuʃ] *nf* (**a**) **en tenir une couche** to have nothing between one's ears, *Br* to be as thick as two short planks, *Am* to have rocks in one's head (**b**) **en remettre une couche** to lay it on thick

coucheries [kuʃri] *nfpl* sleeping around, casual sex□

couchette [kuʃɛt] *nf Can* **être fort sur la couchette** to sleep around

coucou [kuku] *nm (avion)* **un vieux coucou** an old crate

couenne [kwan] *nf* skin□ ▶ *see also* **sucer**

couillave [kujav], **couillaver** [kujave] *vt Cités* to screw, to shaft *(swindle)*

couille [!!] [kuj] *nf* (**a**) *(testicule)* ball, nut, *Br* bollock; **avoir des couilles (au cul)** to have (a lot of) balls; **baiser à couilles rabattues** to fuck like rabbits; **casser les couilles à qn** *Br* to get on sb's tits, *Am* to break sb's balls; **se faire des couilles en or** to make a bundle *or Br* a packet; **partir en couille** to go down the tubes *or Br* pan; **c'est de la couille (en barre)** it's a load of balls *or Br* bollocks; **mes couilles!** my *Br* arse *or*

Spotlight on:

Le corps

There are names for virtually every body part in French slang, and not only for private parts (for which readers are invited to consult the panel on "sexe" on p.168). At the top is your **caboche**, **cafetière**, **calebasse** or **caillou** (head), adorned by your **tifs** or **douilles** (hair) – unless of course you have **une casquette en peau de fesse** (ie you are bald; literally the expression means "to be wearing a cap made of buttock skin"). On your **tronche**, **bobine** or **tirelire** (face) are your **châsses**, **mirettes** or **quinquets** (eyes), your **tarin**, **pif** or **blaire** (nose) and your **gueule**, **goulot** or **clapet** (mouth), in which your **crocs**, **quenottes** or **ratiches** (teeth) can be found as well your **bavarde** or **menteuse** (tongue), while ears are known as **esgourdes** or **portugaises**. Further down, women have a pair of **roberts**, **nibards**, **nichons**, **lolos**, **roploplos**... the list goes on. Small breasts are often referred to as **des œufs sur le plat** (fried eggs). The belly is **le bide**, and people with a pot belly are said to be **gras du bide** or to have **de la brioche**, though most men would much prefer to have a **tablette de chocolat** (six-pack). Unsurprisingly, love handles are **poignées d'amour**. Hands may be known as **paluches** or **pognes**. Below all this is your **cul**, **pétard** or **valseur** (bottom), then come **les guibolles**, **les cannes** or **les pattes** (legs); very big thighs are known as **jambonneaux** (literally "knuckles of ham"). Finally, spare a thought for your **panards**, **arpions**, **pinglots** or **pinceaux** (feet), which have to carry all of the above...

Am ass!; **couille molle** wimp, *Br* big girl's blouse (**b**) *(erreur) Br* cock-up, balls-up, *Am* ball-up (**c**) *(ennui)* problem□; **il m'arrive une couille** I'm in deep shit ▸ *see also* **battre, potage**

couillon, -onne [!] [kujɔ̃, -ɔn] **1** *adj* *Br* bloody *or Am* goddamn stupid
2 *nm,f Br* arsehole, twat, tosser, *Am* asshole, dumbass; **faire le couillon** *Br* to arse about, to piss about, *Am* to screw around

couillonnade [!] [kujɔnad] *nf* (**a**) *(discours stupide)* **dire des couil-** **lonnades** to talk crap *or* bull *or Br* bollocks (**b**) *(acte stupide)* **faire des couillonnades** *Br* to cock *or* balls things up, *Am* to ball things up

couillonner [!] [kujɔne] *vt* to screw, to rip off; **se faire couillonner** to get screwed *or* ripped off

coulant, -e [kulɑ̃, -ɑ̃t] **1** *adj (arrangeant)* easy-going
2 *nm (fromage)* = very ripe cheese, particularly Camembert

coule [kul] *nf* **être à la coule** to know the tricks of the trade, to know the ropes, to know what's what

couler [kule] **1** vt (**a**) (discréditer) **couler qn** to bring sb down, to ruin sb (**b**) **se la couler douce** to take things easy

2 vi (entreprise) to go under ▸ see also **bronze**

couleur [kulœr] nf **annoncer la couleur** (déclarer ses intentions) to lay one's cards on the table; (au restaurant, au café) = to say what one is having; **allez, annonce la couleur!** what's it to be, then? ▸ see also **voir**

coup [ku] nm (**a**) (boisson) drink□; **boire un coup** to have a drink□; **un coup de rouge** a glass of red wine□ (**b**) (acte criminel) job, operation; **il m'a fait le coup de la panne** he tried to pull the old "car won't start" routine on me; **coup fourré** dirty trick (**c**) **un bon coup** [**!**] (partenaire sexuel) a good lay or screw or Br shag (**d**) **avoir le coup (pour faire qch)** to have the knack (of doing sth); **être dans le coup** (être au courant) to know what's going on; (être dans la confidence) to be in on it; **mettre qn dans le coup** to fill sb in, to put sb in the picture; **en mettre un coup** to pull out all the stops; **coup dur** setback□; **en deux coups les gros** in a jiffy, in next to no time ▸ see also **tirer**

coupe-choux [kupʃu] nm inv (rasoir) cut-throat razor□

couper [kupe] **1** vt **ça te la coupe, hein?** you weren't expecting that one, were you!, that shut you up, didn't it?

2 vi **couper à qch** (éviter) to get out of sth ▸ see also **chique, sifflet**

courailler [kuraje] vi Can to chase after women

courailleur [kurajœr] nm Can womanizer, skirt-chaser

courante [kurɑ̃t] nf **la courante** the runs, the trots

courber [kurbe] vt Suisse **courber l'école** to skip school, Br to skive or bunk off, Am to play hookey

coureur, -euse [kurœr, -øz] **1** adj (homme) womanizing; (femme) man-eating

2 nm,f (homme volage) womanizer, skirt-chaser; (femme volage) man-eater

courge [kurʒ] nf Br pillock, plonker, Am meathead, bonehead

courir [kurir] **1** vt **tu commences à me courir!** you're starting to bug me or Br do my head in or Am give me a pain!

2 vi **tu peux toujours courir!** not a chance!, no way!; **tu peux toujours courir pour que je te prête ma caisse!** no way am I lending you my car!; **laisse courir!** forget it!, drop it! ▸ see also **galipote, haricot**

court-jus [kurʒy] nm short-circuit□

cousu [kuzy] adj **c'est du cousu main** (facile) it's in the bag, Br it's a dead cert; (très bien fait) it's a work of art ▸ see also **motus**

couv' [kuv] nf (abbr **couverture**) (de magazine) cover□

couvert [kuvɛr] nm **remettre le couvert** (faire quelque chose à nouveau) to do it again□; (refaire l'amour) to have sex again□; **donne-moi deux minutes pour reprendre mon souffle et puis on remet le couvert, c'est promis** just give me a couple of minutes to get my breath back and I'll be up for round two, promise

couvrante [kuvrɑ̃t] nf blanket□, cover□

crac-crac [krakrak] *nm* **faire crac-crac** to have a bit of nooky *or Br* rumpy-pumpy

cracher [kraʃe] **1** *vt (argent)* to fork out, to cough up

2 *vi* **(a)** *(payer)* to fork out, to cough up **(b) cracher dans la soupe** to bite the hand that feeds one; **il crache pas dessus** he never turns up his nose at it, he never says no to it ▸ *see also* **bassinet, gueule, morceau**

crache-thunes [kraʃtyn] *nm inv (distributeur de billets) Br* hole in the wall, *Am* ATM□

crachoir [kraʃwar] *nm* **tenir le crachoir** to go *or* ramble on and on; **tenir le crachoir à qn** to listen to sb go *or* ramble on and on

crack [krak] *nm* **(a)** *(drogue)* crack **(b)** *(personne douée)* whizz

crackeur [krakœr] *nm* crackhead

cracra [krakra], **crade** [krad] *adj* filthy□

crader [krade], **cradosser** [kradose] *vt (salir)* to muck up, to get dirt all over; **enlève tes godasses, je veux pas que tu me cradosses ma moquette** take your shoes off, I don't want you mucking up my carpet

cradingue [kradɛ̃g], **crado** [krado], **cradoque** [kradɔk] *adj* filthy□

cradosser [kradose] = **crader**

craignos [krɛɲos] *adj* **(a)** *(louche)* shady, *Br* dodgy **(b)** *(laid)* hideous **(c)** *(mauvais)* crap, lousy, the pits

craindre [krɛ̃dr] *vi* **(a)** *(être louche)* to be shady *or Br* dodgy **(b)** *(être laid)* to be hideous **(c)** *(être mauvais)* to be crap, to be the pits, to suck, *Am* to blow **(d) ça craint!** it's crap!, it sucks!

cramé, -e [krame] *adj (ivre)* blitzed,

wasted, *Br* off one's face, *Am* stewed (to the gills)

cramer [krame] **1** *vt* **(a)** *(brûler)* to burn□ **(b)** *(repérer)* to spot□, to clock **2** *vi (brûler)* to burn□

cramouille [!!] [kramuj] *nf* pussy, snatch, twat, *Br* fanny

crampe [krɑ̃p] *nf* **tirer sa crampe** [!] *(s'enfuir)* to beat it, *Br* to piss off, to bugger off, *Am* to book it; *(coïter)* to screw, *Br* to have it off, *Am* to bang

crampon [krɑ̃pɔ̃] *nm (personne importune)* leech; **quel crampon, cette nana, impossible de s'en défaire!** that girl's such a leech, you can't get rid of her!

cran [krɑ̃] *nm* **(a)** *(couteau)* **cran (d'arrêt)** *Br* flick knife□, *Am* switchblade□ **(b) être à cran** to be about to crack up, to have reached boiling point

crâner [krɑne] *vi* to swagger, to show off

crâneur, -euse [krɑnœr, -øz] **1** *adj* swaggering; **être crâneur** to be a show-off *or* a poser **2** *nm,f* show-off, poser

crapahuter [krapayte] *vi (marcher)* to schlep *or* traipse about

crapoter [krapɔte] *vi* = to smoke without inhaling

crapoteux, -euse [krapɔtø, -øz] *adj* filthy□

craquant, -e [krakɑ̃, -ɑ̃t] **1** *adj (personne)* gorgeous, hot, *Br* fit **2** *nm Cités (billet de banque) Br* note□, *Am* bill□

craque [krak] *nf* **(a)** *(mensonge)* lie□, fib, *Br* porky *(pie)* **(b)** [!!] *(sexe de la femme)* crack, gash **(c)** *Can* **avoir une craque** to be off one's rocker

craquer [krake] *vi* **(a)** *(nerveusement)*

to crack up (b) *(succomber)* to crack, to give in°; **finalement j'ai craqué** in the end I couldn't resist°; **craquer pour qn/qch** to fall for sb/sth; **il me fait vraiment craquer** I've got the hots for him, *Br* I really fancy him (c) **faire craquer un cours** *(ne pas y assister)* to *Br* bunk off *or Am* skip a class

craquette [!!] [krakɛt] *nf* pussy, twat, gash, *Br* minge

craqueur [krakœr] = **crackeur**

crasher [kraʃe] **se crasher** *vpr (avion, automobiliste, motard)* to crash°

craspec [kraspɛk] *adj* filthy°

crasse [kras] *nf* **faire une crasse à qn** to play a dirty trick on sb, *Br* to do the dirty on sb, *Am* to do sb dirt

cravacher [kravaʃe] *vi* to work like mad

cravate [kravat] *nf* **c'est de la cravate** it's a load of baloney *or* bull ▸ see also **jeter**

crécher [kreʃe] *vi (habiter)* to live°; **il crèche dans une piaule près de la gare** he's got a place near the station

crémerie [krɛmri] *nf* **changer de crémerie** to go somewhere else°, to move on°

crêpage [krepaʒ] *nf* **crêpage de chignon** catfight

crêper [krepe] **se crêper** *vpr* **se crêper le chignon** to have a catfight

crétin, -e [kretɛ̃, -in] **1** *adj* cretinous **2** *nm,f* cretin

creuser [krøze] **se creuser** *vpr (réfléchir)* to rack *or Am* cudgel one's brains ▸ see also **ciboulot, citron**

crevant, -e [krəvɑ̃, -ɑ̃t] *adj* (a) *(épuisant)* exhausting°, *Br* killing, knack-

ering (b) *(hilarant)* hysterical, side-splitting

crevard, -e [krəvar, -ard] *nm,f (glouton)* pig, *Br* gannet, *Am* hog

crève [krɛv] *nf* **la crève** a stinking cold

crevé, -e [krəve] *adj* (a) *(épuisé) Br* knackered, shattered, *Am* beat (b) *(mort)* dead°

crevée [krəve] *nf Suisse* gaffe°, *Br* boob, *Am* boo-boo

crever [krəve] **1** *vt* (a) *(épuiser)* to wear out°, *Br* to knacker (b) *(tuer)* to kill°, to waste, *Br* to do in (c) **crever la dalle** to be starving *or* ravenous (d) **ça crève les yeux** *(c'est évident)* it sticks out a mile; *(c'est visible)* it's staring you in the face; **c'est lui qui a fait le coup, ça crève les yeux** it's him who did it, it's staring you in the face

2 *vi (mourir)* to kick the bucket, to croak, *Br* to snuff it, *Am* to check out; *Suisse (voiture)* to stall°; **crever de faim/de chaleur** *(avoir faim/chaud)* to be starving/boiling; **à crever de rire** hysterical; **c'était à crever de rire** it was hysterical *or* a scream; **je peux crever la gueule ouverte, t'en as rien à faire!** I could die tomorrow for all you care!; **qu'il crève!** he can go to hell!

3 **se crever** *vpr* (a) *(s'épuiser)* to wear oneself out, *Br* to get knackered (b) *(se donner du mal)* **se crever (à faire qch)** to go out of one's way (to do sth); **se crever le cul (à faire qch) [!]** to bust a gut *or Am* one's ass (doing sth)

Crim', Crime [krim] *nf (abbr* **Brigade Criminelle)** **la Crim'** the crime squad°

criminelle [kriminɛl] *adj f* **elle est criminelle** she's hot, she's a babe

crincrin [krɛ̃krɛ̃] *nm* racket, din *(especially loud music)*

crise [kriz] *nf* **la crise (de rire)!** what a scream *or* hoot!

criser [krize] *vi* to lose it, to go ape, *Br* to go off one's head; **il va criser quand il se rendra compte que tu lui as bousillé son ordinateur** he's going to freak out *or* lose it when he realizes you've wrecked his computer

crisse [kris] *Can Joual* **1** *nmf* bastard; **mon petit crisse** *(à un enfant)* you little bugger!; **être en crisse** to be hopping mad
2 *exclam* for Christ's sake!, shit!

ⓘ This word comes from the word "Christ" as pronounced by a speaker of Joual.

ⓘ Traditionally, French Canadians were deeply Catholic, which explains why several of their most common swearwords are linked to religion: these include "câlice" (derived from "calice", meaning "chalice"), "ciboire", "tabernacle", "hostie" and "criss" (derived from "Christ")

croco [krɔko] *nm* (*abbr* **crocodile**) crocodile (skin)□; **un sac en croco** a crocodile handbag□

crocs [kro] *nmpl* (a) *(dents)* teeth□, *Br* gnashers, *Am* choppers (b) **avoir les crocs** *(avoir faim)* to be hungry□

croire [krwar] **1** *vt* **j'te crois!** *(je suis d'accord)* absolutely!, *Br* too right!; *Ironic* yeah right!, *Br* I believe you (thousands wouldn't)!
2 se croire *vpr* **s'y croire** to think a lot of oneself, *Br* to fancy oneself

croquenots [krɔkno] *nmpl* shoes□, clodhoppers

croqueuse [krɔkøz] *nf* **croqueuse de diamants** gold-digger

croquignolet, -ette [krɔkiɲɔlɛ, -ɛt] *adj Ironic* flaky, off-the-wall

crosser [!!] [krɔse] **se crosser** *vpr Can* to jerk off, *Br* to wank, to have a wank

crosses [krɔs] *nfpl* **chercher des crosses à qn** to try to pick a fight with sb

crouille [kruj] *nm Offensive* = racist term used to refer to a North African Arab

croulant, -e [krulɑ̃, -ɑ̃t] *nm,f* old codger, *Br* wrinkly, *Am* geezer

croupion [krupjɔ̃] *nm* behind, rear (end), rump; **elle marche en ondulant du croupion** she wiggles her butt *or Br* bum when she walks

croûte [krut] *nf* (a) *(tableau)* bad painting□, daub (b) **casser la** *ou* **une croûte** to have a snack□ *or* a bite to eat (c) **gagner sa croûte** to earn a *or* one's crust

croûter [krute] *vi (manger)* to eat□, to chow

croûton [krutɔ̃] *nm* **vieux croûton** old fossil, *Br* crumbly, *Am* geezer

cruche [kryʃ] **1** *adj* dense
2 *nf (imbécile) Br* plonker, pillock, *Am* goof

cube [kyb] *nm* **un gros/petit cube** a big/small bike

cucul [kyky] *adj inv* **cucul (la praline)** *(personne, air)* cutesy, *Br* twee; *(film, livre)* corny

cueillir [kœjir] *vt (arrêter)* to pick up, *Br* to lift

cuiller, cuillère [kɥijɛr] *nf* **elle n'y va pas avec le dos de la cuiller** she doesn't go in for half measures, she doesn't do things by halves; **être à ramasser à la petite cuiller** to be completely Br shattered or Am beat; **en deux** ou **trois coups de cuiller à pot** in next to no time, in two shakes (of a lamb's tail)

cuir [kɥir] nm (a) *(peau)* skin□; **tanner le cuir à qn** to tan sb's hide (b) *(blouson)* leather jacket□ (c) *(homosexuel)* leatherboy

cuisiner [kɥizine] vt *(interroger)* to grill

cuisse [kɥis] nf **avoir la cuisse légère** to sleep around, to be an easy lay; **il y a de la cuisse!** there's plenty of babes or Br talent or totty!

cuistot [kɥisto] nm cook□

cuit, -e [kɥi, -it] adj (a) **être cuit** *(être pris)* to have had it, to be done for; *(être ivre)* to be wasted or plastered or smashed; **c'est cuit** I've/we've/etc had it (b) **c'est du tout cuit** it's in the bag, Br it's a dead cert, Am it's a lock (c) **les carottes sont cuites** the game's up

cuite [kɥit] nf **il tient une sacrée cuite** he's totally wrecked or wasted or Br legless or pissed; **prendre une cuite** to get wrecked or wasted or Br legless or pissed; **tu te souviens de ta première cuite?** do you remember the first time you got wrecked or wasted or Br legless or pissed?

cuiter [kɥite] **se cuiter** vpr to get wrecked or wasted or Br legless or pissed

cul [ky] nm (a) [!] *(postérieur)* Br arse, Am ass; **en avoir plein le cul (de)** *(en avoir assez)* to be pissed off or Am pissed (with); **en avoir plein le cul** *(être fatigué)* to be Br shagged or Am beat; **l'avoir dans le cul** [!!] to have been screwed or shafted; **tu peux te le mettre au cul!** [!!] shove it up your Br arse or Am ass!; **lécher le cul à qn** [!!] Br to lick or kiss sb's arse, Am to kiss sb's ass;

trouer le cul à qn [!!] to flabbergast sb, to knock sb sideways; **avoir qn au cul** to have sb on one's tail; **en rester sur le cul** to be flabbergasted or Br gobsmacked; **avoir le cul bordé de nouilles** to be a lucky bastard; **et mon cul, c'est du poulet?** Br you're taking the piss, aren't you!, Am gimme a break!; **parle à mon cul, ma tête est malade** [!!] *(personne ne m'écoute)* I might as well talk to the fucking wall; *(laisse-moi tranquille)* fuck off!, (talk to the hand cos the face ain't listening); **mon cul!** [!!] no fucking way!, my Br arse or Am ass!; **être comme cul et chemise** to be as thick as thieves; **avoir le cul entre deux chaises** to be in an awkward position; **il y a des coups de pied au cul qui se perdent** somebody needs a good kick Br up the arse or Am in the ass; Can **n'avoir rien que le cul et les dents** to be at rock bottom

(b) [!] *(sexe)* screwing, Br shagging; **un film de cul** a porn movie, Am a skin flick; **un magazine de cul** a porn or skin or girlie mag; **il s'intéresse qu'au cul** all he thinks about is sex□, Br he's got sex on the brain

(c) *(chance)* **avoir du cul** [!] to be a lucky bastard

(d) Pej **cul béni** [!] Bible-basher, Bible-thumper, Am holy Joe

(e) *(camion)* **un gros cul** Br a juggernaut, Am a semi, an eighteen-wheeler

(f) **faire cul sec** to down one's drink in one; **cul sec!** down in one! ▶ see also **carrer, casser, coller, couille, crever, doigt, feu, geler, magner, peau, péter, ras, taper, tête, tirer, tortiller, trou**

culbute [kylbyt] nf **faire la culbute** *(faire faillite)* to go bust or under

culbuter [!] [kylbyte] *vt (posséder sexuellement)* to screw, to shaft, *Br* to shag

culot [kylo] *nm* cheek, nerve; **avoir du culot** to have a lot of nerve, *Br* to have a brass neck; **y aller au culot** to brazen *or* bluff it out

culotte [kylɔt] *nf* **poser culotte** to *Br* have *or Am* take a dump *or* a crap ▸ *see also* **pisser**

culotté, -e [kylɔte] *adj* **être culotté** to have a lot of nerve, *Br* to have a brass neck

cul-terreux [kytɛrø] *nm Pej* yokel, peasant, *Am* hick, hayseed

cureton [kyrtɔ̃] *nm Pej* priest□

curie [kyri] *nm Formerly (billet de cinq cents francs)* five-hundred franc note□

ⓘ A "curie" was so called because a picture of Pierre and Marie Curie used to feature on the banknote.

cuti [kyti] *nf* **virer sa cuti** to change one's whole lifestyle□; *(changer d'opinion)* to switch allegiances□; *(devenir homosexuel)* to turn gay

cuver [kyve] **1** *vt* **cuver son vin/sa bière** to sleep it off
2 *vi* to sleep it off

Dd

dab, dabe [dab] *nm* old man *(father)*

dac [dak] **1** *adv* **je suis/je ne suis pas dac** I agree/don't agree▫
2 *exclam* OK!

d'acodac [dakodak] *exclam* OK!

dalle [dal] *nf* **avoir la dalle** to be hungry▫; **avoir la dalle en pente** to be fond of the bottle, to like a drink; **se rincer la dalle** to have a drink▫ or *Br* a bevvy ▸ *see also* **crever, que dalle**

damer [dame] *vt* **damer le pion à qn** to go one better than sb, to out-do sb▫; **se faire damer le pion** to be outdone▫

dard [!!] [dar] *nm* dick, prick, cock ▸ *see also* **pomper**

dare-dare [dardar] *adv* at or on the double, double quick, pronto; **t'as intérêt à rappliquer dare-dare: le patron veut te voir et il est pas content...** you'd better get here pronto, the boss wants to see you and he's not a happy bunny or camper...

daron [darɔ̃] *nm* old man *(father)*

daronne [darɔn] *nf* old lady, *Br* old dear *(mother)*

dass [das] *nm Cités (verlan* **sida)** the virus

daube [dob] *nf* **(a)** *(chose de mauvaise qualité)* **de la daube** (a load of) garbage or *Br* rubbish; **son dernier**

film, c'est une vraie daube his last film is a pile of crap **(b)** *Suisse (personne stupide)* jerk, *Br* pillock, *Am* jackass

dauber [dobe] **1** *vi* to stink, *Br* to pong, to hum
2 *vt (critiquer)* to badmouth, *Br* to slag off

dauffer [!!] [dofe] *vt* **dauffer qn** to bugger sb, to fuck sb up the *Br* arse or *Am* ass

dawa(h) [dawa] *nm Cités* havoc; **ils arrêtent pas de foutre le dawa en classe** they're always creating havoc in class

deal [dil] *nm* (drug) deal; **il fait de la taule pour deal d'héro** he's doing time for dealing smack

dealer¹ [dilœr] *nm* (drug) dealer

dealer² [dile] *vt & vi* to deal *(drugs)*

deb [dɛb] *adj (abbr* **débile)** daft, *Am* dumb

déballer [debale] *vt (avouer)* to pour out, to spill, to come clean about; **il a tout déballé aux flics** he spilled everything to the cops

débander [!!] [debɑ̃de] *vi* to lose one's hard-on

débarquer [debarke] *vi* **tu débarques?** where have you been?, what planet have you been on? ▸ *see also* **Anglais**

débarrasser [debarase] *vt* **débarrasser le plancher** to hit the road, to be off, to make tracks, *Am* to book it; **tu vas me faire le plaisir de me débarrasser le plancher!** would you kindly get lost!

dèbe [dɛb] *adj* (*abbr* **débile**) daft, *Am* dumb

débecter [debɛkte] *vt* **débecter qn** to make sb sick

débile [debil], **débilos** [debilos] **1** *adj* daft, lame, *Am* dumb
  2 *nmf* dope, *Br* divvy, *Am* dork

débine [debin] *nf* **être dans la débine** to be totally broke *or Br* skint *or* strapped

débiner [debine] **1** *vt Br* to bitch about, to slag off, to badmouth
  2 se débiner *vpr* to take off, to make oneself scarce, *Br* to scarper, *Am* to bug out

débiter [debite] *vt* (*dire*) to come out with, to trot out

débloquer [deblɔke] *vi* (**a**) (*ne plus avoir toute sa tête*) to be off one's rocker, to be not all there, *Br* to be away with the fairies (**b**) (*dire n'importe quoi*) to talk crap *or* bull (**c**) (*ne pas fonctionner correctement*) *Br* to be on the blink, *Am* to be on the fritz

débouler [debule] *vi* to show up, to turn up; **ils ont déboulé chez moi sans prévenir** they showed up at my place without any warning; **les flics ont déboulé dans le café** the cops burst into the bar

débourrer [!!] [debure] *vi* to *Br* have *or Am* take a dump *or* a crap

déboussolé, -e [debusɔle] *adj* lost□, disorientated□; **il est complètement déboussolé depuis que sa femme l'a larguée** he's really lost the plot since his wife left him

débrancher [debrãʃe] *vt Hum* **débranchez-le!** shut him up, will you!

débris [debri] *nm* **un vieux débris** an old codger, an old fogey, *Am* a geezer

dec [dɛk] (*abbr* **déconner**) **sans dec** *adv* **sans dec!** (*je t'assure*) no kidding!, *Br* straight up!; **sans dec?** (*est-ce vrai?*) no kidding?, yeah?, *Br* straight up?

décalcifier [dekalsifje] **se décalcifier** *vpr Hum* to take one's *Br* trousers *or Am* pants off□, *Br* to get one's keks off

---

ⓘ This verb derives its humour from the pun on the word "calcif" – slang for "caleçon" – and the literal translation of the verb "to become decalcified".

---

décalqué, -e [dekalke] *adj* crazy, off one's rocker

décamper [dekãpe] *vi* to clear off, to make oneself scarce, to take off

décaniller [dekanije] *vi* to clear off, to make oneself scarce, to take off

décarcasser [dekarkase] **se décarcasser** *vpr* to sweat blood, to bust a gut (**pour** over); **se décarcasser pour faire qch** to sweat blood *or* bust a gut to do sth

décarrer [dekare] *vi* (*partir*) to make tracks, to hit the road; (*s'enfuir*) to beat it, to clear off, *Am* to book it

décharger [!!] [deʃarʒe] *vi* (*éjaculer*) to shoot one's load

dèche [dɛʃ] *nf* poverty□; **être dans la dèche** to be broke *or Br* skint *or* strapped; **en ce moment c'est la dèche chez nous** we're broke *or Br* skint *or* strapped at the moment

déchiqueté, -e [deʃikte] *adj Cités* (*ivre*) plastered, wasted, *Br* off one's face; (*drogué*) high, wrecked, loaded

déchiré, -e [deʃire] *adj* (*ivre*) plas-

Le symbole □ indique que la traduction n'est pas argotique.

tered, wasted, *Br* off one's face; *(drogué)* wrecked, ripped, loaded; *(drogué avec du cannabis)* stoned

déchirer [deʃire] *vi* **ça déchire!** it rocks!, it's wicked!

déchiros [deʃiros] *nm* weirdo, *Am* wacko

décoiffant, -e [dekwafɑ̃, -ɑ̃t] *adj* mind-blowing

décoiffer [dekwafe] *vi* **ça décoiffe** it's mind-blowing

décoller [dekɔle] *vi* **(a)** *(partir)* to be off, to get going, to make a move; **il ne décolle plus de chez nous** we can't get rid of him, he's constantly round our place **(b)** *(maigrir)* to lose weight□, to slim down□

déconnade [dekɔnad] *nf* **quelle déconnade!** what a hoot!, what a laugh!

déconner [dekɔne] *vi* **(a)** *(dire n'importe quoi)* to talk crap *or* bull *or Br* bollocks; **sans déconner!** *(je t'assure)* no kidding!, *Br* straight up!; **sans déconner?** *(est-ce vrai?)* no kidding?, yeah?, *Br* straight up? **(b)** *(faire le clown)* to fool around **(c)** *(ne pas fonctionner correctement) Br* to be on the blink, *Am* to be on the fritz **(d)** *(ne plus avoir toute sa tête)* to be off one's rocker, to be not all there, *Br* to be away with the fairies **(e)** *(ne pas être raisonnable)* **allez, déconne pas, viens avec nous!** come on, don't be like that, come with us!□ **(f)** *Vulg (sortir du vagin)* to pull out

déconneur, -euse [dekɔnœr, -øz] **1** *adj* **être déconneur** to be a clown *or* a troublemaker
    2 *nm,f* clown, troublemaker

décor [dekɔr] *nm* **la voiture est allée dans le décor** *(hors de la route)* the car went off the road□; **envoyer qn dans le décor** *(le faire tomber)* to send sb flying

décrocher [dekrɔʃe] **1** *vt (obtenir)* to land, to snag; **son frangin a décroché un super boulot** his brother's landed *or* snagged this great job
    2 *vi (drogué)* to kick the habit, to get clean

décuiter [dekɥite] *vi* to sober up□; **ça fait trois jours qu'il décuite pas** he's been wasted *or Br* bladdered for three days

déculottée [dekylɔte] *nf* hammering, trouncing; **prendre une déculottée** to get hammered *or* trounced

défait, -e [defɛ, -ɛt] *adj (ivre)* wasted, wrecked, *Br* slaughtered, *Am* tanked; *(drogué)* wasted, wrecked, loaded

défendre [defɑ̃dr] **se défendre** *vpr (avoir un niveau honorable)* to get by, to hold one's own; **c'est pas un champion mais il se défend** he's not brilliant but he gets by ▸ *see also* **bifteck**

défonce [defɔ̃s] *nf* **(a)** **la défonce** *(le fait de se droguer)* getting stoned; **à part la défonce, rien ne l'intéresse** the only thing he's interested in is getting stoned **(b)** **le concert des Red Hot, c'était vraiment la défonce intégrale** *(extraordinaire)* the Chili Peppers gig was totally mind-blowing *or* totally rocked *or* kicked ass

défoncé, -e [defɔ̃se] *adj* **(a)** *(drogué)* stoned, wasted, out of it **(b)** *Can (affamé)* starving□; **manger comme un défoncé** to wolf down one's food

défoncer [defɔ̃se] **1** *vt* **défoncer la gueule à qn** to smash sb's face in, *Br* to punch sb's lights out, *Am* to punch sb out
    2 **se défoncer** *vpr* **(a)** *(se droguer)* to get stoned *or* wrecked *or* wasted **(b)** *(faire des efforts)* to sweat blood, to bust a gut ▸ *see also* **rondelle**

défriser [defrize] *vt* **et alors, ça te défrise?** have you got a problem with that?

défroquer [defʀɔke] **se défroquer** *vpr* to take one's *Br* trousers *or Am* pants off□, *Br* to get one's keks off

dég [deg] *adj inv* (*abbr* **dégueulasse**) disgusting□, gross

dégager [degaʒe] *vi* (a) (*sentir mauvais*) to stink, *Br* to pong, to hum (b) (*produire un effet puissant*) (*musique*) to be mind-blowing, to kick ass; (*plat, épice*) to blow the top of one's head off, to pack a punch (c) (*partir*) to clear off, to get moving; **allez, dégage!** get out of here!, get lost!, beat it!, *Am* take a hike!

dégaine [degɛn] *nf* strange appearance□; **il a vraiment une dégaine pas possible!** he looks like nothing on earth *or* like something from another planet!

dégelée [deʒle] *nf* thrashing, hiding; **foutre une dégelée à qn** to give sb a thrashing *or* a hiding; **prendre une dégelée** to get a thrashing *or* a hiding

déglingue [deglɛ̃g] *nf* decay□; **il est en pleine déglingue** he's completely fallen apart

déglingué, -e [deglɛ̃ge] *adj* (a) (*cassé*) falling apart, bust, *Br* knackered (b) (*ivre*) wrecked, *Br* off one's face, *Am* fried

dégobiller [degɔbije] *vi* to throw up, to puke, *Br & Austr* to chunder, *Am* to barf

---

ⓘ This word derives from the verb "gober" (to swallow), which is also the origin of the English word "gob".

---

dégoiser [degwaze] **1** *vt* to come out with, to trot out; **qu'est-ce qu'il peut dégoiser comme conneries!**

he can really come out with the biggest load of crap!

2 *vi* **dégoiser sur qn** *Br* to bitch about sb, to slag sb off, to badmouth sb

dégommer [degɔme] *vt* (a) (*tuer*) to blow away, to gun down (b) (*tirer sur*) to shoot at□ (c) (*évincer*) to kick out, to boot out

dégonflard, -e [degɔ̃flar, -ard], **dégonflé, -e** [degɔ̃fle] *nm,f* chicken (*person*)

dégonfler [degɔ̃fle] **se dégonfler** *vpr* to chicken out, *Br* to bottle out, to lose one's bottle

dégoter, dégotter [degɔte] *vt* to unearth, to stumble upon; **où est-ce que tu as dégoté ce bouquin?** where did you get hold of this book?; **il faudrait que je réussisse à dégoter une bonne bagnole d'occasion** I need to get my hands on a good second-hand car

dégoûté, -e [degute] *adj* (*découragé*) bummed (out), *Br* gutted; **putain, je suis trop dégoûté!** what a bummer!, *Br* I'm gutted *or* as sick as a parrot!

dégringoler [degʀɛ̃gɔle] *vi* (a) (*personne*) to tumble□ (b) (*entreprise*) to collapse□; (*prix, cours*) to slump□ (c) (*pleuvoir*) **ça dégringole** it's raining cats and dogs, *Br* it's bucketing down, it's chucking it down

dégrouiller [degʀuje] **se dégrouiller** *vpr* to get a move on, to shake a leg, *Am* to get it in gear

dégueu [degø] *adj inv* (*abbr* **dégueulasse**) (*sale*) disgusting□, gross; (*mauvais*) crappy, lousy, *Br* poxy; **pas dégueu** (*bon*) pretty good

dégueulasse [degœlas] **1** *adj* (a) (*sale*) disgusting□, gross; (*mauvais*) crappy, lousy, *Br* poxy; **pas dégueulasse** (*bon*) pretty good (b) *(moralement)* rotten

2 *nm,f* (**a**) *(sale)* filthy *Br* pig *or Am* hog (**b**) *(moralement) Br* swine, *Am* stinker

dégueulasser [degœlase] *vt* to dirty□, to mess up

dégueuler [!] [degœle] *vi* to throw up, to puke, *Br & Austr* to chunder, *Am* to barf ► *see also* **tripes**

dégueulis [!] [degœli] *nm* puke, vom, *Am* barf

déguster [degyste] *vi (souffrir)* to have a hellish time of it, to have a hell of a time

déj [deʒ] *nm (abbr* **déjeuner**) **petit déj** breakfast□, *Br* brekkie

déjanté, -e [deʒɑ̃te] *Cités* **1** *adj* wacko, *Br* mental, *Am* gonzo

2 *nm,f* headcase, *Br* headbanger

déjanter [deʒɑ̃te] *vi* to flip one's lid, to lose it, *Br* to lose the plot

ⓘ The image behind this verb is that of a tyre being dislodged from its rim.

delacroix [dəlakrwa] *nm Formerly* one-hundred franc note□

ⓘ A "delacroix" was so called because a picture of the painter Eugène Delacroix used to feature on the banknote.

délire [delir] *nm (moment amusant)* **le délire!** it was *Br* wicked *or Am* awesome!; **on s'est tapés un super délire!** we had a blast!, we had *Br* a wicked *or Am* an awesome time!

délirer [delire] *vi (s'amuser)* to have a blast, to have *Br* a wicked *or Am* an awesome time

déloquer [delɔke] **1** *vt* to undress□

2 se déloquer *vpr* to get un-dressed□, *Br* to get one's kit off

démago [demago] **1** *adj (abbr* **démagogique**) crowd-pleasing□

2 *nmf (abbr* **démagogue**) crowd-pleaser□

déménager [demenaʒe] *vi* (**a**) *(être fou)* to be off one's rocker *or* trolley, to have lost it, *Br* to have lost the plot (**b**) *(produire un effet puissant) (musique)* to be mind-blowing, to kick ass; *(plat, épice)* to blow the top of one's head off, to pack a punch

dément, -e [demɑ̃, -ɑ̃t] *adj (excellent)* brilliant, *Br* wicked, *Am* awesome

démerdard, -e [demɛrdar, -ard] **1** *adj* resourceful□; **il est vachement démerdard** he can wangle *or Br* blag *or Am* finagle anything

2 *nm,f* **être un démerdard** to know a trick or two

démerde [demɛrd] *nf* **dans ce pays, tout marche à la démerde** you have to use your wits to get anything done in this country

démerder [demɛrde] **se démerder** *vpr* (**a**) *(se débrouiller)* to manage□, to get by□; **t'en fais pas, je me démerderai tout seul** don't worry, I'll manage on my own; **tu ne voulais pas que je t'aide, maintenant démerde-toi!** you didn't want me to help you, so you can manage on your own now!; **je sais pas comment il se démerde, il casse tout ce qu'il touche** I don't know how he does it, he breaks everything he lays his hands on (**b**) *(dans une discipline)* to manage□, to get by□ (**c**) *(se dépêcher)* to get a move on, *Am* to get it in gear

demi-portion [dəmipɔrsjɔ̃] *nf* weed, squirt

démolir [demɔlir] *vt (battre)* to thrash, to batter

dent [dɑ̃] *nf* **avoir la dent** to be

starving; **avoir la dent dure** to be scathing[□]; **avoir les dents longues, avoir les dents qui rayent le parquet** to be extremely ambitious[□], to aim for the top

dentelle [dɑ̃tɛl] *nf* **ne pas faire** *ou* **donner dans la dentelle** to be really unsubtle[□] *or* in your face

dep [dɛp] *nm Offensive* (*verlan* **pédé**) queer, *Br* poof, *Am* fag

dépaqueter [depakte] **se dépaqueter** *vpr Can Joual* to sober up[□]

dépatouiller [depatuje] **se dépatouiller** *vpr* to manage[□], to get by[□]; **se dépatouiller de qch** to get (oneself) out of sth

déplumé, -e [deplyme] *adj* bald[□]

déplumer [deplyme] **se déplumer** *vpr* to go bald[□]

dépogner [depɔɲe] **se dépogner** *vpr Can* to chill (out)

dépoiler [depwale] **se dépoiler** *vpr* to strip off, *Br* to get one's kit off

dépoter [depɔte] *vi (aller très vite)* to go like a bomb

dépouiller [depuje] *vt* (a) *(voler)* **dépouiller qn** to rob sb, *Br* to do sb over; **se faire dépouiller** to get robbed, *Br* to get done over (b) *(scandaliser)* **ça me dépouille!** it's an outrage *or* a scandal!

dépuceler [depysle] *vt* **dépuceler qn** to deflower sb[□], to pop sb's cherry; **dépuceler une bouteille** to crack open a bottle

dérailler [deraje] *vi (tenir des propos insensés)* to talk drivel, to ramble

derche [!] [dɛrʃ] *nm* butt, *Br* bum, *Am* fanny; **se magner le derche** to move one's butt *or Br* bum; **un faux derche** a two-faced *Br* swine *or Am* stinker

dérouillée [deruje] *nf (correction,*

défaite) thrashing, hammering; **flanquer une dérouillée à qn** to thrash *or* hammer sb; **prendre une dérouillée** to get thrashed *or* hammered

dérouiller [deruje] **1** *vt (battre)* **dérouiller qn** to thrash sb, to hammer sb

2 *vi (se faire battre)* to get thrashed *or* hammered; *(souffrir)* to go through hell, to have a hellish time of it

derrière [dɛrjɛr] *nm* behind, backside; **c'était à se taper le derrière par terre** it was hysterical, it was a scream *or* a hoot

désaper [desape] **se désaper** *vpr* to get undressed[□], *Br* to get one's kit off; **allez, désape-toi et viens me faire un gros câlin!** come on, get your clothes off *or Br* get your kit off and come and give me a cuddle!

descendre [desɑ̃dr] *vt* (a) *(tuer)* to blow away, to blast (b) *(boire)* to put away, to knock back, *Am* to inhale; **qu'est-ce qu'il descend!** he can really put it away *or* knock it back! (c) *(critiquer)* **descendre qn en flammes** to shoot sb down in flames, to crucify sb

descente [desɑ̃t] *nf* **il a une bonne** *ou* **sacrée descente** he can really put it away *or* knock it back

dessin [desɛ̃] *nm* **tu veux que je te fasse un dessin?** do you want me to draw you a map?, do I have to spell it out for you?

dessouder [desude] *vt* to kill[□], to waste, *Br* to do in

destroy [dɛstrɔj] *adj (musique)* hardcore; *(personne)* self-destructive[□]; *(jean)* ripped[□]; *(voiture)* beat up, wrecked, *Br* knackered

dételer [detle] *vi (arrêter de travailler)* to knock off; **sans dételer** non-stop

détente [detɑ̃t] nf **être long** ou **dur à la détente** to be a bit slow on the uptake

déterré, -e [detere] nm,f **avoir une mine de déterré** to look like death warmed up

deuche [dœʃ], **deudeuche** [dœdœʃ] nf Citroën 2CV□

deuil [dœj] nm Hum **il a les ongles en deuil** his nails are filthy, you could grow potatoes under his nails

deux [dø] pron **en moins de deux** in less than no time, in two shakes; **cette bagnole de mes deux [!]** that Br bloody or Am goddamn car; **les ordinateurs et moi, ça fait deux** I don't know the first thing about computers; **lui et moi, ça fait deux** he and I are two different people; **il est radin comme pas deux** he's as stingy or Br tight as they come; **il est menteur comme pas deux** he's an out-and-out liar

deux-pattes [døpat] nf Citroën 2CV□

deuz, deuze [døz] (abbr **deuxième**) **1** adj second□; **je suis deuze!** I'm second!
2 nmf second□

deuzio [døzjo] adv secondly□

devanture [dvɑ̃tyr] nf (a) **se faire refaire la devanture** (un lifting) to have a face-lift□, to have some work done; (se faire battre) to get one's face wasted or one's features rearranged (b) Can (seins) jugs, knockers, rack

déveine [devɛn] nf rotten luck; **être dans la déveine** to have a run of bad luck□

dévierger [!] [devjɛrʒe] vt Can **dévierger qn** to deflower sb□, to pop sb's cherry

dézinguer [dezɛ̃ge] vt (a) (détruire) to wreck (b) (critiquer) to pull to pieces, to slam (c) (tuer) to bump off

diam [djam] nm (abbr **diamant**) sparkler, rock

dico [diko] nm (abbr **dictionnaire**) dictionary□

dingo [dɛ̃go] **1** adj crazy, bonkers, Br barking (mad), Am bonzo
2 nmf maniac, nutcase

dingue [dɛ̃g] **1** adj (a) (fou) crazy, crackers, off one's rocker or Br head (b) (frappant) unreal, incredible□, crazy; **c'est dingue ce qu'il fait chaud!** it's unreal or incredible how hot it is!; **en ce moment j'ai un boulot dingue!** the amount of work I have at the moment is unreal or crazy!
2 nmf headcase, nutcase, Br nutter; **il va finir chez les dingues** he's going to end up in the nuthouse or the loony bin

dinguer [dɛ̃ge] vi **envoyer dinguer qch** (jeter brutalement) to send sth flying; **envoyer dinguer qn** (le faire tomber) to send sb flying; (l'éconduire) to tell sb where to go or where to get off, Br to send sb packing

dire [dir] vt **je te dis pas!** I can't describe it!, you wouldn't believe it!; **il s'est foutu dans une colère, je te dis pas!** he went absolutely ballistic, you wouldn't have believed it!

direct [dirɛkt], **directo(s)** [dirɛkto(s)] adv (abbr **directement**) right away, Br straight; **si tu continues à faire le con comme ça, tu vas te retrouver en taule direct** if you keep pissing about or Br arsing about like that, you'll be going straight to the slammer

dirlo [dirlo] nm Br headmaster□, head, Am principal□

discrétos [diskretos] *adv* on the quiet, on the q.t.

discutailler [diskytɑje] *vi* to quibble

disjoncter [disʒɔ̃kte] *vi (devenir fou)* to crack up, to go round the bend, to lose it, *Br* to lose the plot

disque [disk] *nm* **change de disque!** *(change de sujet)* change the record!

dissert, disserte [disɛrt] *nf (abbr* **dissertation)** essay□

djeun(e) [dʒœn] *Ironic* **1** *adj* young and hip□

2 *nmf* young hip person□, hipster

ⓘ This is the spelling of the word "jeune" as if it were an English word. This can be viewed as an ironic comment on the fact that today's youth culture is dominated by American products and values.

djig [dʒig] *nf Cités* chick, *Br* bird

djos [!] [dʒo] *nmpl Can* tits, jugs

doc [dɔk] *nf (abbr* **documentation)** info

doigt [dwa] *nm* (a) **faire qch les doigts dans le nez** to do sth standing on one's head *or* with one's eyes closed (b) **s'enlever les doigts du cul [!!]** to pull one's finger out (c) **faire un doigt d'honneur à qn** to give sb the finger, *Am* to flip sb the bird (d) **se mettre** *ou* **se fourrer le doigt dans l'œil (jusqu'au coude)** to be barking up the wrong tree (e) **avoir les doigts de pied en éventail** *(paresser)* to laze around; *(avoir un orgasme)* to come

domper [dɔ̃pe] *vt Can Joual (laisser tomber)* to dump

dondon [dɔ̃dɔ̃] *nf* **grosse dondon** fat lump, fatty

donner [dɔne] **1** *vt* (a) *(dénoncer)* to squeal on, *Br* to grass on, to shop, *Am* to rat on (b) **j'ai déjà donné** been there, done that(, got the T-shirt)

2 *vi* **ça donne** it's something else!, it's *Br* wicked *or Am* awesome!

3 se donner *vpr* (a) **s'en donner** to have the time of one's life, to have a blast (b) **se la donner** to show off, to pose

donneur [dɔnœr] *nm Br* grass, *Am* fink

donneuse [dɔnøz] *nf Br* grass, *Am* fink

ⓘ "Donneuse" is not used as the feminine form of "donneur" – both terms always refer to a man. The use of the feminine form in this way makes the term sound even more pejorative. See also the entry **salope (b)**.

donzelle [dɔ̃zɛl] *nf* little madam

dope [dɔp] *nf* dope, stuff, *Br* gear

dort-en-chiant [dɔrɑ̃ʃjɑ̃] *nm Br* slowcoach, *Am* slowpoke

dos [do] *nm* **l'avoir dans le dos** to get done *or* conned; **en avoir plein le dos** *(être épuisé)* to be *Br* knackered *or* shattered *or Am* beat *or* pooped; *(être excédé)* to be hacked off *or* cheesed off; **avoir qn sur le dos** to have sb on one's back; **je l'ai tout le temps sur le dos** she's always on *or* never off my back; **il a bon dos, le métro!** blame it on the *Br* underground *or Am* subway, why don't you!; **faire un enfant dans le dos à qn** to stab sb in the back ▸ *see also* **bête, cuiller**

dose [doz] *nf* (a) **en avoir sa dose** to have had one's fill, to have had it up to here (b) **en tenir une dose** to have nothing between one's ears, *Br* to be as thick as two short planks, *Am* to have rocks in one's head

doser [doze] *vi* **ça dose!** cool!, *Br* wicked!, *Am* awesome!

douce [dus] **en douce** *adv* **faire qch en douce** to do sth on the quiet *or* on the q.t. ▸ *see also* **couler**

douiller [duje] **1** *vt (payer)* to fork out for, to cough up for
　2 *vi* **(a)** *(être cher)* to cost a bundle *or* an arm and a leg *or Br* a bomb **(b)** *(souffrir)* to go through hell, to have a hellish time of it

douilles [duj] *nmpl (cheveux)* hair◻, mop, *Br* barnet; **se faire couper les douilles** to get one's hair◻ *or Br* barnet cut

douleur [dulœr] *nf* **si je le chope, il va comprendre sa douleur** if I catch him, he'll get what's coming to him *or* his worst nightmares will come true

douloureuse [dulurøz] *nf (addition)* *Br* bill◻, *Am* check◻

drague [drag] *nf Br* chatting people up, *Am* hitting on people; **ce mec-là, c'est un pro de la drague** that guy's a bit of a charmer, he's a bit of a pro at *Br* chatting up *or Am* hitting on women, that guy; **c'est un lieu de drague idéal** it's an ideal place for *Br* chatting people up *or Am* hitting on people

draguer [drage] **1** *vt* to come on to, *Br* to chat up, *Am* to hit on

2 *vi* to be *Br* on the pull *or Am* on the make; **il est parti draguer en boîte** he went out *Br* on the pull *or Am* cruising to a club

dragueur, -euse [dragœr, -øz] **1** *adj* **il est très dragueur** he's always *Br* chatting up *or Am* hitting on women; **il n'a jamais été très dragueur** he's never been one for *Br* chatting up *or Am* hitting on women
　2 *nm,f* **c'est un dragueur** he's always *Br* chatting up *or Am* hitting on women

drauper [droper] *nm (verlan* **perdreau***) (policier)* cop

drepou [drəpu] *nf (verlan* **poudre***) (héroïne)* smack, scag, skag; *(cocaïne)* coke, snow, charlie

Duchnoque [dyʃnɔk] *nm* his lordship, *Br* his nibs; *(terme d'adresse) Br* pal, matey, *Am* bud, buddy

Ducon [!] [dykɔ̃], **Ducon-la-joie [!]** [dykɔ̃laʒwa] *nm* shit-for-brains, dick face

dur, -e [dyr] **1** *nm (train)* train◻
　2 *nm,f* **un dur à cuire, une dure à cuire** a hard nut
　3 *exclam* **dur dur!** bummer!, what a drag! ▸ *see also* **coup, détente, feuille**

duraille [dyrɑj] *adj* tough

durite [dyrit] *nf* **péter une durite** *(se mettre en colère)* to go ape *or* ballistic, to hit the *Br* roof *or Am* ceiling

Ee

eau, -x [o] *nf* (**a**) **finir** *ou* **partir en
eau de boudin** *(mal se terminer)* to
end in tears; *(échouer)* to go down
the tubes (**b**) **il n'a pas inventé l'eau
chaude** *ou* **tiède** he's no rocket scientist, *Br* he'll never set the Thames
on fire, he's not the sharpest knife
in the drawer (**c**) **dans ces eaux-là**
thereabouts□, more or less□ (**d**) **il y a
de l'eau dans le gaz** there's trouble
brewing ▶ *see also* **pomme**

échauffer [eʃofe] *vt* **échauffer les
oreilles à qn** to bug sb, *Br* to do sb's
head in, to get up sb's nose, *Am* to
give sb a pain (in the neck)

éclate [eklat] *nf* **c'est l'éclate** it's a
laugh *or* a hoot; **c'est pas l'éclate**
it's not exactly a barrel of laughs

éclater [eklate] **1** *vt* **éclater qn,
éclater la gueule à qn** to smash
sb's face in, to waste sb's face
   2 s'éclater *vpr* to have a blast

éclaterie [eklatri] *nf* **c'est l'éclaterie!** it's a laugh *or* a hoot!

écluser [eklyze] *vt* to knock back,
to down, to sink; **il a éclusé vingt
bières dans la soirée** he knocked
back *or* downed *or* sank twenty
beers over the course of the evening

écolo [ekolo] *adj & nmf* (*abbr* **écolo-
giste**) green

éconocroques [ekɔnɔkrɔk] *nfpl* sav-
ings□

écoper [ekɔpe] *vi* **écoper d'une
amende/de cinq ans de prison** to
get *or* cop a fine/five years in prison

écorcher [ekɔrʃe] *vt (faire trop payer)* to fleece, *Am* to soak

écrase-merdes [ekrazmɛrd] *nmpl*
shoes□, clodhoppers

écraser [ekraze] **1** *vt* **en écraser** to
sleep like a log
   2 *vi* **écrase!** shut up!, *Br* belt up!
   3 s'écraser *vpr* to shut up, *Br* to
belt up

écroulé, -e [ekrule] *adj* **être écroulé
(de rire)** to be doubled up (with
laughter), to be killing oneself (laughing), to be in stitches

ecsta [ɛksta] *nf* (*abbr* **ecstasy**) E

écumoire [ekymwar] *nf* **transformer qn en écumoire** to pump sb
full of lead

effeuilleuse [efœjøz] *nf* stripper

emballer [ɑ̃bale] **1** *vt* (**a**) *(enthou-
siasmer)* **ça ne m'a pas emballé** I
wasn't wild about it *or Br* mad keen
on it, it didn't do much for me; **ça
l'a vraiment emballé** he was really
taken with it (**b**) *(séduire) Br* to pull,
Am to pick up (**c**) *(embrasser) Br* to
snog, to get off with, *Am* to make
out with
   2 s'emballer *vpr* to get carried
away

emberlificoter [ɑ̃berlifikɔte] **1** *vt* to
hoodwink; **se laisser emberlifico-
ter** to let oneself be hoodwinked

2 s'emberlificoter *vpr* to tie oneself in knots; **s'emberlificoter dans ses explications** to get tangled up *or* tied up in one's explanations

embobiner [ãbɔbine] *vt* **embobiner qn** to take sb in, to con sb; **ne te laisse pas embobiner par ce filou** don't let that rogue take you in

embouché, -e [ãbuʃe] *adj* **être mal embouché** *(être de mauvaise humeur)* to be in a foul mood; *(être grossier)* to have a mouth like a sewer, to be a potty-mouth *or Am* a sewermouth

embrayer [ãbreje] *vi* to spit it out, to get to the point; **bon, qu'est-ce que tu as à nous dire, allez, embraye!** come on then, what have you got to say to us? spit it out!; **embrayer sur qch** to get going *or* started on sth; **quand il embraye sur ce sujet, plus moyen de l'arrêter** once he gets going *or* started on that subject, there's no stopping him

embringuer [ãbrẽge] **1** *vt* **embringuer qn dans qch** to get sb mixed up in sth; **il s'est laissé embringuer dans une histoire de trafic de voitures volées** he got himself mixed up in some scam involving stolen cars

2 s'embringuer *vpr* **s'embringuer dans qch** to get mixed up in sth; **il s'est embringué dans une sale affaire** he got himself mixed up in some nasty *or Br* dodgy business

embrouille [ãbruj] *nf* **(a)** *(situation confuse)* muddle; **il s'est foutu dans une embrouille** he got himself into a real muddle **(b)** *(problème)* **tenez-vous tranquilles, je veux pas d'embrouilles!** keep quiet, I don't want any trouble *or* hassle!; **je vois venir les embrouilles** I can see trouble ahead

embrouiller [ãbruje] *vt (duper)*
to confuse[□]; **n'essaye pas de m'embrouiller, je sais très bien que tu me dois encore du fric** don't try to pull the wool over my eyes, I'm well aware that you still owe me some cash; **ni vu ni connu je t'embrouille** no one is/was/*etc* any the wiser

éméché, -e [emeʃe] *adj* tipsy, merry

emmanché [ãmãʃe] *nm* useless idiot, *Br* pillock, *Am* jerk

emmerdant, -e [!] [ãmɛrdã, -ãt] *adj* **être emmerdant** to be a pain in the *Br* arse *or Am* ass, to be damn *or Br* bloody annoying

emmerde [!] [ãmɛrd] *nm or nf* trouble[□], hassle; **avoir des emmerdes** to have a hell of a lot of problems; **en ce moment, j'ai que des emmerdes** at the moment, it's just one damn *or Br* bloody thing *or* hassle after another; **j'ai encore eu un emmerde avec la bagnole** I've had more damn *or Br* bloody trouble with the car

emmerdé, -e [!] [ãmɛrde] *adj* **être emmerdé** to be in a real *or Br* right mess; **avoir l'air emmerdé** to look worried[□] *or* stressed; **je suis emmerdé, je lui avais promis de l'aider à déménager mais les enfants insistent pour que je les emmène au cinéma** I'm in a real mess, I'd promised to help him move but the kids are insisting I take them to the cinema; **il était super emmerdé: il a emprunté la caisse de son père mais il l'a eraflée contre un poteau** he was really stressed: he'd borrowed his dad's car but scraped it against a post

emmerdement [!] [ãmɛrd(ə)mã] *nm* = **emmerde**

emmerder [!] [ãmɛrde] **1** *vt* **(a)** *(contrarier)* **emmerder qn** to bug sb to death, to get up sb's nose, *Br* to piss sb off; **ça m'emmerde de devoir aller à cette réunion** it's a damn *or Br* bloody nuisance having to go to this meeting

(b) *(ennuyer)* **emmerder qn** to bore sb stiff *or* rigid

(c) *(mépriser)* **le directeur, je l'emmerde!** the manager can go to hell *or Br* bugger *or* sod off!

2 s'emmerder *vpr* **(a)** *(s'ennuyer)* to be bored stiff *or* rigid; **s'emmerder à cent sous de l'heure** to be bored shitless

(b) *(se donner du mal)* **s'emmerder à faire qch** to go to the bother *or* trouble of doing sth; **pourquoi s'emmerder à laver par terre alors que les gamins vont tout dégueulasser quand ils rentreront avec leurs godasses pleines de boue?** why bother cleaning the floor when the kids are just going to muck it all up coming in with their muddy shoes?

(c) tu t'emmerdes pas! *(tu ne te refuses rien)* you're very good to yourself!; *(tu as du culot)* you've got a *Br* bloody *or Am* goddamn nerve!
▸ *see also* **rat**

emmerdeur, -euse [!] [ɑ̃mɛrdœr, -øz] *nm,f* pain in the *Br* arse *or Am* ass, damn *or Br* bloody nuisance

empaffé [!!] [ɑ̃pafe] *nm* dickhead, prick, *Br* wanker

empailler [ɑ̃pɑje] **s'empailler** *vpr* *(se quereller)* to lay into each other, *Br* to have a slanging match *or* a barney; **la circulation étaient bloquée car deux automobilistes étaient en train de s'empailler sur la chaussée** the traffic was held up by two drivers laying into each other *or Br* having a slanging match in the middle of the road

empapaouté [!] [ɑ̃papaute] *nm*

arsehole, *Am* asshole

empapaouter [!] [ɑ̃papaute] *vt* to bugger, to take up the *Br* arse *or Am* ass; **va te faire empapaouter!** go to hell!, *Br* bugger off!, sod off!

emperlousé, -e [ɑ̃pɛrluze] *adj* dripping with pearls; **l'opéra était plein de vieilles emperlousées** the opera was full of old dears dripping with pearls

empiffrer [ɑ̃pifre] **s'empiffrer** *vpr* to stuff oneself *or* one's face, to pig out

empiler [!] [ɑ̃pile] *vt* to screw, to fleece; **se faire empiler** to get screwed *or* fleeced

emplafonner [ɑ̃plafɔne] *vt* to crash *or* smash into◻; **il s'est fait emplafonner par un abruti en camionnette** some idiot in a van smashed into him

emplâtre [ɑ̃plɑtr] *nm* slacker, *Br* waster

empoté, -e [ɑ̃pɔte] *nm,f* clumsy *or Br* cack-handed idiot, *Am* klutz

en [ɑ̃] *pron* **en être** *(être homosexuel)* to be one of THEM, to bat for the other side *or* team

encadrer [ɑ̃kadre] *vt* **(a)** *(rentrer dans)* to smash *or* crash into◻; **si tu continues à rouler comme un dingue tu vas finir par encadrer un lampadaire** if you keep driving like a maniac you're going to end up smashing into *or* wrapping yourself round a lamppost **(b) je peux pas l'encadrer** I can't stand (the sight of) him, *Br* I can't stick him

encaisser [ɑ̃kɛse] **1** *vt* *(tolérer)* to stand, *Br* to stick; **je peux pas l'encaisser** I can't stand (the sight of) him, *Br* I can't stick him

2 *vi* *(supporter les coups)* **il sait encaisser** he can take a lot of punish-

---

Le symbole ◻ indique que la traduction n'est pas argotique.

ment; **qu'est-ce qu'il a encaissé!** he took a real hammering or pasting!

encaldosser [!!] [ākaldɔse] vt to bugger, to fuck up the Br arse or Am ass

enculage [!!] [ākylaʒ] nm (a) (sodomisation) buggery (b) **de l'enculage de mouches** hair-splitting□, nit-picking

enculé [!!] [ākyle] nm prick, Br arsehole, wanker, Am asshole; **c'est cet enculé de Michel qui m'a piqué ma mob** that prick Michel pinched my moped ▸ see also **mère**

enculer [!!] [ākyle] vt (a) (sodomiser) to bugger, to fuck up the Br arse or Am ass; **va te faire enculer!** fuck off!, go (and) fuck yourself! (b) (duper) to screw, to shaft (c) **enculer les mouches** to split hairs□, to nit-pick

enculeur, -euse [!!] [ākylœr, -øz] **1** nm,f **enculeur de mouches** hair-splitter□, nit-picker

2 nm (homosexuel actif) top (gay man who gives rather than receives anal sex)

enfant [āfā] nm Can **enfant de chienne** [!] son-of-a-bitch; **cet enfant de chienne m'a fait perdre mon boulot** I lost my job because of that son-of-a-bitch; **être en enfant de chienne** to be fuming, Br to be spitting

enfarinée [āfarine] adj **arriver la gueule enfarinée** to turn up like an idiot or quite unsuspecting

enfer [āfɛr] nm (a) **c'est l'enfer** it's hell (on earth) (b) **d'enfer** (excellent) great, wicked, Br fab, Am awesome ▸ see also **look**

enfiler [āfile] **1** [!!] vt to fuck, to screw, Br to shag

2 s'enfiler vpr (a) (nourriture) to scoff; (boisson) to guzzle, to down,

to sink (b) [!!] (coïter) to fuck, to screw, Br to shag

enfirouâper [āfirwape] vt Can (a) (tromper) to con, to rip off; (mettre enceinte) to knock up; **se faire enfirouâper** (se faire rouler) to get conned or ripped off; (se faire mettre enceinte) to get knocked up (b) (nourriture) to gulp down, to wolf down

enflé [!] [āfle] nm prick, Br arsehole, wanker, Am asshole

enflure [!] [āflyr] nf prick, Br arsehole, wanker, Am asshole

enfoiré, -e [!!] [āfware] nm,f (homme) bastard, fucker; (femme) bitch

engin [!] [āʒē] nm (pénis) prick, tool

engrosser [!] [āgrose] vt **engrosser qn** to knock sb up, Br to get sb up the duff; **elle s'est fait engrosser par un mec rencontré en boîte** she got knocked up by some guy she met in a club

engueulade [āɡœlad] nf bawling out, roasting, earful; **se prendre une engueulade** to get bawled out, to get a roasting or an earful

engueuler [āɡœle] **1** vt **engueuler qn** to bawl sb out, to give sb hell or a roasting; **se faire engueuler** to get bawled out, to get a roasting

2 s'engueuler vpr to be at each other's throats, Br to have a slanging match; **ses parents n'arrêtent pas de s'engueuler** his parents are always at each other's throats ▸ see also **poisson**

enguirlander [āɡirlāde] vt **enguirlander qn** to read sb the riot act; **se faire enguirlander** to get read the riot act

enquiquinant, -e [ākikinā, -āt] adj (a) (ennuyeux) deadly dull (b) (con-

trariant) **être enquiquinant** to be a pain

enquiquiner [ãkikine] *vt* **(a)** *(ennuyer)* to bore stiff *or* rigid **(b)** *(contrarier)* **enquiquiner qn** to bug sb, *Br* to get up sb's nose, to do sb's head in, *Am* to give sb a pain

enquiquineur, -euse [ãkikinœr, -øz] *nm,f* pain (in the neck), pest, nuisance

enrhumer [ãryme] *vt* to overtake at top speed; **t'aurais vu comme je l'ai enrhumé, ce blaireau, avec sa caisse pourrie!** you should have seen the speed I overtook that jerk in his old banger!

entourloupe [ãturlup] *nf* dirty trick

entourlouper [ãturlupe] *vt* **entourlouper qn** to play a dirty trick on sb, *Br* to do the dirty on sb, *Am* to do sb dirty

entourloupette [ãturlupɛt] = **entourloupe**

entraver [ãtrave] *vt* to understand□, to get; **j'entrave que dalle** I don't understand a damn *or Br* bloody thing

entuber [!] [ãtybe] *vt (flouer)* to screw, to shaft; **se faire entuber** to get screwed *or* shafted

envapé, -e [ãvape] *adj* out of it, wasted, loaded

enviandé [!!] [ãvjãde] *nm* prick, *Br* arsehole, wanker, *Am* asshole; **c'est cet enviandé d'Alex qui m'a piqué ma mob** that prick Alex pinched my moped

enviander [!!] [ãvjãde] *vt* to fuck up the *Br* arse *or Am* ass

envoyer [ãvwaje] **1** *vi (être remarquable)* **ça envoie!** it rocks!
2 s'envoyer *vpr* **(a)** *(absorber) (nourriture)* to scoff; *(boisson)* to guzzle, to down, to sink; *(livre)* to

devour **(b)** [!] *(avoir des relations sexuelles avec) Br* to bonk, to have it off with, *Am* to ball; **s'envoyer en l'air (avec qn)** *Br* to bonk (sb), to have it off (with sb), *Am* to ball (sb)
▸ *see also* **balader, bouler, chier, décor, dinguer, paître, péter, pisser, promener, rose, valdinguer, valser, vanne**

épais [epɛ] *adv* **il y en a pas épais** there isn't much/aren't many; **en avoir épais (sur le cœur)** to be feeling down

épate [epat] *nf* **c'est de l'épate** it's just showing off, it's all an act; **faire de l'épate** to show off

épingler [epɛ̃gle] *vt (arrêter)* to nab, *Br* to lift, *Am* to nail; **se faire épingler** to get nabbed *or Br* lifted *or Am* nailed

éponge [epɔ̃ʒ] *nf* **(a)** *(ivrogne)* lush, alky, boozer, *Am* juicer **(b) éponges** lungs□; **avoir les éponges mitées** = to have a disease of the lungs such as tuberculosis or silicosis

éreinter [erɛ̃te] *vt (critiquer sévèrement)* to pull to pieces, to pan, *Br* to slag off, to slate; **la critique a éreinté son dernier film** the critics pulled his last film to pieces

esbigner [ɛsbiɲe] **s'esbigner** *vpr* to clear off, to take off, *Am* to book it; **il s'est esbigné discrètement** he sloped off

esbroufe, esbrouffe [ɛsbruf] *nf* showing off; **faire de l'esbroufe** to show off; **décrocher un boulot à l'esbroufe** to bluff *or Br* blag one's way into a job; **il a eu l'oral à l'esbroufe** he bluffed his way through the oral

esgourde [ɛsgurd] *nf* ear□, *Br* lug, lughole

esgourder [ɛsgurde] *vt (entendre)* to

hear□; *(écouter)* to listen□

espèce [ɛspɛs] *nf* **espèce de con! [!]** you *Br* arsehole *or Am* asshole!; **espèce de menteur!** you filthy liar!; **c'est une espèce d'empoté!** he's a *Br* cack-handed idiot *or Am* klutz!; **il s'est marié avec une espèce de pouffiasse [!]** he married some old tart *or Br* slapper

espingouin [ɛspɛ̃gwɛ̃] *Offensive* **1** *adj* Dago
2 *nm* **Espingouin** Dago *(from Spain)*

ⓘ Depending on the context and the tone of voice used, this term may be either offensive or affectionately humorous. It is nonetheless inadvisable to use it unless one is quite sure of the reaction it will receive.

esquinter [ɛskɛ̃te] *vt* (a) *(endommager)* to wreck, to bust, *Br* to knacker (b) *(blesser)* to smash up; **se faire esquinter** to get smashed up

estomaquer [ɛstɔmake] *vt* to stagger, to flabbergast; **il a été estomaqué** he was staggered *or* flabbergasted *or Br* gobsmacked

estourbir [ɛsturbir] *vt* (a) *(assommer)* to knock out (b) *(tuer)* to kill□, *Br* to do in

étendre [etɑ̃dr] *vt* (a) *(faire tomber)* to floor, to deck (b) *(tuer)* to kill□, *Br* to do in (c) **se faire étendre (à un examen)** *(échouer)* to fail□ *or Am* flunk (an exam)

Étienne [etjɛn] *npr* **à la tienne, Étienne!** cheers(, Big Ears)!

étonner [etɔne] *vt* *Ironic* **tu m'étonnes!** you're telling ME!, you

DO surprise me!; **il s'est barré au moment de régler l'addition? alors là, tu m'étonnes!** he took off as soon as it was time to pay the bill? what a surprise!

étriper [etripe] **s'étriper** *vpr* to make mincemeat of each other

étron [etrɔ̃] *nm* turd

exam [ɛgzam] *nm (abbr* **examen)** exam□

exciter [ɛksite] **s'exciter** *vpr (s'énerver)* to get worked up *or* excited; **t'excite pas, je vais te le rendre ton fric!** calm down *or* don't get worked up, I'll give you your money back!

exhibo [ɛgzibo] *nmf (abbr* **exhibitionniste)** exhibitionist□

exo [ɛgzo] *nm (abbr* **exercice)** exercise□

expliquer [ɛksplike] *vt* **je t'explique pas** I can't describe it, you wouldn't believe it; **on s'est pris un de ces savons, je t'explique pas** you wouldn't have believed the telling-off we got

exploser [ɛksploze] **1** *vt* (a) *(battre)* **exploser qn** to kick sb's head in, to smash sb's face in (b) **être explosé (de rire)** to be killing oneself (laughing), to be cracking up, to be in stitches
2 *vi* **ils ont explosé sur la scène rock il y a vingt ans** they burst onto the rock scene twenty years ago

expo [ɛkspo] *nf (abbr* **exposition)** exhibition□

exta [ɛksta] *nf (abbr* **ecstasy)** E

extra [ɛkstra] *adj inv* great, fantastic, *Br* wicked, *Am* awesome

---

The symbol [!] denotes a very familiar term, [!!] a vulgar one.

Spotlight on:

Les influences étrangères

A substantial proportion of French slang terms come from foreign languages, which is hardly surprising when one considers that one of the main purposes of slang has always been to be intelligible only to restricted circles of people. Moreover, one might argue that from a geographical point of view France is ideally placed for absorbing foreign influences, as it shares a border with so many countries. Long before English became one of the main sources of new French slang words due to the ubiquity of American culture, English words had been absorbed into French: for instance the word **schlass**, meaning "knife", comes from the English "slash", while **grisbi** (a now slightly dated term for "money") is said to come from the English "crispy" (supposedly because of the crispness of new bank notes). The term **reluquer** (to look at, to ogle) comes from Dutch via Walloon, and the words **flic** (policeman), **schlinguer** (to stink) and **mouise** (poverty) all come from German. The terms **basta** (meaning "that's enough!") and **scoumoune** (bad luck) come from Italian, and the terms **gouape** (thug), **caboche** (head) and **tchatcher** (to chat) all come from Spanish. Gypsy languages have also contributed quite a few terms to French slang, such as **surin** (knife) and its derivative **suriner** (to knife), **chou-raver** (to steal) and **pillaver** (to drink). Finally, many words from Arabic (and particularly its North African dialects) have become part of French slang over two main periods. Firstly, during France's period of colonial expansion in North Africa in the 19th century, French soldiers who were stationed there picked up words from local dialects which they started using among themselves, and these words then became part of mainstream slang when the soldiers returned to the mainland. Words such as **gourbi** (hovel), **smala** (family, large group), **un chouïa** (a little) and **clebs** (dog) were all absorbed into French slang during that time. More recently, after the Second World War, large numbers of North Africans moved to France in search of work and a better life and more Arabic words were added to the French slang lexicon, particularly in the "banlieues": words such as **kiffer** (to like, to enjoy), **chouf!** (look!) and **dawah** (mess, disorder).

Ff

fac [fak] *nf* (*abbr* **faculté**) *Br* uni, *Am* school□

façade [fasad] *nf* **se ravaler la façade** to put one's face on, to put on one's warpaint; **se faire ravaler la façade** to have a face-lift□

face [fas] *nf* **face de rat** ratbag, *Am* ratfink; *Can* **avoir une face de bœuf** (*avoir l'air fâché*) to look pissed off *or Am* pissed; (*avoir l'air abruti*) to look spaced-out *or* out of it; **maudite face de bœuf!** you moron!

ⓘ Note that the word "bœuf" in the expression "face de bœuf" is pronounced [bø] even though it is in the singular and so would normally be pronounced [bœuf].

facho [faʃo] *adj & nmf* fascist□

facile [fasil] *adv* easily□, no problem, *Br* no probs

fada [fada] **1** *adj* crazy, crackers, off one's rocker, *Am* wacko
2 *nmf* nutcase, *Br* nutter, *Am* wacko

fadé, -e [fade] *adj* **être fadé** to take the *Br* biscuit *or Am* cake; **habituellement, ses films cassent pas des briques, mais le dernier est particulièrement fadé** his films usually aren't much to write home about, but his last one really takes the *Br* biscuit *or Am* cake

fader [fade] **se fader** *vpr* **se fader qn/qch** to get landed with sb/sth

faf¹ [faf] *adj & nmf* (*fasciste*) fascist□

faf², faffe [faf], **fafiot** [fafjo] *nm* (**a**) (*billet de banque*) *Br* banknote□, *Am* greenback (**b**) **fafs, faffes, fafiots** (*papiers d'identité*) ID

fagoté, -e [fagɔte] *adj* **être mal/ bizarrement fagoté** to be badly/ weirdly dressed ▸ *see also* **as**

ⓘ This term comes from the word "fagot" (bundle of wood). The image is one of a badly assembled bundle of wood.

faire [fɛr] **1** *vt* (**a**) **on ne me la fait pas, à moi!** you can't fool me!, there's no flies on me! (**b**) **faire son affaire à qn** to bump sb off, *Br* to do sb in (**c**) **ça le fait** it's way cool *or Am* awesome; **ça le fait pas** it's just not done; **ça le fait pas de se pointer avec une heure de retard le premier jour** it looks crap to show up an hour late on your first day
2 **se faire** *vpr* (**a**) **se faire qn [!]** (*avoir des rapports sexuels avec*) to screw *or Br* shag sb; (*battre*) to beat the shit out of sb (**b**) (*supporter*) **celui-là, il faut se le faire!** he's a total pain (in the neck)! (**c**) **va te faire!** get out of here!, *Br* sling your hook!, eff off!, *Am* bug off! (**d**) **on se fait un film/un resto chinois?** do you

fancy going to see a film/going for a Chinese?

fait, -e [fɛ, fɛt] *adj (ivre)* wrecked, wasted, *Br* pissed, *Am* tanked

falloir [falwar] *v imp* **il l'a remis à sa place, comme il faut** he put him well and truly in his place; **ils leur ont mis la pâtée, comme il faut** they absolutely hammered *or* thrashed them

falzar [falzar] *nm Br* trousers□, keks, *Am* pants□

famille [famij] *nf* **on s'est pris une engueulade des familles** we got a *Br* right *or* *Am* real roasting; **un petit gueuleton des familles** a nice little meal□ ► *see also* **bijou**

fana [fana] *(abbr* **fanatique)** **1** *adj* **être fana de football** to be into soccer *or Br* football, to be a soccer *or Br* football fan *or* nut

2 *nmf* fan; **un fana de football** a soccer *or Br* football fan *or* nut

farcir [farsir] **se farcir** *vpr* **(a)** *(consommer)* to scoff, to guzzle; **il s'est farci toute la pizza à lui tout seul** he scoffed the whole pizza himself **(b)** *(supporter)* to have to put up with; **celui-là, il faut se le farcir!** he's a total pain! **(c)** *(faire)* **se farcir qch** to get stuck *or Br* lumbered *or* landed with sth; **c'est encore moi qui me suis farci toute la vaisselle** I got stuck with doing all the dishes again **(d)** **[!!]** *(posséder sexuellement)* to screw, *Br* to have it off with, *Am* to ball

fard [far] *nm* **piquer un fard** to go bright red

farine [farin] *nf (héroïne)* smack, scag, skag; *(cocaïne)* coke, charlie, snow

farter [farte] *vi* **ça farte?** wazzup? how's things?

fashion [faʃœn] *adj* trendy

fastoche [fastɔʃ] *adj Br* dead *or Am*

real easy; **c'était hyper fastoche** it was *Br* dead easy, it was a walk in the park *or Br* a doddle

fauche [foʃ] *nf* thieving□, pinching, *Br* nicking; **à chaque fois, il y a de la fauche** things get pinched *or Br* nicked every time

fauché, -e [foʃe] *adj* broke, *Br* skint, strapped (for cash)

faucher [foʃe] *vt (voler)* to pinch, *Br* to nick

Faucheuse [foʃøz] *nf* **la Faucheuse** *(la mort)* the Grim Reaper

fauteuil [fotœj] *nm* **arriver dans un fauteuil** to win hands down, *Br* to walk it

faux [fo] *adv* **avoir tout faux** *(se tromper)* to have got it all wrong ► *see also* **derche, jeton**

faux-cul [foky], **faux-derche** [foderʃ] *nm* two-faced *Br* swine *or Am* stinker

fax [faks] *nm* **c'est un vrai fax, cette fille!** *(elle a une petite poitrine)* she's as flat as a pancake!

ⓘ This humorous expression probably originates in the image of a flat-chested woman being able to pass through a fax machine.

fayot [fajo] *nm* **(a)** *(personne)* crawler, *Br* creep **(b)** *(haricot)* bean□

fayoter [fajɔte] *vi* to crawl, *Br* to creep; **c'est dingue ce qu'il peut fayoter en classe!** he can be such a crawler *or Br* creep in class!

féca [feka] *nm (verlan* **café)** coffee□, *Am* java

fèche [fɛʃ] *exclam* what a drag!

ⓘ This term is a shortened form of the expression "fait chier!" and was popularized by the comic strip character Agrippine, a rebellious teenager created by the cartoonist Claire Brétécher.

---

feeling [filiŋ] *nm* **faire qch au feeling** to do sth by intuition□ *or* gut feeling; **on n'a pas vraiment planifié nos vacances; on va faire ça au feeling** we haven't really planned our holiday, we'll just play it by ear

feignasse [fɛɲas] *nf* lazy so-and-so; **son bonhomme est une vraie feignasse** her old man is a real lazy so-and-so

feignasser [fɛɲase] *vi* to lounge *or* laze around

feinter [fɛ̃te] *vt (duper)* to take in, to con

fêlé, -e [fele] *adj (fou)* crackers, nuts, *Br* barking (mad), *Am* wacko

femmelette [famlɛt] *nf* wimp, drip, sissy, *Br* big girl's blouse

fendant, -e [fɑ̃dɑ̃, -ɑ̃t] *adj* hysterical, side-splitting

fendante [fɑ̃dɑ̃t] *nf* **quelle fendante!, la fendante!** what a scream *or* hoot!

fendard, -e [fɑ̃dar, -ard] **1** *adj (amusant)* hysterical, side-splitting; **c'est fendard** it's hysterical *or* side-splitting
  2 *nm (pantalon) Br* trousers□, keks, *Am* pants□

fendre [fɑ̃dr] **se fendre** *vpr* **(a)** *(rire)* **se fendre (la gueule** *ou* **la poire** *ou* **la pêche** *ou* **la pipe)** to kill oneself (laughing), to crack up, to split one's

---

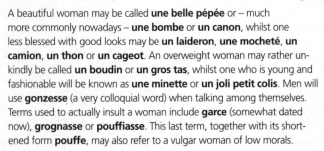

Spotlight on:
Les femmes

Many slang terms are used to refer to women, several of are, perhaps unsurprisingly, used only by men. There are, however, some less sexist terms which people of both genders may use, such as **nana** (a shortening of "Anne", and popularized by the Zola novel) and **nénette**, although since the 1990s both of these have been overtaken in popularity by **meuf** (the verlan term for "femme").

A beautiful woman may be called **une belle pépée** or – much more commonly nowadays – **une bombe** or **un canon**, whilst one less blessed with good looks may be **un laideron**, **une mocheté**, **un camion**, **un thon** or **un cageot**. An overweight woman may rather unkindly be called **un boudin** or **un gros tas**, whilst one who is young and fashionable will be known as **une minette** or **un joli petit colis**. Men will use **gonzesse** (a very colloquial word) when talking among themselves. Terms used to actually insult a woman include **garce** (somewhat dated now), **grognasse** or **pouffiasse**. This last term, together with its shortened form **pouffe**, may also refer to a vulgar woman of low morals.

The symbol [!] denotes a very familiar term, [!!] a vulgar one.

sides (**b**) **se fendre de qch** to come up with sth; **je me suis fendu de cinquante euros** I coughed up *or* forked out fifty euros; **il s'est pas fendu** he wasn't exactly generous, it didn't cost him much; **il s'est même pas fendu d'un sourire** he didn't even crack a smile (**c**) Can **se fendre le cul en quatre [!]** *(travailler beaucoup)* to work one's *Br* arse *or Am* ass off; *(se donner beaucoup de mal)* to bust a gut, *Am* to bust one's ass

fente [!!] [fɑ̃t] *nf (sexe de la femme)* crack, gash

fer [fɛr] *nm* **se retrouver les quatre fers en l'air** to fall flat on one's back

fermer [fɛrme] *vt* **ferme ta gueule!, la ferme!, ferme-la!** shut your face *or* mouth!, shut it!, *Br* belt up! ▶ *see also* **clapet**

ferraille [fɛrɑj] *nf (petite monnaie)* small change□, *Br* coppers, shrapnel

fesse [fɛs] *nf* (**a**) *(sexe)* sex□, *Br* bonking, shagging; **il s'intéresse qu'à la fesse** he's got a one-track mind, *Br* he's got sex on the brain; **film de fesse** porn movie, blue movie, *Am* skin flick; **magazine de fesse** porn *or* skin *or* girlie mag; Can **jouer aux fesses [!!]** to screw, *Br* to shag (**b**) **s'occuper de ses fesses** to mind one's own business ▶ *see also* **chaud, feu, peau**

fêtard, -e [fetar, -ard] *nm, f* party animal

fête [fɛt] *nf* **faire sa fête à qn** to give sb a hammering, *Br* to do sb over; **ça va être ma/ta/etc fête** I'm/you're/*etc* in for it

feu, -x [fø] *nm* (**a**) *(pistolet)* shooter, *Am* piece (**b**) **avoir le feu au cul [!]** *ou* **aux fesses** *(être pressé)* to be in a hell of a rush; *(aimer les plaisirs charnels)* to be horny as hell *Br* to be

gagging for it (**c**) *Cités* **mettre le feu** to knock 'em dead; **je suis allé voir Kanye West en concert, il a vraiment mis le feu à la salle** I went to see Kanye West in concert, he really took the roof off *or* set the place on fire (**d**) Can **prendre le feu** to blow a gasket *or* a fuse; **prendre le feu au cul [!!]** to go apeshit ▶ *see also* **péter, plancher¹**

feuille [fœj] *nf* (**a**) **être dur de la feuille** to be hard of hearing□ (**b**) *(billet de banque)* note□, *Am* greenback

feuj [føʒ] *(verlan juif)* **1** *adj* Jewish□ **2** *nmf* Jew□

fiasse [fjas] *nf* (**a**) *(prostituée)* whore, hooker (**b**) *(femme aux mœurs légères)* slut, tart, tramp, *Br* slapper (**c**) *(femme désagréable)* bitch, *Br* cow

---

ⓘ This word is an abbreviation of the word "pouffiasse".

---

ficelé, -e [fisle] *adj* (**a**) *(habillé)* **être mal ficelé** *Br* to be dressed like a scarecrow *or* a tramp, *Am* to look like a bum (**b**) *(structuré) (histoire, scénario)* **bien/bizarrement ficelé** well/strangely structured□

fiche [fiʃ], **ficher** [fiʃe] **1** *vt (faire)* to do□; **mais qu'est-ce qu'il fiche?** what on earth is he doing?
2 *se fiche, se ficher vpr* **se fiche** *ou* **se ficher de qn/qch** not to give a damn about sb/sth; **je m'en fiche pas mal!** I don't give a damn, I couldn't care less!; **tu te fiches de moi?** are you making a fool of me *or Br* taking the mickey?

fichu, -e [fiʃy] *adj* (**a**) *(hors d'usage)* **être fichu** to have had it, to be done for, *Br* to be knackered
(**b**) *(condamné à une mort certaine)*

être fichu to be done for, to have
had it

(**c**) *(dépréciatif)* *Br* blasted, *Am*
darn(ed); **il a un fichu caractère** he's
so *Br* blasted *or Am* darn(ed) difficult

(**d**) *(fait)* **être bien/mal fichu** to
have/not to have a great bod; **elle
est bien fichue, votre cuisine** your
kitchen's really well designed◻; **un
roman bien fichu** a well-structured
novel◻

(**e**) **mal fichu** *(malade)* under the
weather, *Br* off-colour

(**f**) *(capable)* **être fichu de faire qch**
to be quite capable of doing sth◻; **il
est pas fichu de le faire** he can't do
it ▸ *see also* **as**

fier-pet [fjɛrpɛ] *Can* **1** *adj* pomp-
ous◻, conceited◻
    2 *nm* pompous ass

fiesta [fjɛsta] *nf* wild party◻; **faire la
fiesta** to party

fieu [fjø] *nm* *Belg* sonny

fifi [fifi] *nm* *Can* (**a**) *(petit garçon efféminé)* sissy (**b**) *Offensive (homosexuel)* pansy, *Br* poof, *Am* fag

fifille [fifij] *nf* girl◻, chick, *Am* bird

fifine [fifin] *nf* *Can Offensive (lesbienne)* dyke, *Br* lezzie, lesbo

fifty-fifty [fiftififti] *adv* fifty-fifty

filer [file] **1** *vt (donner)* to give◻; **file-
moi une clope** give me a *Br* fag *or
Am* cig; **filer une baffe à qn** to
smack *or* clout sb
    2 *vi (partir)* to get going *or* moving;
il faut que je file I must be off, I
have to get going; **allez, file, tu vas
être en retard!** go on, off you go,
you're going to be late!

film [film] *nm* **se faire un film** to be
living in a dream world

filoche [filɔʃ] *nf* shadowing, tailing

filocher [filɔʃe] **1** *vt (suivre)* to shadow, to tail

2 *vi (se dépêcher)* to get a move on,
to move it, to get one's skates on,
Am to get it in gear

fiole [fjɔl] *nf* (**a**) *(visage)* face◻, mug
(**b**) *(tête)* head◻, nut

fion [!] [fjɔ̃] *nm* (**a**) *(postérieur)* *Br*
arse, *Am* ass; **se casser le fion (pour
faire qch)** to bust a gut *or Am* one's
ass (doing sth) (**b**) *(anus)* *Br* arsehole,
Am asshole; **l'avoir dans le fion** *(se
faire avoir)* to get screwed *or* shafted
(**c**) *(chance)* luck◻; **avoir du fion** to
be lucky◻ *or Br* jammy; **ne pas avoir
de fion** to have rotten luck

fiotte [!!] [fjɔt] *nf Offensive* queer,
Br poof, *Am* fag

fissa [fisa] *adv* **faire fissa** to get a
move on, to get one's skates on, *Am*
to get it in gear

fix, fixe [fiks] *nm* fix *(of drug)*

fixette [fiksɛt] *nf* **faire une fixette
sur qn/qch** to be obsessed with sb/
sth◻, *Br* to have sb/sth on the brain

flag [flag] **en flag** *adv (abbr* **en fla-
grant délit)** **être pris en flag** to
get caught red-handed *or* with one's
pants down

flagada [flagada] *adj inv* washed-out;
**je me sens tout flagada depuis
quelques jours** I've been feeling all
washed-out for several days

flamber [flɑ̃be] **1** *vt (dépenser)*
to blow; **il flambe un fric fou** he
blows huge amounts of cash, he
spends money like water
    2 *vi* (**a**) *(jouer avec passion)* to be
a heavy gambler◻ *or* a gambling nut
(**b**) *(se donner des airs)* to show off

flambeur, -euse [flɑ̃bœr, -øz] *nm,f*
(**a**) *(joueur)* heavy gambler◻, gambling nut (**b**) *(personne qui se donne
des airs)* show-off

flan [flɑ̃] *nm* (**a**) **en rester comme
deux ronds de flan** to be flabber-

gasted *or Br* gobsmacked (**b**) **c'est du flan** it's a load of nonsense *or Br* rubbish

flancher [flɑ̃ʃe] *vi (abandonner)* to chuck it in, to throw in the towel; **son cœur a flanché** his heart gave out; **j'ai la mémoire qui flanche** my memory's going

flanc-mou [flɑ̃mu] *nm Can Br* skiver, *Am* goldbrick

flanquer [flɑ̃ke] **1** *vt* **flanquer une claque/un coup à qn** to smack/ punch sb; **flanquer qch par terre** *(en le faisant exprès)* to chuck or fling sth on the floor; *(accidentellement)* to knock sth onto the floor[□]; **flanquer qn à la porte** to kick sb out; **flanquer la trouille à qn** to put the wind up sb, to scare sb stiff *or* witless
2 *se flanquer vpr* **se flanquer (la gueule) par terre** to fall flat on one's face

flapi, -e [flapi] *adj* dead beat, bushed, *Br* knackered

flash [flaʃ] *nm* rush *(after taking drugs)*

flasher [flaʃe] *vi* (**a**) *(après absorption de drogue)* to get a rush (**b**) **flasher sur qn** to fall for sb; **flasher sur qch** to fall in love with sth

flèche [flɛʃ] *nm* **j'ai pas un flèche** I'm totally broke *or Br* skint *or* strapped

flémingite [flemɛ̃ʒit] *nf Hum* laziness[□], lazyitis; **être atteint de flémingite aiguë** to suffer from acute laziness *or* lazyitis

flemmard, -e [flɛmar, -ard] **1** *adj* lazy[□]
2 *nm,f* lazy so-and-so

flemmarder [flɛmarde] *vi* to laze *or* lounge about

flemme [flɛm] *nf* laziness[□]; **j'ai**

la flemme I can't be bothered doing anything, I don't feel like doing anything; **j'ai la flemme de le faire maintenant** I can't be bothered doing it just now; **je me traîne une de ces flemmes depuis quelque temps** I haven't felt like doing anything *or* I've been feeling really lazy for a while now

flic [flik] *nm* cop, *Br* plod, *Am* flatfoot

ⓘ This term comes from the word "Fliege", a German translation of the French word "mouche" (fly), which used to mean "policeman" in French slang.

---

flicage [flikaʒ] *nm* police surveillance[□]; **ils craignent le flicage du courrier électronique par la direction** they're scared that the management are monitoring *or* policing their e-mails[□]

flicaille [flikaj] *nf* **la flicaille** the cops, the pigs, *Br* the filth

flingue [flɛ̃g] *nm* shooter, *Am* piece

ⓘ This term comes from the Bavarian word "Flinke", a variant of the German word "Flinte" (itself related to the English word "flint"), which means "shotgun".

---

flinguer [flɛ̃ge] **1** *vt* (**a**) *(tuer)* to blow away (**b**) *(casser)* to wreck, to bust, *Br* to knacker
2 *se flinguer vpr* to blow one's brains out

flip [flip] *nm* (**a**) *(déprime)* **être en plein flip** to be on a real downer; **c'est le flip!** what a downer! (**b**) *(après l'absorption de drogue)* depression[□], downer *(as the after-effect of taking cocaine or amphetamines)*

flippant, -e [flipᾶ, -ᾶt] *adj (déprimant)* depressing□; **être flippant** to be a downer

flipper [flipe] *vi* (a) *(être angoissé)* to feel down, to be on a downer; **faire flipper qn** to get sb down (b) *(avoir peur)* to be scared□, to be freaking out *or Br* bricking it (c) *(après absorption de drogue)* to feel down *(as the after-effect of taking cocaine or amphetamines)* ▶ *see also* **mère**

fliqué, -e [flike] *adj* crawling *or* heaving with cops

fliquer [flike] *vt Pej* (a) *(population, employés)* to keep under surveillance□; **il flique complètement sa femme** he watches his wife like a hawk (b) *(quartier)* to police□

flo [flo] *nmf Can (adolescent)* teenager□, teen

flopée, floppée [flɔpe] *nf* **une flopée (de)** a whole bunch (of), loads (of), tons (of)

flotte [flɔt] *nf (eau)* water□; **prendre la flotte** to get soaked *(in the rain)*; **tomber à la flotte** to fall in□; **t'as pas autre chose que de la flotte à nous proposer?** have you got nothing better than water to offer us?□

flotter [flɔte] *vi (pleuvoir)* to rain□

flouse, flouze [fluz] *nm* cash, dough, *Br* dosh, *Am* bucks

ⓘ This term comes from an Arabic word meaning "money".

flûte [flyt] *nf* (a) *(mensonges)* lies□, fibs, *Br* porkies (b) **jouer de la flûte [!!], tailler une flûte [!!]** to give sb a blow job, to suck sb off, to give sb head

flûter [flyte] *vi (dire des mensonges)* to tell lies□ *or* fibs *or Br* porkies

flûteur, -euse [flytœr, -øz] *nm,f* liar□, fibber

flyé, -e [flaje] *Can Joual* **1** *adj* spaced-out
2 *nm,f (paumé)* space cadet; *(drogué)* junkie

flyer [flajœr] *nm (prospectus de club)* flier□, flyer□

foies [fwa] *nmpl* **avoir les foies** to be scared stiff *or* to death *or* out of one's wits

foin [fwɛ̃] *nm* (a) **faire du foin** *(du tapage)* to make a racket; *(du scandale)* to make waves, to cause a stink (b) *Can* **avoir du foin** *(être riche)* to be loaded *or Br* rolling in it; **il a du foin à vendre** *(sa braguette est ouverte)* his flies are undone□, he's flying low

foire [fwar] *nf* (a) *(désordre)* chaos□, *Br* bedlam; **c'est la foire, là-dedans!** it's a madhouse *or Br* it's bedlam in there! (b) **faire la foire** to have a wild time; **il ne pense qu'à faire la foire** all he thinks about is having a good time

foirer [fware] **1** *vt (rater)* to make a *Br* cock-up *or* balls-up *or Am* ball-up of; **j'ai complètement foiré l'interro d'anglais** I made a complete *Br* cock-up *or* balls-up *or Am* ball-up of the English exam
2 *vi* (a) *(échouer)* to be a *Br* cock-up *or* balls-up *or Am* ball-up; **le coup a complètement foiré** the job was a complete *Br* cock-up *or* balls-up *or Am* ball-up (b) **[!!]** *(déféquer)* to shit, to crap; **il a foiré dans son froc tellement il a eu la trouille** he was so scared he shat himself

foireux, -euse [fwarø, -øz] *adj* useless, lousy; **j'en ai marre de lui et de ses plans foireux** I've had it up to here with him and his lousy schemes

foldingue [fɔldɛ̃g] *adj* crazy, loopy, *Br* mental, *Am* wacko

ⓘ This is a conflation of the words "fol" (variant of "fou") and "dingue".

folichon, -onne [fɔliʃɔ̃, -ɔn] *adj* **pas folichon** not much fun; **ça n'a rien de folichon** it's no fun

folkeux, -euse [fɔlkø, -øz] *nm,f (amateur de musique folklorique)* folkie

folklo [fɔlklo] *adj inv (abbr* **folklorique**) bizarre, weird and wonderful; *(personne)* eccentric□, off-the-wall, *Am* kooky

folle [fɔl] *nf (homosexuel)* queen; **c'est vraiment une folle perdue ce mec-là, on croirait qu'il sort tout droit de "La Cage aux folles"** that guy really is a screaming queen, he's like something out of "La Cage aux folles"

foncedé, -e [fɔ̃sde] *adj Cités (verlan* **défoncé**) stoned, wrecked

fondu, -e [fɔ̃dy] *adj (fou)* round the bend, out to lunch, off one's rocker *or* trolley

fonsdé, -e [fɔ̃sde] *adj Cités (verlan* **défoncé**) stoned, wrecked

foot [fut] *nm (abbr* **football**) *Br* football□, footie, *Am* soccer□,

footeux [futø] *nm (amateur de football) Br* footie fan, *Am* soccer fan□

foqué, -e [!!] [fɔke] *Can Joual* **1** *adj* fucked-up
    2 *nm,f* fuck-up

ⓘ This word comes from the English word "fuck".

foquer [!!] [fɔke] *vt Can Joual (voi-*

ture) to fuck, *Br* to bugger, *Am* to total; *(personne, famille, vie)* to fuck up

ⓘ This word comes from the English word "fuck".

fort [fɔr] **1** *adj* **c'est fort** that's quite something; **c'est un peu fort (de café)** that's a bit much *or* rich
    2 *adv* (**a**) **y aller un peu fort** to go a bit over the top *or Br* OTT; **tu y es allé un peu fort avec le poivre** you overdid it a bit *or* you were a bit heavy-handed with the pepper (**b**) **faire fort** to do really well□, to excel oneself□ ▸ *see also* **gueule**

fortiche [fɔrtiʃ] *adj* clever□, smart□; **il est fortiche aux échecs, mon cousin** my cousin's brilliant at chess

fortifs [fɔrtif] *nfpl (abbr* **fortification**) = the old defence works around Paris, once a favourite area for criminals

fossile [fɔsil] *nm (individu rétrograde)* fossil

fouetter [fwɛte] *vi (sentir mauvais)* to stink, *Br* to pong

foufoune [!] [fufun] *nf* (**a**) *(sexe de la femme)* pussy, *Br* fanny, snatch (**b**) *Can* **foufounes** *(fesses)* buns, butt

fouille [fuj] *nf (poche)* pocket□

fouille-merde [!] [fujmɛrd] *nmf inv* busybody, *Br* nosey parker

fouiller [fuje] **se fouiller** [!] *vpr* **tu peux toujours te fouiller!** you haven't a hope in hell!

fouiner [fwine] *vi* to nose *or* ferret about (**dans** in)

fouler [fule] **se fouler** *vpr* **se fouler (la rate)** to strain *or* overexert oneself□; **t'aurais pu te fouler un peu plus!** you could have made a bit more of an effort!; **tu t'es vraiment**

Le symbole □ *indique que la traduction n'est pas argotique.*

pas foulé (la rate)! you didn't exactly strain *or* overexert yourself!

foultitude [fultityd] *nf* **une foultitude (de)** masses (of), loads (of), tons (of)

ⓘ This term is a conflation of the words "foule" (crowd) and "multitude".

---

foune [!] [fun] *nf* pussy, *Br* fanny, snatch; **avoir de la foune** *(avoir de la chance) (habituellement)* to have the luck of the devil; *(ponctuellement)* to have a stroke of luck◻

four [fur] *nm (échec)* flop, *Br* washout, *Am* bomb, turkey; **faire un four** to be a flop *or Br* a washout, *Am* to bomb

fourbi [furbi] *nm* **(a)** *(désordre)* shambles, mess **(b)** *(affaires)* stuff, *Br* gear

fourguer [furge] *vt* **(a)** *(vendre)* to flog; *(placer)* to unload, to palm off; **fourguer qch à qn** *(vendre)* to flog sth to sb; *(placer)* to unload sth on sb, to palm sth off on sb **(b)** *(dénoncer)* to squeal on, *Br* to grass on, to shop, *Am* to rat on

fourmi [furmi] *nf (petit revendeur de drogue)* (small-time) dealer

fourrer [fure] *vt* **(a)** *(mettre)* to stick, to shove **(b)** [!!] *(posséder sexuellement)* to screw, to shaft, to poke; *Can Joual* **fourrer le chien** *(perdre son temps)* to fuck around ► *see also* **doigt**

foutage [futaʒ] *nm* **c'est du foutage de gueule** you/they/*etc* gotta be kidding!, *Br* that's just taking the piss!

foutaise [futɛz] *nf* **de la foutaise, des foutaises** crap, bull; **raconter des foutaises** to talk crap *or* bull

fouteur, -euse [futœr, -øz] *nm,f* **fouteur de merde** [!] shit-stirrer

foutoir [futwar] *nm* shambles; **quel foutoir dans sa chambre!** her room's a complete pigsty *or* tip!

foutraque [futrak] *adj* nuts, *Br* crackers

foutre [futr] **1** *vt* **(a)** [!] *(faire)* to do◻; **ne rien foutre, ne pas en foutre une** to do damn all *or Br* bugger all *or* sod all; **j'en ai rien à foutre!** I don't give a shit!; **qu'est-ce qu'il fout?** what the hell is he doing?; **qu'est-ce que tu veux que ça me foute?** what the hell do I care?, what the hell does it matter to me?; **qu'est-ce que j'ai bien pu foutre de mes clés?** what the hell can I have done with my keys?

(b) [!] *(mettre)* to stick, to dump, *Br* to bung; **il sait pas où il a foutu les clés** he doesn't know what the hell he's done with the keys; **il peut pas bouffer sans en foutre partout** he can't eat without getting his food everywhere; **foutre qch par terre** *(en le faisant exprès)* to dump *or* chuck sth on the floor; *(accidentellement)* to knock sth onto the floor◻; **foutre qn à la porte** to chuck *or* kick sb out; **foutre son poing dans la gueule à qn** to give sb a punch in the face; **foutre la paix à qn** to get off sb's back; **ça la fout mal** it doesn't look too good; **foutre qn dedans** to mislead sb◻; **j't'en foutrais, moi, de l'esprit d'équipe!** team spirit, I'll give you *Br* bloody *or Am* goddamn team spirit!; **qui est-ce qui m'a foutu un empoté pareil?** how the hell did I end up with such a total *Br* arsehole *or Am* asshole?

(c) va te faire foutre [!!] fuck off!; **qu'il aille se faire foutre!** [!!] he can fuck right off *or* get to fuck!

2 *vi* **foutre sur la gueule à qn** [!] to smash sb's face in, to waste sb's face

---

The symbol **[!]** denotes a very familiar term, **[!!]** a vulgar one.

3 se foutre [!] *vpr* **(a)** *(se mettre)* **se foutre à faire qch** to start doing sth[□]; **il s'est foutu de l'encre partout** he got ink all over himself[□]; **s'en foutre plein les poches** to rake it in; **se foutre par terre, se foutre la gueule par terre** [!!] to fall flat on one's face; **se foutre dedans** to screw up, to blow it
(b) se foutre de qch not to give a shit about sth; **se foutre de qn** *(être indifférent)* not to give a a shit about sb; *(se moquer)* to make a fool of sb, *Br* to take the piss out of sb; **une montre en or! elle s'est pas foutue de toi!** a gold watch! she doesn't do things by halves!, *or* she doesn't mess about, does she?
4 [!!] *nm* spunk, come, cum ▸ *see also* **air, camp, gueule**

foutrement [!] [futrəmɑ̃] *adv* damn(ed), *Br* bloody

foutu, -e [!] [futy] *adj* **(a)** *(hors d'usage)* **être foutu** to have had it, to be done, *Br* to be knackered *or* buggered
(b) *(condamné à une mort certaine)* **être foutu** to have had it, to be done for
(c) *(sans espoir)* **c'est foutu, jamais on n'y arrivera** we're screwed *or Br* buggered, we'll never do it
(d) *(dépréciatif)* damn(ed), godawful, *Br* bloody; **elle a un foutu caractère** she's so damn(ed) *or Br* bloody difficult
(e) *(fait)* **être bien/mal foutu** to have/not to have a great bod; **elle est bien foutue, votre cuisine** your kitchen's really well designed[□]; **un roman bien foutu** a well-structured novel[□]
(f) mal foutu *(souffrant)* under the weather, *Br* off-colour
(g) *(capable)* **être foutu de faire qch** to be quite capable of doing sth[□]; **ne pas être foutu de faire**

qch to be incapable of doing sth[□]
▸ *see also* **as**

fracasse [frakas], **fracassé, -e** [frakase] *adj Cités* smashed, wrecked, wasted

fraîche [frɛʃ] *nf (argent)* cash, dough, *Br* dosh, *Am* bucks

frais¹ [frɛ] *nm* **mettre qn au frais** to put sb inside *or* away *or* behind bars

frais² [frɛ] *nmpl* **(a) aux frais de la princesse** *(aux frais de l'État)* at the taxpayer's expense[□]; *(aux frais d'une société)* at the company's expense[□]
(b) arrêter les frais to throw in the towel *or* sponge

frais-chié, -e [!] [frɛʃje] *nm,f Can (homme)* cocky bastard; *(femme)* cocky bitch

fraise [frɛz] *nf* **ramener sa fraise** *(arriver)* to turn up, to show (up), to show one's face; *(intervenir inopportunément)* to stick one's oar in; **mais je t'ai rien demandé! pourquoi il faut toujours que tu ramènes ta fraise?** I didn't ask you, why do you always have to stick your oar in?; **ramène ta fraise!** get over here! ▸ *see also* **sucrer**

franchouillard, -e [frɑ̃ʃujar, -ard] **1** *adj* typically French[□]
2 *nm,f* typical Frenchman, *f* Frenchwoman[□]

ⓘ This word, whilst not overly pejorative, describes the average French person complete with the stereotypical characteristics of narrow-mindedness and jingoism.

franco [frɑ̃ko] *adv* **vas-y franco!** *(pour encourager quelqu'un)* go for it!; **vas-y franco si tu veux que ça rentre** you'll have to hit/push/*etc* it hard for it to go in; **il y est allé franco avec le piment** he didn't hold back with the chilli; **elle lui a dit ce qu'elle pensait de lui et elle y est allé franco** she told him what she thought of him and she didn't mince her words

frangibus [frɑ̃ʒibys] *nm* brother□, bro

frangin [frɑ̃ʒɛ̃] *nm* brother□, bro

frangine [frɑ̃ʒin] *nf* (a) *(sœur)* sister□, sis (b) *(femme, fille)* chick, *Br* bird

frappadingue [frapadɛ̃g] *adj* crazy, nuts, *Br* bonkers

ⓘ This is a conflation of the words "frappé" and "dingue".

---

frappe [frap] *nf* **une (petite) frappe** a (little) hoodlum *or Am* hood

frappé, -e [frape] *adj (fou)* crazy, nuts, *Br* bonkers

frapper [frape] **se frapper** *vpr* **ne pas se frapper** not to get worked up; **te frappe pas** take it easy!, chill (out)!

frérot [frero] *nm* brother□, bro

fric [frik] *nm* cash, dough, *Br* dosh, *Am* bucks

frichti [friʃti] *nm* cooked meal□; **ça sent bon le frichti** there's a nice smell of cooking□

ⓘ This word comes from an Alsatian word similar to the German word "Frühstück", which means "breakfast".

---

fricot [friko] *nm* food□, chow, grub

fricoter [frikɔte] **1** *vt* **qu'est-ce qu'il fricote?** what's he up to?

2 *vi* **fricoter avec qn** *(avoir des relations sexuelles)* to have a thing with sb; *(avoir des relations)* to have shady *or Br* dodgy dealings with sb;

il paraît que ce politicien fricote avec la Mafia apparently this politician has some shady *or Br* dodgy dealings with the Mafia

Fridolin [fridɔlɛ̃] *nm Offensive* Kraut, Boche

ⓘ This term is somewhat dated now and is normally used in the context of Franco-German conflicts, such as the two World Wars. Depending on the context and the tone of voice used, it may be either offensive or affectionately humorous.

---

frigo [frigo] *nm (abbr* **Frigidaire®)** fridge

frime [frim] *nf* (a) *(fanfaronnade)* **les lunettes noires, c'est pour la frime** dark glasses are just for posing in; **bon, t'arrête ta frime?** will you stop showing off!; **tu l'aurais vu avec son nouveau cuir, la frime!** you should have seen him in his new leather jacket, what a poser! (b) *(comportement trompeur)* **c'est de la frime** it's all an act, it's all put on

frimer [frime] *vi* to show off

frimeur, -euse [frimœr, -øz] *nm,f* show-off

fringale [frɛ̃gal] *nf* hunger□; **avoir la fringale** to have the munchies

fringue [frɛ̃g] *nf* piece of clothing□; **j'ai plus une fringue à me mettre** I've got nothing to wear□; **des fringues** clothes□, threads, *Br* gear

fringuer [frɛ̃ge] **se fringuer** *vpr* to get dressed□; **être bien/mal fringué** to be well-/badly-dressed□; **elle aime bien se fringuer pour sortir** she likes to get all dressed up to go out; **il sait pas se fringuer** he's got no dress sense□; **elle se fringue très seventies** she wears really seventies clothes, she dresses really seventies

fripé, -e [fripe] *adj Can* bushed, *Br* knackered, shattered

friqué, -e [frike] *adj* loaded, *Br* rolling in it, *Am* rolling in dough

Frisé [frize] *nm Offensive (Allemand)* Kraut, Boche

ⓘ This term is somewhat dated now and is normally used in the context of Franco-German conflicts, such as the two World Wars. Depending on the context and the tone of voice used, it may be either offensive or affectionately humorous.

frisquet, -ette [friskɛ, -ɛt] *adj* chilly□, *Br* nippy, parky; **il fait frisquet ce matin** it's a bit chilly or *Br* nippy this morning

frite [frit] *nf* (**a**) *(énergie)* **avoir la frite** to be on top form, to have loads of energy (**b**) *(coup)* flick; **faire une frite à qn** to flick sb on the bottom (**c**) *(visage)* face□, mug; **se fendre la frite** to crack up, to howl (with laughter)

friter [frite] **1** *vt (battre)* **friter qn** to beat sb up, to kick sb's head in

2 se friter *vpr* to have a *Br* punch-up or *Am* fist fight; **il y avait deux mecs en train de se friter dans la rue** there were two guys having a *Br* punch-up or *Am* fist fight in the street

fritz [frits] *nm Offensive* Kraut, Boche

ⓘ This term is somewhat dated now and is normally used in the context of Franco-German conflicts, such as the two World Wars. Depending on the context and the tone of voice used, it may be either

offensive or affectionately humorous.

froc [frɔk] *nm (pantalon) Br* trousers□, keks, *Am* pants□; **faire dans son froc** *(déféquer, avoir peur)* to shit or crap oneself; **baisser son froc** to demean oneself□; **il a encore baissé son froc devant le patron** he let the boss walk all over him again ▸ *see also* **chier, pisser**

from [frɔm] *nmf (abbr* **fromage blanc**) *(Français de souche)* = French person of native stock as opposed to immigrants or their descendants

fromage [frɔmaʒ] *nm* (**a**) **il n'y a pas de quoi en faire tout un fromage** there's no need to make such a big deal or a song and dance about it, *Am* there's no need to make a federal case out of it (**b**) **fromage blanc** *(Français de souche)* = French person of native stock as opposed to immigrants or their descendants

fromgi [frɔmʒi], **frometon** [frɔmtɔ̃] *nm* cheese□

frotte-manche [frɔtmɑ̃ʃ] *nmf Belg* bootlicker

frotter [frɔte] *vt Belg* **frotter la manche à qn** to butter sb up

frotteur [frɔtœr] *nm* = pervert who enjoys rubbing himself against women in crowded places

froussard, -e [frusar, -ard] *adj & nm,f* chicken *(person)*

frousse [frus] *nf* **avoir la frousse** to be scared stiff, *Br* to be bricking it; **foutre la frousse à qn** to scare the living daylights out of sb

frusques [frysk] *nfpl* clothes□, threads, *Br* gear

fufute [fyfyt] *adj* **elle n'est pas fufute** she's no rocket scientist, *Br* she's not the sharpest knife in the drawer

Le symbole □ indique que la traduction n'est pas argotique.

fumant, -e [fymã, -ãt] *adj* **un coup fumant** a masterstroke°

fumantes [fymãt] *nfpl (chaussettes)* socks°

fumasse [fymas] *adj* fuming, livid

fumer [fyme] *vt* (**a**) *(battre)* to clobber, to thump (**b**) *(tuer)* to kill°, *Br* to do in

fumette [fymɛt] *nf* getting stoned; **c'est un habitué de la fumette** he's always getting stoned, he's a stoner; **il y a que la fumette qui l'intéresse** all he's interested in is getting stoned

fumier [!] [fymje] *nm* bastard, shit; **espèce de fumier!** you bastard!

fumiste [fymist] **1** *adj (attitude, personne)* lazy°; **il est un peu fumiste** he's a bit of a shirker

2 *nmf* shirker, *Br* layabout; **c'est un fumiste** he doesn't exactly kill himself working

fumisterie [fymistəri] *nf* sham, farce; **une vaste fumisterie** an absolute farce

fun [fœn] **1** *adj inv* fun°

2 *nm* fun°; **faire qch pour le fun** to do sth just for fun *or* for the fun of it

furax [fyraks], **furibard, -e** [fyribar, -ard] *adj* seething, livid

fusée [fyze] *nf* **lâcher une fusée** *(vomir)* to throw up, to puke, *Br & Austr* to chunder, *Am* to barf; *(faire un pet)* to fart, *Br* to let off

fusiller [fysije] *vt (briser)* to wreck, to bust, *Br* to knacker; **baisse le volume, autrement tu vas fusiller tes enceintes** turn it down or you'll wreck *or Br* knacker your speakers

futal [fytal], **fute** [fyt] *nm Br* trousers°, keks, *Am* pants°

fute-fute [fytfyt] *adj* **elle n'est pas fute-fute** she's no rocket scientist, *Br* she's not the sharpest knife in the drawer

Gg

G [ʒe] *nm Belg (abbr* **GSM**) *(téléphone portable) Br* mobile, *Am* cell

gadin [gadɛ̃] *nm* **prendre** *ou* **se ramasser un gadin** to fall flat on one's face

gadji [gadʒi] *nf Cités* chick, *Br* bird

ⓘ This is a Romany term that originally referred to a non-gypsy married woman.

gadjo [gadʒo] *nm Cités* guy, *Br* bloke

ⓘ This is a Romany term that originally referred to a non-gypsy married man.

gaffe [gaf] *nf* (a) *(bévue)* gaffe, blunder, *Br* boob, *Am* boo-boo; **faire une gaffe** to put one's foot in it, to boob, *Am* to make a boo-boo, to goof (b) **fais gaffe, tu risques de glisser!** watch out, you might slip!; **faire gaffe à qch** *(y prendre garde)* to be careful of sth, to watch out for sth; **fais gaffe à toi!** *(prends soin de toi)* take care of yourself!; *(menace)* be careful!, watch it!; **fais gaffe à ce que tu dis!** be careful *or* watch what you say!

gaffer [gafe] *vi* to put one's foot in it, *Br* to boob, *Am* to make a boo-boo, to goof

gaffeur, -euse [gafœr, -øz] **1** *adj* **être gaffeur** to be always putting one's

foot in it *or Am* putting one's foot in one's mouth

2 *nm,f* **c'est un gaffeur** he's always putting his foot in it *or Am* putting his foot in his mouth

gaga [gaga] *adj* gaga, *Br* away with the fairies

gagedé [gaʒde] *exclam Cités (verlan* **dégage**) get out of here!, get lost!

galère [galɛr] **1** *adj* **c'est galère** what a pain *or* hassle; **lui et ses plans galères!** him and his lousy ideas!

2 *nf (situation pénible)* pain, hassle; **c'est la galère!, quelle galère!** what a pain *or* hassle!; **se foutre dans une galère** to get oneself into a mess; **être en galère** to be in a mess *or* a pickle; **il est en galère de thunes en ce moment** he's a bit short of cash *or Br* strapped for cash at the moment

ⓘ The slang terms "galère" (a messy situation) and "galérer" (to have a hard time) come from Molière's play *Les Fourberies de Scapin* (1671). In one scene, a valet is trying to get some money out of a man by telling him that his son is a galley-slave on a Turkish ship, and can only be freed on payment of a ransom. The father just keeps repeating "Que diable allait-il faire dans cette galère?" ("What the devil was he doing in that galley?").

galérer [galere] *vi* to have a hard time (of it); **tu vas galérer pour trouver à te garer dans le quartier** you're going to have a hard time *or* a lot of hassle finding a parking space in the area; **il a beaucoup galéré dans sa jeunesse** he had a really hard time of it when he was young

galette [galɛt] *nf* (**a**) *(argent)* cash, dough, *Br* dosh, *Am* bucks (**b**) *(disque)* record□

galipote [galipɔt] *nf Can* **courir la galipote** to be a skirt-chaser *or* a womanizer

galoche [galɔʃ] *nf* French kiss, *Br* snog; **rouler une galoche à qn** to French-kiss sb, *Br* to snog sb, *Am* to make out with sb

galure [galyr], **galurin** [galyrɛ̃] *nm* hat□

gamberger [gɑ̃bɛrʒe] *vi* (**a**) *(réfléchir)* to think hard□ (**b**) *(ruminer)* to brood□

gambette [gɑ̃bɛt] *nf* leg□, pin ▸ *see also* **tricoter**

ⓘ This term is a Northern French variant of the word "jambette"; its root is the same as the English word "gammon" and the verb "to gambol".

---

gamelle [gamɛl] *nf* (**a**) *(baiser)* French kiss, *Br* snog; **rouler une gamelle à qn** to French-kiss sb, *Br* to snog sb, *Am* to make out with sb (**b**) **prendre une gamelle** to fall flat on one's face

ganache [ganaʃ] *nf Br* divvy, wally, *Am* dork

gâpette [gɑpɛt] *nf* (flat) cap□

garage [garaʒ] *nm Hum* **garage à bites [!!]** nympho, sex maniac; **c'est un vrai garage à bites [!!]**
she's the town bike, she's seen more ceilings than Michelangelo

garce [gars] *nf* bitch, *Br* cow

garde-à-vous [gardavu] *nm Hum* **être au garde-à-vous** *(avoir une érection)* to have a hard-on *or* boner

garetteci [garɛtsi] *nf Cités (verlan* **cigarette**) *Br* fag, *Am* cig

garot [garo] *Br* fag, *Am* cig

garrocher [garɔʃe] *Can* **1** *vt* to chuck, to fling
2 se garrocher *vpr* to get a move on, to move it, *Am* to get it in gear

gaspard [gaspar] *nm* rat□

gastos [gastos] *nm (bistrot)* bar□, *Br* boozer

ⓘ This term is derived from the German word "Gasthaus" (inn).

---

gâteau [gɑto] *nm* **c'est pas du gâteau** *(c'est pénible)* it's no picnic, it's no walk in the park; *(ça demande un effort intellectuel)* it's no walkover, it's not as easy as it looks, *Am* it's no cakewalk

gâterie [gɑtri] *nf Hum* **faire une gâterie à qn [!]** *(fellation)* to go down on sb, to suck sb off, to give sb a blow-job; *(cunnilingus)* to go down on sb, to lick sb out; **se faire faire une petite gâterie** to get some oral; *(fellation)* to get a blow-job

gatter [gate] *vt Suisse (cours)* to skip, to cut; **gatter l'école** *Br* to bunk off, to skive off, *Am* to play hooky

gauche [goʃ] *nf* **mettre de l'argent à gauche** to stash some money away; **jusqu'à la gauche** totally□, completely□; **il s'est fait entuber jusqu'à la gauche** he got totally *or* completely screwed ▸ *see also* **arme**

gaucho [goʃo] *nmf* leftie, lefty

gaufre [gofr] *nf (chute)* fall□; **se prendre une gaufre** to go flying, *Am* to take a spill

gaufrer [gofre] **se gaufrer** *vpr (faire une chute)* to go flying, *Am* to take a spill

gaule [gol] *nf* **avoir la gaule [!!!]** to have a hard-on *or* a boner

gaulé, -e [gole] *adj* **être bien/mal gaulé** to have/not to have a great bod

gauler [gole] *vt (attraper)* to nab, *Br* to nick; **se faire gauler** to get nabbed *or Br* nicked

gaulois, -e [golwa, -az] *nm,f Cités* = French person of native stock, as opposed to immigrants or their descendants

gaver [gave] *vt (importuner)* **gaver qn** to bug sb, *Br* to do sb's head in, to get up sb's nose, *Am* to give sb a pain (in the neck); **putain, qu'est-ce qu'il peut me gaver avec ses questions!** fucking hell, he *Br* does my head in *or Am* gives me a real pain with all his questions!

gay [gɛ] *adj & nm* gay□

gaz [gaz] *nm* **être dans le gaz** to be out of it

gazer [gaze] *v imp* **ça gaze?** how's it going?, how's things?; **ça gaze** everything's fine

GDB [ʒedebe] *nf (abbr* **gueule de bois)** hangover□

géant, -e [ʒeɑ̃, -ɑ̃t] *adj (excellent)* cool, *Br* wicked, *Am* awesome

gégène [ʒeʒɛn] **1** *adj* brilliant, fantastic

2 *nf* **la gégène** = torture by electric shock

ⓘ Sense 2 is derived from the word "génératrice" (generator).

gelé, -e [ʒəle] *adj Can (drogué)* wasted, wrecked, out of it

geler [ʒ(ə)le] **se geler** *vpr* to freeze to death; **se geler le cul [!]**, **se les geler [!]** to freeze one's *Br* arse *or Am* ass off

gencives [ʒɑ̃siv] *nfpl* **qu'est-ce qu'il s'est pris dans les gencives!** he really got it in the neck!; **elle lui a envoyé dans les gencives que…** she told him straight to his face that…

genhar [ʒɑ̃ar] *nm (verlan* **argent)** cash, dough, *Br* dosh, *Am* bucks

génial, -e [ʒenjal] *adj (excellent)* great, brilliant, fantastic

genre [ʒɑ̃r] *nm* (a) *(environ)* **ça fait genre 200 euros** it's something like *or* somewhere around 200 euros (b) *(type)* **son copain c'est un mec genre hippie** her boyfriend's the hippie type

géo [ʒeo] *nf (abbr* **géographie)** geography□, geog

gerbant, -e [ʒɛrbɑ̃, -ɑ̃t] *adj* **je trouve ça gerbant, la tequila** tequila makes me want to puke; **c'est gerbant, la façon dont ils l'ont traité** it makes me sick, the way they treated him

gerbe [ʒɛrb] *nf (vomissement)* puke, vom, *Am* barf; **foutre la gerbe à qn** *(donner envie de vomir)* to make sb want to puke *or Am* barf; *(dégoûter)* to make sb sick; **avoir la gerbe** to want to puke *or Am* barf; **ça me fout la gerbe de voir un tel étalage de luxe alors qu'il y a des gens qu'arrivent à peine à se nourrir** it makes me sick to see such a show of wealth when there are people who can barely afford to eat

gerber [ʒɛrbe] *vi* to throw up, to puke, *Br & Austr* to chunder, *Am* to barf; **gerber sur qch** *(en dire du mal)* to slate, *Br* to slag off; **la critique a carrément gerbé sur le film** the critic tore the film to shreds

gicler [ʒikle] *vi* to be off, to push off, *Am* to split

giga [ʒiga] *adj inv* great, *Br* wicked, *Am* awesome

gigue [ʒig] *nf* **une grande gigue** a beanpole, *Am* a stringbean

girond, -e [ʒirɔ̃, -ɔ̃d] *adj* gorgeous, hot, *Br* fit

givré, -e [ʒivre] *adj (fou)* crackers, crazy, *Br* bonkers

glamour [glamur] *adj inv* glam

gland [!] [glɑ̃] *nm (imbécile)* dick, prick

glander [glɑ̃de] **1** *vt* **qu'est-ce que tu glandes?** what the hell are you doing?; **j'en ai rien à glander** I don't give a damn *or Br* a toss
2 *vi* to hang around, to bum around

glandes [glɑ̃d] *nfpl* **avoir les glandes** *(être énervé)* to be hacked off *or* cheesed off; *(être triste)* to be upset[□]; **foutre les glandes à qn** *(énerver)* to hack *or* cheese sb off; *(attrister)* to upset sb[□]

glandeur, -euse [glɑ̃dœr, -øz] *nm,f* layabout, *Am* goldbrick

glandouiller [glɑ̃duje] = **glander**

glandouilleur, -euse [glɑ̃dujœr, -øz] = **glandeur**

glandu [glɑ̃dy] *nm* dope, *Br* plonker, *Am* flamer

glaouis [glawi] ▸ = **claouis**

glauque [glok] *adj (personne, endroit)* shady, *Br* dodgy; *(ambiance)* creepy

glaviot [!] [glavjo] *nm* spit[□], *Br* gob

glavioter [!] [glavjɔte] *vi* to spit[□], *Br* to gob; **il est constamment en train de glavioter, c'est dégueulasse!** he's always spitting *or Br* gobbing everywhere, it's gross!

gnangnan [ɲɑ̃ɲɑ̃] *adj inv (personne, air)* drippy; *(film, livre)* corny; **ce qu'elle peut m'agacer celle-là avec son air gnangnan!** she's so drippy it really gets on my nerves!

gnaque, gniac [ɲjak] *nf* fighting spirit[□], drive; **avoir la gniac, être plein de gniac** to have plenty of drive

gnognotte [ɲɔɲɔt] *nf* **de la gnognotte** junk, trash, *Br* rubbish; **c'est pas de la gnognotte** it's quite something

gnole, gnôle [ɲol] *nf* firewater, *Am* alky

gnon [ɲɔ̃] *nm* thump, clout; **donner** *ou* **mettre un gnon à qn** to thump *or* clout sb

gnouf [ɲuf] *nm* glasshouse *(prison)*

go [go] *vi* **on y go?** shall we go?, shall we head?

gober [gɔbe] **1** *vt* **(a)** *(croire)* to swallow; **il gobe tout ce qu'on lui raconte** he swallows everything you tell him **(b)** *(supporter)* **j'ai jamais pu la gober, celle-là!** I've never been able to stand *or Br* stick her! **(c)** **mais reste donc pas là à gober les mouches!** don't just stand there gawping!, don't just stand there like a *Br* lemon *or Am* lump!
2 *vi (prendre un cachet d'ecstasy)* to drop an E
3 se gober *vpr* to fancy oneself

ⓘ Interestingly, the English slang word "gob" is derived from this verb.

godasse [gɔdas] *nf* shoe[□], clodhopper

ⓘ This is a variant of the word
"godillot" (see that entry).

gode [!] [gɔd] *nm* (*abbr* **godemiché**)
dildo

godet [gɔdɛ] *nm* **prendre un godet**
to have a drink□ *or Br* a bevvy

godiche [gɔdiʃ] **1** *adj* (*maladroit*)
ham-fisted, *Br* cack-handed; (*niais*)
daft, *Am* dumb

  2 *nf* **c'est une godiche** she's a
ham-fisted *or Br* cack-handed idiot
or Am klutz

godillot [gɔdijo] *nm* (**a**) (*chaussure*)
shoe□, clodhopper (**b**) (*personne*)
yes-man

ⓘ This word was originally the
name of a shoemaker (Alexis Godillot) who supplied the French army
in the 19th century.

gogo [gogo] *nm* sucker, *Br* mug, *Am*
patsy

gogol [gɔgɔl] = **gol**

gogolerie [gɔgɔlri] *nf* (**a**) (*acte stupide*) **faire une gogolerie** to do a *Br*
bloody *or Am* goddamn stupid thing;
bon, tu arrêtes tes gogole-ries?
will you stop clowning around *or Br*
pissing about? (**b**) (*remarque stupide*)
dire *ou* **raconter des gogoleries** to
talk crap *or* bullshit

goguenots [gɔgno], **gogues** [gɔg]
nmpl Br bog, *Am* john

ⓘ The word "goguenots" (often
abbreviated to "gogues"), meaning "toilet", comes from a Norman-
dy dialectal word meaning "cider
pot".

goinfre [gwɛ̃fr] *nmf* pig, *Br* greedy-

guts, gannet, *Am* hog

goinfrer [gwɛ̃fre] **se goinfrer** *vpr*
to stuff oneself *or* one's face, to pig
out

gol [gɔl] *nmf* (*abbr* **mongolien,
-enne**) spaz, *Br* mong

ⓘ This term is used as a mild re-
proach to someone silly, but because of its origins it is somewhat
politically incorrect.

goldo [gɔldo] *nf* = Gauloise® cigarette

gomme [gɔm] *nf* **mettre la gomme**
(*en voiture*) to step on it, *Br* to put
one's foot down, *Am* to step on the
gas; **à la gomme** useless, pathetic

gommé [gɔme] *nm* (*boisson*) =
lager with a dash of lemon-flavoured
syrup

gommer [gɔme] **se gommer** *vpr*
Cités to clear off, *Am* to split; **allez,
gomme-toi!** get out of here!, get
lost!, beat it!, *Am* take a hike!

gondoler [gɔ̃dɔle] **se gondoler**
vpr (*rire*) to fall about laughing, to
crack up; **qu'est-ce que vous avez
à vous gondoler?** what's so hilari-
ous?

gonflant, -e [gɔ̃flɑ̃, -ɑ̃t] *adj* maddening; **être gonflant** to be a pain (in
the neck)

gonflé, -e [gɔ̃fle] *adj* **être gonflé** to
have a cheek *or* a nerve; **je le trouve
gonflé de me demander de lui
prêter ma caisse** I think he's got a
cheek *or* a nerve asking me to lend
him my car

gonfler [gɔ̃fle] *vt* (*ennuyer*) **gonfler
qn** to bug sb, *Br* to get up sb's nose,
to do sb's head in, *Am* to tick sb off;
**bon, t'arrêtes de me gonfler avec
tes questions?** look, will you stop

bugging me with your questions?

gonflette [gɔ̃flɛt] *nf* pumping iron; **faire de la gonflette** to pump iron; **il a de gros muscles, mais c'est de la gonflette** he's got big muscles, but that's coz he pumps iron

gonze [gɔ̃z] *nm* guy, *Br* bloke

① This term comes from the Italian word "gonzo", which means "simpleton".

gonzesse [gɔ̃zɛs] *nf* chick, *Br* bird

gorgeon [gɔrʒɔ̃] *nm* drink□, *Br* bevvy

gosse [gɔs] **1** *nmf* kid; **beau/belle gosse** good-looking guy/girl
2 *nm* **gosses** [!] *Can (testicules)* balls, nuts, *Br* bollocks

gossebo [gɔsbo] *nm (verlan **beau gosse**)* hottie, stud (muffin), *Br* fit lad

gosser [gɔse] *vt Can* to whittle□

gouape [gwap] *nf* hoodlum, *Am* hood

① This term comes from the Spanish word "guapo", which means "handsome" in standard Spanish but "ruffian" in Spanish slang.

goudou [!] [gudu] *nf Offensive* dyke, *Br* lezzie, lesbo

gougnafier [guɲafje] *nm (individu grossier)* yokel, peasant, *Am* hick; *(bon à rien)* good-for-nothing, *Br* waster, *Am* slacker; *(mauvais ouvrier)* careless workman□, *Br* cowboy

gouine [!!] [gwin] *nf Offensive* dyke, *Br* lezzie, lesbo

goulot [gulo] *nm* mouth□, *Br* gob; **repousser** *ou* **refouler du goulot** to have rotten breath *or* dogbreath

goupiller [gupije] **1** *vt (arranger)* to cook up, to set up
2 se goupiller *vpr (se passer)* to turn out, to work out; **finalement, tout s'est bien goupillé** everything turned out fine in the end

gourbi [gurbi] *nm* dump, hole

① This word is derived from an Algerian Arabic word referring to a rudimentary type of hut. It entered the French language at the time of the colonial expansion in North Africa.

gourdasse [gurdas] *nf* dope, *Br* muppet, *Am* dumbass

gourde [gurd] **1** *adj* dopey, thick
2 *nf (personne)* dope, *Br* muppet, *Am* dumbass; **c'est une vraie gourde!** he's such a dope!

gourdin [!!] [gurdɛ̃] *nm (pénis)* dick, prick, *Br* knob; **avoir le gourdin** to have a hard-on *or* a boner

gourer [gure] **se gourer** *vpr* (**a**) *(se tromper) Br* to boob, *Am* to goof (up); **je me suis gouré de train** I got the wrong train□; **se gourer de jour** to get the day wrong□; **je me suis gouré dans les horaires** I got the times mixed up□ (**b**) *(se douter)* **je m'en gourais!** I thought as much!

gourmandise [!] [gurmɑ̃diz] *nf Hum (fellation)* blow-job; **faire une gourmandise à qn** to give sb a blow-job, to go down on sb, to suck sb off

gousse [!!] [gus] *nf Offensive* dyke, *Br* lezzie, lesbo

goutte [gut] *nf* **boire la goutte** to have a drop *or* a nip of brandy

grabuge [grabyʒ] *nm* trouble, *Br* aggro; **tirons-nous d'ici, je sens qu'il**

va y avoir du grabuge let's get out of here, I think there's trouble brewing

graff [graf] *nm* graffiti□

graffeur, -euse [grafœr, -øz] *nm,f* graffiti artist□

graillaver [grɑjave] *vi Cités* to eat□, to chow down

graille [grɑj] *nf* (**a**) *(aliments)* food□, chow, grub (**b**) *(repas)* meal□; **faire la graille** to do the cooking□

graillé [!] [grɑje] *adj Can* well-hung

grailler [!] [grɑje] *vt & vi* to eat□, to chow down

graillon [grɑjɔ̃] *nm* **sentir le graillon** to smell of burnt fat□; **avoir un goût de graillon** to taste of burnt fat□

graillonner [grɑjɔne] *vi* to clear one's throat noisily□

grain [grɛ̃] *nm* **avoir un grain** to be not all there, to be not right in the head, to have a screw loose

graine [grɛn] *nf* (**a**) **casser la graine** to have a bite to eat; **de la graine de voyou** a hooligan in the making, *Br* a future yob; **graine de con** [!] *Br* bloody *or Am* goddamn fool; **c'est de la mauvaise graine** he's a bad egg; **prends-en de la graine!** take note!, take a leaf out of his/her book! (**b**) [!] *Can (pénis)* dick, prick, cock

grand-duc [grɑ̃dyk] *nm* **la tournée des grands-ducs** a big night out on the town *or Br* the tiles; **faire la tournée des grands-ducs** to go for a big night out on the town *or Br* the tiles

grand-mère [grɑ̃mɛr] *nf* **et ta grand-mère, elle fait du vélo?** mind your own business!

graph [graf] = **graff**

grapheur, -euse [grafœr, -øz] = **graffeur**

grappe [grap] *nf* **lâcher la grappe à qn** to get off sb's back *or* case

grappin [grapɛ̃] *nm* **mettre le grappin dessus à qn** *(arrêter)* to collar *or Br* lift *or* nick sb; *(accaparer)* to get one's hands on sb, to corner sb; **mettre le grappin sur qch** to get one's hands□ *or* mitts on sth

gras [grɑ] **1** *nm* **discuter le bout de gras** to chew the fat *or* the rag
2 *adv* **il y a pas gras de monde dans les rues aujourd'hui** there's not many people out today

gratin [gratɛ̃] *nm (élite)* **le gratin** high society□, *Br* the upper crust; **le gratin du monde du spectacle** the A-list, the showbiz elite

gratiné, -e [gratine] *adj* over the top, *Br* OTT

gratos [gratos] *adv* free (of charge)□, for nothing□; **on a réussi à entrer gratos** we managed to get in for nothing

gratte [grat] *nf* guitar□, *Br* axe, *Am* ax

gratter [grate] **1** *vt (devancer)* to overtake□; **personne n'arrive à le gratter au démarrage** nobody can beat him off the mark when the lights turn green
2 *vi (travailler)* to work□
3 se gratter *vpr* **tu peux toujours te gratter!** no way!, *Br* nothing doing!

gratteux [gratø] *nm (guitariste)* guitarist□

grave [grav] **1** *adj (dérangé)* **il est grave** he's not all there, he's off his rocker *or Br* head
2 *adv* seriously, majorly, big time; **il me prend la tête grave** he seriously bugs me, *Br* he does my head

in big time; **grave de chez grave** seriously, majorly, big time

Grecs [grɛk] nmpl **va te faire voir chez les Grecs! [!]** go to hell!, Br sod off!, Am take a hike!

greffier [grefje] nm (chat) puss, kitty, Br moggy

grelot [grəlo] nm (a) (téléphone) **un coup de grelot** a phone call□; **filer un coup de grelot à qn** to give sb a buzz or Br a bell (b) **grelots [!]** (testicules) balls, nuts, Br bollocks

greluche [grəlyʃ] nf chick, Br bird

greum [grœm] adj Cités (verlan **maigre**) thin□, skinny

grillé, -e [grije] adj **il est grillé** he's had it

griller [grije] **1** vt (a) **griller qn** (devancer) to leave sb standing, to leave sb for dead; **jamais tu réussiras à me griller au démarrage!** you'll never beat me off the mark when the lights turn green! (b) (compromettre) to land sb in it; **vous avez grillé notre indic avec vos indiscrétions** you've landed our Br grass or Am rat right in it with your blabbing (c) **en griller une** to have a smoke or Br a fag

2 se griller vpr (se démasquer) **il s'est grillé en disant cela** he gave himself away by saying that; **se griller auprès de qn** to blot one's copybook with sb

grimpant [grɛ̃pɑ̃] nm Br trousers□, keks, Am pants□

grimper [!] [grɛ̃pe] vt (posséder sexuellement) to screw, to ride, Br to shag

grimpion, -onne [grɛ̃pjɔ̃, -ɔn] nm,f Suisse careerist□; **il n'y a que des grimpions dans mon service** everyone in my department's desperate to get to the top

gringue [grɛ̃g] nm **faire du gringue à qn** to come on to sb, Br to chat sb up, Am to hit on sb

grisbi [grisbi] nm cash, dough, Br dosh, Am bucks

griveton [grivtɔ̃] nm private (soldier)□, Br squaddie, Am grunt

groggy [grɔgi] adj inv (épuisé, sous l'effet de l'alcool) out of it; (étourdi) dazed

grognasse [grɔɲas] nf Pej (fille) tart, Br slapper; (copine) girlfriend□, (main) squeeze, Br bird

grolle [grɔl] nf shoe□

gros, grosse [gro, gros] nm,f **un gros/une grosse plein(e) de soupe** a tub of lard

gros-cul [groky] nm (camion) Br large lorry□, Am large truck□

grouiller [gruje] **se grouiller** vpr to get a move on, Br to shake a leg, Am to get it in gear; **allez, grouille-toi** ou **grouille!** come on, get a move on!

grue [gry] nf (a) (fille facile) Br tart, slapper, Am hooker (b) **faire le pied de grue** to hang about or around

gruger [gryʒe] **1** vi (tricher) to cheat□; **pas la peine d'acheter de tickets de métro, on n'aura qu'à gruger!** no need to buy metro tickets, we'll just jump the barrier!

2 vt **gruger la place de qn** to push in front of sb

guèche [gɛʃ] nmf Portuguese□

ⓘ This term comes from shortening the word "portuguèche", a pronunciation of "portugais" that mimics the "sh" sound characteristic of the Portuguese language. Depending on the context and the tone of voice used, this term may be either offensive or affectionately humorous. It is nonetheless inadvisable to use it unless one is quite sure of the reaction it will receive.

---

gueudin [gødɛ̃] **1** adj (verlan **dingue**) crazy, nuts, Br mental

2 nmf nutcase, Br nutter; **c'est un truc de gueudin** it's mental

guenon [gənɔ̃] nf (femme laide) dog, boot, Br minger, Am beast

guêtres [gɛtr] nfpl **traîner ses guêtres quelque part** to wander about or around◻; **j'en ai plein les guêtres** (après une marche) I'm Br knackered or Am bushed; (j'en ai assez) I've had it up to here

gueulante [gœlɑ̃t] nf **pousser une gueulante** to kick up a stink, to hit the Br roof or Am ceiling

gueulard, -e [gœlar, -ard] nm,f **(a)** (personne qui parle fort) **quel gueulard!** he's got a voice like a foghorn! **(b)** (protestataire) grouch, whinger

gueule [!] [gœl] nf **(a)** (bouche) mouth◻, Br gob; **emporter** ou **arracher la gueule** to take the roof of one's mouth off; **puer de la gueule** to have rotten breath or dogbreath; **une grande gueule** a loudmouth; **être fort en gueule** to be a loudmouth, to have too much to say for oneself; **ta gueule!** shut your mouth or face!, shut it!; **pousser un coup de gueule** to kick up a stink, to hit the roof
(b) (visage) face◻, mug; **avoir une sale gueule** (personne) (avoir l'air antipathique) to look shady or Br dodgy; (avoir l'air malade) to look under the weather or Br off-colour; (plat, aliment) to look gross or Br minging; **il s'est fait arrêter pour délit de sale gueule** he got arrested just because they didn't like the look of him; **prendre un coup dans la**

gueule ou **sur le coin de la gueule** to get hit in the face◻; **il s'est pris le ballon en pleine gueule** the ball hit him right in the face◻; **en mettre plein la gueule à qn** (critiquer) to give sb a mouthful; (frapper) to smash sb's face in; **en prendre plein la gueule (pour pas un rond)** (se faire critiquer) to get a real mouthful; (se faire frapper) to get one's face smashed in; **ça va me retomber sur la gueule** it's all going to come back on me, I'm going to get the blame for it all◻; **se foutre sur la gueule** to go for each other; **foutre sur la gueule à qn** to sock sb in the face; **faire** ou **tirer la gueule** to be in a huff; **faire une gueule d'enterrement** to have a face like a wet weekend; **il en fait une gueule, qu'est-ce qu'il a?** he looks really down, what's wrong with him?; **faire la gueule à qn** to be in a huff with sb; **cracher à la gueule de qn** to spit in sb's face; **gueule de bois** hangover◻; **avoir la gueule de bois** to have a hangover◻, to be hungover◻; **avoir de la gueule** (avoir du style) to have something; **cette bagnole a de la gueule** that's some car, that car's quite something, Br that's a car and a half; **gueule de con** Br arsehole, Am asshole; **gueule de raie** fishface **(c)** (individu) **ma/ta/etc gueule** me/you/etc◻; **se fiche** ou **se foutre de la gueule de qn** to make a fool of sb, Br to take the piss out of sb; **du coq au vin! elle s'est pas foutue de notre gueule!** coq au vin! she doesn't do things by halves or Br she's really pushed the boat out!; **se foutre de la gueule du monde** to treat people like idiots, Br to take the piss; **c'est pour ma gueule** it's for me ▶ see also **arracher, bourrer, casser, crever, défoncer, éclater, enfarinée, fendre, fermer, flan-**

Le symbole ◻ indique que la traduction n'est pas argotique.

quer, foutre, ouvrir, péter, soûler

gueuler [gœle] *vi* (a) *(crier)* to yell (one's head off) (b) *(protester)* to kick up a fuss *or* stink

gueuleton [gœltɔ̃] *nm* blowout, feast, feed; **je vous ai préparé un petit gueuleton dont vous me direz des nouvelles** I've made a bit of a feast for you, I think you'll like it

gugus [gygys] = **gus**

guibolle [gibɔl] *nf* leg□, pin; **j'en ai plein les guibolles** my legs are killing me; **elle a des guibolles de rêve** she's got a lovely pair of pins on her

guidoune [gidun] *nf Can* slut, *Br* tart, slapper

guignard, -e [giɲar, -ard] *nm,f* unlucky person□, *Am* schmo

guigne [giɲ] *nf* rotten luck□; **avoir la guigne** to have a run of bad luck□

guignol [giɲɔl] *nm (personne ridicule)* clown, joker; **faire le guignol** to play the fool, to clown around; **mais qui est-ce qui m'a fichu un guignol pareil?** how on earth did I get landed with such a clown?

guimbarde [gɛ̃bard] *nf (voiture)* heap, *Br* banger, *Am* jalopy

guincher [gɛ̃ʃe] *vi* to dance□, to bop, to groove

guindaille [gɛ̃daj] *nf Belg* student party□; **il adore faire la guindaille** he loves to party

guindailler [gɛ̃daje] *vi Belg* to go to a student party□

guindailleur, -euse [gɛ̃dajœr, -øz] *nm,f Belg* = student who likes to party; **c'est un sacré guindailleur** he's a real party animal

gus, gusse [gys] *nm* guy, *Br* bloke

Hh

H ['aʃ] *nm (haschisch)* hash, *Br* blow

habiller ['abije] *vt* **habiller qn** to badmouth sb, *Br* to slag sb off

haine [ɛn] *nf* **avoir la haine** to be full of rage□

ⓘ This expression was brought to a wider audience by the 1995 film *La Haine* by Mathieu Kassovitz. Describing the lives of three teenagers of different backgrounds living in a deprived Paris suburb, it used a lot of slang vocabulary, and in particular "verlan" (see panel p.398). See also the panel **l'argot des banlieues** p.219.

---

hallu [aly] *nf (abbr* **hallucination**) hallucination□; **je dois avoir des hallus!** I must be seeing things!

halluciner [alysine] *vi* **c'est pas vrai, j'hallucine!** I must be seeing things!

hardeux, -euse ['ardø, -øz] *nm,f* **(a)** *(fan)* metalhead; *(musicien)* (hard) rocker **(b)** *(acteur, actrice de films pornographiques)* porn star

hardos ['ardos] *nm (musicien de hard-rock)* (hard) rocker; *(amateur de hard-rock)* (hard) rocker, metalhead

haricot ['ariko] *nm* **courir sur le haricot à qn** *Br* to get on sb's wick *or* up sb's nose, *Am* to tick sb off; **c'est la fin des haricots** I've/we've/

etc had it now; **des haricots!** not a chance!; **travailler pour des haricots** to work for peanuts

harponner ['arpɔne] *vt (retenir)* to corner, to waylay

hasch ['aʃ] *nm (abbr* **haschisch**) hash

haute ['ot] *nf* **la haute** high society□, *Br* the upper crust

hebdo [ɛbdo] *nm (abbr* **hebdomadaire**) weekly (magazine)□

herbe [ɛrb] *nf (marijuana)* grass, weed

héro [ero] *nf (abbr* **héroïne**) smack, scag, skag

hétéro [etero] *adj & nmf (abbr* **hétérosexuel, -elle**) straight, hetero

heure [œr] *nf* **à pas d'heure** at an ungodly hour; **elle est rentrée à pas d'heure** she didn't get home until some ungodly hour

hic ['ik] *nm* **il y a un hic** there's a snag

histoire [istwar] *nf* **(a)** **qu'est-ce que c'est que cette histoire?** what the hell is going on? **(b)** **faire qch histoire de rigoler** to do sth just for a laugh; **je l'ai fait histoire de me changer les idées** I did it just to take my mind off things

homme [ɔm] *nm* Can **un homme aux hommes** *(un homosexuel)* a gay man□

homo [omo] (*abbr* **homosexuel, -elle**) **1** *adj* gay▢
   2 *nmf* gay▢

ⓘ In French, the word "homo" has no pejorative or homophobic connotations and is therefore not used in the same way as the English word "homo".

honte [ʒt] *nf* **avoir la honte, se taper la honte** to be embarrassed▢ or mortified; **(c'est) la honte!** the shame of it!

horreur [ɔrœr] *nf* **c'est l'horreur** it's the pits, it sucks, *Am* it blows; **il y avait une de ces circulations en ville, c'était l'horreur!** there was so much traffic in town, it was horrendous or a total nightmare!

hostie [!] [ɔsti] *exclam Can* fucking hell!, for fuck's sake!

ⓘ Traditionally, French Canadians were deeply Catholic, which explains why several of their most common swearwords are linked to religion: these include "câlice" (derived from "calice", meaning "chalice"), "ciboire", "tabernacle",

"hostie" and "criss" (derived from "Christ").

hosto [ɔsto] *nm* (*abbr* **hôpital**) hospital▢

hotte [ɔt] *nf* **en avoir plein la hotte** to be bushed or *Br* knackered or *Am* beat

HP [aʃpe] *nm* (*abbr* **hôpital psychiatrique**) psychiatric hospital▢, nuthouse, *Br* loony bin; **elle tourne pas rond, ça m'étonnerait pas qu'elle finisse en HP** she's not all there, it wouldn't surprise me if she ended up in the nuthouse or *Br* loony bin

HS [aʃes] *adj* (*abbr* **hors service**) **(a)** *(objet)* bust, *Br* knackered **(b)** *(personne)* bushed, *Br* knackered, shattered, *Am* beat

hublots ['yblo] *nmpl* specs

huile [ɥil] *nf (personnage important)* big shot, big cheese, big enchilada
  ▶ *see also* **pomme**

hyper [ipɛr] *adv* mega, *Br* dead, *Am* real; **on s'est hyper bien amusés** we had a blast, we had or *Br* a wicked or *Am* an awesome time

hypra [ipra] *adv* mega, *Br* dead, *Am* real

Ii

iech [!], ièche [!] [jɛʃ] *vi (verlan chier)* **faire iech qn** *Br* to piss sb off, to get on sb's tits, *Am* to break sb's balls; **se faire iech** to be bored shitless

illico [iliko] *adv* pronto

imbibé, -e [ɛ̃bibe] *adj (ivre)* plastered, *Br* tanked up, *Am* tanked

imbitable [ɛ̃bitabl] *adj* incomprehensible□; **il est imbitable, son article** I can't make head nor tail of his article

imbuvable [ɛ̃byvabl] *adj (insupportable)* unbearable□; **je le trouve imbuvable, ce mec** I can't stand (the sight of) that guy, I can't stomach *or Br* stick that guy

impasse [ɛ̃pas] *nf (sujet non étudié)* **faire une impasse** = to miss out part of a subject when revising

impayable [ɛ̃pɛjabl] *adj (amusant)* priceless

impec [ɛ̃pɛk] **1** *adj (abbr* **impeccable)** *(très propre)* spotless; *(parfait)* perfect□
2 *adv (abbr* **impeccablement)** perfectly□; **tout s'est passé impec** everything went off like a dream *or* without a hitch; **ils nous ont reçus impec** they made us incredibly welcome; **c'est du travail de pro, il a fait ça impec** it's a really professional job, his work was faultless

in [in] *adj inv* in, cool, hip

incendier [ɛ̃sɑ̃dje] *vt* **incendier qn** *(le réprimander)* to give sb hell, to haul sb over the coals; **il s'est fait incendier par ses parents** he caught hell from his parents

incruste [ɛ̃kryst] *nf* **si on l'invite, il va encore taper l'incruste** if we invite him, we'll never get rid of him; **il a tapé l'incruste à ma boum** he gatecrashed my party

incruster [ɛ̃kryste] **s'incruster** *vpr* **j'espère qu'il va pas s'incruster** I hope he doesn't overstay his welcome□, I hope we can manage to get rid of him; **il s'est incrusté à ma boum** he gatecrashed my party

indé [ɛ̃de] *adj (abbr* **indépendant)** indie; **le rock indé** indie (rock)

indic [ɛ̃dik] *nm (abbr* **indicateur)** squealer, *Br* grass, *Am* rat

infichu, -e [ɛ̃fiʃy] *adj* **être infichu de faire qch** to be incapable of doing sth□

info [ɛ̃fo] *nf (abbr* **information)** **(a)** **une info** a piece of info **(b)** **les infos** *(les nouvelles)* the news□

infoutu, -e [ɛ̃futy] *adj* **être infoutu de faire qch** to be incapable of doing sth□

inquiéter [ɛ̃kjete] **s'inquiéter** *vpr* **t'inquiète!** don't worry!□, take it easy!

instit [ɛ̃stit] *nmf (abbr* **instituteur, -trice)** (primary school) teacher□

Spotlight on:

Les insultes

Abuse is perhaps the purest form of slang, and is certainly the most direct, as it is always meant to be rude. Some of the more typical patterns found in French insults are given below. The simplest insult of all is a noun used as an exclamation (see the noun column below). This can itself be reinforced by a slang adjective (from the adjective column below). The table below shows this pattern with some of the most common words. Although some "mixing and matching" is possible, note that some combinations work better than others.

ADJECTIVE	NOUN	TAG
pauvre	**andouille**	**de merde**
sale	**idiot(e)**	
espèce de (sale)	**con (conne) [!]**	
	connard (connasse) [!]	
	salaud (salope) [!]	
	enfoiré(e) [!!]	
	pouffiasse [!!]	
	enculé [!!]	

Speakers of "banlieue"-type slang (see panel **L'argot des banlieues** p.219) often favour "tags" such as **de ta race** or **de ta mère** (eg: **espèce d'enculé de ta race** or **de ta mère!**). Many more colourful insults using a verbal expression begin with "va ...", eg:

va voir ailleurs si j'y suis!

va te faire cuire un œuf!

va te faire voir (chez les Grecs)! [!]

va te faire mettre! [!!]

va te faire foutre! [!!]

va te faire enculer! [!!]

All of the above imperatives with the structure "va te faire…" can be modified into "tu peux aller te faire... ! "

The symbol [!] denotes a very familiar term, [!!] a vulgar one.

intello [ɛ̃telo] (*abbr* **intellectuel, -elle**) **1** *adj* intellectual□, highbrow□ **2** *nmf* egghead, brain

interpeller [ɛ̃tɛrpəle] *vt* **ça m'interpelle (quelque part)** I can relate to that

interro [ɛ̃tɛro] *nf* (*abbr* **interrogation**) test□ *(at school)*

intox [ɛ̃tɔks] *nf* (*abbr* **intoxication**)

de l'intox brainwashing□

inventer [ɛ̃vɑ̃te] *vt* **il n'a pas inventé l'eau chaude** *ou* **le fil à couper le beurre** *ou* **la poudre** he's no rocket scientist, *Br* he's not the sharpest knife in the drawer

invite [ɛ̃vit] *nf* (*abbr* **invitation**) invite

iroquoise [irɔkwaz] *nf* (*coupe de cheveux*) mohican

Jj

jacasser [ʒakase] *vi* to chatter, to yap, *Br* to witter (on), to natter

jacky [ʒaki] *nm Br* petrolhead, *Am* gearhead

ⓘ The "jacky" (derived from the name "Jacques") is a man who loves his car above everything else.

Jacques [ʒak] *npr* **faire le Jacques** to play the fool, to clown around

jacter [ʒakte] *vi* to chatter, to yap, *Br* to witter (on), to natter

jaffe [ʒaf] *nf (nourriture)* food□, grub, chow; *(repas)* meal□

jaffer [ʒafe] *vi* to eat□, to chow down

jaja [ʒaʒa] *nm* wine□, vino, *Br* plonk

jambe [ʒãb] *nf* (**a**) **tenir la jambe à qn** to drone on and on at sb (**b**) **faire une partie de jambes en l'air** [!] to have a bit of nooky, *Br* to have a bonk (**c**) **ça me fait une belle jambe!** a fat lot of good that does me! (**d**) **en avoir plein les jambes** to be *Br* knackered *or* shattered *or Am* beat *or* pooped

jambonneaux [ʒãbɔno] *nmpl (cuisses)* thunderthighs; **elle a une sacrée paire de jambonneaux** she's a real thunderthighs!

jap [ʒap] *Offensive* **1** *adj (abbr* **japonais, -e**) Jap

2 *nmf* **Jap** *(abbr* **Japonais, -e**) Jap, Nip

jaquette [ʒakɛt] *nf Offensive* **la jaquette flottante [!]** *(les homosexuels) Br* poofs, *Am* fags; **être** *ou* **refiler de la jaquette (flottante) [!]** to be a *Br* poof *or Am* fag

jaspiner [ʒaspine] *vi* to chat, to yak, *Br* to natter

jaune [ʒon] *nm* (**a**) *(apéritif anisé)* pastis□ (**b**) *(ouvrier non gréviste)* strikebreaker□, scab, *Br* blackleg

java [ʒava] *nf (fête)* party□, bash, *Br* do; **faire la java** to party

jean-foutre [!] [ʒãfutr] *nm inv* loser, no-hoper, *Br* waster

jeannette [ʒanet] *nf Belg Offensive (homosexuel)* queer, *Br* poof, *Am* fag

je-m'en-foutisme [ʒmãfutism] *nm* couldn't-care-less attitude

jeté, -e [ʒəte] *adj (fou)* crazy, off one's rocker, *Br* barking (mad), *Am* wacko

jeter [ʒ(ə)te] **1** *vt* (**a**) *(abandonner) (personne)* to chuck, to dump; **il s'est fait jeter par sa gonzesse** his chick *or Br* bird dumped him (**b**) *(chasser)* to throw *or* chuck out, *Am* to eighty-six; **se faire jeter** to get thrown *or* chucked out, *Am* to get eighty-sixed (**c**) **jeter du jus, en jeter** to be quite *or* really something, to be something else (**d**) **n'en jetez plus (la cour est pleine)!** give it a rest!, pack it in!

Slang sleuth

Javanais

More a source of amusement for French schoolchildren than a true form of slang, "javanais" is formed by inserting the syllable "-av-", "-va-" or "-ag-" immediately after each consonant or group of consonants. "Chatte", for example, becomes **chagatte** and "pute" becomes **pavute**. It is probably so called because the word "javanais" contains the syllable "-av-" and suggests an exotic, secret language.

2 se jeter *vpr* **s'en jeter un (derrière la cravate)** to have a drink□

jeton [ʒətɔ̃] *nm* (**a**) **être un faux jeton** to be two-faced (**b**) **avoir les jetons** to be scared□, to be spooked, *Br* to be bricking it; **foutre les jetons à qn** to give sb a fright□, to spook sb, *Br* to put the wind up sb

jeune [ʒœn] *adj* (*insuffisant*) **ça fait un peu jeune** it's cutting it a bit fine, it's pushing it a bit; **trois bouteilles de vin pour vingt personnes, ça fait un peu jeune** three bottles of wine for twenty people, that's cutting it a bit fine *or* that's pushing it a bit

jeunot [ʒœno] *nm* lad, youngster□

job [dʒɔb] *nm* job□

jobard, -e [ʒɔbar, -ard] **1** *adj* gullible□

2 *nm,f* sucker, *Br* mug, *Am* patsy

jobine [ʒɔbin], **jobinette** [ʒɔbinɛt] *nf* *Can* casual job□; **faire des jobines** *ou* **des jobinettes** to do odd jobs

joint [ʒwɛ̃] *nm* joint, spliff

jojo [ʒoʒo] **1** *adj inv* (*beau, correct*) **pas jojo** not very nice□; **il est pas jojo son petit ami** her boyfriend's no oil painting; **c'est pas jojo ce qu'il a fait là** that wasn't a very nice

thing for him to do

2 *nm* **un affreux jojo** a little horror *or* monster, a holy terror

jos-connaissant [djokɔnɛsɑ̃] *nm Can Br* know-all, *Am* know-it-all

jouasse [ʒwas] *adj* pleased□, *Br* chuffed; **qu'est-ce t'as, t'es pas jouasse?** got a problem?; **il avait pas l'air jouasse** he didn't look too pleased *or Br* chuffed

jouer [ʒwe] **1** *vt* **où t'as vu jouer ça?** are you mad?, have you got a screw loose?, are you off your rocker?

2 se jouer *vpr* **se la jouer** to show off, to pose ▸ *see also* **caïd, touche-pipi, tripes**

joueur, -euse [ʒwœr, -øz] *nm,f* **petit joueur, petite joueuse** lightweight

joufflu [ʒufly] *nm Hum* (*postérieur*) butt, *Br* bum, *Am* fanny

jouir [ʒwir] *vi* (**a**) (*atteindre l'orgasme*) to come (**b**) *Ironic* (*souffrir*) to go through hell; **j'ai joui quand je me suis foutu un coup de marteau sur les doigts** it hurt like hell *or Br* like buggery *or* like a bastard when I whacked my fingers with the hammer; **qu'est-ce qu'il m'a fait jouir ce salaud de dentiste!** that bastard dentist put me through hell!

jouissif, -ive [ʒwisif, -iv] *adj* (**a**) (*qui*

procure un grand plaisir) orgasmic **(b)** *Ironic (douloureux)* Br bloody or Am goddamn painful; **s'écraser le petit orteil, c'est jouissif!** stubbing your little toe is a real barrel of laughs!

journaleux, -euse [ʒurnalø, -øz] *nm,f Pej* hack

joyeuses [!] [ʒwajøz] *nfpl (testicules)* balls, nuts, Br bollocks

JT [ʒite] *nm (abbr journal télévisé)* TV news□

juif, -ive [ʒɥif, -iv] *nm,f* **(a)** *(avare)* tightwad, skinflint **(b) le petit juif** the funny bone

ⓘ This term as used in category **(a)**, although not overtly racist, is nonetheless very politically incorrect and should be used with extreme caution.

Jules [ʒyl] *npr* boyfriend□, man, *Br* bloke; **elle est venue avec son Jules** she came with her man or *Br* bloke; **elle se cherche un Jules** she's trying to find a man or *Br* bloke

Julie [ʒyli] *npr* girlfriend□, (main) squeeze, *Br* bird

jus [ʒy] *nm* **(a)** *(eau)* **tomber au jus** to fall in□ **(b)** *(café)* coffee□, *Am* java; **jus de chique** *ou* **de chaussette** dishwater **(c)** *(courant électrique)* juice; **prendre le jus** to get a shock; **être au jus** to be in the know ▸ *see also* **jeter**

jusque-là [ʒyskəla] *adv* **(a) s'en mettre jusque-là** to stuff oneself *or* one's face, to pig out **(b) en avoir jusque-là (de)** to have had it up to here (with); **j'en ai jusque-là de tes imbécilités** I've had it up to here with your stupid behaviour

juter [!!] [ʒyte] *vi (éjaculer)* to come, to shoot one's load, to spurt

juteux¹ [ʒytø] *nm (adjudant) Br* ≃ warrant officer class II□, *Am* ≃ warrant officer (junior grade)□

juteux², -euse [ʒytø, -øz] *adj (fructueux)* lucrative□; **une affaire juteuse** a goldmine, *Br* a nice little earner

---

Slang sleuth

Joual

Joual is the traditional working-class variant of French used in Quebec. The word "joual" is derived from the vernacular French Canadian pronunciation of the word "cheval". Although initially derided by purists as a bastardized and highly anglicized form of French, the reputation of "joual" was rehabilitated in the sixties when it was championed by Quebec intellectuals as a symbol of Québécois identity. Many words bear a close resemblance to their English equivalents, such as **badloqué** (from "bad luck"), **bomme** (from "bum") and **crisse** (from "Christ").

The symbol [!] denotes a very familiar term, [!!] a vulgar one.

Kk

kakou [kaku] *nmf* **faire le/la kakou** to act smart

kaput [kaput] *adj* kaput; **la téloche est kaput; impossible de regarder le match!** the TV's kaput, we can't watch the match!

kawa [kawa] *nm* coffee□, *Am* java

ⓘ This word is derived from an Algerian Arabic word meaning "coffee". It entered the French language at the time of the colonial expansion in North Africa.

---

kebla [kəbla] *nmf Cités (verlan* **black**) Black

kéblo [keblo] *adj Cités (verlan* **bloqué**) hung-up, full of hang-ups

kébra [kebra] *vt Cités (verlan* **braquer**) *(banque, bijouterie)* to hold up; **kébra qch à qn** to pinch or *Br* nick sth from sb

ken [!] [kɛn] *vt (verlan* **niquer**) (**a**) *(posséder sexuellement)* to screw, to shaft, *Br* to shag, *Am* to bang (**b**) *(endommager)* to bust, *Br* to knacker, to bugger (**c**) *(duper)* to rip off, *Am* to rook (**d**) *Cités (attraper)* to nab, to collar; **se faire ken** to get nabbed or collared

kepa [kepa] *nm (verlan* **paquet**) *(de cocaïne)* bindle

késako [kezako] = **quès aco**

keuf [kœf] *nm (verlan* **flic**) cop, pig

keum [kœm] *nm Cités (verlan* **mec**) guy, *Br* bloke

keupon [kœpɔ̃] *nm (verlan* **punk**) punk

keusse [køs] *nm Formerly Cités (verlan* **sac**) ten francs□

kif [kif] *nm* kif, kef

kiffer [kife] *Cités* **1** *vt* (**a**) *(prendre du plaisir à)* to get a kick out of (**b**) *(aimer)* to be crazy about; **je la kiffe trop, cette fille** I'm totally crazy about this girl

2 *vi (prendre du plaisir)* to get off; **nous, on fait de la musique pour faire kiffer les gens** we make music for people to get off on

kif-kif [kifkif] *adv* **c'est kif-kif** it's six of one and half a dozen of the other, it's six and two threes

kiki [kiki] *nm* (**a**) *(cou)* neck□; *(gorge)* throat□; **serrer le kiki à qn** to wring sb's neck□ (**b**) *(type d'homosexuel)* = gay man who habitually wears jeans, a bomber jacket and baseball boots, and whose hair is either shaved or worn with a Tintin-style quiff (**c**) **c'est parti mon kiki** here we go!

kil [kil] *nm* **un kil de rouge** a bottle of red wine□

kisdé [kisde] *nm Cités (policier)* cop, pig

klébard [klebar], **klebs** [klɛps] *nm* mutt

ⓘ These words are derived from an Arabic word meaning "dog". They entered the French language at the time of the colonial expansion in North Africa.

klondike [klɔ̃dajk] *nm Can* plum job, cushy number

kopeck [kɔpɛk] *nm* **pas un kopeck** not a bean *or Am* a red cent; **il me reste plus un kopeck** I haven't got a bean *or Am* a red cent

kro [kro] *nf* Kronenbourg® beer

kroumir [krumir] *nm* **(vieux) kroumir** old fogey, codger, *Am* geezer

ⓘ This is the name of a nomadic tribe in Tunisia.

L1

là [la] *adv* **il est un peu là, il se pose là** *(il est remarquable)* he makes his presence felt□; **elle se pose là comme cuisinière** she's a mean cook, she's some cook; *Ironic* she's a mean cook…not!, she's a mean cook, I don't think!; **comme emmerdeur/menteur, il se pose là!** he's a total pain in the butt/liar!

labo [labo] *nm* (*abbr* **laboratoire**) lab

lâcher [laʃe] **1** *vt* (**a**) *(laisser tranquille)* **lâche-moi!** leave me alone!, get off my back *or* case! (**b**) *(abandonner)* *(emploi)* to quit, *Br* to chuck *or* pack in; *(famille, associé)* to walk out on; *(amant)* to chuck, to dump (**c**) **les lâcher** *(payer)* to cough up, to fork out; **il les lâche pas facilement** he's a real tightwad, he's really tight-fisted (**d**) **en lâcher une** [!] to fart, *Br* to let off, *Am* to lay one
2 [!] *vi* (émettre des gaz intestinaux) to fart, *Br* to let off, *Am* to lay one ► *see also* **basket, caisse, fusée, grappe, louise, morceau, perle, perlouse, rampe**

lambin, -e [lãbɛ̃, -in] *nm,f Br* slowcoach, *Am* slowpoke

lambiner [lãbine] *vi* to dawdle

lambineur, -euse [lãbinœr, -øz], **lambineux, -euse** [lãbinø, -øz] *nm,f Can Br* slowcoach, *Am* slowpoke

lampe [lãp] *nf* **s'en mettre** *ou* **s'en foutre** [!] **plein la lampe** to stuff oneself *or* one's face, to pig out

lance-pierres [lãspjɛr] *nm inv* **manger avec un lance-pierres** to wolf one's food down; **payer qn avec un lance-pierres** to pay sb peanuts

lancequiner [!] [lãskine] *vi* (**a**) *(pleuvoir)* **il lancequine** it's pissing down (**b**) *(uriner)* to pee, to piss, to take a leak, *Br* to have a slash

lapin [lapɛ̃] *nm* (**a**) **poser un lapin à qn** to stand sb up (**b**) **baiser comme des lapins** [!!] to fuck like rabbits ► *see also* **cage, chaud, pet¹, tirer**

lard [lar] *nm* **un gros lard** a big fat slob, a tub of lard; **rentrer dans le lard à qn** to lay into sb, to go for sb; **faire du lard** to sit around and get fat

lardon [lardɔ̃] *nm* (enfant) kid; **il a préféré venir sans ses lardons** he preferred to come without his kids

lardu [lardy] *nm* cop, *Am* flatfoot

larfeuil, larfeuille [larfœj] *nm Br* wallet□, *Am* billfold□

largeur [larʒœr] *nf* **dans les grandes largeurs** totally□, majorly, big time, way; **ils se sont fait entuber dans les grandes largeurs** they got totally *or* majorly ripped off, they got ripped off big time

Slang sleuth

Largonji

Largonji is a type of slang formed by replacing the initial consonant of a word with the letter "l" and moving the original consonant to the end of the word, where it is followed by a vowel to aid pronunciation. "À poil" thus becomes **à loilpé**, "en douce" becomes **en loucedé** and "cher" becomes **lerche** (in the expression "il y en a pas lerche", meaning "there isn't much"). The word "largonji" is itself the result of this procedure applied to the word "jargon".

---

largué, -e [large] *adj* **être largué** to be lost, not to have a clue

larguer [large] **1** *vt (abandonner) (emploi)* to quit, *Br* to chuck or pack in; *(famille, associé)* to walk out on; *(amant)* to chuck, to dump; **il s'est fait larguer par sa nana** his chick or *Br* bird dumped him
2 [!] *vi (émettre des gaz intestinaux)* to fart, *Br* to let off, *Am* to lay one ► *see also* **caisse**

larmichette [laʁmiʃɛt] *nf* tiny drop□; **tu me remets une larmichette de vin?** will you pour me another smidgen of wine?

larve [laʁv] *nf (personne faible)* wimp, wuss, *Br* big girl's blouse

larver [laʁve] *vi (ne rien faire)* to veg (out); **j'ai passé le week-end à larver devant la télé** I spent the weekend vegging (out) in front of the TV or *Br* telly

lascar [laskaʁ] *nm Cités (voyou)* lout, *Br* yob, ≈ chav

latino [latino] *adj & nmf (abbr* **latino-américain, -e)** Latino

latte [lat] *nf (chaussure)* **un coup de latte** a kick□, a boot; **il m'a filé un coup de latte** he gave me a kick or a boot, he kicked or booted me; **ils lui ont défoncé la gueule à coups de lattes** they kicked or booted his head in

latter [late] *vt* to kick□, to boot, *Br* to put the boot into

lavasse [lavas] *nf* **de la lavasse** *(café, bière)* dishwater

lavette [lavɛt] *nf (personne)* wimp, wuss, *Br* big girl's blouse; **quand sa femme l'a traité de lavette, il a failli lui répondre quelque chose** when his wife called him a wimp, he almost answered her back

lèche [lɛʃ] *nf* **faire de la lèche** to be a bootlicker; **faire de la lèche à qn** to lick sb's boots

lèche-bottes [lɛʃbɔt] *nmf inv* bootlicker

lèche-cul [!!] [lɛʃky] *nmf inv* brownnose, *Br* arse-licker, *Am* ass-licker

lécheur, -euse [leʃœʁ, -øz] *nm,f* bootlicker

lèdge [lɛdʒ], **lège** [lɛʒ] *adj (abbr* **léger)** *(insuffisant) (excuse)* weak; **deux bouteilles pour quatre, ça va faire un peu lèdge, non?** two bottles for four people, that's cutting it a bit fine, isn't it?

légitime [leʒitim] *nf* **ma légitime** my old lady, *Br* the missus, her indoors

---

The symbol **[!]** denotes a very familiar term, **[!!]** a vulgar one.

lerche [lɛrʃ] *adv* **il y en a pas lerche** there isn't much□/aren't many□

ⓘ This word is in fact the word "cher", after it has been given the "largonji" treatment (see panel).

lerga [lɛrga] *nf Cités (verlan* **galère)** pain, hassle

lesbos [!!] [lɛsbos] *nf Offensive* dyke, *Br* lezzie, lesbo

lessivé, -e [lesive] *adj (épuisé)* washed out, wiped

lever [ləve] *vt* (**a**) *(séduire)* to pick up, *Br* to pull, to get off with (**b**) **lever le pied** *(ralentir)* to slow down□; **lève le pied, il y a un radar par ici** slow down, there's a speed camera round here (**c**) **lever le coude** *(boire)* to bend one's elbow

levrette [ləvrɛt] **en levrette** *adv* doggy-style

lézard [lezar] *nm (difficulté)* **il y a pas de lézards** no problem, no sweat, *Br* no prob *or* probs

lézarder [lezarde] *vi* to soak up the sun, to catch some rays

ligne [liɲ] *nf* (**a**) *(dose de cocaïne)* line; **se faire une ligne** to do a line (**b**) **sur toute la ligne** from beginning to end□

limace [limas] *nf (chemise)* shirt□

ⓘ This word derives from the word "lime" (file), apparently because of the way a shirt rubs against the wearer's back.

limer [!!] [lime] *vt (posséder sexuellement)* to hump, to screw, *Br* to shag

limite [limit] *adj inv* **je me suis pas mis en colère, mais c'était limite**

I didn't lose my temper, but it was a near thing; **question propreté, c'était limite** it certainly wasn't the cleanest place in the world; **ses blagues sont un peu limite** his jokes are a bit close to the bone *or* near the knuckle; **j'hésite à me déchausser, mes chaussettes sont un peu limite** I'm not sure whether I should take my socks off, they're a bit iffy *or Br* dodgy

linge [lɛ̃ʒ] *nm* **du beau linge** high society□, *Br* the upper crust; **il y avait que du beau linge à la réception** the upper crust were out in force at the reception

liquette [likɛt] *nf* shirt□; **mouiller sa liquette** to work up a sweat; **il se fatigue pas trop celui-là, pas de danger qu'il mouille sa liquette** he doesn't exactly tire himself out, there's not much chance of him breaking a sweat

liquider [likide] *vt* (**a**) *(tuer)* to bump off, to liquidate (**b**) *(nourriture)* to scoff, to guzzle; *(boisson)* to sink, to down, *Am* to inhale

litron [litrɔ̃] *nm* bottle of red wine□

locdu [lɔkdy] = **loquedu**

loche [lɔʃ] *nf (sein)* tit, boob; **regarde un peu la paire de loches!** check out those tits!, check out the rack on that!

loilpé [lwalpe] **à loilpé** *adv* in the buff, *Br* starkers

ⓘ This word is in fact the expression "à poil", after it has been given the "largonji" treatment (see panel p.314).

lolo [lolo] *nm* (**a**) *(sein)* tit, boob (**b**) *(lait)* milk□

longe [lɔ̃ʒ] *nf (année)* year□

ⓘ This term is never used when referring to people's ages.

longuet, -ette [lɔ̃gɛ, -ɛt] adj longish, on the long side; **j'ai trouvé le film un peu longuet** I found the film a bit on the long side

look [luk] nm look, image; **avoir un look d'enfer** to look fantastic or Br wicked or Am awsome

looké, -e [luke] adj **être looké punk/grunge** to have a punky/grungy look or image

lope [lɔp], **lopette** [lɔpɛt] nf (a) Offensive (homosexuel) queer, Br poof, Am fag (b) (lâche) wimp, wuss, Br big girl's blouse

loquedu [lɔkdy] nm (a) (bon à rien) good-for-nothing, loser, no-hoper, Br waster (b) (individu méprisable) scumbag, Br swine, Am stinker

loser [luzœr] nm loser

lot [lo] nm (femme) **un joli (petit) lot** a babe, a knockout, Br a bit of all right

loub [lub] nm (abbr **loubard**) hooligan⁰, Br yob, Am hood

loubard [lubar] nm hooligan⁰, Br yob, Am hood

loucedé [lusde] **en loucedé** adv on the quiet or sly

ⓘ This word is in fact the expression "en douce", after it has been given the "largonji" treatment (see panel p.314).

louche [luʃ] nf (main) hand⁰, mitt, paw; **serrer la louche à qn** to shake hands with sb⁰

loucher [luʃe] vi **loucher sur qch** to eye sth up, to have one's eye on sth

louf [luf], **loufedingue** [lufdɛ̃g] adj crazy, Br barking (mad), off one's head, Am wacko

ⓘ The term "louf" is in fact the word "fou", after it has been given the "largonji" treatment (see panel p.314).

loufe [luf] nm (pet) fart

loufer [!], **loufier [!]** [lufe] vi to fart, Br to let off, Am to lay one

loufiat [lufja] nm waiter⁰ (in a café)

louise [lwiz] nf fart; **lâcher une louise** to fart, Br to let off, Am to lay one

loulou, -oute [lulu, -ut] nm,f (a) (personne) hoodlum, hooligan⁰ (b) (appellation affectueuse) **mon loulou, ma louloute** sweetheart, honey, babe

louper [lupe] **1** vt (examen) to fail⁰, Am to flunk; (train, cible) to miss⁰

2 vi **j'étais sûr qu'il pleuvrait, et ça n'a pas loupé!** I was sure that it would rain, and sure enough it did!

3 se louper vpr (a) (échouer dans une tentative de suicide) to bungle one's suicide attempt⁰; **il s'est coupé les cheveux tout seul et il s'est pas loupé!** he cut his own hair and made some job of it!; **je me suis blessé avec l'ouvre-boîte – dis-donc, tu t'es pas loupé!** I've cut myself on the tin-opener – you have, haven't you! (b) **vous vous êtes loupés de peu** you just missed each other⁰ ▸ see also **une**

loupiot [lupjo] nm kid

loupiote [lupjɔt] nf lamp⁰, light⁰

lourd, -e [lur, lurd] **1** adj (sans subtilité) unsubtle⁰, in your face, Br OTT

2 adv **il en fiche pas lourd** he

doesn't exactly overtax himself, he doesn't kill himself with overwork; **il en reste pas lourd** there's not that much/many left◻

lourde [lurd] *nf (porte)* door◻

lourder [lurde] *vt* **(a)** *(lourder)* **lourder qn** to give sb the boot, to kick sb out; **ils l'ont lourdé quand ils se sont rendu qu'il piquait dans la caisse** they gave him the boot when they found out he had his hand in the till **(b)** *(agacer)* **lourder qn** to piss sb off, *Br* to do sb's head in; **tu commences à me lourder avec tes histoires** you're starting to piss me off *or Br* do my head in with your nonsense; **ça me lourde de l'attendre** I'm getting pissed off waiting for him, *Br* it's doing my head in waiting for him

lourdingue [lurdɛ̃g] *adj* unsubtle◻, in your face, *Br* OTT; **il est vraiment lourdingue avec ses blagues de cul** he's so in your face with his dirty jokes

louse [luz] **de la louse** *adj* **c'est de la louse** it sucks

loustic [lustik] *nm* **(a)** *(individu)* guy, *Br* bloke **(b)** *(farceur)* clown, joker; **c'est un sacré loustic** he's quite a character, he's a real case

loute [lut] *nf* chick, *Br* bird

louzeda [luzda] *nf Cités* **avoir la louzeda** to be starving◻

ⓘ This is the "verlan" of "avoir la dallouze", which is itself a variant of "avoir la dalle".

LSD [!] [ɛlɛsde] *nf Hum (femme de petite taille)* shorty, squirt, *Br* short-arse

---

ⓘ This humorous but somewhat vulgar expression comes from a pun on LSD the drug and LSD, the initial letters of "elle (L) suce debout", meaning "she sucks standing up". The image is thus of a woman who is short enough to perform oral sex on a man while in a standing position.

---

luc [!] [lyk] *nm (verlan* **cul***) Br* arse, *Am* ass

luette [lɥɛt] *nf Can* **se mouiller** *ou* **se rincer la luette** *(prendre un verre)* to wet one's whistle, *Br* to have a couple of jars; *(se soûler)* to get plastered *or* wasted *or Br* ratted *or* legless

lugée [lyʒe] *nf Suisse (échec)* failure◻; **il s'est pris une fameuse lugée** he failed miserably, *Am* he bombed

luger [lyʒe] *Suisse* **1** *vi (échouer)* to fail◻, *Am* to flunk
2 se luger *vpr (échouer)* to fail◻

lune [lyn] *nf (derrière)* butt, *Br* bum, *Am* fanny; **se faire taper dans la lune** [!] to take it up the *Br* arse *or Am* ass ▸ *see also* **con**

luné, -e [lyne] *adj* **être bien/mal luné** to be in a good/bad mood◻

Mm

maboul, -e [mabul] *adj* crazy, *Br* mental, bonkers, *Am* wacko

ⓘ This word is derived from an Arabic word meaning "crazy". It entered the French language at the time of the colonial expansion in North Africa.

mac [mak] *nm* (*abbr* **maquereau**) pimp, *Am* mack

macache [makaʃ] *exclam* **macache (bono)!** no way (José)!, no chance!, *Br* nothing doing!

ⓘ This word is derived from an Arabic word meaning "there isn't any". It entered the French language at the time of the colonial expansion in North Africa.

macadam [makadam] *nm* **faire le macadam** to walk the streets, *Br* to be on the game, *Am* to hustle

macaroni [makarɔni] *nm Offensive* (*Italien*) wop, Eyetie, *Am* guinea

ⓘ Depending on the context and the tone of voice used, this term may be either offensive or affectionately humorous. It is nonetheless inadvisable to use it unless one is quite sure of the reaction it will receive.

macchabée [makabe] *nm* stiff (*corpse*)

machin, -e [maʃɛ̃, -in] **1** *nm* (**a**) (*chose*) thing◻, thingy (**b**) **espèce de vieux machin!** you old fool!
  2 *npr* **Machin, Machine** (*personne*) thingy, what's-his-name, *f* what's-her-name

maganer [magane] *vt Can* (*personne*) to beat up; (*objet*) to wreck

magner [maɲe] **se magner** *vpr* **se magner (le train** *ou* **le popotin)** to get a move on, to get one's skates on, *Am* to get it in gear; **se magner le cul [!]** to move *or* shift one's *Br* arse *or Am* ass

magnéto [maɲeto] *nm* (*abbr* **magnétophone**) tape recorder◻, cassette player◻

magot [mago] *nm* stash, hoard, pile; **il se souvient plus où il a planqué le magot** he can't remember where he hid the stash

magouille [maguj] *nf* scheme; **magouilles électorales** vote-rigging; **se livrer à des magouilles** to scheme, to do some wheeling and dealing

magouiller [maguje] *vi* to scheme, to do some wheeling and dealing

magouilleur, -euse [magujœr, -øz] *nm,f* schemer, wheeler-dealer

mahous, -ousse [maus] = **maous**

maigrichon, -onne [megriʃɔ̃, -ɔn] *adj* skinny

maille [maj] *nf Cités (argent)* cash, *Br* dosh, *Am* bucks

ⓘ Originally, a "maille" was a coin used in France in the Middle Ages.

maison [mezɔ̃] *adj inv* **une engueulade/une râclée maison** an almighty telling-off/thrashing

mal [mal] *nm* **ça me ferait mal!, ça me ferait mal aux seins [!]** it would kill me!; **ça te ferait mal de t'excuser?** it wouldn't hurt you to apologize!

malabar [malabar] *nm* hulk; **il s'est retrouvé nez à nez avec un malabar qui lui barrait le passage** he found himself nose to nose with some big hulk who was blocking his way

malade [malad] **1** *adj (inconscient)* crazy, crackers, *Br* mental, *Am* gonzo
2 *nmf* (**a**) *(inconscient)* maniac, headcase, *Br* nutter, *Am* screwball; **il conduit comme un malade** he drives like a maniac; **bosser comme un malade** to work like crazy *or* like mad; **il a flippé comme un malade** he totally flipped *or* freaked out (**b**) *(fanatique)* nut, freak

malaise [malɛz] *nm* **il y a comme un malaise** there's a bit of a snag *or* a hitch

mal-baisée [!!] [malbeze] *nf* **c'est une mal-baisée** she needs a good fuck *or Br* a good seeing-to

maldonne [maldɔn] *nf* **il y a maldonne** something's gone wrong somewhere

malengueulé, -e [malɑ̃gœle] *Can* **1** *adj* vulgar□, uncouth□; **être malengueulé** to have a mouth like a sewer, to be a potty-mouth *or Am* a sewermouth
2 *nm,f* **être un malengueulé** to have a mouth like a sewer, to be a potty-mouth *or Am* a sewermouth

malle [mal] *nf* **se faire la malle** *(partir)* to beat it, *Br* to clear off, *Am* to book it; *(se détacher)* to fall off□

manche [mɑ̃ʃ] **1** *adj (maladroit)* ham-fisted, *Br* cack-handed
2 *nm (personne maladroite) Br* cack-handed idiot, *Am* klutz; *(personne incapable)* useless idiot, *Br* prat, *Am* dork, lamo; **tu t'y prends comme un manche** you're making a real mess of it; **il conduit comme un vrai manche** he's a lousy *or* hopeless driver ▸ *see also* **paire**

manche-à-balle [mɑ̃ʃabal] *nm Belg* crawler, bootlicker

mandale [mɑ̃dal] *nf* clout, slap; **filer une mandale à qn** to clout *or* slap sb

manettes [manɛt] *nfpl* **à fond les manettes** at full speed, *Br* like the clappers, *Am* like sixty

manger [mɑ̃ʒe] **se manger** *vpr* **se manger qch** *(percuter)* to go head-first into sth; **il s'est mangé un sapin en pleine tronche** he went head-first into a fir tree

manif [manif] *nf (abbr* **manifestation)** demo

manip [manip] *nf (abbr* **manipulation)** process□; **tu veux que je te réexplique ou tu as compris la manip?** do you want me to explain it to you again or do you get the idea?

manitou [manitu] *nm* **un grand manitou** a big shot *or* cheese *or* enchilada

maous, -ousse [maus] *adj* ginormous, humongous, massive

maqué, -e [make] *adj* **être maqué(e)** *(avoir une copine)* to have a woman;

(avoir un copain) to have a man or Br a bloke; **ils sont maqués** they're an item

maquer [make] **se maquer** *vpr (se marier)* to get hitched or spliced, to tie the knot; *(s'établir en couple)* to shack up together; **se maquer avec qn** *(se marier avec)* to get hitched or spliced to sb; *(s'établir en couple avec)* to shack up with sb

maquereau, -x [makro] *nm (proxénète)* pimp, *Am* mack

maquerelle [makrɛl] *nf* **(mère) maquerelle** madam *(in brothel)*

marave[1] [marav] *nf* scuffle, *Br* punch-up, scrap, *Am* slugfest

marave[2]**, maraver** [marave] *vt* **(a)** *(battre)* **marave qn** to smash sb's face in, to waste sb's face **(b)** *(tuer)* to kill□, to waste, *Br* to bump off

---

ⓘ This term comes from a Romany word meaning "to hit".

---

marcel [marsɛl] *nm Hum (maillot de corps sans manches)* Br vest□, *Am* undershirt□, wifebeater; **il se balade toujours en marcel** he's always walking around Br in his vest or *Am* in a wifebeater

marcher [marʃe] *vi* **(a)** *(croire naïvement quelque chose)* to fall for it, to swallow it; **faire marcher qn** to pull sb's leg, *Br* to wind sb up, *Am* to yank sb's chain; **il a pas marché, il a couru** he fell for it or swallowed it hook, line and sinker **(b)** *(accepter)* **je marche** count me in, I'm up for it; **je marche pas** count me out, I'm not up for it **(c)** *(fonctionner)* **il marche au whisky/aux speeds** he runs on whisky/speed ▸ *see also* **pompe, radar**

margoulette [margulɛt] *nf* **casser la margoulette à qn** to smash sb's

face in, to waste sb's face; **se casser la margoulette** to fall flat on one's face

margoulin [margulɛ̃] *nm* **(a)** *(escroc)* con man, crook, *Am* grifter **(b)** *(incompétent)* prat, *Br* pillock, *Am* lamo

Marie-Chantal [mariʃɑ̃tal] *npr inv* Br ≃ Sloane (Ranger), *Am* ≃ preppy

Marie-couche-toi-là [marikuʃtwala] *nf inv* trollop, slut

marie-jeanne [mariʒan] *nf inv (cannabis)* Mary Jane, pot

mariole, mariolle [marjɔl] *nmf* clever dick, wise guy; **faire le mariole** to act smart

marlou [marlu] *nm (voyou)* hooligan, thug, *Br* yob□; *(proxénète)* pimp, *Am* mack

marmaille [marmɑj] *nf* brood, kids; **elle est venue avec toute sa marmaille** she came with her whole brood

marmot [marmo] *nm* kid

marner [marne] *vi* to slog, to sweat blood, to bust a gut; **il nous fait marner** he keeps us hard at it or slaving away

maronner [marɔne] *vi* **(a)** *(protester)* to grumble, to grouch, to gripe **(b)** *(attendre)* to hang about or around; **il nous fait toujours maronner** he always has us hanging about or around waiting

marrant, -e [marɑ̃, -ɑ̃t] **1** *adj (amusant, bizarre)* funny; **c'est marrant, j'aurais pourtant juré qu'il était homo** that's funny, I could have sworn he was gay; **t'es marrant toi, comment veux-tu que j'entre si j'ai pas la clef?** very funny, how am I meant to get in if I don't have the key?; **t'es pas marrant!** you're no fun!

2 *nm,f* **être un marrant** to be fun, to be a laugh *or* a riot; **son père, c'est pas un marrant** his dad's not much fun *or* not much of a laugh

marre [mar] *adv* **en avoir marre (de)** to be fed up (with) *or* hacked off (with) *or* sick and tired (of); **en avoir marre de faire qch** to be fed up with *or* hacked off with *or* sick and tired of doing sth; **j'en ai marre de tes jérémiades** I'm sick and tired of your moaning; **c'est marre!** that's enough!, that'll do!

marrer [mare] **se marrer** *vpr* to have a laugh; **on s'est bien marré hier soir avec les potes** we had a good laugh last night with the guys *or Br* lads; **il nous a bien fait marrer avec ses histoires de régiment** he gave us a good laugh with his army stories; *Ironic* **alors là, je me marre!** that's a laugh!, don't make me laugh!; **tu me fais marrer avec tes histoires de télépathie!** you make me laugh with all your stuff about telepathy!

marron [marɔ̃] **1** *adj* (**a**) *(qui exerce clandestinement)* unqualified⁰ (**b**) *(dupé)* **être marron** to have been taken in, to have been taken for a ride, *Am* to have been rooked; **faire qn marron** to take sb in, to take sb for a ride, *Am* to rook sb

2 *nm (coup)* belt, wallop; **coller un marron à qn** to belt *or* wallop sb one

marteau [marto] *adj (fou)* **être marteau** to be not right in the head *or* not all there, to have a screw loose

maso [mazo] *(abbr* **masochiste) 1** *adj* masochistic⁰

2 *nmf* masochist⁰

masquer [maske] *vi (bouder)* to be in a *or* the huff

masse [mas] *nf* (**a**) **être à la masse** to be off one's head, to be *Br* barking (mad) *or Am* wacko (**b**) **il y en a pas des masses** there isn't much/aren't many⁰

mastard [mastar] *nm* hulk; **c'est un sacré mastard, le copain de ma cousine** my cousin's boyfriend is a huge hulk of a guy

mastoc [mastɔk] *adj inv* (**a**) *(énorme)* ginormous, humongous, massive (**b**) *Belg (fou)* crazy, *Br* barking (mad), *Am* wacko

mat' [mat] *nm (abbr* **matin) deux/ trois heures du mat'** two/three a.m.⁰ *or* in the morning⁰

mater¹ [mate] *vt* to check out; *(avec concupiscence)* to eye up; **mate-moi ça!** check it out!, *Br* get a load of that!

mater² [matɛr], **maternelle** [matɛrnɛl] *nf* old lady, *Br* old dear *(mother)*

mateur, -euse [matœr, -øz] *nm,f* **c'est un sacré mateur** he's always eyeing up women

maton, -onne [matɔ̃, -ɔn] *nm,f* screw *(prison warder)*, *Am* hack, bull

matos [matos] *nm* stuff, gear; **les musiciens se sont fait piquer leur matos pendant leur tournée** the band got all their gear pinched *or Br* nicked while they were on tour

maudit, -e [!] [modi, -it] *Can* **1** *adj (très)* **c'est une maudite belle fille** she's a hell of a good-looking girl, *Br* she's bloody good-looking; **être en maudit** to be fuming *or Br* spewing; **c'est un beau film en maudit** it's a damn *or Br* bloody good film; **il court vite en maudit** he's a damn *or Br* bloody fast runner

2 *exclam* shit!, *Br* bloody hell!

mauditement [moditmɑ̃] *adv Can* damn, *Br* bloody; **mauditement**

cher damn or Br bloody expensive

mauvaise [movɛz] adj **l'avoir** ou **la trouver mauvaise** to be hacked off or bummed

mauviette [movjɛt] nf wimp, wuss, Br big girl's blouse

max [maks] nm (abbr **maximum**) **un max de monde/de voitures** tons or a ton of people/cars; **assurer un max** to do brilliantly; **sur scène ils assurent un max** they really kick ass on stage

maxi [maksi] adv (abbr **maximum**) **on sera vingt maxi** there'll be twenty of us max or tops; **ça prendra deux heures maxi** it'll take two hours max or tops

mec [mɛk] nm (a) (individu) guy, Br bloke; **salut les mecs!** hi, guys! (b) (compagnon) boyfriend□, man, Br bloke; **elle est venue sans son mec** she came without her man or Br bloke

meca [məka] nf Cités (verlan **came**) drugs□, stuff, Br gear

méchamment [meʃamɑ̃] adv (très, beaucoup) really□, Am real

méchant, -e [meʃɑ̃, -ɑ̃t] adj (remarquable) amazing, terrific

mecton [mɛktɔ̃] nm guy, Br bloke

médoc [medɔk] nm medicine□; **il est dépressif et bourré de médocs** he suffers from depression and he's drugged up to the eyeballs or he's a walking pharmacy

mégalo [megalo] (abbr **mégalomane**) **1** adj megalomaniac□, power-crazed
   2 nmf megalomaniac□, power maniac, control freak

mégoter [megɔte] vi to skimp (**sur** on); **arrête de mégoter, achète du vrai Champagne!** stop being stingy or Br tight, get real champagne!; **il**

a pas mégoté sur le piment he didn't skimp on the chilli

meilleure [mejœr] nf **ça c'est la meilleure!** that just tops it all!

mélanger [melɑ̃ʒe] **se mélanger** vpr Hum (avoir des rapports sexuels) to exchange bodily fluids

mêler [mele] **se mêler** vpr **de quoi je me mêle?** what's that got to do with you/him/etc?

mêle-tout [mɛltu] nmf inv busybody, Br nosey parker

mélo [melo] **1** adj (abbr **mélodramatique**) melodramatic□, over-the-top, Br OTT
   2 nm (abbr **mélodrame**) melodrama□

melon [məlɔ̃] nm (a) Offensive (Maghrébin) = racist term used to refer to a North African Arab (b) **choper le melon** to get bigheaded

membré [mɑ̃bre] adj **être bien/mal membré** to be/not to be well-hung

mémèrage [memeraʒ] nm Can gossip□

mémère [memɛr] **1** nf (femme d'un certain âge) old biddy, Br old dear
   2 adj frumpy, frumpish; **faire mémère** to look frumpy, to look like an old granny ▸ see also **pousser**

mémérer [memere] vi Can to gossip□

méninges [menɛ̃ʒ] nfpl **se remuer les méninges** to rack or Am cudgel one's brains

menteuse [mɑ̃tøz] nf (langue) tongue□

merde [!] [mɛrd] **1** nf (a) (excrément) shit, crap; **être dans la merde** to be in the shit, to be up shit creek (without a paddle); **traîner qn dans la merde** to drag sb's name through the mud; **ne pas se pren-**

dre pour de la merde to think one's shit doesn't stink, *Br* to think the sun shines out of one's arse; **il a de la merde dans les yeux** he never sees a thing, he can't see what's going on right in front of him

(**b**) *(individu méprisable)* shit

(**c**) *(chose de mauvaise qualité)* **c'est une merde cet ordinateur** this computer's (a load of) shit *or* crap; **de la merde** (a load of) shit *or* crap; **c'est de la merde ce rasoir!** this razor's (a load of) shit *or* crap!; **un boulot/un quartier de merde** a shit *or* shitty job/area; **tu vas l'éteindre, ta radio de merde, oui?** will you turn that *Br* bloody *or Am* goddamn radio off!

(**d**) *(désordre)* **semer** *ou* **foutre la merde** to create havoc; **c'est la merde dans le pays en ce moment** the country's a *Br* bloody *or Am* goddamn mess *or* shambles at the moment; **c'est la merde pour circuler dans Paris en ce moment** driving in Paris is a *Br* bloody *or Am* goddamn nightmare at the moment

(**e**) *(problème)* problem□; **et si il nous arrivait une merde?** what if we ended up in the shit?; **il m'est arrivé une merde** something shit's happened, I'm in the shit

2 *exclam* (**a**) *(pour exprimer l'exaspération)* shit!; **dire merde à qn** to tell sb to piss off *or Br* bugger off; **alors, tu viens, oui ou merde?** are you coming or not, for Christ's sake?; **avoir un œil qui dit merde à l'autre** to have a squint□

(**b**) *(pour souhaiter bonne chance)* break a leg! ▸ *see also* **bordel, fouteur**

merder [!] [mɛrde] **1** *vt (rater)* to screw up, *Br* to cock up, to balls up, *Am* to ball up

2 *vi (personne)* to screw up, *Br* to cock up; *(situation)* to be a *Br* cock-

up *or* balls-up *or Am* ball-up; **le coup a complètement merdé** the job was a complete *Br* cock-up *or* balls-up *or Am* ball-up

merdeux, -euse [!] [mɛrdø, -øz] **1** *adj (coupable)* **se sentir merdeux** to feel shit *or* shitty

2 *nm,f* (**a**) *(personne méprisable)* shit (**b**) *(enfant)* kid

merdier [!] [mɛrdje] *nm Br* bloody *or Am* goddamn mess *or* shambles

merdique [!] [mɛrdik] *adj* shit, shitty

merdouille [!] [mɛrduj] *nf* (**a**) *(situation déplaisante) Br* bloody *or Am* goddamn mess *or* shambles; **être dans la merdouille** to be in the shit (**b**) *(chose sans valeur)* **de la merdouille** (a load of) shit

merdouiller [!] [mɛrduje], **merdoyer** [!] [mɛrdwaje] *vi* to screw up, *Br* to cock up, to balls up, *Am* to ball up

mère [mɛr] *nf Cités* **ta mère!** [!] *Br* piss off!, *Am* take a hike!; **enculé de ta mère!** [!!] you fucking prick *or Br* arsehole *or* wanker *or Am* asshole!; **niquer sa mère à qn** [!!] to kick sb's fucking head in, to waste sb's fucking face, *Br* to punch sb's fucking lights out; **flipper sa mère** to be scared stiff, *Br* to be absolutely bricking it; **ouah! il est beau sa mère ce mec!** wow! that guy is a total babe *or* hottie!, *Br* that guy's well fit! ▸ *see also* **maquerelle, niquer**

ⓘ The word "mère", literally translated as "mother", appears in numerous slang expressions of the "banlieues" (see panel **L'argot des banlieues** p.219) and functions as an intensifier.

---

mérinos [merinos] *nm Hum* **laisser**

pisser le mérinos to let things take their course□

merlan [mɛrlɑ̃] nm (**a**) (coiffeur) hairdresser□ (**b**) **regarder qn avec des yeux de merlan frit** (sans comprendre) to gaze blankly at sb□, to gape at sb□; (amoureusement) to make sheep's eyes at sb

métèque [metɛk] nmf Offensive = racist term used to refer to any dark-skinned foreigner living in France, especially one from the Mediterranean; **sa fille s'est mise en ménage avec un métèque** his daughter's shacked up with some Dago-looking guy or some swarthy type

métro [metro] nm (**a**) **il a toujours un métro de retard** he's always the last one to know what's going on (**b**) **métro, boulot, dodo** the daily grind, the nine-to-five routine

mettable [!!] [mɛtabl] adj fuckable, Br shaggable

mettre [mɛtr] **1** vt (**a**) [!!] (posséder sexuellement) to fuck, to screw, Br to shag; **va te faire mettre!** up yours!, fuck off!, go (and) fuck yourself! (**b**) **les mettre, mettre les bouts** to make tracks, to hit the road, Am to book it

2 se mettre vpr (**a**) **son contrat, il peut se le mettre quelque part!** [!!] he can shove his contract up his Br arse or Am ass! (**b**) **s'en mettre jusque-là** to stuff oneself or one's face, to pig out; **qu'est-ce qu'on s'est mis!** we really stuffed ourselves or our faces!, we really pigged out! (**c**) **qu'est-ce qu'ils se sont mis!** (dans une bagarre) they really laid into each other!, they were going at it hammer and tongs! ▶ see also **coup, grappin, nez, paquet, veilleuse, voile, vue**

meuf [mœf] nf (verlan **femme**) (**a**) (fille) chick, Br bird (**b**) (compagne) girlfriend□, woman, Br bird

meule [møl] nf (**a**) (moto) (motor)bike□ (**b**) **meules** (postérieur) butt, Br bum, Am fanny (**c**) Suisse (personne ou chose fastidieuse) drag

mézigue [mezig] pron yours truly, Br muggins (here)

mic [majk] nm Cités mike

miches [miʃ] nfpl (**a**) (postérieur) butt, Br bum, Am fanny (**b**) (seins) boobs, knockers

micheton [miʃtɔ̃] nm Br punter, Am john (prostitute's client)

ⓘ This word comes from the man's name "Michel".

michetonner [miʃtɔne] vi (**a**) (avoir recours à une prostituée) to go to a hooker (**b**) (se prostituer) to turn tricks, Br to be on the game

mickey [mikɛ] nm nobody□, nonentity□

micmac [mikmak] nm muddle, shambles

midi [midi] nm (**a**) **chercher midi à quatorze heures** to look for complications (where there are none)□; **pas besoin de chercher midi à quatorze heures pour expliquer son départ** no need to look too far to understand why he left (**b**) **marquer midi** [!!] (avoir une érection) to have a hard-on or a boner

millefeuille [!!] [milfœj] nm (sexe de la femme) pussy, beaver, snatch

mimi [mimi] **1** adj inv cute□

2 nm (**a**) (baiser) kiss□ (**b**) (chat) puss, Br moggy (**c**) [!] (sexe de la femme) pussy, Br fanny

mimine [mimin] nf (main) hand□, mitt; **lave-toi les mimines, mon**

coco wash your hands, sweetie□

minable [minabl] **1** *adj* **(a)** *(mesquin, pauvre)* shabby, grotty **(b)** *(incompétent, insuffisant)* pathetic, lousy
2 *nmf* loser, no-hoper, *Br* waster

mince [mɛ̃s] *exclam (pour exprimer l'exaspération)* blast!, sugar!, *Am* shoot!, *Br* pants!; *(pour exprimer la surprise)* wow!, *Br* blimey!, strewth!, *Am* gee (whiz)!

minch [minʃ] *nf* Cités **(a)** *(femme)* chick, *Br* bird **(b)** [!] *(sexe de la femme)* pussy, beaver, snatch

mine [min] *nf* **prendre** *ou* **se mettre une mine** to get smashed *or* wasted *or Br* pissed

minet, -ette [minɛ, -ɛt] **1** *nm* **(a)** *(chat)* puss, moggy **(b)** [!] *(sexe de la femme)* pussy, beaver, snatch
2 *nm,f (jeune personne à la mode)* trendy, hipster
3 [!] *nf (sexe de la femme)* pussy, beaver, snatch; **faire minette (à qn)** to go down (on sb), to give (sb) head

minou [minu] *nm* **(a)** *(chat)* puss, moggy **(b)** [!] *(sexe de la femme)* pussy, beaver, snatch

mioche [mjɔʃ] *nmf* kid

mirettes [mirɛt] *nfpl* eyes□, peepers; **en mettre plein les mirettes à qn** to blow sb's mind

miro [miro] *adj* short-sighted□; **il est complètement miro** he's as blind as a bat; **elles sont devant ton nez, tes clés; t'es miro ou quoi?** your keys are right under your nose, are you blind?

mitan [mitɑ̃] *nm* **le mitan** the underworld, gangland

mitard [mitar] *nm* disciplinary cell□, cooler; **se retrouver au mitard** to end up in solitary

miteux, -euse [mitø, -øz] **1** *adj*

(costume, chambre, hôtel) shabby, grotty; *(personne)* seedy-looking, shabby; *(situation, salaire)* pathetic
2 *nm,f (indigent)* bum, *Br* dosser

mitraille [mitrɑj] *nf (petite monnaie)* small change□, *Br* coppers, shrapnel

mob [mɔb] *nf (abbr* **mobylette)** moped□

moche [mɔʃ] *adj* **(a)** *(laid)* ugly□, hideous, *Br* minging **(b)** *(moralement répréhensible)* rotten, lousy; **c'est moche ce qu'il a fait** that was a rotten *or* lousy thing he did **(c)** *(regrettable)* rotten!; **c'est moche ce qui lui est arrivé** it was rotten *or* terrible what happened to him

mocheté [mɔʃte] *nf* **(a)** *(femme laide)* dog, moose, *Br* boot, minger, *Am* beast; *(homme laid)* horror, *Br* minger **(b)** *(chose laide)* eyesore

modeux, -euse [mɔdø, -øz] *nm,f* fashionista

mofflé, -e [mɔfle] *nm,f Belg* failed (exam) candidate□

moffler [mɔfle] *vi Belg* **j'ai été mofflé** I failed my exam□, *Am* I flunked my exam

moine [!!!] [mwan] *nm Can (pénis)* prick, dick, cock

moisir [mwazir] **1** *vi* **on va pas moisir ici, tirons-nous!** we're not hanging around here for ever, let's get out of here!
2 *vt* **moisir qn** to badmouth sb, *Br* to slag sb off

moite-moite [mwatmwat] *adv* fiftyfifty, half-and-half

molard [!], **mollard** [!] [mɔlar] *nm* spit□, *Br* gob of spit

molarder [!], **mollarder** [!] [mɔlarde] *vi* to spit□, *Br* to gob

mollasson, -onne [mɔlasɔ̃, -ɔn] **1** *adj* slow□, sluggish□

2 *nm,f* lazy so-and-so, slob

mollo [molo] **1** *adv* **y aller mollo** to go easy, to take it easy; **vas-y mollo avec la sauce** go easy on the sauce **2** *exclam* take it easy!

môme [mom] **1** *nmf (enfant)* kid **2** *nf* **(a)** *(fille)* chick, *Br* bird **(b)** *(compagne)* girlfriend□, *(main)* squeeze, *Br* bird

monaco [monako] *nm* = drink consisting of beer, grenadine syrup and lemonade

monnaie [monɛ] *nf (argent)* cash, dough, *Br* dosh, *Am* bucks

monstre [mɔ̃str] *adj* ginormous, humongous, massive; **j'ai un boulot monstre!** I've got loads *or* tons *or* piles of work to do!; **il a un culot monstre** he's got a damned nerve *or* *Br* a bloody cheek

monté [mɔ̃te] *adj* **être bien monté** to be well-hung; **être monté comme un âne** *ou* **un bourricot** *ou* **un taureau** [!] to be hung like a horse *or* *Br* a donkey *or* *Am* a mule

montesquieu [mɔ̃tɛskjø] *nm* Formerly *(billet de deux cents francs)* two-hundred franc note□

ⓘ The "montesquieu" was so called because a picture of the writer Charles Montesquieu used to feature on the banknote.

---

morbac, morbaque [morbak] *nm* **(a)** [!] *(pou du pubis)* crab **(b)** *(enfant)* kid

morceau, -x [morso] *nm* **(a)** *(personne)* **un beau morceau** a babe, a hottie, *Br* a bit of all right; **un sacré morceau** a big bruiser **(b)** **casser** *ou* **cracher** *ou* **lâcher** *ou* **manger le morceau** to spill the beans, to let the cat out of the bag **(c)** **casser le**

morceau à qn to give sb a piece of one's mind **(d)** **emporter** *ou* **enlever le morceau** to get one's own way

mordache [mordaʃ] *nf Suisse* **avoir la mordache** to have the gift of the gab

mordicus [mordikys] *adv* stubbornly□; **il soutient mordicus que c'est vrai** he swears blind that it's true

mordu, -e [mordy] **1** *adj (amoureux)* madly in love, completely smitten **2** *nm,f* fan, fanatic□; **un mordu de football** a *Br* football *or* *Am* soccer fan *or* fanatic□

morfale [morfal] **1** *adj* greedy□ **2** *nmf* pig, *Br* greedy-guts, gannet, *Am* hog

morfler [morfle] **1** *vt* **(a)** *(recevoir)* to get□; **il a morflé une claque dans la tronche** he got a slap in the face **(b)** *(se voir infliger une peine de)* to get□, to cop **2** *vi* **(a)** *(être abîmé)* to get smashed up; *(être blessé)* to get injured□; **les suspensions de la voiture ont drôlement morflé** the car suspension's totally wrecked *or* *Br* knackered **(b)** *(être sévèrement puni)* to catch it, *Br* to cop it

moricaud, -e [moriko, -od] **1** *adj* dark-skinned□, swarthy□ **2** *nm,f Offensive* **(a)** *(personne de race noire)* nigger, *Br* wog **(b)** *(personne à la peau foncée)* dark-skinned *or* swarthy person□

morlingue [morlɛ̃g] *nm (porte-monnaie)* *Br* purse□, *Am* change purse□; *(portefeuille)* *Br* wallet□, *Am* billfold□; **avoir des oursins dans le morlingue** *(être très avare)* to be a total skinflint *or* tightwad, *Br* to have moths in one's wallet

mornifle [mornifl] *nf* **(a)** *(argent)* cash, dough, *Br* dosh, *Am* bucks **(b)** *(gifle)* slap, cuff

---

The symbol [!] denotes a very familiar term, [!!] a vulgar one.

morpion [mɔrpjɔ̃] nm (a) *(pou du pubis)* crab (b) *(enfant)* kid

mort, -e [mɔr, mɔrt] **1** adj (a) *(hors d'usage)* **être mort** to be dead, to have had it, to be kaput or Br knackered (b) *(fatigué)* dead, Br knackered, done in, Am beat (c) **être mort de rire** to be killing oneself (laughing); **être mort de trouille** to be scared to death

2 à mort adv **freiner à mort** to slam on the brakes; **déconner à mort** [!] to talk complete crap or bull or Br bollocks; **bander à mort** [!!] to have a raging hard-on ▸ see also **rat**

mortel, -elle [mɔrtɛl] **1** adj (a) *(excellent)* cool, Br wicked, Am awesome (b) *(très mauvais)* hellish, Am gnarly (c) *(ennuyeux)* deadly boring

2 adv **on s'est éclatés mortel!** we had a blast!, we had Br a wicked or Am an awesome time!; **on s'est fait chier mortel** [!!] we were bored shitless

3 exclam cool!, Br wicked!, Am awesome!

mortibus [mɔrtibys] adj dead□

morue [!] [mɔry] nf (a) *(prostituée)* whore, hooker (b) *(femme)* slut, tart, Br slapper

morveux, -euse [mɔrvø, -øz] **1** adj snotty-nosed

2 nm,f (a) *(enfant)* kid (b) *(jeune prétentieux)* snotty little upstart

motte [!!] [mɔt] nf *(sexe de la femme)* pussy, snatch, Br minge, twat; **s'astiquer la motte** to finger oneself, to play with oneself

motus [mɔtys] exclam **motus (et bouche cousue)!** not a word!, mum's the word!

mou [mu] **1** adv *(doucement)* **y aller mou** to go easy, to take it easy; **vas-y mou avec le piment** go easy on

2 nm (a) **bourrer le mou à qn** to pull the wool over sb's eyes (b) **c'est du mou** *(c'est faux)* it's a load of garbage or Br rubbish (c) **rentrer dans le mou à qn** *(agresser qn)* to go for sb, to lay into sb ▸ see also **bourrage, chique**

mouais [mwɛ] exclam well, yeah; **alors, t'as aimé le film? – mouais, j'ai vu pire...** did you like the movie, then? – well, yeah, I've seen worse

mouchard, -e [muʃar, -ard] nm,f squealer, Br grass, Am rat; *(à l'école)* snitch, Br sneak, tell-tale, Am tattle-tale

moucharder [muʃarde] **1** vt to squeal on, Br to grass on, to shop, Am to rat on; *(à l'école)* to snitch on, Br to sneak on, to tell tales on

2 vi to squeal, Br to grass, Am to rat; *(à l'école)* to snitch, Br to sneak, to tell tales, Am to tattle

mouflet, -ette [muflɛ, -ɛt] nm,f kid

moufter [mufte] vi **ne pas moufter** to keep one's mouth shut, Br to keep schtum

mouille [!!] [muj] nf *(sécrétions vaginales)* lube, love juice; *(sexe de la femme)* pussy, snatch, Br fanny, twat, minge

mouiller [muje] **1** vt (a) *(compromettre)* to involve□, to drag in (b) Can *(fêter)* **il va falloir mouiller ça!** we'll have to have a drink to celebrate!□, this calls for a celebration!□

2 vi (a) [!] *(avoir peur)* to wet oneself, to piss oneself (b) [!!] *(être excitée sexuellement)* to be wet

3 se mouiller vpr (a) *(se compromettre)* to stick one's neck out (b) Can **se mouiller la dalle** ou **le gargoton** ou **le canayen** to get smashed or wasted or Br pissed ▸ see also **liquette**

mouise [mwiz] *nf (misère)* poverty□; *(ennuis)* grief, hassle, *Br* aggro; **être dans la mouise** *(être dans la misère)* to be hard up *or* broke *or* *Br* skint; *(avoir des ennuis)* to be in a hole, *Am* to be behind the eightball

moule [‼] [mul] *nf (sexe de la femme)* pussy, snatch, *Br* fanny, twat, minge; **avoir de la moule** *(de la chance) (ponctuellement)* to be lucky□ *or* *Br* jammy; *(toujours)* to have the luck of the devil

moumoune [mumun] *nf Can Offensive* fairy, queer, *Br* poof, *Am* fag

moumoute [mumut] *nf* wig□, rug, *Br* syrup

mourir [murir] *vi* **plus débile/macho, tu meurs!** they don't come any more stupid/macho than that!

mouron [murɔ̃] *nm* **se faire du mouron** to worry oneself sick

mousse [mus] *nf* (a) *(bière)* beer□; **on se boit une mousse?** fancy a *Br* pint *or* *Am* brew? (b) **se faire de la mousse** to worry oneself sick

moutard [mutar] *nm* kid

mouv' [muv] *nm (abbr* **mouvement)** **c'est dans le mouv'** it's way cool, it's dead hip

moyen [mwajɛ̃] *nm* **y'a moyen!** can do!

muflée [myfle] *nf* **prendre une muflée** to get wrecked *or* wasted *or* *Br* pissed; **il tenait une sacrée muflée** he was totally wrecked *or* wasted *or* *Br* legless *or* pissed

mule [myl] *nf (passeur de drogue)* mule

mur [myr] *nm* **tenir le mur** to bum around all day *(because one is unemployed)*

murge [myrʒ] *nf* **prendre une murge** to get wrecked *or* wasted *or* *Br* pissed; **il tenait une sacrée murge** he was totally wrecked *or* wasted *or* *Br* legless *or* pissed

murger [myrʒe] **se murger** *vpr* to get wrecked *or* wasted *or* *Br* pissed

muscu [mysky] *nf (abbr* **musculation)** body-building□; **faire de la muscu** to do body-building

musiciens [myzisjɛ̃] *nmpl (haricots)* beans□

musicos [myzikos] *nm (musicien)* muso

must [mœst] *nm* must; **c'est un must** it's a must

mytho [mito] *nmf (abbr* **mythomane)** (a) *(menteur)* compulsive liar□ (b) *Cités (mensonge)* lie□, fib, *Br* porky (pie)

Nn

nager [naʒe] *vi (ne rien comprendre)* to be totally lost, not to have a clue

nana [nana] *nf (femme)* chick, *Br* bird; *(petite amie)* girlfriend□, (main) squeeze, *Br* bird

nanar [nanar] *nm* (a) *(marchandise sans valeur)* junk, trash, garbage (b) *(mauvais film)* lousy film, *Am* turkey

NAP [nap] *(abbr* **Neuilly-Auteuil-Passy)** **1** *adj Br* ≃ Sloany, *Am* ≃ preppy
2 *nmf Br* ≃ Sloane (Ranger), *Am* ≃ preppy

ⓘ Neuilly, Auteuil and Passy are areas in the west of Paris, and are among the wealthiest and most middle-class in the city, although strictly speaking Neuilly is not part of Paris, but in the adjoining département Hauts-de-Seine. A "NAP" is typically rich, expensively dressed, and politically to the right.

nase [naz] = **naze**

naseaux [nazo] *nmpl (narines)* nostrils□; **on a pris toute la fumée dans les naseaux** all the smoke went right up our noses

navet [navɛ] *nm (mauvais film)* lousy film, *Am* turkey

naze [naz] **1** *adj* (a) *(épuisé) Br* knackered, shattered, *Am* beat (b) *(hors d'usage)* kaput, bust, *Br* knackered, clapped-out (c) *(stupide)* thick, dense, *Am* dumb (d) *(de mauvaise qualité)* crap, crappy, lousy, *Br* poxy
2 *nmf* useless idiot, loser

nèfles [nɛfl] *nfpl* **des nèfles!** no way!, no chance!

négatif [negatif] *exclam* no!□, nope!

negifran [nəʒifrã] *nf (verlan* **frangine)** chick, *Br* bird

négro [negro] *nm Offensive* nigger

neige [nɛʒ] *nf (cocaïne)* snow, coke, charlie

nénés [nene] *nmpl* tits, boobs, knockers, *Am* hooters

nénette [nenɛt] *nf* (a) *(femme, fille)* chick, *Br* bird (b) *(tête)* **se casser la nénette (à faire qch)** to go to a lot of bother (to do sth); **te casse pas la nénette** don't worry about it, don't let it bother you

nerfs [nɛr] *nmpl* **avoir les nerfs** to be hacked off; **foutre les nerfs à qn** to hack sb off, to get sb's back up
► *see also* **paquet**

net, nette [nɛt] *adj* **pas net** *(louche)* shady, *Br* dodgy; *(ivre, drogué)* wasted, wrecked, *Am* off one's face; *(pas complètement sain d'esprit)* not all there, not right in the head, *Br* one sandwich short of a picnic

nettoyer [netwaje] *vt* (a) *(dépouiller)* to clean out, to take to the cleaners (b) *(tuer)* tp wipe out, *Br* to bump off, *Am* to rub out

neuf-trois [nœftrwa] *nm (département de la Seine-Saint-Denis)* Seine-Saint-Denis□

ⓘ This term comes from the two-digit number of the Seine-Saint-Denis département, which is located on the outskirts of Paris and contains many impoverished housing estates.

neuneu [nønø] *adj* daft, *Am* dumb

neutu [nœty] *nf Cités (verlan* **thune)** cash, dough, *Br* dosh, *Am* bucks

nez [ne] *nm* (**a**) **avoir un coup dans le nez** to have had one too many, to be the worse for wear (**b**) **elle m'a dans le nez** she can't stand *or* stomach *or Br* stick me, *Br* I get right up her nose (**c**) **mettre à qn le nez dans son caca** *ou* **dans sa merde** [!!] to call sb to order□, to pull sb up ▸ *see also* **doigt, pendre, tirer**

niac [njak] *nmf Offensive (Asiatique)* slant, *Am* gook

niacoué, -e [njakwe] *nm,f Offensive (Asiatique)* slant, *Am* gook

ⓘ This term comes from the Vietnamese word "niah-koué", meaning "farmer".

niaiser [njɛze] *Can* **1** *vt* **niaiser qn** *(faire perdre patience à)* to drive sb crazy; *(se moquer de)* to laugh at sb, *Br* to wind sb up, *Am* to razz sb; *(raconter des histoires à)* to pull sb's leg, *Br* to wind sb up, *Am* to yank sb's chain
2 *vi (ne rien faire)* to hang around

niaiseux, -euse [njɛzø, -øz] *Can* **1** *adj* thick, dense, *Am* dumb
2 *nm,f* moron, jerk

niaque [njak] = **gnaque**

nibards [!] [nibar] *nmpl* tits, knockers

nichons [niʃɔ̃] *nmpl* boobs, tits

nickel [nikɛl] **1** *adj inv* (**a**) *nickel ou* **nickel chrome** *(très propre)* spotless□, gleaming□ (**b**) *(parfait)* perfect□, just the thing, *Br* spot-on; **c'est nickel, comme appareil, pour se mettre à la photo** it's the perfect camera for someone just taking up photography□; **ça s'est super bien passé, l'organisation et l'ambiance étaient nickel!** it went really well, it was brilliantly organized and the atmosphere was perfect□ *or Br* spot-on!
2 *adv* **faire qch nickel** *ou* **nickel chrome** to do sth really well□

nickelé [nikle] *adj* **avoir les pieds nickelés** *(être trop paresseux pour marcher)* to be too lazy to walk anywhere□; *(avoir de la chance)* to be lucky□ *or Br* jammy

niet [njɛt] *exclam* no way!, not a chance!

nimportenawaque [nɛ̃pɔrtnawak] *adv Cités* crap, *Br* pants, *Am* BS; **ce film, je te raconte pas, c'était nimportenawaque!** that film, my God, what a load of crap *or Br* pants *or Am* BS!

nipper [nipe] **se nipper** *vpr* to get dressed□; **il sait pas se nipper** he's got no dress sense□

nippes [nip] *nfpl* clothes□, gear, *Br* threads

nique [nik] *nf* **faire la nique à qn** to thumb one's nose at sb

niquer [!!] [nike] **1** *vt* (**a**) *(posséder sexuellement)* to fuck, to screw, *Br* to shag, *Am* to bang; **va te faire niquer!, nique ta mère!** fuck off!, go (and) fuck yourself!
(**b**) *(endommager)* to fuck up, *Br* to

knacker, to bugger; **il m'a niqué ma mob** he's fucked up *or Br* knackered *or* buggered my moped; **il s'est niqué le genou** he's fucked up *or Br* knackered *or* buggered his knee; **je vais lui niquer sa gueule!** I'm going to kick his fucking head in *or* waste his fucking face *or Br* punch his fucking lights out!; *Cités* **niquer sa mère** *ou* **sa race à qn** to smash sb's face in, to waste sb's face

(c) *(attraper)* to nab, to collar; **il s'est fait niquer par les contrôleurs** he got nabbed *or* collared by the ticket collectors

(d) *(duper)* to screw, to shaft, **c'est un faux, tu t'es fait niquer!** it's a fake, you've been screwed *or* shafted!

2 *vi* to fuck, to screw, *Br* to shag, *Am* to bang

niquet [nikɛ] *nm Belg* snooze, nap, *Br* kip; **faire un niquet** to have a snooze *or* a nap *or Br* a kip

noce [nɔs] *nf* **(a)** **faire la noce** to live it up **(b)** **être à la noce** to have the time of one's life, to have a whale of a time; **on n'était pas à la noce** it was no picnic

nœud [!!!] [nø] *nm (pénis)* cock, dick, prick; **à la mords-moi le nœud** lousy, crappy, *Br* poxy ▸ *see also* **tête**

nœud-pap [nøpap] *nm (abbr* **nœud papillon)** bow tie□

noiche [nwaʃ] *nmf Cités (verlan* **chinois)** Chinese□, Chink, Chinky

noir, -e [nwar] **1** *adj (ivre)* plastered, smashed, wasted

2 *nm* **un petit noir** a black coffee□

noircir [nwarsir] **se noircir** *vpr (s'enivrer)* to get plastered *or* smashed *or* wasted

noisettes [!] [nwazɛt] *nfpl (testi-* cules) balls, nuts, *Br* bollocks

noix [nwa] *nf* **à la noix (de coco)** lousy, *Br* poxy

nom [nɔ̃] **1** *nm* **nom à coucher dehors** mouthful; **il a un nom à coucher dehors** his name's a real mouthful; **petit nom** first name□

2 *exclam* **nom de nom!, nom d'un petit bonhomme!, nom d'une pipe!** for goodness' *or* heaven's sake!, *Br* blimey!, *Am* gee (whiz)!; **nom d'un chien!** hell!; **nom de Dieu!** for Christ's sake!, Christ (Almighty)!

nono, -ote [nono, nonɔt] *nm,f Can* jerk, *Br* pillock, plonker, *Am* schmuck

noraf [nɔraf], **nordaf** [nɔrdaf] *nm Offensive* = racist term used to refer to a North African Arab

nouba [nuba] *nf* party□; **faire la nouba** to party

nougats [nuga] *nmpl (pieds)* feet□, *Br* plates, *Am* dogs

nouille [nuj] *nf* **(a)** *(personne stupide)* dope, *Br* berk, divvy, *Am* meathead **(b)** [!] *(pénis)* dick, prick, *Br* knob, *Am* schlong; **égoutter la nouille** to *Br* have *or Am* take a piss, to take a leak, *Br* to have a slash

nuigrave [nɥigrav] *nf* smoke, *Br* fag

ⓘ This term is a contraction of the words "nuit gravement à la santé", the government health warning which appears on every cigarette pack in France.

nul, nulle [nyl] **1** *adj* crap, garbage, *Br* rubbish; *(personne)* useless, hopeless, clueless; **il est nul en anglais** he's crap *or* useless *or* hopeless at English; **c'est nul de pas l'avoir invité à ta boum** it was crap not to invite him to your party; **nul à chier [!!]** fucking awful

    2 *nm,f* useless idiot, loser

nullache [nylaʃ] *adj* (*abbr* **nul à chier**) godawful, *Br* bloody awful; **son dernier skeud, il est nullache** his latest record is godawful *or Br* bloody awful

nullard, -e [nylar, -ard] **1** *adj* crap, lousy

    2 *nm,f* useless idiot, loser

nullissime [nylisim] *adj* totally useless, pathetic

nullité [nylite] *nf (personne)* useless idiot, loser

nullos [nylos] **1** *adj* useless

    2 *nmf* useless idiot, loser; **mais qui est-ce qui m'a fichu une bande de nullos pareille?** how did I get stuck with such a bunch *or of* useless idiots?

numéro [nymero] *nm* (**a**) *(personne originale)* character, case; **quel numéro!** what a character *or* case!; **c'est un drôle de numéro!** he's a strange character!, *Br* he's a right one! (**b**) **avoir tiré le bon numéro** to have found Mr/Miss Right

nunuche [nynyʃ] *adj* daft, *Am* dumb

nympho [nɛ̃fo] *nf (abbr* **nymphomane**) nympho, *Br* goer

Oo

occase [ɔkaz] *nf* (*abbr* **occasion**)
(**a**) (*opportunité*) chance◻, opportunity◻; **c'est le genre d'occase à
ne pas laisser passer** you shouldn't
let an opportunity like that pass you
by◻; (**b**) (*affaire*) *Br* snip, *Am* steal
profites-en, c'est une occase!
make the most of it, it's a real *Br*
snip *or Am* steal! (**c**) **d'occase** second-hand◻; **je n'achète que des
voitures d'occase** I only buy second-hand cars

occuper [ɔkype] **s'occuper** *vpr*
t'occupe! mind your own business!,
keep your nose out!, butt out! ▶ *see
also* **oignon**

-oche [ɔʃ] *suffix* **baloche** local
dance◻; **cantoche** canteen◻; **cinoche** *Br* pictures, flicks, *Am* movies;
fastoche easy as pie, *Br* dead *or Am*
real easy

ⓘ This suffix is found at the end
of many French slang nouns and
adjectives and is used for either pejorative or humorous effect.

œil [œj] *nm* **mon œil!** my eye!, my
foot!; **faire de l'œil à qn** to give
sb the eye; **œil au beurre noir**
black eye◻, shiner; **à l'œil** free (of
charge)◻; **avoir qn à l'œil** to have
one's eye on sb, to keep an eye on
sb ▶ *see also* **battre, doigt, rincer,
taper, tourner, yeux**

œuf [œf] *nm* (**a**) **va te faire cuire un
œuf!** take a running jump!, go and
jump in the lake!, *Am* take a hike!
(**b**) *Hum* **œufs sur le plat** (*seins*)
fried eggs

oigne [!!] [waɲ] *nm Br* arsehole,
Am asshole; **l'avoir dans l'oigne** to
have been screwed *or* shafted

oignon [ɔɲɔ̃] *nm* (**a**) [!!] (*anus*) *Br*
arsehole, *Am* asshole; **l'avoir dans
l'oignon** to have been screwed *or*
shafted (**b**) **s'occuper de ses oignons** to mind one's own business;
c'est pas tes oignons! it's none
of your business! (**c**) **aux petits oignons** great, fantastic ▶ *see also*
carrer

oilpé [walpe] = **loilpé**

oinj [wɛ̃ʒ] *nm* (*verlan* **joint**) joint,
spliff

oiseau, -x [wazo] *nm* **un drôle
d'oiseau** an odd character, a funny old bird; **se donner des noms
d'oiseaux** to hurl insults *or* abuse at
each other

olé olé [ɔleɔle] *adj inv* **être un peu
olé olé** (*de mœurs légères*) to be a
bit loose; (*peu respectueux*) to be a
bit too laid back; **il a raconté des
blagues un peu olé olé devant les
gosses** he told some pretty dirty *or*
racy *or Br* dodgy jokes in front of the
kids; **il y avait quelques scènes olé
olé dans le film** there were some
raunchy *or* steamy bits in the film

ombre [ɔ̃br] *nf* (**a**) **être à l'ombre** *(en prison)* to be behind bars *or* inside; **mettre qn à l'ombre** to put sb behind bars *or* inside (**b**) **marche à l'ombre!** *(conseil)* keep a low profile!; *(menace)* stay out of my sight!

ordure [ɔrdyr] *nf (individu méprisable)* scumbag, *Br* rotter, *Am* stinker

orphelines [!] [ɔrfəlin] *nfpl (testicules)* balls, nuts, *Br* bollocks

os [ɔs] *nm* (**a**) *(problème)* snag, hitch; **il y a un os** there's a snag *or* a hitch; **tomber sur un os** to hit a snag (**b**) **l'avoir dans l'os** [!] to get screwed *or* shafted; **jusqu'à l'os** totally□, completely□ ▸ *see also* **sac**

-os [ɔs] *suffix* **chicos** classy, smart; *Offensive* **portos** Dago *(from Portugal)*; **nullos** useless idiot; **rapidos** pronto; **ringardos** uncool, unhip, square

ⓘ This suffix is found at the end of many French nouns and adjectives and often indicates that the word is rather pejorative.

oseille [ozɛj] *nf (argent)* cash, dough, *Br* dosh, *Am* bucks

ostrogoth [ostrogo] *nm* boor, pig, Neanderthal

où [u] **d'où** *adv Cités* **d'où tu me parles comme ça, toi?** who do you think you're talking to?

ouais [wɛ] *exclam* yeah!; **elle m'a même pas invité à sa teuf, je suis trop dégoûté, ah ouais!** she didn't even invite me to her party, I'm really *Br* gutted *or Am* bummed, y'know!

oublier [ublije] *vt* **oublie-moi!** get off my back *or* case!

ouf [uf] **1** *adj (verlan* **fou***)* crazy, *Br* mental, barking (mad), *Am* wacko
2 *nm (verlan* **fou***)* nutcase, *Br* nutter, *Am* screwball; **c'est un truc de ouf** it's mental
3 *exclam* phew!; **il n'a pas eu le temps de dire ouf** he didn't even have time to catch his breath

ouïe [wi] *nf Can (oreille)* ear□, *Br* lug, lughole

-ouille [uj] *suffix* **magouille** scheme; **merdouille** cock-up; *Pej* **pedzouille** yokel, peasant, *Am* hick

ⓘ This suffix is found at the end of many French nouns and adjectives and often indicates that the word is rather pejorative.

-ouse [uz] *suffix* **bagouse** ring□; **partouse** orgy; **perlouse** pearl□; **piquouse** shot, *Br* jab; *Offensive* **tantouse** queer, *Br* poof, *Am* fag

ⓘ This suffix is found at the end of many French nouns and adjectives and often indicates that the word is rather pejorative.

outil [uti] *nm Hum (pénis)* tool ▸ *see also* **remballer**

outillé [utije] *adj Hum* **être bien outillé** to be well-hung

ouvrir [uvrir] *vt* **l'ouvrir, ouvrir sa gueule** [!] *(parler)* to open one's big mouth

-ouze [uz] = **-ouse**

Pp

pacson [paksɔ̃] *nm* (**a**) *(paquet)* parcel□, package□ (**b**) **toucher le pacson** *(dans une affaire)* to make a bundle *or Br* a packet; *(au jeu)* to win a bundle *or Br* a packet

paddock [padɔk] *nm (lit)* bed□, *Br* pit

paf [paf] **1** *adj inv* smashed, plastered, sozzled
2 [!] *nm (pénis)* dick, cock, *Br* knob, *Am* schlong

pagaïe, pagaille [pagaj] *nf* (**a**) *(désordre)* mess, shambles (**b**) **il y en a en pagaïe** there's loads *or* tons of it/them

page [paʒ], **pageot** [paʒo] *nm (lit)* bed□, *Br* pit

pager [paʒe], **pagnoter** [paɲɔte] **se pager, se pagnoter** *vpr* to hit the sack *or* the hay *or Am* the rack

paillasse [pajas] *nf (ventre)* stomach□, belly, gut; **trouer la paillasse à qn** to knife sb in the belly

paillasson [pajasɔ̃] *nm (personne servile)* doormat; **traiter qn comme un paillasson** to treat sb like a doormat

paille [paj] *nf* (**a**) **être/finir sur la paille** to be/end up completely broke *or Br* on one's uppers *or Am* without a dime (**b**) *Ironic (petite somme)* **il a perdu vingt mille euros à la roulette – une paille!** he lost twenty thousand euros at the roulette table

– chickenfeed!, peanuts!

pain [pɛ̃] *nm* (**a**) *(coup)* belt, smack; **coller un pain à qn** to belt *or* smack sb (**b**) **ça mange pas de pain** it won't do any harm ► *see also* **planche**

paire [pɛr] *nf* (**a**) **se faire la paire** *(s'enfuir)* to take off, to make oneself scarce, *Br* to scarper; *(s'évader)* to break out□; *(faire une fugue)* to run away□, *Br* to do a bunk (**b**) **c'est une autre paire de manches** that's a different kettle of fish, that's a whole different ball game (**c**) **en glisser une paire à qn** [!] to give sb one, to slip it to sb

paître [pɛtr] *vi* **envoyer qn paître** to tell sb where to go, *Br* to send sb packing

paix [pɛ] *nf* **fiche-moi** *ou* **fous-moi** [!] **la paix!** get off my back *or* case!; **la paix!** shut up!

pâle [pɑl] *adj* (**a**) **se faire porter pâle** to call in sick□ *(when one is well enough to work)*, *Br* to take *or* pull a sickie (**b**) **être pâle des genoux** to be *Br* knackered *or* shattered *or Am* beat

paletot [palto] *nm* **tomber sur le paletot à qn** to jump on sb, to go for sb; **mettre la main sur le paletot à qn** to nab *or Br* nick *or* lift sb

pâlichon, -onne [paliʃɔ̃, -ɔn] *adj* a bit pale□ *or* pasty, on the pale side□

pallot [!] [palo] *nm* French kiss,

Br snog; **rouler un pallot à qn** to French-kiss sb, *Br* to snog sb, *Am* to make out with sb

palmée [palme] *adj Hum* **les avoir palmées** to be bone idle *or* a complete layabout

ⓘ This expression literally means "to have webbed hands", a condition that would, obviously, make work somewhat difficult.

palper [palpe] *vi (toucher de l'argent)* to get one's money□, to collect; **t'en fais pas pour lui, il a déjà palpé** don't worry about him, he's already got his share

palpitant [palpitã] *nm (cœur)* ticker

paluche [palyʃ] *nf* hand□, mitt, paw

palucher [!] [palyʃe] **1** *vt* to grope, to feel up, to touch up
    2 se palucher *vpr* to play with oneself, to touch oneself up

panade [panad] *nf* **être dans la panade** to be broke *or Br* on one's uppers *or Am* without a dime

panais [!!] [panɛ] *nm* **tremper son panais** to dip one's wick

Paname [panam] *npr* = nickname given to Paris

panard [panar] *nm* (a) *(pied)* foot□, *Br* plate, *Am* dog (b) *(plaisir intense)* **quel panard!** great!, cool!, *Br* wicked!; **prendre son panard** *(éprouver un grand plaisir)* to get one's kicks; *(atteindre l'orgasme)* to come, to get off

panier [panje] *nm* (a) *(derrière)* **mettre la main au panier à qn** to goose sb, to feel sb's *Br* bum *or Am* butt (b) **panier à salade** *Br* Black Maria, *Am* paddy wagon

panouille [panuj] *nf* (a) *(personne stupide)* idiot, fool (b) *(petit rôle)* bit-part

pantouflard, -e [pãtuflar, -ard] **1** *adj* **être pantouflard** to be a real stay-at-home *or* homebody
    2 *nm,f* stay-at-home, homebody

papa [papa] **à la papa** *adv* leisurely□; **on va faire ça à la papa** we'll take it easy, we'll do it at our own pace

papelard [paplar] *nm* (a) *(papier)* paper□ (b) *(article de journal)* (newspaper) article□, piece (c) **papelards** *(papiers d'identité)* ID; **les flics lui ont demandé ses papelards** the cops asked to see his ID

papi [papi] *nm (homme âgé)* granddad, grandpa

papier-cul, papier Q [papjeky] *nm Br* bog roll, *Am* TP

papillon [papijɔ̃] *nm (contravention)* (parking) ticket□; **on m'a encore collé un papillon** I've got another parking ticket

papoter [papɔte] *vi* to chat, to yak, *Br* to natter

papouilles [papuj] *nfpl* **faire des papouilles à qn** to stroke sb□, to caress sb□; **c'est un gamin qui aime bien qu'on lui fasse des papouilles** he's a very cuddly child

pâquerette [pɑkrɛt] *nf* **voler au ras des pâquerettes** *(conversation, plaisanterie)* to be pretty lowbrow□, not to be very sophisticated□

paquet [pakɛ] *nm* (a) **mettre le paquet** to pull out all the stops, to go all out (b) **tout un paquet de** a pile *or* stack of; **il m'a montré sa collection de CD et je peux te dire qu'il y en a pour un paquet de fric!** he showed me his CD collection and I can tell you it must be worth a bundle *or Br* a packet! (c) **un paquet de nerfs** a bag of nerves

parachuter [paraʃyte] *vt (faire venir de l'extérieur)* to parachute in□; **per-**

sonne ne le connaît, il a été para-chuté d'une autre boîte no one knows him, he's been parachuted in from another company

parano [parano] **1** adj (abbr **paranoïaque**) paranoid[□]

2 nmf (abbr **paranoïaque**) paranoid person[□]

3 nf (abbr **paranoïa**) paranoia[□]; **personne ne veut ta peau, t'es en pleine parano!** nobody's after you, you're just being paranoid!

pardon [pardɔ̃] exclam **qu'est-ce qu'on a bien bouffé, alors là, pardon!** you should have seen how well we ate, it was something else!; **elle a une paire de lolos, pardon!** you should see the boobs or the rack she's got on her!; **Sophia Loren, ah pardon! ça c'est une femme!** Sophia Loren, now THAT'S what I call a woman!

pare-chocs [parʃɔk] nmpl Hum (seins) bumpers, knockers

parfum [parfœ̃] nm **être au parfum** to be in the know; **mettre qn au parfum** to fill sb in, to put sb in the picture

parigot, -e [parigo, -ɔt] **1** adj Parisian[□]

2 nm,f **Parigot, Parigote** Parisian[□]; **Parigot, tête de veau!** stuck-up city type! (insult used by country people towards Parisians)

parler [parle] vi **tu parles!** (absolument) you're telling me!, absolutely!, Br too right!; (absolument pas) you must be joking!, are you kidding!; **tu parles d'une cuisinière! elle est pas fichue de faire cuire un œuf…** some cook she is, she can't even boil an egg!

parlote, parlotte [parlɔt] nf chat, chitchat

parole [parɔl] exclam cross my heart!, I swear to God!

parti, -e [parti] adj (ivre) wasted, plastered, Br legless, Am bombed

partie [parti] nf **partie fine** orgy; **partie carrée** foursome

partousard, -e [partuzar, -ard] nm,f = person who takes part in an orgy

partouse [partuz] nf orgy

partouser [partuze] vi = to take part in an orgy

partouzard, -e [partuzar, -ard] = **partousard**

partouze [partuz] = **partouse**

partouzer [partuze] = **partouser**

pascal [paskal] nm Formerly (billet de cinq cents francs) five-hundred franc note[□]

ⓘ The "pascal" was so called because a picture of the writer and philosopher Blaise Pascal used to feature on the banknote.

passe [pɑs] nf (d'une prostituée) trick; **faire une passe** to turn a trick

passe-lacet [pɑslasɛ] nm **raide comme un passe-lacet** completely broke or Br skint or strapped (for cash)

passer [pɑse] vi (a) **y passer** to croak, Br to snuff it, Am to kick off, to cash in (b) Hum **il y a que le train qui lui soit pas passé dessus** she's the town bike, she's seen more ceilings than Michelangelo ▸ see also **arme, as, billard, casserole, pommade, savon, sentir, tabac**

passoire [pɑswar] nf (a) **transformer qn en passoire** to pump sb full of lead, to riddle sb with bullets (b) (mauvais gardien de but) **c'est une vraie passoire, ce gardien** this goalie lets everything in (c) **ma mémoire est une vraie passoire** I've got a memory like a sieve

pastaga [pastaga] *nm (pastis)* pastis□

patapouf [patapuf] *nm* **gros patapouf** fatso, fatty

pataquès [patakɛs] *nm* mess, shambles; **faire un pataquès** to cause a stink, to set tongues wagging

patate [patat] *nf* (**a**) *(pomme de terre)* potato□, spud (**b**) *(coup)* thump, clout (**c**) *(dans les jeux de balle)* powerful shot□, whack (**d**) *Formerly (dix mille francs)* ten thousand francs□ (**e**) **en avoir gros sur la patate** to be down in the mouth (**f**) *(imbécile)* dope, *Br* divvy, wally, *Am* meathead (**g**) *Can* **lâche pas la patate!** hang in there!

patati [patati] *exclam* **et patati et patata** blah blah blah, and so on and so forth, *Am* yada yada yada

patatras [patatra] *exclam* crash!

patauger [patoʒe] *vi* **patauger (dans la semoule)** to be totally lost; **je ne comprends rien à ces histoires de logarithmes, je patauge** I don't understand the first thing about this logarithm nonsense, I'm totally lost

pâte [pɑt] *nf* **être bonne pâte** to be a good sort

pâtée [pɑte] *nf* thrashing, hammering; **foutre la pâtée à qn** *(correction, défaite)* to give sb a thrashing *or* a hammering

patelin [patlɛ̃] *nm (village)* village□; *(petite ville)* small town□

pater [patɛr], **paternel** [patɛrnɛl] *nm (père)* old man, *Br* pater

patin [patɛ̃] *nm* (**a**) **[!]** *(baiser)* French kiss, *Br* snog; **rouler un patin à qn** to French-kiss sb, *Br* to snog sb, *Am* to make out with sb (**b**) **donner** *ou* **filer un coup de patin** *(un coup de frein)* to slam on the brakes

patraque [patrak] *adj* out of sorts, under the weather, *Br* off-colour

patron, -onne [patrɔ̃, -ɔn] *nm,f* other half; *(conjoint)* old man; *(conjointe)* old lady, *Br* missus; **j'en sais rien, demande à la patronne** I've no idea, ask my old lady *or Br* the missus

patte [pat] *nf* (**a**) *(jambe)* leg□, pin; **tirer dans les pattes à qn** to cause trouble for sb; **retomber sur ses pattes** to land on one's feet; **un pantalon pattes d'eph'** a pair of flares *or Br* lionels *or* Tonys; **en avoir plein les pattes** to be *Br* knackered *or Am* beat (**b**) *(main)* hand□, mitt, paw; **tomber dans les pattes de qn** to fall into sb's clutches; **graisser la patte à qn** to grease sb's palm; **bas les pattes!** paws off!, keep your paws to yourself! ▸ *see also* **casser**

paturon [patyrɔ̃] *nm* foot□, *Br* plate, *Am* dog

paumé, -e [pome] **1** *adj* (**a**) *(reculé)* godforsaken; **il habite une ferme dans un coin paumé** he lives on a farm in the middle of nowhere (**b**) *(perdu, embrouillé)* lost

2 *nm,f* loser, dropout, *Br* waster, *Am* slacker

paumer [pome] **1** *vt* to lose□

2 se paumer *vpr* to get lost□

pavé [pave] *nm* (**a**) *(livre épais)* doorstop (**b**) *(dent)* tooth□, *Br* gnasher

paveton [pavtɔ̃] *nm (pavé)* paving stone□

pavute [!] [pavyt] *nf* whore, hooker

> ⓘ This word is in fact the word "pute", after it has been given the "javanais" treatment (see box on "javanais" p.309).

paye [pɛj] *nf* **ça fait une paye** it's

been ages *or Br* yonks

payer [peje] **se payer** *vpr* **il a brûlé un feu rouge et s'est payé un piéton** he went through a red light and hit a pedestrian[□]; **il s'est payé un arbre en moto** he crashed *or* smashed his motorbike into a tree[□]; **si il continue à m'énerver, celui-là, je vais me le payer!** if he carries on annoying me, I'm going to swing for him *or* thump him one!; **se payer la tête** *ou* **la tronche [!] de qn** *Br* to take the mick *or* mickey out of sb, to take the piss out of sb, *Am* to razz sb; **il s'est payé une crève carabinée** he came down with a stinking cold *or Br* some hideous lurgy; **se payer du bon temps, s'en payer** to have a blast, to have *Br* a wicked *or Am* an awsome time ▸ *see also* **tranche**

peau, -x [po] *nf* **faire la peau à qn** to bump sb off, *Br* to do sb in; **trouer la peau à qn** to fill *or* pump sb full of lead; **avoir qn/qch dans la peau** to be mad *or* crazy about sb/sth; **avoir le rythme dans la peau** to have rhythm in one's blood; **il sait pas quoi faire de sa peau** he doesn't know what to do with himself; **coûter la peau des fesses** *ou* **du cul [!]** to cost an arm and a leg; **peau de balle** *ou* **de zébi!** no way (José)!, no chance!, *Br* nothing doing!; **peau d'âne** diploma[□]; **peau de vache** *(homme)* scumbag, *Br* swine, *Am* stinker; *(femme)* bitch, *Br* cow

pébroc, pébroque [pebrɔk] *nm* umbrella[□], *Br* brolly

pêche [pɛʃ] *nf* **(a)** *(coup)* thump, wallop; **prendre une pêche** to get thumped *or* walloped **(b)** **avoir la pêche** to be on (top) form, to be full of go **(c)** **poser une pêche [!]** to *Br* have *or Am* take a dump, to drop a

log ▸ *see also* **fendre**

pécho [peʃo] *vt (verlan* **choper)** **(a)** *(saisir)* to grab[□] **(b)** *(surprendre)* to catch[□], to nab; **se faire pécho** to get caught *or* nabbed **(c)** *(maladie, coup de soleil)* to catch[□], to get

pêchu, -e [pɛʃy] *adj* on (top) form, full of go

pécore [pekɔr] *nmf Pej* yokel, peasant, *Am* hick

pécos [pekos] *nm* joint, spliff

pécu [peky] *nm Br* bog roll, *Am* TP

pédale [pedal] *nf* **(a)** *Offensive (homosexuel)* queer, *Br* poof, *Am* fag; **être de la pédale** to be a queer *or Br* poof *or Am* fag **(b)** **perdre les pédales** to lose one's marbles, *Br* to lose the plot; **s'emmêler les pédales** to get all mixed up, to get hopelessly lost

pédaler [pedale] *vi* **pédaler dans la choucroute** *ou* **dans la semoule** *ou* **dans le yaourt** to get nowhere

pédé [!!] [pede] *Offensive (abbr* **pédéraste) 1** *adj* queer, *Br* bent; **pédé comme un phoque** *Br* as bent as a nine-bob note *or* as a three-pound note, *Am* as queer as a three-dollar bill

2 *nm* queer, *Br* poof, *Am* fag

pédégé [pedeʒe] *nm Hum Br* MD[□], *Am* CEO[□]

ⓘ This expression comes from the humorous spelling of "P-DG", the abbreviation of "président-directeur général", as it is pronounced.

pédibus [pedibys] *adv* on foot[□]; **il y est allé pédibus** he went on foot[□], he hoofed it

pedzouille [pedzuj] *nmf Pej* yokel, peasant, *Am* hick

Le symbole [□] indique que la traduction n'est pas argotique.

péfli [pefli] *vi Cités (verlan* **flipper**) to be scared□, to be freaking out *or Br* bricking it

peigne-cul [pɛɲky] *nm (individu méprisable)* jerk, *Br* tosser; *(individu grossier)* pig, boor, *Am* hog

peignée [peɲe] *nf* thrashing, hiding, hammering; **flanquer une peignée à qn** to give sb a thrashing *or* hiding *or* hammering; **recevoir une peignée** to get a thrashing *or* hiding *or* hammering

peinard, -e [penar, -ard] **1** *adj* **(a)** *(tranquille)* **être peinard** to have it easy, to have an easy time of it, *Am* to be on easy street; **ils sont peinards dans leur nouvelle baraque** they're nice and comfy in their new place; **il a trouvé un coin peinard pour pioncer** he found a quiet corner to crash out; **tiens-toi peinard!** keep your nose clean! **(b)** *(peu fatigant)* **un boulot peinard** a cushy number
 2 *adv (tranquillement)* in peace□, peacefully□; **on va rouler peinard, pas besoin de faire la course, on est en vacances** we'll just drive *or* potter along at our own pace, it's not a race, we're on holiday

pékin [pekɛ̃] *nm (individu)* guy, *Br* bloke

pelant, -e [pəlɑ̃, -ɑ̃t] *adj Belg (agaçant)* annoying□; *(assommant)* deadly dull; **c'est pelant!** *(agaçant)* it's a real pain (in the neck) *or* a real nuisance!; *(assommant)* it's a real drag!

pelé [pəle] *nm* **il y avait trois pelés et un tondu** there was hardly a soul there

peler [pəle] **1** *vi* to be freezing (cold); **ça pèle** it's freezing (cold) *or Br* baltic *or* brass monkeys
 2 se peler *vpr* **se (les) peler** to be

freezing one's *Br* arse *or Am* ass off

pèlerin [pɛlrɛ̃] *nm (individu)* guy, *Br* bloke

pelle [pɛl] *nf* **(a)** [!] *(baiser)* French kiss, *Br* snog; **rouler une pelle à qn** to French-kiss sb, *Br* to snog sb, *Am* to make out with sb **(b)** **à la pelle** in spades, by the bucketload; **des nanas comme elle, il y en a à la pelle** there's loads of chicks *or Br* birds like her **(c)** **(se) prendre** *ou* **(se) ramasser une pelle** *(tomber)* to fall flat on one's face; *(subir un échec)* to come unstuck ▸ *see also* **rond**

pelloche [pelɔʃ] *nf* film□ *(for camera)*

pélo [pelo] *nm (individu)* guy, *Br* bloke

pelote [!!] [plɔt] *nf Can (sexe de la femme)* pussy, snatch, *Br* fanny; *(femme)* a bit of *Br* skirt *or Am* pussy *or* tail

peloter [plɔte] **1** *vt* to grope, to feel up, to touch up
 2 se peloter *vpr* to grope each other, to feel *or* touch each other up

pelouse [pluz] *nf (marijuana)* grass, weed

pelure [plyr] *nf (manteau)* coat□

pendouiller [pɑ̃duje] *vi* to dangle□, to hang down□

pendre [pɑ̃dr] *vi* **ça te pend au nez** you've got it coming to you; **être toujours pendu au téléphone** to be never off the phone, to spend one's life on the phone

péniches [peniʃ] *nfpl (grandes chaussures)* shoes□, clodhoppers

péno [peno] *nm (abbr* **penalty)** penalty□, *Br* pen *(in football)*

penser [pɑ̃se] *vt* **il peut se le mettre où je pense** he knows where he can stick it, he can stick it you know where; **elle lui a fichu un coup de pied où je pense** she gave him a kick up the you-know-where

people [pipɔl] **1** adj **un magazine people** a celeb or gossip magazine
2 nm (célébrité) celeb; **les people** celebs

pépé [pepe] nm (homme âgé) grand-dad, grandpa

pépée [pepe] nf chick, Br bird

pépère [pepɛr] **1** adj (a) (tranquille) relaxing□ (b) (peu fatigant) **un boulot pépère** a cushy number
2 adv leisurely□; **on a fait ça pépère** we took it easy, we did it at our own pace
3 nm (a) (homme âgé) granddad, grandpa (b) **un gros pépère** a big fatty or fatso

pépètes, pépettes [pepɛt] nfpl (a) (argent) cash, dough, Br dosh, Am bucks (b) Belg **avoir les pépètes** to be scared stiff or witless, Br to be bricking it

pépin [pepɛ̃] nm (a) (problème) hitch, snag; **avoir un pépin** to have a problem□ (b) (parapluie) umbrella□, Br brolly

péquenaud, -e [pekno, -od] nm,f Pej yokel, peasant, Am hick

péquenot [pekno] nm Pej yokel, peasant, Am hick

perche [pɛrʃ] nf (a) **grande perche** (personne) beanpole, Am stringbean (b) **tendre la perche à qn** to throw sb a line, to give sb a helping hand

percuter [pɛrkyte] vi (comprendre) to catch on, to get it

perdreau, -x [pɛrdro] nm (policier) cop

perfecto® [pɛrfɛkto] nm biker jacket

périf, périph' [perif] nm (abbr **bou-**levard périphérique) **le périf** = the ring road around Paris

perle [!] [pɛrl] nf (a) (pet) fart; **lâcher une perle** to fart, Br to let off, Am to lay one (b) (faute grossière) howler; **il collectionne les perles de ses élèves** he collects the howlers that his pupils come out with (c) **enfiler des perles** to mess around; **bon, faudrait peut-être se mettre au boulot, on n'est pas là pour enfiler des perles** right, it's maybe time to get to work, we're not here to twiddle our thumbs

perlouse, perlouze [pɛrluz] nf (a) (perle) pearl□ (b) [!!] (pet) fart; **lâcher une perlouse** to fart, Br to let off, Am to lay one

perm, perme [pɛrm] nf (abbr **permission**) leave□

Pérou [peru] npr **c'est pas le Pérou** it won't break the bank

perpète [pɛrpɛt] **à perpète** adv (abbr **à perpétuité**) (a) (pour toujours) **être condamné à perpète** to get life (b) (très loin) miles away; **n'y va pas à pied, c'est à perpète** don't walk there, it's miles away

perroquet [pɛrɔke] nm (cocktail) = drink consisting of pastis and mint-flavoured syrup

perso [pɛrso] adv (abbr **personnellement**) **être** ou **jouer perso** to hog the ball

personne [pɛrsɔn] pron **quand il s'agit de faire la vaisselle/de payer, il n'y a plus personne** when it's time to do the dishes/to pay, you can't see anyone for dust

pervenche [pɛrvɑ̃ʃ] nf (contractuelle) Br (female) traffic warden□, Am meter maid□

pèse [pɛz] = **pèze**

pet¹ [pɛ] nm (a) (gaz intestinaux) fart;

Le symbole □ indique que la traduction n'est pas argotique.

ça vaut pas un pet de lapin it's not worth a monkey's fart; **celui-là, il a toujours un pet de travers** there's always something up with him (b) **faire le pet** *(faire le guet)* to keep watch□ or a lookout□

pet² [pɛt] = **pète**

pétage [petaʒ] *nm* **pétage de plombs** *(fait de se mettre en colère)* going ballistic, hitting the roof or *Am* ceiling, blowing one's top or *Am* stack; *(fait de craquer nerveusement)* cracking up; **le patron nous a fait un pétage de plombs maison quand il s'est aperçu de ce qui s'était passé** the boss went totally ballistic or totally hit the roof or *Am* ceiling when he saw what had happened; **il faut que je prenne des vacances parce que là je suis au bord du pétage de plombs** I need to take a holiday coz I'm on the verge of cracking up

pétant, -e [petã, -ãt] *adj* **à cinq heures pétantes** at five sharp or on the dot

Pétaouchnock [petauʃnɔk] *npr* = imaginary distant place; **ils l'ont envoyé à Pétaouchnock** they sent him to some place in the back of beyond or to Timbuktu

pétard [petar] *nm* (a) *(cigarette de cannabis)* joint, spliff (b) **être en pétard** *(en colère)* to be fuming or livid; **se mettre en pétard** to go ballistic, to hit the roof or *Am* ceiling, to blow one's top or *Am* stack (c) *(pistolet)* shooter, *Am* piece (d) *(postérieur)* butt, *Br* bum, *Am* fanny (e) *Can (belle fille)* babe, hottie, *Br* stunner (f) **faire du pétard** *(du bruit)* to make a racket or a din; *(du scandale)* to kick up a fuss, to cause a stink

pétasse [petas] *nf* (a) *(femme vulgaire)* slut, tart, *Br* slapper (b) *(prostituée)* whore, hooker

pète [pɛt] *nm (trace de coup)* dent□, bash□

pété, -e [!] [pete] *adj (ivre)* shit-faced, *Br* rat-arsed, pissed

pète-dans-le-sable [pɛtdãlsabl] *nmf* runt, squirt, shorty

péter [pete] **1** *vt* (a) *(briser)* to break□; *(mettre hors d'usage)* to bust, *Br* to knacker, to bugger; **péter la gueule à qn** to smash sb's face in, to waste sb's face (b) **péter le feu** *ou* **des flammes** to be bursting with energy (c) **la péter** *(avoir très faim)* to be starving or ravenous□ (d) **se la péter, péter sa frime** to show off, to pose
2 *vi* (a) [!] *(émettre des gaz intestinaux)* to fart; **péter plus haut que son cul** to think one's shit doesn't stink, *Br* to think the sun shines out of one's arse; **péter dans la soie** to live in the lap of luxury; **envoyer qn péter** to tell sb where to go or where to get off (b) *(casser)* to break□, to bust (c) **tu vas la fermer? j'en ai rien à péter de tes histoires!** will you shut up? I don't give *Br* a monkey's or a toss or *Am* a rat's ass about your nonsense
3 se péter *vpr* (a) *(se casser)* **se péter le poignet/la cheville** to break one's wrist/ankle□; **la poutre s'est pétée en deux** the beam broke in two□ (b) **se péter la gueule** *(tomber)* to fall flat on one's face; **se péter (la gueule)** [!!] *(s'enivrer)* to get shit-faced or *Br* rat-arsed or pissed ► *see also* **durite, plomb, sous-ventrière**

pète-sec [pɛtsɛk] **1** *adj inv* abrupt□, snippy
2 *nmf inv* abrupt□ or snippy person

péteux, -euse [petø, -øz] **1** *adj* (a) *(lâche)* chicken, yellow-bellied (b) *(prétentieux)* stuck-up, snooty
2 *nm,f* (a) *(lâche)* chicken (b) *(prétentieux)* upstart

pétochard, -e [petɔʃar, -ard] *adj & nm,f* chicken *(coward)*

pétoche [petɔʃ] *nf* fear□; **avoir la pétoche** to be scared stiff *or* witless, *Br* to be bricking it

pétocher [petɔʃe] *vi* to be scared stiff *or* witless, *Br* to be bricking it

pétoire [petwar] *nf Hum* old rifle□

peton [pɔtɔ̃] *nm* foot□, *Br* plate, *Am* dog

pétouiller [petuje] *vi Suisse* to dither *or* faff about

pétrin [petrɛ̃] *nm* **être/se mettre dans le pétrin** to be in/get into a fix *or* a mess

pétrolette [petrɔlɛt] *nf Hum (cyclomoteur)* moped□

peu [pø] *nm* **un peu (mon neveu)!** you bet!, sure thing!, *Br* too right!; **il est un peu bête, ce mec – un peu beaucoup!** the guy's a bit stupid – more than a bit!; **pas qu'un peu** more than a little

peuple [pœpl] *nm* (a) *(monde)* **il y avait du peuple** there were tons of people there (b) **que demande le peuple?** what more could you ask for?

peupons [pøpɔ̃] *nfpl (verlan* **pompes**) shoes□, clodhoppers

pèze [pɛz] *nm* cash, dough, *Br* dosh, *Am* bucks

philo [filo] *nf (abbr* **philosophie**) philosophy□

phosphorer [fɔsfɔre] *vi* to think hard□; **il faut trouver une solution, alors c'est le moment de phosphorer, les mecs!** we need to find a solution, so let's put our heads together *or* get our thinking caps on, guys!

photo [foto] *nf* **tu veux ma photo?** what are YOU staring at?; **y'a pas photo** there's no two ways about it; **des deux frangines, c'est elle la mieux roulée, y'a pas photo** of the two sisters, that one's got the best body, no two ways about it

---

① The expression "y a pas photo" comes from the world of horseracing, where a photo-finish decides the result of a race in which it has been impossible to see which horse won.

---

piaf [pjaf] *nm (oiseau)* bird□; *(moineau)* sparrow□

piailler [pjɑje] *vi (criailler)* to squeal□; **on entendait la marmaille en train de piailler dans la cour de récré** you could hear the kids squealing in the playground

piane-piane [pjanpjan] *adv* slowly□; **vas-y piane-piane!** take your time!, there's no rush!

piano [pjano] **1** *adv* **piano(-piano)** *(doucement)* slowly□; **vas-y piano-piano!** take your time!, there's no rush!
2 *nm* **piano du pauvre, piano à bretelles** squeezebox

piasse [pjas] *nf Can* dollar□, buck

piastre [pjastr] *nf Can* dollar□, buck

piaule [pjol] *nf* (bed)room□

picaillons [pikɑjɔ̃] *nmpl* cash, dough, *Br* dosh, *Am* bucks

pichtegorne [piʃtəgɔrn] *nm* wine□, vino, *Br* plonk

picole [pikɔl] *nf* boozing; **la picole, il n'y a que ça qui l'intéresse** boozing's the only thing he/she's interested in

picoler [pikɔle] **1** *vt* to knock back
2 *vi* to booze, to knock it back

picoleur, -euse [pikɔlœr, -øz] *nm,f* boozer, alky, *Br* pisshead, *Am* booze-hound

picrate [pikrat] *nm* wine□, vino, *Br* plonk

pièce [pjɛs] *nf* (a) **une belle pièce** *(femme)* a babe, *Br* a bit of all right (b) **on n'est pas aux pièces** we're not on piecework, there's no great hurry

pied [pje] *nm* **prendre son pied** *(atteindre l'orgasme)* to come, to get off; *(prendre du plaisir)* to get one's kicks; **c'est le pied** it's great *or* fantastic *or Br* wicked *or Am* awesome; **il a fait ça comme un pied** he made a dog's breakfast *or* dinner *or Br* a pig's ear of it; **il chante/conduit comme un pied** he can't sing/drive to save his life; **être bête comme ses pieds** *Br* to be thick (as two short planks), to be as daft as a brush, *Am* to have rocks in one's head ▸ *see also* **grue, lever, nickelé**

piège [pjɛʒ] *nm* **piège à cons** con, scam

piercé, -e [pirse] **1** *adj* pierced□ *(part of body)*
2 *nm,f* = person with body piercings

pierrot [pjero] *nm (moineau)* sparrow□

pieu, -x [pjø] *nm (lit)* bed□, *Br* pit; **se mettre au pieu** to hit the sack *or* the hay *or Am* the rack ▸ *see also* **affaire**

pieuter [pjøte] **1** *vi* to crash, *Br* to kip
2 se pieuter *vpr* to hit the sack *or* the hay *or Am* the rack

pif [pif] *nm* (a) *(nez) Br* conk, hooter, *Am* schnozzle; **je l'ai dans le pif** I can't stand *or* stomach *or Br* stick him, *Br* he gets right up my nose (b)

(abbr **pifomètre**) **faire qch au pif** to do sth by guesswork

pifer, piffer [pife] *vt* **je ne peux pas le piffer** I can't stand *or* stomach *or Br* stick him, *Br* he gets right up my nose

pifomètre, piffomètre [pifɔmɛtr] *nm* **faire qch au piffomètre** to do sth by guesswork

pige [piʒ] *nf* year□; **il a au moins soixante-dix piges** he's at least seventy□

pigeon [piʒɔ̃] *nm (dupe)* sucker, *Br* mug, *Am* patsy

pigeonner [piʒɔne] *vt* **pigeonner qn** to take sb for a ride, to take sb in, *Am* to rook sb

piger [piʒe] *vt* to get it, to catch on; **il est pas question que je te prête ma caisse, tu piges?** no way am I lending you my car, got it?

pignoler [piɲɔle] **se pignoler** [!] *vpr* to jerk off, to beat off, *Br* to toss oneself off, to have a wank

pignouf [piɲuf] *nm* slob, boor

pile [pil] **pile-poil!** *adv* great!, cool!

ⓘ This expression was popularized in *Les Guignols de l'Info*, a television programme in the form of a satirical puppet show.

piler [pile] *vi* to slam on the brakes

pillave [pijav], **pillaver** [pijave] *vi* to booze, to knock it back

ⓘ This term comes from a Romany word meaning "to drink".

pilule [pilyl] *nf* **dorer la pilule à qn** to *Br* sugar *or Am* sweeten the pill for sb; **se dorer la pilule** to catch some rays; **il a dit ça pour faire passer la**

pilule he said it to *Br* sugar *or Am* sweeten the pill

pinailler [pinɑje] *vi* to split hairs□, to nit-pick

pinard [pinar] *nm* wine□, vino, *Br* plonk

pince [pɛ̃s] *nf* (a) *(main)* hand□, mitt, paw; **serrer la pince à qn** to shake hands with sb□ (b) **aller à pinces** to go on foot□, to hoof it ▸ *see also* **chaud**

pinceaux [pɛ̃so] *nmpl (pieds)* feet□, *Br* plates, *Am* dogs; **s'emmêler les pinceaux** *(trébucher)* to trip up□, to stumble□; *(s'embrouiller)* to tie oneself in knots

pincer [pɛ̃se] 1 *vt* (a) *(arrêter)* to collar, to nab; **se faire pincer** to get collared *or* nabbed (b) **en pincer pour qn** to be crazy about sb, to have the hots for sb, *Br* to fancy the pants off sb

2 *v imp* **ça pince** *(il fait froid)* it's chilly *or Br* nippy *or* parky

pincettes [pɛ̃sɛt] *nfpl* **ne pas être à prendre avec des pincettes** to be like a bear with a sore head

pine [!!] [pin] *nf* dick, prick, cock; **rentrer la pine sous le bras** to go home without getting laid *or Br* without getting one's oats

piner [!!] [pine] *vt & vi* to fuck, to screw, *Br* to shag

pinglot [pɛ̃glo] *nm* foot□, *Br* plate, *Am* dog

pinté, -e [pɛ̃te] *adj* smashed, plastered, trashed

pinter [pɛ̃te] **se pinter** *vpr* to get smashed *or* plastered *or* trashed

pinteur, -euse [pɛ̃tœr, -øz] *nm,f Belg & Suisse* boozer, alky

pintocher [pɛ̃tɔʃe] *vi Suisse* to booze, to knock it back

pion, pionne [pjɔ̃, pjɔn] *nm,f (surveillant)* supervisor□ *(student paid to supervize pupils outside class hours)* ▸ *see also* **damer**

pioncer [pjɔ̃se] *vi* to sleep□, to crash, *Br* to kip; **tu peux rester pioncer chez moi si tu veux** you can crash *or Br* kip at mine if you like; **à trois heures de l'après-midi il était toujours en train de pioncer** he was still crashed out at three in the afternoon

pipe [pip] *nf* (a) [!!] *(fellation)* blowjob; **tailler** *ou* **faire une pipe à qn** to give sb a blow-job, to suck sb off, to go down on sb (b) **casser sa pipe** to croak, to kick the bucket, *Br* to snuff it, *Am* to check out (c) *(cigarette)* smoke, *Br* fag, ciggy ▸ *see also* **fendre, nom, tailleuse**

pipeau [pipo] *nm* **c'est du pipeau** it's a load of garbage *or Br* rubbish

pipeauter [pipote] *vi* to talk crap *or* bull

pipelette [piplɛt] *nf* chatterbox, gasbag

pipette [pipɛt] *nf Suisse* **ça ne vaut pas pipette** it's not worth a bean *or Am* a red cent

pipi [pipi] *nm* (a) *(urine)* pee; **faire pipi** to pee, to have a pee (b) **du pipi de chat** *(boisson insipide)* dishwater, gnat's piss

pipi-room [pipirum] *nm Br* loo, *Am* bathroom□, little boys'/girls' room

pipole [pipɔl] *nmf* celeb; **c'est un bar fréquenté par les pipoles** the bar is a popular celeb hang-out

piqué, -e [pike] *adj* (a) *(fou)* crazy, loopy, *Br* bonkers, barking *(mad)*, *Am* wacko (b) **un film pas piqué des vers** *ou* **des hannetons** a heck of a good film; **un rhume pas piqué des vers** *ou* **des**

hannetons a stinking cold

piquer [pike] **1** vt (**a**) (voler) to pinch, Br to nick (**b**) (surprendre) to nab, Br to nick (**c**) (faire) **piquer une colère** to go ballistic, to hit the roof or Am ceiling, to blow one's top or Am stack; **piquer un cent mètres** to sprint off�; **piquer une tête** (plonger) to dive in⌐; (se baigner) to have a dip

2 se piquer vpr (se droguer) to shoot up, to hit it up, to jack up ▶ see also **fard, ronflette, roupillon, ruche**

piquette [pikɛt] nf (**a**) (défaite) thrashing, pasting; **foutre la piquette à qn** to thrash or paste sb (**b**) (vin de mauvaise qualité) cheap wine⌐, Br plonk

piquouse, piquouze [pikuz] nf shot, Br jab; **c'est un adepte de la piquouse** he's into shooting up

pire [pir] adj (excellent) Br wicked, Am awesome; **il faut que tu ailles le voir, c'est un pire film!** you have to go and see it, it's Br a wicked film or Am an awesome movie!

pisse [!] [pis] nf piss; **c'est de la pisse d'âne, ta bière!** your beer's like (gnat's) piss!

pisse-copie [piskɔpi] nmf inv hack

pisse-froid [pisfrwa] nmf inv cold fish

pissenlit [pisãli] nm **manger les pissenlits par la racine** (être mort) to be pushing up the daisies

pisser [pise] **1** vt (**a**) **pisser du sang** [!] to piss blood; **pisser des lames de rasoir** [!] (souffrir au cours de la miction) to piss razor blades (**b**) **son bras pissait le sang** blood was pouring or gushing from his arm

2 vi (**a**) [!] (uriner) to piss; **c'est comme si je pissais dans un violon**

it's a complete waste of time, it's like pissing in the wind; **laisse pisser!** forget it!, drop it!; **c'était à pisser de rire** it was an absolute scream; **pisser dans sa culotte** ou **son froc** to piss oneself or one's pants; **ils en pissaient dans leur culotte** ou **froc** they were pissing themselves (laughing); **envoyer pisser qn** to tell sb to piss off; **ça lui a pris comme une envie de pisser** the urge just came over him; **ça pisse pas loin** it's no great shakes, it's not up to much; **pisser à la raie à qn** [!!] not to give a shit about sb (**b**) (fuir) to leak⌐ ▶ see also **mérinos, sentir**

pissette [pisɛt] nf Can (pénis) dick, prick, cock

pisseuse¹ [pisøz] nf little girl⌐

pisseux, -euse² [pisø, -øz] adj (couleur) washed-out

pissodrome [!] [pisodrom] nm Belg public urinal⌐

pissotière [pisɔtjɛr] nf (public) urinal⌐

pissou [pisu] nm Can wimp, wuss, Br big girl's blouse

pistoche [pistɔʃ] nf swimming pool⌐

pistolet [pistɔlɛ] nm **un drôle de pistolet** a shady or Br dodgy character; Can **être en pistolet** to be fuming or Br spewing

piston [pistɔ̃] nm (népotisme) string-pulling; **avoir du piston** to have friends in the right places; **il a eu son job au piston** he got his job by having friends in the right places

pistonner [pistɔne] vt **pistonner qn** to pull strings for sb; **il s'est fait pistonner** he got someone to pull strings for him

pitonner [pitɔne] vi Can (zapper) to zap, to (channel-)surf; (sur un clavier, une calculatrice) to tap away⌐

placard [plakar] *nm (prison)* slammer, clink, *Br* nick, *Am* pen; **mettre qn au placard** *(en prison)* to put sb behind bars *or* inside *or* away; *(l'écarter)* to sideline sb□

placardisation [plakardizasjɔ̃] *nf* sidelining□

placardiser [plakardize] *vt* to sideline□

placer [plase] *vt* **ne pas pouvoir en placer une** to be unable to get a word in (edgeways)

placoter [plakɔte] *vi Can* to chew the fat *or* the rag

placoteur, -euse [plakɔtœr, -øz], **placoteux, -euse** [plakɔtø, -øz] *nm,f Can* gossip□, gossipy person□

plafond [plafɔ̃] *nm* (a) **être bas de plafond** to be a bit slow on the uptake (b) **avoir une araignée au plafond** to have bats in the belfry

plaire [plɛr] *vi Ironic* **il commence à me plaire, celui-là!** he's starting to bug me *or Br* do my head in *or* get up my nose *or Am* give me a pain (in the neck)

plan [plɑ̃] *nm* (a) *(projet)* plan□; **lui et ses plans foireux!** him and his lousy plans!; **on se fait un plan ciné/resto?** shall we go to the *Br* pictures *or* flicks *or Am* movies□/go out for a meal?□; **y'a pas plan** no can do; **je t'aurais bien accompagné, vieux, mais là, vraiment, y'a pas plan!** I'd have gone with you, pal, but no can do (b) **laisser qn en plan** to leave sb in the lurch; **tout laisser en plan** to drop everything

planant, -e [planɑ̃, -ɑ̃t] *adj (drogue)* relaxing□; *(musique)* mellow□, chilled-out

planche [plɑ̃ʃ] *nf* (a) **avoir du pain sur la planche** to have a lot on one's plate (b) **c'est une vraie planche à pain** *ou* **à repasser** *(elle a de petits seins)* she's as flat as a pancake *or* as an ironing-board

plancher¹ [plɑ̃ʃe] *nm* (a) **le plancher des vaches** dry land□, terra firma□ (b) **avoir un feu de plancher** to be wearing ankle-swingers ▸ *see also* **débarrasser**

plancher² [plɑ̃ʃe] *vi* to be tested□, to have a test□ *(at school)*

planer [plane] *vi* (a) *(être sous l'influence d'une drogue)* to be flying, to be high (as a kite), to be spaced out (b) *(ne pas avoir le sens des réalités)* to always have one's head in the clouds, to be a space cadet; *(penser à autre chose)* to be miles away, to have one's head in the clouds

plan-plan [plɑ̃plɑ̃] *adj* routine□, humdrum; **il a une vie tout ce qu'il y a de plus plan-plan** he has the most humdrum life imaginable

planque [plɑ̃k] *nf* (a) *(cachette)* hiding place□, hidey-hole (b) *(surveillance)* stakeout; **ils étaient en planque autour de la maison** they were staking out the house (c) *(emploi tranquille)* cushy number

planqué, -e [plɑ̃ke] *nm,f* person with a cushy number

planquer [plɑ̃ke] **1** *vt* to hide□, to stash

2 se planquer *vpr* (a) *(se cacher)* to hide□ (b) *(se protéger)* to take cover□

planter [plɑ̃te] **1** *vt (tuer à l'arme blanche)* to stab□ *or* knife to death; *(blesser à l'arme blanche)* to stab□, to knife, *Am* to shank, to shiv

2 *vi (ordinateur)* to go down□, to crash□

3 se planter *vpr* (a) *(se tromper)* to get it wrong□, *Br* to boob, *Am* to goof (b) *(avoir un accident de la*

route) to have a crash□ **(c)** *(échouer)* to fail□, *Am* to flunk; **il s'est planté à son examen** he failed□ *or Am* flunked his exam

plaque [plak] *nf* **(a) être à côté de la plaque** to be wide of the mark, to be off target, to be barking up the wrong tree **(b)** *Formerly (dix mille francs)* ten thousand francs□

plaquer [plake] *vt (emploi)* to quit, *Br* to chuck *or* pack in; *(famille)* to walk out on; *(amant)* to dump, to chuck; **tout plaquer** *Br* to chuck *or* pack it all in, *Am* to chuck everything

plastoc, plastoque [plastɔk] *nm* plastic□

plat [pla] *nm* **(a) faire du plat à qn** *Br* to chat sb up, *Am* to hit on sb **(b) faire tout un plat de qch** to make a big song and dance *or* a big fuss about sth **(c) il en fait un plat** *(il fait très chaud)* it's a scorcher, *Br* it's roasting ▸ *see also* **œuf**

platiniste [platinist] *nmf* DJ□, spinner

plâtrée [platre] *nf* huge helping□; **une plâtrée de nouilles** a huge helping of noodles□

plein, -e [plɛ̃, plɛn] *adj (ivre)* **être plein (comme une barrique), être fin plein** to be plastered, to have had a skinful ▸ *see also* **as, botte, cul, dos, hotte, jambe**

pli [pli] *nm* **ça ne fait pas un pli** there's no doubt about it□, it's bound to happen□; **je me doutais qu'il se blesserait, et ça n'a pas fait un pli** I was just waiting for him to hurt himself, and sure enough he did

plié, -e [plije] *adj* **être plié (de rire), être plié en quatre** to be doubled up *or* bent double (with laughter)

plier [plije] *vt (voiture)* to smash up, to wreck, *Am* to total

plomb [plɔ̃] *nm* **péter les plombs** *(se mettre en colère)* to go ballistic, to hit the roof *or Am* ceiling, to blow one's top *or Am* stack; *(craquer)* to crack up; **la pression était tellement forte au boulot que j'ai cru que j'allais péter les plombs** the pressure was so bad at work that I thought I was going to crack up ▸ *see also* **casquette**

plombe [plɔ̃b] *nf* hour□; **il nous a encore fait attendre trois plombes** he kept us waiting for ages again□

plombé, -e [!] [plɔ̃be] *adj (atteint par une MST)* **être plombé** to have a dose

plomber [plɔ̃be] *vt* **(a)** *(tuer à l'aide d'une arme à feu)* to fill sb with lead, to pump sb full of lead **(b)** *(transmettre une MST à)* **plomber qn [!]** to give sb a dose **(c)** *(compromettre)* to compromise□, to jeopardize□; **les négociations ont été plombées par les récentes grèves** the negotiations have been compromised by the recent strikes **(d) plomber qn** *(démoraliser)* to get sb down; *(ennuyer)* to bore sb to tears *or* to death

plonge [plɔ̃ʒ] *nf* **faire la plonge** to wash dishes□ *(in a restaurant)*, to be a washer-upper

plonger [plɔ̃ʒe] *vi* **(a)** *(être envoyé en prison)* to be put inside *or* away, *Br* to be sent down **(b)** *(prendre une décision importante)* to take the plunge, to go for it

plouc [pluk] *nmf* yokel, peasant, *Am* hick, hayseed

ⓘ The word "plouc" (meaning "country bumpkin") comes from the name of many Breton villages and towns starting with the sound "Plou-" (as in "Plougastel" or "Ploumanac'h"). Over a long period of time many people from Brittany emigrated to Paris, where they were considered uncouth and ignorant by the locals.

---

pluie [plyi] *nf* **pluie d'or** [!] *(pratique sexuelle)* golden showers

plumard [plymar], **plume¹** [plym] *nm (lit)* bed□, *Br* pit

plume² [plym] *nf* (a) [!!] *(fellation)* blow-job; **tailler une plume à qn** to give sb a blow-job, to suck sb off, to go down on sb (b) *(cheveux)* **perdre ses plumes** to go thin on top (c) **il y a laissé des plumes** he didn't come out of it unscathed□ (d) **voler dans les plumes à qn** to go for sb, to lay into sb (e) **on a eu chaud aux plumes** we had a narrow escape, it was a close call ▸ *see also* **tailleuse**

plumer [plyme] *vt (escroquer)* to fleece

pochard, -e [poʃar, -ard] *nm,f* alky, boozer, *Br* pisshead, *Am* boozehound

poche [poʃ] *nf* **c'est dans la poche** it's in the bag; **faire les poches à qn** to go through sb's pockets; **mets ça dans ta poche (et ton mouchoir par-dessus)!** put that in your pipe and smoke it!; **ne pas avoir les yeux dans sa poche** to have eyes in the back of one's head; **s'en mettre** *ou* **s'en foutre** [!] **plein les poches** to rake it in

pochetron [poʃtrɔ̃] *nm* alky, boozer, *Br* pisshead, *Am* boozehound

pochette-surprise [poʃetsyrpriz] *nf* **tu l'as eu dans une pochette-surprise, ton permis?** where did you get your licence, in a cornflakes packet *or* in a Christmas cracker?

pogne [poɲ] *nf* hand□, paw, mitt; **se**

faire une pogne [!!] to jerk off, to beat off, *Br* to have a wank

pogner [!!] [poɲe] **1** *vi Can (se caresser mutuellement)* to neck, *Am* to make out; *(avoir des relations sexuelles)* to screw, *Br* to shag

2 se pogner *vpr* (a) to jerk off, to beat off, *Br* to have a wank (b) *Can* **se pogner le cul** *(se caresser mutuellement)* to neck, *Br* to snog, *Am* to make out; *(avoir des relations sexuelles)* to screw, *Br* to shag

pognon [poɲɔ̃] *nm* cash, dough, *Br* dosh, *Am* bucks

pogo [pogo] *nm* pogo *(dance)*

pogoter [pogote] *vi* to pogo

poignée [pwaɲe] *nf* **poignées d'amour** love handles

poil [pwal] *nm* **à poil** in the buff, *Br* starkers; **torse poil** *(homme)* barechested□; *(femme)* topless□; **être au (petit) poil** to be just the ticket; **tomber au poil** to arrive just at the right moment□; **au (petit) poil!** great!, terrific!; **il a raté le train à un poil près** he missed the train by a hair's breadth *or* by a whisker; **son analyse est juste, à un poil près** his analysis is correct apart from one or two small details□; **avoir un poil dans la main** to be bone idle; **être de bon/mauvais poil** to be in a good/bad mood□; **rentrer dans qch au quart de poil** to fit into sth perfectly□; **démarrer au quart de poil** to start right away *or* first time□; **tomber sur le poil à qn** to jump on sb, to go for sb ▸ *see also* **tarte**

poilant, -e [pwalɑ̃, -ɑ̃t] *adj* hysterical, side-splitting

poiler [pwale] **se poiler** *vpr (rire)* to kill oneself (laughing), to laugh one's head off, to split one's sides; *(s'amuser)* to have a ball *or Am* a blast

---

point [pwɛ̃] *nm* **point barre** end of story, *Br* end of; **tu rentres à minuit ou bien tu n'y vas pas; point barre** you'll be home by midnight or you're not going at all and that's it, end of story *or Br* end of

pointer [pwɛ̃te] **se pointer** *vpr* to turn up, to show up

pointure [pwɛ̃tyr] *nf (personne remarquable en son genre)* **une (grosse) pointure** a big name; **tous les musiciens qui l'accompagnent sont des pointures** all his/her backing musicians are big names in their own right

poire [pwar] *nf* (a) *(visage)* face▭, mug, *Am* map; **il s'est pris le ballon en pleine poire** the ball hit him right in the face (b) *(personne facile à duper)* **une (bonne) poire** a sucker, *Br* a mug, *Am* a patsy ▶ *see also* **fendre**

poireau, -x [pwaro] *nm* (a) **[!!]** *(pénis)* dick, cock, prick; **souffler dans le poireau à qn** to give sb a blow-job, to suck sb off, to give sb head (b) **faire le poireau** to hang about *or* around

poireauter [pwarote] *vi* to hang about *or* around; **faire poireauter qn** to keep sb hanging about *or* around; **ça fait presque une heure que je poireaute!** I've been hanging about *or* around for nearly an hour!

poiscaille [pwaskaj] *nm (poisson)* fish▭

poisse [pwas] *nf (malchance)* bad luck▭; **avoir la poisse** to be unlucky▭; **porter la poisse** to bring bad luck▭

poisson [pwasɔ̃] *nm* **engueuler qn comme du poisson pourri** to bite sb's head off, to bawl sb out, to jump down sb's throat

poivré, -e [pwavre] *adj (ivre)* wasted, trashed, *Br* legless, *Am* tanked

poivrer [pwavre] **se poivrer** *vpr* to get wasted *or* trashed *or Br* legless *or Am* tanked

poivrot, -ote [pwavro, -ɔt] *nm,f* alky, boozer, *Br* lush, *Am* boozehound

Polac, Polack [pɔlak] *nmf Offensive* Polack; **être soûl comme un Polack** to be as drunk as a skunk, to be wasted *or Br* ratted

---

ⓘ Depending on the context and the tone of voice used, this term may be either offensive or affectionately humorous. It is nonetheless inadvisable to use it unless one is quite sure of the reaction it will receive.

---

polar [pɔlar] *nm* whodunnit

polichinelle [pɔliʃinɛl] *nm* **avoir un polichinelle dans le tiroir** to have a bun in the oven, *Br* to be up the spout *or* the duff, *Am* to be knocked up

pommade [pɔmad] *nf* **passer de la pommade à qn** *(flatter)* to butter sb up

pomme [pɔm] *nf* (a) **tomber dans les pommes** to pass out▭, to keel over (b) **aux pommes** *(excellent)* great, fantastic (c) **pomme (à l'eau ou à l'huile)** *(personne naïve)* sucker, *Br* mug, *Am* patsy (d) **ma pomme** *(moi)* yours truly; **ta/sa pomme** *(toi/lui ou elle)* you/him/her▭ ▶ *see also* **sucer**

pompe [pɔ̃p] *nf* (a) **avoir un coup de pompe** to suddenly feel *Br* knackered *or* shattered *or Am* beat (b) *(chaussure)* shoe▭; **un coup de pompe** a kick▭; **être ou marcher à côté de ses pompes** to be screwed

---

The symbol **[!]** *denotes a very familiar term,* **[!!]** *a vulgar one.*

Spotlight on:

La police

As slang was originally the coded language of criminals and delinquents, it is not surprising that there are literally dozens of French slang terms which refer to the police and to policemen. The most common term for a policeman is **un flic** and, to a lesser extent, **un poulet** (literally "a chicken"). Collectively the police are known as **la flicaille, la poulaille** (a word derived from "poulet"), **la bleusaille** (because of the colour of their uniforms), **les bourres** and **les vaches**. Other terms include **un cogne, un flicard, un keuf** (which is the verlan of "flic") and **un condé**. A corrupt policeman is **un ripou** (verlan of "pourri", which means "rotten"). A more recent term for policeman used in the "banlieues" is **kisdé**, an abbreviation of the phrase "qui se déguise" (ie "someone who puts on a disguise", a reference to plain-clothes policemen). Policemen on motorcycles are known as **vaches à roulettes** (cows on wheels), while policemen on bicycles used to be known as **hirondelles à roulettes** (meaning "swallows on wheels" due to the black capes they used to wear, which were reminiscent of wings). The police department that specializes in narcotics is called **la brigade des stups** ("stup" being the abbreviation of "stupéfiant"). A police informer is **un indic** (which is the abbreviation of "indicateur"). To denounce someone is **balancer quelqu'un**; to confess is **se mettre à table** and **manger** or **casser le morceau**.

Expressions for being arrested include **se faire alpaguer, se faire coincer** and **se faire pincer**. A prison cell is known as **le gnouf** and to be in prison is **être en taule, être au frais** (literally "to be in a cool place", similar to the English "to be in the cooler"), **être à l'ombre** (literally "to be in the shade") as well as the euphemistic **être en voyage** (to be away travelling). To be sentenced to life imprisonment is **être condamné à perpète**. Prisoners who manage to **se faire la belle** (escape) are said to be **en cavale** (on the run). The police will be keen to catch them and bring them back in **les bracelets** (handcuffs).

up (**c**) **à toute pompe** like lightning, *Br* like the clappers, *Am* like sixty (**d**) *(aide-mémoire) Br* crib, *Am* trot (**e**) **un soldat de deuxième pompe,**

un deuxième pompe *Br* a squaddie, *Am* a grunt (**f**) *(seringue)* hype, hypo ▸ *see also* **cirer**

pompé, -e [pɔ̃pe] *adj (épuisé) Br*

knackered, shattered, *Am* beat

pomper [pɔ̃pe] **1** *vt* **(a) pomper qn, pomper l'air à qn** *(l'importuner)* to get on sb's nerves, to bug sb, *Br* to get on sb's wick, to do sb's head in, *Am* to give sb a pain **(b)** *(copier)* to copy◻, to crib; **il a pompé tout ça dans une encyclopédie** he copied◻ *or* cribbed it all out of an encyclopedia **(c)** *(boire)* to knock back; **qu'est-ce qu'il pompe!** he can really knock it back *or* put it away! **(d)** *(épuiser)* to wear out, *Br* to knacker, to do in **(e) pomper qn [!!], pomper le dard à qn [!!]** *(lui faire une fellation)* to give sb a blow-job, to suck sb off, to go down on sb

2 *vi* *(copier)* to copy◻, to crib; **pomper sur qn/dans qch** to copy◻ *or* crib from sb/sth

pompette [pɔ̃pɛt] *adj* tipsy, merry

pompier [!!] [pɔ̃pje] *nm* *(fellation)* blow-job; **faire un pompier à qn** to give sb a blow-job, to suck sb off, to go down on sb

pompon [pɔ̃pɔ̃] *nm* **c'est le pompon!** that's the limit!; **avoir** *ou* **décrocher** *ou* **tenir le pompon** to take the *Br* biscuit *or Am* cake; **j'ai connu des gens de mauvaise foi mais toi, vraiment, tu tiens le pompon!** I've known insincere people before, but you really take the *Br* biscuit *or Am* cake!

pondeuse [pɔ̃døz] *nf Hum (femme très féconde)* **c'est une sacrée pondeuse** she breeds like a rabbit, she's like a battery hen

pondre [pɔ̃dr] *vt* **(a)** *(mettre au monde)* to produce◻, to drop; **sa bonne femme lui a encore pondu un marmot** his old lady's had another kid, *Br* his missus has dropped another sprog **(b)** *(produire)* to produce◻, to come up with; **il pond deux romans par an** he churns

out two novels a year

Popaul [!!] [pɔpol] *npr (pénis)* dick, prick, cock; **étrangler Popaul** to beat one's meat, to bang *or Br* bash the bishop

popof [pɔpɔf] = **popov**

popote [pɔpɔt] **1** *adj inv* overly houseproud◻
   2 *nf* cooking◻; **faire la popote** to do the cooking◻

popotin [pɔpɔtɛ̃] *nm* butt, *Br* bum, *Am* fanny ▸ *see also* **magner**

popov [pɔpɔf] **1** *adj inv* Russian◻
   2 *nmf inv* **Popov** Russki

poppers [pɔpœrz] *nmpl* poppers

populo [pɔpylo] *nm* **(a)** *(peuple)* **le populo** the plebs, the riff-raff, the rabble **(b)** *(monde)* crowd◻; **il y avait un de ces populos en ville** the town was jam-packed *or Br* chock-a-block *or* heaving

poquer [pɔke] *vt Can Joual (contusionner)* to bruise◻; *(emboutir)* to dent◻, to bump◻; *(érafler)* to scratch◻; *(frapper)* to hit◻; **se faire poquer la gueule** to get one's face smashed in *or* wasted

porno [pɔrno] **1** *adj (abbr* **pornographique)** porn, porno
   2 *nm (abbr* **pornographie) (a)** *(genre)* porn **(b)** *(film)* porn movie *or Br* film, blue movie, *Br* skin flick

porte [pɔrt] *nf* **Lyon, ce n'est pas la porte à côté** it's a fair way to Lyons; **il n'habite pas la porte à côté** he doesn't exactly live round the corner

portenawak [pɔrtnawak] *exclam Cités* garbage!, *Br* rubbish!

porte-poisse [pɔrtpwas] *nm inv* jinx◻

portillon [pɔrtijɔ̃] *nm* **(a) ça se bouscule au portillon** he/she/*etc* can't get his/her/*etc* words out **(b) ça**

se bouscule pas au portillon *(il y a peu de monde)* people are staying away in droves

portos [pɔrtos] *nmf Offensive* Dago *(from Portugal)*

ⓘ Depending on the context and the tone of voice used, this term may be either offensive or affectionately humorous. It is nonetheless inadvisable to use it unless one is quite sure of the reaction it will receive.

portrait [pɔrtrɛ] *nm (visage)* **abîmer le portrait à qn** to waste sb's face, to rearrange sb's features; **se faire tirer le portrait** to have one's photo taken□

portugaises [pɔrtygɛz] *nfpl (oreilles)* ears□, *Br* lugs, lugholes; **avoir les portugaises ensablées** to be as deaf as a post

ⓘ "Portugaises" are so called after the variety of oyster with the same name whose shape resembles an ear.

positiver [pozitive] *vi* to think positive, to look on the bright side□; **arrête donc de te morfondre comme ça, essaye de positiver!** stop moping around like that, try to look on the bright side!

ⓘ This term originated in an advertising campaign for Carrefour (a chain of French supermarkets); the slogan used was "avec Carrefour, je positive!"

posse [pɔsi] *nf (bande)* posse

pot [po] *nm* **(a)** *(chance)* (good) luck□; **avoir du pot** to be lucky□ *or Br*

jammy; **manque de pot, la banque était fermée** as (bad) luck would have it, the bank was closed

(b) *(boisson)* drink□; **prendre un pot** to go for a drink□; **je suis invité à un pot ce soir** I've been invited out for drinks□ *or Br* to a drinks do tonight

(c) *(postérieur)* butt, *Br* bum, *Am* fanny

(d) **plein pot** *(à toute vitesse) Br* like the clappers, *Am* like sixty

(e) **être sourd comme un pot** to be as deaf as a post

(f) **être un vrai pot de peinture** *(très maquillée)* to wear make-up an inch thick, to trowel on one's make-up on; **quel pot de colle, ce mec, impossible de s'en défaire!** he sticks to you like glue, that guy, you just can't get rid of him!

potable [pɔtabl] *adj (passable)* reasonable□, just about OK

potache [pɔtaʃ] *nm* schoolboy□, schoolkid; **des plaisanteries de potaches** schoolboy jokes *or* humour

potage [pɔtaʒ] *nm* **(a)** **être dans le potage** *(être évanoui)* to be out cold; *(être dans une situation pénible)* to be in the soup **(b)** **il y a une couille dans le potage** *(un problème)* there's a bit of a glitch

potasser [pɔtase] **1** *vt Br* to swot up on, *Am* to bone up on; **il a potassé ses leçons d'histoire pendant toute la nuit** he *Br* swotted up on *or Am* boned up on his history all night

2 *vi Br* to swot, *Am* to bone up

pote [pɔt] **1** *adj* **être pote avec qn** to be pally with sb; **ils sont très potes** they're very pally

2 *nm* pal, *Br* mate, *Am* buddy; **salut mon pote!** hi pal *or Br* mate *or Am* buddy!

poteau, -x [pɔto] *nm* pal, *Br* mate, *Am* buddy

potin [pɔtɛ̃] *nm* racket, din

pou, -x [pu] *nm* **chercher des poux dans la tête à qn** to pick a quarrel with sb

poubelle [pubɛl] *nf (voiture)* heap, rustbucket, *Br* banger, *Am* jalopy

pouce [pus] *nm Can* **faire du pouce** to thumb a *Br* lift *or Am* ride ▸ *see also* **tourner**

poudre [pudr] *nf (héroïne)* smack, skag, H; *(cocaïne)* coke, charlie, *Am* nose candy ▸ *see also* **inventer**

pouffe [!!] [puf], **poufiasse [!!]**, **pouffiasse [!!]** [pufjas] *nf* **(a)** *(prostituée)* whore, hooker **(b)** *(femme aux mœurs légères)* slut, tart, *Br* slapper, slag **(c)** *(femme désagréable)* bitch, *Br* cow

poulaille [pulɑj] *nf* **la poulaille** the cops, *Br* the pigs, the filth

poule [pul] *nf* **(a)** *(prostituée)* whore, hooker **(b)** *(femme)* slut, tart, *Br* slapper, slag **(c)** *(terme d'affection)* sweetheart, honey, babe

poulet [pulɛ] *nm (policier, gendarme)* cop, pig

poulette [pulɛt] *nf* **(a)** *(fille, femme)* chick, *Br* bird **(b)** *(terme d'affection)* sweetheart, honey, babe

poumons [pumɔ̃] *nmpl Hum (seins)* tits, knockers, jugs, *Am* hooters; **elle a des sacrés poumons** she's got a great pair of lungs on her

poupée [pupe] *nf (femme, fille)* babe, doll; **comment ça va, poupée?** how are you doing, babe?

poupoule [pupul] *nf* **ma poupoule** sweetheart, honey, babe

pourave [purav] *adj* crap, garbage, *Br* rubbish; **une bagnole pourave** a heap, *Br* a banger, *Am* a jalopy

pourliche [purliʃ] *nm* tip□ *(money)*

pourri, -e [puri] **1** *adj* **(a)** *(en mauvais état)* falling apart, *Br* clapped-out, knackered **(b)** *(mauvais)* rotten, lousy; **il a fait un temps pourri** the weather was rotten *or* lousy **(c)** *(de mauvaise qualité)* crappy, *Br* rubbish, *Am* rinky-dink **(d)** *(corrompu)* rotten to the core, *Br* bent

2 *nm,f (homme méprisable)* scumbag, *Br* swine, *Am* stinker; *(femme méprisable)* bitch, *Br* cow ▸ *see also* **poisson**

pourrir [purir] *vt (dire du mal de)* to badmouth, *Br* to slag off

pousse-au-crime [pusokrim] *nm inv* firewater, rotgut

pousser [puse] *vt* **(a)** **faut pas pousser (mémé ou mémère dans les orties)** that's pushing it a bit **(b)** **pousser la chansonnette, en pousser une** to sing a song□

PQ [peky] *nm Br* bog roll, *Am* TP

praline [pralin] *nf* **(a)** *(coup)* belt, wallop **(b)** *(balle d'arme à feu)* bullet□, slug **(c)** **[!!]** *(clitoris)* clit

précieuses [!] [presjøz] *nfpl Hum (testicules)* crown *or* family jewels, *Br* (wedding) tackle

première [prəmjɛr] **de première** *adj* first-class; **c'est un crétin de première** he's a first-class *or* prize idiot

prems [prɛms] = **preums**

prendre [prɑ̃dr] *vt* **(a)** **qu'est-ce qu'il a pris!** he really caught it! **(b)** **ça prend pas!** give me a break!, yeah right!, *Br* pull the other one!

pression [presjɔ̃] *nf* **mettre la pression à qn** to pressurize sb□, to put pressure on sb□

preums [prɛms] *(abbr* **premier, -ère)** **1** *adj* first□ **2** *nmf* first□

primo [primo] *adv* first of all⁰, for starters

privé [prive] *nm* (*abbr* **détective privé**) private eye, *Am* shamus

pro [pro] *nmf* (*abbr* **professionnel, -elle**) pro

prof [prɔf] *nmf* (*abbr* **professeur**) teacher⁰

professionnelle [prɔfɛsjɔnɛl] *nf* (*prostituée*) pro, streetwalker

profonde [prɔfɔ̃d] *nf* (*poche*) pocket⁰

projo [prɔʒo] *nm* (*abbr* **projecteur**) projector⁰

prolo [prɔlo] (*abbr* **prolétaire**) **1** *adj* plebby
  2 *nmf* prole, pleb

promener [prɔmne] **1** *vi* **envoyer promener qn** (*l'éconduire*) to send sb packing, to tell sb where to go; **tout envoyer promener** *Br* to chuck *or* pack it all in, *Am* to chuck everything
  2 se promener *vpr* (*éprouver de la facilité*) **il se promène en maths** maths is a walk in the park *or* a push-over for him

promo [promo] *nf* (*abbr* **promotion**) promotion⁰, promo

pronto [prɔ̃to] *adv* pronto; **tu vas me débarrasser ton bordel pronto, OK?** get your shit out of here pronto, OK?

proprio [prɔprijo] *nmf* (*abbr* **propriétaire**) landlord, *f* landlady⁰

prose [prɔz] = **proze**

protal [prɔtal] *nm Br* headmaster⁰, head, *Am* principal⁰

prout [prut] *nm* (**a**) (*pet*) fart; **faire un prout** to fart, *Br* to let off, *Am* to lay one (**b**) **prout, ma chère!** (*pour singer un homosexuel*) ≃ fabulous, sweetie!

prout-prout [prutprut] *adj* snobby, snooty, *Br* up oneself; **qu'est-ce qu'elle peut être prout-prout, sa gonzesse!** his girlfriend can be such a snob *or* so up herself!

provo [provo] *nm* (*abbr* **proviseur**) *Br* headmaster⁰, head, *Am* principal⁰

provoc [prɔvɔk] *nf* (*abbr* **provocation**) provocation⁰; **il ne pense pas vraiment ce qu'il dit, c'est de la provoc** he doesn't really believe what he's saying, he's just trying to *Br* wind you up *or Am* yank your chain

proxo [prɔkso] *nm* (*abbr* **proxénète**) pimp, *Am* mack

proze [!] [prɔz], **prozinard** [!] [prɔzinar] *nm* butt, *Br* bum, *Am* fanny

prune [pryn] *nf* (**a**) (*coup de poing*) punch⁰, thump, clout (**b**) **pour des prunes** (*pour rien*) for nothing⁰ (**c**) (*contravention*) fine⁰

pruneau, -x [pryno] *nm* (*balle d'arme à feu*) bullet⁰, slug; **il s'est pris un pruneau dans la jambe** he took a bullet in the leg

pseudo [psødo] *nm* (*abbr* **pseudonyme**) alias⁰

psy [psi] *nmf* (*abbr* **psychanalyste**) shrink

puant, -e [pɥɑ̃, -ɑ̃t] **1** *adj* (*très vaniteux*) cocky, full of oneself; **c'est le genre de mec qui n'arrête pas de se faire mousser, je le trouve puant** he's the kind of guy who's always blowing his own trumpet, he's so full of himself
  2 *nm* (*fromage*) smelly cheese⁰

puceau, -x [pyso] *nm* virgin⁰

pucelage [pyslaʒ] *nm* virginity⁰; **c'est avec lui qu'elle a perdu son pucelage** she lost her cherry to him

Le symbole ⁰ indique que la traduction n'est pas argotique.

pucelle [pysɛl] *nf* virgin□

pucier [pysje] *nm (lit)* bed□, *Br* pit

pue-la-sueur [pylasɥœr] *nm inv Pej* workman□, *Br* workie

puer [pɥe] *vi* **ça pue!** it sucks!

puissant, -e [pɥisɑ̃, -ɑ̃t] *adj (remarquable)* great, *Br* wicked, *Am* awesome

punaise [pynɛz] *exclam* heck!, sugar!, *Br* pants!, *Am* shoot!

punkette [pœnkɛt] *nf* punkette

pur, -e [pyr] *adj (excellent)* cool, *Br* wicked, *Am* awesome

purée [pyre] **1** *nf* **balancer la purée [!!]** *(éjaculer)* to shoot one's load; **balancer la purée [!]** *(tirer avec une arme à feu)* to open fire□

2 *exclam* heck!, sugar!, *Br* pants!, *Am* shoot!

putain [!] [pytɛ̃] **1** *nf (prostituée)* whore, hooker; *(femme aux mœurs légères)* tart, slut, *Br* slapper, slag; **faire la putain** *(chercher à plaire)* to prostitute oneself; **putain de bagnole/de temps!** fucking car/weather!

2 *exclam* fuck!, fucking hell!

putassier, -ère [!] [pytasje, -ɛr] *adj* (**a**) *(vulgaire)* tarty, slutty (**b**) *(servile, obséquieux)* ingratiating□, *Br* arse-licking, *Am* ass-licking

pute [!!] [pyt] *nf (prostituée)* whore, hooker; *(femme facile)* tart, slut, *Br* slapper, slag; **faire la pute** *(chercher à plaire)* to prostitute oneself; **fils de pute** son-of-a-bitch, son-of-a-whore

Qq

quadra [kadra] *nmf* (*abbr* **quadra-génaire**) person in his/her forties□, forty-something; **être quadra** to be in one's forties□, to be forty-something; **c'est un quadra** he's in his forties□, he's forty-something

quart [kar] *nm* **quart de brie** (*nez*) beak, *Br* conk, hooter, *Am* schnozzle ▸ *see also* **poil**

quatre [katr] *adj inv* **un de ces quatre (matins)** one of these days ▸ *see also* **fer**

quat'zyeux [katzjø] **entre quat'-zyeux** *adv* in private□; **il a demandé à me voir entre quat'zyeux** he asked to see me in private

quebri [kəbri] *nf Formerly* (*verlan* **brique**) ten thousand francs□

que dalle [kədal] *pron* zilch, *Br* bugger all, sod all, sweet FA; **j'y comprends que dalle** I don't understand a damn *or Br* bloody thing

quelque chose [kɛlkəʃoz] *pron* (a) **il s'est viandé, quelque chose de bien** he got smashed up something awful; **il lui a passé un savon, quelque chose de bien** he gave him an almighty telling-off; **il tenait quelque chose comme cuite!** he was totally plastered *or* wasted!; **il y a quelque chose comme vent dehors** it's blowing a gale out there (b) **mais c'est quelque chose!** that's a bit much!

quelque part [kɛlkəpar] *adv* **il lui a mis son pied quelque part** (*au derrière*) he gave him a kick up the you-know-what; **elle lui a foutu un coup de genou quelque part** (*dans les testicules*) she kneed him in the you-know-where *or* where it hurts

quenotte [kənɔt] *nf* tooth□, *Br* gnasher

quenouilles [kənuj] *nfpl Can* (*jambes*) long skinny legs□, matchstick legs

que pouic [kəpwik] *pron* zilch, *Br* bugger all, sod all, sweet FA; **j'y comprends que pouic** I don't understand a damn *or Br* bloody thing

quéquette [kekɛt] *nf* willy, *Am* peter, johnson

quès aco [kezako] *adv* what's that?□, wozzat?

question [kɛstjɔ̃] *nf* (a) **question soleil, on n'a pas été gâtés** we didn't see much in the way of sunshine; **question argent, j'ai pas à me plaindre** moneywise, I can't complain (b) **alors, tu te magnes le cul? question!** so, are you going to move your *Br* arse *or Am* ass or what?

que tchi [kətʃi] *pron* zilch, *Br* bugger all, sod all, sweet FA; **il y comprend que tchi** he doesn't understand a damn *or Br* bloody thing

queude [kœd] = **que dalle**

queue [kø] *nf* (**a**) [!!] *(pénis)* dick, prick, cock; **se faire** *ou* **se taper une queue** to jerk off, *Br* to wank, to have a wank (**b**) **il y en avait pas la queue d'un/d'une** there wasn't a single one, there wasn't one to be seen; **ne pas en avoir la queue d'un** to be broke *or Br* skint *or* strapped (**c**) **des queues!** [!] no way!, no chance! ▸ *see also* **rond**

queutard [!!] [køtar] **1** *adj* horny as fuck
  2 *nm* horny bastard

queuter [!!] [køte] *vt* to screw, to shaft

quiche [kiʃ] *nf (personne médiocre)* **je suis une quiche en anglais** I'm totally crap at English, I suck at English

quillard [kijar] *nm Formerly* = soldier about to be discharged or nearing the end of his national service

quille [kij] *nf* (**a**) *(jambe)* leg□, pin; **jouer des quilles** to beat it, to leg it (**b**) *(petite fille)* little girl□ (**c**) *(fin de service militaire, démobilisation)* discharge□, *Br* demob

quincaillerie [kɛ̃kajri] *nf* (**a**) *(armes à feux)* weapons□ (**b**) *(bijoux)* jewellery□, bling, ice

quinquets [kɛ̃kɛ] *nmpl (yeux)* eyes□, peepers; **ouvre bien grand tes quinquets** open your eyes wide□

ⓘ This term comes from the name of an 18th century pharmacist who designed a type of oil lamp.

---

quiquette [kikɛt] = **quéquette**

Rr

rab [rab], **rabiot** [rabjo] *nm* (**a**) *(excédent)* leftovers□, extra□; **il y a du rab de poulet** there's some chicken left over□; **qui veut du rab?** who wants seconds?; **t'aurais pas une clope en rab?** can I *Br* cadge a fag *or Am* bum a smoke?, have you got a spare smoke *or Br* fag?; **vous auriez pas un oreiller en rab?** do you have a spare pillow?□ (**b**) **faire du rab** *(au travail)* to put in a bit of overtime *or* a few extra hours; *(à l'armée)* to serve extra time□

rabioter [rabjɔte] **1** *vt (obtenir en supplément)* to wangle
2 *vi* to skimp; **rabioter sur qch** to skimp on sth

râble [rɑbl] *nm* **tomber sur le râble à qn** to lay into sb, to go for sb

rabza [rabza] *nmf (verlan* **arabe)** = person of North African origin

racaille [rakɑj] *nf* (**a**) **la racaille** *(voyous)* trash, louts, *Br* yobs, ≃ chavs; **la racaille de banlieue** *Br* ≃ council estate yobs, *Am* ≃ hoods from the projects (**b**) **une racaille** *(voyou)* a lout, *Br* a yob, ≃ a chav

raccrocher [rakrɔʃe] **1** *vt* **raccrocher le client** *(prostituée)* to solicit□, *Am* to hustle, to hook
2 *vi (cesser une activité)* to pack it in, *Am* to hang it up

raccuser [rakyze] *vt Belg* to snitch on, *Br* to sneak on

raccusette [rakyzɛt] *nf Belg* snitch, *Br* sneak

race [ras] *nf Cités* **ta race!** [!] *Br* piss off!, *Am* take a hike!; **enculé de ta race!** [!!] you fucking prick *or Br* arsehole *or* wanker *or Am* asshole!; **défoncer** *ou* **faire** *ou* **éclater sa race à qn** to smash sb's face in, *Br* to punch sb's lights out, *Am* to punch sb out ▸ *see also* **niquer**

ⓘ The word "race" appears in numerous slang expressions of the "banlieues" (see panel **L'argot des banlieues** p.219) and functions as an intensifier. See also the entry for **mère**, which has a similar function.

---

racho [raʃo] *(abbr* **rachitique)** **1** *adj (personne, arbre)* weedy, scrawny; *(portion)* mean, stingy
2 *nmf* scrawny person

raclée [rakle] *nf (correction, défaite)* thrashing, hammering; **flanquer une raclée à qn** to give sb a thrashing *or* a hammering; **prendre une raclée** to *Br* get *or Am* take a thrashing *or* a hammering

racli [rakli] *nf Cités* chick, *Br* bird

ⓘ This term is derived from a Romany word for a non-gypsy girl.

---

raclo [raklo] *nm Cités* guy, *Br* bloke

ⓘ This term is derived from a Romany word for a non-gypsy boy.

raclure [!] [raklyr] *nf (homme méprisable)* bastard, *Am* son-of-a-bitch; *(femme méprisable)* bitch, *Br* cow

raconter [rakɔ̃te] *vt* (a) **je te raconte pas!** you can't imagine!; **on s'est pris une de ces cuites, je te raconte pas...** you can't imagine how plastered we got (b) **se la raconter** to show off

radar [radar] *nm* **marcher** *ou* **être au radar** *(ne pas être bien réveillé)* to be on automatic pilot

radasse [!!] [radas] *nf* (a) *(prostituée)* whore, hooker (b) *Pej (femme)* tart, slut, *Br* slapper, slag

rade¹ [rad] *nm (café)* bar□, *Br* boozer

rade² [rad] **en rade** *adv* (a) *(en panne)* **être en rade** to have broken down□ *or* conked out, to be *Br* on the blink *or Am* on the fritz; **tomber en rade** to break down□, to conk out (b) *(abandonné)* stranded□; **laisser qn en rade** to leave sb stranded□ *or* in the lurch

radin, -e [radɛ̃, -in] **1** *adj* stingy, tight-fisted, *Br* tight
2 *nm,f* skinflint, tightwad

radiner [radine] **1** *vi* to turn up, to show up, to roll up; **alors, tu radines?** are you coming, then?
2 se radiner *vpr* to turn up, to show up, to roll up; **il se radine toujours quand on l'attend pas, celui-là!** he always turns up when you least expect him to!

radis [radi] *nm (sou)* **j'ai plus un radis** I haven't got a bean *or Am* a red cent; **sans un radis** broke, *Br* skint

raffut [rafy] *nm* (a) *(bruit)* racket, din; **c'est pas bientôt fini ce raffut?** is this racket *or* din going to go on for much longer? (b) *(scandale)* **faire du raffut** to cause a stink, to set tongues wagging

rafiot [rafjo] *nm* old tub *(boat)*

rageant, -e [raʒɑ̃, -ɑ̃t] *adj* maddening□, infuriating□; **c'est vraiment rageant, j'ai loupé le train à trente secondes près** it's really maddening, I missed the train by thirty seconds

ragnagnas [!] [raɲaɲa] *nmpl* **avoir ses ragnagnas** to have one's period□, to be on, to be on the rag

raide [rɛd] *adj* (a) *(drogué)* high, wasted, out of it; *(ivre)* plastered, *Br* off one's face, legless, *Am* tanked (b) *(sans argent)* broke, *Br* skint (c) **elle est raide, celle-là!** that's a bit far-fetched *or* hard to swallow! ▸ *see also* **passe-lacet**

raie [rɛ] *nf* **taper dans la raie à qn** [!!] *(sodomiser)* to fuck sb up the *Br* arse *or Am* ass, to bugger sb ▸ *see also* **gueule, pisser**

rail [raj] *nm (de cocaïne)* line; **se faire un rail** to do a line

ralléger [raleʒe] *vi (venir)* to come□; *(revenir)* to come back□

ramasser [ramase] **1** *vt* (a) *(recevoir)* to get□; **ramasser une gifle/un coup/un PV** to get a slap/a clout/a parking ticket (b) **se faire ramasser** *(se faire emmener par la police)* to get picked up *or Br* lifted *or* nicked; *(subir un échec)* to come unstuck, *Br* to come a cropper
2 *vi (recevoir une correction)* to get it, to catch it
3 se ramasser *vpr* (a) *(tomber)* to fall flat on one's face, to go flying (b) *(échouer)* to come unstuck, *Br* to come a cropper (c) *(recevoir)* **se ramasser une gifle/un coup/un PV**

to get a slap/a clout/a parking ticket ▶ *see also* **bûche, cuiller, gadin, pelle**

rambo [rãmbo] *nm Cités* = security officer patrolling the Parisian railway network or underground

ramdam [ramdam] *nm* racket, din; **faire du ramdam** to make a racket *or* a din

① This word comes from "ramadan", the Muslim festival during which people fast during the day and tend to be active at night.

rame [ram], **ramée** [rame] *nf* **ne pas en fiche** *ou* **en foutre [!] une rame** *ou* **une ramée** to do zilch *or Br* bugger all *or* sod all

ramener [ramne] **1** *vt* **la ramener** *(intervenir de façon intempestive)* to stick one's oar in; *(se vanter)* to show off; **il faut toujours qu'il la ramène quand on lui demande rien** he always has to stick his oar in when nobody's asked him anything
2 se ramener *vpr* to turn up, to show up, to roll up ▶ *see also* **fraise**

ramer [rame] **1** *vt* **ne pas en ramer une** to do zilch *or Br* bugger all *or* sod all
2 *vi (éprouver des difficultés)* to have a hard time of it; **ramer pour faire qch** to sweat blood *or* to bust a gut to do sth

ramier [ramje] **1** *adj (fainéant)* lazy◻, bone idle
2 *nm (fainéant)* lazybones, lazy so-and-so

ramollo [ramolo] **1** *adj* washed out, wiped; **je me sens tout ramollo aujourd'hui** I feel like a wet rag today
2 *nmf* wet rag *(person)*

ramoner [!!] [ramɔne] *vt (posséder*

sexuellement) to screw, to shaft, to hump, *Br* to shag

rampe [rãp] *nf* **lâcher la rampe** *(mourir)* to croak, to kick the bucket, *Br* to snuff it, *Am* to check out

ramponneau, -x [rãpɔno] *nm* clout, thump, *Br* wallop

① This term comes from the name of an innkeeper from a town near Paris, whose strength was legendary.

rancard [rãkar] = **rencard**

rancarder [rãkarde] = **rencarder**

rancart [rãkar] *nm* **mettre** *ou* **jeter qn au rancart** to throw sb on the scrap heap; **mettre** *ou* **jeter qch au rancart** *(objet)* to chuck sth out; *(projet)* to scrap sth

ranger [rãʒe] **se ranger** *vpr* **se ranger des voitures** to settle down; *(criminel)* to go straight; **être rangé des voitures** to have settled down; *(criminel)* to have gone straight

raousse [raus] *exclam* (get) out!, *Br* on your bike!, *Am* take a hike!

① This term comes from the German "heraus", meaning "out". It entered the French language during the Second World War, when France was occupied by Germany.

râpe [rɑp] *nf* **(a)** *(guitare)* guitar◻, *Br* axe, *Am* ax **(b)** *Suisse (avare)* skinflint, tightwad

râpé [rɑpe] *adj* **c'est râpé** we've/ you've *etc* had it; **c'est râpé pour nos vacances en Australie!** bang goes our holiday in Australia!, that's our holiday in Australia out the window!

rapiat, -e [rapja, -at] **1** *adj* stingy,

tight-fisted, *Br* tight
  2 *nm,f* skinflint, tightwad

rapido [rapido], **rapidos** [rapidos] *adv* quickly□; **boire un coup rapidos** to have a quick drink; **on se fait une petite partie rapidos?** shall we have a quick game?

raplapla [raplapla] *adj inv* washed out, wiped

rappliquer [raplike] *vi (arriver)* to come□; *(revenir)* to get back□; **ma belle-mère rapplique ce week-end** my mother-in-law's descending on us this weekend

raquer [rake] **1** *vt* to cough up, to fork out; **combien t'as raqué pour ton blouson?** how much did your jacket set you back?
  2 *vi* to pay up, to cough up

ras [rɑ] *adv* **en avoir ras le bol** *ou* **ras la casquette** *ou* **ras le cul [!]** to have had it up to here, to be fed up (to the back teeth) ▸ *see also* **pâquerette**

rasant, -e [razɑ̃, -ɑ̃t] *adj* deadly dull; **c'était rasant** it was a real drag

rasdep [!] [rasdɛp] *Offensive (verlan* **pédéraste) 1** *adj* queer, *Br* bent
  2 *nm* queer, *Br* poof, *Am* fag, faggot

rase-bitume [razbitym] *nmf inv* runt, squirt

raser [raze] **1** *vt* (**a**) *(ennuyer)* **raser qn** to bore sb stiff *or* to tears (**b**) **comme la société a eu de bons résultats cette année, on aura peut-être droit à une prime... – oui, c'est ça, et demain on rase gratuit!** since the company has done well this year maybe we'll get a bonus – yeah right, dream on!
  2 se raser *vpr (s'ennuyer)* to be bored stiff *or* to tears

raseur, -euse [razœr, -øz] *nm,f* bore;

quel raseur! what a bore *or* drag!

rasibus [razibys] *adv* (**a**) *(court)* short□, very close□; **il s'est fait couper les cheveux rasibus** he's been scalped (**b**) *(très près)* very close□; **la balle est passée rasibus** the bullet whizzed past

rasif [razif] *nm* razor□; **ils se sont battus à coups de rasif** they were going at each other with open razors

rasoir [razwar] *adj* deadly dull; **ce qu'il peut être rasoir!** he's such a drag! ▸ *see also* **pisser**

rassis [rasi] *nm* **se taper un rassis [!!]** to jerk off, to beat off, *Br* to have a wank

rasta [rasta] *nmf (abbr* **rastafari)** Rasta

rat [ra] **1** *adj (avare)* stingy, tight-fisted, *Br* tight
  2 *nm* (**a**) *(avare)* skinflint, tightwad (**b**) **s'emmerder** *ou* **se faire chier comme un rat mort [!]** to be bored shitless ▸ *see also* **face**

rata [rata] *nm* food□, grub, chow; **s'endormir sur le rata** to fall asleep on the job

ratatiner [ratatine] *vt (vaincre)* **ratatiner qn** to thrash *or* hammer sb, *Am* to kick sb's ass

rate [rat] *nf* (**a**) **se dilater la rate** to be in stitches, to kill oneself (laughing), to split one's sides (**b**) *(femme)* chick, *Br* bird ▸ *see also* **fouler**

râteau [rato] *nm* (**a**) *(peigne)* comb□ (**b**) **mettre un râteau à qn** *(rejeter qn)* to turn sb down, *Br* to knock sb back; **se prendre un râteau** *(être rejeté)* to get turned down□; *Br* to get a knockback (**c**) *Suisse* stingy, tight-fisted, *Br* tight

râtelier [ratəlje] *nm* (**a**) *(dentier)* dentures□, false teeth□ (**b**) **manger**

à tous les râteliers to have a finger in every pie

ratiboiser [ratibwaze] *vt* (a) **ratiboiser qn** *(au jeu)* to clean sb out, to take sb to the cleaners; **ratiboiser qch à qn** *(au jeu)* to clean sb out of sth; *(le lui voler)* to pinch *or Br* nick sth from sb (b) **se faire ratiboiser (la colline)** *(se faire couper les cheveux)* to get scalped

ratiche [ratiʃ] *nf* tooth□, *Br* gnasher

raton [ratɔ̃] *nm Offensive* = racist term used to refer to a North African Arab

ravagé, -e [ravaʒe] *adj (fou)* crazy, nuts, bonkers, *Br* barking (mad), *Am* wacko

rave [rɛiv] *nf* rave

raymond [rɛmɔ̃] *adj & nm* square, uncool

ⓘ This term comes from the first name "Raymond", which is nowadays considered rather unfashionable.

rayon [rɛjɔ̃] *nm* **c'est/c'est pas mon rayon** that's/that's not my department *or Am* turf; **en connaître un rayon** to know a thing or two, to be well clued-up

réac [reak] *adj & nmf (abbr réactionnaire)* reactionary□

rebelote [rəbəlɔt] **1** *nf* **faire rebelote** to do it again□; **la dernière fois le service était nul donc je préfère essayer ailleurs, j'ai pas envie de faire rebelote** last time the service was crap so I'd rather try elsewhere, I don't want to go there again; **leur premier album était excellent, et ils ont fait rebelote avec le deuxième** their first album was excellent and they've done it

again with their second one
2 *exclam* here we go again!

rebeu [rəbø] *nmf (verlan beur)* = person born and living in France of North African immigrant parents

ⓘ "Beur" is itself the "verlan" term for "Arabe". "Rebeu", then, is an example of a word which has been "verlanized" twice. See the panel at **verlan** (p.398).

rébou [rebu] *adj (verlan bourré)* plastered, trashed, *Br* pissed, *Am* wasted

récré [rekre] *nf (abbr récréation) Br* break time□, *Am* recess□

rectifier [rɛktifje] **1** *vt* (a) *(casser)* to break□ (b) *(tuer)* to bump off, *Br* to do in (c) *(dépouiller)* to rob□, to mug, *Br* to do over
2 se rectifier *vpr (s'enivrer)* to have a skinful, to get wasted

recui [rəkɥi] *nm (verlan cuir)* leather jacket□

récup' [rekyp] *nf (abbr récupération)* (a) **de la récup'** *(matériaux)* scrap (b) *(récupération idéologique)* exploitation□

redescendre [r(ə)desɑ̃dr] *vi (après une prise de drogue)* to come down

refaire [r(ə)fɛr] **1** *vt (duper)* to do, to have, to con; **j'ai été refait!** I've been done *or* had *or* conned!; **je me suis fait refaire de cinquante euros** I've been done out of fifty euros
2 se refaire *vpr (regagner une somme perdue)* to recoup one's losses□ ▸ *see also* **devanture**

refiler [r(ə)file] *vt* (a) *(donner)* to give□; **il m'a refilé son vieux blouson** he gave me his old jacket□ (b) *(transmettre)* to give□; **le salaud, il m'a refilé son rhume! [!]** the bastard's given me his cold! (**c**) **refiler de la jaquette [!]** *ou* **de la dossière [!!], en refiler [!!]** to take it up the *Br* arse *or Am* ass ▸ *see also* **chouette**

refouler [!!] [r(ə)fule] *vi (sentir mauvais)* to stink□, *Br* to pong, to niff ▸ *see also* **goulot**

refroidir [r(ə)frwadir] *vt (tuer)* to ice, to bump off, to liquidate

regarder [r(ə)garde] *vt* **non mais tu m'as bien regardé?, tu m'as pas regardé?** what do you take me for?; **non mais tu t'es regardé?** who do you think you are?

réglo [reglo] **1** *adj inv (personne)* straight, on the level; *(opération, transaction)* legit, kosher

2 *adv* by the book, fair and square; **il a intérêt à jouer réglo** he'd better play fair; **on fait ça réglo, hein?** we'll do it by the book, OK?

régulière [regyljɛr] **1** **à la régulière** *adv* fair and square; **ils se sont battus à la régulière** they had a good, clean fight

2 *nf* (**a**) *(épouse)* old lady, *Br* missus (**b**) *(maîtresse)* mistress□, fancy woman, *Br* bit on the side

relax [rəlaks] **1** *adj* laid-back

2 *adv* **faire qch relax** to take it easy doing sth; **on a fait ça relax** we took it easy

3 *exclam* **relax, Max!** take it easy!, chill out!

relooker [r(ə)luke] **1** *vt* to revamp

2 se relooker *vpr* to change one's image□, to have a makeover□

reloquer [r(ə)lɔke] **se reloquer** *vpr* to put one's clothes back on□, *Br* to get one's kit back on

relou [rəlu] *adj (verlan lourd)* (**a**) *(qui manque de subtilité)* unsubtle□, in-your-face, over the top, *Br* OTT; **ce que tu peux être relou avec tes blagues de cul!** you can be so in-your-face with your dirty jokes! (**b**) *(stupide)* thick, daft, *Am* dumb

reluire [rəlɥir] *vi (atteindre l'orgasme)* to come

reluquer [r(ə)lyke] *vt* to eye up, to check out, *Am* to scope (out); **sa bonne femme n'aime pas qu'il reluque les gonzesses** his other half doesn't like him checking out other chicks *or Br* birds

ⓘ Interestingly, this verb shares a common origin with the English verb "to look".

remballer [rɑ̃bale] *vt Hum* **remballer ses outils** to put one's *Br* trousers□ *or* keks *or Am* pants□ back on

rembarrer [rɑ̃bare] *vt* **rembarrer qn** to tell sb where to go *or* where to get off, *Br* to knock sb back; **se faire rembarrer** to get told where to go *or* where to get off, *Br* to get knocked back

remettre [r(ə)mɛtr] *vt* (**a**) *(reconnaître)* to recognize□, to place; **tu me remets?** can you place me? (**b**) **remettre ça** *(recommencer)* to start again□; *(prendre un autre verre)* to have another one□ ▸ *see also* **couvert**

rempiler [rɑ̃pile] *vi (se rengager)* to sign up again□

remplumer [rɑ̃plyme] **se remplumer** *vpr* (**a**) *(reprendre du poids)* to put a bit of weight *or* a few pounds back on□ (**b**) *(améliorer sa situation financière)* to improve one's cash flow□, to get back on one's feet

renauder [r(ə)node] *vi* to whinge, to moan

rencard [rɑ̃kar] *nm* (**a**) *(rendez-vous)*

appointment[]; *(amoureux)* date; **avoir un rencard avec qn** to have an appointment/a date with sb; **filer un rencard à qn** to fix an appointment/a date with sb **(b)** *(renseignement)* tip-off

rencarder [rɑ̃karde] **1** *vt* **rencarder qn** *(renseigner)* to tip sb off; *(donner rendez-vous à)* to arrange to meet sb

2 se rencarder *vpr (se renseigner)* to get information[]

renifler [r(ə)nifle] *vi (sentir mauvais)* to stink, *Br* to pong, to niff

reniflette [rəniflɛt] *nf (cocaïne)* coke, charlie

renoi [rənwa] *Cités (verlan* **noir) 1** *adj* black[]
2 *nmf* Black

renps [rɑ̃p(s)] *nmpl (verlan* **parents)** folks, *Br* old dears, *Am* rents, olds

rentre-dedans [rɑ̃tdədɑ̃] *nm* **faire du rentre-dedans à qn** to come on to sb, *Br* to chat sb up, *Am* to hit on sb

repasser [r(ə)pase] **1** *vt (escroquer)* to do, to rip off

2 *vi* **tu repasseras!** no way!, no chance!, not on your life!; **il peut toujours repasser** he hasn't got a hope in hell, he's got another think coming ▸ *see also* **planche**

repiquer [r(ə)pike] **1** *vt (classe)* to repeat[]

2 *vi* **(a)** *(redoubler une classe)* to repeat a *Br* year *or Am* grade[] **(b)** **repiquer au truc** *(reprendre une activité ou une habitude)* to be at it again

replonger [r(ə)plɔ̃ʒe] *vi* **(a)** *(retourner en prison)* to go back inside **(b)** *(reprendre une habitude)* to be at it again

répondant [repɔ̃dɑ̃] *nm* **avoir du**

répondant *(avoir des économies)* to have plenty of cash stashed away

repousser [r(ə)puse] *vi (sentir mauvais)* to stink, *Br* to pong, to niff ▸ *see also* **goulot**

restau [rɛsto] *nm (abbr* **restaurant)** restaurant[]; **restau-U** university cafeteria *or Br* canteen *or* refectory[]

resté, -e [rɛste] *adj Can (épuisé) Br* knackered, shattered, *Am* beat

resto [rɛsto] = **restau**

resucée [rəsyse] *nf* **(a)** *(quantité supplémentaire)* **une resucée** some more[]; **t'en prendras bien une petite resucée?** will you have a bit more?[] **(b)** *(copie)* rehash

résultat [rezylta] *nm* **résultat des courses,...** the upshot was...[], as a result,...[]; **résultat des courses, on s'est retrouvés au poste** the whole thing ended up with us in the police station

rétamé, -e [retame] *adj* **(a)** *(ivre)* wasted, trashed, *Br* legless, *Am* fried **(b)** *(épuisé) Br* knackered, shattered, *Am* beat, bushed **(c)** *(hors d'usage)* wrecked, bust, *Br* knackered, clapped-out

rétamer [retame] **1** *vt* **(a)** *(rendre ivre)* **rétamer qn** to get sb wasted *or* trashed *or Br* legless *or Am* fried **(b)** *(épuiser)* to wear out, *Br* to knacker **(c)** *(mettre hors d'usage)* to wreck, to bust, *Br* to knacker

2 se rétamer *vpr (tomber)* to go flying, to take a tumble; *(échouer)* to fail[], *Am* to flunk; **elle s'est rétamée à l'oral** she failed[] *or Am* flunked the oral

retape [rtap] *nf* **(a)** **faire la retape** *(en parlant de prostituées) Br* to be on the game, *Am* to hustle **(b)** **faire de la retape pour qch** to plug sth for all it's worth; **ça fait bizarre de**

voir ce soit-disant comédien alternatif faire de la retape pour une marque de lessive it's weird seeing a so-called alternative comedian plugging a brand of washing powder for all it's worth

retourne [rturn] *nf* **les avoir à la retourne** to be bone idle

rétro [retro] *nm* (*abbr* **rétroviseur**) rear-view mirror▫

reuch [rœʃ] *adj* Cités (*verlan* **cher**) expensive▫, pricey

reuf [rœf] *nm* Cités (*verlan* **frère**) brother▫, bro

reum [rœm] *nf* Cités (*verlan* **mère**) old lady, *Br* old dear

reunoi [rœnwa] = **renoi**

reup [rœp] *nm* Cités (*verlan* **père**) old man

reur [rør], **reureu** [rørø] *nm* Cités (*RER*) = express rail network serving Paris and its suburbs

reuss [rœs] *nf* Cités (*verlan* **sœur**) sister▫, sis

reviens [rəvjɛ̃] *nm* **je te prête mon dico mais il s'appelle reviens** I'll lend you my dictionary but I'll need it back▫

revoyure [rvwajyr] *nf* **à la revoyure!** see you!

revue [rvy] *nf* **être de la revue** to have to go without▫

ⓘ This expression has its origins in military slang: the soldiers selected to take part in a military parade had to endure many hours of training for the event during what would have been their free time.

ribambelle [ribãbɛl] *nf* **une ribambelle de** tons of, loads of

ricain, -e [rikɛ̃, -ɛn] (*abbr* **américain,**

-**e**) **1** *adj* Yank, *Br* Yankee

2 *nm,f* **Ricain, Ricaine** Yank, *Br* Yankee

richard, -e [riʃar, -ard] *nm,f* money-bags

riche [riʃ] *adj* **baiser à la riche [!!]** (*pratiquer la sodomie*) to have anal sex▫; **il l'a baisée à la riche** he fucked her up the *Br* arse *or Am* ass

ⓘ This expression comes from the fact that this type of intercourse doesn't produce children and all the expenses that they inevitably involve.

ric-rac [rikrak] *adv* **c'était ric-rac** it was touch and go, it was a close call *or* a near thing

rideau [rido] *exclam* enough!, that'll do!

rien [rjɛ̃] *adv* (a) (*très*) seriously, majorly, *Br* well, *Am* real; **elle est rien moche, sa copine** his girlfriend's a real dog *or Br* a total minger *or Am* a real beast (b) **c'est rien de le dire** you can say that again, you said it ▸ *see also* **casser**

rififi [rififi] *nm* trouble, *Br* aggro; **il va y avoir du rififi** there's going to be trouble *or Br* aggro, *Br* it's going to kick off

riflard [riflar] *nm* umbrella▫, *Br* brolly

riflette [riflɛt] *nf* (*guerre*) war▫

rigolade [rigɔlad] *nf* (a) (*amusement*) **quelle rigolade!** what a hoot *or* a scream!; **prendre qch à la rigolade** (*avec humour*) to see the funny side of sth, to treat sth as a joke; (*avec légèreté*) not to take sth too seriously▫ (b) **c'est de la rigolade!** (*facile*) it's a piece of cake!, it's a walkover!; **c'est pas de la rigolade!** it's no picnic!

rigoler [rigɔle] *vi* to laugh□; **histoire de rigoler, pour rigoler** for a laugh, for fun; **fais ce que je te dis, je ne rigole pas!** do as you're told, I'm not kidding *or* joking!; **tu rigoles?** are you kidding *or* joking?, *Br* are you having a laugh?; **ils rigolent pas avec la sécurité dans cet aéroport** they don't mess about *or* take any chances with security at this airport; *Ironic* **tu me fais rigoler, tiens!** you make me laugh!, don't make me laugh!

rigolo, -ote [rigɔlo, -ɔt] **1** *adj* funny□ **2** *nm,f* **(a)** *(personne amusante)* hoot, scream **(b)** *(personne peu sérieuse)* clown, joker

rikiki [rikiki] = **riquiqui**

rincée [rɛ̃se] *nf (averse)* downpour□

rincer [rɛ̃se] **1** *vt* **se faire rincer** to get caught in a downpour□
2 *vi (offrir à boire)* to get the drinks in; **c'est moi qui rince!** I'll get the drinks in!, the drinks are on me!; **c'est le patron qui rince!** the drinks are on the house!
3 se rincer *vpr* **se rincer l'œil** to get an eyeful ▸ *see also* **dalle**

ringard, -e [rɛ̃gar, -ard] **1** *adj* tacky, *Br* naff
2 *nm,f* geek, nerd, *Br* anorak

ringardise [rɛ̃gardiz] *nf* tackiness, *Br* naffness; **la déco était d'une ringardise, je te dis pas!** the decor was unbelievably tacky *or Br* naff!

ringardiser [rɛ̃gardize] *vt* to make tacky

ringardissime [rɛ̃gardisim] *adj* incredibly tacky *or Br* naff

ringardos [rɛ̃gardos] = **ringard**

ripatons [ripatɔ̃] *nmpl* feet□, *Br* plates, *Am* dogs

riper [ripe] *vi* to beat it, to push off, *Am* to beat feet, to book it

ripoliné, -e [ripoline] *adj (maquillé à l'excès)* **sa copine était pas mal roulée, mais elle était tellement ripolinée qu'on aurait dit un clown** her friend wasn't bad looking, but she'd trowelled on so much make-up *or Br* slap she looked like a clown

ripoliner [ripoline] **se ripoliner** *vpr (se maquiller à l'excès)* to trowel *or* pile on the make-up *or Br* the slap

ripou, -x [ripu] *nm (verlan* **pourri**) *Br* bent *or Am* bad cop

ⓘ This expression was popularized by Claude Zidi's 1984 comedy film about corruption in the police force, *Les Ripoux*.

riquiqui [rikiki] *adj inv* teenyweeny

rital, -e [rital] *Offensive* **1** *adj* wop, Eyetie
2 *nm (langue)* Italian□
3 *nm,f* **Rital, Ritale** wop, Eyetie

ⓘ Depending on the context and the tone of voice used, this term may be either offensive or affectionately humorous. It is nonetheless inadvisable to use it unless one is quite sure of the reaction it will receive.

roberts [!] [rɔbɛr] *nmpl (seins)* tits, knockers, jugs

ⓘ This term comes from a once famous make of baby's bottle.

robineux [rɔbinø] *nm Can* tramp, *Am* hobo

rodéo [rɔdeo] *nm (en voiture volée)* joyride

rogne [rɔɲ] *nf* anger□, rage□; **être en rogne** to be fuming *or* hopping mad; **se mettre en rogne** to go crazy *or* ballistic *or Br* mental

rognons [!!] [rɔɲɔ̃] *nmpl (testicules)* balls, nuts, *Br* bollocks

roi [rwa] *nm* **c'est le roi des cons [!]/des poivrots** he's a complete prick/alky

roille [rɔj] *nf Suisse* downpour□; **pleuvoir à la roille** to bucket down, *Br* to chuck it down

roiller [rwaje] *vi Suisse (pleuvoir)* to bucket down, *Br* to chuck it down

romano [rɔmano] *nmf Pej (abbr* **romanichel, -elle)** gypsy□, gippo

rombière [rɔ̃bjɛr] *nf* (a) *(femme désagréable)* **(vieille) rombière** stuck-up old cow (b) *(épouse)* other half, old lady; *Br* missus *(maîtresse)* mistress□, fancy woman, *Br* bit on the side

rond, -e [rɔ̃, rɔ̃d] **1** *adj (ivre)* wasted, loaded, *Br* pissed, *Am* bombed; **rond comme une queue de pelle** *ou* **comme un boudin** *Br* as pissed as a newt, *Am* stewed to the gills

2 *adv* **ne pas tourner rond** *(machine)* to be on the blink, *Am* to be on the fritz; *(personne)* to be not all there, to be not right in the head, to have a screw loose

3 *nm* (a) *(argent)* **ne pas avoir un rond** *Br* not to have a penny to one's name, *Am* not to have a red cent; **t'as des ronds sur toi?** got any cash on you? (b) **prendre** *ou* **filer du rond [!!]** to take it up the *Br* arse *or Am* ass ▶ *see also* **flan, gueule**

rondelle [!!] [rɔ̃dɛl] *nf (anus)* ring, ringpiece, *Br* arsehole, *Am* asshole; **défoncer** *ou* **casser la rondelle à**

qn to fuck sb in the *Br* arse *or Am* ass; **se faire taper dans la rondelle** to get fucked in the *Br* arse *or Am* ass

ronflette [rɔ̃flɛt] *nf* **piquer une ronflette** to have a nap *or* a snooze *or Br* a kip

roploplos [!] [roploplo] *nmpl* tits, knockers, jugs

Rosbif [rɔsbif] *nmf Offensive (Britannique)* Brit

ⓘ This term originates in the stereotypical notion among the French that the British consume large quantities of roast beef. Depending on the context and the tone of voice used, this term may be either offensive or affectionately humorous.

rose [roz] *nf* (a) **ça sent pas la rose** it stinks *or Br* pongs a bit, *Br* it's a bit whiffy (b) **envoyer qn sur les roses** to send sb packing, to tell sb where to go *or* where to get off

rosette [!] [rozɛt] *nf (anus)* ring, ringpiece, *Br* arsehole, *Am* asshole

roteuse [rɔtøz] *nf (bouteille de champagne)* bottle of bubbly *or Br* champers

rotin [rɔtɛ̃] *nm (sou)* **ne pas avoir un rotin** *Br* not to have a penny to one's name, *Am* not to have a red cent

rotoplots [rotoplo] = **roploplos**

rotule [rɔtyl] *nf* **être sur les rotules** to be wiped (out) *or Br* knackered *or* shattered *or Am* beat; **mettre qn sur les rotules** to wipe sb out, *Br* to knacker sb

roubignoles, roubignolles [rubiɲ-ɔl] = **roupettes**

rouflaquettes [ruflakɛt] *nfpl* sideburns□

rouge [ruʒ] *nm (vin rouge)* red wine□; **une bouteille de rouge** a bottle of red; **un coup de rouge** a glass of red wine□; **du gros rouge** cheap red wine□

roulée [rule] *adj* **bien roulée** *(femme)* curvy

rouler [rule] **1** *vt* (a) **rouler les mécaniques** to walk with a swagger (b) **rouler une pelle** *ou* **une galoche** *ou* **un pallot** *ou* **un patin à qn** [!] to French-kiss sb, *Br* to snog sb, *Am* to make out with sb

2 *vi* (a) *(aller bien)* **ça roule** everything's OK *or* cool, it's all good (b) **rouler pour qn** *(agir pour son compte)* to be in sb's pay□

3 se rouler *vpr* (a) **s'en rouler une** to roll a smoke *or Br* a fag (b) **se les rouler** to twiddle one's thumbs ▶ *see also* **bosse**

roulottier [rulɔtje] *nm (voleur)* = thief who robs parked cars

roulure [!] [rulyr] *nf* (a) *(prostituée)* hooker, whore (b) *(homme méprisable)* bastard, *Am* son-of-a-bitch; *(femme méprisable)* bitch, *Br* cow

roupettes [!] [rupɛt], **roupignolles** [!] [rupiɲɔl] *nfpl* balls, nuts, *Br* bollocks

roupiller [rupije] *vi* to sleep□, to snooze, *Br* to kip; **il faudrait que tu arrêtes de roupiller en classe** you need to stop snoozing in class

roupillon [rupijɔ̃] *nm* snooze, nap, *Br* kip; **piquer un roupillon** to have a snooze *or* a nap *or Br* a kip

rouquin [rukɛ̃] *nm (vin rouge)* red wine□

rouscailler [ruskɑje] *vi* to whinge, to moan

rouspétance [ruspetɑ̃s] *nf* `**pas de rouspétance!** I don't want to hear any whingeing *or* moaning!

rouspéter [ruspete] *vi* to whinge, to moan

rouspéteur, -euse [ruspetœr, -øz] *nm,f* moan, whinge

rousse [rus] *nf* **la rousse** *(la police)* the cops, the pigs, *Br* the filth

rouste [rust] *nf* thrashing, hammering; **flanquer une rouste à qn** to give sb a thrashing *or* a hammering

roustons [!] [rustɔ̃] *nmpl* balls, nuts, *Br* bollocks

royaumer [rwajome] **se royaumer** *vpr Suisse* to lounge about

RU [ry] *nm (abbr* **restaurant universitaire**) university cafeteria *or Br* canteen *or* refectory□

ruche [ryʃ] *nf* **se piquer la ruche** to get wasted *or* trashed *or Br* pissed *or Am* bombed

ruper [rype] *vt Suisse (manger)* to stuff oneself with, to pig out on

rupin, -e [rypɛ̃, -in] **1** *adj (personne)* loaded, *Br* rolling in it, *Am* rolling in dough; *(quartier)* upmarket□, *Br* posh

2 *nm,f* moneybags

Ruskoff [ryskɔf] *nmf Offensive* Russki

ⓘ Depending on the context and the tone of voice used, this term may be either offensive or affectionately humorous. It is nonetheless inadvisable to use it unless one is quite sure of the reaction it will receive.

Ss

sabrer [sɑbʀe] *vt* (**a**) *(couper) (texte)* to slash (**b**) *(noter sévèrement) (personne)* to give a lousy mark to (**c**) *(refuser) (candidat)* to failᵃ, *Am* to flunk (**d**) **[!]** *(posséder sexuellement)* to poke, *Br* to shaft

sac [sak] *nm* (**a**) *Formerly (dix francs)* ten francsᵃ; **dix/vingt sacs** a hundred/two hundred francs (**b**) **sac d'os** *(personne maigre)* bag of bones

ⓘ In sense (**a**), "sac" used to be used in multiples of ten.

sacquer [sake] *vt* (**a**) *(congédier)* to fire, to sack (**b**) **je ne peux pas le sacquer** I can't stand *or Br* stick him

sacrant, -e [sakʀɑ̃, -ɑ̃t] *adj Can* (**a**) *(fâcheux)* annoyingᵃ; **cet accident est bien sacrant!** this accident is a real pain! (**b**) **au plus sacrant** *(au plus vite)* as quickly as possibleᵃ, asap

sacré, -e [sakʀe] *adj* **un sacré con [!]** a total *Br* wanker *or* arsehole *or Am* asshole; **un sacré fouteur de merde [!]** a hell of a shit-stirrer; **c'est un sacré numéro** he's a real character *or* case!; **cette sacrée bagnole est encore en panne** the damn *or Br* bloody car's broken down again; **c'est un sacré veinard** he's a lucky *or Br* jammy devil

sacrément [sakʀemɑ̃] *adv* damn, *Br* bloody; **il s'est sacrément foutu de notre gueule [!]** he made a total damn *or Br* bloody fool of us; **il est sacrément radin celui-là!** he's so damn *or Br* bloody tight!; **il fait sacrément froid** it's damn *or Br* bloody cold

sado [sado] *nmf* (*abbr* **sadique**) sadistᵃ

sado-maso [sadomazo] (*abbr* **sado-masochiste**) **1** *adj* SM, S & M
2 *nmf* sado-masochistᵃ

sagouin, -e [sagwɛ̃, -in] *nm,f* *(personne malpropre)* filthy slob, pig; **du travail de sagouin** sloppy work

saigner [seɲe] **1** *vt (tuer à l'arme blanche)* to stabᵃ *or* knife to death
2 *vi* **ça va saigner** there's going to be trouble, *Br* it's going to kick off

sainte-nitouche [sɛ̃tnituʃ] *nf* goody-two-shoes; **avec ses airs de sainte-nitouche** looking as though butter wouldn't melt in his/her mouth

ⓘ This term is a corruption of "sainte", meaning "saint", and "ne pas y toucher", meaning "not to touch", suggesting someone who avoids any activities of a sexual nature.

saint-frusquin [sɛ̃fʀyskɛ̃] *nm* **tout le saint-frusquin** the whole (kit and) caboodle, *Br* the full monty, *Am* the whole enchilada

Saint-Glinglin [sɛ̃glɛ̃glɛ̃] *nf* **attendre jusqu'à la Saint-Glinglin** to wait forever *or* until doomsday; **c'est maintenant qu'il faut le faire, pas à la Saint-Glinglin** it has to be done now, not whenever

salade [salad] *nf* (a) *(situation embrouillée)* muddle, mess; **quelle salade!** what a muddle *or* mess! (b) **vendre sa salade** to make a pitch▯, to try to sell an idea▯ (c) **raconter des salades** to tell fibs *or Br* porkies ▸ *see also* **panier**

salamalecs [salamalɛk] *nmpl* bowing and scraping

ⓘ This term from the Arabic greeting "salam 'alayk", which means "peace be with you".

salaud [!] [salo] **1** *adj* **c'est salaud de faire/dire ça** that's a really shitty thing to do/say, that's a bastard of a thing to do/say; **il a été salaud avec elle** he's been a real bastard to her **2** *nm* bastard, *Am* son-of-a-bitch

sale [sal] *adj* **pas sale** pretty good, not bad; **il est pas sale, ton pinard** this wine of yours is pretty good

salé, -e [sale] *adj* (a) *(élevé) (note, addition)* steep (b) *(osé)* steamy, X-rated

salement [salmã] *adv (beaucoup)* badly▯, seriously; *(très) Br* dead, *Am* real; **salement blessé** badly injured; **salement déçu** *Br* dead *or Am* real disappointed, *Br* gutted; **il a salement vieilli** he's seriously aged

saleté [salte] *nf* (a) *(en injure)* **saleté!** *(à un homme)* swine!, bastard!; *(à une femme)* bitch!, *Br* cow!; **c'est une vraie saleté** he's a total bastard (b) **saleté de bagnole/de temps!** this blasted *or Am* darn car/weather!

saligaud [!] [saligo] *nm (individu malpropre)* filthy pig; *(individu méprisable)* bastard, *Am* son-of-a-bitch

salingue [!] [salɛ̃g] **1** *adj* filthy **2** *nmf* filthy pig

salopard [!] [salɔpar] *nm* bastard, *Am* son-of-a-bitch

salope [!] [salɔp] *nf* (a) *(femme méprisable)* bitch, *Br* cow; *(femme aux mœurs légères)* tart, slut, *Br* slapper (b) *(homme méprisable)* bastard, *Am* son-of-a-bitch

saloper [salɔpe] *vt* (a) *(salir)* to dirty▯, to mess up (b) *(mal exécuter)* to make a dog's breakfast *or* dinner *or Br* a pig's ear of

saloperie [salɔpri] **1** *nf* (a) *(acte méprisable)* dirty trick; **faire une saloperie à qn** to play a dirty trick on sb, *Br* to do the dirty on sb, *Am* to do sb dirty (b) *(marchandise de mauvaise qualité)* garbage, junk, *Br* rubbish; **saloperie de bagnole/d'ordinateur!** this blasted *or Am* darn car/computer! (c) *(maladie, virus)* something nasty; **il a attrapé une saloperie en vacances** he caught something nasty on *Br* holiday *or Am* vacation; **c'est une vraie saloperie, ce nouveau virus** this new virus is really nasty (d) *(homme méprisable)* bastard, *Am* son-of-a-bitch **2 saloperies** *nfpl* (a) *(saletés)* crud, crap, *Br* muck (b) *(propos orduriers)* filthy language▯; **dire des saloperies** to use filthy language (c) *(aliments malsains)* junk (food), garbage, *Br* rubbish; **il bouffe que des saloperies** he just eats garbage *or* junk *or Br* rubbish

salsifis [salsifi] *nmpl (doigts)* fingers▯

sang [sã] *nm* **bon sang!** *(de surprise) Br* blimey!, *Am* gee (whiz)!;

(de colère) blast it!, hell! ▸ *see also* **pisser**

sans [sɑ̃] *prep* **sans un** broke, *Br* skint, strapped ▸ *see also* **dec, déconner**

santé [sɑ̃te] **1** *nf* **avoir de la santé** *(avoir de l'audace)* to have a nerve *or Br* a brass neck

2 *exclam* cheers! ▸ *see also* **voleuse**

santiags [sɑ̃tjag] *nfpl* cowboy boots□

saper [sape] **1** *vt* to dress□

2 **se saper** *vpr (s'habiller)* to get dressed□; *(s'habiller chic)* to get all dressed up□; **être bien/mal sapé** to be well/badly dressed□; **elle aime bien se saper pour sortir** she likes to get all dressed up to go out□; **il sait pas se saper** he's got no dress sense□; **elle se sape très seventies** she wears really seventies clothes, she dresses really seventies

sapes [sap] *nfpl* clothes□, threads, *Br* gear

sapeur [sapœr] *nm* = young, well-dressed African man

sapin [sapɛ̃] *nm Hum* **ça sent le sapin** he's/she's/etc on his/her/etc last legs; **une toux qui sent le sapin** a worryingly unhealthy cough□, a death-rattle of a cough

saquer [sake] = **sacquer**

saton [satɔ̃] *nm* **coup de saton** kick□, boot; **donner des coups de saton à qn/dans qch** to boot sb/sth, to give sb/sth a kicking

satonner [satɔne] *vt* **satonner qn/qch** to boot sb/sth, to give sb/sth a kicking

saturer [satyre] *vi* to have had enough, to have had as much as one can take

sauce [sos] *nf* (**a**) *(pluie)* rain□;

prendre la sauce to get soaked *or* drenched□ (**b**) **mettre la sauce** to pull out all the stops, to go all out (**c**) **balancer la sauce [!!]** *(éjaculer)* to shoot one's load *or* wad

saucée [sose] *nf* downpour□; **prendre une saucée** to get drenched□ *or* soaked

saucer [sose] *vt* **se faire saucer** to get soaked *or* drenched□

sauciflard [sosiflar] *nm* (dried) sausage□

saucisse [sosis] *nf* **grande saucisse** *(personne)* beanpole, *Am* stringbean; **saucisse à pattes** sausage dog

saucissonné, -e [sosisɔne] *adj* trussed up; **il était tout saucissonné dans son pardessus** he was trussed up like a turkey in his overcoat

saucissonner [sosisɔne] **1** *vt (ligoter)* to tie up□

2 *vi* to grab a quick snack *or* bite

saumâtre [somatr] *adj* **il l'a trouvée saumâtre** he didn't appreciate it at all□, he wasn't amused *or* impressed□

saute-au-paf [!] [sotopaf] *nf inv* nympho, *Br* goer

sauter [sote] **1** *vt* (**a**) **[!!]** *(posséder sexuellement)* to fuck, to screw, *Br* to shag (**b**) **la sauter** *(avoir faim)* to be starving

2 *vi* (**a**) **se faire sauter la cervelle** *ou* **le caisson** to blow one's brains out (**b**) **et que ça saute!** jump to it!, make it snappy! (**c**) *(perdre son emploi)* to get fired *or Br* sacked

sauterelle [sotrɛl] *nf (fille, femme)* chick, *Br* bird

sauterie [sotri] *nf* party□, get-together, *Br* do

sauvage [sovaʒ] *adj (excellent)* wild, unreal

The symbol [!] denotes a very familiar term, [!!] a vulgar one.

savate [savat] *nf* **(a)** **il chante comme une savate** he can't sing to save his life, *Br* he can't sing for toffee **(b)** **traîner la savate** to be completely broke *or Br* skint *or Am* without a dime

savater [savate] *vt* to kick◻, to boot

savon [savɔ̃] *nm* **passer un savon à qn** to give sb a roasting, to bawl sb out, *Am* to chew sb out; **se faire passer** *ou* **prendre un savon** to get a roasting, to get bawled out *or Am* chewed out

savonnette [savɔnɛt] *nf (de cannabis)* = 250-gramme block of hashish

SBAB [!!] [zbab] *nf (abbr* **super bonne à baiser***)* fuckable *or Br* shaggable woman

scato [skato] *adj (abbr* **scatologique***) (blague)* disgusting◻, gross; **humour scato** toilet humour

schizo [skizo] *adj & nmf (abbr* **schizophrène***)* schizo, *Am* schiz

schlass[1] [ʃlas] *nm (couteau)* knife◻, blade, *Am* shiv

ⓘ This term comes from the English word "slash".

schlass[2], **schlasse** [ʃlas] *adj (ivre)* sozzled, trashed, wasted

schlinguer [ʃlɛ̃ge] = **chlinguer**

schlof [ʃlɔf] *nm* bed◻, *Br* pit; **se mettre au schlof** to hit the sack *or* the hay *or Am* the rack

ⓘ This word comes from an Alsatian word related to the German "schlafen", meaning "to sleep".

schmilblick [ʃmilblik] *nm* **faire avancer le schmilblick** to make progress◻, to get somewhere; **tout ça, ça fait pas avancer le schmilblick** that's not getting us any further forward

ⓘ This expression comes from a radio quiz show of the early 1970s, in which the contestants had to identify the mystery object (the "schmilblick") by asking the presenter a series of questions to which he could answer only yes or no. "Faire avancer le schmilblick" thus signified asking a question which gave the contestant additional clues to the object in question. The expression was popularized by the comedian Coluche, who performed a famous sketch based on this show.

schmitt [ʃmit] *nm* cop, *Am* flatfoot

schneck [!!] [ʃnɛk] *nm Cités* pussy, snatch, *Br* fanny, twat

schnock, schnoque [ʃnɔk] *nm* halfwit, dope, *Br* divvy, *Am* goober; **un vieux schnock** an old fogey, an old codger, *Am* a geezer

schnouf, schnouffe [ʃnuf] = **chnouf**

schtarbé, -e [ʃtarbe] = **chtarbé**

schwartz [ʃwarts] *nm* **(a)** *(policier)* cop, *Am* flatfoot **(b)** *(Noir)* Black

scier [sje] *vt* **(a)** *(surprendre)* to amaze◻, to stagger, to flabbergast, *Am* to knock for a loop; **ça m'a scié d'apprendre que...** I was staggered *or Br* gobsmacked *or Am* knocked for a loop to find out that... **(b)** *Suisse* **scier du bois** to snore like a pig

scotché, -e [skɔtʃe] *adj* **(a)** *(stupéfait)* **je suis resté scotché** I was staggered *or Br* gobsmacked **(b)** **être scotché devant la télé** to be glued to the TV

Le symbole ◻ indique que la traduction n'est pas argotique.

scotcher [skɔtʃe] vt (stupéfaire) to stagger, flabbergast; **ça m'a vraiment scotché!** I was staggered or Br gobsmacked!

scoumoune [skumun] nf rotten luck; **avoir la scoumoune** to be jinxed

scratch [skratʃ] nm (en musique) scratching

scratcher [skratʃe] **1** vi (en parlant d'un DJ) to scratch▫
2 se scratcher vpr to go off the road▫; **il s'est scratché avec la moto de son frère** he went off the road on his brother's motorbike▫

sec [sɛk] adv (a) (beaucoup) a lot▫; **il boit sec** he can really knock it back or put it away; **ils ont dérouillé sec pendant la guerre** they went through total hell during the war (b) **l'avoir sec** to be bummed (out) or Br gutted (c) **être à sec** to be broke or Br skint ▸ see also **cinq**

sèche [sɛʃ] nf (cigarette) smoke, Br fag, ciggy

sécher [seʃe] **1** vt (ne pas assister à) (cours) Br to bunk off, to skive off, Am to skip
2 vi (ne pas aller en classe) Br to bunk off, to skive, Am to play hookey

sécoin [sekwɛ̃] (verlan coincé) **1** adj uptight
2 nmf **c'est une vraie sécoin cette bonne femme** she's so uptight, that woman!

sécot [seko] adj (a) (sec) dry▫ (b) (maigre) skinny, lanky

secoué, -e [skwe] adj (fou) off one's head or rocker, Br crackers, Am nutso

secouer [s(ə)kwe] vt (a) **j'en ai rien à secouer** [!] I don't give a damn or Br a toss or Am a rat's ass (b) **secouer les puces à qn** Br to have a go at sb, to tell sb off, Am to chew sb out

Sécu [seky] nf (abbr **Sécurité sociale**) Br ≃ Social Security▫, Am ≃ welfare▫

sensass [sɑ̃sas] adj inv (abbr **sensationnel**) sensational, terrific, Br smashing

sentiment [sɑ̃timɑ̃] nm **la faire au sentiment à qn** to get round sb

sentir [sɑ̃tir] **1** vt (a) **je ne peux pas la sentir** I can't stand or Br stick her; **je le sens pas bien, ce mec-là** there's something about that guy I don't like (b) **je l'ai senti passer!** (à propos d'une douleur, d'une facture, d'une réprimande) I certainly knew about it!
2 se sentir vpr Hum **ne plus se sentir** (se comporter de façon étrange) to have taken leave of one's senses; **ne plus se sentir (pisser)** (être vaniteux) to be too big for one's Br boots or Am britches ▸ see also **rose, sapin**

sérieux [serjø] **1** adv (sérieusement) seriously; **ils se sont foutus sur la gueule sérieux** they seriously went for each other; **sérieux?** seriously?
2 nm (chope de bière) litre of beer▫

séropo [seropo] (abbr **séropositif, -ive**) **1** adj HIV-positive▫
2 nmf HIV-positive person▫

serre-la-piastre [sɛrlapjastr] nm Can (avare) stingy, tight-fisted, Br tight

serre-patte [sɛrpat] nm sergeant▫

serrer [sere] vt (arrêter) Br to nick, to lift, Am to bust ▸ see also **kiki, louche, pince, vis**

service [sɛrvis] nm Hum **entrée de service** [!] (anus) back door, tradesman's entrance

Spotlight on:

La séduction

In French slang, to look for a sexual partner is known as **draguer**, the activity is known as **la drague**, and someone who is a regular practitioner of the activity is known as **un dragueur** or **une dragueuse**, depending on their gender. A man who is very successful with the ladies is known as **un tombeur**. Expressions for "chatting someone up" are **faire du gringue** or **faire du plat à quelqu'un**. To be successful is **faire une touche** (an expression normally used in angling, when a fish has taken the bait) or **emballer**; to go all the way is **conclure**. To get rebuffed is **se prendre une veste** or **un vent** or **un râteau**. A man who fails to get what he came for is sometimes humorously (but somewhat vulgarly) said to **rentrer la pine sous le bras** (literally "to come back with one's dick under one's arm"); to go without is **faire tintin**. Someone who ends up on his or her own at a party or nightclub while other people pair off is said to **tenir la chandelle** (literally, "to hold the candle"). A French kiss is known as **une pelle**, **un pallot** or **une galoche**, and to give someone a French kiss is **rouler une pelle** or **un pallot** or **une galoche à quelqu'un**. People kissing are said to **se bécoter** (from **un bécot**, a kiss) and to feel each other up is **se peloter**. An attractive person, man or woman, can be described using the adjectives **craquant(e)** or **bandant(e)** (the latter term being considerably more vulgar than the former). To speak about a particularly attractive woman, the young men of today will say **elle est chaude** (she's hot) or **elle est bonne**. A woman with a good body is **bien roulée** or **bien bousculée**. The word **bombe** is only used for very attractive women whereas **canon** can be used for both men and women.

seulabre [sǝlɑbr] *adj* alone[□], *Br* on one's tod

sévère [sevɛr] *adv (gravement)* severely, seriously; **il déjante sévère en ce moment** he's severely *or* seriously lost it at the moment; **on a morflé sévère** we went through total hell

SF [ɛsɛf] *nf (abbr* **science fiction)** sci-fi, SF

shit [ʃit] *nm* hash, shit, *Br* blow

shoot [ʃut] *nm (de drogue)* fix, shot; **se faire un shoot** to shoot up, to jack up

shooté, -e [ʃute] **1** *adj* (**a**) *(drogué)*

Le symbole [□] indique que la traduction n'est pas argotique.

Spotlight on:

Le sexe

There are countless slang terms used to describe the male sex organ, among the most common of which are **bite**, **queue** and **pine**. **Bout** is also encountered in the extremely vulgar expressions **s'astiquer le bout** and **se mettre quelqu'un sur le bout**. The female equivalent is usually referred to as **la chatte**. **Couilles** is the most frequently used term for testicles, but it has several synonyms, including the humorous-sounding **coucougnettes**, **roubignolles** and **valseuses**, a term popularized by the 1974 Bertand Blier film *Les Valseuses*. A man with an erection is said to **bander (comme un taureau)** or to **avoir la gaule** or **la trique**. The verb "to have sex" also has many slang equivalents. The most common is **baiser**, which originally meant "to kiss", but is no longer used to mean this; fortunately so, as the potential for misunderstandings would be great. **Baiser** has several related words: **baise**, **baiseur** or **baiseuse** and **baisable**, together with more humorous inventions such as **baisodrome** (a place where much sexual activity takes place) and **baise-en-ville** (used to mean an overnight bag, a much less vulgar term than the others). The verb **tirer** is also used to refer to sex, on its own or in the expression **tirer un coup**. By extension, a good sexual partner is **un bon coup**. Transitive verbs meaning "to have sex with" include **s'enfiler**, **s'envoyer**, **se faire**, **sauter** and **bourrer** (an especially vulgar expression). **Niquer** and a more recent coinage, **bouillaver**, are often used by young people in the Parisian "banlieues". It is interesting to note that unlike similar English verbs, the above terms can only have a man as their subject. Fellatio has several colourful slang expressions: the most frequently encountered are **tailler une pipe**, **une plume** or **une flûte** and **faire une turlute**. The verbs **enculer** and, less frequently, **empapaouter** or **empaffer**, refer to sodomy. The passive voice of some verbs referring to sex often have a more figurative use. The expression **se faire baiser** thus means "to get swindled", similar to the notion in English of getting screwed or shafted. It is worth noting that **foutre** used to refer to the sex act but has now lost any erotic connotation, although it has kept its meaning of "semen".

être shooté to be a druggie or a junkie **(b)** *(fou)* crazy, *Br* barking (mad), *Am* wacko
2 *nm,f* **(a)** *(drogué)* druggie, junkie **(b)** *(fou)* headcase, nutcase, *Br* nutter, *Am* wacko

shooter [ʃute] **se shooter** *vpr* to shoot up, to jack up

shooteuse [ʃutøz] *nf* hype, hypo

sifflard [siflar] *nm* (dried) sausage□

ⓘ This term is derived from another slang word, "sauciflard", which is itself derived from "saucisson".

siffler [sifle] **1** *vt (boire)* to sink, to down, to knock back
2 **se siffler** *vpr* **il s'est sifflé un litre de rouge à lui tout seul** he sank or downed or knocked back a whole litre of red wine on his own

sifflet [siflɛ] *nm* **couper le sifflet à qn** to leave sb speechless, to shut sb up

sinoque [sinɔk] = **cinoque**

siphonné, -e [sifɔne] *adj (fou)* crazy, bonkers, *Br* barking (mad)

situasse [sityas] *nf (abbr* **situation)** situation□, *Br* sitch

six-quatre-deux [siskatdø] **à la six-quatre-deux** *adv* **faire qch à la six-quatre-deux** to do sth any old how

skeud [skœd] *nm* Cités *(verlan* **disque)** record□

skin [skin] *nm (abbr* **skinhead)** skin, skinhead

slibar [slibar] *nm* boxers, *Am* shorts, skivvies

smack [smak] *nm* smack, scag, skag

smala, smalah [smala] *nf* family□, tribe, clan

sniffer [snife] *vt* to sniff, *Am* to huff; *(cocaïne)* to snort, to sniff, *Am* to huff

snobinard, -e [snɔbinar, -ard] **1** *adj* stuck-up, snobby, lah-di-dah
2 *nm,f* snob□

snul [snyl] *nm Belg* cretin, *Br* dipstick

socialo [sɔsjalo] *adj & nmf (abbr* **socialiste)** socialist□, leftie, lefty

sœur [sœr] *nf* **(a)** *(femme)* chick, *Br* bird **(b)** **et ta sœur?** mind your own business!

soft [sɔft] *nm* soft porn

soif [swaf] *nf* **(a)** **jusqu'à plus soif** to one's heart's content **(b)** **il fait soif** I'd kill for a drink, *Br* I could murder a drink

soiffard, -e [swafar, -ard] *nm,f* alky, lush, boozer, *Br* pisshead, *Am* booze-hound

soigné, -e [swaɲe] *adj (remarquable en son genre)* **une engueulade soignée** a hell of a telling-off; **il lui a fichu une raclée, quelque chose de soigné!** he thrashed him to within an inch of his life!; **l'addition était soignée** the *Br* bill or *Am* check was exorbitant

soigner [swaɲe] *vt* **faut te faire soigner!** you need your head examined!, you need help!

soixante-neuf [swasɑ̃tnœf] *nm (position)* sixty-nine

sonné, -e [sɔne] *adj* **(a)** *(fou)* crazy, nuts, *Br* bonkers, barking (mad), *Am* wacko **(b)** *(étourdi)* groggy

sonner [sɔne] *vt* **(a)** *(assommer)* to knock out **(b)** **sonner les cloches à qn** to bawl sb out, to give sb what-for **(c)** **toi, on t'a pas sonné!** nobody asked you!

sono [sɔno] *nf (abbr* **sonorisation)** sound system□

sortable [sɔrtabl] *adj* **il n'est pas sortable** you can't take him anywhere

sortir [sɔrtir] **1** *vt* *(dire)* to come out with; **ce qu'il peut sortir comme conneries!** [!] he can come out with some real crap *or* bullshit!

2 *vi* **d'où tu sors?** where have you been?, what planet have you been on?; **il me sort par les trous de nez** *ou* **par les yeux** I can't stand the sight of him

souçaille [susaj] *nm (souci)* **pas de souçailles!, no souçailles!** no worries!

ⓘ This word originated in the satirical TV programme *Les Guignols de l'Info*, and is supposed to sound like the anglicized form of the French word "souci" (meaning "worry").

souci [susi] *nm* **il n'y a pas de soucis!** no worries!

souffler [sufle] **1** *vt* **(a)** *(surprendre)* to amaze□, to stagger, to flabbergast, *Am* to knock for a loop; **ça m'a soufflé d'apprendre ça** I was staggered *or Br* gobsmacked to hear that **(b)** *(dérober)* **souffler qch à qn** to pinch *or Br* nick sth from sb

2 *vi* **souffler dans les bronches à qn** to bawl sb out, to give sb hell, *Am* to chew sb out ▸ *see also* **ballon, poireau**

souk [suk] *nm (désordre)* mess; **c'est le souk dans sa piaule!** his/her room's an absolute bombsite *or* pigsty!; **foutre le souk (dans)** *(mettre en désordre)* to make a mess (of); **il fout le souk en classe** he creates havoc in the classroom

ⓘ This is a pejorative usage of an Arabic word which means "market". Interestingly, the word "bazar" is also used in French to describe a state of disorder.

soulager [sulaʒe] **1** *vt* **soulager qn de qch** *(lui voler quelque chose)* to relieve sb of sth

2 **se soulager** *vpr* **(a)** *(uriner, déféquer)* to relieve oneself **(b)** *(se masturber)* to give oneself relief

soûlard, -e [sular, -ard] *nm,f* alky, boozer, *Br* lush *Am* boozehound

soûler [sule] *vpr* **se soûler la gueule** [!] *Br* to get pissed *or* rat-arsed, *Am* to hang *or* tie one on

soûlon [sulɔ̃] *nm Can & Suisse (ivrogne)* alky, boozer, *Br* lush, *Am* boozehound

soûlot, -ote [sulo, -ɔt] *nm,f* alky, boozer, *Br* lush, *Am* boozehound

soupe [sup] *nf* **(a)** **par ici la bonne soupe!** that's the way to make money□, ker-ching! **(b)** **faire la soupe à la grimace** to sulk□, to be in a huff **(c)** **à la soupe!** grub's up! **(d)** **être soupe au lait** to fly off the handle easily **(e)** *(musique insipide)* supermarket *or* elevator music ▸ *see also* **cheveu, cracher**

souper [supe] *vi* **en avoir soupé de qn/qch** to have had enough of sb/sth, to be fed up (to the back teeth) with sb/sth

sourdingue [surdɛ̃g] *adj* deaf as a post

souris [suri] *nf (femme)* chick, *Br* bird

sous-fifre [sufifr] *nm* underling□, minion□

sous-marin [sumarɛ̃] *nm* **(a)** *(véhicule de surveillance)* = converted van used for police surveillance **(b)** *(boisson)* = cocktail consisting of a pint of beer with a shot glass of tequila in the bottom of the beer glass, served with a straw

sous-merde [!] [sumɛrd] *nf* nobody[□], nonentity[□]; **traiter qn comme une sous-merde** to treat sb like shit

sous-off [suzɔf] *nm* (*abbr* **sous-officier**) non-commissioned officer[□]

soussaille [susaj] = **souçaille**

sous-ventrière [suvɑ̃trijɛr] *nf* **manger à s'en faire péter la sous-ventrière** to stuff oneself *or* one's face, to pig out

soutif [sutif] *nm* bra[□]

speed [spid] **1** *adj* (*nerveux*) hyper **2** *nm* (*amphétamine*) speed

speedé, -e [spide] *adj* (**a**) (*nerveux*) hyper (**b**) (*drogué aux amphétamines*) **être speedé** to be speeding

speeder [spide] *vi* (**a**) (*être sous l'effet d'amphétamines*) to be speeding (**b**) (*se dépêcher*) to get a move on, *Am* to get it in gear; **il va falloir speeder si on veut pas arriver à la bourre** we're going to have to get a move on *or Am* get it in gear if we don't want to be late (**c**) (*être hyperactif*) to be hyper; **mais arrête donc de speeder comme ça, détends-toi!** stop being so hyper, relax!

splif [splif] *nm* spliff, joint

sport [spɔr] *nm* (**a**) **il va y avoir du sport** this is going to be fun (**b**) *Hum* **sport en chambre** (*rapports sexuels*) bedroom sports, sexual athletics

squatter [skwate] **1** *vt* (**a**) (*monopoliser*) to take over, to hog; **il squatte toujours la télécommande quand on regarde un film** he always hogs the remote control when we're watching a film; **arrête de squatter le joint, fais tourner!** stop bogarting that joint, pass it round! (**b**) *Cités* (*vivre aux*

dépens de) to scrounge off **2** *vi* to squat; **ça fait trois semaines qu'il squatte chez moi** he's been squatting at mine for three weeks now

starsky [starski] *nm* cop, *Am* flatfoot

ⓘ This term comes from *Starsky and Hutch*, the popular 1970s American TV series about two policemen.

---

stick [stik] *nm* (thin) joint *or* spliff

stonba [stɔ̃ba] *nf Cités* (*verlan* **baston**) scuffle, *Br* scrap, punch-up, *Am* slugfest

stone [ston], **stoned** [stond] *adj* stoned

student [stydɛnt] *nm Belg* student[□]

stups [styp] *nmpl* **la Brigade des stups, les stups** the Drug Squad, *Am* the narcs

suant, -e [sɥɑ̃, -ɑ̃t] *adj* (*fâcheux*) **être suant** to be a pain (in the neck)

subclaquant, -e [sybklakɑ̃, -ɑ̃t] *adj* **être subclaquant** to be on one's last legs, to have one foot in the grave

sucer [syse] *vt* (**a**) [!!] **sucer qn** (*pratiquer la fellation sur*) to go down on sb, to give sb head, to suck sb off; (*pratiquer le cunnilinctus sur*) to go down on sb, to give sb head, *Br* to lick sb out (**b**) **sucer la pomme** *ou* **la couenne à qn** *Br* to snog sb, *Am* to make out with sb; **se sucer la pomme** *ou* **la couenne** *Br* to snog, *Am* to make out, to suck face (**c**) **il suce pas que de la glace** he drinks like a fish (**d**) (*essence*) to guzzle; **il faudrait que je me trouve une bagnole qui suce un peu moins d'essence** I need to find a car that guzzles a bit less gas *or* that's a bit less thirsty

sucette [sysɛt] *nf* **partir en sucette** to go down the tubes *or* pan

suceur [!] [sysœr] *nm (flatteur) Br* arse-licker, *Am* ass-licker

suceuse [!!] [sysøz] *nf (femme qui pratique la fellation)* **c'est une sacrée suceuse** she gives a great blow-job, she gives great head

sucre [sykr] *vt* **casser du sucre sur le dos de qn** to bad-mouth sb, *Br* to slag sb off

sucrer [sykre] **1** *vt* (**a**) *(supprimer) (permis, licence)* to take away◻; *(permission, prime)* to cancel◻; *(argent de poche)* to stop◻ (**b**) **sucrer les fraises** to have shaky hands
  2 se sucrer *vpr (s'octroyer un bénéfice)* to line one's pockets

suer [sɥe] *vi* (**a**) **faire suer qn** *(l'embêter)* to bug sb, *Br* to get up sb's nose, to do sb's head in, to get on sb's wick, *Am* to tick sb off (**b**) **faire suer le burnous** to be a real slavedriver

suif [sɥif] *nm* **faire du suif** to kick up a fuss

sulfateuse [sylfatøz] *nf (mitraillette)* submachine gun◻

① In standard French a "sulfateuse" is used to spray vines.

sup [syp] *adj inv (abbr* **supplémentaire**) **heures sup** overtime◻

super [sypɛr] **1** *adj inv* great, fantastic, terrific
  2 *adv* super, mega, *Br* dead, *Am* real; **un bouquin super chiant** a *Br* dead *or Am* real boring book; **on s'est super bien marrés** we had a blast, we had *Br* a wicked *or Am* an awesome time

① This is by far the most common word used to describe the excellence of someone or something. "Super" and its accompanying term are often written as one word, eg "supernana", "superplan", "superchiant".

surgé [syrʒe] *nmf (abbr* **surveillant général**) head supervisor◻ *(in charge of school discipline)*

surin [syrɛ̃] *nm* knife◻, blade, *Am* shiv, shank

suriner [syrine] *vt (blesser avec un couteau)* to knife, *Am* to shiv; *(tuer avec un couteau)* to stab to death◻

survêt [syrvɛt] *nm (abbr* **survêtement**) tracksuit◻, trackie

sympa [sɛ̃pa] *adj (abbr* **sympathique**) nice◻; **c'est quelqu'un de très sympa** he's/she's really nice; **j'ai dégoté un petit resto très sympa** I've found a really nice little restaurant

syphilo [sifilo] *nmf (abbr* **syphilitique**) = syphilis sufferer

système [sistɛm] *nm* (**a**) **taper sur le système à qn** *Br* to get on sb's wick, to get up sb's nose, to do sb's head in, *Am* to give sb a pain (in the neck) (**b**) **le système D** resourcefulness◻; **le système D, ça le connaît** he knows how to use his wits

Tt

tabac [taba] *nm* (**a**) **faire un tabac** to be a big hit (**b**) **passer qn à tabac** to beat sb up, to give sb a hammering *or* pasting; **passage à tabac** beating up, hammering *or* pasting (**c**) **c'est le même tabac** it's the same difference, it amounts to the same thing ▸ *see also* **blague**

tabasser [tabase] *vt* **tabasser qn** to beat sb up, to give sb a hammering *or* pasting; **se faire tabasser** to get beaten up, to *Br* get *or* *Am* take a hammering *or* pasting

tabernacle [tabɛrnakl] *exclam Can* damn!

ⓘ Traditionally, French Canadians were deeply Catholic, which explains why several of their most common swearwords are linked to religion: these include "câlice" (derived from "calice", meaning "chalice"), "ciboire", "tabernacle", "hostie" and "criss" (derived from "Christ").

---

table [tabl] *nf* **se mettre** *ou* **passer à table** *(faire des aveux)* to spill the beans, to let the cat out of the bag; **on a encore mangé à la table qui recule** we had to go without food again[□]

tablette [tablɛt] *nf* **tablette de chocolat** *(abdominaux)* six-pack

---

ⓘ This expression derives from the fact that a set of well-toned stomach muscles is somewhat resembles of the squares of a bar of chocolate.

---

tablier [tablije] *nm Hum* **tablier de sapeur** *ou* **de forgeron** [!] *(poils pubiens)* bush, beaver

tache [taʃ] *nf* (**a**) *(personne nulle)* nonentity[□], loser, no-hoper; **quelle tache ce mec-là!** that guy's such a loser *or* no-hoper! (**b**) **faire tache** *(jurer)* to stand *or* stick out like a sore thumb

tacot [tako] *nm* (**a**) *(vieille voiture)* heap, rustbucket, *Br* banger, *Am* jalopy (**b**) *(taxi)* taxi[□], cab, *Am* hack

taf [taf] *nm (travail)* work[□]; *(tâche, emploi)* job[□]

taffe [taf] *nf* drag, puff

taffer [tafe] *vi (travailler)* to work[□]

tag [tag] *nm* tag *(piece of graffiti)*

tagger¹ [tage] *vt* to cover in graffiti[□]

tagger² [tagœr] *nm* graffiti artist[□], tagger, *Am* writer

taguer [tage] = **tagger**¹

tagueur, -euse [tagœr, -øz] *nm,f* = **tagger**²

tailler [tɑje] **1** *vt* (**a**) **tailler une pipe** *ou* **une plume** *ou* **une flûte à qn** [!!] to give sb a blow-job, to suck sb off, to give sb head (**b**) **tailler un costard à qn** *Br* to slag sb off, *Am* to badmouth sb (**c**) **tailler la route** *(parcourir beaucoup de chemin)* to eat up the miles; *(partir)* to beat it, *Br* to scarper, *Am* to book it

  2 se tailler *vpr (partir)* to beat it, *Br* to scarper, *Am* to book it ▸ *see also* **bavette**

tailleuse [tɑjøz] *nf* **c'est une sacrée tailleuse de pipes** *ou* **de plumes** [!!] she gives a great blow-job, she gives great head

talbin [talbɛ̃] *nm Br* banknote□, *Am* greenback; **qu'est-ce que t'as foutu des talbins?** what have you done with the cash *or* dough *or Br* dosh *or Am* bucks?

taloche [talɔʃ] *nf* clout, cuff; **flanquer une taloche à qn** to clout *or* cuff sb

talocher [talɔʃe] *vt* to clout, to cuff

tambouille [tɑ̃buj] *nf* food□, grub, chow; **faire la tambouille** to do the cooking□

tamponne [tɑ̃pɔn] *nf Belg* (drinking) binge; **prendre une tamponne** to get trashed *or* wasted

tamponner [tɑ̃pɔne] **se tamponner** *vpr* (**a**) **s'en tamponner (le coquillard)** not to give a damn *or Br* a toss *or* a monkey's *or Am* a rat's ass (**b**) *Belg* to get trashed *or* wasted

tanche [tɑ̃ʃ] *nf* jerk, *Br* plonker, *Am* meathead

tangente [tɑ̃ʒɑ̃t] *nf* **prendre la tangente** to slip off *or* away, to make oneself scarce

tango [tɑ̃go] *nm (boisson)* = drink consisting of beer and grenadine syrup

tannant, -e [tanɑ̃, -ɑ̃t] *adj* (**a**) *(importun)* annoying□; *(énervant)* maddening□; **ce que tu peux être tannant**

avec tes questions! you're a real pain with all these questions! (**b**) *(remuant)* rowdy

tanné, -e [tane] *adj Can* **être tanné** *(en avoir assez)* to be fed up (to the back teeth), to have had it up to here; **je suis tannée à faire le ménage** I'm fed up *or* I've had it up to here with housework

tannée [tane] *nf (correction, défaite)* thrashing, hammering; **filer une tannée à qn** to thrash *or* hammer sb, to give sb a thrashing *or* a hammering; **prendre une tannée** to get thrashed *or* hammered

tanner [tane] *vt (importuner)* to pester, to badger, to bug ▸ *see also* **cuir**

tante [tɑ̃t], **tantouse, tantouze** [tɑ̃tuz] *nf Offensive (homosexuel)* queer, fairy, *Br* poof, *Am* fag

tapant, -e [tapɑ̃, -ɑ̃t] *adj* **à cinq heures tapantes** at five o'clock sharp *or* on the dot

tapé, -e [tape] *adj (fou)* nuts, *Br* bonkers, barking (mad), *Am* wacko

tapecul, tape-cul [tapky] *nm (véhicule)* boneshaker

tapée [tape] *nf* **(toute) une tapée de** loads of, tons of

taper [tape] *vt* (**a**) *(emprunter)* to bum, to cadge, to scrounge; **taper qch à qn, taper qn de qch** to bum *or* cadge *or* scrounge sth off sb, to hit sb for sth; **il m'a tapé dix euros** he bummed *or* cadged *or* scrounged ten euros off me, he hit me for ten euros
(**b**) *(atteindre)* **taper le cent/le deux cents** to hit a hundred/two hundred (kilometres an hour)
(**c**) **elle lui a tapé dans l'œil** *(elle lui a plu)* he was really taken with her, he took quite a shine to her
(**d**) *(faire)* **taper la frime** to show

off; **taper la discussion** to chew the fat *or* the rag, to shoot the breeze

2 se taper *vpr* (a) *(subir)* **on s'est tapé ses parents tout le week-end** we got stuck *or Br* landed *or* lumbered with his/her parents all weekend; **se taper le ménage/les courses** to get stuck *or Br* landed *or* lumbered with the housework/the shopping; **on s'est tapé de la pluie pendant trois semaines** we had rain every day for three weeks; **on s'est tapé deux heures d'embouteillages** we got stuck in traffic jams for two hours; **se taper la honte** to be totally mortified

(b) *(absorber) (nourriture)* to guzzle, to scoff; *(boisson)* to sink, to down, to knock back; **je me taperais bien une pizza!** I'd kill for *or Br* I could murder a pizza!; **il a fallu que je me tape tout Proust pour l'examen** I had to get through the complete works of Proust for the exam

(c) [!!] *(posséder sexuellement)* **se taper qn** to fuck *or* screw *or Br* shag sb

(d) [!] *(se désintéresser)* **je m'en tape** I don't give a shit *or Br* a toss *or Am* a rat's ass

(e) **à se taper le derrière** *ou* **le cul** [!] **par terre** hysterical, side-splitting
► *see also* **carton, cloche, colonne, honte, incruste, lune, queue, raie, rassis, système**

tapette¹ [tapɛt] *nf Offensive (homosexuel)* queer, fairy, *Br* poof, *Am* fag

tapette² *nf (bagou)* **il a une bonne** *ou* **fière tapette!** he's a real chatterbox!

tapeur, -euse [tapœr, -øz] *nm,f* sponger, scrounger, *Am* moocher

tapin [tapɛ̃] *nm* **faire le tapin** to walk the streets, *Br* to be on the game, *Am* to hustle

tapiner [tapine] *vi* to walk the streets, *Br* to be on the game, *Am* to hustle; **elle tapine du côté du port** she walks the streets *or Am* hustles down at the port

tapineur, -euse [tapinœr, -øz] *nm,f* streetwalker

tapocher [tapɔʃe] *vt Can (frapper)* to tap□; *(battre)* to beat up

taponner [tapɔne] *Can* **1** *vt (tâter)* to touch□, to feel□; *(sexuellement)* to grope, to feel up
2 *vi (ne rien faire)* to hang around

tarba [tarba] *nm (verlan* **bâtard**) bastard

taré, -e [tare] **1** *adj* crazy, off one's head *or* rocker, *Br* barking (mad), *Am* wacko
2 *nm,f* nutcase, headcase, *Br* nutter, *Am* wacko

targettes [tarʒɛt] *nfpl* (a) *(pieds)* feet□, *Br* plates, *Am* dogs (b) *(chaussures)* shoes□, clodhoppers

tarin [tarɛ̃] *nm Br* conk, hooter, *Am* schnozzle

tarlouze [tarluz] *nf Offensive (homosexuel)* queer, fairy, *Br* poof, *Am* fag

tarpé [tarpe] *nm (verlan* **pétard**) joint, spliff, reefer

tarte [tart] **1** *adj* (a) *(ridicule)* ridiculous□, *Br* naff, *Am* dorky (b) *(stupide)* *Br* dim, thick, *Am* dumb
2 *nf* (a) *(coup)* clout, wallop; **flanquer une tarte à qn** to clout *or* wallop sb (b) **c'est pas de la tarte** *(c'est difficile)* it's no walkover, it's no picnic (c) **tarte aux poils** [!!] *(sexe de la femme)* bush, beaver, muff; **bouffer de la tarte aux poils** to go muffdiving

Tartempion [tartɑ̃pjɔ̃] *npr* thingy, what's-his-name, *f* what's-her-name

tartignol, tartignolle [tartiɲɔl] *adj*

ridiculous□, *Br* naff, *Am* dorky

tartine [tartin] *nf* (a) *(pied)* foot□, *Br* plate, *Am* dog (b) *(chaussure)* shoe□, clodhopper (c) *(texte long)* **en mettre une tartine** *ou* **des tartines** to write screeds, to waffle on

tartiner [tartine] **1** *vt* (a) *(écrire)* to churn out (b) *(enduire en grande quantité)* **tartiner qn/qch de qch** to cover sb/sth in sth□
2 se tartiner *vpr* **se tartiner de qch** to cover oneself in sth□, to get covered in sth□

tartir [tartir] *vi* **se faire tartir** [!] to be bored shitless

tas [tɑ] *nm* (a) **tas de ferraille** *(voiture en mauvais état)* rusty old heap *or Br* banger *or Am* jalopy, rustbucket (b) **un tas** *ou* **des tas de** *(un grand nombre de, une grande quantité de)* a lot of□; **tas de paresseux/menteurs!** you bunch of lazybones/liars!, *Br* you lazy/lying lot! (c) **un gros tas** *(gros individu mou)* a big fat lump; *(grosse fille laide)* a fat old bag *or* boot

tasse [tɑs] *nf* (a) **boire la tasse** *(avaler de l'eau)* to get a mouthful of water□ (b) **tasses** *(urinoirs)* street urinals□

tassé, -e [tɑse] *adj* **il a la cinquantaine bien tassée** he's fifty if he's a day, he's on the wrong side of fifty

tassepé [!] [taspe] *nf (verlan* **pétasse**) (a) *(fille)* slut, tart, *Br* slapper, slag (b) *(prostituée)* whore, hooker

tata [tata] *nf* Offensive *(homosexuel)* queer, fairy, *Br* poof, *Am* fag

tatane [tatan] *nf* shoe□, clodhopper

tataner [tatane] *vt* **tataner qn/qch** to give sb/sth a kicking

taulard, -e [tolar, -ard] *nm,f* jailbird, con

taule [tol] *nf* (a) *(prison)* slammer,

clink, *Br* nick, *Am* pen; **faire de la taule** to do time, to do a stretch (b) *(lieu de travail)* workplace□ (c) *(chambre)* room□

taulier, -ère [tolje, -ɛr] *nm,f* (a) *(d'un hôtel)* boss (b) *(logeur)* landlord, *f* landlady□

taupe [top] *nf* **avoir la taupe au bord du trou** [!!] to be dying for a shit

tauper [tope] *vt* Suisse **tauper qch à qn** *(emprunter)* to scrounge *or* to sponge *or* to cadge sth from sb; *(soustraire)* to do *or* to con sb out of sth

taxer [takse] *vt* (a) *(emprunter)* **taxer qch à qn** to scrounge *or* to sponge *or* to cadge sth from sb (b) *(voler)* to pinch, *Br* to nick; **je me suis fait taxer mon cuir par une bande de skins** I got my leather jacket pinched *or Br* nicked by a bunch of skinheads

TBM [tebeɛm] *adj (abbr* **très bien monté**) hung like a horse *or Br* a donkey *or Am* a mule

tchatche [tʃatʃ] *nf* **de la tchatche** the gift of the gab; **tout ça c'est de la tchatche** that's just a lot of talk

tchatcher [tʃatʃe] *vi* to chat□

ⓘ This word and its derivatives come from the Spanish verb "chachaear", meaning "to chat".

---

tchatcheur, -euse [tʃatʃœr, -øz] *nm,f* smooth talker

techi [tœʃi] *nm (verlan* **shit**) shit, hash, *Br* blow

tehon [tœɔ̃] *nf (verlan* **honte**) **avoir** *ou* **se taper la tehon** to be embarrassed□ *or* mortified; **(c'est) la tehon!** the shame of it!

tèj [tɛʒ] *vt (verlan* **jeter**) *(chasser)* to

throw *or* chuck out, *Am* to eighty-six; *(abandonner)* to dump, to chuck; **il s'est fait tèj par sa meuf** his woman *or Br* bird dumped *or* chucked him

téléphoné, -e [telefɔne] *adj* **c'était téléphoné** you could see it coming (a mile off); **un gag téléphoné** a joke you can see coming (a mile off)

téloche [telɔʃ] *nf* TV, *Br* telly, box, *Am* tube

tendance [tɑ̃dɑ̃s] *adj* trendy, cool

tendu *adj (difficile, juste)* tight; **ça va être tendu pour ce soir, je préfère remettre à un autre jour** it's going to be a bit tight for tonight, I'd rather put it off till another day; **avec le retard que le train a pris, ça va être très tendu pour avoir notre correspondance** with the train being late, it's going to be tight getting our connection *or* we'll be cutting it fine for our connection; **nous jouons contre une excellente équipe, ça va être tendu** we're playing an excellent team, it's going to be tough

tenir [tənir] *vt* **tenir une bonne cuite** to be totally wrecked *or* wasted *or Br* legless *or* pissed; **qu'est-ce qu'il tient!** *(il est vraiment stupide)* what a jerk *or Br* tosser!; *(il est complètement ivre)* he's totally wrecked *or* wasted *or Br* legless *or* pissed! ▸ *see also* **bavarde, bout, chandelle, côte, couche, crachoir, dose, jambe**

tension [tɑ̃sjɔ̃] *nf* **avoir deux de tension** to be all sluggish

terre [tɛr] *nf* **ne plus toucher terre** to be run off one's feet; *Can* **être à terre** *(déprimé)* to be *or* feel down

têtard [tetar] *nm (enfant)* kid, brat

tête [tɛt] *nf* **être une tête** to be brainy, to be a brain; **tête de con**

[!], **tête de nœud** [!] dickhead; *Can Pej* **tête carrée** English-speaking Canadian◻; **quelle tête à claques ce mec!** he's got a face you just want to slap!; **c'est quinze euros par tête de pipe** it's fifteen euros a head; **prendre la tête à qn** *Br* to get up sb's nose, to do sb's head in, to get on sb's wick, *Am* to give sb a pain; **prise de tête** pain (in the neck); **tomber sur la tête** to go off one's rocker, to lose it, *Br* to lose the plot; **non mais t'es tombé sur la tête ou quoi?** were you dropped on your head as a baby or something?; **ça va pas la tête?** are you mad *or* off your head?, have you lost your mind?; **avoir** *ou* **attraper la grosse tête** to have a big head, to be bigheaded; **faire une (grosse) tête** *ou* **une tête au carré à qn** to smash sb's face in, *Br* to punch sb's lights out, *Am* to punch sb out; **avoir la tête dans le cul** [!] to be out of it ▸ *see also* **cul, payer, piquer, pou, yeux**

téter [tete] *vi (boire avec excès)* to knock it back, to put it away

tétons [tetɔ̃] *nmpl (seins)* tits, boobs, knockers

teuch¹ [tœʃ] *nm (verlan* **shit***)* shit, hash, *Br* blow

teuch² [!!] [tœʃ] *nf Cités (verlan* **chatte***)* pussy, snatch, *Br* fanny, twat

teuf [tœf] *nf (verlan* **fête***)* **(a)** *(soirée)* party◻, *Br* do **(b)** *(rave)* rave◻

teufer [tœfe] *vi* to party◻

teufeur [tœfœr] *nm* **(a)** *(dans une soirée)* party animal **(b)** *(dans une rave)* raver◻

teup [!] [tœp] *nf Cités (verlan* **pute***)* **(a)** *(prostituée)* whore, hooker **(b)** *(femme facile)* tart, slut, *Br* slapper, slag

Le symbole ◻ indique que la traduction n'est pas argotique.

teuté [tœte] *nf Cités (verlan* **tête)** head□, *Br* nut

texto [tɛksto] *adv (abbr* **textuellement)** word for word□

thon [tɔ̃] *nm (femme laide)* dog, moose, *Br* boot, minger, *Am* beast

thune [tyn] *nf* **(a)** *(argent)* cash, dough, *Br* dosh, *Am* bucks; **ils ont de la thune dans sa famille** his/her family's loaded *or Br* rolling in it; **être pété de thunes** to be loaded **(b)** *(pièce)* **j'ai plus une thune** I haven't got a bean *or Am* a red cent

tiags [tjag] *nfpl (abbr* **santiags)** cowboy boots□

ticket [tikɛ] *nm* **avoir le ticket (avec qn)** to be in there; **profites-en, je crois que t'as le ticket avec elle** go for it, I think you're well in with her

tickson [tiksɔ̃] *nm* ticket□

tiéquar [tjekar] *nm Cités (verlan* **quartier)** neighbourhood□

tifs [tif] *nmpl* hair□, *Br* barnet; **il faut que j'aille me faire couper les tifs** I must go and get my hair *or Br* barnet cut

tige [tiʒ] *nf* **(a)** *(cigarette)* smoke, *Br* fag, cig **(b)** **[!!]** *(pénis)* dick, prick, cock ▶ *see also* **brouter**

tignasse [tiɲas] *nf (cheveux)* mane, mop

ⓘ This word is related to "teigne", which means "ringworm".

---

tilt [tilt] *nm* **ça a fait tilt** the penny dropped, it clicked

timbré, -e [tɛ̃bre] *adj (fou)* nuts, crazy, *Br* bonkers, barking (mad), *Am* wacko

tintin [tɛ̃tɛ̃] *nm* **(a)** **tintin!** no way (José)!, no chance!, *Br* nothing doing! **(b)** **faire tintin** to go without□

tintouin [tɛ̃twɛ̃] *nm* **(a)** *(vacarme)* racket, din **(b)** *(souci)* grief, hassle, *Br* aggro; **elle me donne bien du tintouin** she's giving me so much trouble *or* hassle *or Br* aggro; **tous ces invités, ça fait du tintouin** all these guests is just a lot of hassle

tip-top [tiptɔp] *adj* tip-top

tiquer [tike] *vi* to wince□; **il a pas tiqué** he didn't bat an eyelid *or* turn a hair; **ça l'a fait tiquer** it gave him a shake *or* a jolt

tire [tir] *nf (voiture)* car□, *Br* motor, *Am* ride

tire-au-cul [!] [tiroky], **tire-au-flanc** [tiroflɑ̃] *nm inv Br* skiver, *Am* goldbrick

tirée [tire] *nf* haul, trek; **ça fait une tirée d'ici à là-bas** it's a bit of a haul *or* trek from here

tire-jus [!] [tirʒy] *nm* snot-rag

tire-larigot [tirlarigo] **à tire-larigot** *adv* **boire à tire-larigot** to drink like a fish; **il y en a à tire-larigot** there's loads *or* tons of them

tirelire [tirlir] *nf* **(a)** *(visage)* face□, mug; **se fendre la tirelire** to split one's sides (laughing), *Br* to kill oneself laughing **(b)** *(tête)* head□, nut

tire-moelle [!] [tirmwal] *nm inv* snot-rag

tirer [tire] **1** *vt* **(a)** *(voler)* **tirer qch à qn** to pinch *or Br* nick sth from sb **(b)** *(prendre pour cible)* **ils tiraient les passants comme des lapins** they were picking off passers-by one by one
(c) [!!] *(posséder sexuellement)* to fuck, to screw, to hump, *Br* to shag **(d) [!!]** **tirer un coup** to get laid, to have a fuck *or* a screw *or Br* a shag; **ça fait des semaines que j'ai pas tiré mon coup** I haven't got laid in weeks

---

The symbol **[!]** denotes a very familiar term, **[!!]** a vulgar one.

(e) *(passer)* **il est en train de tirer dix piges pour vol à main armée** he's doing ten years *or* a ten-year stretch for armed robbery; **encore deux mois à tirer avant les vacances** another two months to get through before the *Br* holidays *or Am* vacation

(f) **tirer les vers du nez à qn** to worm *or* drag it out of sb

2 *vi* **tirer au flanc** *ou* **au cul [!]** to shirk, *Br* to skive

3 se tirer *vpr* (a) *(partir)* to hit the road, to get going, to make tracks; *(se sauver)* to beat it, *Br* to clear off, *Am* to book it

(b) **se tirer sur l'élastique [!]** to jerk off, to beat off, *Br* to wank, to have a wank ▸ *see also* **crampe, gueule, numéro, patte, portrait**

tiroir [tirwar] *nm (ventre)* stomach☐, belly, gut ▸ *see also* **polichinelle**

tise [tiz] *nf Cités* boozing

tiser [tize] **1** *vt* to sink, to down, to knock back

2 *vi* to booze, to knock it back

tis-jos-connaissant [tiʒokɔnɛsã] *nm Can Br* know-all, *Am* know-it-all

titi [titi] *nm* = Parisian street urchin

tocante [tɔkãt] *nf* watch☐

tocard, -e [tɔkãr, -ard] **1** *nm,f (personne insignifiante)* nonentity☐, no-hoper, loser

2 *nm (mauvais cheval de course)* rank outsider☐

tof, toffe [tɔf] *adj Belg* great, fantastic

toile [twal] *nf* (a) **se faire une toile** to go to the *Br* pictures *or* flicks *or Am* movies (b) **toiles** *(draps)* sheets☐; **se mettre dans les toiles** to hit the sack *or* the hay *or Am* the rack

tomate [tɔmat] *nf (cocktail)* = drink consisting of pastis and grenadine syrup

tombeau [tɔ̃bo] *nm* **à tombeau ouvert** at breakneck speed

tomber [tɔ̃be] **1** *vt* (a) *(séduire)* to pick up, *Br* to pull (b) *(enlever)* to take off☐; **il a tombé la veste** he took his jacket off☐

2 *vi* (a) *(être arrêté)* to get nabbed *or Br* lifted *or* nicked (b) *(pleuvoir)* to rain☐; **qu'est-ce qu'il est tombé hier soir!** it was raining cats and dogs *or Br* bucketing down *or* chucking it down last night! (c) **laisse tomber!** forget it!, drop it! (d) *Belg* **tomber dans l'œil de qn** to catch sb's eye ▸ *see also* **carafe, cordes, jus, os, paletot, patte, poil, pomme, râble, rade², tête**

tombeur [tɔ̃bœr] *nm* (a) *(séducteur)* womanizer, ladies' man (b) *(vainqueur)* **c'est lui le tombeur du champion du monde** he's the man who defeated the world champion☐

-ton [tɔ̃] *suffix* **biffeton** *(billet de banque)* note☐, *Am* greenback; *(de transport, de spectacle)* ticket☐; **cureton** priest☐; **frometon** cheese☐; **mecton** guy, *Br* bloke

ⓘ This suffix is found at the end of many French nouns and is used for either humorous or pejorative effect.

top [tɔp] **1** *adj* great, *Br* wicked, top, *Am* awesome

2 *adv (très) Br* dead, *Am* real; **putain, sa gonzesse elle est top bonne!** fuck me, his girlfriend is seriously hot *or Br* bloody gorgeous!

3 *nm* **c'est le top (du top)** it's the best there is, *Br* it's the business!

topo [topo] *nm* report☐; **faire un topo à qn sur qch** to give sb the lowdown on sth, *Am* to hip sb to sth; **tu vois (un peu) le topo?** (you) see what I mean?; **c'est toujours le même topo** it's always the same old story

toqué, -e [tɔke] **1** adj crazy, nuts, Br mental, Am gonzo

2 nm,f nutcase, Br nutter, Am wacko

torche [tɔrʃ] nf Can (grosse femme) fat cow

torche-cul [!] [tɔrʃ(ə)ky] nm (journal) rag; (texte) trash, Br rubbish

torchée [tɔrʃe] nf (correction) thrashing, hammering; **filer une torchée à qn** to thrash or hammer sb

torcher [tɔrʃe] **1** vt (a) (faire en vitesse) to knock off, to dash off; **j'ai torché ma dissert en une heure** I knocked off my essay in an hour; **bien torché** well put-together (b) [!!] (essuyer le derrière de) **torcher (le cul de) qn** to wipe sb's Br arse or Am ass

2 se torcher vpr (a) (se battre) to knock lumps out of each other, to have a Br punch-up or Am slugfest (b) [!!] (s'essuyer) **se torcher (le cul)** to wipe one's Br arse or Am ass; **je m'en torche!** I don't give a shit or a (flying) fuck or Am a rat's ass! (c) [!] (s'enivrer) to get shit-faced or Br pissed or rat-arsed

torchon [tɔrʃɔ̃] nm (mauvais journal) rag; (devoir mal présenté) dog's breakfast or dinner

tordant, -e [tɔrdɑ̃, -ɑ̃t] adj (amusant) hysterical, side-splitting

tord-boyaux [tɔrbwajo] nm inv gutrot, rotgut, Am alky

tordre [tɔrdr] **se tordre** vpr **se tordre (de rire)** to be in stitches, to kill oneself (laughing), to be doubled up (with laughter)

tordu, -e [tɔrdy] nm,f nutcase, headcase, Br nutter, Am wacko

torgnole [tɔrɲɔl] nf (gifle) clout, wallop; **flanquer une torgnole à qn** to clout or wallop sb

torrieu [tɔrjø] exclam Can oh hell!

tortiller [tɔrtije] vi **y a pas à tortiller, y a pas à tortiller du cul pour chier droit** [!!] there's no getting away from it, there are no two ways about it

tortore [tɔrtɔr] nf cooking▫; **elle fait de la vachement bonne tortore** she makes really great food▫ or Br scran

tos [tɔs] nmf Offensive Dago (from Portugal)

ⓘ Depending on the context and the tone of voice used, this term may be either offensive or affectionately humorous. It is nonetheless inadvisable to use it unless one is quite sure of the reaction it will receive.

tosser [tɔse] vi to get stoned

total [tɔtal] adv total, **j'ai perdu mon boulot/il a fallu que je recommence** the upshot is, I lost my job/I had to start again

totale [tɔtal] nf **quand il m'a demandée en mariage, il m'a fait la totale** when he proposed to me, he really went all out; **on a eu droit à la totale: verglas, embouteillages, barrages de routiers** black ice, traffic jams, lorry drivers' road blocks, you name it, we had it

ⓘ This expression originates from "la totale" meaning a hysterectomy. It is used to abbreviate a long list and may have either positive or negative connotations.

toto [toto] *nm* louse◻, *Am* cootie

toubab [tubab] *nmf Cités* = French person of native stock, as opposed to immigrants or their descendants

toubib [tubib] *nm* doctor◻, doc

ⓘ This word comes from Arabic. It entered the French language at the time of the French colonial expansion in North Africa.

touche [tuʃ] *nf* (**a**) *(aspect)* look◻; **il a une de ces touches avec sa veste à franges!** he looks like something from another planet with that fringed jacket of his! (**b**) *(personne séduite)* conquest◻; **faire une touche** to score, *Br* to pull (**c**) *Can* **tirer** *ou* **prendre une touche** *(fumer)* to have a smoke

touche-pipi [tuʃpipi] *nm inv* **jouer à touche-pipi** to play at doctors and nurses

toucher [tuʃe] **1** *vi* (**a**) *(être doué)* to be brilliant (**en/à** at) (**b**) *(recevoir de l'argent)* to collect

2 se toucher *vpr* (**a**) **[!!]** *(se masturber)* to play with oneself, *Br* to touch oneself (up) (**b**) **se toucher (la nuit)** to fool oneself, to kid oneself on ▸ *see also* **bille, pacson**

touffe [!!] [tuf] *nf (toison pubienne)* bush, pubes; **une jupe ras la touffe** a micro mini-skirt◻, *Br* a bumfreezer

touiller [tuje] *vt* to stir◻

toupie [tupi] *nf* **une vieille toupie** an old crone *or Br* bag

tournant [turnɑ̃] *nm* **attendre qn au tournant** to be waiting for a chance to get even with sb

tournante [turnɑ̃t] *nf (viol collectif)* gang-rape◻, gang-bang

tourner [turne] **1** *vi* (**a**) *(devenir)* **tourner homo** to turn gay; **tourner hippie; tourner hippie** to become or turn into a hippy (**b**) **tourner de l'œil** to pass out◻, to keel over

2 se tourner *vpr* **se tourner les pouces, se les tourner** to twiddle one's thumbs ▸ *see also* **rond**

tournicoter [turnikɔte] *vi* to wander around aimlessly

toutim, toutime [tutim] *nm et* **tout le toutim** the works, the whole enchilada, *Br* the full monty

toutou [tutu] *nm* doggy, doggie

touzepar [tuzpar] *nf (verlan* **partouze)** orgy

toxico [tɔksiko] *nmf (abbr* **toxicomane)** addict◻, junkie, *Am* hophead

trace [tras] *nf* **traces de pneu** *(sur un slip)* skidmarks

tracer [trase] *vi (aller vite)* to belt along, to bomb along; *(déguerpir)* to beat it, *Br* to clear off, *Am* to book it

traduc [tradyk] *nf (abbr* **traduction)** translation◻

train [trɛ̃] *nm (postérieur)* backside, *Br* bum, *Am* fanny; **filer le train à qn** to shadow *or* tail sb ▸ *see also* **botter, magner, passer**

traînailler [trɛnaje] *vi* (**a**) *(être lent)* to dawdle (**b**) *(perdre son temps)* to hang about, *Br* to faff about

traînard, -e [trɛnar, -ard] *nm,f Br* slowcoach, *Am* slowpoke

traîne [trɛn] *nf* **être à la traîne** to lag behind

traînée [!] [trɛne] *nf (femme)* tart, *Br* slapper, scrubber

traîner [trɛne] *vi (être posé)* to lie around, to hang around ▸ *see also* **guêtres, merde, savate**

traîne-savates [trɛnsavat] *nm inv*

down-and-out, *Br* dosser, *Am* bum

traîneux [trɛnø] *nm Can* slob, waster

traiter [trɛte] *vt (insulter) Br* to slag off, *Am* to bad-mouth

tralala [tralala] *nm* **et tout le tralala** the works, *Br* the full monty, *Am* the whole enchilada

tranche [trɑ̃ʃ] *nf* **s'en payer une tranche** to have a ball *or Am* a blast

tranquillos [trɑ̃kilos] *adv (tranquillement)* **vas-y tranquillos, inutile de faire des excès de vitesse** take your time, there's no need to break the speed limit; **ils étaient dans le canapé en train de siroter mon whisky, tranquillos** they were on the sofa sipping away at my whisky, without a care in the world

transbahuter [trɑ̃sbayte] *vt* to shift, to hump, to lug; **comment on va faire pour transbahuter tout ton bordel?** how are we going to shift all your mess?

transfo [trɑ̃sfo] *nm (abbr* **transformateur)** transformer◻

transpirer [trɑ̃spire] *vi Cités* **transpirer sa race** to be crapping oneself, *Br* to be bricking it

trappe [trap] *nf Can (bouche)* trap, *Br* gob

trapu, -e [trapy] *adj* **(a)** *(difficile)* tough, tricky **(b)** *(expert)* brainy, brilliant **(en/à** at)

travail [travaj] *nm* **et voilà le travail!** and that's all there is to it!, *Br* and Bob's your uncle!; **qu'est-ce que c'est que ce travail?** what's going on here?, what's this all about?

travelo [travlo] *nm* drag queen, TV, *Br* tranny

traviole [travjɔl] **de traviole** *adv* **marcher de traviole** to be staggering all over the place; **être de traviole** to be lopsided *or* skew-whiff

trèfle [trɛfl] *nm* **(a)** *(argent)* cash, dough, *Br* dosh, *Am* bucks **(b)** *(foule)* crowd◻; **qu'est-ce qu'il y avait comme trèfle en ville!** the town was totally jam-packed *or Br* heaving *or* chock-a-block

tremblement [trɑ̃bləmɑ̃] *nm* **et tout le tremblement** the works, *Br* the full monty *Am* the whole enchilada

tremblote [trɑ̃blɔt] *nf* **avoir la tremblote** *(de peur)* to have the jitters; *(de froid, à cause de la fièvre)* to have the shivers; *(à cause d'une maladie)* to have the shakes; *(vieillard)* to be shaky

trempe [trɑ̃p] *nf (correction)* thrashing, pasting; **prendre une trempe** to *Br* get *or Am* take a thrashing *or* a pasting; **flanquer une trempe à qn** to give sb a thrashing *or* a pasting

tremper [trɑ̃pe] *vi* **tremper dans qch** to be mixed up in sth ► *see also* **biscuit, panais**

trempette [trɑ̃pɛt] *nf* **faire trempette** to have a dip

trente-six [trɑ̃tsis] *adj* **tous les trente-six du mois** once in a blue moon; **il y en a pas trente-six** there aren't that many of them; **des raisons, je pourrais t'en citer trente-six** I could give you umpteen reasons; **il y a pas trente-six solutions** there's no getting away from it, there are no two ways about it; **voir trente-six chandelles** to see stars

trente-sixième [trɑ̃tsizjɛm] *adj* **être au trente-sixième dessous** to be in a tight spot

tricard, -e [trikar, -ard] **1** *adj* = prohibited from entering a certain area **2** *nm,f* = ex-convict prohibited from entering a certain area

trichlo [triklo] nm (abbr **trichlo-réthylène**) trichloroethylene$^\square$ (used as a drug)

tricoter [trikɔte] vi (marcher vite) **tricoter (des gambettes)** to leg it, to belt along

trifouiller [trifuje] **1** vt (a) (fouiller) to rummage through (b) (toucher à) to fiddle with, to tinker with

2 vi **trifouiller dans qch** to rummage around in sth

Trifouillis-les-Oies [trifujilezwa] npr = fictional name for the archetypal isolated, dull village

trimarder [trimarde] vi to be on the road

trimardeur [trimardœr] nm tramp, Am hobo

trimballer [trɛ̃bale] **1** vt (a) (transporter) to hump, to schlep, to lug around; **il trimballe sa famille partout où il va** he has his family in tow everywhere he goes (b) **qu'est-ce qu'il trimballe!** what a total halfwit or Br tosser or Am klutz!

2 se **trimballer** vpr to schlep around, to trail around

trimer [trime] vi to slog away, to slave away; **faire trimer qn** to keep sb hard at it, to keep sb's nose to the grindstone; **qu'est-ce qu'ils peuvent nous faire trimer dans cette boîte!** they really keep us hard at it in this company!

tringler [!!] [trɛ̃gle] vt to fuck, to screw, Br to shag

trinquer [trɛ̃ke] vi (subir un désagrément) to be the one who suffers$^\square$, to pay the price

trip [trip] nm (a) (centre d'intérêt) kick; **il est en plein trip écolo en ce moment** he's on some environmental kick at the moment; **c'est vraiment pas mon trip, ce genre de truc** I'm not really into that kind of thing, it's not my scene, that kind of thing (b) (produit par la drogue) trip

tripaille [tripaj] nf innards, guts

tripant, -e [tripɑ̃, -ɑ̃t] adj Can great, terrific

tripatouiller [tripatuje] vt (a) (truquer) (document) to tamper with$^\square$; (chiffres, résultats) Br to fiddle, Am to doctor; **tripatouiller les comptes** to cook the books (b) (modifier) (texte) to alter$^\square$ (c) (tripoter) (personne) to paw, to feel up; (cheveux) to play or fiddle with; (bouton) to pick at

triper [tripe] vi to trip (after taking drugs); **ça me fait vraiment triper, ce genre de musique** this type of music just blows me away

tripes [trip] nfpl (a) **jouer avec ses tripes** to give it one's all (b) **rendre ou vomir ou dégueuler tripes et boyaux** to be as sick as a dog, Br to spew one's guts up

tripette [tripɛt] nf **ça ne vaut pas tripette** it's a load of tripe or dross, Am it's not worth diddly

tripotée [tripɔte] nf (a) **une tripotée (de)** tons (of), loads (of) (b) (correction, défaite) thrashing, hammering; **filer une tripotée à qn** to thrash or hammer sb, to give sb a thrashing or a hammering; **prendre une tripotée** to get thrashed or hammered

tripoter [tripɔte] **1** vt (a) (toucher) to fiddle with, to play with (b) (se livrer à des attouchements sur) to feel up, to grope, Br to touch up

2 se **tripoter** [!] vpr to touch oneself up, to play with oneself

trique [!!] [trik] nf (érection) hard-on, boner; **avoir la trique** to have a hard-on or a boner

triquer [!!] [trike] *vi* to have a hard-on *or* a boner

triso [trizo] *Offensive (abbr* **triso-mique)** **1** *adj* spazzy, *Br* mong
2 *nmf* spaz, *Br* mong

trisser [trise] **1** *vi* to hightail it, to scoot, *Am* to split
2 se trisser *vpr* to hightail it, to scoot, *Am* to split

tristounet, -ette [tristune, -ɛt] *adj* sad⊐, down⊐; **il a l'air un peu tris-tounet** he looks a bit down

trogne [trɔɲ] *nf (visage)* face⊐, mug, *Am* map

trognon [trɔɲɔ̃] **1** *adj (mignon)* cute, sweet
2 *nm* **jusqu'au trognon [!]** well and truly; **il s'est fait avoir jusqu'au trognon [!]** he's been well and truly had *or* shafted

trom [trɔm] *nm (verlan* **métro)** *Br* underground⊐, *Am* subway⊐

trombine [trɔ̃bin] *nf* face⊐, mug

trombiner [!!] [trɔ̃bine], **trom-boner [!!]** [trɔ̃bɔne] *vt (posséder sexuellement)* to fuck, to screw, to shaft, *Br* to shag

tromé [trome] = **trom**

tronc [trɔ̃] *nm* **se casser le tronc** to worry⊐, *Br* to get one's knickers in a twist

tronche [trɔ̃ʃ] *nf* **(a)** *(visage)* face⊐, mug; **il a une drôle de tronche** he looks really odd, he's really odd-looking; **faire la tronche** to sulk⊐, to be in a *or* the huff; **t'en fais une tronche, qu'est-ce qui t'arrive?** you look really down, what's up?; **une tronche de cake** *(personne)* a complete jerk **(b)** *(personne intelli-gente)* brain, brainy person; **ce mec-là, c'est une tronche!** that guy's a real brain *or* so brainy! ▸ *see also* **payer**

troncher [!!] [trɔ̃ʃe] *vt* to fuck, to screw, *Br* to shag

trône [tron] *nm Hum* **être sur le trône** *(aux toilettes)* to be on the throne

trop [tro] **1** *adj inv (incroyable)* too much, unreal
2 *adv (très)* **j'étais trop dégoûté** I was so bummed *or Br* gutted; **il est trop mortel, son plan** his plan's so *or* too brilliant; **j'étais trop mort de rire** I was absolutely killing myself; **ah ouais, je l'ai vu, ce film, il est trop bien!** oh yeah, I've seen that film, it was really *Br* fab *or* top *or Am* awesome!

troquet [trɔkɛ] *nm* bar⊐, *Br* boozer

trotte [trɔt] *nf* hike, stretch, schlep; **il y a** *ou* **ça fait une trotte d'ici à là-bas** it's quite a hike *or* stretch *or* schlep from here

trottoir [trɔtwar] *nm* **faire le trot-toir** to walk the streets, *Br* to be on the game, *Am* to hustle

trou [tru] *nm* **(a)** *(prison)* slammer, clink, *Br* nick, *Am* pen **(b)** *(endroit isolé)* hole; **il n'est jamais sorti de son trou** he's never been out of his own backyard **(c)** **boire com-me un trou** to drink like a fish **(d)** **trou de balle [!], trou du cul [!!]** *Br* arsehole, *Am* asshole **(e)** **c'est le trou du cul du monde** it's the armpit *or Br* arsehole *or Am* asshole of the universe ▸ *see also* **taupe, yeux**

trouduc [!] [trudyk], **trou-du-cul [!]** [trudyky] *nm (imbécile) Br* arse-hole, *Am* asshole

troufignon [!] [trufiɲɔ̃] *nm (anus) Br* arsehole, *Am* asshole

troufion [trufjɔ̃] *nm* **(a)** *(simple sol-dat) Br* squaddie, *Am* grunt **(b) [!]** *(postérieur) Br* arse, *Am* ass

trouillard, -e [trujar, -ard] *nm,f* chicken *(person)*

trouille [truj] *nf* fear□; **avoir la trouille** to be scared stiff; **foutre la trouille à qn** to scare the living daylights out of sb, to scare sb stiff

trouillomètre [trujɔmɛtr] *nm* **avoir le trouillomètre à zéro** to be scared stiff

trouilloter [!] [trujɔte] *vi* (**a**) *(avoir peur)* to be scared shitless, to be shit-scared (**b**) *(sentir mauvais)* to stink, *Br* to pong

trousser [!] [truse] *vt (posséder sexuellement)* to hump, *Br* to have it away *or* off with

truander [tryɑ̃de] **1** *vt* to swindle, to rip off, to con, *Am* to rook; **se faire truander** to get swindled *or* ripped off *or* conned *or Am* rooked
   2 *vi (tricher)* to cheat□ (**à** in); *(resquiller)* to sneak in

truanderie [tryɑ̃dri] *nf* con, scam

truc [tryk] *nm* thing□; **c'est pas mon truc** it's not my thing *or* bag *or Br* cup of tea; **c'est tout à fait son truc** it's just his/her sort of thing, *Br* it's right up his/her street

trucider [tryside] *vt* to bump off, to ice, to waste

Trucmuche [trykmyʃ] *npr* thingy, what's-his-name, *f* what's-her-name

truffe [tryf] *nf (imbécile) Br* divvy, dipstick, *Am* lamebrain, schmuck

trumeau, -x [trymo] *nm (femme laide)* dog, *Br* boot, *Am* beast

truster [trœste] *vt (monopoliser)* to monopolize□, to hog

tubard, -e [tybar, -ard] **1** *adj* **être tubard** to have TB
   2 *nm,f* TB sufferer

tuber [tybe] *vt (téléphoner à)* **tuber qn** to give sb a buzz *or Br* a bell

tuer [tɥe] *vt* **ça me tue!** it kills me!; **ça tue!** it's a killer!

tuile [tɥil] *nf (problème)* hassle; **il m'arrive une tuile** I'm in a bit of a mess

tune [tyn] = **thune**

turbin [tyrbɛ̃] *nm* work□

turbine [tyrbin] *nf* **turbine à choco-lat [!!]** *Br* arsehole, *Am* asshole, dirtbox

turbiner [tyrbine] *vi* (**a**) *(travailler)* to slog *or* slave away (**b**) *(se livrer à la prostitution)* to turn tricks, *Br* to be on the game

turbo [tyrbo] *nm* **mettre le turbo** to get a move on, to get one's skates on, *Am* to get it in gear

turbo-prof [tyrboprɔf] *nmf* = teacher who works in a town in the provinces and commutes there from Paris every day

turf [tyrf] *nm* (**a**) *(prostitution)* prostitution□; **faire le turf** to turn tricks, *Br* to be on the game (**b**) *(travail)* work□; *(lieu de travail)* workplace□

turista [turista] *nf* **la turista** *Br* Delhi belly, *Am* the Aztec two-step

turlupiner [tyrlypine] *vt* to bother□, to bug

turlute [!] [tyrlyt] *nf* blow-job; **faire une turlute à qn** to give sb a blow-job, to go down on sb, to give sb head

turne [tyrn] *nf* room□

ⓘ This word is derived from an Alsatian word meaning "prison".

tuyau, -x [tɥijo] *nm* (**a**) *(conseil)* tip, hint, pointer; *(aux courses)* tip; *(renseignement)* tip-off; **un tuyau percé** a useless tip/tip-off (**b**) **la famille tuyau de poêle** incestuous family

tuyauter [tɥijɔte] *vt (renseigner)* to tip off

tuyauterie [tɥijɔtri] *nf (organes de la digestion)* innards, guts; *(poumons)* lungs□

type [tip] *nm* guy, *Br* bloke; **un chic type** a good guy *or Br* bloke, *Am* a mensch; **un sale type** a bad egg, a nasty piece of work; **un pauvre type** a sad *or* pathetic individual, *Br* a saddo

Uu

une [yn] *adj* **et d'une** for a start, for starters; **ne faire ni une ni deux** not to think twice; **il n'en loupe** *ou* **rate pas une** he's always screwing up

uni [yni], **unif, univ** [ynif] *nf Belg Br* uni, *Am* school▫

unité [ynite] *nf Formerly (dix mille francs)* ten thousand francs▫

urger [yrʒe] *vi* to be urgent▫

uro [yro] *nf (urolagnie)* water sports

usiner [yzine] **1** *vi (travailler dur)* to slog *or* slave away, to be hard at it

   2 s'usiner *vpr* to jerk off, *Br* to wank, to have a wank

Vv

vacciné, -e [vaksine] *adj* **être vacciné** to have learnt one's lesson; **être vacciné au vinaigre** to be in a foul mood; **être vacciné à la merde [!]** to be in a shit mood

vachard, -e [vaʃar, -ard] *adj* rotten, mean, nasty

vache [vaʃ] **1** *adj* (**a**) *(méchant)* rotten, mean, nasty; **ce qu'elle peut être vache!** she can be so bitchy *or* such a bitch! (**b**) *(remarquable)* **il a un vache (de) coquard** he's got a hell of a black eye *or* a shiner; **il a eu une vache d'idée** he had a hell of a good idea

2 *nf* (**a**) *(homme méchant)* *Br* swine, *Am* stinker; *(femme méchante)* bitch, *Br* cow; **elle lui a fait un coup en vache** she played a dirty trick on him, *Br* she did the dirty on him, *Am* she did him dirty; **elle a dit ça en vache** she just said that to be bitchy *or* a bitch (**b**) **manger** *ou* **bouffer de la vache enragée** to have a hard *or* tough time of it (**c**) **la vache!** *(de surprise)* God!, *Br* blimey!, *Am* gee (whiz)!; *(d'admiration)* wow! (**d**) **mort aux vaches!** *(à bas la police)* kill the pigs! ► *see also* **peau, plancher**[1]

vachement [vaʃmɑ̃] *adv* really[□], *Br* dead, *Am* real; **on s'est vachement bien marrés** we had a blast, we had *Br* a wicked *or* *Am* an awesome good time; **il y a vachement de monde en ville** there are loads *or* tons of people in town

vacherie [vaʃri] *nf* (**a**) *(méchanceté)* meanness[□], nastiness[□] (**b**) *(action méchante)* dirty trick; **faire une vacherie à qn** to play a dirty trick on sb, *Br* to do the dirty on sb, *Am* to do sb dirt (**c**) *(parole blessante)* nasty remark[□]; **il m'a dit un tas de vacheries** he said loads of nasty things to me

vachté [vaʃte] *adv* really[□], *Br* dead, *Am* real

va-comme-je-te-pousse [vakɔmʒtəpus] **à la va-comme-je-te-pousse** *adv* **faire qch à la va-comme-je-te-pousse** to do sth any old how

vadrouille [vadruj] *nf* wander[□]; **être en vadrouille** to be wandering *or* roaming around[□]; **il est rarement à son bureau, il est toujours en vadrouille** he's hardly ever at his desk, he's always wandering around somewhere

vadrouiller [vadruje] *vi* to wander *or* roam around[□]; **il est constamment en train de vadrouiller dans le bureau** he's always wandering around the office

valda [valda] *nf (balle d'arme à feu)* bullet[□], slug

ⓘ This term comes from the name of a famous brand of throat pastilles, the shape of which is reminiscent of that of a bullet.

valdinguer [valdɛ̃ge] *vi* to go flying; **envoyer valdinguer qn/qch** to send sb/sth flying

valise [valiz] *nf* (a) **valises** *(poches sous les yeux)* bags (under one's eyes) (b) *Can* sucker, mug

valoche [valɔʃ] *nf* (a) *(valise)* suitcase▫, case▫ (b) **valoches** *(poches sous les yeux)* bags (under one's eyes)

valse [vals] *nf* (a) *(correction)* hammering, thrashing; **foutre une valse à qn** to give sb a hammering *or* a thrashing (b) *(cocktail)* = drink consisting of beer with a dash of mint-flavoured syrup

valser [valse] *vi* (a) *(perdre l'équilibre)* **il est allé valser contre la porte** he went flying into the door; **envoyer valser qch** to send sth flying; **envoyer valser qn** *(l'éconduire)* to send sb packing, to show sb the door; *(pousser)* to send sb flying (b) *(abandonner)* **j'ai envie de tout envoyer valser!** I feel like packing it all in *or Br* jacking it all in *or Am* chucking everything!

valseur [valsœr] *nm* *(postérieur)* butt, *Br* bum, *Am* fanny

valseuses [!] [valsøz] *nfpl* *(testicules)* balls, nuts, *Br* bollocks

ⓘ This word became popular after the success of Bertrand Blier's 1974 film *Les Valseuses*, which told the story of two young dropouts, one of whom was played by Gérard Depardieu.

vanne [van] *nf* (a) *(remarque désobligeante)* snide remark▫, dig, jibe, *Am* zinger; **envoyer des vannes à qn** to make digs at sb, *Am* to zing sb (b) *(plaisanterie)* joke▫, crack

vanné, -e [vane] *adj* worn out, *Br* knackered, shattered, *Am* beat

vanner [vane] *vt* *(se moquer de)* to make digs at, *Am* to zing

vapes [vap] *nfpl* **être dans les vapes** to be out of it *or* in a daze; **tomber dans les vapes** to pass out▫, to keel over

variétoche [varjetɔʃ] *nf* middle-of-the-road music, MOR

vaser [vɑze] *v imp* to pour with rain, *Br* to bucket down, to chuck it down

vaseux, -euse [vɑzø, -øz], **vasouillard, -e** [vɑzujar, -ard] *adj* (a) *(mauvais)* **plaisanterie/excuse vaseuse** feeble *or* pathetic joke/excuse; **raisonnement vaseux** woolly *or Br* dodgy reasoning (b) *(mal en point)* under the weather, out of sorts, *Br* off-colour

vasouiller [vɑzuje] *vi* to flounder

vautrer [votre] **se vautrer** *vpr* *(tomber)* to go flying

va-vite [vavit] *nm Can* **avoir le va-vite** to have the runs *or* the trots

veau, -x [vo] *nm (véhicule poussif)* = hairdrier on wheels

vécés [vese] *nmpl Br* loo, *Am* john

veille [vɛj] *nf* **c'est pas demain la veille** that's not going to happen in a hurry; **c'est pas demain la veille qu'ils te proposeront un boulot** they're not going to be offering you a job in a hurry

veilleuse [vɛjøz] *nf* **la mettre en veilleuse** to shut up, to put a sock in it

veinard, -e [vɛnar, -ard] **1** *adj* lucky▫, *Br* jammy
2 *nm,f* lucky *or Br* jammy devil

veine [vɛn] *nf (chance)* luck▫; **avoir de la veine** to be lucky▫ *or Br* jammy
▶ *see also* **cocu**

Slang sleuth

Verlan

Verlan is the most frequently used form of slang among young French people, particularly in the impoverished areas of large cities. It is formed by inverting the syllables of the word and making any spelling changes necessary to aid pronunciation. The word "verlan" is itself the inverted form of "l'envers" meaning "the other way round". Some verlan terms have passed into spoken French generally and are used or understood by a great many speakers, eg **laisse béton** (laisse tomber) – popularized by the singer Renaud many years ago – **ripou** (pourri) and **meuf** (femme). It is, however, an extremely generative form of slang and any word can, in theory, be "verlanized". Some examples: "pétard" becomes **tarpé**, "bizarre" becomes **zarbi**, and "pute" becomes **teupu** which is then shortened to **teup**. Monosyllabic words can also be "verlanized", eg "chaud" becomes **auch**; an "e" is frequently added to aid pronunciation, eg "flic" becomes **keufli** which is shortened to **keuf**, "mère" becomes **reumé** which is in turn shortened to **reum**. A term may even be "verlanized" twice – the term **rebeu**, for example, comes from the verlan for "Arabe" – **beur** – which is then "re-verlanized" to give **rebeu**. See also the panel at **L'argot des banlieues**, p.219.

vélo [velo] *nm* **avoir un petit vélo dans la tête** to be off one's rocker, to be not all there, to have a screw loose ▸ *see also* **grand-mère**

vénère [venɛʀ] *Cités* **1** *adj* (*verlan* **énervé**) *Br* wound up, *Am* ticked off

2 *vt* (*verlan* **énerver**) **vénère qn** to bug sb, *Br* to wind sb up, to do sb's head in, *Am* to tick sb off

vent [vɑ̃] *nm* (**a**) **avoir du vent dans les voiles** to be three sheets to the wind (**b**) **du vent!** clear off!, buzz off!, get lost! (**c**) **se prendre un vent** (*être rejeté*) to get turned down□, *Br* to get a knockback (**d**) **je me suis pris un vent, je lui ai parlé pendant un bon quart d'heure et** elle a rien écouté it was like talking to a brick wall, I was talking to her for a good quarter of an hour and she didn't listen to a word I was saying...

ventre [vɑ̃tʀ] *nm* **en avoir dans le ventre, avoir quelque chose dans le ventre** to have guts; **ne rien avoir dans le ventre** to be gutless

verni, -e [vɛʀni] *adj* (*qui a de la chance*) lucky□, *Br* jammy

vérole [veʀɔl] *nf* (**a**) (*syphilis*) **la vérole** the pox (**b**) **quelle vérole!** what a pain!

verrat [!] [veʀa] **1** *nm Can* (*homme méprisable*) swine, bastard, *Am* son-of-a-bitch; **en verrat** really□, *Br* dead, *Am* real; **un beau film en verrat** a

The symbol [!] denotes a very familiar term, [!!] a vulgar one.